PHILOSOPHY OF PSYCHOLOGY

Philosophy of Psychology: Contemporary Readings is a comprehensive anthology that includes classic and contemporary readings from leading philosophers. Addressing in depth most major topics within philosophy of psychology, the editor has carefully selected articles under the following headings:

- pictures of the mind
- commonsense psychology
- representation and cognitive architecture

Articles by the following philosophers are included:

Bermúdez	Evans	Lewis	Sejnowski
Carruthers	Fodor	McLeod	Simon
Paul Churchland	Garon	Marr	Sterelny
Patricia Churchland	Goldman	Newell	Stich
Cosmides	Gordon	Plunkett	Tienson
Cummins	Harman	Ramsey	Tooby
Currie	Horgan	Rey	van Gelder
Davidson	Hornsby	Rolls	Van Gulick
Dennett			

Each section includes a helpful introduction by the editor which aims to guide the student gently into the topic. The book is highly accessible and provides a broad-ranging exploration of the subject, including discussion of the leading philosophers in the field. Ideal for any student of philosophy of psychology or philosophy of mind.

José Luis Bermúdez is Professor of Philosophy and Director of the Philosophy-Neuroscience-Psychology Program at Washington University in St Louis, USA. He is series editor of New Problems in Philosophy (Routledge) and author of *The Paradox of Self-Consciousness* (1998), *Thinking without Words* (2003), and *Philosophy of Psychology: A Contempoary Introduction* (Routledge, 2005).

Routledge Contemporary Readings in Philosophy

Series Editor: Paul K. Moser,
Loyola University of Chicago

Routledge Contemporary Readings in Philosophy is a major new series of philosophy anthologies aimed at undergraduate students taking core philosophy disciplines. It is also a companion series to the highly successful *Routledge Contemporary Introductions to Philosophy*. Each book of readings provides an overview of a core general subject in philosophy offering students an accessible transition from introductory to higher-level undergraduate work in that subject. Each chapter of readings will be carefully selected, edited, and introduced. They will provide a broad overview of each topic and will include both classic and contemporary readings.

Philosophy of Science
Yuri Balashov and Alex Rosenberg

Metaphysics
Michael J. Loux

Epistemology
Michael Huemer with introduction by Robert Audi

Philosophy of Mind
Timothy O'Connor and David Robb

Ethics
Harry Gensler, Earl Spurgin, and James Swindal

Philosophy of Psychology
José Luis Bermúdez

PHILOSOPHY OF PSYCHOLOGY

Contemporary Readings

Edited by
José Luis Bermúdez

Routledge
Taylor & Francis Group

NEW YORK AND LONDON

First published 2006
in the USA and Canada
by Routledge
270 Madison Ave, New York, NY 10016

Simultaneously published in the UK
by Routledge
2 Park Square, Milton Park, Abingdon, Oxon, OX14 4RN

*Routledge is an imprint of the Taylor & Francis Group,
an informa business*

© 2006 selection and editorial matter José Luis Bermúdez
individual chapters © the authors

Typeset in Sabon and Trade Gothic by
Florence Production Ltd, Stoodleigh, Devon
Printed and bound in Great Britain by
MPG Books Ltd, Bodmin

All rights reserved. No part of this book
may be reprinted or reproduced or utilized in any form
or by any electronic, mechanical, or other means, now known or
hereafter invented, including photocopying and recording,
or in any information storage or retrieval system, without
permission in writing from the publishers.

British Library Cataloguing in Publication Data
A catalogue record for this book is available from
the British Library

Library of Congress Cataloging in Publication Data
A catalog record has been requested

ISBN10: 0–415–36861–8 (hbk)
ISBN10: 0–415–36862–6 (pbk)
ISBN10: 0–203–02895–3 (ebk)

ISBN13: 978–0–415–36861–2 (hbk)
ISBN13: 978–0–415–36862–9 (pbk)
ISBN13: 978–0–203–02895–7 (ebk)

CONTENTS

CONTENTS

CONTENTS

ACKNOWLEDGMENTS

Part I

IA

D. Dennett, "Personal and sub-personal levels of explanation", in *Content and Consciousness*, Routledge, 1969. Reproduced by kind permission of the author and publisher.

D. Davidson, "Psychology as philosophy", in *Essays on Actions and Events*, Oxford University Press, 1980. Reproduced by kind permission of the publisher.

J. Hornsby, "Physicalist thinking and conceptions of behaviour", in P. Pettit and J. McDowell (eds), *Subject, Thought and Context*, Oxford University Press, 1986. Reproduced by kind permission of the publisher.

IB

D. Lewis, "Reduction of mind", in S. Guttenplan (ed.), *Companion to the Philosophy of Mind*, Blackwell, 1994. Section 2 has been omitted. Reproduced by kind permission of the publisher.

R. Van Gulick, "Functionalism, information and content" *Nature and System* 2, 1980. Reproduced by kind permission of the author.

R. Cummins, "'How does it work?' Versus 'What are the laws?'", in F.C. Keil and R.A. Wilson (eds), *Explanation and Cognition*, MIT Press. Copyright © 2000 Massachusetts Institute of Technology. Sections 6, 7, and 8 have been omitted. Reproduced with permission.

IC

J. Fodor, "First approximations", in *The Language of Thought*, MIT Press, 1975. Reproduced with permission.

G. Rey, "A not 'merely empirical' argument for a language of thought", in *Philosophical Perspectives* 9, 1995. Reproduced with permission.

ID

P.S. Churchland and T.J. Sejnowski, "Neural representation and neural computation", in Lynn Nadel, Lynn Cooper, Peter W. Culicover, and Robert N. Harnish (eds), *Neural Connections, Mental Computations*, MIT Press. Copyright © 1989 Massachusetts Institute of Technology. Reproduced with permission.

P. McLeod, K. Plunkett, and E.T. Rolls, "The attraction of parallel distributed processing for understanding cognition", in *Introduction to Connectionist Modelling of Cognitive Processes*, Oxford University Press, 1998.

Part II

IIA

J. Fodor, "The persistence of the attitudes", in *Psychosemantics*, MIT Press. Copyright © 1987 Massachusetts Institute of Technology. Reproduced with permission.

S.P. Stich, "Autonomous Psychology and the Belief–Desire Thesis", in *The Monist* 61, 4, 1978, pp. 573–91. Copyright © 1978, *The Monist: An International Quarterly Journal of General Philosophical Enquiry*, Peru, Illinois, 61354. Reprinted by permission.

IIB

W. Ramsey, S. Stich, and J. Garon, "Connectionism, eliminativism, and the future of folk psychology", in *Philosophical Perspectives* 4, 1990. Reproduced with permission of the publisher and the authors.

D. Dennett, "Real Patterns", in *The Journal of Philosophy* 88, 1991. Reproduced by kind permission of the journal and author.

IIC

P.M. Churchland, "Folk psychology and the explanation of human behaviour", in *Philosophical Perspectives* 3, 1989. Reproduced with permission.

A. Goldman, "Interpretation psychologized", in *Mind and Language* 4, 1989. Reproduced with permission.

ACKNOWLEDGMENTS

R. Gordon, "Simulation without introspection or inference from me to you", in M. Davies and T. Stone (eds), *Mental Simulation*, Blackwell, 1995. Reproduced with permission.

Part III

IIIA

D. Marr, *Vision*, W.H. Freeman, 1982; selection and editorial matter R. Cummins and D. Cummins (eds), *Minds, Brains, and Computers*, Blackwell, 2000. Reproduced with permission.

A. Newell and H.A. Simon, "Computer science as empirical inquiry: Symbol and search", in *Mind Design 2*, MIT Press, 1997. Copyright © 1997 Massachusetts Institute of Technology. Reproduced with permission.

D. Dennett, "Cognitive wheels: The frame problem of AI", in C. Hookway (ed.), *Minds, Machines and Evolution: Philosophical Studies*, 1984. Copyright © Cambridge University Press. Reproduced with permission.

IIIB

T. Horgan and J. Tienson, "Levels of description in non-classical cognitive science", in C. Hookway and D. Petersen (eds), *Philosophy and Cognitive Science*, 1993. Copyright © Cambridge University Press. Reproduced with permission.

T. van Gelder, "Compositionality: A connectionist variation on a classical theme", in *Cognitive Science* 14, 1990. Reproduced by kind permission of The Cognitive Science Society and the author.

IIIC

J. Fodor, "Précis of *The Modularity of Mind*", in *Behavioral and Brain Sciences* 8, 1985. Copyright © Cambridge University Press. Reproduced with permission.

G. Currie and K. Sterenly, "How to think about the modularity of mind-reading", in *Philosophical Quarterly* 50, 2000. Reproduced with permission.

L. Cosmides and J. Tooby, "Origins of domain specificity: The evolution of functional organization", in L.A. Hirschfeld and S.A. Gelman (eds), *Mapping the Mind: Domain Specificity in Cognition and Culture*, 1994. Copyright © Cambridge University Press. The final two sections have been omitted. Reproduced with permission.

ACKNOWLEDGMENTS

IIID

S. Stich, "Belief and subdoxastic states", in *Philosophy of Science* 45, 1978. Reproduced with permission.

G. Evans. "Semantic theory and tacit knowledge", in *Collected Papers*, Oxford University Press, 1985. Reproduced by kind permission of the publisher.

IIIE

G. Harman, "Language, thought, and communication", in *Reasoning, Meaning and Mind*, Oxford University Press, 1999. Reproduced by kind permission of the publisher.

P. Carruthers, "The cognitive functions of language", in *Behavioral and Brain Sciences* 25, 2002. Copyright © Cambridge University Press. Sections 6 and 7 have been omitted. Reproduced with permission.

J.L. Bermúdez, "Language and thinking about thoughts", in *Thinking without Words*, Oxford University Press, 2003. Reproduced by kind permission of the publisher.

The index was compiled by Santiago Amaya.

PART I

PICTURES OF THE MIND

INTRODUCTION

The articles in this section introduce four influential but very different ways of thinking about the mind/brain. Each picture of the mind offers a conceptual framework both for thinking about some of the key problems in the philosophy of psychology and for thinking about how to integrate the many different disciplines studying the mind/brain. We can view these four ways of thinking about the mind/brain as offering different responses to what I have elsewhere termed the *interface problem* (Bermúdez 2005).

The interface problem arises because we can study the mind/brain at many different levels. Philosophers typically think about the mind in very high-level ways. They are concerned with mental states such as beliefs and desires, hopes and fears, and their aim is to understand what these mental states are; how they are related to each other; and how they are realized by, or instantiated, in the brain. Psychologists, in contrast, often work at a somewhat lower level of analysis. Their interest is in the different capacities that we have for finding out about the world (both physical and social), for thinking about it, and for acting upon it. Psychologists want to understand both what these capacities are and what mechanisms underlie them. Moving still further down the hierarchy of explanation, neuroscientists study individual neurons and populations of neurons, trying to make sense of the structure and organization of the brain. These are all complementary investigations, and one of the most fundamental problems in the philosophy of psychology is working out how, if at all, they can be fitted together to form a unified theoretical perspective on the mind/brain.

Traditional philosophy of mind concerns itself with various versions of the so-called mind–body problem. The mind–body problem is standardly formulated at the level of individual mental states. How are individual mental states related to physical states? Philosophers of mind have answered this question in many different ways. According to behaviorists such as Ryle, mental states are complicated behavioral dispositions, so that a person's mental life is ultimately determined by how they are behaving and how they are disposed to behave. Identity theorists, on the other hand, take mental states to be identical to brain states, while functionalists argue that mental states stand to neural states in the same relation that software programs stand to the computer hardware that implements them.

3

In contrast to the traditional mind–body problem, which in effect asks about the physical basis for individual mental states such as particular beliefs and desires, the interface problem asks about the physical basis for our practices of commonsense psychological explanation – of explaining why people do what they do in terms of how they take the world to be (the beliefs that they have) and how they want things to turn out (the desires that they have). The interface problem is the problem of determining how commonsense psychological explanation is to be integrated with levels of explanation lower down in the hierarchy.

The interface problem: How does commonsense psychological explanation interface with the explanations of cognition and mental operations given by scientific psychology, cognitive science, cognitive neuroscience and the other levels in the explanatory hierarchy?

Each of the four pictures of the mind that are introduced in this section gives a very different response to the interface problem. The four views together form a spectrum.

At one end of the spectrum is the picture of the *autonomous mind*, which holds that the interface problem is not really a problem at all. Autonomy theorists make much of the distinction between *personal* and *subpersonal* levels of explanation (introduced by Dennett in Chapter 1) and argue that there is a fundamental discontinuity between explanations given at the personal level of commonsense psychology and explanations given at the various subpersonal levels of explanation explored by psychologists and neuroscientists. The picture of the autonomous mind understands the mind in terms of an autonomous and independent type of explanation that has no application to the non-psychological world and that interfaces only indirectly with the types of explanation applicable in the non-psychological realm.

According to the picture of the *functional mind*, however, there is no such fundamental distinction between personal and subpersonal levels of explanation. Commonsense psychological explanations are a species of causal explanation, no more and no less mysterious than the various types of causal explanation with which we are familiar both from science and from our everyday experience of the physical world. Mental states have associated with them a determinate causal role, specifying what normally gives rise to them and how they themselves typically give rise to other mental states and to behavior. This allows us to understand the mental states that feature in commonsense psychological explanation in terms of their causal dimension.

The picture of the *representational mind* shares with the functional picture the view that the essence of the mind is given by the causal dimension of mental states, but takes a rather different approach to the interface problem. The key idea behind the representational picture is that psychological states should be understood as relations to sentences in an internal language of thought, where the language of thought is a physically realized medium of thought that has many of the properties of a natural language. This allows representational theorists to think about thinking in terms of operations that act directly only on the physical properties of those inner sentences, but in a way that is sensitive to the semantic relations between those inner sentences (to the relations that hold between their meanings). The causal transitions between states of the representational mind are purely formal in a way that exactly mirrors the transitions between states of a digital computer. In fact, representationalists effectively claim that the mind can best be modeled as a digital computer.

At the other end of the spectrum from the conception of the autonomous mind lies the picture of the *neurocomputational mind*. Like representational theorists, proponents of the neurocomputational mind are deeply influenced by the requirements of modeling the mind, but they are inspired by a fundamentally different paradigm. Whereas the picture of the representational mind is motivated by the idea that the mind is a digital computer and can be studied as a piece of software, in complete independence of the hardware in which it is implemented, neurocomputational theorists are inspired by research into artificial neural networks, which are computer models of different types of cognitive ability explicitly designed to reflect certain features of how the brain is thought to process information. Neural networks do not seem to accommodate many of the features of commonsense psychological explanations, and this inspires proponents of the neurocomputational mind to stress the discontinuities between personal-level explanation and the neuroscientific explanations occurring at the bottom of the hierarchy. They propose a *co-evolutionary* model, on which our understanding of commonsense psychology coevolves with our understanding of the neural basis of cognition.

IA   The autonomous mind

Theorists of the autonomous mind, such as Donald Davidson, John McDowell, Jennifer Hornsby, and (in some of his incarnations) Daniel Dennett, seek to make a principled distinction between the activities and practices of commonsense psychological explanation, on the one hand, and the many different explanatory projects in the social, behavioral, and neural sciences. Although they each do so for very different reasons, these theorists all think that the enterprise of making sense of the thoughts and behavior of other people is a fundamentally different type of explanatory project from the enterprise of trying to understand the neural and psychological basis of cognition and behavior. The three papers in this section each offer a different way of motivating this distinction between different explanatory projects.

Daniel Dennett's "Personal and Subpersonal Levels of Explanation", drawn from his first book *Content and Consciousness*, gives a clear formulation of this basic distinction between two types of explanation, which he terms the distinction between *personal* and *subpersonal* levels of explanation. There is, Dennett argues, a fundamental difference between the activities and states characteristic of persons, on the one hand, and the activities and states characteristic of parts of persons, on the other. He claims that it is a mistake to think that questions about what a person does (questions formulated at the personal level) can be answered by appeal to operations and mechanisms at the subpersonal level. The example he gives is our ability to locate sensations – to scratch an itch, for example, or to reach to the location of a pain. Although there are of course afferent pathways that carry information to the brain about the location of painful stimuli on the body, it would be a mistake, Dennett thinks, to appeal to these afferent pathways and associated neural mechanisms in answer to the question of how we locate our sensations. Locating sensations is something that we as persons just do. At the personal level there is nothing more to be said. Moving to the subpersonal level does not provide further explanation. It merely changes the subject.

The second paper in this section is **Donald Davidson**'s "Psychology as Philosophy". Davidson's sophisticated version of the picture of the autonomous mind is derived from his well-known doctrine of *anomalous monism*. Anomalous monism combines the token-identity of mental and physical events (the idea that every mental event is identical to some physical event) with the denial that there can be any strict laws defined over mental states (where Davidson's paradigm of a strict law are the laws to be found in fundamental physics). It is this second claim (the so-called *anomalism of the mental*) that makes Davidson an autonomy theorist and that is explored and defended in this paper. The impossibility of strict laws involving mental states derives, according to Davidson, from the role of considerations of rationality in psychological explanation. When we try to make sense of other people's behavior, we are constrained to interpret them so that their behavior comes out as rational. We have to credit them with a psychological profile that rationalizes the way they behave, which forces us to see human behavior as taking place within a coherent and consistent psychological frame. Often enough, Davidson notes, "we must warp the evidence to fit this frame" (p. 29). There is, Davidson thinks, nothing corresponding to these requirements of rationality, coherence, and consistency when we move outside the realm of commonsense psychological explanation. This is what makes psychological explanation at the person level so fundamentally different from, and irreducible to, the various forms of explanation at the subpersonal level.[1]

In "Physicalist Thinking and Conceptions of Behaviour," **Jennifer Hornsby**, who has been much influenced by Dennett and Davidson, offers a different perspective on the distinction between personal and subpersonal levels of explanation. Whereas both Dennett and Davidson stress differences in the style of the two different explanatory projects and the constraints that govern them, Hornsby emphasizes what she takes to be the very different *explananda* (things to be explained) of the two explanatory projects. In very broad terms, both personal and subpersonal explanation can be seen as exploring the processes by which information arriving at the sensory periphery is processed and transformed in a manner that leads ultimately to behavior. This apparent similarity, however, obscures a fundamental point of difference. According to Hornsby, the concept of behavior is understood very differently in the two different explanatory projects. At the personal level, the behavior that is being explained is understood in a broad sense,

6

in terms of *actions* that are carried out *intentionally* for a *purpose*. At the subpersonal level, in contrast, the behavior that is being explained is understood narrowly, in terms of bodily movements/motor responses. Only if we equivocate between these two ways of understanding behavior does it seem possible to assimilate the two types of explanation. But, Hornsby argues, when we see how different they are, and that it is impossible to assimilate one to the other, we will appreciate that it is a mistake to try to explain facts at the personal level in terms of facts at the subpersonal level.

IB   The functional mind

Whereas supporters of the autonomous mind argue that, from the perspective of personal-level explanation, the connections between mental states and between mental states and behavior have to be understood in fundamentally rational terms, and hence as very different from the "ordinary" relations that hold between non-minded physical objects, the picture of the functional mind sees the connections between mental states and between mental states and behavior as being primarily causal. We understand behavior in terms of its causal antecedents, just as we understand everyday physical occurrences in terms of their causal antecedents. There is no basic difference of kind between explanation at the personal level and explanation at the subpersonal level. From this perspective, the key to understanding the mind is understanding the complex network of causal relations that hold between perceptual inputs and mental states; between different mental states; and between mental states and behavior. Commonsense psychology is itself a (partial) model of this complex network. The generalizations of commonsense psychology to which we appeal, either explicitly or implicitly, in psychological explanation are generalizations about causal relations within the network.

David Lewis's "Reduction of Mind" illustrates one way of resolving the interface problem on the picture of the functional mind, in the context of a global reductionism set out in the first few pages of the paper. Lewis envisages commonsense (or folk) psychology as a theory about the causal relations between perceptual stimuli, mental states, and motor responses. This theory allows us to think of mental states in terms of their *causal role*, where the causal role of a mental state is given by the causal generalizations in which it features. Causal roles are discoverable at the personal level, by processes of conceptual analysis. Truths about causal roles are, Lewis thinks, analytic truths. Once we have an understanding of these analytic truths about causal roles we resolve the interface problem by looking to psychology and neuroscience to tell us about the subpersonal states that *realize* or *implement* these causal roles. According to Lewis, empirical investigations at the subpersonal level will uncover a causal network of physical states that is isomorphic to the commonsense psychological theory arrived at on the basis of conceptual analysis.

In "Functionalism, Information and Content" **Robert Van Gulick** explores one key aspect of the functional picture. If we are to think of mental states as the occupiers of causal roles, then we have to explain how every aspect of a mental state can be derived from its causal role. In this context, it is helpful to bear in mind the distinction, originating with Frege, between the force and the content of a particular mental state. The force of my belief that, say, the cat is on the mat is the fact that it is a belief (as opposed to a desire, or a hope). Its content is the proposition that the cat is on the mat – a proposition that could equally be the content of the desire that the cat be on the mat. It is relatively straightforward to see how the force of a mental state can be understood in causal terms. The causal role of a belief is fundamentally different from the causal role of a desire in ways that are relatively easy to specify. If I believe that p, then I will act on the basis that p is the case, while if I desire that p, I will act in ways that I think likely to bring p about. But it is far more difficult to see how the content of a belief can be understood in causal terms. This is the problem that Van Gulick addresses. Van Gulick sets out to explain what makes a particular state an *informational* state. He offers an account in terms of notions of goal directedness and adaptiveness of the causal role that a mental state must play in order to qualify as a processing information for the organism. The basic idea is that states are informational just if they operate in ways that lead to adaptive modification of the organism's behavior in appropriate circumstances. The paper spells out how "adaptive modification" and "appropriate circumstances" are to be understood.

The picture of the functional mind, as presented by Lewis and other "functionalist" philosophers of mind, makes two very strong claims about the nature of psychological explanation. The first, which is one of the claims sharply distinguishing the functional mind from the autonomous mind, is the claim that personal level psychological explanation is ineliminably law-governed. As we might expect, given that the functional roles of mental states are fixed by the causal laws holding over those states, psychological explanation is essentially a matter of subsuming behavior under the relevant causal generalizations. This brings with it a second claim, this time about the nature of psychological explanation at the subpersonal level. It is a key tenet of the functional picture that we will be able to identify realizers at the subpersonal level for the functional roles defined at the personal level. But this seems to require a structural isomorphism between personal level and subpersonal explanation, which in turn demands that appropriate causal generalizations be identifiable at the subpersonal level. Both of these claims about psychological explanation have been challenged.

Proponents of the simulationist approach to commonsense psychology take issue with the first claim (see Part IIC), while the second claim is disputed in **Robert Cummins**'s "'How does it work?' versus 'What are the laws?'" Cummins argues that scientific psychology is not in the business of identifying laws. Such laws as there are in psychology are really effects that need to be explained – as opposed to laws that are capable of providing explanatory leverage in the way that the laws of physics are explanatory. According to Cummins, who is putting forward a version of the functional picture that is sometimes termed *homuncular functionalism*, psychological explanation is essentially an enterprise of *functional analysis*. In functional analysis, psychological capacities are analyzed in terms of

8

organized complexes of less sophisticated capacities. There is no single distinction between role and realizer (as on the Lewis-style functional picture), but rather a multitude of different levels of explanation, each of which can be seen as a realization of the level above it and each of which is itself realized by the next level down. The process of psychological explanation comes to an end when we "bottom out" in capacities that no longer count as psychological. This is a very different way of developing the functional picture from that proposed by Lewis but, Cummins would argue, one that is much closer to the actual practices of psychologists and neuroscientists.

IC   The representational mind

As we saw in Van Gulick's paper in Part IB, the standard way of developing the picture of the functional mind holds that both the force and the content of mental states are to be illuminated in terms of causal functional role. What makes the belief that *p* is a belief is the fact that it fulfills a particular role in the cognitive economy. And the fact that it fulfills this role is, moreover, what makes it a belief with the content *p*. On the picture of the representational mind, these two aspects of mental states come apart. Representational theorists are happy to explain the force of a mental state in terms of its causal role, but they do not extend this explanatory strategy to the content of mental states. We can see representational theorists as stressing a fundamentally different direction of explanation from functional theorists. Whereas the functional picture takes the causal role of psychological states as a given and accounts for their content on the basis of their causal role, representational theorists are motivated by the (arguably) more fundamental problem of how mental states can be causally efficacious in virtue of their contents in the first place. Psychological explanations work because they identify mental states that cause behavior in virtue of how they represent the world. But the fact that mental states can do this is itself puzzling.

Jerry Fodor's version of the representational theory offers a robust solution to this puzzle (see also "The Persistence of the Attitudes" in Part IIA). Psychological explanations, he argues, are computational explanations. That is, they presuppose that agents act the way they do as a result of sequences of computations carried out within a representational system. According to Fodor this has significant implications for how we think about the realizers of those mental states. In brief, Fodor thinks of computation as requiring a language-like representational medium (hence the label of the representational mind). This leads him to think of mental states as sentences in an internal language of thought, where a sentence in the language of thought has constituents corresponding to the logically relevant constituents of the content of the relevant mental state. The sentence in the language of thought that is the vehicle of my belief that Springfield is the capital of Illinois has constituents corresponding to the proper names "Springfield" and "Illinois" and to the two-place predicate "– is the capital of –". As he makes clear in other writings (see, for example, Fodor 1987), this allows him to resolve the puzzle of causation by content. Computations are mechanical processes sensitive only to the *formal* properties of representational states. The analogy in the background here is with operations in logical languages such as the first order predicate calculus – operations that can be viewed as operating solely on the "shape" of formulae in the logical language. Just as the *soundness* of a logical language ensures that syntactic transformations on well-formed formulae are truth preserving, the architecture of the mind is configured in such a way that causal relations between sentences in the language of thought track the semantic relations between the contents of those sentences.

In "The Language of Thought: First Approximations" Fodor is concerned to establish the first part of his argument. He considers three different types of explanatory project in psychology and argues that each only makes sense on the assumption that there is an internal language of thought. The three domains he considers are "considered action" (which he thinks requires organisms to compare the possible outcomes of different courses of action), concept learning, and perception (both of which he takes to involve processes of hypothesis formation and testing). Each domain, he argues, involves computations that are defined over language-like representations. And, since these basic forms of cognition are widespread among non-linguistic creatures (both non-human animals and prelinguistic children), Fodor concludes that the representational format cannot be an internalized public language. It must be a dedicated language of thought (Mentalese).

A different way of arguing for the language of thought hypothesis and the picture of the representational mind is to be found in **Georges Rey**'s "A Not 'Merely Empirical' Argument for a Language of Thought". Whereas Fodor's argument in the chapter reprinted here begins with what he takes to be basic explanatory practices in psychology (while his other writings explore some of the empirical constraints imposed by the possibility of causation by content), Rey explores the far more abstract question of what it is for a creature to count as being capable of rational thought. According to Rey, only creatures that are capable of making logical transitions between thoughts can be capable of rational thought. Logical transitions between thoughts are distinguished from transitions based upon association or conditioning. But what is involved in making such logical transitions? According to Rey, making logical transitions in thought requires being sensitive to the logical properties of thoughts. For some logical transitions (e.g. truth-functional transitions grounded in the logical properties of logical operators such as "and" and "or") these logical properties hold between individual thoughts. For other logical transitions, such as those codified in the predicate calculus, the logical properties in question are internal to individual thoughts. If I infer from the thought that the pen is on the table to the thought that there is at least one thing on the table, then I am exploiting the internal structure of the thought (since I am applying the form of inference that allows me to conclude from Fa that $\exists x\ Fx$). This, Rey thinks, means that the internal structure of the thought must be represented in a manner that is causally available, since transitions between thoughts must, in the last analysis, be causal transitions. But the hypothesis that the internal structure of a thought is causally accessible just is the language of thought hypothesis.

ID   The neurocomputational mind

Each of the three pictures of the mind we have been considering holds that we can only understand the mind by abstracting away from the details of how the brain works. On the picture of the autonomous mind it is a "category mistake" to look to subpersonal displines such as neuroscience to illuminate personal-level thought and behavior. The functional and representational pictures, on the other hand, are essentially *top-down* in orientation. Both pictures of the mind hold that commonsense psychology offers a privileged level of description for cognitive abilities and capacities. Once commonsense psychology has fixed the things that are to be explained at the subpersonal level, we work downwards through the hierarchy of different disciplines, identifying the realizers for causal roles, or the physical structures that implement sentences in the language of thought. Our fourth and final picture of the mind rejects this top-down model for understanding the mind. It is a fundamental tenet of the picture of the neurocomputational mind that our thinking about commonsense psychology must *coevolve* with our thinking about the neural basis of cognition. Whereas the top-down model of explanation rests on the assumption that we can understand any given level in the hierarchy independent of the levels below it, the neurocomputational picture is based on the idea that the boundaries between disciplines and levels of explanation are fluid and malleable, so that we need to see personal and subpersonal explanations as interlocking and interacting. In particular, we cannot hope to understand the mind without understanding the brain, since the way the brain works imposes important constraints upon our understanding of higher-level cognition and ordinary commonsense psychology.

Patricia Churchland and **Terence Sejnowski**'s "Neural Representation and Neural Computation" begins by presenting a clear statement of the co-evolutionary approach to studying the mind and cognition. They reject some of the standard arguments for what they call *theory dualism* (the view that we can understand the mind without understanding the brain), devoting particular attention to the language of thought hypothesis (which they term *sententialism*). Churchland and Sejnowski present a number of empirical considerations for thinking that cognition should not be understood in terms of computations defined over language-like symbolic structures in the way that the language of thought hypothesis holds. They observe, for example, that the brain is a parallel system, with huge numbers of simultaneous connections between neurons, rather than a serial processor, carrying out single algorithmic steps one at a time, as (they argue) it would have to be were the language of thought hypothesis to be correct. Nor, they suggest, do neurons operate sufficiently quickly for even the simplest serial computations to take place within a realistic framework. So how then should we think about neural computation?

We do not have the technology to study neural computation directly, despite recent advances in detailed knowledge of how the brain works. Techniques such as *functional magnetic resonance imaging* (fMRI) and *positron emission tomography* (PET) have allowed neuroscientists to begin establishing large-scale correlations between specific brain areas and particular cognitive tasks, while other techniques have made it possible to study brain activity at the level of the single neuron. Yet, although a functional map of the brain can tell us what cognitive tasks are carried out by which brain areas, it has nothing to say about *how* those tasks are carried out. And it is natural to think that neural computation requires the interaction of populations of neurons, rather than taking place at the level of individual neurons. The most promising strategy for understanding neural computation is to develop models of populations of neurons and then to investigate how they carry out particular cognitive tasks. Whereas the picture of the representational mind takes the mind to operate essentially like a digital computer, Churchland and Sejnowski propose looking to *connectionist* models (also known as *parallel distributed* models and *neural network* models) to illuminate how computation takes place in the brain. The final section of the paper shows how network modeling can be used to pursue the co-evolutionary research agenda.

Whereas Churchland and Sejnowski discuss specific neural network models such as NETtalk, **Peter McLeod**, **Kim Plunkett**, and **Edmund Rolls** in "The Attractions of Parallel Distributed Processing for Understanding Cognition" give a clear presentation of some of the general characteristics of neural network models, where they understand neural networks in very general terms as computational models in which information is distributed across many processing units and where computations take place in parallel across these processing units. As they bring out with reference to McClelland's well-known Jets and Sharks network, one of the distinguishing features of neural network models is that information is stored in them in a content-addressable manner. That is, if a connectionist network is given some part of a body of information it can recover the remaining parts. This is in opposition to ordinary digital computers, in which information is accessed through an *address* (much as the information in an encyclopedia entry can only be accessed through the keyword of the entry). As McLeod, Plunkett, and Rolls bring out, content-addressable connectionist networks display a number of the characteristics of human memory. In particular, they operate in ways that generate *typicality effects* (when "asked" to produce a random member of some collection they will produce a typical member). This is just one of the features of connectionist networks that have been thought to be biologically realistic. Another such feature that they discuss (and that Churchland and Sejnowski mention as something that serial processing models cannot accommodate) is the damage resistance and fault tolerance of neural networks. Since the output of a neural network model is determined by the "best fit" between current input and previously received information, they "degrade gracefully" when damaged, rather than suddenly cease to function in the manner of a damaged digital computer. They are also much more tolerant of noisy input.

Notes

1   In "Psychology as Philosophy" and elsewhere in his writings, Davidson is concerned with the basic distinction between commonsense psychological expla-

nation and explanation in the physical sciences, but the arguments he gives are really arguments for a principled distinction between explanations that involve propositional attitudes subject to constraints of rationality and consistency and explanations that do not – or, in other words, to a principled distinction between personal- and subpersonal-level explanations.

FURTHER READING

Survey texts

Bermúdez, J.L. (2005) *Philosophy of Psychology: A Contemporary Introduction*, New York: Routledge.

Braddon-Mitchell, D. and Jackson, F. (1996) *Philosophy of Mind and Cognition*, Oxford: Blackwell.

Dawson, M.R.W. (1998) *Understanding Cognitive Science*, Oxford: Blackwell.

Heil, J. (1998) *Philosophy of Mind: A Contemporary Introduction*, London: Routledge.

Kim, J. (1993) *Philosophy of Mind*, Oxford: Westview Press.

Rey, G. (1997) *Contemporary Philosophy of Mind*, Oxford: Blackwell.

Useful anthologies

Block, N. (ed.) (1980) *Readings in Philosophy of Psychology*, Cambridge, Mass.: Harvard University Press.

Haugeland, J. (1997) *Mind Design II*, Cambridge, Mass.: MIT Press.

Heil, J. (ed.) (2004) *Philosophy of Mind: A Guide and Anthology*, New York: Oxford University Press.

Lycan, W. (ed.) (1990/1999) *Mind and Cognition: A Reader*, Oxford: Blackwell. (1st edition 1990, 2nd edition 1999.)

IA   The autonomous mind

Davidson, D. (1970) "Mental Events". Reprinted in *Essays on Actions and Events*, Oxford: Clarendon Press (1980).

Dennett, D. (1969) *Content and Consciousness*, London: Routledge and New York: Humanities Press.

—— (1971) "Intentional Systems", *Journal of Philosophy* 68: 87–106. Reprinted in *Brainstorms: Philosophical Essays on Mind and Psychology*, Cambridge, Mass.: MIT Press (1981).

—— (1981) "True Believers: The Intentional Strategy and Why it Works", in *The Intentional Stance*, Cambridge: Cambridge University Press.

McDowell, J. (1994) "The Content of Perceptual Experience" *Philosophical Quarterly* 44: 196–205.

Ryle, G. (1949) *The Concept of Mind*, London: Penguin.

IB   The functional mind

Cummins, R. (1983) *The Nature of Psychological Explanation*, Cambridge, Mass.: MIT Press.

PART I: PICTURES OF THE MIND

Jackson, F. (1998) *From Metaphysics to Ethics. A Defence of Conceptual Analysis*, Oxford: Clarendon Press.

Kim, J. (1993) *Philosophy of Mind*, Oxford: Westview Press, Ch. 5.

Lewis, D. (1972) "Psychophysical and Theoretical Identifications", *Australasian Journal of Philosophy* 50: 249–58.

Shoemaker, S. (1981) "Some Varieties of Functionalism". Reprinted in *Identity, Cause, and Mind*, Cambridge: Cambridge University Press (1984).

IC   The representational mind

Copeland, J. (1993) *Artificial Intelligence: A Philosophical Introduction*, Oxford: Blackwell. Particularly Chs 4–5.

Dawson, M.R.W. (1998) *Understanding Cognitive Science*, Oxford: Blackwell, Ch. 2.

Fodor, J. (1987) *Psychosemantics*, Cambridge, Mass.: MIT Press.

Haugeland, J. (1998) "The Nature and Plausibility of Cognitivism", in *Having Thought Essays in the Metaphysics of Mind*, Cambridge, Mass.: Harvard University Press.

Pylyshyn, Z.W. (1980) "Cognition and Computation: Issues in the Foundations of Cognitive Science", *Behavioral & Brain Science* 3(1): 154–69.

Sterelny, K. (1990) *The Representational Theory of Mind*, Oxford: Blackwell.

ID   The neurocomputational mind

Bechtel, W. and Abrahamsen, A. (1991) *Connectionism and the Mind*, Oxford: Blackwell. (2nd edition 2001.)

Churchland, P.S. (1986) *Neurophilosophy: Toward a Unified Science of the Mind/Brain*, Cambridge, Mass.: MIT Press/Bradford Books.

Clark, A. (1993) *Associative Engines: Connectionism, Concepts and Representational Change*, Cambridge, Mass.: MIT Press/Bradford Books.

—— (1997) *Being There: Putting Brain, Body and World Together Again*, Cambridge, Mass.: MIT Press/Bradford Books.

Rumelhart, D.E. (1989) "The Architecture of Mind: A Connectionist Approach", in M. Posner (ed.), *Foundations of Cognitive Science*, Cambridge, Mass.: MIT Press. Reprinted in Haugeland (1997).

IA

THE AUTONOMOUS MIND

1

D.C. Dennett, "Personal and Sub-personal Levels of Explanation"

The physiology of pain is relatively well understood. When a pain is felt, neural impulses travel from the area in which the pain is felt along an anatomically distinct neural network for the transmission of pain stimuli. In many instances there is a peripheral reflex arc that triggers withdrawal, but there are also other as yet unanalysed effects in the central areas of the brain.

It is appropriate for an organism to heed the most pressing demands of survival, and the imminence of injury or death is as pressing as a demand can be, so it is altogether to be expected that a strongly entrenched pain network, essentially including appropriate responses of withdrawal, should be inherited. Moreover, as personal experience reveals, the behavioural reactions to pain are more difficult to overrule than any other behavioural tendencies. Genuine pain behaviour is compulsive, involuntary, and only with great 'will power' or special training can man or beast keep from reactions to pain. Whether or not such inherited afferent-efferent networks are a *sufficient* condition for the existence of the 'phenomenon of pain', it is safe to say they are a necessary condition. That is, it would be a very mysterious view that held that the bare phenomenon of pain could occur on the evolutionary scene before there were organisms that reacted appropriately to stimuli that were harbingers of injury. Pain could not appear until organisms began avoiding it. The question before us now is whether pain is something (some *thing*) in addition to the physical operations of the pain-network.

An analysis of our ordinary way of speaking about pains shows that no events or processes could be discovered in the brain that would exhibit the characteristics of the putative 'mental phenomena' of pain, because talk of pains is essentially non-mechanical, and the events and processes of the brain are essentially mechanical. When we ask a person why he pulled his hand away from the stove, and he replies that he did so because it hurt, or he felt pain in his hand, this looks like the beginning of an answer to a question of behavioural control, the question being how people know enough to remove their hands from things that can burn them. The natural 'mental process' answer is that the person has a 'sensation' which he identifies as pain, and which he is some-how able to 'locate' in his fingertips, and this 'prompts' him to remove his hand. An elaboration of this answer, however, runs into culs-de-sac at every turning.

17

The first unanswered question is how a person distinguishes a painful sensation from one that is not painful. It is no answer to say that painful sensations are just those that hurt, for then the question becomes how a person distinguishes sensations that hurt from sensations that do not. If this question is seen as asking for a criterion for sensations that hurt, a criterion used by the person to distinguish these sensations, the question admits of no answer, for one does not distinguish the sensations that hurt or are painful by applying some criterion; one simply distinguishes them. Their only distinguishing characteristic is painfulness, an unanalysable quality that can only be defined circularly. Moreover, a person's ability to distinguish this quality in sensations is ensured; one simply *can tell* when a sensation is painful (excluding cases where one's doubt is over whether the word 'pain' is too strong for the occasion). When trying to explain the discrimination of pains, appeal to the quality of painfulness is no advance over the question; it tells us nothing we did not already know. When one is asked how one tells an *x* from a *y* and answers that *x*'s have an indefinable characteristic which one is simply able to recognize but not describe, all one is saying is: I can tell – that's all.

The *mechanical* question, how is it done? is blocked. It is blocked not because the reply is that one is in the dark about how one distinguishes painful sensations from others, but because the reply is that no mechanical answer would be appropriate in this context. Pains or painful sensations are 'things' discriminated *by people*, not, for example, by brains (although brains might discriminate other things related to pains), and the question is: how do *you* (the person) distinguish pains from other sensations? The question admits of no answer because the *person* does not *do* anything in order to distinguish pains; he just distinguishes them. Distinguishing pains is not a personal *actvity*, and hence no answer of the form, first I do A and then I do B, makes any sense at all. But if this is so, the appeal to a quality of these discriminated sensations is gratuitous. A quality, to do any work in a theory, must be identified, but this means it must either be described or ostended. Description presupposes analysis, and in this instance analysis presupposes personal activity; where discrimination occurs without personal activity, no description of a discriminated quality is possible. Then, if the quality is to be identified at all, it must be ostended, but ostension of the quality in this instance cannot be separated from ostension of the discriminating. Where discriminating is an analysable personal activity, like discriminating good apples from bad by checking for colour and crispness, we can distinguish the qualities from the discriminating of them, but in the case of distinguishing sensations as painful, the act of discrimination itself is the only clue to the localization (in space and time) of the presumed quality. Insisting that, above and beyond our ability to distinguish sensations as painful, there is the quality of painfulness, is thus insisting on an unintelligible extra something.

The first cul-de-sac, then, is that a *person*'s power to discriminate painful sensations is a brute fact subject to no further questions and answers. The next question concerns the location of these pains, and meets the same fate. We do

18

not locate our pains with the aid of any independently describable qualities or 'local signs' provided us by the sensations; we just *can* locate them. Whatever the brain may be 'doing' when one locates a pain, the person does not do anything in the process of locating his pains, for there is no such process that a person could engage in. One could engage in the process of locating another person's pains, by asking him questions, poking around until he screams and so forth, but not in the process of locating one's own pains.

The third question left unanswered has already been shown to have no answer. What is there about painfulness that prompts us to avoid it, withdraw our hand, attempt to eliminate it? The question is dead because there is nothing *about* painfulness at all; it is an unanalysable quality. We simply do abhor pain, but not in virtue of anything (but its painfulness). If, in our attempt to build an explanatory bridge between sensation and action here, we invoke the appreciation of an unanalysable quality of painfulness, we are forced to choose between two non-explanations. We can either take it as a contingent fact that painfulness is something we dislike, but a contingent fact that admits of no explanation since painfulness is unanalysable; or we can take painfulness as necessarily abhorrent – something which by definition we withdraw from or avoid – in which case there is no room for explanation since 'we avoid pains' is then analytic, and cannot take the 'because' of causal explanation after it.

When we have said that a person has a sensation of pain, locates it and is prompted to react in a certain way, we have said all there is to say within the scope of this vocabulary. We *can* demand further explanation of how a person happens to withdraw his hand from the hot stove, but we cannot demand further explanations of terms of 'mental processes'. Since the introduction of unanalysable mental qualities leads to a premature end to explanation, we may decide that such introduction is wrong, and look for alternative modes of explanation. If we do this we must abandon the explanatory level of people and their sensations and activities and turn to the *sub-personal* level of brains and events in the nervous system. But when we abandon the personal level in a very real sense we abandon the subject matter of pains as well. When we abandon mental process talk for physical process talk we cannot say that the mental process analysis of *pain* is wrong, for our alternative analysis cannot be an analysis of pain at all, but rather of something else – the motions of human bodies or the organization of the nervous system. Indeed, the mental process analysis of pain is correct. Pains are feelings, felt by people, and they hurt. People can discriminate their pains and they do this not by applying any tests, or in virtue of any describable qualities in their sensations. Yet we do talk about the qualities of sensations and we act, react and make decisions in virtue of these qualities we find in our sensations.

Abandoning the personal level of explanation is just that: *abandoning* the pains and not bringing them along to identify with some physical event. The only sort of explanation in which 'pain' belongs is non-mechanistic; hence no identification of pains or painful sensations with brain processes makes sense,

2010
G. Press

and the physical, mechanistic explanation can proceed with no worries about the absence in the explanation of any talk about the discrimination of unanalysable qualities. What is the physical explanation to be? Something like this. When a person or animal is said to experience a pain there is afferent input which produces efferent output resulting in certain characteristic modes of behaviour centring on avoidance or withdrawal, and genuine pain behaviour is distinguished from feigned pain behaviour in virtue of the strength of the afferent-efferent connections – their capacity to overrule or block out other brain processes which would produce other motions. That is, the *compulsion* of genuine pain behaviour is given a cerebral foundation. Now would this account of pain behaviour suffice as an account of *real* pain behaviour, or is there something more that must be going on when a person is really in pain? It might be supposed that one could be suddenly and overwhelmingly compelled to remove one's finger from a hot stove without the additional 'phenomenon' of pain occurring. But although simple withdrawal may be the basic or central response to such stimulation, in man and higher animals it is not the only one. Could any sense be made of the supposition that a person might hit his thumb with a hammer and be suddenly and overwhelmingly compelled to drop the hammer, suck the thumb, dance about, shriek, moan, cry, etc., and yet *still* not be experiencing pain? That is, one would not be acting in this case, as on a stage; one would be compelled. One would be physically incapable of responding to polite applause with a smiling bow. Positing some horrible (but otherwise indescribable) quality or phenomenon to accompany such a compelled performance is entirely gratuitous.[1]

In one respect the distinction between the personal and sub-personal levels of explanation is not at all new. The philosophy of mind initiated by Ryle and Wittgenstein is in large measure an analysis of the concepts we use at the personal level, and the lesson to be learned from Ryle's attacks on 'para-mechanical hypotheses' and Wittgenstein's often startling insistence that explanations come to an end rather earlier than we had thought is that the personal and sub-personal levels must not be confused. The lesson has occasionally been misconstrued, however, as the lesson that the personal level of explanation is the *only* level of explanation when the subject matter is human minds and actions. In an important but narrow sense this is true, for as we see in the case of pain, to abandon the personal level is to stop talking about pain. In another important sense it is false, and it is this that is often missed. The recognition that there are two levels of explanation gives birth to the burden of relating them, and this is a task that is not outside the philosopher's province. It cannot be the case that there is *no* relation between pains and neural impulses or between beliefs and neural states, so setting the mechanical or physical questions off-limits to the philosopher will not keep the question of what these relations are from arising. The position that pains and beliefs are in one category or domain of inquiry while neural events and states are in another cannot be used to isolate the philosophical from the mechanical questions, for, as we have seen, different categories are no better than different Cartesian substances unless they are construed as different ontolog-ical categories, which is to say: the *terms* are construed to be in different categories and only one category of terms is referential. The only way to foster the proper separation between the two levels of explanation, to prevent the contamination of the physical story with unanalysable qualities or 'emergent phenomena', is to put the fusion barrier between them. Given this interpreta-tion it is in one sense true that there is no relation between pains and neural impulses, because there are no pains; 'pain' does not refer. There is no way around this. If there is to be *any* relation between pains and neural impulses, they will have to be related by either identity or non-identity, and if we want to rule out both these relations we shall have to decide that one of the terms is non-referential. Taking this step does not answer all the philosophical ques-tions, however, for once we have decided that 'pain'-talk is non-referential there remains the question of how each bit of the *talk* about pain is related to neural impulses or talk about neural impulses. This and parallel questions about other phenomena need detailed answers even after it is agreed that there are different sorts of explanation, different levels and categories. There is no one general answer to these questions, for there are many different sorts of talk in the language of the mind, and many different phenomena in the brain.

Notes

1   Cf. L. Wittgenstein: '"And yet you again and again reach the conclusion that the sensation itself is a nothing." Not at all. It is not a *something*, but not a *nothing* either! The conclusion was only that a nothing would serve just as well as a some-thing about which nothing could be said.' *Philosophical Investigations*, trans. G. E. M. Anscombe, Oxford, 1953, i 304.

2

D. Davidson,
"Psychology as Philosophy"

Not all human motion is behaviour. Each of us in this room is moving eastward at about 700 miles an hour, carried by the diurnal rotation of the earth, but this is not a fact about our behaviour. When I cross my legs, the raised foot bobs gently with the beat of my heart, but I do not move my foot. Behaviour consists in things we do, whether by intention or not, but where there is behaviour, intention is relevant. In the case of actions, the relevance may be expressed this way: an event is an action if and only if it can be described in a way that makes it intentional. For example, a man may stamp on a hat, believing it is the hat of his rival when it is really his own. Then stamping on his own hat is an act of his, and part of his behaviour, though he did not do it intentionally. As observers we often describe the actions of others in ways that would not occur to them. This does not mean that the concept of intention has been left behind, however, for happenings cease to be actions or behaviour only when there is no way of describing them in terms of intention.

These remarks merely graze a large subject, the relation between action and behaviour on the one hand, and intention on the other. I suggest that even though intentional action, at least from the point of view of description, is by no means all the behaviour there is, intention is conceptually central; the rest is understood and defined in terms of intention. If this is true, then any considerations which show that the intentional has traits that segregate it conceptually from other families of concepts (particularly physical concepts) will apply *mutatis mutandis* to behaviour generally. If the claim is mistaken, then the following considerations apply to psychology only to the extent that psychology employs the concepts of intention, belief, desire, hope, and other attitudes directed (as one says) upon propositions.

Can intentional human behaviour be explained and predicted in the same way other phenomena are? On the one hand, human acts are clearly part of the order of nature, causing and being caused by events outside ourselves. On the other hand, there are good arguments against the view that thought, desire and voluntary action can be brought under deterministic laws, as physical phenomena can. An adequate theory of behaviour must do justice to both these insights and show how, contrary to appearance, they can be reconciled.

By evaluating the arguments against the possibility of deterministic laws of behaviour, we can test the claims of psychology to be a science like others (some others).

When the world impinges on a person, or he moves to modify his environment, the interactions can be recorded and codified in ways that have been refined by the social sciences and common sense. But what emerge are not the strict quantitative laws embedded in sophisticated theory that we confidently expect in physics, but irreducibly statistical correlations that resist, and resist in principle, improvement without limit. What lies behind our inability to discover deterministic psychophysical laws is this. When we attribute a belief, a desire, a goal, an intention or a meaning to an agent, we necessarily operate within a system of concepts in part determined by the structure of beliefs and desires of the agent himself. Short of changing the subject, we cannot escape this feature of the psychological; but this feature has no counterpart in the world of physics.

The nomological irreducibility of the psychological means, if I am right, that the social sciences cannot be expected to develop in ways exactly parallel to the physical sciences, nor can we expect ever to be able to explain and predict human behaviour with the kind of precision that is possible in principle for physical phenomena. This does not mean there are any events that are in themselves undetermined or unpredictable; it is only events as described in the vocabulary of thought and action that resist incorporation into a closed deterministic system. These same events, described in appropriate physical terms, are as amenable to prediction and explanation as any.

I shall not argue here for this version of monism, but it may be worth indicating how the parts of the thesis support one another. Take as a first premise that psychological events such as perceivings, rememberings, the acquisition and loss of knowledge, and intentional actions are directly or indirectly caused by, and the causes of, physical events. The second premise is that when events are related as cause and effect, then there exists a closed and deterministic system of laws into which these events, when appropriately described, fit. (I ignore as irrelevant the possibility that microphysics may be irreducibly probabilistic.) The third premise, for which I shall be giving reasons, is that there are no precise psychophysical laws. The three premises, taken together, imply monism. For psychological events clearly cannot constitute a closed system; much happens that is not psychological, and affects the psychological. But if psychological events are causally related to physical events, there must, by premise two, be laws that cover them. By premise three, the laws are not psychophysical, so they must be purely physical laws. This means that the psychological events are describable, taken one by one, in physical terms, that is, they are physical events. Perhaps it will be agreed that this position deserves to be called *anomalous monism*: monism, because it holds that psychological events are physical events; anomalous, because it insists that events do not fall under strict laws when described in psychological terms.

My general strategy for trying to show that there are no strict psychophysical laws depends, first, on emphasizing the holistic character of the cognitive field. Any effort at increasing the accuracy and power of a theory of behaviour forces us to bring more and more of the whole system of the agent's beliefs and motives directly into account. But in inferring this system from the evidence, we necessarily impose conditions of coherence, rationality, and consistency. These conditions have no echo in physical theory, which is why we can look for no more than rough correlations between psychological and physical phenomena.

Consider our common-sense scheme for describing and explaining actions. The part of this scheme that I have in mind depends on the fact that we can explain why someone acted as he did by mentioning a desire, value, purpose, goal, or aim the person had, and a belief connecting the desire with the action to be explained. So, for example, we may explain why Achilles returned to the battle by saying he wished to avenge the death of Patroclus. (Given this much, we do not need to mention that he believed that by returning to the battle he could avenge the death of Patroclus.) This style of explanation has many variants. We may adumbrate explanation simply by expanding the description of the action: 'He is returning to battle with the intention of avenging the death of Patroclus.' Or we may more simply redescribe: 'Why is he putting on his armour?' 'He is getting ready to avenge Patroclus' death.' Even the answer, 'He just wanted to' falls into the pattern. If given in explanation of why Sam played the piano at midnight, it implies that he wanted to make true a certain proposition, that Sam play the piano at midnight, and he believed that by acting as he did, he would make it true.

A desire and a belief of the right sort may explain an action, but not necessarily. A man might have good reasons for killing his father, and he might do it, and yet the reasons not be his reasons in doing it (think of Oedipus). So when we offer the fact of the desire and belief in explanation, we imply not only that the agent had the desire and belief, but that they were *efficacious* in producing the action. Here we must say, I think, that causality is involved, i.e., that the desire and belief were causal conditions of the action. Even this is not sufficient, however. For suppose, contrary to the legend, that Oedipus, for some dark oedipal reason, was hurrying along the road intent on killing his father, and, finding a surly old man blocking his way, killed him so he could (as he thought) get on with the main job. Then not only did Oedipus want to kill his father, and actually kill him, but his desire caused him to kill his father. Yet we could not say that in killing the old man he intentionally killed his father, nor that his reason in killing the old man was to kill his father.

Can we somehow give conditions that are not only necessary, but also sufficient, for an action to be intentional, using only such concepts as those of belief, desire and cause? I think not. The reason, very sketchily stated, is this. For a desire and a belief to explain an action in the right way, they must cause it in the right way, perhaps through a chain or process of reasoning that meets standards of rationality. I do not see how the right sort of causal process can be distinguished without, among other things, giving an account of how a decision is reached in the light of conflicting evidence and conflicting desires. I doubt whether it is possible to provide such an account at all, but certainly it cannot be done without using notions like evidence, or good reasons for believing, and these notions outrun those with which we began.

What prevents us from giving necessary and sufficient conditions for acting on a reason also prevents us from giving serious laws connecting reasons and actions. To see this, suppose we had the sufficient conditions. Then we could say: whenever a man has such-and-such beliefs and desires, and such-and-such further conditions are satisfied, he will act in such-and-such a way. There are no serious laws of this kind. By a serious law, I mean more than a statistical generalization (the statistical laws of physics are serious because they give sharply fixed probabilities, which spring from the nature of the theory); it must be a law that, while it may have provisos limiting its application, allows us to determine in advance whether or not the conditions of application are satisfied. It is an error to compare a truism like 'If a man wants to eat an acorn omelette, then he generally will if the opportunity exists and no other desire overrides' with a law that says how fast a body will fall in a vacuum. It is an error, because in the latter case, but not the former, we can tell in advance whether the condition holds, and we know what allowance to make if it doesn't. What is needed in the case of action, if we are to predict on the basis of desires and beliefs, is a quantitative calculus that brings all relevant beliefs and desires into the picture. There is no hope of refining the simple pattern of explanation on the basis of reasons into such a calculus.

Two ideas are built into the concept of acting on a reason (and hence, the concept of behaviour generally): the idea of cause and the idea of rationality. A reason is a rational cause. One way rationality is built in is transparent: the cause must be a belief and a desire in the light of which the action is reasonable. But rationality also enters more subtly, since the way desire and belief work to cause the action must meet further, and unspecified, conditions. The advantage of this mode of explanation is clear: we can explain behaviour without having to know too much about how it was caused. And the cost is appropriate: we cannot turn this mode of explanation into something more like science.

Explanation by reasons avoids coping with the complexity of causal factors by singling out one, something it is able to do by omitting to provide, within the theory, a clear test of when the antecedent conditions hold. The simplest way of trying to improve matters is to substitute for desires and beliefs more directly observable events that may be assumed to cause them, such as flashing lights, punishments and rewards, deprivations, or spoken commands and instructions. But perhaps it is now obvious to almost everyone that a theory of action inspired by this idea has no chance of explaining complex behaviour unless it succeeds in inferring or constructing the pattern of thoughts and emotions of the agent.

The best, though by no means the only, evidence for desires and beliefs is action, and this suggests the possibility of a theory that deals directly with the relations between actions, and treats wants and thoughts as theoretical constructs. A sophisticated theory along these lines was proposed by Frank Ramsey.[1] Ramsey was primarily interested in providing a foundation in behaviour for the idea that a person accords one or another degree of credence to a proposition. Ramsey was able to show that if the pattern of an individual's preferences or choices among an unlimited set of alternatives meets certain conditions, then that individual can be taken to be acting so as to maximize expected utility, that is, he acts as if he assigns values to the outcomes on an interval scale, judges the plausibility of the truth of propositions on a ratio scale, and chooses the alternative with the highest computed expected yield.

Ramsey's theory suggests an experimental procedure for disengaging the roles of subjective probability (or degree of belief) and subjective value in choice behaviour. Clearly, if it may be assumed that an agent judges probabilities in accord with frequencies or so-called objective probabilities, it is easy to compute from his choices among gambles what his values are; and similarly one can compute his degree of belief in various propositions if one can assume that his values are, say, linear in money. But neither assumption seems justified in advance of evidence, and since choices are the resultant of both factors, how can either factor be derived from choices until the other is known? Here, in effect, is Ramsey's solution: we can tell that a man judges an event as likely to happen as not if he doesn't care whether an attractive or an unattractive outcome is tied to it, if he is indifferent, say, between these two options:

	Option 1	Option 2
If it rains you get:	$1,000	a kick
If it doesn't rain:	a kick	$1,000

Using this event with a subjective probability of one half, it is possible to scale values generally, and using these values, to scale probabilities.

In many ways, this theory takes a long step towards scientific respectability. It gives up trying to explain actions one at a time by appeal to something more basic, and instead postulates a pattern in behaviour from which beliefs and attitudes can be inferred. This simultaneously removes the need for establishing the existence of beliefs and attitudes apart from behaviour, and takes into systematic account (as a construct) the whole relevant network of cognitive and motivational factors. The theory assigns numbers to measure degrees of belief and desire, as is essential if it is to be adequate to prediction, and yet it does this on the basis of purely qualitative evidence (preferences or choices between pairs of alternatives). Can we accept such a theory of decision as a scientific theory of behaviour on a par with a physical theory?

Well, first we must notice that a theory like Ramsey's has no predictive power at all unless it is assumed that beliefs and values do not change over time. The theory merely puts restrictions on a temporal cross-section of an agent's dispositions to choose. If we try experimentally to test the theory, we run into the difficulty that the testing procedure disturbs the pattern we wish to examine. After spending several years testing variants of Ramsey's theory on human subjects, I tried the following experiment (with Merrill Carlsmith). Subjects made all possible pairwise choices within a small field of alternatives, and in a series of subsequent sessions, were offered the same set of options over and over. The alternatives were complex enough to mask the fact of repetition, so that subjects could not remember their previous choices, and pay-offs were deferred to the end of the experiment so that there was no normal learning or conditioning. The choices for each session and each subject were then examined for inconsistencies – cases where someone had chosen *a* over *b*, *b* over *c*, and *c* over *a*. It was found that as time went on, people became steadily more consistent; intransitivities were gradually eliminated; after six sessions, all subjects were close to being perfectly consistent. This was enough to show that a static theory like Ramsey's could not, even under the most carefully controlled conditions, yield accurate predictions: merely making choices (with no reward or feedback) alters future choices. There was also an entirely unexpected result. If the choices of an individual over all trials were combined, on the assumption that his 'real' preference was for the alternative of a pair he chose most often, then there were almost no inconsistencies at all. Apparently, from the start there were underlying and consistent values which were better and better realized in choice. I found it impossible to construct a formal theory that could explain this, and gave up my career as an experimental psychologist.

Before drawing a moral from this experiment, let me return to Ramsey's ingenious method for abstracting subjective values and probabilities simultaneously from choice behaviour. Application of the theory depends, it will be remembered, on finding a proposition with a certain property: it must be such that the subject does not care whether its truth or its falsity is tied to the more attractive of two outcomes. In the context of theory, it is clear that this means, *any* two outcomes. So, if the theory is to operate at all, if it is to be used to measure degrees of belief and the relative force of desire, it is first necessary that there be a proposition of the required sort. Apparently, this is an empirical question; yet the claim that the theory is true is then a very sweeping empirical claim. If it is ever correct, according to the theory, to say that for a given person a certain event has some specific subjective probability, it must be the case that a detailed and powerful theory is true concerning the pattern of that person's choice behaviour. And if it is ever reasonable to assert, for example, that one event has a higher subjective probability than another for a given person, then there must be good reason to believe that a very strong theory is true rather than false.

From a formal point of view, the situation is analogous to fundamental measurement in physics, say of length, temperature, or mass. The assignment of numbers to measure any of these assumes that a very tight set of conditions holds. And I think that we can treat the cases as parallel in the following respect. Just as the satisfaction of the conditions for measuring length or mass may be viewed as constitutive of the range of application of the sciences that employ these measures, so the satisfaction of conditions of consistency and rational coherence may be viewed as constitutive of the range of applications of such concepts as those of belief, desire, intention, and action. It is not easy to describe in convincing detail an experiment that would persuade us that the transitivity of the relation of *heavier than* had failed. Though the case is not as extreme, I do not think we can clearly say what should convince us that a man at a given time (without change of mind) preferred *a* to *b*, *b* to *c*, and *c* to *a*. The reason for our difficulty is that we cannot make good sense of an attribution of preference except against a background of coherent attitudes.

The significance of the experiment I described a page or so back is that it demonstrates how easy it is to interpret choice behaviour so as to give it a consistent and rational pattern. When we learn that apparent inconsistency fades with repetition but no learning, we are apt to count the inconsistency as merely apparent. When we learn that frequency of choice may be taken as evidence for an underlying consistent disposition, we may decide to write off what seem to be inconsistent choices as failures of perception or execution. My point is not merely that the data are open to more than one interpretation, though this is obviously true. My point is that if we are intelligibly to attribute attitudes and beliefs, or usefully to describe motions as behaviour, then we are committed to finding, in the pattern of behaviour, belief, and desire, a large degree of rationality and consistency.

A final consideration may help to reinforce this claim. In the experiments I have been describing, it is common to offer the subject choices verbally, and for him to respond by saying what he chooses. We assume that the subject is choosing between the alternatives described by the experimenter, i.e. that the words used by subject and experimenter have the same interpretation. A more satisfying theory would drop the assumption by incorporating in decision theory a theory of communication. This is not a peripheral issue, because except in the case of the most primitive beliefs and desires, establishing the correctness of an attribution of belief or desire involves much the same problems as showing that we have understood the words of another. Suppose I offer a person an apple and a pear. He points to the apple, and I record that he has chosen the apple. By describing his action in this way, I imply that he intended to point to the apple, and that by pointing he intended to indicate his choice. I also imply that he believed he was choosing an apple. In attributing beliefs we can make very fine distinctions, as fine as our language provides. Not only is there a difference between his believing he is choosing an apple and his believing he is choosing a pear. There is even a difference between his believing he is choosing the best apple in the box and his believing he is choosing the largest apple, and this can happen when the largest is the best.

All the distinctions available in our language are used in the attribution of belief (and desire and intention); this is perhaps obvious from the fact that we can attribute a belief by putting any declarative sentence after the words, 'He believes that'. There is every reason to hold, then, that establishing the correctness of an attribution of belief is no easier than interpreting a man's speech. But I think we can go further, and say that the problems are identical. Beliefs cannot be ascertained in general without command of a man's language; and we cannot master a man's language without knowing much of what he believes. Unless someone could talk with him, it would not be possible to know that a man believed Fermat's last theorem to be true, or that he believed Napoleon had all the qualities of a great general.

The reason we cannot understand what a man means by what he says without knowing a good deal about his beliefs is this. In order to interpret verbal behaviour, we must be able to tell when a speaker holds a sentence he speaks to be true. But sentences are held to be true partly because of what is believed, and partly because of what the speaker means by his words. The problem of interpretation therefore is the problem of abstracting simultaneously the roles of belief and meaning from the pattern of sentences to which a speaker subscribes over time. The situation is like that in decision theory: just as we cannot infer beliefs from choices without also inferring desires, so we cannot decide what a man means by what he says without at the same time constructing a theory about what he believes.

In the case of language, the basic strategy must be to assume that by and large a speaker we do not yet understand is consistent and correct in his beliefs – according to our own standards, of course. Following this strategy makes it possible to pair up sentences the speaker utters with sentences of our own that we hold true under like circumstances. When this is done systematically, the result is a method of translation. Once the project is under way, it is possible and indeed necessary, to allow some slack for error or difference of opinion. But we cannot make sense of error until we have established a base of agreement.

The interpretation of verbal behaviour thus shows the salient features of the explanation of behaviour generally: we cannot profitably take the parts one by one (the words and sentences), for it is only in the context of the system (language) that their role can be specified. When we turn to the task of interpreting the pattern, we notice the need to find it in accord, within limits, with standards of rationality. In the case of language, this is apparent, because understanding it is *translating* it into our own system of concepts. But in fact the case is no different with beliefs, desires, and actions.

The constitutive force in the realm of behaviour derives from the need to view others, nearly enough, as like ourselves. As long as it is behaviour and not something else we want to explain and describe, we must warp the evidence to fit this frame. Physical concepts have different constitutive elements. Standing ready, as we must, to adjust psychological terms to one set of standards and physical terms to another, we know that we cannot insist on a sharp and law-like connection between them. Since psychological phenomena do not constitute a closed system, this amounts to saying they are not, even in theory, amenable to precise prediction or subsumption under deterministic laws. The limit thus placed on the social sciences is set not by nature, but by us when we decide to view men as rational agents with goals and purposes, and as subject to moral evaluation.

Notes

1   'Truth and Probability'. Ramsey's theory, in a less interesting form, was later, and independently, rediscovered by von Neumann and Morgenstern, and is sometimes called a theory of decision under uncertainty, or simply decision theory, by economists and psychologists.

3

J. Hornsby, "Physicalist Thinking and Conceptions of Behaviour"

1. I start from two pictures. One presents a view of what is involved when we ascribe propositional attitudes to one another. The other presents a view of what is involved when the scientist treats a human being as a physical thing – of what a neurophysiologist sees as going on when he concerns himself with the stimulations of sense organs, with the motor responses in a person's body, and with events and states that intervene between such stimulations and responses.

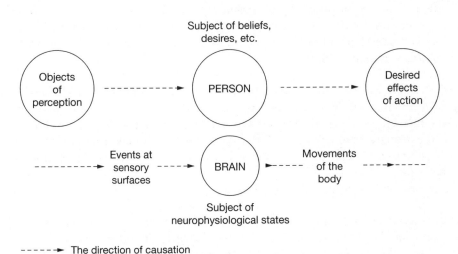

The direction of causation

One has only to look at these two picture to be tempted to make a superimposition. Two considerations may combine to make the temptation irresistible. First, the brain and central nervous system is a part of a person whose proper functioning is a necessary condition of that person's having the effects on the world she desires to have. Second, the causal chains that lead up to and away from a person's psychological states apparently pass through the events depicted in the area that circumscribes the neurophysiologist's study.

If you extend the causal chains of the representation of the brain backwards and forwards, what you reach is the elements standing at the left and right of the representation of the person. The dependence of the person's functioning on the functioning of her brain may make one think of the brain as a mechanism inside the person which is responsible for producing the effects in virtue of which she has her distinctive effects on the world. But then the common properties of the brain's states and of the person's mental states – states of each sort being seen as causal intermediaries – may make one think that in placing the brain inside the person one locates the propositional–attitude states there. Many will therefore feel compelled to say that particular beliefs and desires *are* the neurophysiological states of a person.

This line of thought gives a very quick argument for a version of physicalism. Perhaps no one wishes to acknowledge that he takes such a direct or simple route. But I think that there is a widespread presumption that if beliefs and desires have any place in the physical world, then they are internal states of persons, or of their brains; and I think that this presumption can be created by the sort of high-level comparison of pictures I have just imagined. My project in this paper is to question certain versions of physicalism the quick argument may seem to recommend, by challenging the envisaged superimposition of the two pictures. More particularly, I shall challenge the use to which a certain conception of *behaviour* is put. According to this conception, *behaviour* subsumes both a brain's outputs and a person's outputs, and thus provides an area common to both pictures.

2. Naively we think that we can become informed about people's answers to such questions as 'Why did she keep to the edge of the pond?' or 'Why did she turn on the burner?'. And we suppose that such answers give psychological explanations of behaviour. But it is often said nowadays that any account of psychological explanatory states is bound to use a purely bodily notion of behaviour.

Consider, for example, Kim's claims:[1]

> [An] action of turning on the burner, insofar as this is thought to involve the burner going on, is not an action that it is the proper business of psychological theory to explain or predict. . . . It is not part of the object of *psychological* explanation to explain why the burner went on. . . . The job of psychological explanation is done once [psychological theory] has explained the bodily action of turning a knob; whether or not this action results in my also turning on the stove, my starting cooking the dinner . . . is dependent on facts quite outside the province of psychology, [which] are not the proper concern of psychological theory.

Kim and others believe, then, that we ought to recognize psychology's proper business to be much narrower than we naively take it to be.

Kim's claim that psychological states cannot serve to explain (for example) why Kim turned on the burner is rested on the premiss that such states do not serve to explain why the burner went on. Both the premiss and the argument here may be questioned. In order to question the premiss, one must take a relaxed view about psychological explanation. Then it will seem that it can be psychologically explained (for example) why a burner went on. 'Why did the burner go on? Is the switch faulty?' 'No: Jane turned it on, she wanted to make some tea'.

To question the argument, one may take a less relaxed view and start with the assumption that any psychological explanation has as its explanandum why some person did what she did. The principle underlying the argument would then seem to be something like this:

> Even if the explanation why p appears to be the fact that z, still if q and r are necessary for p and the fact that z does not explain why q, then the fact that z can only really explain why r.

But such a principle is surely unacceptable. Suppose that we thought that we could explain why the window broke by saying that a heavy stone hit it at speed. We then notice that the window's breaking required that the window be situated at p and that p be on the stone's trajectory, and that the stone's hitting the window at speed does not explain why the window is situated at p. We do not conclude that after all the stone's hitting the window at high speed cannot really explain why the window broke.[2]

It is a question how narrow the province of what is psychologically explained would become if one endorsed Kim's argument wholeheartedly. Kim himself speaks as if *turning a knob*, unlike *turning on the burner*, were an admissible object of psychological explanation. Yet *turning a knob* is surely proscribed for him: it seems no more to be 'part of the object of psychological explanation' to explain why a knob turned than it is to explain why the burner went on. And we may wonder whether in fact Kim's principle does not rule out psychological explanations even of 'bodily actions' – of why someone moved her finger, say; for it is by no means obvious that someone's moving her finger is not 'dependent on facts which are not the proper concern of psychological theory'. (I return to this at the end of section 3.)

Of course Kim's conclusion about the objects of psychological explanation may not be meant to rely on the principle alone. It may rely on a prior view of psychological states – as internal states of people which are the immediate causal ancestors of movements of their bodies. This view is certainly held by functionalists. And the functionalists' conception of behaviour may be supposed to recommend itself on the merits of functionalism. So it will be worth discovering whether the attractions of functionalism can survive scrutiny of the particular notion of behaviour that that doctrine employs.

3. Functionalists think that the defining feature of any type of mental state is given by describing the causal relations that its instances bear (a) to the

environment's effects on a person, (b) to mental states of other types, and (c) to a person's effects on the environment. And they think that mental terms can be simultaneously implicitly defined in a total psychological theory of all the types of mental states. Such a theory contains terms of two sorts, which David Lewis has called the T-terms and the O-terms. The T-terms are, intuitively, mental terms, to be thought of as receiving implicit definition; in a functional theory, their denotations are accorded functional roles that are specified using only the non-mental O-terms. The functionalist thinks of the functional theory (abstracted, as it were, from the psychological theory) as true of, or realized by, the physical states of individuals: physical states occupy the functional roles of mental states.[3]

Functionalism is to be understood here as a thesis in the philosophy of mind, which treats of those states and events that in the ordinary way we attribute to one another, for example in explaining action. We can ask then 'What does the functionalist have to say about the role of the propositional–attitude states in producing action?'. Put in the functionalist's own terms, this is a question about output generalizations ((c) above), which are meant to give an account of the systematic ways in which such states as beliefs lead, as it is said, to behaviour.

We are told that behaviourism is the ancestor of functionalism, and that functionalism inherits the virtues of behaviourism. But the functionalist's notion of behaviour is very much more restrictive than that which some of the behaviourists employed. When functionalists speak of behaviour, they speak, like Kim, of bodily movements, or else they speak of motor responses.[4] When Ryle spoke about behaviour, he meant such characterizations of people's actions as these: 'telling oneself and others that the ice is thin, skating warily, shuddering, dwelling in imagination on possible disasters, warning other skaters, keeping to the edge of the pond'.[5] (It is true that some behaviourists were reductionists, and that they used a narrower conception of behaviour than Ryle. But if one is allowed to think of functionalism as inheriting its attractions from a non-reductionist position, then Ryle's everyday use of 'behaviour' ought not to be legislated into invisibility.)

There are two important differences here between the (Rylean) behaviourist and the functionalist. The behaviourist makes allusion to things beyond the agent's body in his specifications of behaviour, but the functionalist does not. And the behaviourist's behavioural items are actions (that is, events of people doing things such as moving their bodies), whereas the functionalist's behavioural items are apparently not actions, but movements of people's bodies (which are either effects of actions, or proper parts of actions, depending upon your views).[6] We need to understand why the functionalists should depart from the behaviourists in these two ways and employ the particular conception that they do.

The functionalist's stated objection to behaviourism is familiar enough: the behaviourist said that to believe something (for instance) is to be disposed to certain behaviour, whereas the functionalist insists that belief cannot be defined in terms of behaviour alone, because allowance has to be made for the simultaneous determination of behaviour by many different mental states. In this point alone, however, there is nothing that evidently constrains one to used a bodily conception of behaviour. And we need to notice something else, which is seldom stated very explicitly by functionalists; the behaviourists' neglect of the interdependencies between mental things was not in fact the only defect of behaviourism that the functionalist needed to correct for. Certainly, if your belief that it is going to rain is to lead you to take your umbrella, then you need (for example) to want not to get wet and to believe that umbrellas keep the rain off, and to have no other countervailing desires or interfering beliefs. But equally certainly, if your belief that it is going to rain is to lead you to take your umbrella, then you need to believe of something that is your umbrella *that* it is your umbrella. Not only can it not be left out of account what desires a person has (as the behaviourist seemed to suppose), it also cannot be taken for granted that what people believe is true. Avoiding taking this for granted, one might say that someone who believes that *p* is (very roughly) someone who would, *given that p*, realize such desires as prevailed given her other desires and beliefs. But there is a problem about incorporating this into a functionalist psychological theory as it stands. For this does not tell us, in behavioural terms however broadly construed, what someone with a certain belief would ever unconditionally *do*.

There are two ways in which the functionalist might try to make allowance for the fact that it is only where other relevant beliefs of the agent are true that behaviour as we naturally and widely conceive it is predictably matched with particular desires and beliefs. First, he might settle for using what one could call a world-conditioned notion of behaviour, saying, at the behavioural end of an output generalization, that a person would do things of this sort: such-and-such-if-the-world-is-as-it-would-be-if-relevant-beliefs-of-the-agent-were-true. (I return to this idea in section 5.) Second, he might restrict the notion of behaviour, so that something counts as a description of behaviour only if an agent can be expected to satisfy it irrespective of whether her beliefs are true. In talking about behaviour, he then confines himself to those things that an agent would do no matter whether the world were as she believed it to be – things, one might say, that she is *simply able* to do.

This provides the real explanation of why the functionalist should go back to the body in describing behaviour. And perhaps we can now also understand the functionalist's other deviation from the behaviourist – his not treating actions themselves as behavioural items. Even if a person's beliefs about what it is to ϕ are false, she will at least *try* to ϕ if she has overwhelming reason to ϕ (or so a functionalist may say). It seems then that the notion of *trying* or *attempting* can be introduced if one wants a means of saying in 'purely psychological' terms what someone's beliefs and desires in conjunction do produce. One then arrives at a two-stage account of action production, such as can be found in some functionalist writings.[7] At the first stage, one says how beliefs and desires modify one another and mediate the production of attempts; so much is 'pure psychology', in the language of the T-terms. At the second stage, one says what attempts to do things would actually bring about, whatever the truth values of the beliefs that led to those attempts; the idea is that a sufficiently motivated agent who is *simply able* to do something will do that thing. This second stage takes one from the T-terms to the O-terms; and it is here that one is constrained to use the bodily movement vocabulary for describing behaviour, and to speak (not of actions themselves, but) only of things that are the most immediate, bodily effects of a person's attempts.

Something like this functionalist view of action production is presumably shared by Kim (section 2). But what one now gets at the second stage of the account of action production will be instances of

a tries to ϕ & a is *simply able* to ϕ → there occurs a ϕ-type movement

(where to be a 'ϕ-type movement' is, intuitively, to be a movement of the type associated with actions of ϕ-ing). And this means that, unless we are prepared to say that an agent's being *simply able* to do something is a 'proper concern of psychological theory', the argument that Kim gave in order to encourage us to suppose that only 'bodily action' is genuinely psychologically explicable could he used again now to show that even movements of bodies are not things 'that it is the proper business of psychological theory to explain or predict'. But an agent's being *simply able* to move a part of her body is constituted by the integrity and functioning of the relevant bits of her motor system and the absence of constraints on her body itself, and such things are in no obvious or intuitive sense psychological and would seem to be quite on a par with (for instance) the burner's being such as to light when the knob is turned. Following through on Kim's argument, then, the province of psychological explanation would become even more circumscribed than Kim allowed: the proper objects of psychological explanation could only be events described as agents' *trying* to do things.[8]

4. Functionalists for their part will probably be happy to allow that conditions relating to agents' *simple abilities* have to be specified using T-terms and be caught up with psychological theory. Their aim is to show how some of the brain's complexity can be seen to mirror the complexity of the propositional–attitude scheme. And it might seem that the use of purely bodily O-terms for describing people's outputs is in no way inimical to that aim. Although a bodily motion of behaviour is more restricted than an everyday one, there is much that can be said about people's bodies' movements, and it may seem that functionalists can avail themselves of anything that can be said about them and proceed to an interesting psychological theory.

But it must not be forgotten that functionalist output generalizations are still meant to be got from what we all know about action-explanation in knowing common-sense psychology. One thing that we know is that ϕ-ing is a proper explanandum of the common-sense psychological scheme only if agents have some beliefs in the ascription of which ϕ -ing could be mentioned. So functionalists are not in fact entitled to use whatever bodily movement terms they like; their resources can include only such terms as could be used in giving the contents of agents' mental states. It seems, then, that they must refrain from using any very detailed bodily movement terms.

In fact it will be controversial exactly how much detail can enter into the bodily movement descriptions of common-sense psychology. If someone turns on a light (say), how detailed can a bodily description be of what she intentionally does, or tries to do? What beliefs about the movements of their bodies do people in practice employ? My own view is that hardly any detail can enter. When we engage in the practice of skills that require the manipulation of objects, for instance, it is unclear that we employ any beliefs which concern purely and simply the movements of our hands. It seems that a person can act as a result of having beliefs and desires, while having next to nothing in the way of beliefs about how her body moves when she acts.[9] And if this is right, then the functionalist, in confining himself to bodily movements, confines himself to an extremely impoverished notion of behaviour indeed.

What is certain is that functionalists don't in fact envisage using a notion of behaviour that would strike us as at all impoverished. Even if common-sense bodily movement descriptions can be richer than I have just suggested, we may still doubt that they can be as rich as those that functionalists actually want to employ. In functionalist writings, one often finds what appear to be gestures towards great complication in accounts of behaviour. Armstrong spoke of 'making certain motions with the hand and so on'; he remarked that this was vague, and said that 'the matter might be investigated in a time-and-motion study for instance'.[10] Lewis speaks of 'Karl's fingers moving on certain trajectories and exerting certain forces'.[11] It can seem as if the functionalists, feeling that the complexity of the propositional–attitude scheme must indeed demand some richness in the specification of behaviour, simply ignore the common-sense character of the truths about propositional attitudes that they represent themselves as beginning from.

It will be no good saying that, since every bodily movement does have some detailed description of which a student of time-and-motion or a physiologist could become apprised, any detail that the functionalist's aims require can always be introduced into functionalist theories. For one thing, the student of time-and-motion may discover that the sorts of bodily movements that agents think of themselves as going in for are not connected in systematic ways with the sorts of motions his studies concern.[12] And although it is surely right that there are, occasion by occasion, identities between the (coarse) bodily movement effects of actions and the (refined) bodily movement effects of finely discriminated states of the nervous system, it is unclear that this can help the functionalist who is trying to avoid a notion of behaviour that strikes him as too crude for the use to which he wants to put it. Someone who hoped to use physiological knowledge occasion by occasion to pin down the neurophysiological states that caused some effect of some action would have lost sight of one of the functionalists' aspirations – to use our knowledge of interpersonal psychology to define types of mental state.

5. I suggest that some of the allure of functionalism has resulted from failure to keep track of the use of the simple term 'behaviour'. The elements of common sense that give rise to the idea of a psychological theory seem correct when 'behaviour' is understood in Ryle's way, as including all the many things an agent does. The idea of a functional theory realized in neurophysiological states seems correct when 'behaviour' is understood in (say) the physiologist's way, as an agent's moving her body in all kinds of complex fashions. These two notions of behaviour overlap, and when 'bodily movements' is used to catch them both, they are made to appear to coincide. But the two notions do not coincide. And if one wants to preserve both common sense and the idea about functional theories, then one can only conclude that there is a complexity in propositional–attitude psychology that does not derive from any complexity in people's bodily movements conceived in ways available to common-sense psychology.[13]

No doubt many functionalists will say that theoretical psychology has to be enlisted in the service of common-sense psychology. They would make proposals about how theoretical psychological findings could be brought to bear on common-sense psychological states, and they would claim that the proposals will enable us to discover states that must be counted as beliefs and desires even though common-sense psychology unaided would never have recognized them as such.[14] It is as if common-sense psychology had a hidden complexity that the theoretical psychologist could uncover experimentally; as if the superimposition of the picture of the person on the picture of the brain could reveal a sort of complexity in the picture of the person which ordinarily goes unheeded. But why should we think that common-sense psychology, in order to achieve what we can all achieve using it, must really be capable of achieving a great deal more that non-theoreticians will never know about? If common-sense psychology has no concern with how exactly we move our fingers when we turn on lights (say), then this is because we do not have to try to move our fingers in the exact way in which we actually move them in order to turn on a light when we want to. But where the details of bodily movements are not within common-sense psychology's province, how can that which bears on the details have a bearing on common-sense psychological states? How can theoretical psychology dictate to common sense answers to questions that it is in the nature of common sense not to ask?

Instead of resorting to theoretical psychology, we could suppose that the picture of the brain cannot be superimposed on the picture of the person because the picture of the person has its own fine points which are not such as to be exposed in the structure of the brain. What we should then have to exploit in understanding the felt complexity of propositional–attitude psychology is not the brain's complexity, but our knowledge that common-sense psychology enables us to explain so much more than why there are the movements of people's bodies that there are. The step from a Rylean sort of behaviourism to functionalism will then seem to have been, in a way, a retrograde step. If mental states are to be thought of as dispositions of any sort (or, if you prefer, as states that are parts of systems that exhibit an overall structure), then, to the extent that they are dispositions to behave (or states connected systematically with ways of behaving), the relevant notion of behaviour is the broad one that the philosopher behaviourists used and the functionalists left behind.

If we do employ the ordinary and richer conception of behaviour in specifying the upshots of mental states, we cannot hope to circumscribe mental states in anything like the way that the functionalist envisages. Recall what was wrong with the old behaviourist's conception from the functionalist's point of view. Using that conception, one cannot leave the truth or falsity of agents' beliefs out of account. We imagined that this point might be accommodated by using a 'world-conditioned' notion of behaviour, but left this suggestion rather vague (section 3). Now the ramified character of the interdependencies between mental states, which the functionalist is so anxious to take account of, ensures that any worldly conditions incorporated in a notion of behaviour would ramify in any theory that attempted to accommodate that notion. A person can be expected to do what she tries to do on occasion only if certain beliefs that explain her then trying to do that are true. But the interdependencies between mental things ensure that for any desire or belief whose causal role we might think to define, it is possible that almost any belief might interact with it in the production of some possible event of trying.[15] Thus if the world-conditioned notion of behaviour is introduced by the functionalist, and from case to case he makes it explicit which beliefs are such that their truth or falsity on occasion is relevant to what behaviour is produced, his task turns into the project of giving an account of the structure of rational thought and practice, any exemplification of which is conditioned by a simultaneous view of the world as a subject confronts it. This is not the project of providing descriptions, however abstract, of the brain.

6. It is not a novel claim that explanation in the rational mode cannot be converted into science. As Davidson has said:

> Any effort at increasing the accuracy and power of a theory of behaviour forces us to bring more and more of the whole system of the agent's beliefs and motives directly into account. But in inferring this system from the evidence, we necessarily impose conditions of coherence, rationality, and consistency. These conditions have no echo in physical theory.[16]

I take the mismatch Davidson sees between the mental and the scientific physical to show up in the fact that an attempt to incorporate conditions of rationality in a physicalist theory, using a conception of behaviour that is

bodily but constrained by common-sense psychology, seems to leave something out. Even to its proponents it seems to leave something out, and they
proceed by injecting some extra detail into bodily behavioural descriptions (cf.
Armstrong and Lewis). But there is no warrant for the extra detail.[17]

Davidson himself thinks that the mismatch between the mental and the
scientific physical shows up in two particular ways at the level of what can be
said about people's 'outputs'. First, 'Practical reasoning . . . may simply fail to
occur'. Second, 'Wanting to do something . . . may cause someone to do [the]
thing, and yet the causal chain may operate in such a manner that the act is
not intentional'.[18] These two claims surely reveal an immediate and insuper-
able obstacle to constructing functionalists' output generalizations. But I have
allowed the argument to progress, believing that the superficial plausibility of
the functionalists' contrary claims derives in large part from their free use of
a quite schematic notion of *behaviour*.

The idea upon which the arguments here have traded is present in Davidson
too, of course – in the claim that the mental is not a closed system. The felt
complexity of propositional–attitude psychology will be accommodated only
when 'the constitutive role of rationality' is properly acknowledged, and the
attempt to see the patterns in a person's mental states embodied in the states
of physical science is duly abandoned.[19]

7. The fundamental assumption that has been in dispute is that, in stating the
causal powers of mental states, one can prescind from all but the most immediate effects of the actions they produce, and ignore almost everything under
the head of 'desired effects of actions' in the picture of the person (section 1).
This assumption underlay the physicalist line of thought sketched at the outset.
And we shall see now that it is the same assumption which leads people to
accept the supervenience of the mental on the neurophysiological, and which
gives rise to another physicalist view of intentional states of mind.

To many it seems (a) that a difference of mental state between two people
requires some difference in their behavioural dispositions, and (b) that a difference in the behavioural dispositions of two animal bodies requires some
difference in their internal physical machinery. They think, then, that if one
were to allow that there could be a mental difference without a difference in
brain state, one would be denying that the brain was responsible for the
production of behaviour.[20]

Their argument is guilty of the same equivocation on 'behaviour' as the
functionalists rely on. Premiss (a) requires for its truth a broad and everyday
conception of a behavioural disposition; (b) requires a narrow one. (a) is true
if we take it to mean that a change in mental state affect the proper explananda
of psychological explanations; (b) is true if we take it to mean that only a
change in brain state could affect how a creature moves itself. Nothing in the
argument holds these two conceptions of a behavioural disposition together.[21]

Of course it is well known that there are counterexamples to a thesis of the
supervenience of the psychological on the neurophysiological. Putnam's Twin

Earth examples show that there can be variations in the objects of *de re* states of mind that are not reflected in any dispositions to move the body one way rather than another.[22]

Some proponents of the supervenience thesis try to show that these examples do their thesis only negligible damage, as if the existence of *de re* states posed some special, local problem. But we saw that the so-called holism of the mental is apt to embrace all of those worldly facts which a person's attitudes concern and which her bodily movements confront: the problem for supervenience is not a problem specifically about *de re* states of mind.

In some physicalist writings, this last point is acknowledged, and it is agreed that propositional–attitude states cannot be characterized as the functionalist envisages; but it is then said that these states must nevertheless have causal–explanatory *components*, which components may be seen to coincide with brain states. According to this new view, the picture of a person from which we begin is not itself something upon which any picture of the brain can be superimposed; but the picture of the person can, as it were, be split into two, and one of the resultant parts – the 'internal side' of a person, which is supposed to incorporate explanatory states – is suited to having some picture of the brain fitted on to it.[23]

Yet it is hard to see how anyone is in a position to claim that there are states whose ascription to people is explanatory of their behaviour unless he can demonstrate that the ascription of such states does, or would, cast light upon behaviour. We know of course that such states as we ascribe – beliefs having contents, for instance – do cast light. But it is no help then to be told that there must be states which lurk behind the states we ascribe and which carry their explanatory force. It is a strange idea that the satisfaction yielded by common-sense explanations has its source in something of which the parties to the explanation are quite ignorant – as if light had been cast through a medium that we cannot yet see through. But it would be a quite baffling idea that the explanatory force of an explanation resides in something that is not capable of illuminating anything for us – as if we could be sure that light will one day pass through a medium that is always opaque.

Not only can the picture of the brain not be superimposed upon the person, then: we have no reason to believe in any picture of a person's non-worldly aspect for it to be superimposed upon instead.

8. These conclusions ought not to surprise anyone who accepts that our reason for believing that mental states are occupants of causal roles is given by pointing to the place of mental states in causal explanation. For nothing in the argument here is hostile to the thought that causal roles are constitutive of at least some mental concepts. It can be true that the explanatory task that propositional–attitude ascription serves is a causal one; and it can be true that we cast all the light we can on propositional–attitude concepts by saying (not in functionalist theories, but in the available ways) what explanatory task their ascriptions serve.

It will be said that there is a puzzle here, however. How can the propositional–attitude states be thought of as mediating causally between inputs to and outputs from persons, although nothing with the appropriate causal powers of mental states can be found by scrutiny of a person's interior? Does not our conception of causality compel us to see the states which are cited in causal explanations of (*inter alia*) movements of a body as states which are located on causal chains that can be traced through space and time and that run through space–time volumes incorporating movements of that body? But then are we not obliged to see bodily movements as somehow primary among the explananda of action explanations? (Some line of thought such as this must be what lends plausibility to arguments like Kim's in section 2.)

One will feel tremendous pressure to accept this if one adopts a paradigm of causal explanations, got (say) from the picture of the brain, and takes it that the causal explanations obtained in viewing a person as a person must also conform to that paradigm. But if the causal–explanatory powers of mental states cannot be specified in such a way that a scientist could be led to recognize states that are the subjects of his studies as having those powers, then the belief that common-sense psychological states conform to the paradigm is undermined. The impossibility of specifying the causal–explanatory powers of mental states in ways that would suit a scientist is revealed in the difficulty of finding a notion of behaviour which is both available to common-sense psychology and rich enough to define states that are explanatory according to the paradigm even while they share in the complexities of common-sense psychological states.

9. Why is the idea that propositional–attitude states can be fitted to the scientific paradigm so compelling? I suspect that an unacknowledged allegiance to principles of positivist epistemology must take a share of the blame.

If one begins with a distinction between psychological terms and non-psychological terms, and dresses this up in a distinction between T-terms and O-terms such as Lewis's (section 3), then one comes to think of the O-terms as conveying all the data from which psychological theories could be constructed. Application of the O-terms seems then to be independent of anything one knows about people (*per se*), and common-sense psychology begins to seem to be a theory of such observables as the O-terms describe, a theory distinctive only in its particular concepts.

But reflection on the practice of psychological explanation shows what an extraordinary myth this is.[24] Someone required to explain why some agent has done something has to show how the psychological facts about the agent are consistent with what she ostensibly did. This may require him to become clearer about what went on in the world even as he speculates about her mental states. (Equally of course he may learn about the world by learning of her states of mind.[25]) It is not, as the model of theory and observation might suggest, that he has to arrive at a view about what went on in the agent's head which coheres with some prior account of what happened at the place where her body meets the world.

We ought not then to expect to find any notion of behaviour ('the observable') that is suited to reductionist claims. Certainly Rylean talk of skaters' dispositions to warn other skaters seems laughable if it is read as offering any reduction of believing that the ice is thin. And there is reason to suppose that the features of Ryle's behavioural term which contaminate them psychologically must in fact be present equally in any terms that figure in any account of mental things. There are two (related) ways in which the application of everyday behavioural terms is caught up with the application of psychological terms. First, bits, or items, of behaviour, as described by behavioural concepts, are the effects of mental states; but it is impossible to divide behaviour up into bits in such a way that the bits correspond to things that have a psychological history unless we know something about the mental states that actually produce the behaviour. Second, Ryle's descriptions tell us of things that the agent intentionally did; and one is not in a position to take a view of which things are intentionally done by people unless one has some view of their mental states. These two features are bound to be inherited by any behavioural descriptions that are fit for inclusion in an account of mental states: their application must presuppose (a) a psychologically informed method for articulating the events that flow from a person, and (b) a sense of what is psychologically relevant among the events thus articulated.[26]

If one rests content with a naive conception of psychology's province, one cannot then construe 'observable' in positivist spirit and think of behaviour, the objects of psychological explanation, as 'observable'. Helping oneself to 'observable' behaviour, on the other hand, is only a way of ensuring that one ignores the truth about psychological explanation.

10. Section 9 is no doubt inadequate as a diagnosis of the attractions of present-day physicalist accounts of intentional phenomena. Here I suspect that the whole history of the subject is to the point. Philosophers of mind have come to see Cartesian dualism as the great enemy, but have underestimated what they have to contend with. Taking the putatively immaterial character of minds to create the only problem that there is for Descartes' account, they marry up the picture of the person with the picture of her brain, and settle for a view of mind which, though material in its (cranial) substance, is Cartesian in its essence.[27]

Of course the acceptance of immaterial substance *was* one of Descartes' errors. But it does not take a scientific materialism to remedy that error. After all, it has not been said that there are elements of the person picture that science fails to deal with because they are ethereal and unnatural, but only that we have to look for the source of common-sense psychology's complexity elsewhere than at the junction between the central nervous system and the world.

Notes

1   Jaegwon Kim, 'Psychophysical Supervenience', *Philosophical Studies*, xli (1982), 64. (I have changed the order of Kim's sentences.) For a similar argument, given in the course of a defence of functionalism, see Brian Loar, *Mind and Meaning* (CUP, Cambridge, 1981), 88.

2   It may be said that this counterexample is importantly different from the examples that were Kim's concern, because in the counterexample it is only in the presence of the explanans that we come to be able to separate necessary conditions for the obtaining of the explanandum. But this feature may also be present in psychological cases. We can know that someone turned on the burner (and that there is a psychological explanation of that) without knowing what sort of bodily movement on her part resulted in the burner's being on.

3   David Lewis, 'Psychophysical and Theoretical Identifications', *Australasian Journal of Philosophy*, 1(1972), 249–58. (Where Lewis uses 'state' I use 'type of state', because, unlike Lewis, I reserve the word 'state' for particulars; and I make no assumption that functionalists are committed to any type identities of Lewis's sort.)

4   'Bodily movements' is used by Loar and others; 'motor responses' by Lewis in 'Psychophysical and Theoretical Identifications'.

5   *The Concept of Mind* (Hutchinson, London, 1949), 129.

6   There is little here that is uncontroversial. (For an account of the controversy, see my 'Bodily Movements, Actions and Mental Epistemology', in *Midwest Studies in Philosophy*, vol. IX (1985).) What I assume now is that we can distinguish the denotations of descriptions such as '*a*'s raising her arm', which are actions, from the denotations of such descriptions as '*a*'s arm's rising', which are not actions.

7   See *Mind and Meaning*, 86–91. Loar uses a technical, theoretical psychological notion of *willing*, where my exposition uses *trying*. Loar's view of theoretical psychology is discussed in section 5. For arguments (in effect) that 'try' has many of the properties needed for the two-stage account of action production, see Chapters 3 and 4 of my *Actions* (Routledge and Kegan Paul, London, 1980).

8   Loar's argument for narrowing down psychological explanation (see n. 1) introduces *basic actions*, which Loar calls 'primary explananda'. He says that non-basic things are explained by 'independent facts', that is facts that are not themselves psychologically explained. The question for Loar is quite parallel to that for Kim: is the reason offered for extricating 'independent facts' from non-basic things not also a reason for extricating non-psychological facts even from basic things?

There are two points about Loar's terminology. (a) I have spoken of *basic things* (*done*), rather than *basic actions*, because actions themselves, assuming these are particulars, do not stand to one another in relations of relative basicness. (See *Actions*, Chapter 5, where the relation *more basic than* is taken to hold between descriptions of actions, or, better, my 'Action and Ability', in R Haller (ed.), *Language, Logic and Philosophy* (Reidel, Dordrecht, 1981), where the relation is taken to hold between the things a person does.) (b) It may be that Loar himself does not distinguish actions from bodies' movements, as my exposition of functionalism has suggested functionalists do.

I state the second stage of a functionalist's account of output as I do because I think that (on occasion) an agent's ϕ-ing is the same as her trying to ϕ and not the same as a movement of the ϕ-type. Still the consequent of the conditional might read 'a ϕs' – only then the conditional cannot be supposed to take one from cause to effect (unless one denies that, on occasion, events of trying simply are actions). At any rate, the argument addressed to Kim and Loar requires only that some condition relating to the agent's body's functioning, as well as some condition relating to the agent's mind, is necessary for the occurrence of an action. To accept this much, no stand needs to be taken on the controversy mentioned in n. 6, or on the details of a correct formulation of the two-stage account of action production.

9 See my discussion of what I there called *teleologically* basic descriptions of actions in Chapter 6 of *Actions*. And notice that I make no assumption to the effect that all beliefs are linguistically expressible by their possessors.

   If bodily movement descriptions of actions are not basic, then there will be some *non-bodily* basic descriptions for functionalists to use in describing outputs. But if the functionalist does use output O-terms which touch on regions beyond the agent's body, then (a) it will become more implausible that his 'simple ability' conditions are 'purely psychological', and (b) this will do nothing to supply the richness that functionalists seem to want to find in their notion of behaviour (see below).

10 D. M. Armstrong, *A Materialist Theory of The Mind* (Routledge and Kegan Paul, London, 1968), 147.

11 David Lewis, 'Radical Interpretation', at p. 114 in the reprinting in his *Philosophical Papers*, vol. I (Clarendon Press, Oxford, 1983), quoted more fully at n. 26. Many functionalists speak of behaviour in a purely schematic way.

12 I am relying here on such claims as are made for example by P. F. Strawson and G. J. Warnock in D. F. Pears (ed), *Freedom and the Will* (Macmillan, London, 1963): our system of classifying actions is grounded in quite different interests from any system of bodily movement classification. I do not conclude, as they did, that actions are not bodily movements; but I do take their claim to show the irreducibility of movements-classified-by-someone-interested-in-action to movements-classified-by-the-scientist-interested-in-movements-*per-se*.

13 It may be pointed out that complexity could be derived from complexity in descriptions of *inputs*. (Functionalists insist that stimulus terms as well as behavioural ones are needed to characterize the mental ones: this is a respect in which functionalists are thought to differ from behaviourists which I have not singled out for attention.) But I think that there are things to be said about *perception* which lead in the same direction as the things I have said about *action* and which would show that the functionalist cannot make anything of this point. And the argument I actually give is meant to rely on the fact that my opponents themselves believe that more detail is needed in *output* specifications than (so I say) they are entitled to.

14 This explains the technicalities in Loar's account (see n. 7). Loar's suggestion is that if a theory well confirmed by experiments in theoretical psychology and neurophysiology were true of a person, and certain of the functional states of the theory satisfied the full complement of the constraints imposed by common sense as necessary conditions of having beliefs and desires, then it would be correct to count those functional states as beliefs and desires.

15 The 'certain' beliefs are (intuitively, and leaving out modifications that would be required to accommodate fortuitously false beliefs) those whose truth is required for the agent's trying to ϕ to result in the agents ϕ-ing.

It is easy to miss the point about the ramification of worldly conditions if one thinks about explanation as we know it and forgets about the predictive aspirations of functionalists' output generalizations. When we know the explanation of an agent's doing something, we are in a position to specify a small number of beliefs which enter the explanation of her doing that, and only some of these are beliefs whose truth values bear on whether she has actually done the thing. But this is not the position of someone who hopes for a general, predictive theory of what agents would do. Consider a functionalist who hoped to derive actual mental/physical identities for the case of a particular person at a particular time. He might start with a list of types of state which were instantiated in the person at that time. For any type of state on that list, he will say (counterfactually) that its instance would interact thus and so *if* . . .; for any type of state not on that list, he will say (doubly counterfactually, as it were) that *if* there were an instance of it, then it would interact thus and so *if*. . . . Thus *possible* events of trying must be seen (at *t*) as such as to be produced in a person (at a time later than *t*) by way of beliefs that that person may lack (at *t*). (Some people seem to forget that a functionalist's psychological theory must make mention of all the types of mental state there are. I have put the matter as I have here only because it may help to remind one of this.)

16 This is from 'Psychology as Philosophy'; see Donald Davidson, *Essays on Actions and Events* (Clarendon Press, Oxford, 1980), 231. This volume, 24.

17 I say that there is no warrant for the detail. But I should acknowledge that I have an argument only in so far as I am in a position to ask (rhetorically) 'What reason could there be for supposing that the detail is warranted?' ('What reason could there be for supposing that theoretical psychology can dictate to common sense?'). Of course the committed proponent of scientific materialism thinks that there are reasons where I see none: he supposes that metaphysical principles provide the warrant. I try to engage with his position in sections 8–10.

18 The quotations are from 'Freedom to Act', at pp. 77 and 78 in *Essays on Actions and Events*.

19 John McDowell also argues that if expositions such as Loar's seem to undermine Davidson's claims about the mental's anomalousness, then that could only be an illusion. He focuses attention on 'internal constraints', where I have focused on 'output generalizations'. See 'Functionalism and Anomalous Monism', in Ernest Le Pore and Brian McLaughlin (eds.), *The Philosophy of Donald Davidson: Perspectives on Actions and Events* (Blackwell, Oxford, 1986).

20 The argument is in Colin McGinn, *The Character of Mind* (Oxford University Press, Oxford, 1982), 29; though McGinn would not endorse the argument just as it stands (see n. 23).

21 Of course anyone can if he wants, put common-sense descriptions of behaviour together with scientific descriptions of behaviour, and call what he arrives at descriptions of behaviour. What cannot be guaranteed, however, is that, having assembled a notion of behaviour by reference to two explanatory schemes, one has then accorded some stable sense to 'explanation of behaviour' or 'behavioural disposition'. (I have not said that no one is entitled to the functionalists' conception of behaviour; I have only questioned whether one is entitled to suppose that it can be put to the use to which functionalists put it.)

22 See Hilary Putnam 'The Meaning of "Meaning"', in his *Mind, Language and Reality* (CUP, Cambridge, 1975).

23 See for example Colin McGinn, 'The Structure of Content' in Andrew Woodfield (ed.), *Thought and Object* (Clarendon Press, Oxford, 1982). McGinn himself argues that the notion of *content* is decomposable into explanatory and truth-conditional aspects. The explanatory states he envisages do not have semantic content by virtue of their explanatory role, and the arguments below apply to his position inasmuch as this is so.

24 The story that mental terms were actually introduced as theoretical terms is called a myth by David Lewis (op. cit. n. 3). In support of the idea that it is a good myth (sc. that our terms for mental states mean just what they would if the myth were true), Lewis says that if it were a good myth, it would explain the appeal of Rylean behaviourism. But the appeal of Rylean behaviourism cannot be separated from its use of a broad and everyday notion of behaviour; and this is a notion which ought not to be available to one who tells the mythical story. (See below, and n. 26 on Lewis on behaviour.)

25 That this is a point about psychological explanation, rather than about 'head/world correlations', will be apparent only if one takes a relaxed view of psychological explanation; see section 2.

26 Lewis is sensitive to the fact that intentional notions must be precluded from accounts of behaviour if they are to be put to a theoretical use. He wrote (loc. cit. n. 11):

> There is an ambiguity in the term 'behaviour'. . . . I am using it to refer to raw behaviour – body movements and the like – . . .; not to behaviour specified partly in terms of the agent's intentions. . . . That Karl's fingers move on certain trajectories and exert certain forces is what I call 'behaviour'; that he signs a cheque is not.

What Lewis seems to want to rule out from 'raw' behavioural descriptions is only instances of 'ϕ' such that any event of someone's ϕ-ing is an event of her intentionally ϕ-ing. There is no need to deny that this ruling can give us a notion of behaviour. What I do deny is that such a ruling provides us with a notion that might have been used by someone ignorant of all common-sense psychological truths. I deny, then, that Lewis has found a notion fit for his 'good myth'. (Of course there *is* a notion of behaviour (or anyway of *output*) that we can imagine applied in utter independence of any interest in persons; but with this (very raw) notion, we return to one on which we get no real purchase when we state common-sense psychological accounts.)

27 What Descartes's commentators are typically most anxious to remind us of is that Descartes should not have held both that mind and body are substances whose essences are distinct, and that mind and body causally interact. Bernard Williams is an exception: he describes a difficulty which is independent of Descartes's treating the mind as soul-like, and depends only upon Descartes's thinking that all the transactions between the mental and the physical happen, as it were, at an interface. See the discussion of *terminal* interactionism (as Williams says we might call it) in *Descartes: The Project of Pure Enquiry* (Penguin, Harmondsworth, 1978), 288–92.

IB

THE FUNCTIONAL MIND

4

D. Lewis, "Reduction of Mind"

I am a realist and a reductive materialist about mind. I hold that mental states are contingently identical to physical – in particular, neural states. My position is very like the 'Australian materialism' of Place, Smart, and especially Armstrong. Like Smart and Armstrong, I am an ex-Rylean, and I retain some part of the Rylean legacy. In view of how the term is contested, I do not know whether I am a 'functionalist'.

Supervenience and analysis

My reductionism about mind begins as part of an *a priori* reductionism about everything. This world, or any possible world, consists of things which instantiate fundamental properties and which, in pairs or triples or . . ., instantiate fundamental relations. Few properties are fundamental: the property of being a club or a tub or a pub, for instance, is an unnatural gerrymander, a condition satisfied by miscellaneous things in miscellaneous ways. A fundamental, or 'perfectly natural', property is the extreme opposite. Its instances share exactly some aspect of their intrinsic nature. Likewise for relations.[1] I hold, as an *a priori* principle, that every contingent truth must be made true, somehow, by the pattern of coinstantiation of fundamental properties and relations. The whole truth about the world, including the mental part of the world, supervenes on this pattern. If two possible worlds were exactly isomorphic in their patterns of coinstantiation of fundamental properties and relations, they would thereby be exactly alike *simpliciter*.[2]

It is a task of physics to provide an inventory of all the fundamental properties and relations that occur in the world. (That's because it is also a task of physics to discover the fundamental laws of nature, and only the fundamental properties and relations may appear in the fundamental laws.[3]) We have no *a priori* guarantee of it, but we may reasonably think that present-day physics already goes a long way toward a complete and correct inventory. Remember that the physical nature of ordinary matter under mild conditions is very well understood.[4] And we may reasonably hope that future physics can finish the job in the same distinctive style. We may think, for instance, that mass and charge are among the fundamental properties; and that whatever fundamental properties remain as yet undiscovered are likewise instantiated by very small things that come in very large classes of exact duplicates. We may further think that the very same fundamental properties and relations, governed by the very same laws, occur in the living and the dead parts of the world, and in the sentient and the insentient parts, and in the clever and the stupid parts. In short: if we optimistically extrapolate the triumph of physics hitherto, we may provisionally accept that all fundamental properties and relations that actually occur are physical. This is the thesis of materialism.

(It was so named when the best physics of the day was the physics of matter alone. Now our best physics acknowledges other bearers of fundamental properties: parts of pervasive fields, parts of causally active spacetime. But it would be pedantry to change the name on that account, and disown our intellectual ancestors. Or worse, it would be a tacky marketing ploy, akin to British Rail's decree that second class passengers shall now be called 'standard class customers'.)

If materialism is true, as I believe it is, then the *a priori* supervenience of everything upon the pattern of coinstantiation of *fundamental* properties and relations yields an *a posteriori* supervenience of everything upon the pattern of coinstantiation of fundamental *physical* properties and relations. Materialist supervenience should be a contingent matter. To make it so, we supply a restriction that makes reference to actuality. Thus: if two worlds were physically isomorphic, and if no fundamental properties or relations alien to actuality occurred in either world, then these worlds would be exactly alike *simpliciter*. Disregarding alien worlds, the whole truth supervenes upon the physical truth. In particular, the whole mental truth supervenes. So here we have the common core of all materialist theories of the mind.[5]

A materialist who stops here has already said enough to come under formidable attack. An especially well-focused version of the attack comes from Frank Jackson.[6] Mary, confined in a room where all she can see is black or white, studies the physics of colour and colour vision and colour experience (and any other physics you might think relevant) until she knows it all. Then she herself sees colour for the first time, and at last she knows what it's like to see colour. What is this knowledge that Mary has gained? It may seem that she has eliminated some possibilities left open by all her previous knowledge; she has distinguished the actual world from other possible worlds that are exactly like it in all relevant physical respects. But if materialist supervenience is true, this cannot be what has happened.

Materialists have said many things about what does happen in such a case. I myself, following Nemirow, call it a case of know-how: Mary gains new imaginative abilities.[7] Others have said that Mary gains new relations of acquaintance, or new means of mental representation; or that the change in her is just that she has now seen colour. These suggestions need not be taken as rival alternatives. And much ink has been spent on the question whether these various happenings could in any sense be called the gaining of 'new knowledge', 'new belief, or 'new information'. But for a materialist, the heart of the matter is not what *does* happen but what *doesn't*: Mary does not distinguish the actual world from other worlds that are its physical duplicates but not its duplicates *simpliciter*.

Imagine a grid of a million tiny spots – pixels – each of which can be made light or dark. When some are light and some are dark, they form a picture, replete with interesting intrinsic gestalt properties. The case evokes reductionist comments. Yes, the picture really does exist. Yes, it really does have those gestalt properties. However, the picture and the properties reduce to the arrangement of light and dark pixels. They are nothing over and above the pixels. They make nothing true that is not made true already by the pixels. They could go unmentioned in an inventory of what there is without thereby rendering that inventory incomplete. And so on.

Such comments seem to me obviously right. The picture reduces to the pixels. And that is because the picture supervenes on the pixels: there could be no difference in the picture and its properties without some difference in the arrangement of light and dark pixels. Further, the supervenience is asymmetric: not just any difference in the pixels would matter to the gestalt properties of the picture. And it is supervenience of the large upon the small and many. In such a case, say I, supervenience is reduction. And the materialist supervenience of mind and all else upon the arrangement of atoms in the void – or whatever replaces atoms in the void in true physics – is another such case.

Yet thousands say that what's good about stating materialism in terms of supervenience is that this avoids reductionism! There's no hope of settling this disagreement by appeal to some uncontested definition of the term 'reductionism'. Because the term *is* contested, and the aim of some contestants is to see to it that whatever position they may hold, 'reductionism' shall be the name for something else.

At any rate, materialist supervenience means that for anything mental, there are physical conditions that would be sufficient for its presence, and physical conditions that would be sufficient for its absence. (These conditions will include conditions saying that certain inventories are complete: an electron has only so-and-so quantum numbers, for instance, and it responds only to such-and-such forces. But it's fair to call such a condition 'physical', since it answers a kind of question that physics does indeed address.) And no matter how the world may be, provided it is free of fundamental properties or relations alien to actuality, a condition of the one sort or the other will obtain. For all we know so far, the conditions associated with a given mental item might be complicated and miscellaneous – even infinitely complicated and miscellaneous. But so long as we limit ourselves just to the question of how this mental item can find a place in the world of fundamental physics, it is irrelevant how complicated and miscellaneous the conditions might be.

It may seem unsatisfactory that physical conditions should always settle whether the mental item is present or absent. For mightn't that sometimes be a vague question with no determinate answer? A short reply to this objection from vagueness is that if it did show that the mental was irreducible to fundamental physics despite supervenience, it would likewise show that boiling was irreducible to fundamental physics – which is absurd. For it is a vague matter just where simmering leaves off and boiling begins.

A longer reply has three parts. (1) If the physical settles the mental insofar as anything does, we still have materialist supervenience. Part of what it means for two physically isomorphic worlds to be just alike mentally is that any mental indeterminacy in one is exactly matched by mental indeterminacy in the other. (2) Whenever it is a vague question whether some simplistic mental classification applies, it will be determinate that some more subtle classification applies. What's determinate may be not that you do love him or that you don't, but rather that you're in a certain equivocal state of mind that defies easy description. (3) If all indeterminacy is a matter of semantic indecision,[8] then there is no indeterminacy in the things themselves. How could we conjure up some irreducible mental item just by failing to decide exactly which reducible item we're referring to?

It may seem that when supervenience guarantees that there are physical conditions sufficient for the presence or absence of a given mental item, the sufficiency is of the wrong sort. The implication is necessary but not *a priori*. You might want to say, for instance, that black-and-white Mary really did gain new knowledge when she first saw colour; although what she learned followed necessarily from all the physics she knew beforehand, she had remained ignorant because it didn't follow *a priori*.

A short reply to this objection from necessity *a posteriori* is that if it did show that the mental was irreducible to fundamental physics, it would likewise show that boiling was irreducible to fundamental physics – which is absurd. For the identity between boiling and a certain process described in fundamental physical terms is necessary *a posteriori* if anything is.

(A longer reply, following Jackson, is founded upon the 'two-dimensional' analysis of necessity *a posteriori*.[9] Two-dimensionalism says that there is no such thing as a necessary *a posteriori* proposition. However, one single sentence ϕ may be associated in two different ways with two different propositions, one of them necessary and the other one contingent; and the contingent one can be known only *a posteriori*. Suppose we choose to adopt a conception of meaning under which our conventions of language sometimes fix meanings only as a function of matters of contingent fact – for example, a conception on which the meaning of 'boils' is left dependent on which physical phenomenon turns out to occupy the boiling-role. Then if we interpret a sentence ϕ using the meanings of its words as fixed in world W_1, we get proposition H_1; using the meanings as fixed in W_2, we get H_2; and so on. Call these the propositions *horizontally expressed* by ϕ at the various worlds; and let H be the proposition horizontally expressed by φ at the actual world. The proposition *diagonally expressed* by φ is the proposition *D* that holds at any world *W* iff the proposition horizontally expressed by φ at *W* is true at *W*. So if we know *D*, we know that φ horizontally expresses some truth or other, but we may not know which truth. Sentence φ is necessary *a posteriori* iff *H* is necessary but *D* is knowable only *a posteriori*. Likewise, a proposition *P* *necessarily implies* that φ iff *P* implies *H*; but *P* *a priori implies* that φ iff *P* implies *D*. Our worry was that when φ was about the mind, and *P* was a premise made true by fundamental physics, *P* might imply that φ necessarily but not *a priori*. But if so, and if you think it matters, just take another proposition *Q*: let *Q* be true at exactly those worlds where φ horizontally expresses the same proposition *H* that it actually does. *Q* is true. Given the materialist supervenience of everything, *Q* as well as *P* is made true by fundamental physics. *P* and *Q* together imply *a priori* that φ. So the gap between physical premises and mental conclusion is closed. Anyone who wants to reopen it – for instance, in order to square materialist supervenience with Mary's supposed ignorance – must somehow show that the two-dimensional analysis of necessity *a posteriori* is inadequate.)

If we limit ourselves to the question how mind finds a place in the world of physics, our work is done. Materialist supervenience offers a full answer. But if we expand our interests a little, we'll see that among the supervenient features of the world, mind must be very exceptional. There are countless such features. In our little toy example of the picture and the pixels, the supervenient properties number 2 to the power: 2 to the millionth power. In the case of materialist supervenience, the number will be far greater. The infinite cardinal beth-3 is a conservative estimate. The vast majority of supervenient features of the world are given only by miscellaneously infinite disjunctions of infinitely complex physical conditions. Therefore they are beyond our power to detect, to name, or to think about one at a time. Mental features of the world, however, are not at all beyond our ken. Finite assemblies of particles – us – can track them. Therefore there must be some sort of simplicity to them. Maybe it will be a subtle sort of simplicity, visible only if you look in just the right way. (Think of the Mandelbrot set: its overwhelming complexity, its short and simple recipe.) But somehow it must be there. Revealing this simplicity is a job for conceptual analysis.

Arbiters of fashion proclaim that analysis is out of date. Yet without it, I see no possible way to establish that any feature of the world does or does not deserve a name drawn from our traditional mental vocabulary. We should repudiate not analysis itself, but only some simplistic goals for it. We should allow for semantic indecision: any interesting analysandum is likely to turn out vague and ambiguous. Often the best that any one analysis can do is to fall safely within the range of indecision. And we should allow for semantic satisficing: analysis may reveal what it would take to deserve a name perfectly, but imperfect deservers of the name may yet deserve it well enough. (And sometimes the perfect case may be impossible.) If so, there is bound to be semantic indecision about how well is well enough.

I offer not analyses, but a recipe for analyses. We have a very extensive shared understanding of how we work mentally. Think of it as a theory: folk psychology. It is common knowledge among us; but it is tacit, as our grammatical knowledge is. We can tell which particular predictions and explanations conform to its principles, but we cannot expound those principles systematically.[10] Folk psychology is a powerful instrument of prediction. We are capable of all sorts of behaviour that would seem bizarre and unintelligible, and this is exactly the behaviour that folk psychology predicts, rightly, will seldom occur. (But we take a special interest in questions that lie beyond the predictive power of folk psychology; wherefore ingrates may fairly complain of a lack of *interesting* predictions!) Folk psychology has evolved through thousands of years of close observation of one another. It is not the last word in psychology, but we should be confident that so far as it goes – and it does go far – it is largely right.

Folk psychology concerns the causal relations of mental states, perceptual stimuli, and behavioural responses. It says how mental states, singly or in combination, are apt for causing behaviour; and it says how mental states are apt to change under the impact of perceptual stimuli and other mental states. Thus it associates with each mental state a typical causal role. Now we have our recipe for analyses. Suppose we've managed to elicit all the tacitly known general principles of folk psychology. Whenever M is a folk-psychological name for a mental state, folk psychology will say that state M typically occupies a certain causal role: call this the M-role. Then we analyse M as meaning 'the state that typically occupies the M-role'. Folk psychology implicitly defines the term M, and we have only to make that definition explicit.

Since the causal roles of mental states involve other mental states, we might fear circularity. 'The remedy is due in its essentials to Ramsey.[11] Suppose, for instance, that folk psychology had only three names for mental states: L, M, N. We associate with this triplet of names a complex causal role for a triplet of states, including causal relations within the triplet: call this the LMN-role. Folk psychology says that the states L, M, N jointly occupy the LMN-role. That implies that M occupies the derivative role: coming second in a triplet of states that jointly occupy the LMN-role. Taking this as our M-role, we proceed as before. Say that the names L, M, N are *interdefined*, The defining of all three via the LMN-role is a package deal.

We might fear circularity for another reason. The causal roles of mental states involve responses to perceptual stimuli. But the relevant feature of the stimulus will often be some secondary quality – for instance, a colour. We cannot replace the secondary quality with a specification of the stimulus in purely physical terms, on pain of going beyond what is known to folk psychology. But if we analyse the secondary quality in terms of the distinctive mental states its presence is apt to evoke, we close a definitional circle. So we should take interdefinition further. Let folk psychology include folk psycho-physics. This will say, for instance, that the pair of a certain colour and the corresponding sensation jointly occupy a complex causal role that consists in part, but only in part, of the former being apt to cause the latter. Now we have a derivative role associated with the name of the colour, and another associated with the name of the sensation: the role of coming first or coming second, respectively, in a pair that jointly occupies this complex role.

We might worry also about the behaviour that mental states are apt for causing. Often we describe behaviour in a mentally loaded way: as action. To say that you kicked the ball to your teammate is to describe your behaviour. But such a description presupposes a great deal about how your behaviour was meant to serve your desires according to your beliefs; and also about the presence of the ball and the playing surface and the other player, and about the social facts that unite players into teams. More threat of circularity? More need for interdefinition? I don't know how such further interdefinition would work; and anyway, it would be well to call a halt before folk psychology expands into a folk theory of the entire *Lebenswelt*!

Describing the behaviour in purely physical terms – the angle of the knee, the velocity of the foot – would get rid of those presuppositions. But, just as in the case of the stimuli, it would go beyond what is known to folk psychology. Further, these descriptions would never fit the behaviour of space aliens not of humanoid shape; and yet we should not dismiss out of hand the speculation that folk psychology might apply to aliens as well as to ourselves.

Fortunately there is a third way to describe behaviour. When you kicked the ball, your body moved in such a way that *if* you had been on a flat surface in Earth-normal gravity with a suitably placed ball in front of you and a suit-ably placed teammate some distance away, *then* the impact of your foot upon the ball would have propelled the ball onto a trajectory bringing it within the teammate's reach. That description is available to the folk. They wouldn't give it spontaneously, but they can recognize it as correct. It presupposes nothing about your mental states, not even that you have any; nothing about whether the ball and the playing field and the gravity and the teammate are really there; nothing about your humanoid shape, except that you have some sort of foot. It could just as well describe the behaviour of a mindless mechanical contrap-tion, in the shape of a space alien (with a foot), thrashing about in free fall.

(I don't say that we should really use these 'if – then' descriptions of behav-iour. Rather, my point is that their availability shows how to unload the presuppositions from our ordinary descriptions.)

If *M* means 'the state that typically occupies the *M*-role' and if that role is only imperfectly occupied, what are we to do? – Satisfice: let the name *M* go to a state that deserves it imperfectly. And if nothing comes anywhere near occupying the *M*-role? – Then the name *M* has no referent. The boundary between the cases is vague. To take an example from a different term-intro-ducing theory, I suppose it to be indeterminate whether 'dephlogisticated air' refers to oxygen or to nothing. But folk psychology is in far better shape than phlogiston theory, despite scare stories to the contrary. We can happily grant that there are no perfect deservers of folk-psychological names, but we shouldn't doubt that there are states that deserve those names well enough.

What to do if the M-role, or the LMN-role, turns out to be doubly occupied? I used to think that in this case too the name M had no referent.[12] But now I think it might be better, sometimes or always, to say that the name turns out to be ambiguous in reference. That follows the lead of Field; and it is consistent with, though not required by, the treatment of Carnap.[13] Note that we face the same choice with phrases like 'the moon of Mars'; and in that case too I'd now lean toward ambiguity of reference rather than lack of it.

My recipe for analyses, like Rylean analytic behaviourism, posits analytic truths that constrain the causal relations of mental states to behaviour. (We have no necessary connections between distinct existences, of course; the necessity is verbal. The state itself could have failed to occupy its causal role, but would thereby have failed to deserve its mental name.) But the constraints are weak enough to be credible. Because the state that typically occupies a role need not occupy it invariably, and also because a state may deserve a name well enough in virtue of a role that it occupies imperfectly, we are safe from the behaviourist's bugbears. We have a place for the resolute deceiver, disposed come what may to behave as if his mental states were other than they really are. We have a place for the total and incurable paralytic with a rich mental life and no behavioural dispositions whatever. We even have a place for a madman whose mental states are causally related to behaviour and stimuli and one another in a totally haywire fashion.[14] And yet not anything goes. At some point – and just where that point comes is a matter of semantic indecision – weird tales of mental states that habitually offend against the principles of folk psychology stop making sense; because at some point the offending states lose all claim to their folk-psychological names. To that extent, analytic behaviourism was right. To quote my closest ally in these matters, '. . . outward physical behaviour and tendencies to behave do in some way enter into our ordinary concept of mind. Whatever theory of mind is true, it has a debt to pay, and a peace to be made, with behaviourism.'[15]

When we describe mental state M as the occupant of the M-role, that is what Smart calls a topic-neutral description.[16] It says nothing about what sort of state it is that occupies the role. It might be a non-physical or a physical state, and if it is physical it might be a state of neural activity in the brain, or a pattern of currents and charges on a silicon chip, or the jangling of an enormous assemblage of beer cans. What state occupies the M-role and thereby deserves the name M is an a posteriori matter. But if materialist supervenience is true, and every feature of the world supervenes upon fundamental physics, then the occupant of the role is some physical state or other – because there's nothing else for it to be. We know enough to rule out the chip and the cans, and to support the hypothesis that what occupies the role is some pattern of neural activity. When we know more, we shall know what pattern of neural activity it is. Then we shall have the premises of an argument for psychophysical identification:[17]

mental state M = the occupant of the M-role (by analysis),
physical state P = the occupant of the M-role (by science),
therefore $M = P$.

That's how conceptual analysis can reveal the simple formula – or anyway, the much less than infinitely complicated formula – whereby, when we know enough, we can pick out a mental feature of the world from all the countless other features of the world that likewise supervene on fundamental physics.

The causal-role analyses would still hold even if materialist supervenience failed. They might even still yield psychophysical identifications. Even if we lived in a spook-infested world, it might be physical states that occupied the causal rules (in us, if not in the spooks) and thereby deserved the folk-psychological names. Or it might be non-physical states that occupied the roles. Then, if we knew enough parapsychology, we would have the premises of an argument for psycho-*non*physical identification.

When our argument delivers an identification $M = P$, the identity is contingent. How so? – All identity is self-identity, and nothing could possibly have failed to be self-identical. But that is not required. It's contingent, and it can only be known *a posteriori*, which physical (or other) states occupy which causal roles. So if M means 'the occupant of the M-role' it's contingent which state is the referent of M; it's contingent whether some one state is the common referent of M and P; so it's contingent whether $M = P$ is true.

Kripke vigorously intuits that some names for mental states, in particular 'pain', are rigid designators: that is, it's not contingent what their referents are.[18] I myself intuit no such thing, so the non-rigidity imputed by causal-role analyses troubles me not at all.

Here is an argument that 'pain' is not a rigid designator. Think of some occasion when you were in severe pain, unmistakable and unignorable. All will agree, except for some philosophers and faith healers, that there is a state that actually occupies the pain role (or near enough); that it is called 'pain'; and that you were in it on that occasion. For now, I assume nothing about the nature of this state, or about how it deserves its name. Now consider an unactualized situation in which it is some different state that occupies the pain role in place of the actual occupant; and in which you were in that different state; and which is otherwise as much like the actual situation as possible. Can you distinguish the actual situation from this unactualized alternative? I say not, or not without laborious investigation. But if 'pain' is a rigid designator, then the alternative situation is one in which you were not in pain, so you could distinguish the two very easily. So 'pain' is not a rigid designator.

Philosophical arguments are never incontrovertible – well hardly ever. Their purpose is to help expound a position, not to coerce agreement. In this case, the controverter might say that if the actual occupant of the pain role is not a physical state, but rather is a special sort of non-physical state, then indeed you can distinguish the two situations. He might join me in saying that this would not be so if the actual occupant of the role were a physical state – else neurophysiology would be easier than it is – and take this together with intuitions of rigidity to yield a *reductio* against materialism. Myself, I don't see how the physical or non-physical nature of the actual occupant of the role has anything to do with whether the two situations can be distinguished. Talk of 'phenomenal character' and the like doesn't help. Either it is loaded with question-begging philosophical doctrine, or else it just reiterates the undisputed fact that pain is a kind of experience.[19]

If there is variation across worlds with respect to which states occupy the folk-psychological roles and deserve the folk-psychological names (and if this variation doesn't always require differences in the laws of nature, as presumably it doesn't) then also there can be variations within a single world. For possibility obeys a principle of recombination: roughly, any possible kind of thing can coexist with any other.[20] For all we know, there may be variation even within this world. Maybe there are space aliens, and maybe there will soon be artificial intelligences, in whom the folk-psychological roles are occupied (or near enough) by states very different from any states of a human nervous system. Presumably, at least some folk-psychological roles are occupied in at least some animals, and maybe there is variation across species. There might even be variation within humanity. It depends on the extent to which we are hard-wired, and on the extent of genetic variation in our wiring.

We should beware, however, of finding spurious variation by overlooking common descriptions. Imagine two mechanical calculators that are just alike in design. When they add columns of numbers, the amount carried goes into a register, and the register used for this purpose is selected by throwing a switch. Don't say that the carry-seventeen role is occupied in one machine by a state of register A and in the other by a state of register B. Say instead that in both machines alike the role is occupied by a state of the register selected by the switch. (Equivalently, by a state of a part of the calculator large enough to include the switch and both registers.) If there is a kind of thinking that some of us do in the left side of the brain and others do in the right side, that might be a parallel case.

If M means 'the occupant of the M-role' and there is variation in what occupies the M-role, then our psychophysical identities need to be restricted: not plain $M = P$, but M-in-$K = P$ where K is a kind within which P occupies the M-role. Human pain might be one thing, Martian pain might be something else.[21] As with contingency, which is variation across worlds, so likewise with variation in a single world: the variability in no way infects the identity relation, but rather concerns the reference of the mental name.

The threat of variation has led many to retreat from 'type–type' to 'token–token' identity. They will not say that $M = P$, where M and P are names for a state that can be common to different things at different times – that is, for a property had by things at times. But they will say that $m = p$, where m and p are mental and physical names for a particular, unrepeatable event. Token–token identities are all very well, in their derivative way, but the flight from type–type identities was quite unnecessary. For our restricted identities, of the form M-in-$K = P$, are still type–type.

But don't we at least have a choice? Couldn't our causal role analyses be recast in terms of the causal roles of tokens, and if they were, would they not then yield token–token identities? After all, the only way for a type to occupy a causal role is through the causes and effects of its tokens. The effects of pain are the effects of pain-events – I think, following Jackson, Pargetter, and Prior, that this recasting of the analyses would not be easy.[22] There are more causal relations than one. Besides causing, there is preventing. It too may figure in folk-psychological causal roles; for instance, pain tends to prevent undivided attention to anything else. Prevention cannot straightforwardly be treated as a causal relation of tokens, because the prevented tokens do not exist – not in this world, anyway. It is better taken as a relation of types.

If a retreat had been needed, a better retreat would have been to 'subtype–subtype' identity. Let MK name the conjunctive property of being in state M and being of kind K; and likewise for PK. Do we really want psychophysical identities of the form $MK = PK$? – Close, but I think not quite right. For one thing, M-in-K is not the same thing as MK. The former but not the latter can occur also in something that isn't of kind K. For another thing, it is P itself, not PK, that occupies the M-role in things of kind K.

Non-rigidity means that M is different states in different possible cases; variation would mean that M was different states in different actual cases. But don't we think that there is *one* property of being in the state M – one property that is common to all, actual or possible, of whatever kind, who can truly be said to be in state M? – There is. It is the property such that, for any possible X, X has it just in case X is in the state that occupies the M-role for X's kind at X's world.[23] The gerund 'being in M' can be taken, at least on one good disambiguation, as a rigid designator of this property. However, this property is not the occupant of the M-role. It cannot occupy that or any other causal role because it is excessively disjunctive, and therefore no events are essentially havings of it.[24] To admit it as causally efficacious would lead to absurd double-counting of causes. It would be like saying that the meat fried in Footscray cooked because it had the property of being either fried in Footscray or boiled in Bundoora – only worse, because the disjunction would be much longer and more miscellaneous.

Since the highly disjunctive property of being in M does not occupy the M-role, I say it cannot be the referent of M. Many disagree. They would like it if M turned out to be a rigid designator of a property common to all who are in M. So the property I call 'being in M', they call simply M; and the property that I call M, the occupant of the M-role, they call 'the realisation of M'. They have made the wrong choice, since it is absurd to deny that M itself is causally efficacious. Still, their mistake is superficial. They have the right properties in mind, even if they give them the wrong names.

It is unfortunate that this superficial question has sometimes been taken to mark the boundary of 'functionalism'. Sometimes so and sometimes not – and that's why I have no idea whether I am a functionalist.

Those who take 'pain' to be a rigid designator of the highly disjunctive property will need to controvert my argument that 'pain' is not rigid, and they will not wish to claim that one can distinguish situations in which the pain-role is differently occupied. Instead, they should controvert the first step, and deny that the actual occupant of the pain-role is called 'pain'. I call that denial a *reductio*.

Notes

1 See David Lewis, 'New Work for a Theory of Universals', *Australasian Journal of Philosophy* 61 (1983), pp. 343–377; and David Lewis, *On the Plurality of Worlds* (Blackwell, 1986), pp. 59–69.

2 See David Lewis, 'Critical Notice of D. M. Armstrong, *A Combinational Theory of Possibility*', *Australasian Journal of Philosophy* 70 (1992), pp. 211–224.

3 Lewis, 'New Work for a Theory of Universals', pp. 365–370.

4 Gerald Feinberg, 'Physics and the Thales Problem', *Journal of Philosophy* 66 (1966), pp. 5–13.

5 Lewis, 'New Work for a Theory of Universals', pp. 361–365.

6 Frank Jackson, 'Epiphenomenal Qualia', *Philosophical Quarterly* 32 (1982), pp. 127–136.

7 Laurence Nemirow, 'Physicalism and the Cognitive Role of Acquaintance' and David Lewis, 'What Experience Teaches', both in *Mind and Cognition: A Reader*, ed. by W. G. Lycan (Blackwell, 1990).

8 Lewis, *On the Plurality of Worlds*, pp. 212–213.

9 Frank Jackson, 'Armchair Metaphysics', in *Philosophy in Mind*, ed. by J. O'Leary Hawthorne and M. Michael (Kluwer, 1994); Robert Stalnaker, 'Assertion', *Syntax and Semantics* 9 (1978), pp 315–332; M. K. Davies and I. L. Humberstone, 'Two Notions of Necessity', *Philosophical Studies* 38 (1980), pp. 1–30; and Pavel Tichý, 'Kripke on Necessity *A Posteriori*', *Philosophical Studies* 43 (1983), pp. 225–241.

10 Pace David Lewis, 'Psychophysical and Theoretical Identifications', *Australasian Journal of Philosophy* 50 (1972), pp. 249–258, eliciting the general principles of folk psychology is no mere matter of gathering platitudes.

11 F. P. Ramsey, 'Theories' in Ramsey, *The Foundations of Mathematics*. (Routledge & Kegan Paul, 1931), pp. 212–236; Rudolf Carnap, 'Replies and Expositions' in *The Philosophy of Rudolf Carnap*, ed. by P. A. Schilpp (Cambridge University Press, 1963), pp. 958–966. See also David Lewis, 'How to Define Theoretical Terms', *Journal of Philosophy* 67 (1970), pp. 427–446, reprinted in Lewis, *Philosophical Papers*, Vol. 1 (Oxford University Press, 1983); and Lewis, 'Psychophysical and Theoretical Identifications'.

12 David Lewis, 'How to Define Theoretical Terms' and 'Psychophysical and Theoretical Identifications'.

13 Hartry Field, 'Theory Change and the Indeterminacy of Reference', *Journal of Philosophy* 70 (1973), pp. 462–481; Carnap *loc. cit.*

14 David Lewis, 'Mad Pain and Martian Pain', in *Readings in Philosophy of Psychology*, Vol. 1, ed. by N. Block (Harvard University Press, 1980), reprinted with postscript in Lewis, *Philosophical Papers*, Vol. 1 (Oxford University Press, 1983).

15 D. M. Armstrong, *A Materialist Theory of Mind* (Routledge & Kegan Paul, 1968), p. 68.

16 J. J. C. Smart, 'Sensations and Brain Processes', *Philosophical Review*, 68 (1959), pp. 141–156.

17 See David Lewis, 'An Argument for the Identity Theory', *Journal of Philosophy* 63 (1966), pp. 17–25, reprinted with additions in Lewis, *Philosophical Papers*, Vol. 1 (Oxford University Press, 1983); and Lewis, 'Psychophysical and Theoretical Identifications'. See Armstrong, *A Materialist Theory of the Mind*, for an independent and simultaneous presentation of the same position, with a much fuller discussion of what the definitive causal roles might be.

18 Saul Kripke, *Naming and Necessity* (Blackwell, 1980), pp. 147–148.

19 The controverter just imagined would agree with the discussion in Kripke, *Naming and Necessity*, pp. 144–155. But I don't mean to suggest that Kripke would agree with him. At any rate, the words I have put in his mouth are not Kripke's.

20 Lewis, *On the Plurality of Worlds*, pp. 86–92.

21 Lewis, 'Mad Pain and Martian Pain'.

22 Frank Jackson, Robert Pargetter, and Elizabeth Prior, 'Functionalism and Type–type Identity Theories', *Philosophical Studies* 42 (1982), pp. 209–225.

23 In 'How to Define Theoretical Terms' I called it the 'diagonalized sense' of *M*.

24 David Lewis, 'Events' in Lewis, *Philosophical Papers*, Vol. 2 (Oxford University Press, 1986).

5

R. Van Gulick, "Functionalism, Information and Content"

Human beings are physical systems and thus in principle their activity can be described within the language of physical science. Yet it is clear that such descriptions will not suffice for every practical or explanatory purpose.[1] Among the theoretical perspectives which seem required for an adequate psychology of human action or behavior are those which describe human beings as acquiring information about their environment as well as storing, interrelating and using that information. Indeed, so large a role do such factors play in human behavior that many cognitive psychologists have adopted the notion of an *information processing system* as the dominant model in constructing theories of human psychological function.[2] However, despite the widespread popularity of the information processing approach, there is considerable theoretical unclarity about the notions of information and cognitive representation which are employed in formulating such theories. Various uses of the term 'information' drawn from computer science, communication theory, traditional psychology and common sense are often distinguished only inexactly, if at all.

Functionalism and content My intent below will be to provide an analytic, though nonrigorous,[3] treatment of the related concepts of information and content from a basically functionalist perspective, where functionalism is understood as the philosophic view that psychological states are type individuated by their distinctive role within a complex network of states mediating the perceptual conditions and behavior of organisms or systems.[4] States, including contentful states, are held to be of a given psychological type in virtue of their functional role within such a network. Thus the functionalist is obliged to explain how content is to be unpacked by reference to functional role.

The class of contentful states includes beliefs, desires, states of perceptual awareness in lower as well as higher animals, and at least some so-called "memory states" in digital computers. Roughly speaking, a contentful state is any state of a system whose adequate description requires a specification of its content. A particular belief state, for example, must be a state of believing that p or believing that q. Particular desires and intentions similarly require a specification of their content in order to be adequately characterized; we must say what is desired or intended and under what description.

The basic functionalist thesis is that psychological state types are to be characterized in terms of the functional roles which those states play in a structure of internal states, mediating stimulus inputs and behavioral outputs (leaving aside for now any further claims about the conceptual resources which will suffice to specify those roles.[5] Considerations of functional role are held to differentiate not only among general psychological state types such as beliefs, desires, and intentions, but also among subtypes such as *believing that p* and *believing that q*. A state has whatever content it does on the basis of its functional role.

Informational states In accord with our primary interest in the concept of information, I will focus on those contentful states which can be thought of as informational states of their respective systems. Systems realize informational states in the relevant sense when they can be said to possess the information or to have stored it in a manner allowing them to make use of it. It is the idea of *information possession* which is crucial here. For while representations and symbols can be thought of as representing or encoding certain bits of information, it would make no sense to think of them as themselves possessing that information. The information is present in those representations to be retrieved by any person or system capable of interpreting them. But when we attribute to an agent the belief that p (a belief being a type of informational state), we clearly attribute to him also the ability to understand and utilize that information. The distinction corresponds to Dennett's between intelligent and nonintelligent information storage,[6] for the crucial feature with respect to both intelligent information storage and informational states is that the relevant information is information *for the system* storing it or being in that state. Our task is to say what functional role or relation to input and output a state must realize if it is to constitute a system's possessing information.

Input Let us consider input relations first. Much contemporary psychological work on human and animal perception treats organic sensory structures as systems for extracting information from the physical stimuli impinging on the organism.[7] The processes are usually complex, involving first level transducers which convert physical stimuli in patterns of neural activity, followed by many levels of "analysis" performed on those neural patterns. In the retina, optic nerve, and cortex the pattern of neural firing is continually modified as it passes upward. The firing rates of neurons at upper levels are determined according to sometimes complex functions by the firing rates of neurons connecting to them from below. The firing of neurons from below has sometimes a facilitory and sometimes an inhibitory effect on neurons to which it inputs, but the details of these processes need not concern us here. What is relevant is that using this dual system of inhibition and excitement it is possible to build up structures, where neurons at the upper level are more and more selective in their response to features of the sensory stimuli. Thus using these so-called "perceptron" system[8] we can construct sophisticated feature extractors or pattern recognition devices; for example, selectively firing cortical neurons which alter their firing rate only if a line of light is present on the retina, or a line of a certain width, or of a certain width, length and orientation.

Such perceptron systems are often spoken of as "extracting information" from the initial pattern of light falling on the retina. But in what sense can the firing of the relevant cortical neuron be thought of as recognition of the presence of a horizontal line or as the realization of an informational state whose content is that a horizontal line is present? 'Information' is being used here in a manner much as in communications theory, where we talk of the nonrandom covariance between the properties of two communicating system.[9] In the visual perception system there is a nonrandom correlation between the presence or absence of various features in the initial stimuli and the firing of cortical neurons.

Given the correlations and its causal ties to the stimulus conditions, the firing of the relevant cortical neuron might seem to represent the presence of a horizontal line. But for whom or for what system does it represent such? The relevant system in this case must surely be the organism, but we are not justified in attributing to it the possession of information about the horizontal line purely on the basis of the sorts of input analysis described above.

Output In order to possess that information, the organism must be able to *utilize* it. The possession of the information must make a difference in the organism's actual or counterfactual behavior. For the content of any given state is a matter not only of its relations to input but also of its relations to the outputs of the system of which it is a part. Unless the system is in some way disposed to act differentially with respect to the stimulus, or in consequence of the state occasioned by the stimulus, no sense could be made of the system's attaching any significance to that stimulus. There would be nothing about the system which would constitute its taking the stimulus to be of a certain sort. Thus we could assign no content to the supposed representational state. Such a system would be only a passive or nonintelligent storer of information. The point is not an epistemological one about our inability to assign or discover the contents of internal states in the absence of behavioral manifestations of those states, but rather a conceptual claim. For a state may well have content though it never in fact manifests itself in behavior. Its influence on the organism's behavior may remain purely potential in the absence of the appropriate circumstances for activating its effects. However, even in the case of such never activated structures, it is the difference which they *would* make to behavior which provides the basis for assigning them informational content.

Of course not all the influences which a system's states have on its behavior are relevant to determining what content, if any, those states realize for the system. There are many ways in which a system's inputs can alter its output which are not properly thought of as involving the acquisition of information. This point should emerge clearly if we consider two general classes of constraints which apply in relating behavior regulating role to content. The first consists of constraints which concern adaptivity and the specificity of a response's adaptive value. The others involve rationality and interstate relations.

Adaptivity Speaking somewhat loosely, a system's states may be thought of as informational states or states of possessing information whenever the presence of those states leads to *adaptive modification* of the system's behavior; that is, modification which enhances the system's survival or the realization of its goals. To see a system as using information, we need not suppose that there is some separate store of information which it "consults" prior to acting to regulate its behavior. Rather in so far as structures within the system adaptively modify the behavioral responses of the system to changing environmental conditions, the very presence of those structures should be thought of as the possession of information by the system. For the likelihood that random behavioral changes occasioned by environmental conditions would be benefi-cial to the system is sufficiently low, that any structures which generally modify behavior in adaptive ways must be thought of as nonrandom and as consti-tuting information possessed by the system about its environment. The point is put somewhat more strongly by the ethologist Konrad Lorenz when writing of organic adaptation. He argues:

> "Adaptation" is the process which molds the organism so that it fits its environment in a way achieving survival. ... Any molding of the organism to its environment is a process so akin to that of forming within organic structure an image of the environment that it is completely correct to speak of information concerning the environment being acquired by the organism.[10]

Specificity This general characterization of information possession in terms of any adaptive structure is of course overly broad. It is at this point that consid-erations of specificity apply. The modifications of behavior brought about must be responsive to specific features of the changing environmental situation in order to justify the attribution of informational content to the structure. By running regularly a man may increase the strength of his legs, and the resul-tant increase in endurance and speed may well be considered adaptive. Yet we would not normally consider the organic changes in his musculature as the acquisition of information. What is missing in such a case is the development of structures regulating behavior which fit that behavior to the particular and specific circumstances of the environmental situation. We are in a strong position to attribute content to an internal state of a given system when the presence of that state is causally correlated with the presence of a particular environmental feature and the presence of the state modifies the behavior of the system in ways specifically adaptive to that particular environmental feature (for example, the cortical states of a frog which are excited only by small moving objects in its visual field and which produce "fly-catching" movements of its tongue). In very complex informational systems, the links between an informational state and adaptive behavior may be quite indirect. It may be difficult, for example, to locate any adaptive difference in behavior which connects with the average science student's true beliefs about the speed of light. But such cases can arise only within the context of a rich network of interconnected states. Specific adaptivity of response seems an essential element in the primary or basic cases of information possession.[11] Only where some states of a system have acquired content on such a basis can other states perhaps acquire content derivatively by relation to those states, without themselves having any specific adaptive consequences.[12]

Having introduced the notion of specific adaptivity, we cannot go further without discussing the idea of a system's *having goals* or being *goal directed*. Many philosophers and psychologists find such notions objectionably teleo-logical, but properly understood their use need not involve us in any excessive metaphysical commitments. Moreover, there seems no hope of giving any satisfactory account of active information possession without using goal-based concepts. In as far as informational states have the contents that they do in virtue of the adaptive modifications of behavior which they bring about, we must be prepared to attribute goals and goal directedness to any system to which we wish to attribute informational states. For otherwise, the notion of adaptivity could have no application. A system could not have informational states in the interesting sense of actively possessing information unless that system also had goals whose achievement could be enhanced by the utilization of that information. Thus possessing information presupposes having goals. Moreover, a proper understanding of goal directed systems will show that the converse also holds; that is, any system which is goal directed in an interesting sense must also be a system possessing information, a system with informational states.

Goal directedness To establish these connections, let us consider the generally plausible account of goal directedness offered by Ernest Nagel in his 1976 John Dewey lectures.[13] On Nagel's analysis which is fundamentally in keeping with general systems theory, a goal-directed system is one which tends toward a fixed state, and whose behavior in tending toward that state is persistent and plastic in the face of disturbing influences but (causally) orthogonal to those disturbing forces. The conditions of persistence and plasticity build in the notion of variable response to changing environmental conditions and thus exclude as non-goal-directed any systems which uniformly proceed toward some equilibrium state in too simple a manner, exhibiting no substantial degree of correction or self regulation. Operationalizing or making more specific how one might measure variability or plasticity would be no easy matter, but the general notions are I hope sufficiently clear as is their applicability to the concept of goal directedness.

The requirement of orthogonality is needed to rule out cases where the character of the system's corrective responses are direct and simple causal consequences of the nature of the disturbing influences operating. Explaining the system's persistence in tending toward the fixed end state in such cases does not require appeal to any internal behavior regulating structures, but is a simple direct causal consequence of direct input/output relations. Here again there are difficulties in spelling out the constraint. How indirect must the link between disturbance and response be to count as orthogonal? And how might one measure directness? We surely cannot require that there be *no* causal link between disturbance and response without danger of depriving all physical systems of goal-directed status.[14] What is important is that the organizational structure of the system play an essential role in determining the behavioral response, and that *ceteris paribus* the more that response depends on the complex and systematic interaction of component structures within the system, the more basis there is for treating the behavior as goal directed. Still in many cases there will be an element of choice involved in our attribution of goal directedness, choices dependent on our explanatory aims and on the larger systematic context within which the structure or component we are describing occurs. If we understand what the causal determinants of that item's response to its environment are, the issue of whether or not to regard it as goal directed is not one of adding further causal factors or causal factors of a different sort to our story. It is rather a matter of choosing that descriptive framework which, consistent with the causal facts, meets our need to explain and understand the item in question and its behavior. The teleological description might be apt in cases where we wish to explain why this structure rather than some other came to be (or to be perpetuated), by appeal to the selective advantage of the goals it secures. The teleological view may also bring out similarities between the item in question and other structures which emerge only when we depart from their causal details and consider them in terms of the goals toward which they can be seen as directed. In so far as characterizing any item X as of a given sort F is not a matter independent of taking it to be like or unlike other things (in some variety of respects), it may be necessary to exhibit those of X's similarities to other items which emerge only under a teleological description in order to achieve the sort of understanding of X which we aim at in a given situation. At the level of detailed causal structure X may bear little resemblance to Y and Z, though we may enhance our understanding of X if we recognize the affinities between X, Y, and Z considered teleologically. For example, they might all be seen to function as feedback devices regulating some growth process within their respective containing systems.

In consequence of this context dependence, we may find much better grounds to regard one of two very similar items as more goal directed than another, merely on the basis of its role within the system of which it is a component. We cannot restrict our attention to the component's input/output relations alone nor even to the causal determinants of its behavior. Of two structures acting similarly to achieve changes in the ionization balance internal and external to themselves, one may be more aptly thought of as goal directed, if its achieving such an effect can be seen to contribute to larger more clearly goal-directed behaviors in its containing system. Imagine perhaps that one structure is an isolated randomly occurring molecular structure and the other is a neural membrane of some vertebrate. In the latter case, we are more likely to derive explanatory value from describing the membrane in goal-directed terminology so as to fit its activity within the larger context of the organism's goal-directed processes. In doing so we do not attribute to its activity a different causal structure than that attributed to the isolated molecule, but rather focus attention on ways of relating the membrane and its behavior to other systematically related items.[15] The conditions which justify the description of some system as goal directed will not be independent of the pragmatic and explanatory context in which the description is to be used. This contextual dependence should emphasize that nothing said above is intended to provide a strict operational definition of what it is to be a goal-directed system.

Holism Despite its somewhat open and pragmatic character, our basic account establishes important links between the notions of goal directedness and information possession. Modification of behavior which is specifically adaptive to changing environmental circumstances is a crucial element in both analyses. The sorts of internal structures which must be present regulating behavior to provide sufficient plasticity and orthogonality of behavior to justify the attribution of goal directedness to a system are of the same sort required to attribute the possession of information to the system. Just as possessing information presupposes the having of goals, so also no system could adapt its behavior in the ways required by our analysis of goal directedness without *ipso facto* possessing information. The two notions are analytically interdependent; indeed they might be thought of as merely two aspects of a single functional characteristic of complex systems, that of having structures which adaptively mold or fit the system to its environment and which manifest an understanding of that environment and its causal structure in their regulation of the system's behavior.[16] The existence of such conceptual connections will come as no surprise to those sympathetic to the claims of mental holism, though the conceptual interdependence for which I have argued above seems both more intimate and more general in scope than in standard discussions of holism.[17] The oft alleged mutual interdependence of belief and desire can now be seen as merely a special case of a more general link between informational and goal-direction states. The considerations which so intimately tie belief and desire are not peculiar to any given theory of human or common-sense psychology, but would apply equally with respect to any psychological theory which employed the concepts of information or goal directedness in explaining behavior.

To adequately display the importance of holistic considerations in characterizing such systems, we must go on to discuss the second general class of constraints which apply to their functional organizations. For holistic interdependencies arise also within the fine-grained relations among large classes of particular contentful states, all of which may be of the same general state type. For example, the realization of a particular informational state will typically require the realization of a structure of other related informational states. If the state is a belief, it is clear that to have one belief, the believer must have many. And the beliefs which he has must be interconnected and interrelated in appropriate ways manifesting a rational order. Taking account of this holism requires us to expand our list of the constraints which must be honored in relating a state's content to its behavioral role by adding constraints which concern the nature and degree of the state's *interconnection or functional interaction* with other internal behavior regulating states, with special emphasis on connections of rationality.

Interconnection In considering constraints of interconnection it is important to distinguish between two sorts of reasons for attending to interstate relations in developing an account of content – one practical, the other more conceptual. As a practical matter, most of the systems to which we would wish to attribute informational states, are ones in which the behavior of the system can rarely if ever be explained by appeal to the influence of a single state acting in isolation. Rather it is characteristic of such systems that their behavior is the product of complex and multiple interactions involving many internal structures. Any adequate specification of the role which a given state or structure plays with respect to the system's behavior will have to be in terms of the partial contributions which that state makes to the determination of behavior in conjunction with a wide variety of internal state combinations. Thus as a practical matter, if we wish our account of content as a function of behavioral role to cover such systems, as we surely do, then we must be prepared to accommodate these interrelations. On the conceptual side, a stronger claim is suggested. For a high degree of interstate connection may be more than accidentally present in the actual systems of interest to us. Such rich connections among informational (or contentful) states may be necessary for possessing many sorts of information. If so, no system lacking such interstate connections within its functional organization could satisfy the conditions for possessing the relevant information.

To see how this might be so, we must note how the range of information which a system can possess is constrained by the character of its internal functional organization. In so far as content is understood as a function of functional role, relations among items of content must in some way be reflected in relations among functional structures. Now recognizing relations among items of content will be a pervasive and necessary feature of sophisticated information possessing systems. For given our sense of active information possession, a system cannot possess the information that a certain situation obtains or that some item satisfies a given description unless the system can in some sense "understand" what it would be for that situation to obtain or that description to apply. But achieving this understanding in most cases will require of the system that it 'recognize' how this particular fact links up with other facts. To understand what an individual fact comes to, the system will have to place it within a larger organized structure of facts (some analog of a theory). Thus in order to satisfy the conditions for possessing the one item of information, it must also realize in its functional organization the conditions for possessing those related items of content as well as reflecting their interrelations. The holism of the cognitive field at the level of content must be mirrored at the level of functional organization if content is as we suppose a function of functional organization. At some level of description, there must be an *isomorphism* between the logical and relational structure of the information possessed and the functional organization of states which constitutes the possession of that information.[18]

Unfortunately our use of isomorphism is likely to remain vague here, though it can perhaps be made a bit more specific by looking at its application in particular cases. Suppose for example that we wish our system to possess information about the relative volumes of a group of cylinders. The ordering of cylinders by relative volume will be transitive, and this transitivity should be reflected in our system's representation of those volumes. Now one need not suppose that the states of the system realizing the possession of information about the volumes of particular cylinders should themselves evidence some transitive *physical* ordering, far less an ordering in terms of relative volume. But the transitive ordering must somehow be embodied in the interactive relations between those states in virtue of which the behavior of the system is determined. The structure must be such that if the system is asked to select the member greater in volume from each of the three pairs of cylinders A and B, B and C, and C and A, it will not make any such intransitive selections as A, B, C, respectively. Thus the isomorphic relation which mirrors the transitive ordering of the cylinders' volumes may not be any simple physical relation, but rather a relation which emerges only at the level of the functional roles which the contentful states play in regulating the system's behavior. In such cases, the isomorphism between informational structure and functional structure can be established only when the functional organization is described in terms of its actual behavior regulating role. That the relevant isomorphism might be a mapping from a structure of informational items onto a structure of behavior regulating operations or procedures in no way undercuts the demand for some sort of 'mirroring' as an essential condition for possessing the relevant information. We must just avoid too narrow a conception of 'mirroring.'

The line of support for our conceptual claim should now be obvious. A system can actively possess information about a given fact only if it can understand that fact by placing it in a context. Thus to realize the initial informational state a system must also realize a structure of other interrelated states which constitute its possession of information about those related facts which form the necessary context for understanding the original fact. Holism is inescapable with respect to information possession, and the more sophisticated is the information possessed, the greater become the demands for functional interconnection.

If we remember that the relevant context of understanding for active information possession is a real world context and not a merely symbolic one, a second argument can be made for the necessity of interconnection by appeal to behavioral roles. The idea of information possession is essentially bound up with that of adaptive modification of behavior. However, with respect to many of the contents we might wish to use in specifying the information possessed by a system there is no simple or isolated set of behavioral routines or responses which would manifest its possession of just that information. The sorts of facts about a system's behavior which could count as its understanding and possessing such items of information would have to involve its realizing patterns of complex *conditional* response sensitive as well to a great many other environmental features or parameters. In such cases, then, the realization by any system of a functional structure which constituted its possession of the initial information would require its also realizing functional structures constituting the possession of a great deal of other information as well, information about those other factors.[19] Thus the argument from treating content as a function of behavioral role reaches the same holistic result as the argument from understanding. Indeed, the two are closely tied in so far as achieving greater understanding involves establishing more finely tuned adaptive behavior regulation.

Sententially specified content This can be illustrated in an especially clear way by considering the special conditions which a system must satisfy to justify us in using the sentential mode to specify the contents of its informational states. By "sentential mode" or "sentential idiom" here I mean the use of *that*-clauses to specify content, as when we say of someone or something that it knows *that* or believes *that the door is open*. When we employ this method, we attribute to the system whose informational states we are specifying a degree of understanding very much like our own. We treat the informational state as the system's possession of the same sort of information which we would possess if we knew the declarative sentence portion of the *that*-clause to be true.[20] Thus possessing such information requires of a system that it realize a large network of richly and rationally interconnected states. The demands of holism are especially great when the sentential mode is to be employed.

Consider again our selectively firing cortical neuron which responds only to the presence on the retina of a horizontal line of light. We saw that to count the state of that neuron's firing as the recognition of a horizontal line's presence, that state would have to make an appropriate difference to the system's behavior, where "appropriate" was left to be spelled out in detail. In moving to the sentential mode of content specification we face increased requirements which must be met for a state to qualify as the recognition or awareness *that* a horizontal line is present. Here the appropriate behavior cannot be merely some limited set of responses which are apt given the line's presence. Rather we require of the system that it evidence the variety of differences in behavior which might result when a human possesses the equivalent belief. There will not be any easy or simple way to spell out the relevant behavior influencing role, since the number of effects which such recognition might have on the behavior of a human or other fully rational agent is virtually limitless and crucially dependent on the totality of his other psychological states.

A system's realizing a sententially specified informational state cannot be a matter of its realizing a state which merely produces some small repertoire of fixed adaptive behaviors. The behavioral role played by such a state will be considerably more abstract and involve the state's making a partial contribution to a great many different behavior regulating processes. The differences of response which the presence or absence of the given state produces in each of these many cases enables the system to exhibit an overall pattern of selective variation in its behavior which may be counted as its realizing the possession of the relevant abstract information.

Moreover, the possession of such information could be realized *only* via structures functioning in such relatively global ways. A system's possessing the information *that* X obtains, where X is some sententially specified state of affairs, could not be merely a matter of S's having a structure which causes it to act in certain ways *toward* X. Rather possessing such information will involve the system's acting in highly selective and differential ways toward a great many environmental features other than X, but in ways which can be seen as manifesting the information it possesses about X. That is, the system can understand and possess information about X's obtaining only in virtue of realizing structures modifying its behavior toward some Ys and Zs in ways which are selectively adaptive given X. These behaviors most be counted among the responses which S makes *with respect to* X, though not (directly) *toward* X.

Both types of behaviour are relevant to a state's content determining functional role, and in systems realizing sententially specified informational states it is often responses of the former sort which figure the largest in fixing content. If we wish to attribute to some system the possession of the information *that* the can before it contains blue paint or *that* five times seven equals thirty-five, we must suppose that the system realizes structures to utilize this information in a great many diverse applications. Thus a high degree of holistic interaction among functional states turns out to be an essential characteristic of any system which realizes contentful states of the abstract sort specified in the sentential mode. Holism, abstraction, and sentential content go naturally together. Thus the holism of common-sense psychology is not a peculiarity of that theory. The degree of interactive complexity among informational states which we find in the common-sense model will have to be a necessary feature of any system to which we might wish to attribute the sorts of contents specifiable by use of the sentential idiom. No system which was substantially less holistic in its system of possessing information could have states informationally equivalent to those of sententially specified systems. But of course it is not just the *degree* of interaction among states which matters, but also the *character* of that interaction. Not just any interconnections will suffice. For in addition to the richness of their interstate connections, sententially specified systems are distinguished by the degree to which those relations must satisfy what we may term the *constraints of rationality*.[21]

Rationality In so far as we wish to use the sentential idiom in characterizing the informational contents of a system's states, the contents which we attribute to that system must on the whole form a relatively consistent and coherent set. We cannot meaningfully attribute to a system a set of contents whose members are grossly incompatible in terms of their deductive or inductive relations. Nor can we suppose a system to have states with a particular set of sentential contents, C, while lacking any states whose contents correspond to the obvious inductive and deductive consequences of C.

We need not assume that a system's set of informational states satisfies the demands of strict closure under the consequence relation just as we do not expect human agents to be ideally rational or to draw all the consequences of their beliefs. Nonetheless, a certain minimal but hardly insignificant degree of rationality is built into the very notion of a sentential state. For a system cannot possess information in our sense about matters it cannot understand. At the level of sententially specified content, this entails that a person or system cannot believe or possess the information that a *particular proposition p obtains* unless it understands what the truth of *p* would amount to. Now such understanding will have to consist in large part of linking *p* with other propositions. For surely no system could be said to understand *p* while failing to connect *p* with any reasonable number of its deductive and inductive consequences.

Moreover, the rationality of the system must be reflected not only in the overall consistency and coherence of its set of contents *at a time*, but also in the procedures which govern the transitions in the system's set of states *over time*. The manner in which states are added to or deleted from the system's set should more often than not correspond to patterns of sound inference between the sententially characterized contents of those states.

The constraints of rationality are not merely methodological guides to be used in effectively employing the sentential mode of content specification. Rather, they are elements essential to viewing any system as realizing sentential states. As such they are a special case of the general requirement noted earlier for an information possessing system to mirror or preserve the relational structure of the information which it possesses. The notion of a set of propositions is essentially bound up with the logical relations among the members of that set. To possess the information that a given set of propositions obtains, a system must embody in the structure of its informational states the relations among those propositions. I do not wish to claim that to understand a given proposition, there is some well defined and explicit set of other propositions which the system must also understand and to which it must connect the original proposition. We surely must allow for individual differences, but that a system should be able to understand that a proposition p obtains while "recognizing" virtually none of p's relations to other propositions is incoherent. Just as a sentence has meaning only within the context of a language, so too a state can have a content specified by a sententially generated *that*-clause only within the context of a network of rationally interconnected states. A grossly inconsistent set of sentences does not constitute a theory as it provides no coherent account of what it might be taken to describe. Similarly, one could not think of an informational system as realizing an overall set of contentful states with just the contents specified by such a set of inconsistent sentences. The set of sentences we use to specify the information possessed by a system must exhibit that minimal degree of rationality required to justify the use of the intentional idiom.

There are three elements present here which while differentiable must not be thought of as independent: the system's realizing a set of contentful or informational states, the interconnections or functional interactions between those states in regulating behavior, and the system's understanding of the relevant sorts of content. No one of these phenomena should be thought of as an independent element which comes about as a causal consequence of the others. Neither the interconnections between states nor the system's utilization of the information contained in those states should be thought of as a causal consequence of the system's understanding the relevant information. Rather its understanding *consists in* its having the structure of interactive relations among its states in regulating behavior which it does. It is also in virtue of those functional relations that the states have the contents that they do, but their content is not a *causal* consequence of those relations. Rather, that the system of states has the functional structure that it does and that the states have the contents that they do are one and the same state of affairs differently described; or perhaps the former could be said to constitute or realize the latter. Thus the two phenomena of a system's achieving understanding and its having contentful states turn out to be interdependent and mutually presupposing. Either both or neither will be present, and where they are present they will be so in virtue of the structure of interactive behavior regulating mechanisms which constitute their joint realization by the system.

Sentential and nonsentential content Given the rough conditions that have been laid out for realizing sententially specified content, we can see that states justifying specification of their content in the sentential mode will be a limited subset of contentful states. While we often use the sentential idiom in attributing information to non-human animals, it seems that many such attributions are unjustified or justified only in so far as we are speaking loosely or metaphorically. The informational states which are the resultants of a frog's visual perception system, for example, cannot be literally described as states of recognizing *that there is a fly to the front*. We know that the frog is unable to discriminate between the presence of a moving fly and the presence of any roughly fly-sized moving object before it, no matter how unfly-like it might be in shape, color, or edibility.[22] The restricted range of input analysis clearly makes the use of the human concept of 'a fly' inappropriate in describing the information obtained by those processes. Might we describe the informational state as the frog's recognition *that a roughly half-inch sized object is moving to the front?* Again the answer must be negative, but not in this case due to the frog's limited abilities to discriminate among inputs. The deficiency lies rather in the limited nature of the differences which the frog's perceptual state can make to its behavior. The perceptual state will trigger the frog to thrust out its tongue and will spatially orient the tongue movements toward the location of the moving object. To the extent that this constitutes the whole of the behavioral influences produced by the presence of the relevant perceptual state, the sentential idiom is not at all appropriate. The state simply fails to interact in the requisite ways with other states to produce complex rational changes in the frog's behavior.

The sentential mode is also limited in its application to humans. For many of the informational states likely to be posited by a theory of human psychology will occur as components of networks not justifying the sentential idiom. An example might be the sort of information about the condition of local muscle fiber groups realized by brain structures regulating voluntary bodily movements.[23] Despite the highly specific character of the input or sensory analysis involved in such cases, it would be mistaken to specify the content of such a cortical state as an awareness *that* such-and-such fibers are fatigued to degree *n*, or *that* such-and-such muscle is bent at an angle of *x* degrees. The contents of those states simply do not enter into the sorts of inferential relations that these sentential characterizations would suggest. The information which is contained in these states of kinaesthetic afferentation is relatively isolated in the sorts of ways it affects behavior, notwithstanding the fineness of regulation it produces with respect to bodily movement. In so far as those neural structures realize an understanding of muscle activity and function, that understanding is opaquely embedded in movement-regulating processes and is not of an explicit sort which would allow for rich inferential connection.

The question of just how the content of such states ought to be specified so that we attribute to the state neither more nor less information than it actually contains is no simple problem once we recognize the impropriety of treating it as analogous to the informational content of our own familiar cognitive states, our conscious beliefs. Whatever methods we employ are likely to have some misleading implications, and caution will require us to keep a close watch on the overall structure of the relevant information systems in discussing the contents of their states.

Motivational states Though our focus has been on informational states, the mutual interdependence of information possession and goal directedness should lead us to expect that the principal features of our account of content specification apply similarly to the contents of motivational or preference states. All the difficulties which confront us in attempting to specify what a given system *takes to obtain* will apply *mutatis mutandis* in specifying what it is the system *aims at* or is *directed toward bringing about*. For simple systems or organisms there is likely to be no natural language specification of the system's goals which characterizes them in a way reflecting the modesty of the system's psychological organization. It is no more appropriate to attribute to a frog a rich and exactly specified preference than it would be to attribute to it a similar belief or perceptual state. It would be wrong to attribute to a frog a preference or desire to ingest small moving objects of such-and-such shape and size, even where such a result is regularly achieved by the frog's behavior. In so far as we want our characterization of the frog's goals to reflect the overall structure of his psychological organization, we must describe those goals at a level of content specification consistent with the sort of awareness attributable to the frog and the sort of interaction present among its psychological states. Where a high level of rational interconnectedness is absent, neither goals nor informational content can be appropriately specified in the sentential mode.

Pragmatics and interest relativity Throughout our account, the general dependence of content on holistic interstate relations has provided the basis for distinguishing many degrees of content sophistication as well as degrees to which any system can be said to understand or be rational. Thus we need draw no sharp lines between those systems which are rational and those which are not. Moreover, attributions of content turn out to involve an element of choice dependent on our explanatory and practical interests. Specifications of content are not arbitrary and functional organization constrains content realization, but there is always discretion to use or forgo description in terms of content, as well as in how content is to be specified.

The way in which our choices in such cases depend pragmatically on our explanatory interests nicely turns our account of content and understanding back on itself. Since possessing information about some item (or understanding it) is to have behavior-regulating mechanisms which allow one to deal with it in a way enhancing the realization of one's goals, what constitutes understanding or information will always be relative to one's goals or interests. Such interest relativity applies as well in those cases where it is information possessing systems themselves which are to be understood. What information we possess about such a system and in what ways we understand it will depend on how we are able to adaptively interact with it. Our understanding will be bound up with our goals and interests relative to it, and different descriptions will likely be appropriate for the various cases in which we wish to predict its behavior, experimentally investigate it, make sense of its actions, manipulate it, construct it, or communicate with it.

It is worth emphasizing this pragmatic element, since the adaptive interest-relative aspect of understanding tends to slip out of sight in considering our own informational states, while conversely the informational character of adaptivity tends to get hidden when we consider very simple systems. We might consider informational states as ordered on a continuum[24] according to the rough account of content sophistication developed above. To one extreme would fall such crude information as that possessed or "understood" by a chameleon about the color of its environment or the value of camouflage. At the other end would come such fully sentential states as the beliefs of a rational human agent, while intermediate would be states of the sort associated with the frog visual system and human fine muscle control. With cases of the one extreme, where adaptivity is a causally direct result of structure, speaking of the chameleon as acquiring information about the color of his surroundings or of the bird's wing and flight mechanisms as "understanding" or embodying the possession of information about the air, we may seem to strain the notion of understanding past its limit. But the prominence and directness of adaptivity in these cases should not blind us to the fact that the presence of such physically improbable structures constitutes the possession of phylogenetically acquired information about the environment.

As we move further along or up our ordering we do not move away from states linked to behavior. We move only away from states whose content lies in their connection with a single fixed behavior toward those whose content consists in their larger (or potentially infinite) number of links to behavior. As we move toward states with richer and more varied behavior influencing roles, the instrumentally adaptive character of their informational content tends to diffuse, but not diminish. In sophisticated systems, like ourselves, with fully sentential states, the interest-relative dependence of informational content on adaptive value is obscured by the wealth and diversity of interests involved. But one must not mistake cases of multiple use information possession for cases of a basically incoherent sort in which information is possessed in the absence of any even potential effects on goal-directed behavior.

Of course there is an enormous difference between the frog's understanding of its visual environment and a physicist's understanding of the principles of thermodynamics. But this should not lead us to draw a distinction between instrumental and noninstrumental (or purely theoretical) understanding; for given a functionalist analysis of content, understanding is necessarily bound up with instrumental function. The interesting contrast is rather between the sort of implicit understanding which is opaquely embedded in adaptive procedures and the explicit understanding and inferential richness characteristic of theoretical thinking (with many cases in between). It seems plausible to link explicitness and inferential connectedness; for we can view the progression from the frog to the physicist as a move toward systems which become "aware of" (understand or possess information about) the rationales which are implicit or embedded in their functional structures. Making the contents realized by such structures explicit and themselves the objects of understanding

79

would be *ipso facto* to generalize their application and bring them within a wider inferential sphere.

In as far as this progression is toward forms of understanding which provide more open-ended possibilities for successful interaction with what is understood, its direction bears some resemblance to what Thomas Nagel has described as the "direction of objectivity."[25] The movement in each case is toward forms of understanding which abstract from the particular character of the direct causal dealings between the understanding system (or subject) *S* and its object. Coming to have a more objective understanding of *x* is to acquire a capacity for the sorts of indirect dealings with *x* that result from placing it within a larger inferential context. In so doing the system *S* realizes a greater understanding of *x* as an object playing a role in the world independently of *S*. Thus although the construction and use of theoretical representations is likely to be of great value in achieving such objective understanding, we can unpack the notion of objectivity and give an account of what it is to have objective understanding in purely functional terms.

Extending the functionalist account Still, the absence from one functionalist account of any specific discussion of the role of theoretical and symbolic structures in achieving understanding should serve to underscore its status as only a preliminary account of content. It is intended to provide a general framework within which further issues about content may be addressed and elaborated. Thus it seems apt to close by considering how a few important issues about content, neglected above, might be handled in keeping with the main themes of our analysis. Three such areas of concern would be: giving some account of symbolic representation and representational content, the problem of self-conscious and self-understanding systems, and accommodating the social holism of content and meaning. Let us consider these three briefly and in turn.

Representations It is a virtue of the functionalist approach that it allows us to provide an account of contentful states and intelligent information-possessing systems without having to rely on talk of representations or representational content. Still it seems clear that representations and symbolic structures play so large a role in human understanding and information possession that one cannot hope to have a complete or adequate human psychology which fails to include an account of representations and their content.[26]

I suggest the following strategy. In keeping with the guiding ideal of functionalism, the notion of "being a representation" would be analyzed as specifying a functional category. Perhaps the functional class could be better specified as items which "are used as representations by some system *S*" or which "serve as representations for *S*." The content of any such item would depend on its use by or within the relevant system (focusing for present purposes on internally used representations). The notion of a *state*'s having content would be taken as analytically or theoretically more primitive than

80

that of a *representation*'s having content, in that the idea of state content would be used in two ways to account for representational content.

First, representations and processes operating on representations can be understood as *underlying* or *realizing* a system's network of contentful states. That is, the description of the system's operations on representations would be at a lower level of abstraction, or nearer a hardware description than the contentful state description. The relevant system would satisfy the functional condition for possessing certain items of information about its environment on the basis of its internal structure of processes operating on representations. It is important to note that though the representation-based processes causally underlie or instantiate the system's contentful states, they do so only in virtue of realizing the necessary *functional* roles. As regards their own functional roles, the representations have whatever content they do only in virtue of the contentful states which they serve to realize within the system.

Moreover, the notion of state content must figure in a second respect; for not every causal structure which underlies a contentful state does so by functioning as a representation. The hope would be to mark off the special role played by representations by appeal to our theory of contentful states. In brief, representations might be classed as structures which not only underlie contentful states, but do so in virtue of themselves *being taken to have or understood to have content* by the very system within which they occur. The notion of a system's understanding certain features of its own structure or organization to have content would be explicated in terms of the system's having contentful states to that effect (that is, its bearing the appropriate causal functional relations to those features of itself). Of course, we cannot suppose that all of a system's contentful states are realized by representation based processes, if we are to avoid a vicious and infinite regress. But our functionalist theory can easily allow for some understanding which is simply embedded in processes.[27] Such processes could operate on representations and do so in a way which constitutes understanding those items as having content, without embodying that understanding itself in any representations. Though developing these suggestions in detail would be no simple matter, they offer the functionalist a basis for optimism.[28]

Self-consciousneses and self-understanding Our proposal for handling representations also suggests a strategy for developing a functionalist account of self-awareness or self-consciousness. The basic idea is to treat self-aware systems as realizing informational states about their own structure and functional organization.[29] The analysis of information possession would continue to be in terms of adaptive modification of behavior. A self-aware system's understanding of its own features would be a matter of its capacity for adaptive interaction with those features. We have often spoken above of the system's interaction with its environment, but of course the system itself can be a part of its environment, considered as the sphere of its adaptive activity.

81

Moreover, self understanding need not be restricted to its structural features, but might include complex higher-order features of its functional organization as well.

As our discussion of internal representation use should suggest, a capacity for self-understanding may do more than simply allow a system to interact adaptively with itself as it does with other objects. Rather, a system's capacity for self-understanding may greatly enhance its ability to adaptively interact with other non-self portions of the world. Being able to use features of itself as representations of the external environment and being able to make explicit the rationales embedded in its behavioral procedures in a way which allows for their generalization would be just two of the many such possibilities. We also might consider a capacity for learning or self-design[30] as a form of functionally analyzable self-understanding. A system could be said to possess information about or understand the function of a given behavior-regulating mechanism insofar as it realized a set of internal procedures which modified that mechanism in a way enhancing its adaptive value on the basis of environmental feedback. Such understanding need not be explicit; indeed it might be opaquely embedded in the learning procedures. But where the resulting modifications are so apt to the mechanism's function, the procedures guiding that modification should be seen as constituting implicit understanding of that function.

It is unclear just how much can be gotten from our functional account of information possession by constructing systems which turn back on themselves iteratively and reiteratively. Especially lacking is a clear route which would lead us from such iterative structures to an account of the sort of self-consciousness which we associate with conscious human experience. No immediate solutions to different philosophic puzzles about the subjective and phenomenal features of conscious experience seem in the offing.[31] Still the basic functionalist strategy here presents a wealth of opportunities which have barely begun to be exploited.

The social holism of meaning and content Indeed, the functionalist may be confronted with an embarrassment of programmatic riches. For complementary to the strategy of investigating self-conscious or inwardly turning informational systems is the equally promising project of considering information possession systems which are turned outward within a social context or community of interacting informational systems. Our basic functionalist account above focused on cases of isolated individual systems within well-defined nonsocial environments. While such a focus may have been heuristically justified, it clearly will not suffice for constructing an overall account of how social organisms, such as human beings, understand and possess information about their world. However, I believe it is possible to extend our functionalist account to accommodate the social dimension, while preserving its basic analysis of content and information. I hope to make this claim of extendability plausible by discussing in an admittedly quick and simple fashion three ways in which the introduction of the social context would make a difference to the functionalist analysis of content.

First, systems or organisms which live together in genuine communities would of necessity have to possess the ability to understand each other as systems which understand, possess information, and have goals. They would have to possess some *second-order* understanding; that is, they would need to realize contentful states concerned with the realization of contentful states by other systems. Not only would they have contentful states, but they would in some sense "understand" what it is to have contentful states. Of course, their understanding need not be at all like an explicit theoretical understanding of such matters. Indeed all the relevant understanding might be opaquely embedded in mechanisms which regulate the interactions among the members of the community. Given its adaptive value, the presence of a mechanism which puts a sparrow to flight in response to a 'warning call' cannot be regarded as a random fact. Rather it should be seen as constituting the possession of phylogenetically acquired information, part of which is an implicit understanding of other sparrows as perceivers capable of detecting or acquiring information about the presence of predators. Though human beings can understand each other as informational systems in a much more explicit and sophisticated way, the bird example should make clear that on our naturalistic and functionalist view of content, various forms of (at least implicit) second-order understanding are widely realized throughout the biological world.

The second feature of the social which the functionalist must accommodate is the existence of *socially constituted* objects of understanding. Societies bring into existence practices, institutions and states of affairs which could have no reality apart from the regularities of the social context (for example, pecking orders, law courts and ritual ceremonies). Moreover, the members of societies can and must realize informational and other contentful states about those socially constituted phenomena in order to participate in the behavioral regularities which do the constituting. It is this tail-biting aspect of social constitution which prevents us from treating such cases as differing from our standard cases of information possession only in their particular content. It is not like shifting from information about flies to information about sticks. For in the social case, the states of affairs which are taken to exist and about which information is possessed are dependent for their very existence on being recognized or taken to obtain by the members of the society. Thus in talking about content or information possession in such cases, we must complicate the simple picture presented above, in which content was analyzed in terms of causal functional relations obtaining between an informational system and an independently existing set of objects. Socially constituted phenomena do have a reality independent of their recognition by any *particular* informational system or society member, but it is clear that their dependence on the *collective* contentful states of the society's members will demand special attention in accommodating understanding and the possession of information about such phenomena within our functionalist account.

Moreover, reflection on the social cases reveals that in a less radical form such an interdependence between understanding and its objects is yet another form of pervasive holism that applies with respect to *all* contentful states. Such nonsocial objects as trees, rocks, and flies are not dependent upon recognition for their existence or character. But if we wish to specify the contentful states which a system has about such items, our choice of how to describe or classify them will not be independent of their relations to the system in question. Types of objects which might be classed together relative to one system which fails in any way to distinguish among them, might need to be described as of many different kinds relative to some other system. Thus in general our description of the objective component of the functional relations between a contentful system and its environment will not be independent of the character of the informational system or subjective element of the relation.

It is this sort of descriptive holism embracing the environment as well as the informational system which underlies familiar difficulties about specifying the inputs and outputs for human functional psychology. On the one hand, many classes of inputs such as red objects really only constitute a class on the basis of subjective facts; that is, facts about their functional equivalence in affecting the perceptual mechanisms of human subjects.[32] And on the other hand, such disparate outputs as nodding one's head, raising a hand, or uttering 'yes' get classed together only on the basis of all being taken as gestures of assent by the community of subjects. The human cases are not special in this regard but only make more evident the descriptive interdependence of subject and object which arises whenever we turn to specify the functional networks underlying contentful relations.

The third respect in which society makes a difference can be illustrated by again considering the example of the sparrow's warning call. In virtue of their coordinated collective behavior each member of the sparrow community gains perceptual or informational access to portions of its environment beyond the reach of its individual sensory organs.[33] Thus its position within a social group enhances each sparrow's ability to acquire information about nonsocial portions of the world. In analyzing information possession in terms of causal functional relations, we must acknowledge that the necessary connections will often be established only through the mediation of social structures.

Moreover, the social context can do more than merely extend the ability of its members to acquire information of a sort which they could acquire individually. Society can transform the nature of understanding in a more radical manner, such that the social group can be said to understand or possess information of a sort not possessed by any member of the group. Social insects provide clear examples of such more radically social information possession. There are good reasons for attributing to a *colony* of bees information not possessed by any of the individual bees. Collectively their behavior will result in the construction of a well-defined adaptive hive structure Yet no bee possesses the information of how to build a hive. Rather such understanding is embedded in the mechanism which regulates each bee's behavior as a function of what other nearby bees are doing. That is, the individual bee's behavior is not under the control of feedback about the emerging overall structure of the hive. The behavior regulating mechanisms in each bee are under only local feedback control sensitive to its interaction with other nearby bees. Yet the end product of this activity is a completed hive. The presence of mechanisms within the individual bees which produce such a result cannot be treated as a random fact, but should be understood as constituting the possession by the bee colony as a whole of phylogenetically acquired information about how to build a hive. The shaping processes of natural selection in this case have operated at the social level, perpetuating the genetically based social structures which embody the possession of such understanding.

The dramatic character of social understanding in bees and other social insects should not blind us to the presence of similar phenomena in more sophisticated animal societies, including human culture and society. For if we keep our focus on the functional notion of information possession as a capacity for adaptive interaction with the environment, it should be clear that large organized human groups can successfully deal with the environment in ways which manifest an understanding of that environment not possessed by any of their members. It is important to note that in such cases collective action is required not merely to put into action or apply that understanding, but the very understanding itself may be irreducibly collective. Consider a large scientific research program which over time investigates some class of micro-phenomena. A great many specialists with diverse theoretical, computational, and experimental skills will need to collaborate and depend on one another's activities to advance the research effort. It is unreasonable and simply false to believe that each of these research team members has individual cognitive mastery of all the elements of the overall project. Indeed, there is likely to be no such team member. The thought that there *must* be some person who individually possesses all the information probably arises from overrating the understanding of those team members whose contribution to the program derives from their skill in manipulating the theoretical formalism rather than in using its experimental and equipmental analogs of sensory and effector mechanisms. Of course, the theoreticians will have some understanding of the experimental set ups, but it is only the entire organized and intercommunicating scientific group together with its technical devices which can actually carry out the successful dealings with the micro-phenomena in those ways which constitute the acquisition and possession of information. The ability of individual researchers to describe and discuss overall aspects of their research should not lead us to neglect the necessity in such contexts for a social division of epistemological labor.[34]

Despite the wealth of complications and further interdependencies we have encountered in considering the social context, I hope to have offered plausible suggestions for accommodating the social aspects of information possession within our functionalist framework. However, it should also be evident that it would be a very messy affair to construct for even a moderately sophisticated system an explicit account of content which would take us from a physical description of the system and its dealings with the environment to a specification of its informational and other contentful states. Most often we will rather be engaged in attributing a limited range of contentful states to some system of which we have some prior understanding on the basis of its dealing with an environment described in a manner already appropriate to that system's patterns of interacting with it. This is most evident when we deal with other humans whom we assume to be quite like us or with other natural organisms of whose biological nature and needs we are at least partially aware.

Adopting a functionalist approach to content carries no commitment to theoretical reductionism. The functionalist program does not aim to construct an account which would enable us to deduce every fact about a system's contentful states from a physical description of its causal relations to its environment. It does, however, offer a way to think about content which is naturalistic and metaphysically austere, allowing us to discern the continuities which fit facts about content within the natural and biological sphere. Thus it satisfies those of our desires for a unity of science which are reasonable, while providing us with basic guiding ideas to link information, understanding, and adaptive causal interaction in developing accounts of content for the particular systems and situations where we need them.

Notes

I have benefited greatly from discussion of earlier versions of this paper with my colleagues at Rutgers University, especially Robert Matthews, Laverne Shelton, Sarah Stebbins, and Robert Weingard. My work was aided by a research leave granted by the Rutgers University FASP program.

1 The argument against the adequacy of physical description as a universal explanatory framework is made forcefully in Hilary Putnam, "Philosophy and our mental life," in Hilary Putnam, *Mind, Language, and Reality* (Cambridge, 1975), pp. 291–303.
2 For example, see P. Lindsay and D. Norman, *Human Information Processing* (Academic Press, 1972).
3 The account will be nonrigorous in that no attempt will be made to formulate strict necessary and sufficient conditions for key concepts. I do not take this to be a defect of the account. For, as discussed below, the applicability of those concepts appears to depend on pragmatic features of the given explanatory context.
4 The functionalist view is reflected in much contemporary work in the philosophy of mind. For some examples see D. C. Dennett, *Content and Consciousness* (Routledge & Kegan Paul, 1969); and "Intentional systems," *The Journal of Philosophy*, 1971, pp. 87–106; David Lewis, "An argument for the identity theory," *The Journal of Philosophy*, 1966, pp. 17–25; Gilbert Harman, *Thought* (Princeton University Press), pp. 34–53; and Hilary Putnam, ibid., pp. 429–40.
5 For some suggestions in this regard see Putnam, ibid., pp. 362–85, where a proposal in terms of Turing machine specification is offered; and D. K. Lewis, "Psychophysical and theoretical identifications," *Australasian Journal of*

Philosophy, 1972, pp. 249–51, for an account in terms of common-sense causal relations. Criticisms may be found in N. Block and J. Fodor, "What psychological states are not," *Philosophical Review*, 1972, 159–81; and in N. Block, "Troubles with Functionalism," in W. Savage (ed.), *Minnesota Studies in the Philosophy of Science*, vol. IX, 1979 (University of Minnesota Press), pp. 261–325.

6 Dennett, "Intentional Systems."

7 Lindsay and Norman, ibid., pp. 58–114; and J. J. Gibson, *The Senses Considered as Perceptual Systems* (Houghton, 1966).

8 Detailed discussion of such structures, as well as of their limitations, can be found in M. Minsky and S. Pappert, *Perceptrons* (MIT Press), 1969.

9 See, for example, G. Raisbeck, *Information Theory* (MIT Press, 1963), pp. 4–12.

10 K. Lorenz, *Evolution and the Modification of Behavior* (University of Chicago Press, 1965), p. 8.

11 Clearly we can and do attribute to human agents informational states which are on the whole maladaptive. In some cases the maladaptiveness is due to the incorrectness of the state, though in others the state may be nonadaptive even though its content accords with the facts. My point above is that such cases are possible only within the context of a large number of interdependent contentful states, where our basic scheme for fixing the contents of those states accords in general with our principle that information possession produce adaptive behavior. For discussion of a related point concerning veridicality and belief attribution see D. C. Dennett, "Intentional systems," pp. 102–3.

12 Notorious difficulties surround the attempt to account for the meanings of theoretical statements by their relations to nontheoretical or observational statements. No such intent, positivistic or otherwise, is implied by my use of the term 'basic' here. As should be clear below, my view of content is thoroughly holistic rather than foundationalist. What is basic is the general connection between information and adaptivity, not a privileged set of cases where that connection is especially direct or atomistically isolable.

13 Ernest Nagel, "Teleology revisited," *The Journal of Philosophy*, 1977, pp. 261–301.

14 The difficulty here is that the causal influences and responses of a closed causal system will always be nonorthogonal under some sufficiently complex description of the system's causal structure. Thus the weight of the constraint must fall on the complexity and indirectness of a causal link, rather than on its total absence.

15 See also R. Cummins, "Functional analysis," *The Journal of Philosophy*, 1975, pp. 741–65.

16 There is thus more than a punning similarity between the teleological and nonteleological senses in which informational states (or psychological states in general) may be thought of as *functional* states. For the interdependence of information possession and goal directedness entails that it will not be possible to spell out the relevant *causal behavior determining roles* in virtue of which some feature (or state) functions to realize the possession of information, without also characterizing the system's states *vis-à-vis teleological* functions. Adaptivity is a teleological notion in so far as it requires us to attribute goals to the system being considered, and it is a state's causal role in determining adaptive behavior which is crucial to information possession. Thus with respect to information possessing systems the notion of a functional state as specified in terms of its contribution to behavior within a systematic context of interacting components of necessity

merges with the notion of a functional state specified in terms of its adaptive value.

17 As in Donald Davidson, "Mental events," in L Foster and J. W. Swanson (eds), *Experience and Theory* (Massachusetts, 1970); "Psychology as Philosophy," in S. C. Brown (ed.), *Philosophy and Psychology*, (Macmillan, 1974); and D. C. Dennett, "Intentional systems." A somewhat more general account of the interdependence is offered in H. P. Grice, "Method in philosophical psychology," *Proceedings and Addresses of the American Philosophical Association*, 1975, pp. 23–53.

18 For some interesting suggestions on a related point see Stephen Palmer, "Fundamental aspects of cognitive representation," in E. H. Rosch and B. B. Lloyd (eds), *Cognition and Categorization* (Erlbaum Press, 1978).

19 See also in this regard H. P. Grice, "Method in philosophical psychology."

20 This question of when it is appropriate to employ the sentential idiom in specifying content is related to the question raised by Dennett in "Intentional systems" of "What is involved in *treating something as* an intentional system?" However, I am here interested in the further question which Dennett declines to discuss there of "What is it for a system to *actually realize* the possession of sententially specified content, i.e. to *be* an intentional system?"

21 The coiner of this term is to my knowledge Donald Davidson ("Mental events"). My use, however, parallels his only in part. The main differences concern the emphasis placed here on rational connectedness as requisite for *understanding* and the use to which these constraints of rationality are put. I, unlike Davidson, am primarily concerned to distinguish the realization of sententially specified states from other forms of information possession. Moreover, the constraints of rationality function show as constraints on sets of real state transitions, rather than as rules governing the reconstruction of an agent's psychological states from partial samples of his behavior. Understood in the manner described above the constraints seem of little value in support of Davidson's claims about the anomalous nature of the mental.

22 J. Y. Lettvin, H. R. Maturana, W H. Pitts, and W. S. McCulloch, "What the frog's eye tells the frog's brain," *Proceedings of the IRE*, 1959, pp. 1940–51.

23 A. I. Luria, *The Working Brain* (Basic Books, 1973), especially pp. 35–8.

24 I use the term 'continuum' here primarily to suggest the density of the ordering and to emphasize that systems may vary by many subtle degrees in the nature and quality of the information which they possess. I do not wish to imply that there is a simple linear ordering of systems in terms of the sophistication of the contents which characterize their informational states. The construction of a general hierarchy of levels of content specification would not be so simple a matter. For present purposes the rough judgments we can make distinguishing among substantially different levels of content specification should suffice.

25 T. Nagel, *Mortal Questions* (Cambridge University Press, 1978), p. 174. While the resonance between Nagel's remarks and the discussion above is suggestive, their apparent affinity should be regarded cautiously, given Nagel's strongly antifunctionalist bent.

26 For arguments to this effect see J. Fodor, *The Language of Thought*, ch. 2.

27 For discussion on procedural understanding see T. Winograd, "Formalism for knowledge," in *Thinking* (Cambridge University Press, 1977), pp. 62–71.

28 I make some attempt to carry this project a bit further in "Mental representation: A functionalist view," *Pacific Philosophical Quarterly*, 1982, pp. 3–20.

29 See D. C. Dennett's *Brainstorms*, pp. 149–73; and Grice's "Method in philosophical psychology."

30 The description of learning as self-design is Dennett's: *Brainstorms*, pp. 71–89.

31 T. Nagel forcefully presents the case for difficulties in his essay "What is it like to be a bat?" in *Mortal Questions*, pp. 165–80.

32 To get a feel for just how complex and indirect is the relation between an object's light reflecting characteristics and its perceived color see E. H. Land, "The Retinex Theory of color vision," *Scientific American*, Dec. 1977, pp. 108–28.

33 This example and its use to illustrate the view of language as "the extension of the senses" is due to W. V. O. Quine and J. Ullian, *The Web of Belief* (Random House, 1970).

34 Such division of epistemological labor (there called linguistic labor) is discussed in H. Putnam, *Mind, Language, and Reality*, ch. 12, especially pp. 245–7.

6

R. Cummins, "'How Does It Work?' versus 'What Are the Laws?': Two Conceptions of Psychological Explanation"

1 In the beginning

In the beginning there was the deductive nomological (DN) model of explanation, articulated by Hempel and Oppenheim (1948). According to DN, scientific explanation is subsumption under natural law. Individual events are explained by deducing them from laws together with initial conditions (or boundary conditions), and laws are explained by deriving them from other more fundamental laws, as, for example, the simple pendulum law is derived from Newton's laws of motion.

It is well-known that DN is vulnerable to a wide variety of counterexamples (e.g., Kim 1962; Salmon 1998). As a result, DN is not widely defended. But it is, I think, still widely believed that scientific explanation is subsumption under law. This is something of a scandal. Given DN's miserable track record in spite of spirited defense by many ingenious believers, one is led to ask why so many cleave so faithfully to a doctrine that has proved so indefensible?

There are two factors that work to keep DN in place. First, there is the fact that every experimental paper one picks up involves the explanation of some data by appeal to some hypothesis or other. It is tempting to conclude that philosophers' continued failure to articulate this practice in some defensible way is a point against philosophers, not against DN. And second, there is the fact that there is no widely understood and compelling alternative to DN on the market. If cognitive psychology has taught us anything, it is that no one willingly gives up a well-worn idea without having something to put in its place. I propose to examine these two factors in turn.

2 Two pitfalls

In psychology DN gets a spurious plausibility from the fact that data are routinely said to be "explained" or "accounted for" by some hypothesis or other. But this is likely to be misleading in at least two ways.

First, when psychologists talk about explaining or accounting for some percentage of the variance, the "hypothesis" in question is that the experimental treatment will have some real effect. One is looking to reject the null hypothesis in favor of its complement, namely, the hypothesis that whatever differences there are between the treatment group and the control group are not due to chance (random variation). But this sort of hypothesis isn't a law or anything like a law. The word "hypothesis" as it is used in statistical analysis, and the word "hypothesis" as it is used to refer to a conjectured theory or law, are little more than homonyms: They share the element of conjecture and little else. While there is nothing wrong with either use of the word, in the present context, we do well to keep the two senses distinct. With this in mind, I will use "proposed law" to refer to a hypothesis in the second sense.

The second way in which talk of explanation in the context of the statistical analysis of data is likely to be misleading is that, even though experimenters sometimes are attempting to test a theory or an hypothesis in the second sense (i.e., a proposed law or regularity), this is an exercise in confirmation, not explanation. We say that a law or theory accounts for or explains the data, but this simply means that the data *confirm* the law or theory. When a law is confirmed by some data set, this is evidence that the law *describes* the data (to some reasonable approximation). The now classic illustration of this is Balmer's formula (Hempel 1966):

$$\lambda = 3645.6 \, \frac{n^2}{n^2 - 4}$$

This formula specifies the wavelengths of the emission spectrum of hydrogen. Finding spectral lines in the places predicted by the formula confirms the law, but no one thinks the law explains why the lines are where they are.

Defenders of DN concede that Balmer's formula and similar cases are cases in which subsumption under law is not explanatory. They then take their task to be formulating a criterion that will distinguish cases like Balmer's formula from genuinely explanatory laws. There is wide consensus, however, that this has not been done successfully, and the suspicion grows that it *cannot* be done successfully. I think we should take seriously the possibility that it cannot be done because there isn't any difference: No laws are explanatory in the sense required by DN. Laws simply tell us what happens; they do not tell us why or how. Molière, satirizing scholastic appeals to occult properties and "virtues," tweaks the doctors of his time for explaining that opium puts people to sleep because it has a dormitival virtue. But isn't this just what subsumption under law always amounts to? Does the Law of Effect explain why giving a pigeon Pigeon Chow whenever it pecks a key increases the rate of key peeking? Or does it just restate the phenomenon in more general terms? Surely the correct moral to draw here is that the law of effect is an *explanandum*, not an *explanans*.

In science, when a law is thought of as an *explanandum*, it is called an "effect." Einstein received his Nobel prize, not for his work on relativity, but for his explanation of the photo-electric effect. In psychology, such laws as there are are almost always conceived of, and even called, effects. We have the Garcia effect (Garcia and Koelling 1966), the spacing effect (Madigan 1969), the McGurk effect (MacDonald and McGurk 1978), and many, many more. Each of these is a fairly well confirmed law or regularity (or set of them). But no one thinks that the McGurk effect explains the data it subsumes. No one not in the grip of the DN model would suppose that one could *explain* why someone hears a consonant like the speaking mouth appears to make by appeal to the McGurk effect. That just *is* the McGurk effect.

The mistaken idea that accounting for data by subsuming it under law is explanation is also fostered by a confusion between explanation and prediction.[1] A law that predicts a certain data point or data set is said to "explain" it. But prediction and explanation are separable in ways that DN cannot accommodate. It is possible to understand how a mechanism works, and hence to be in a position to explain its behavior and capacities – the *effects* it exhibits – without being able to predict or control its behavior. This is true generally of stochastic or chaotic systems. It is also true of systems whose relevant initial states are unknowable or simply unknown. In possession of a machine table for a Turing machine, I can explain all of its capacities, but, lacking knowledge of its initial state, I may be unable to predict its behavior (Moore 1956). Less interestingly, but just as important, some systems are simply intractable. We can explain the swirling trajectory of a falling leaf, but it would be hopeless to predict it.[2] Finally many systems are well understood in an idealized form, but their actual behavior cannot be predicted because the relevant boundary conditions are seldom or never realized.

So, systems can be well-understood yet unpredictable. What about the converse? Can a system be predictable without being understood? Certainly. For centuries, the tides have been predicted from tide tables. Their predictability was not improved at all by Newton's successful explanation of them.[3] Consider also the plight of the seventeenth-century scientist confronted with the fact that pounding a nail makes it hot. Caloric theory, the going theory of heat at the time, treated changes in heat as diffusion phenomena. Your coffee cools because the caloric in it diffuses into the surrounding cup and air until equilibrium is reached. The fire reheats it because the caloric in the fire diffuses into the pot and surrounding air, and thence to the coffee, and so on. But pounding a nail will make it hot regardless of the temperature of the hammer.[4] This phenomenon – call it the "Galileo effect" after the man who made it famous – is relatively easy to quantify You can be in a position to predict what is going to happen, and even be able to quantify those predictions, yet still have no idea *why* it happens. Conversely, once in possession of the mechanical theory of heat, one sees that pounding a nail is like poking a cube of Jell-O: more vibration equals more heat. But this insight does not improve predictability at all; it explains the Galileo effect, but it is the statement of the effect itself that generates the predictions.

3 Why the Laws of Psychology are *Explananda*

From the perspective I've been urging, it emerges that a substantial proportion of research effort in experimental psychology isn't expended directly in
the explanation business; it is expended in the business of discovering and
confirming effects, An effect, I've been arguing, is an *explanandum*, not an
explanans. In psychology, we are overwhelmed with things to explain, and
somewhat underwhelmed by things to explain them with. Why is that?

I want to begin by mentioning a sociological factor just so it can be set to
one side. The fact is that it is very difficult to publish a paper that simply offers
an explanation of an effect. Must journals want reports of experiments.
Explanation, such as it is, is relegated to the "discussion" section, which is
generally loose and frankly speculative compared to the rest of the paper.
Discussion sections are often not read, and their contents are almost never
reported in other articles. The lion's share of the effort goes into the experiments and data analysis, not into explaining the effects they uncover. Any
other course of action is a quick route to a plot in Tenure Memorial Park.

This is not mere tradition or perversity. It derives from a deep-rooted uncertainty about what it would take to really explain a psychological effect. What,
after all, would a successful explanatory theory of the mind look like?

We can be pretty sore what it wouldn't look like. It wouldn't look like a
Principia Psychologica. Newtonian mechanics was laid out as an axiomatic
system, self-consciously imitating Euclidian geometry, a widely influential
paradigm in the seventeenth century, and has since been the dominant paradigm of an explanatory theory in science. It is arguable whether this is a
really useful paradigm in any science. Certainly mechanics, even Newtonian
mechanics, is never presented that way today. Still, if the goal is to lay out the
fundamental principles of motion, the axiomatic approach makes a kind of
sense. There are, one might suppose, a small number of fundamental principles governing motion, and these, together with some suitable definitions,
might enable the derivations of equations specifying the (perhaps idealized)
behavior of any particular mechanical system: a pendulum, a spring, a solar
system, and so on. What makes this seem a viable approach is the idea that
motion is the same everywhere, whatever moves, wherever and whenever it
moves. It is also this sort of idea that grounds the widespread conviction that
physics is the most fundamental science.

Conversely, what grounds the idea that psychology and geology are not
fundamental sciences is the thought that psychological and geological systems
are special. The principles of psychology and geology and the other so-called
special sciences do not govern nature generally, but only special sorts of
systems. Laws of psychology and geology are laws in situ, that is, laws that
hold of a special kind of system because of its peculiar constitution and organization. The special sciences do not yield general laws of nature, but rather
laws governing the special sorts of systems that are their proper objects of
study. Laws in situ specify effects – regular behavioral patterns characteristic
of a specific kind of mechanism.

Once we see that the laws of a special science are specifications of effects, we see why theories in such sciences could not be anything like Newton's *Principia*. Who would be interested in an axiomatic development of the effects exhibited by the liver or the internal combustion engine? What we want is an explanation of those effects in terms of the constitution and organization of the liver or engine. At the level of fundamental physics, laws are what you get because, at a *fundamental* level, all you can do is say how things are. We don't think of the fundamental laws of motion as effects, because we don't think of them as specifying the behavior of some specialized sort of system that behaves as it does because of its constitution and organization. The things that obey the fundamental laws of motion (everything) do not have some special constitution or organization that accounts for the fact that they obey those laws. The laws of motion just say what motion *is* in this possible world. Special sorts of systems, on the other hand, exhibit distinctive characteristic effects. In general, then, it seems that special sciences like psychology should seek to discover and specify the effects characteristic of the systems that constitute their proprietary domains, and to explain those effects in terms of the *structure* of those systems, that is, in terms of their constituents (either physical or functional) and their mode of organization (see Cummins 1983, chaps. 1, 2, for how this kind of explanation applies to psychology).

4   Effects and Capacities

What I have been calling "psychological effects" are not the only, or even the primary, *explananda* of psychology. I have been concentrating on effects because I have been criticizing the idea that psychological explanation is subsumption under law; and psychological laws specify effects. The primary *explananda* of psychology, however are not effects (psychological laws) but *capacities*: the capacity to see depth, to learn and speak a language, to plan, to predict the future, to empathize, to fathom the mental states of others, to deceive oneself, to be self-aware, and so on. Understanding these sorts of capacities is what motivates psychological inquiry in the first place.

Capacities are best understood as a kind of complex dispositional property. Standard treatments typically assume that dispositions are specified by subjunctive conditionals along the following lines:

Salt is water-soluble = If salt were put in water, then, ceteris paribus, it would dissolve.

This sort of analysis is valuable because it makes it clear that to have a dispositional property is to satisfy a law in situ, a law characterizing the behavior of a certain kind of thing. Capacities and effects are thus close kin.

For this sort of analysis to work, we have to know what precipitating conditions (putting x in water) generate which manifestations (x dissolves). For many psychological capacities, it is a matter of some substance to specify exactly what they are. The specification of a capacity is what Marr (1982) called the "computational problem." This can be extremely nontrivial. How, after all, should we specify the capacity to understand Chinese? Or it can be relatively simple, as in the ease of calculational capacities (the capacity to add or multiply, for example). So one reason we do not think of the capacity to learn a natural language as an effect is just that it is relatively ill specified. As a consequence, the primary *explananda* of psychology – capacities – are not typically specified as laws, nor is it clear they always can be.

But there is a more interesting reason. Many of the things we call "effects" in psychology are in fact incidental to the exercise of some capacity of interest. An analogy will help to clarify the distinction I have in mind. Consider two multipliers, M1 and M2. M1 uses the standard partial products algorithm we all learned in school. M2 uses successive addition. Both systems have the capacity to multiply: given two numerals, they return a numeral representing the product of the numbers represented by the inputs. But M2 also exhibits the "linearity effect": computation is, roughly, a linear function of the size of the multiplier. It takes twice as long to compute 24 × N as it does to compute 12 × N. M1 does not exhibit the linearity effect. Its complexity profile is, roughly, a step function of the number of digits in the multiplier.

The "linearity effect" is incidental to the capacity to multiply in M1. It is, as it were, a side effect of the way M1 exercises its capacity to multiply, and that is why we call this fact about computation time an "effect" and the multiplication a "capacity". Of course, the "linearity effect" might be computed. We could design a system M3 that not only computes products, but computes reaction times as well, timing its outputs to mimic a successive addition machine. M3 might be quite difficult to distinguish from M1 on behavioral grounds, though it need not be impossible. The timing function might be disabled somehow without disabling the multiplier. More subtly, computation of the relevant output times might itself be nonlinear, in which case M3 will not be able to fool us on very large inputs (assuming it can process them at all). Or it might be that the "linearity effect" in M3 is cognitively penetrable (Pylyshyn 1982), in which case it cannot be incidental. Thus it can be a matter of substantive controversy whether we are looking at an exercise of a capacity or an incidental effect. This is precisely what is at issue between the friends of imagery and their opponents. Are the rotation and scanning effects (for example) incidental effects of rotating or scanning a picturelike representation, or is it the exercise of a capacity to estimate rotation or scanning times involving real physical objects? (See, for example, Pylyshyn 1979.)

As primacy *explananda* of psychological theory, capacities typically do not have to be discovered: everyone knows that people can see depth and learn language. But they do have to be specified, and that, to repeat, can be nontrivial. As secondary *explananda*, effects typically *do* have to be discovered. Much more important, however, is the different bearing that explaining effects as opposed to capacities has on theory confirmation. Given two theories or models of the same capacity, associated incidental effects can be used to distinguish between them. This is important for two reasons. First, it is always possible in principle, and often in fact, to construct weakly equivalent models of the same capacity. To take an extreme case, Smolensky, Legendre and Miyata (1992) have shown that, for any parser written in a LISP-like language called "tensor product programming language" (TPPL), it possible [*sic*] to construct a distributed connectionist network that effects the same parses. With respect to parsing per se, then, there is nothing to choose between the two models. However, they predict very different incidental effects. Second, even when two models are not weakly equivalent, they may be on a par empirically, that is, close enough so that differences between them are plausibly attributed to such factors as experimental error, idealization, and the like. Again, incidental effects that may have no great interest as *explananda* in their own right may serve to distinguish such cases.

We can expect, then, to see a good deal of effort expended in the explanation of incidental effects that have little interest in their own right: no one would construct a theory just to explain *them*. But their successful explanation can often be crucial to the assessment of theories or models designed to explain the core capacities that are the primary targets of psychological inquiry.

5 Functional Analysis

A theory may explain a dispositional property by systematic analysis – i.e. analyzing the system that has it, or it may proceed instead by analyzing the disposition itself. I call the application of property analysis to dispositions or capacities "functional analysis."

Functional analysis consists in analyzing a disposition into a number of less problematic dispositions such that programmed manifestation of these analyzing dispositions amounts to a manifestation of the analyzed disposition By "programmed" here, I simply mean organized in a way that could be specified in a program or flowchart. Assembly line production provides a transparent illustration. Production is broken down into a number of distinct and relatively simple (unskilled) tasks. The line has the capacity to produce the product by virtue of the fact that the units on the line have the capacity to perform one or more of these tasks, and by virtue of the fact that when these tasks are performed in a certain organized way – according to a certain program – the finished product results. Schematic diagrams in electronics provide another familiar example. Because each symbol represents any physical object having a certain capacity, a schematic diagram of a complex device constitutes an analysis of the electronic capacities of the device as a whole into the capacities of its components. Such an analysis allows us to explain how the device as whole exercises the analyzed capacity, for it allows us to see exercises on the analyzed capacity as programmed (i.e., organized) exercises of the analyzing capacities.

In these examples, analysis of the disposition goes together in a fairly obvious way with componential analysis of the disposed system, analyzing dispositions being capacities of system components. This sort of direct form-function correlation is fairly common in artifacts because it facilitates diagnosis and repair of malfunctions. Form-function correlation is certainly absent in many cases, however, and it is therefore important to keep functional analysis and componential analysis conceptually distinct. Componential analysis of computers, and probably brains, will typically yield components with capacities that do not figure in the analysis of capacities of the whole system. A cook's capacity to bake a cake analyzes into other capacities of the "whole cook." Similarly Turing machine capacities analyzes into other Turing machine capacities. Because we do this sort of analysis without reference to a realizing system, the analysis is evidently not an analysis of a realizing system but of the capacity itself. Thus functional analysis puts very indirect constraints on componential analysis. My capacity to multiply 27 times 32 analyzes into the capacity to multiply 2 times 7, to add 5 and 1, and so on, but these capacities are not (so far as is known) capacities of my components.

The explanatory interest of functional analysis is roughly proportional to (1) the extent to which the analyzing capacities are less sophisticated than the analyzed capacities; (2) the extent to which the analyzing capacities are different in kind from the analyzed capacities; and (3) the relative sophistication of the program appealed to, that is, the relative complexity of the organization of component parts or processes that is attributed to the system. Item (3) is correlative with (1) and (2): the greater the gap in sophistication and kind between analyzing and analyzed capacities, the more sophisticated the program must be to close the gap.

Ultimately, of course, a complete theory for a capacity must exhibit the details of the target capacity's realization in the system (or system type) that has it. Functional analysis of a capacity must eventually terminate in dispositions whose realizations are explicable via analysis of the target system. Failing this, we have no reason to suppose we have analyzed the capacity as it is realized in that system.

Notes

1   I do not mean to suggest that DN theorists were confused about this. On the contrary , they held that explanation and prediction are just two sides of the same coin. The point is rather that DN conflates explanation and prediction, which are, I claim, orthogonal.

2   Cartwright (1983) denies that we can explain the trajectory of a falling leaf. But all she argues for is that we cannot predict it. She seems to think it follows from this that we have no reason to believe that the laws of mechanics accurately subsume it. A more conservative view is that we understand falling leaves quite well. No one seriously thinks this is an outstanding mystery of nature on a par with the nature of consciousness, say. The problem is just that prediction is intractable.

3   This is an interesting case in a number of ways. Newton's successful explanation in terms of the moon's gravitational influence does not allow prediction, which is done today, as before Newton, by tables. So here we have in a single instance a case where prediction is neither necessary nor sufficient for explanation. Moreover, we have a case where explanation seems to come apart from truth. The Newtonian mechanics on which the explanation is based has been supplanted, yet the explanation is still accepted.

4   Friction was thought to release otherwise bound caloric but this will not help with a cold hammer and nail.

References

Cartwright, N. (1983) *How the Laws of Physics Lie*. Oxford: Clarendon Press.

Cummins, R. (1983) *The Nature of Psychological Explanation*. Cambridge, Mass.: MIT Press.

Garcia, J. and Koelling, R. (1966) "The relation of cue to consequence in avoidance learning." *Psychonomic Science*, 4: 123–4.

Hempel, C. (1966) *Philosophy of Natural Science*. Englewood Cliffs, N.J.: Prentice Hall.

Hempel, C. and Oppenheim, P. (1948) "Studies in the logic of explanation." *Philosophy of Science*, 15: 135–75.

Kim, J. (1962) "On the logical conditions of deductive explanation." *Philosophy of Science*, 30: 286–91.

MacDonald, J. and McGurk, H. (1978) "Visual influences on speech perception processes." *Perception and Psychophysics*, 24: 253–7.

Madigan, S. (1969) "Intraserial repetition and coding processes in free recall." *Journal of Verbal Learning and Verbal Behavior*, 8: 828–35.

Marr, D. (1982) *Vision*. New York: Freeman.

Moore. E. (1956) "Gedanken experiments on sequential machines". In C. Shannon and J. McCarthy (eds), *Automata Studies*, Princeton: Princeton University Press.

Pylyshyn, Z. (1979) "The rate of 'mental rotation' of images: A test of a holistic analogue hypothesis." *Memory and Cognition*, 7: 19–28.

—— (1982) *Computation and Cognition*. Cambridge, Mass.: MIT Press.

Salmon, W. (1998) *Causality and Explanation*. New York: Oxford University Press.

Smolensky, P., Legendre, G., and Miyata, Y. (1992) *Principles for an Integrated Connectionist/Symbolic Theory of Higher Cognition*. Technical Report 92–08. Boulder, CO: University of Colorado, Institute of Cognitive Science.

IC

THE REPRESENTATIONAL MIND

7

J.A. Fodor, "The Language of Thought: First Approximations"

I'm the only president you've got.
Lyndon B. Johnson

The main argument of this book runs as follow:

1 The only psychological models of cognitive processes that seem even remotely plausible represent such processes as computational.
2 Computation presupposes a medium of computation: a representational system.
3 Remotely plausible theories are better than no theories at all.
4 We are thus provisionally committed to attributing a representational system to organisms. 'Provisionally committed' means: committed insofar as we attribute cognitive processes to organisms and insofar as we take seriously such theories of these processes as are currently available.
5 It is a reasonable research *goal* to try to characterize the representational system to which we thus find ourselves provisionally committed.
6 It is a reasonable research *strategy* to try to infer this characterization from the details of such psychological theories as seem likely to prove true.
7 This strategy may actually work: It is possible to exhibit specimen inferences along the lines of item 6 which, if not precisely apodictic, have at least an air of prima facie plausibility.

The epistemic status of these points is pretty various. I take it, for example, that item 3 is a self-evident truth and therefore requires no justification beyond an appeal to right reason. I take it that item 4 follows from items 1–3. Items 5–7, on the other hand, need to be justified *in practice*. What must be shown is that it is, in fact, productive to conduct psychological research along the lines they recommend. Much of the material in later chapters of this book will be concerned to show precisely that. Hence, the discussion will become more intimately involved with empirical findings, and with their interpretations, as we go along.

This chapter, however is primarily concerned with items 1 and 2. I shall argue that, quite independent of one's assumptions about the *details* of psychological theories of cognition, their general structure presupposes underlying computational processes and a representational system in which such processes are carried out. It is often quite familiar facts which, in the first instance, constrain one's models of the mental life, and this chapter is mostly a meditation on a number of these. I shall, in short, discuss some kinds of theories which, I think, most cognitive psychologists would accept in outline, however much they might disagree about specifics. I want to show how, in every case, these theories presuppose the existence and exploitation of a representational system of some complexity in which mental processes are carried out. I commence with theories of choice.

I take it to be self-evident that organisms often believe the behavior they produce to be behavior of a certain kind and that it is often part of the explanation of the way that an organism behaves to advert to the beliefs it has about the kind of behaviour it produces.[1] This being assumed, the following model seems overwhelmingly plausible as an account of how at least some behaviour is decided on.

8 The agent finds himself in a certain situation (S).

9 The agent believes that a certain set of behavioral options ($B_1, B_2, \ldots B_n$) are available to him in S; i,e., given S, B_1 through B_n are things the agent believes that he can do.

10 The probable consequence of performing each of B_1 through B_n are predicted: i.e., the agent computes a set of hypotheticals of roughly the form if B_i is performed in S, then, with a certain probability, C_i. Which such hypotheticals are computed and which probabilities are assigned will, of course, depend on what the organism knows or believes about situations like S. (It will also depend upon other variables which are, from the point of view of the present model, merely noisy: time pressure, the amount of computation space available to the organism, etc.)

11 A preference ordering is assigned to the consequences.

12 The organism's choice of behavior is determined as a function of the preferences and the probabilities assigned.

Two caveats. First, this is not a theory but a theory schema. No predictions about what particular organisms will choose to do on particular occasions are forthcoming until one supplies values for the variables; e.g., until one knows how S is described, which behavioral options are considered, what consequences the exploitation of the options are believed to lead to, what preference ordering the organism assigns to these consequences and what trade-off between probability and preferability the organism accepts. This is to say that, here as elsewhere, a serious theory of the way an organism behaves presupposes extensive information about what the organism knows and values. Items

8–12 do not purport to give such a theory, but only to identify some of the variables in terms of which one would have to be articulated.

Second, it is obvious that the model is highly idealized. We do not always contemplate each (or, indeed, any) of the behavioral options we believe to be available to us in a given situation. Nor do we always assess our options in the light of what we take to be their likely consequences. (Existentialists, I'm told, make a point of never doing so.) But these kinds of departures from the facts do not impugn the model. The most they show is that the behaviors we produce aren't always in rational correspondence with the beliefs we hold. It is sufficient for my point, however, that some agents are rational to some extent some of the time, and that when they are, and to the extent that they are, processes like the ones mentioned by items 8–12 mediate the relation between what the agent believes and what he does.[2]

Insofar as we accept that this model applies in a given case, we also accept the kinds of explanations that it licenses. For example, given the model, we may explain the fact that organism a produced behavior B by showing:

13 That a believed himself to be in situation S.
14 That a believed that producing behavior of the type B_i in S would probably lead to consequence C_i.
15 That C_i was a (or the) highly valued consequence for a.
16 That a believed and intended B to be behavior of the B_i type.

The point to notice is that it is built into this pattern of explanation that agents sometimes take their behavior to be behavior of a certain kind; in the present case, it is part of the explanation of a's behavior that he believed it to be of the B_i kind, since it is behavior of that kind for which highly valued consequences are predicted. To put it briefly, the explanation fails to *be* a (full) explanation of a's behavior unless that behavior was B_i and a believed it to be so.

Items 13–16 might, of course, *contribute* to an explanation of behavior even where B is *not* produced and where the actual behavior is *not* taken by the agent to be B_i behavior. 'Will nobody pat my hiccup?' cried the eponymous Reverend Spooner. We assume that what goes in for B_i is a structural description of the sentence type 'Will nobody pick my hat up?' and that the disparity between the behavior produced and a token of that type is attributable to what the networks call a temporary mechanical failure. In such cases, our confidence that we know what behavior the agent intended often rests upon three beliefs:

17 That items 14 and 15 are true under the proposed substitution for B_i.
18 That items 14 and 15 would be false if we were instead to substitute a description of the type of which the observed behavior was in fact a token. (In the present example, it is plausibly assumed that Spooner would have set no positive utility upon the production of a token of the type 'Will nobody pat my hiccup?'; why on earth should he want to say *that*?)

103

19 That it is plausible to hypothesize mechanisms of the sort whose operations would account for the respects in which the observed and the intended behaviors differ. (In the present case, mechanisms of metathesis.)

It is notorious that if 'psychodynamic' explanations of behavior are true, the mechanisms envisaged by item 19 may themselves be of practically fathomless complexity. My present point, in any event, is that not only accounts of observed behavior, but also attributions of thwarted behavioral intentions, may intimately presuppose the applicability of some such explanatory schema as items 8–12.

I am laboring these very obvious remarks because I think that their immediate consequences are of profound significance for the construction of cognitive theories in general: viz., that this sort of explanation can go through only if we assume that agents have means for representing their behaviors to themselves; indeed, means for representing their behaviors as having certain properties and not having others. In the present case, it is essential to the explanation that the agent intends and believes the behavior he produced to be behavior of a certain kind (viz., of the kind associated with relatively highly valued consequences in S) and not of some other kind (viz., not of the kind associated with relatively low-valued consequences in S). Give this up, and one gives up the possibility of explaining the behavior of the agent by reference to his beliefs and preferences.

The moral I want to draw, then, is that certain kinds of very central patterns of psychological explanation presuppose the availability, to the behaving organism, of some sort of representational system. I have emphasized, for purposes of exposition, the significance of the organism's representation of its own behavior in the explanation of its considered actions. But, once made, the point is seen to be ubiquitous. It was, for example, implicit in the model that the organism has available means for representing not only its behavioral options but also: the probable consequence of acting on those options, a preference ordering defined over those consequences and, of course, the original situation in which it finds itself. To use this sort of model is, then, to presuppose that the agent has access to a representational system of very considerable richness. For, according to the model, deciding is a computational process; the act the agent performs is the consequence of computations defined over representations of possible actions. No representations, no computations. No computations, no model.

I might as well have said that the model presupposes a language. For, a little prodding will show that the representational system assumed by items 8–12 must share a number of the characteristic features of real languages. This is a point to which I shall return at considerable length in chapters 2 and 3. Suffice it to point out here just two of the properties that the putative system of representations must have in common with languages properly so-called (e.g., with natural languages).

In the first place, an infinity of distinct representations must belong to the system. The argument here is precisely analogous to the argument for the nonfiniteness of natural languages: Just as, in the latter case, there is no upper bound to the complexity of a sentence that can be used to make a statement, so in the former case, there is no upper bound to the complexity of the representation that may be required to specify the behavioral options available to the agent, or the situation in which he finds himself, or the consequences of acting one way or another.

This is not, of course, to argue that the *practical* possibilities are *literally* infinite. Just as there is a longest-sentence-that-anyone-can-utter, so there must be a most-complex-situation-that-anyone-can-act-upon. The infinite capacity of the representational system is thus an idealization, but it is not an *arbitrary* idealization. In both cases, the essential point is the organism's ability to deal with *novel* stimulations. Thus, we infer the productivity of natural languages from the speaker/hearer's ability to produce/understand sentences on which he was not specifically trained. Precisely the same argument infers the productivity of the internal representational system from the agent's ability to calculate the behavioral options appropriate to a kind of situation he has never before encountered.

But productivity isn't the only important property common to natural languages and whatever system of representation is exploited in deciding what to do. It is evident, for example, that the notion that the agent can represent to himself salient aspects of the situations in which he finds himself presupposes that such familiar semantic properties as truth and reference are exhibited by formulae in the representational system.[3] We have been supposing that, underlying the capacity for reasoned action, there must be a capacity for the description of real and possible states of affairs. But the notions of description, truth, and reference are inseparable: Roughly, 'D' describes what 'a' refers to iff ('Da' is true iff a is D).

A similar line of thought shows that mechanisms for expressing intentional properties will have to be available to the representational system. In particular, calculated action presupposes decisions between possible (but) nonactual outcomes. So, the representational system recruited for the calculations must distinguish between possible, nonactual states of affairs. Whether one ought to do this by defining preference orderings over propositions (as traditional treatments of intentionality would suggest) or over possible worlds (in the manner of model-theoretic approaches to semantics) is a question I won't even attempt to deal with. My present point is just that *some* such mechanisms must be available to the representational system, and for reasons quite parallel to those that lead us to think that some such mechanisms are available to natural languages.

I have assumed so far in this discussion that anyone reasonable will accept that something like items 8–12 is essential to a theory of the psychology of choice; what I have been doing is just spinning out some of the implications of that assumption. But, notoriously, the assumption isn't true. Behaviorists, for example, don't accept that deciding is a computational process, so behavioristic accounts of action can make do without postulating a system of internal representations. I don't propose to raise the general question of the adequacy of such accounts; it seems to me a dead issue. Suffice it to remark that, in light of our discussion, some of the standard criticisms can be deepened.

It is a point often made against behaviorists that they seek a prima facie implausible reduction of calculated actions to habits. The intended criticism is usually that insofar as actions are viewed simply as trained responses to environmental inputs the productivity of behavior is rendered unintelligible. (For elaboration, see Chomsky, 1959.) But this is not the only thing wrong with construing calculated behaviors as species of conditioned responses. What everyone knows, but the behaviorist's methodology won't allow him to admit, is that at least some actions are choices from among a range of options contemplated by the agent. The behaviorist cannot admit this because he is committed to describing actions as the effects of environmental causes. Since only *actual* states of affairs can be causes, the-possibility-that-*P* cannot be among the determinants of a response. But nor, however, can *contemplations* of possibilities since, though they are presumably real events on any rational ontology, they are not *environmental* events in the behaviorist's proprietary sense of that notion. Looked at either way, the behaviorist is methodologically committed to denying what would seem to be self-evident: that we sometimes act the way we do because that seems the best way to act given what we take to be the options. In short, the behaviorist requires us to view considered behaviors as responses to actual inputs, when what we want to do is view them as responses to possible outcomes.

It is, conversely, one of the great advantages of computational theories of action that they allow us to acknowledge what everybody knows: that deciding what to do often involves considering what might turn out to be the case. To assume a representational system which can distinguish among (viz., assign different representations to) distinct possible states of affairs is precisely to permit oneself to view the behavior that is actually produced as a choice from among those options that the agent regards as 'live'. It is worth emphasizing that the behaviorist literature offers no grounds for rejecting this immensely plausible treatment except the reiterated assertion that it is, somehow, 'unscientific'. So far as I can tell, however, this amounts only to the (correct) observation that one cannot both say what it is plausible to say about actions and adhere to a behavioristic methodology. So much the worse for the methodology.

It will have occurred to the reader that what I am proposing to do is resurrect the traditional notion that there is a 'language of thought' and that characterizing that language is a good part of what a theory of the mind needs to do. This is a view to which, it seems to me, much of the current psychological work on cognition bears a curious and mildly schizoid relation. On the one hand, it seems to be implicit in almost every kind of explanation that cognitive psychologists accept since, as I remarked above, most such explanations treat behavior as the outcome of computation, and computation presupposes a medium in which to compute. But, on the other hand, the assumption of such a medium is relatively rarely made explicit, and the pressing question to which it leads – what properties does the system of internal representations have – is only occasionally taken as the object of sustained research.

I propose, as we go along, to consider a variety of types of evidence that may bear upon the answer to that question. Before doing so, however, I want to explore two more lines of argument which seem to lead, with a fair show of inevitability, to the postulation of a language of thought as a precondition for any sort of serious theory construction in cognitive psychology. My point will be that not only considered action, but also learning and perception, must surely be viewed as based upon computational processes; and, once again, no computation without representation.

Let us first consider the phenomenon that psychologists sometimes call 'concept learning'. I want to concentrate on concept learning not only because it provides a useful illustration of our main thesis (cognitive processes are computational processes and hence presuppose a representational system) but also because the analysis of concept learning bears on a variety of issues that will arise in later chapters.

To begin with, then, concept learning is one of those processes in which what the organism knows is altered as a consequence of its experiences; in particular, as a consequence of its interactions with the environment. But, of course, not *every* case of an environmentally determined alteration in knowledge would count as learning; *a fortiori*, not all such cases count as *concept* learning. So, for example, aphasia is often environmentally induced, but catching aphasia isn't a learning experience. Similarly, if we could somehow induce knowledge of Latin by swallowing blue pills, I suppose that that would be acquiring Latin without learning it. Similarly, imprinting (see Thorpe, 1963) alters what the organism knows as a consequence of its experiences, but is only marginally a learning process if it is a learning process at all. A general theory of concept learning is, at best, *not* a general theory of how experience affects knowledge.

There are, moreover, kinds of *learning* that very probably aren't kinds of concept learning.[4] Rote learning is a plausible example (e.g., the learning of a list of nonsense syllables. However, see Young, 1968). So is what one might call 'sensory learning' (learning what a steak tastes like, learning what middle C sounds like played on an oboe, and so forth). Very roughly, and just by way of marking out the area of our concern, what distinguishes rote learning and sensory learning from concept learning is that, in the former cases, what is *remembered of* an experience typically exhausts what is *learned from* that experience. Whereas concept learning somehow 'goes beyond' the experiential data. But what does *that* mean?

I think that what concept learning situations have in common is fundamentally this: The experiences which occasion the learning in such situations (under their theoretically relevant descriptions) stand in a *confirmation relation* to what is learned (under *its* theoretically relevant description). A short way of saying this is that concept learning is essentially a process of hypothesis formation and confirmation.[5] The best way to see that this is so is to consider the experimental paradigm in terms of which the concept learning 'construct' is, as one used to say, 'operationally defined'.

In the typical experimental situation, the subject (human or infra-human) is faced with the task of determining the environmental conditions under which a designated response is appropriate, and learning is manifested by S's increasing tendency, over time or trials, to produce the designated response when, and only when, those conditions obtain. The logic of the experimental paradigm requires, first, that there be an 'error signal' (e.g., reinforcement or punishment or both) which indicates whether the designated response has been appropriately performed and, second, that there be some 'criterial property' of the experimentally manipulated stimuli such that the character of the error signal is a function of the occurrence of the designated response together with the presence or absence of that property. Thus, in a simple experiment of this kind, S might be asked to sort stimulus cards into piles, where the figures on the cards exhibit any combination of the properties red and black with square and circular, but where the only correct (e.g., rewarded) sorting is the one which groups red circles with black squares. In such a case, the 'designated response' is sorting into the positive pile and the 'criterial property' is *red circle or black square.*

It is possible to use this sort of experimental setup to study the rate of learning as a function of any large number of variables: e.g., the character of the criterial property; S's ability to report the property in terms of which he is sorting; the character of the error signal; the character of the relation (temporal, statistical, etc.) between occurrences of the error signal and instantiations of the criterial property; the character of the subject population (age, species, intelligence, motivation, or whatever); and so on. Much of the experimental psychology of learning in the last thirty years has been concerned with ringing changes on the values of these variables; the paradigm has been central to the work of psychologists who have little else in common as, say, Skinner and Vygotsky.[6]

My present point is that there is only one kind of theory that has ever been proposed for concept learning – indeed, there would seem to be only one kind of theory that is conceivable – and this theory is incoherent unless there is a language of thought. In this respect, the analysis of concept learning is like the analysis of considered choice; we cannot begin to make sense of the phenomena unless we are willing to view them as computational and we cannot begin to make sense of the view that they are computational unless we are willing to assume a representational system of considerable power in which the computations are carried out.

Notice, to begin with, that at any given trial t and in respect of any given property P, the organism's experience in the concept learning paradigm is appropriately represented as a data matrix in which the rows represent trials and the columns represent the performance of the designated response, the presence or absence of P, and the character of the error signal.[7] Thus:

Trial	Designated response performed	Property P present	Value of error signal
1	yes	yes	minus
2	no	no	minus
3	yes	no	plus

Put this way, it seems clear that the problem the organism faces on trial t is that of choosing a value of P for which, in the ideal case, the last column of the matrix is positive when and only when the first two columns are, and which is such that the matrix will continue to exhibit that correspondence for any (reasonable) value of $t_n > t$. This is the sense in which what is learned in concept learning 'goes beyond' what is given in the experiential data. What the organism has to do in order to perform successfully is to extrapolate a generalization (all the positive stimuli are P-stimuli) on the basis of some instances that conform to the generalization (the first n positive stimuli were P-stimuli). The game is, in short, inductive extrapolation, and inductive extrapolation presupposes (a) a source of inductive hypotheses (in the present case, a range of candidate values of P) and (b) a confirmation metric such that the probability that the organism will accept (e.g., act upon) a given value of P at t is some reasonable function of the distribution of entries in the data matrix for trials prior to t.

There are, of course, many many ways of fleshing out the details of this kind of model. For example, there is plenty of reason to believe that the various values of P are typically tested in a determinate order; indeed, that the choices of P may be very subtly determined by the character of the P-values previously assessed and rejected and by the particular configuration of the data matrix for those values. But, however the details go, what seems entirely clear is that the behavior of the organism will depend upon the confirmation relation between the data and the hypothesis, so that accounts of its behavior will require information about how, in the course of learning, the data and the hypotheses are represented.

Why is this entirely clear? Fundamentally, because one of its distinguishing characteristics of concept learning is the *nonarbitrariness* of the relation between what is learned and the character of the experiences that occasion the learning. (Compare the case of acquiring Latin by taking pills.) That is, what a theory of concept learning has to explain is why it is experiences of xs which are F (and not, say, experiences of xs which are G) that leads the organism, eventually, to the belief that all the xs are F. We *can* explain that if we assume (a) that the organism *represents* the relevant experiences as experiences of xs which are F; (b) that one of the hypotheses that the organism can entertain about its environment is the hypothesis that perhaps all xs are F; and (c) that the organism employs, in the fixation of its beliefs, a rule of confirmation which says (*very* roughly) that all the observed xs being F is, *ceteris paribus*, grounds for believing that all the xs are F. To put it mildly, it seems unlikely that any theory radically incompatible with items (a–c) could account for the nonarbitrariness of the relation between what is learned and the experiences that occasion the learning.[8]

In short, concept learning begs for analysis as involving the determination of a confirmation relation between observed and extrapolated reward contingencies, and this is already to commit oneself to a representational system in which the observations and the candidate extrapolations are displayed and the degree of confirmation is computed. There is, however, also a more subtle way in which inductive extrapolation presupposes a representational system, and this point bears considering.

Inductive extrapolation is a form of nondemonstrative inference. For present purposes this means that, at any given trial t, there will be indefinitely many nonequivalent values of P that are 'compatible' with the data matrix up to t. That is, there will be indefinitely many values of P such that, on all trials prior to t, the designated response is rewarded iff P is exhibited by the stimulus, but where each value of P 'predicts' a different pairing of responses and rewards on future trials. Clearly, if the organism is to extrapolate from its experiences, it will need some way of choosing between these indefinitely many values of P. Equally clearly, that choice cannot be made on the basis of the data available up to t since the choice that needs to be made is precisely among hypotheses all of which predict the *same* data up to t.

This is a familiar situation in discussions of inductive inference in the philosophy of science. The classic argument is due to Goodman (1965), who pointed out that, for any fixed set of observations of green emeralds, both the hypothesis that all emeralds are green and the hypothesis that all emeralds are *grue* will be compatible with the data. (One way of defining a *grue*-predicate is: An emerald is *grue* iff it is (in the data sample and green) or (not in the data sample and blue).) It is part of Goodman's point, however, that there are indefinitely many ways of constructing predicates which share the counterinductive properties that *grue* exhibits. Since both hypotheses are compatible with the data, the principle that distinguishes between them must appeal to something other than observations of green emeralds.

The way out of this puzzle is to assume that candidate extrapolations of the data receive an a priori ordering under a *simplicity metric,* and that metric prefers 'all xs are green' to 'all xs are *grue*' as the extrapolation of any body of data compatible with both.[9] In the present case this means that the decision that a given value of P is confirmed relative to a given data matrix must be determined not only by the distribution of entries in the matrix, but also by the relative simplicity of P. This conclusion seems to be irresistible, given the nondemonstrative character of the extrapolations involved in concept learning. It has, however, immediate consequences for the general claim that theories of concept learning are incoherent unless they presuppose that a representational system is available to the organism.

The point is that, so far as anyone can tell, simplicity metrics must be sensitive to the *form* of the hypotheses that they apply to, i.e., to their syntax and vocabulary.[10] That is, so far as anyone can tell, we can get an a priori ordering of hypotheses only if we take account of the way in which the hypotheses are expressed. We need such an ordering if we are to provide a coherent account of the order in which values of P are selected in the concept learning situation. But this means that a theory of concept learning will have to be sensitive to the way that the organism represents its hypotheses. But the notion of the organism representing its hypotheses in one way or another (e.g., in one or another vocabulary or syntax) just *is* the notion of the organism possessing a representational system.

In fact, this argument states the case too weakly. In the formalization of scientific inference a simplicity metric distinguishes between hypotheses that are compatible with the data but make different predictions for *un*observed cases. Our point, thus far, has been that the corresponding remarks presumably hold in the special case where the hypotheses are *P*-values and the data are the observed values of the error signal. There is, however, a respect in which the case of scientific inference differs from the extrapolation involved in concept learning. A simplicity metric used in the evaluation of scientific theories is presumably *not* required to distinguish between *equivalent* hypotheses. To put it the other way around, two hypotheses are identical, for the purposes of formalizing scientific inferences, if they predict the same extrapolations of the data matrix and are equally complex. Pairs of hypotheses that are identical in this sense, but differ in formulation, are said to be 'notational variants' of the same theory.

There is ample evidence, however, that the a priori ordering of *P*-values exploited in concept learning *does* distinguish between hypotheses that are, in this sense, notational variants of each other; i.e., the ordering of *P*-values imposes *stronger* constraints upon the form of hypothesis than simplicity metrics do.

It is, for example, a standard finding the *S*s prefer affirmative conjunctive representations of the data matrix to negative or disjunctive representations. (See Bruner et al., 1956.) Thus, subjects in the concept learning task will typically find it easier to learn to sort all the red triangles together than to learn to sort together all things that *aren't* triangles or all the things that are either triangles or red. Yet, affirmative conjunctive hypotheses are interdefinable with negative disjunctive hypotheses; the subject who is choosing all and only red triangles as instances of positive stimuli is ipso facto choosing all and only things that are (not triangles or not red) as instances of the negative stimuli.[11] What makes the difference in the subject's performance is which of these choices he takes himself to be making; i.e., the way he represents the choices. *S*s who report an affirmative conjunctive hypothesis typically learn faster than those who don't.[12] This is thoroughly intelligible on the assumption that the same hypothesis can receive different internal representations and that the subject's a priori preferences are sensitive to such differences. But it doesn't seem to be intelligible on any other account.

We have been considering some of the ways in which viewing the concept learning task as essentially involving inductive extrapolation commits one to postulating a representational system in which the relevant inductions are carried through. I think it is worth emphasizing that no alternative view of concept learning has ever been proposed, though there are alternative vocabularies for formulating the view just discussed. For example, many psychologists use the notion of habit strength (or strength of association) where I have used the notion of degree of confirmation of a hypothesis. But once it has been recognized that any such construct must be defined over candidate extrapolations of a data matrix (and not over S–R pairings; see note 6) the residual issue is entirely terminological. A theory which determines how habit strength varies as a function of reinforcement (or which determines strength of association as a function of frequency of association, etc.) just *is* an inductive logic, where the confirmation function is articulated by whatever laws of reinforcement/association are assumed.

Similarly, some psychologists would prefer to speak of a theory of attention where I have spoken of a theory which determines the order in which P-values are tested. But again the issue is just terminological. A theory that determines what the organism is attending to at t thereby predicts the stimulus parameter that is extrapolated at t. It must therefore be sensitive to whatever properties of the data matrix, and of the previously contemplated hypotheses, affect the order in which P-values are tested, and to whatever a priori ordering of P-values determines their relative complexity. Whether or not one *calls* this a theory of attention, the function of the construct is precisely to predict what extrapolations of the data matrix the organism will try and in what order it will try them.

Finally, there are psychologists who prefer to describe the organism as 'sampling' the properties of the stimulus rather than as constructing hypotheses abut which such properties are criterial for sorting. But the notion of a property is proprietary in the former kind of theory. In the nonproprietary sense of 'property', every stimulus has an infinity of properties an infinite subset of which are never sampled. The properties that *are* sampled, on the other hand, are of necessity a selection from those that the organism is capable of internally representing. Given that, talking about sampling hypotheses about those properties are two ways of making the same point.

To summarize: So far as anyone knows, concept learning is essentially inductive extrapolation, so a theory of concept learning will have to exhibit the characteristic features of theories of induction. In particular, concept learning presupposes a format for representing the experiential data, a source of hypotheses for predicting future data, and a metric which determines the level of confirmation that a given body of data bestows upon a given hypothesis. No one, so far as I know, has ever doubted this, though I suppose many psychologists have failed to realize what it was that they weren't doubting. But to accept that learning which 'goes beyond the data' involves inductive inference is to commit oneself to a language in which the inductions are carried out, since (a) an inductive argument is warranted only insofar as the observation statements which constitute its premises confirm the hypothesis which constitutes its conclusion; (b) whether this confirmation relation holds between premises and conclusion depends, at least in part, upon the *form* of the premises and conclusion; and (c) the notion of 'form' is defined only for 'linguistic' objects; viz. for representations.

I shall close this chapter by pointing out that the same kinds of morals emerge when one begins to think about the structure of theories of perception.

112

To begin with, there is an obvious analogy between theories of concept learning of the kind I have just been discussing and classical theories of perception in the empiricist vein. According to the latter, perception is essentially a matter of problem solving, where the form of the problem is to predict the character of future sensory experience given the character of past and current sensations as data. Conceived this way, models of perception have the same general structure as models of concept learning: One needs a canonical form for the representation of the data, one needs a source of hypotheses for the extrapolation of the data, and one needs a confirmation metric to select among the hypotheses.

Since some of the empiricists took their project to be the formalization of perceptual *arguments* – viz., of those arguments whose cogency justifies our knowledge claims about objects of perception – they developed fairly explicit doctrines about the kinds of representations that mediate perceptual inferences. It is possible (and it is in the spirit of much of the empiricist tradition) to regard such doctrines as implying theories of the computational processes that underlie perceptual integration. It is notorious, however, that in a number of respects empiricist accounts of perceptual inferences make dubious psychology when so construed. For example, the premises of perceptual inferences were sometimes presumed to be represented in a 'sense datum' language whose formulae were supposed to have some extremely peculiar properties: E.g. that sense datum statements are somehow incorrigible, that all empirical statements have a unique decomposition into sense datum statements; that each sense datum statement is logically independent of any of the rest, and so on.

For many of the empiricists, the defining feature of this data language was supposed to be that its referring expressions could refer only to qualia: If sense datum statements were curious, that was because qualia were curiouser. Conversely, the language in which perceptual hypotheses are couched was identified with 'physical object language', thereby making the distinction between what is sensed and what is perceived coextensive with the distinction between qualia and things. Redescriptions of sensory fields in physical object terms could mediate the prediction of future sensations because, on this view, to accept a description of one's experiences in a physical object language is logically to commit oneself to (at least hypothetical) statements about experiences yet to come. Roughly, sense datum statements provide inductive support for physical object statements, and physical object statements entail statements about further sensations. One thus accepts an 'inductive risk' in inferring from sensations to perceptions, and the problem posed to the perceiver is that of behaving rationally in face of this risk. That is, given a description of experience couched in the sensation language, he must somehow choose that *re*description in physical object terms which the experiences best confirm. Only by doing so can he be rationally assured that most of the expectations about future or hypothetical experiences to which his perceptual judgments commit him are likely to be true.

If, in short, I describe my current experience in terms of color patches, textures, smells, sounds, and so forth, I do not commit myself to predictions about the character of my prior or future experiences. But if I describe it in terms of tables and chairs and their logical kin then I *am* so committed since nothing can be a table or chair unless it performs in a reasonably table-or-chair-wise fashion across the time. So, if I claim that what I see is a table, I am (implicitly) going bond for its past and future behavior; in particular, I am issuing guarantees about the sensations it will, or would, provide. So the story goes.

It is widely known that this account of perception has taken a terrific drubbing at the hands of epistemologists and Gestalt psychologists. It is hard, these days, to imagine what it would be like for the formulae of a representational system to be privileged in the way that formulae in the sense datum language were supposed to be. Nor is it easy to imagine a way of characterizing qualia which would make it turn out that one's perceptual information is all mediated by the sensing of them. Nor does it seem pointful to deny that what one sees are typically *things*; not, in any event, if the alternative is that what one sees are typically color patches and their edges.

This line of criticism is too well known to bear repeating here. I think that it is clearly cogent. But I think, nevertheless, that the core of the empiricist theory of perception is inevitable. In particular, the following claims about the psychology of perception seem to me to be almost certainly true and entirely in the spirit of empiricist theorizing:

1   Perception typically involves hypothesis formation and confirmation.
2   The sensory data which confirm a given perceptual hypothesis are typically internally represented in a vocabulary that is impoverished compared to the vocabulary in which the hypotheses themselves are couched.

Before I say why I think these aspects of the empiricist treatment of perception are right, I want to say something brief about where I think the empiricists went wrong.

I am reading the typical empiricist theory of perception as doing double duty: as an account of the justification of perceptual beliefs and as a psychology of the integration of percepts. I think it is clear that many of the empiricists took their views this way. But it is also pretty clear that when a conflict arose between what the psychology required and what the epistemology appeared to, it was the demands of the latter that shaped the theory.

For example, the claim of incorrigibility for sense datum statements was not responsive to any particular psychological insight, but rather to the presumed need to isolate inductive risk at some epistemic level other than one at which the data were specified. The idea was, roughly, that we could not know physical object statements to be true unless we were certain of the data for those statements, and we could not be *certain* of the data statements if it is possible that some of them are false. Certainty is, as it were, inherited upward from the data to the perceptual judgements they support. Similarly, experiences of qualia have to be conscious events because the statements which such experiences confirm are the premises for arguments whose conclusions are the physical object statements we explicitly believe. If such arguments are to be our justification for believing such statements, their premises had better be available for us to cite.

This is, very probably, mostly muddle. Justification is a far more pragmatic notion that the empiricist analysis suggests. In particular, there is no reason why the direction of all justificatory arguments should be upward from epistemologically unassailable premises. Why should not one of my physical object statements be justified by appeal to another, and that by appeal to a third, and so on? What justificatory argument requires is not that some beliefs be unquestionable but at most that some of them be (de facto) unquestioned. What *can't* be done is to justify all my beliefs *at once*. Well, what can't be done can't be done.

But while I think that the notion of *the* direction of justification is largely confused, the notion that there is a direction of information flow *in perception* is almost certainly well taken, though the arguments are empirical rather than conceptual.

To begin with, it seems clear that causal interactions between the organism and its environment must contribute to the etiology of anything one would want to call *perceptual* knowledge. Insofar as this is right, there is a good deal of empirical information available about the character of these interactions.

So far as anybody knows, any information that the organism gets about its environment as a result of such interactions must be mediated by the activity of one or another *sensory mechanism*. By a sensory mechanism, I mean one which responds to physical properties of environmental events. By a physical property I mean one designated by a natural kind term in some (ideally completed) physical science (for the notion of a natural kind term, see the second part of the introduction). What *mediated by* comes to will take some explaining, but as a first approximation I mean that the operation of a sensory mechanism in responding to a physical property of an environmental event is an empirically necessary condition for the organism's perception of *any* property of that environmental event.

Suppose, for example, that we think of a sensory mechanism as represented by a characteristic function, such that the value of the function is 1 in any case where the mechanism is excited and 0 otherwise. Then, so far as anyone knows, we can develop a theory which predicts the values of that function across time only if we take into account the physical properties of inputs to the mechanism. And we can predict the perceptual analysis that the organism will assign a given environmental event only if we know which physical properties of that event the sensory mechanisms of the organism have responded to. (Thus, for example, to predict the state of excitation of the human auditory system, we need information about the spectrum analysis of impinging wave forms. And to predict the sentence type to which an utterance token will be perceptually assigned, we must know at least which auditory properties of the utterance have been detected.)

I want to stress that this is an *empirical* fact even though it is not a *surprising* fact. We can imagine an organism (say an angel or a clairvoyant) whose perceptual knowledge is *not* mediated by the operation of sensory mechanisms;

only, so far as we know, there are no such organisms, or, if there are any, psychologists have yet to find them. For all the known cases, perception is dependent upon the operation of mechanisms whose states of excitation can be predicted from physical descriptions of their input and not in any other way.

Viewed in terms of information flow, this means that a sensory mechanism operates to associate token physical excitations (as input) with token physical descriptions (as output); i.e., a sensory mechanism is a device which says 'yes' when excited by stimuli exhibiting certain specified values of physical parameters and 'no' otherwise.[13] In particular, it does not care about any property that environmental events *fail* to share so long as the events have the relevant physical properties in common, and it does not care about nonphysical properties that environmental events have in common so long as they fail to share the relevant physical properties. In this sense, the excitation of a sensory mechanism encodes the presence of a physical property. (If the auditory system is a mechanism whose states of excitation are specific to the values of frequency, amplitude, etc., of causally impinging environmental events, then one might as well think of the output of the system as an encoded description of the environment in terms of those values. Indeed, one had better think of it this way if one intends to represent the integration of auditory percepts as a *computational* process.) But if this is true, and if it is also true that whatever perceptual information the organism has about its environment is mediated by the operation of its sensory mechanisms, it follows that perceptual analyses must somehow be responsive to the information about values of physical parameters of environmental events that the sensory mechanisms provide.[14]

That, I suppose, *is* the problem of perception insofar as the problem of perception is a problem in psychology. For though the information provided by causal interactions between the environment and the organism is information about physical properties in the *first* instance, in the *last* instance it may (of course) be information about any property the organism can perceive the environment to have. To a first approximation, the outputs of sensory mechanisms are appropriately viewed as physical descriptions, but perceptual judgments need not be articulated in the vocabulary of such descriptions. Typically they *are* not: A paradigm perceptual judgment is, 'There's a robin on the lawn' or 'I see by the clock that it's time for tea'.

It is, I take it, an empirical question whether psychological processes are computational processes. But if they are, then what must go on in perception is that a description of the environment that is *not* couched in a vocabulary whose terms designate values of physical variables is somehow computed on the basis of a description that *is* couched in such a vocabulary. Presumably this is possible because the perceptual analysis of an event is determined not just by sensory information but also by such background knowledge as the organism brings to the task. The computational processes in perception are mainly those involved in the integration of these two kinds of information. I take it that that is what is left of the classical empiricist view that perception involves the (non-demonstrative) inference from descriptions couched in a relatively impoverished language to conclusions couched in a relatively unimpoverished one.

Almost nothing is left of the empiricist epistemology. For example, the perceptually pertinent description of sensory information is not given in the theory-free language of qualia but rather in the theory-laden language of values of physical parameters. (This is a way of saying what I said above: that, so far as anyone knows, the only way of providing a reasonably compact account of the characteristic function for a sensory mechanism is by taking its inputs under physical description.) Hence, there is no reason to believe that the organism cannot be mistaken about what sensory descriptions apply in any given case. For that matter, there is no reason to believe that organisms are usually conscious of the sensory analyses that they impose.

This distinction – between the notion of a sensory mechanism as the source of a mosaic of conscious experiences out of which percepts are constructed (e g., by associative processes) and the notion of the senses as transducers of such environmental information as affects perceptual integration – is now standard in the psychological literature. It is stressed even by such psychologists as Gibson (1966), whose approach to perception is not, on the whole, sympathetic to the sort of computational views of psychology with which I am primarily concerned. For Gibson, perception involves the detection of invariant (typically relational) properties of impinging stimulus arrays. He apparently assumes that any percept can be identified with such an invariant if only the relevant property is sufficiently abstractly described.[15] But, though Gibson denies that percepts are constructed from conscious sensory data, he does apparently hold that the presence of the relevant stimulus invariant must be inferred from the information output by sensory transducers.

> ... I will distinguish the input to the nervous system that evokes conscious sensation from the input that evokes perception. .... For it is surely a fact that *detecting* something can sometimes occur without the accompaniment of sense impressions. An example is the visual detection of one thing behind another. ... But this does not mean that perception can occur without stimulation of receptors; it only means that organs of perception are sometimes stimulated in such a way that they are not specified in consciousness. Perception cannot be ... without input; it can only be so if that means without awareness of the visual, auditory, or other quality of the input. An example of this is the 'obstacle sense' of the blind, which is felt as 'facial vision' but is actually auditory echo detection. The blind man 'senses' the wall in front of him without realizing what sense has been stimulated. In short there can be sensationless perception, but not informationless perception. (p. 2)

Thus, even for psychologists who think of perceptual distinctions as distinctions between (abstract) stimulus invariants, the problem of how such invariants are themselves detected needs to be solved; and it appears that solving it requires postulating the same sorts of inferences from inputs that empiricist theories assumed. The difference is mainly that contemporary psychologists do not assume that the computations, or the data over which they are defined, must be consciously accessible.[16]

It is worth emphasizing that the claim that the outputs of sensory mechanisms are, in general, not consciously accessible is supposed to be an empirical result rather than a truth of epistemology. There is, for example, quite good empirical evidence that an early representation of a speech signal must specify its formant relations.[17] Yet speaker/hearers have no conscious access to formant structure and, for that matter, very little conscious access to any other acoustic property of speech. It is, in fact, very probably a general truth that, of the various redescriptions of the input that underlie perceptual analyses, the degree of conscious accessibility of a representation is pretty well predicted by the abstractness of its relation to what the sensors specify. This is the kind of point that such philosophers as Cassirer have had in mind when they remark that we 'hear through' an utterance of a sentence to its meaning; one is much better at reporting the syntactic type of which an utterance is a token than at reporting the acoustic properties of the token, and one is much better at reporting those syntactic features which affect meaning than those which don't. One might put it that one does not hear the formant relations in utterances of sentences even though one does hear the linguistic relations and the formant structure (*inter alia*) causally determines *which* linguistic relations one hears. Of course, which descriptions are consciously accessible is to some extent labile. Artists and phoneticians learn consciously to note properties of their sensory experience to which the layman is blind and deaf. This fact is by no means uninteresting.

Where we have gotten to is that the etiology of perceptual analyses involves a series of redescriptions of the environment, and that the initial description in this series specifies perceptually relevant physical properties of the environment. Perception must involve hypothesis formation and confirmation because the organism must somehow manage to infer the appropriate task-relevant description of the environment *from* its physical description together with whatever background information about the structure of the environment it has available. Notoriously, this inference is nondemonstrative: There is typically *no* conceptual connection between a perceptual category and its sensory indicants; an indefinite number of perceptual analyses will, in principle, be compatible with any given specification of a sensory input.[18] On this account, then, perceptual integrations are most plausibly viewed as species of inferences-to-the-best-explanation, the computational problem in perceptual integration being that of choosing the best hypothesis about the distal source of proximal stimulations.

There is, in short, an enormous problem about how to relate the conditions for applying physical descriptions so the conditions for applying such descriptions as 'time for tea'. My present point is that the computational capacities

118

of the organism must constitute a solution to such problems insofar as its perceptual judgments are (a) mediated by sensory information, and (b) true.

It is time to draw the moral, which will by now sound familiar. If one accepts, even in rough outline, the kind of approach to perception just surveyed, then one is committed to the view that perceptual processes involve computing a series of redescriptions of impinging environmental stimuli. But this is to acknowledge that perception presupposes a representational system; indeed, a representational system rich enough to distinguish between the members of sets of properties all of which are exhibited by the same event. If, for example, *e* is a token of a sentence type, and if understanding/perceptually analyzing *e* requires determining which sentence type it is a token of, then on the current view of understanding/perceptually analyzing, a series of representations of *e* will have to be computed. And this series will have to include, and distinguish between, representations which specify the acoustic, phonological, morphological, and syntactic properties of the token. It will have to include all these representations because, so far as anybody knows, each is essential for determining the type/token relation for utterances of sentences. It will have to distinguish among them because, so far as anyone knows, properties of sentences that are defined over any one of these kinds of representation will, ipso facto, be undefined for any of the others.

We are back to our old point that psychological processes are typically computational and computation presupposes a medium for representing the structures over which the computational operations are defined. Instead of further reiterating this point, however, I shall close this part of the discussion by making explicit two assumptions that the argument depends upon.

I have claimed that the only available models for deciding, concept learning, and perceiving all treat these phenomena as computational and hence presuppose that the organism has access to a language in which the computations are carried through. But, of course, this argument requires taking the models literally as at least schemata for explanations of the phenomena. In particular, it requires assuming that if such a model attributes a state to an organism, then insofar as we accept the model we are ontologically committed to the state. Now many philosophers do not like to play the game this way. They are willing to accept computational accounts of cognitive processes if only for lack of viable theoretical alternatives. But the models are accepted only as *façons de parler*, some reductionist program having previously been endorsed.

As I remarked in the introduction, I cannot prove that it is impossible to get the force of computational psychological theories in some framework which treats mental states as (e.g.) behavioral dispositions. But I think it is fair so say that no one has ever given any reason to believe that it is possible, and the program seems increasingly hopeless as empirical research reveals how complex the mental structures of organisms, and the interactions of such structures, really are. I have assumed that one oughtn't to eat the cake unless one is prepared to bite the bullet. If our psychological theories commit us to a language of thought, we had better take the commitment seriously and find out what the language of thought is like.

My second point is that, while I have argued for a language of thought, what I have really shown is at best that there is a language of computation; for thinking is something that *organisms* do. But the sorts of data processes I have been discussing, though they may well go on in the nervous systems of organisms, are presumably not, in the most direct sense, attributable to the organisms themselves.

There is, obviously, a horribly difficult problem about what determines what a person (as distinct from his body, or parts of his body) did. Many philosophers care terrifically about drawing this distinction, and so they should: It can be crucial in such contexts as the assessment of legal or moral responsibility. It can also be crucial where the goal is phenomenology: i.e., the systematic characterization of the *conscious* states of the organism.[19] But whatever relevance the distinction between states of the organism and states of its nervous system may have for *some* purposes, there is no particular reason to suppose that it is relevant to the purposes of cognitive psychology.

What cognitive psychologists typically try to do is to characterize the etiology of behavior in terms of a series of transformations of information. Roughly speaking, information is said to be available to the organism when the neural event which encodes it is one of the causal determinants of the behavior of the organism. 'Behavior' is itself construed broadly (and intuitively) to include, say, thinking and dreaming but not accelerating when you fall down the stairs.

If one has these ends in view, it turns out (again on empirical rather than conceptual grounds) that the ordinary distinction between what the organism does, knows, thinks, and dreams, and what happens to and in its nervous system, does not seem to be frightfully important. The natural kinds, for purposes of theory construction, appear to include some things that the organism does, some things that happen in the nervous system of the organism, and some things that happen in its environment. It is simply no good for philosophers to urge that, since this sort of theory does not draw the usual distinctions, the theory *must* be a muddle. It cannot be an objection to a theory that there are some distinctions it does not make; if it were, it would be an objection to every theory. (Aristotelians thought that it was an argument *against* the Galelean mechanics that it did not distinguish between sublunary and heavenly bodies; that its generalizations were defined for both. This line of argument is now widely held to have been ill-advised.)

In short, the states of the organism postulated in theories of cognition would not count as states of the organism for purposes of, say, a theory of legal or moral responsibility. But so what? What matters is that they should count as states of the organism for *some* useful purpose. In particular, what matters is that they should count as states of the organism for purposes of constructing psychological theories that are true.

To put this point the other way around, if psychological theories fail to draw the usual distinctions between some of the things that happen to organisms and some of the things that organisms do, that does *not* imply that psychologists are committed to denying that there are such distinctions or that they should be drawn for some purposes or other. Nor does it imply that psychologists are (somehow, and whatever precisely this may mean) committed to 'redrawing the logical geography' of our ordinary mental concepts. What is implied (and all that is implied) is just that the distinction between actions and happenings isn't a *psychological* distinction. Lots of very fine distinctions, after all, are not.[20]

Notes

1 I am not supposing that this is, in any technical sense, a *necessary* truth. But I do think it is the kind of proposition that it would be silly to try to confirm (or confute) by doing experiments. One can (just barely) imagine a situation in which it would be reasonable to abandon the practice of appealing to an organism's beliefs in attempts to account for its behavior: either because such appeals had been shown to be internally incoherent or because an alternative theoretical apparatus had been shown to provide better explanations. As things stand, however, no such incoherence has been demonstrated (the operationalist literature to the contrary notwithstanding) and no one has the slightest idea what an alternative theoretical option would be like (the operationalist literature to the contrary notwithstanding). It is a methodological principle I shall adhere to scrupulously in what follows that if one has no alternative but to assume that P, then one has no alternative but to assume that P.

2 It is not, of course, a sufficient condition for the rationality of behavior that processes like items 8–12 should be implicated in its production. For example, behaviors so mediated will generally be *ir*rational if the beliefs involved in item 10 are superstitions, or if the preferences involved in item 11 are perverse, or if the computations involved in items 9–12 are grossly unsound. Nor, so far as I can see, do items 8–12 propose *logically* necessary conditions upon the rationality of behavior. To revert to the idiom of the introduction, the conceptual story about what makes behavior rational presumably requires a certain kind of correspondence between behavior and belief but doesn't care about the character of the processes whereby that correspondence is effected; it is, I suppose, logically possible that angels are rational by reflex. The claim for items 8–12, then, is just that they or something reasonably like them – are *empirically* necessary for bringing about a rational correspondence between the beliefs and the behaviors of sublunary creatures. The short way of saying this is that items 8–12 propose a (schematic) psychological theory.

3 I use the term 'formulae' without prejudice for whatever the vehicles of internal representation may turn out to be. At this point in the discussion it is left open that they might be images, or semaphore signals, or sentences of Japanese. Much of the discussion in succeeding chapters will concern what is known about the character of internal representations and what can be inferred about it from what is known of other things.

4 I regard this as an empirical issue; whether it's true depends on what, in fact, goes on in the various learning processes. It *might* turn out that the mechanism of concept learning is the general learning mechanism, but it would be a surprise if that were true and I want explicitly not to be committed to the assumption that it is. We badly need – and have not got – an empirically defensible taxonomy of kinds of learning.

5 This analysis of concept learning is in general agreement with such sources as Bruner, Goodnow, and Austin (1956), as is the emphasis upon the inferential character of the computations that underlie success in concept learning situations.

6 Though Skinner would not, perhaps, like to see it put this way. Part of the radical behaviorist analysis of learning is the attempt to reduce concept learning to 'discrimination learning'; i.e., to insist that *what* the organism learns in the concept learning situation is *to produce the designated response*. It seems clear, however, that the reduction ought to go the other way around: The concept learning paradigm and the discrimination learning paradigm are the same, but in neither is the existence of a designated response more than a convenience to the experimenter; all it does is provide a regimented procedure whereby S can indicate which sorting he believes to be the right one as a given stage in the learning process.

This is, I take it, not a methodological but an empirical claim. It is clear on several grounds that concept learning (in the sense of learning which categorization of the stimuli is the right one) can, and usually does, proceed in the absence of specific designated responses – indeed, in the absence of any response at all. Nature addicts learn, I'm told, to distinguish oaks from pine trees, and many of them probably do so without being explicitly taught what the distinguishing criteria are. This is true concept learning, but there is no distinctive response that even nature addicts tend to make when and only when they see an oak.

There is, in fact, plenty of experimental evidence on this point. Tolman (1932) showed that what a rat learns when it learns which turning is rewarded in a T-maze is *not* specific to the response system that it uses to make the turn. Brewer (to be published), in a recent survey of the literature on conditioning in human beings, argues persuasively that the designated response can usually be detached from the criterial stimuli simply by instructing the subject to detach it ('From now on, please do *not* sort the red circles with the black squares'). It is, in short, simply not the case that learning typically consists of establishing connections between specific classes of stimuli and specific classes of responses. What *is* the case is (a) that S can often use what he has learned to effect a correspondence between the occurrence of criterial stimulation and the production of a designated response; (b) that it is often experimentally convenient to require him to do so, thereby providing a simple way for E so determine which properties of the stimuli S believes to be criterial; and (c) that Ss will go along with this arrangement providing that they are adequately motivated to do so. Here as elsewhere, what the subject does is determined by his beliefs together with his preferences.

7 One might, ideally, want a three-valued matrix since, on any given trial, the organism may not have observed, or may have observed and forgotten, whether the designated response was performed, whether P was present, or what the value of the error signal was. This is the sort of nicety which I shall quite generally ignore. I mention it only to emphasize that it is the organism's internal representation of its experiences (and not the objective facts about them) that is immediately implicated in the causation of its behavior.

8 I have purposely been stressing the analogies between the theory of inductive confirmation and the theory of the fixation of belief. But I do *not* intend to endorse the view (which examples like item (c) might suggest) that the confirmation of universal hypotheses in science is normally a process of simple generalization from instances. For that matter, I do not intend to endorse the view, embodied in the program of 'inductive logic', that confirmation is normally reconstructable as a 'formal' relation between hypotheses and data. On the contrary, it appears that the level of confirmation of a scientific hypothesis is frequently sensitive to a variety of *in*formal considerations concerning the overall economy, plausibility, persuasiveness and productivity of the theory in which the hypothesis is embedded, to say nothing of the existence of competing theories.

It may well be that the fixation of belief is also sensitive to these sorts of 'global' considerations. Even so, however, the prospects for a formal theory of belief seem to me considerably better than the prospects for an inductive logic. To formalize the relation of inductive confirmation, we should have to provide a theory which picks the *best* hypothesis (the hypothesis that *ought* to be believed), given the available evidence. Whereas, to formalize the fixation of belief, we need only develop a theory which, given the evidence, picks the hypothesis that the organism *does* believe. To the extent that this *cannot* be done, we cannot view learning as a computational process; and it is, for better or for worse, the working assumption of this book that computational accounts of organisms will not break down.

9 I take it that this is common ground among philosophers of science. Where they disagree is on how to characterize the difference between predicates like *grue* (which the simplicity metric doesn't like) and predicates like green (which it does), and also, on how to justify adopting a simplicity metric which discriminates that way.

10 Notions like entrenchment, for example, are defined over the *predicates* of a science, if 'green' is more entrenched than 'grue', that is presumably because there are laws expressed in terms of the former but no laws expressed in terms of the latter. (For discussion, see Goodman, 1965.) One could, of course, try to avoid this conclusion by defining simplicity, entrenchment, and related notions for *properties* (rather than for predicates). But even if that *could* be done it would seem to be a step in the wrong direction: Insofar as one wants psychological processes to turn out to be *computational* processes, one wants the rules of computation to apply formally to the objects in their domains. Once again: my goal in this book is not to *demonstrate* that psychological processes are computational, but to work out the consequences of assuming that they are.

11 The point is, of course, that 'choosing' is opaque in the first occurrence and transparent in the second. Perhaps it's not surprising that what is chosen opaquely is chosen under a representation.

12 For example, Wason and Johnson-Laird (1972) describe an experiment in which Ss were, in effect, presented with data matrices and required to articulate the appropriate extrapolations. The basic prediction, which was confirmed, was that 'concepts which were essentially conjunctive in form would be easier to formulate than concepts which were essentially disjunctive in form, and that whenever a component was negated there would be a slight increase in difficulty' (p. 70). They note that the order of difficulty that they obtained by asking the subject to state the relevant generalization 'conforms to the order obtained when subjects have to *learn* concepts in the conventional manner' (p. 72), i.e., in the concept

learning task. The point to notice is that, since conjunction is interdefinable with negation and disjunction, no concept is, *strictly speaking*, essentially conjunctive or essentially disjunctive. Strictly speaking, concepts don't *have* forms, though representations of concepts do. What Wason and Johnson-Laird mean by a conjunctive concept is, as they are careful to point out, just one which can be expressed by a (relatively) economical formula *in the representational system that the subject is using* (in the present case, in English). What the experiment really shows, then, is that the employment of such a representation facilitates the subject's performance; hence that formulations of a hypothesis which are, in the sense described above, mere notational variants of one another, may nevertheless be differentially available as extrapolations of a data matrix.

13 For purposes of exposition, I am ignoring the (serious) empirical possibility that some or all sensory mechanisms have output values between 0 and 1. Problems about the 'digitalness' of the various stages of cognitive processing are at issue here; but, though these problems are interesting and important, they don't affect the larger issues. Suffice it to say that the question is not just whether the outputs of sensory mechanisms are continuous under physical description, but rather whether intermediate values of excitation carry information that is used in later stages of processing. I don't know what the answer to this question is, and I don't mean to preclude the possibility that the answer is different for different sensory modalities.

14 It bears emphasizing that the present account of sensory systems, like most of the psychological theorizing in this chapter, is highly idealized. Thus, 'from the physical point of view the sensory receptors are transducers, that is, they convert the particular form of energy to which each is attuned into the electrical energy of the nerve impulse' (Loewenstein, 1960). But, of course, it does not follow that the sensors are *perfect* transducers, viz., that their output is predictable *just* from a determination of the impinging physical energies. On the contrary, there is evidence that any or all of the following variables may contribute to such determinations.

i. Cells in sensory systems exhibit a characteristic cycle of inhibition and heightened sensitivity consequent upon each firing. The effects of impinging stimuli are thus not independent of the effects of prior stimulations unless the interstimulus interval is large compared to the time course of this cycle.

ii. Cells on the sensory periphery may be so interconnected that the excitation of any of them inhibits the firing of the others. Such mutual 'lateral' inhibition of sensory elements is usually interpreted as a 'sharpening' mechanism; perhaps part of an overall system of analog-to-digital conversion. (See Ratliff, 1961.)

iii. At any distance 'back' from the periphery of the sensory system one is likely to find 'logic' elements whose firing may be thought of as coding Boolean functions of the primary transducer information. (See Lettvin et al., 1961; Capranica, 1965.)

iv. There may be central 'centripetal' tuning of the response characteristics of the peripheral transducers, in which case the output of such transducers may vary according to the motivational, attentional, etc. state of the organism.

v. Cells in the sensory system exhibit 'spontaneous' activity; viz., firing which is *not* contingent upon stimulus inputs.

A sensory transducer may thus diverge, in all these respects, from the ideal mechanisms contemplated in the text; nor do I wish to claim that this list is complete. But for all that, the main point holds: Insofar as the environment *does* contribute to the etiology of sensory information, it is presumably only under physical description that the uniformities in its contribution are revealed.

Equivalently for these purposes: Insofar as the activity of sensory mechanisms encodes information about the state of the environment, it is the physical state of the environment that is thus encoded.

15 The status of the claim that there are stimulus invariants corresponding to percepts is unclear. On one way of reading it it would seem to be a necessary truth: Since 'perceive' is a success verb, there must be at least one invariant feature of all situations in which someone perceives a thing to be of type *t*; viz., the presence of a thing of type *t*. On the other hand, it is a very strong *empirical* claim that, for any type of thing that can be perceived, there exists a set of *physical* properties such that the detection of those properties is plausibly identified with the perception of a thing of that type. This latter requires that the distinction between things of type *t* and everything else *is a physical distinction*, and, as we saw in the introduction, that conclusion does *not* follow just from the premise that *t*-type objects are physical objects.

The issue is whether there are physical kinds corresponding to perceptual kinds and that, as we have been saying all along, is an empirical issue. My impression of the literature is that the correspondence fails more often than it holds; that perception cannot, in general, be thought of as the categorization of *physical* invariants, however abstractly such invariants may be described. (For a discussion of the empirical situation in the field of speech perception, cf. Fodor et al., 1974.)

16 Gibson sometimes writes as though the problem of how the (presumed) stimulus invariants are detected could be avoided by distinguishing between the stimulus for the *sensory transducers* (viz., physical energies) and the stimulus for the *perceptual organs* (viz., abstract invariants). But this way trivialization lies. If one is allowed to use the notion of a stimulus so as to distinguish the input to the retina (light energy) from the input to the optic system (patterns of light energy which exhibit invariances relevant, e.g., to the explanation of perceptual constancies), why not also talk about the stimulus for the *whole organism* (viz., perceptibles)? Thus, the answer to 'How do we perceive bottles?' would go: 'It is necessary and sufficient for the perception of a bottle that one detect the presence of the stimulus invariant *bottle*.' The trouble with this answer (which, by the way, has a curiously Rylean sound to my ears) is, of course, that the problem of how one detects the relevant stimulus invariant is the *same* problem as how one perceives a bottle, so no ground has been gained overall.

What this shows, I think, is not that the psychological problem of perception is a muddle, but that *stating* the problem requires choosing (and motivating) a proprietary vocabulary for the representation of inputs. I have argued that the vocabulary of values of physical parameters *is* appropriate on the plausible assumption that sensory transducers detect values of physical parameters and that all perceptual knowledge is mediated by the activity of sensory transducers.

17 I have been assuming that the representations of an environmental event that are assigned in the course of perceptual analysis are computed serially. Actually, a weaker assumption will do: viz., that at least *some* information about physical parameters normally 'gets in' before any higher-level representations are computed. I don't suppose this is a claim that any psychologist would wish to deny.

18 Hence the possibility of perceptual illusions. For a discussion of perception that runs along the lines I have endorsed, see Gregory (1966) or Teuber (1960).

19 It is, of course, quite unclear whether the latter undertaking can be carried through in any very revealing way. That will depend upon whether there are generalizations which hold (just) for conscious mental states, and that depends in turn on whether the conscious states of an organism have more in common with one another than with the unconscious states of the nervous system of the organism. It is, in this sense, an open question whether conscious psychological states provide a natural domain for a theory, just as it is an open question whether, say, all the objects in Minnesota provide a natural domain for a theory. One can't have theories of everything under every description, and which descriptions of which things can be generalized is not usually a question that can be settled a priori. I should have thought that, since Freud, the burden of proof has shifted to those who maintain that the conscious states (of human beings) do form a theoretical domain.

20 These remarks connect, in obvious ways, with the ones that concluded the introduction: The various intellectual disciplines typically cross-classify one another's subject matter.

References

Bruner, J.S., Goodnow, J.J., and Austin, G.A. (1956) *A Study of Thinking*. New York: Wiley. (Paperback Wiley Science Editions, 1962.)

Capranica, R.R. (1965) *The Evoked Vocal Response of the Bullfrog: A Study of Communication by Sound*. Cambridge, Mass.: MIT Press.

Chomsky, N. (1959) "Review of Skinner's *Verbal Behavior*." *Language*, 35: 26–58.

Fodor, J.A., Bever, T., and Garrett, M. (1974) *The Psychology of Language: An Introduction to Psycholinguistics and Generative Grammar*. New York: McGraw-Hill.

Gibson, J.J. (1966) *The Senses Considered as Perceptual Systems*: Boston: Houghton.

Goodman, N. (1965) *Fact, Fiction and Forecast*. Indianapolis: Bobbs-Merrill.

Gregory, R.L. (1966) *Eye and Brain: The Psychology of Seeing*. New York: McGraw-Hill.

Lettvin, J., Maturana, H., Pitts, W., and McCulloch, W. (1961). "Two remarks on the visual system of the frog." In *Sensory Communication* (W. Rosenblith, ed.). Cambridge, Mass.: MIT Press.

Loewenstein, W.R. (1960) "Biological transducers." *Scientific American*, August. (Also in *Perception: Mechanisms and Models, Readings from Scientific American* (1972), San Francisco: Freeman.)

Ratliff F. (1961) "Inhibitory interaction and the detection and enhancement of contours." In *Sensory Communication* (W. Rosenblith, ed.). Cambridge, Mass.: MIT Press.

Teuber, H.L. (1960) Perception. In *Handbook of Psychology*, vol. 3 (J. Field, H.W. Magoun, and V.E. Hall, (eds). Washington, DC: Amer. Phys. Soc.

Thorpe, W.H. (1963) *Learning and Instinct in Animals*. London: Methuen.

Tolman, E.C. (1932) *Purposive Behavior in Animals and Men*. New York: Century.

Wason, P.C. and Johnson-Laird, P.N. (1972) *Psychology of Reasoning: Structure and Content*. London: Batsford; Cambridge, Mass.: Harvard University Press.

Young, R.K. (1968) "Serial learning." In *Verbal Behavior and General Behavior Theory* (T. Dixon and D. Horton, eds). Englewood Cliffs, N.J.: Prentice-Hall.

8

G. Rey, "A Not 'Merely Empirical' Argument for a Language of Thought"

I

The "Language of Thought" ("LOT") hypothesis ("LOTH") is the hypothesis that thinking involves states that have (semantically valuable) logico-syntactic constituents that are causally available to the thinker.[1] It has been advanced in recent decades largely as an empirical hypothesis about the character of much human cognition. While this kind of defense of that hypothesis is perfectly reasonable and, I think, very promising, it has the unfortunate side-effect of inviting philosophers to regard the hypothesis as "merely empirical," a kind of Rube-Goldberg conjecture showing (perhaps contrary to Descartes) how a material mind *conceivably might* work, but not a serious hypothesis about how one actually *does* (much less *must*) work. Questions of this latter sort are the business of ("mere") psychologists and computer scientists, not philosophers.

Now, there are, to be sure, "merely empirical issues" in discussions of mind, as in any concrete domain, issues that can be settled only by going out and looking: for example, what strategies people actually use in reasoning, the fallacies to which they are susceptible, how their amygdalas are implicated in anger. But there are also theoretical issues in this domain, as in any other, which I submit are not happily classified as either "purely philosophical" or "merely empirical." They are a mixed bag of methodological reflections, very general constraints on possible theories, and commitments that may turn out to run fairly deep in our understanding of the world. For example, the atomic theory of matter, the theory of natural selection, the theory of genetic inheritance: these theories strike me as too deep to be classified as "merely empirical." For no notion of "observation," however loose and theory-laden, do we just "observe" them to be true. But nor do they all seem to be establishable "by pure reason alone." We can *imagine* some of them being false; they may even be *possibly* false. *Mere* imaginings and possibilities, however, can come to seem idle and uninteresting the more we appreciate the fundamental role these hypotheses play in our general theories and taxonomies of the world.[2]

The LOTH strikes me as just such a case in point. Although there are many "merely empirical" considerations that can be marshalled on its behalf, there

127

are also deeper ones that should not be so regarded. Some philosophers, e.g. Maloney (1989), Davies (1991), Lycan (1993), have already proposed some *a priori*-style arguments (Lycan calls his "deductive"), to many parts of which I'm quite sympathetic. I worry, though, that the premises of their arguments may not be all that *a priori* or unproblematic, and that, in any case, they may be far too strong for many readers.[3] In §II of this paper I want to advance what I believe to be, if not an *a priori*, at least a not "merely empirical" argument of my own, based on weaker premises. Whether it is in fact *a priori* – whether the premises are in some sense analytic or apodeictic or otherwise "philosophical" – is not something I want to decide here. For reasons I discuss elsewhere (Rey 1993), these further philosophical distinctions seem to me highly theoretic ones, whose clarification seems to me to await a more detailed psychology than we yet possess. But I do think the argument I will present is close to many that have been regarded as "purely philosophical" in the past, and is, I hope, based upon extremely weak premises that most anyone on a little reflection ought to accept.

One thing I hope to accomplish by providing such an argument is to indicate just how weak and natural the LOTH need be. Many discussions of the LOTH make it seem as though the issue is whether people are Turing machines; or whether thought isn't often imagistic; whether people's *everyday* mental processes are "formal" and abstract in the fashion of symbolic logic, or somehow more ingrained in their understanding of real examples; whether our brains have a "classical" von Neumann architecture or a connectionist/ "dynamical" one. Many of *these* questions do turn on quite specific empirical details about which a philosopher need and perhaps ought not make any claims. In §III I will show how my argument frees the LOTH from a stand on these further issues, and so can tolerate much of the evidence and argument that has been raised by connectionists and others against a Classical View. It may well be that many people's *actual* mental processes involve images, metaphors, analogies and all manner of computational tricks, as well as massive parallel processing that is distributed far and wide in the brain. My argument will try to establish only that, if people are genuinely thinking things, they must *also* have *available* to them the resources of an LOT.

There is afoot, however, a general resistance to *any* philosophical (or not "merely empirical") conjectures about the internal structures of our brains, a resistance that has its roots in Twentieth Century abhorrence of philosophy committing itself to any substantive claims about the world. This has resulted in what I call a "superficialism" about mental concepts that is evident in much phenomenological, behavioristic and even more recent "commonsense" accounts of such concepts. In §IV I shall argue that the arguments on behalf of these accounts are fallacious, and that they miss the important, internal explanatory role that the phenomena picked out by many mental concepts are designed to play. If this is true, then it can be no objection to my argument for LOTH that it involves speculations about internal structures that are ordinarily hidden from view.

II Argument T

What might be called "the argument from thought" – what I will call "argument T" – proceeds as follows:

1 There are thinking things (e.g. oneself) that are capable of rational thought, involving at least first-order logical thought.
2 Anything that is capable of rational thought is capable of making *logical transitions* in thought; i.e. it is *psychologically possible* that it pass from one thought to another *by virtue of logical properties* of its thought.
3 First-order logical properties are in part constituted by (semantically valuable) logico-syntactic constituent structure.
4 For transitions between thoughts to occur by virtue of logico-syntactic constituent structure, those constituents must be *causally available* features of the thinker.

From these premises, it follows that:

5 A thinking thing is a thing some of whose states have (semantically valuable) logical syntactic constituents that are causally available to the thinker.

and so:

6 There are things (e.g. oneself) some of whose states have (semantically valuable) logico-syntactic constituents that are causally available to it, i.e. there are things whose states entoken sentences in a LOT.

The essential idea is that one can know that there are things (e.g. oneself) that have a language of thought almost as well as one can know that there are things (e.g. oneself) that are *capable* of *processes* of logical thought. I shall discuss the premises one by one.

> *Premise (1)* **There are thinking things (e.g. oneself) that are capable of rational thought, involving at least first-order logical thought.**

'Thinking' can, of course, be used in a loose sense for most any mental process, but presumably a system qualifies for this loose sense only if it is capable of thought in some more specific sense, a sense we often capture ordinarily when we contrast thinking with mere dreaming, free association, rote memorization. At least part of what I think we mean to capture by this more specific sense is *rational thought*, or *reasoning* (and unless otherwise noted I shall have this sense in mind in my uses of 'thought', 'thinking' and related forms[4]).

So understood, premise (1) should, of course, be acceptable to anyone the least bit moved by Descartes. Although he didn't have the resources of modern logic, I take it he and his followers would think those resources do capture an essential *core* of the thoughts of which he thought himself capable by virtue of being a thinking thing – even if they don't capture them *all*. This core includes at least some truth-functional (e.g., "Either I exist or I don't exist") and some quantificational thoughts (e.g., "If I exist, then something exists").[5]

To be sure, Descartes regarded (at least his personal instance of) premise (1) as an absolute certitude on which he hoped to base a great deal of the rest of his knowledge. Argument T has no such ambitions, and can even treat premise (1) as dubitable, at least in principle, even by a live and thinking thing. There might, for example, be some specific feature of the concept [thinking] that could turn out to be problematic (we shall see in discussing the next premise what one such feature might be); or it may be that *no* intentional notion is scientifically or metaphysically respectable. Many philosophers and radical connectionist opponents of the LOTH have, of course, taken this latter view. For example, Daniel Dennett (1978) defines mental (or "intentional") systems as being "stance relative":

> What do two people have in common when they both believe that snow is white? I propose this:
> $$(x)(x \text{ believes snow is white iff } x \text{ can be predictively}$$
> $$\text{attributed the belief that snow is white}). \ (1978\text{: xvii})$$

reiterating a little later: "There is no objectively satisfiable sufficient condition for an entity's *really* having beliefs" (1978: 285). Fine: this then simply denies premise (1), that anything is a thinking thing – that anything (e.g. oneself) *really* is one.[6] The present argument is not addressed to such a person. But I do presume that such a view is extremely implausible, shown to be so by the overwhelming failure of eliminativist efforts (e.g. methodological behaviorism) to explain obvious regularities in much human and animal behavior.[7] That's at least one reason on which one could rely to reassure oneself of premise (1). In any case, if you like, assume premise (1) merely for the sake of my argument (and, if not yourself; since perhaps you find the relevant regularities more easily observable in others, use some other example you find more plausible).

Premise (2) **Anything that is capable of rational thought is capable of making *logical* transitions in thought; i.e. it is *psychologically possible* that it pass from one thought to another *by virtue of logical properties* of its thought.[8]**

The claim here is that it is not enough that a thinking thing *have* logical thoughts: it must be at least *capable* of undergoing a *particular sort of process* (or set of processes). At this point in the development of psychology it would be rash to try to specify precisely what the process(es) must be, as rash as it would have been to try to specify exactly the relevant processes that count as digestion or metabolism prior to an adequate theory of physiology. But, as would have been true in the case of digestion, it's not impossible to suggest some plausible *necessary* conditions.[9]

Rational thought has something to do with *reasoning*, reasoning with the *provision of reasons*; and, as I've already suggested in premise (1), the core cases of reasons are provided by *logic*. But, contrary to behaviorism,[10] not just any process that produces as output logical consequences of input premises would count as thinking or reasoning. As the contrast with rote memorization and free association suggests, someone who merely memorized steps of a proof, or associated premises with conclusions as one does "salt" with "pepper," is not someone who is thinking in our non-loose sense, i.e. *genuinely reasoning*. Nor would it do for the process to consist of merely a "look-up" procedure, whereby a table was consulted in which sentences were paired, one by one, with some consequences.[11] What these examples strongly suggest is that, in a case of genuine thinking, it must also be possible for the thought of the consequences to have come about in a certain way *by virtue* of the thought of the premises; and, then, not by virtue of just *any* arbitrary property of the premises – say, a certain pattern of rhyme – but by virtue of their *logical* properties. It would certainly seem to be the most basic fact about thinking things that they are things that are sensitive to such properties.[12] Transitions between thoughts that occur by virtue of the logical properties I shall call "logical transitions." If something were psychologically *incapable* of making *any* such logical transitions, it is hard to see what point there would be in regarding it as a *genuinely* thinking thing, as opposed to something that, like the objects of Dennett's stances, could be conveniently or instrumentally so regarded.

There are, of course, heaps of problems with spelling out just what the nice phrase "by virtue of" means. I do presume that it is metaphysically legitimate, that premise (2) is as intelligible as "He died by virtue of inhaling the smoke, not by virtue of being consumed by the flames (had there been no smoke he would have escaped in time)." Whatever problems attach to such a phrase, I assume, however, that they are in no way peculiar to the mental, or beg the question of the LOTH. Although I won't hazard a general account, perhaps what I have in mind will become clearer by discussion of related cases, both here and in the discussion of the other premises (particular premise (4)).

Consider, at least by way of analogy, Davidson's (1963) similar insistence on a distinction between *real* and mere *rationalized* reasons:

> [A] person can have a reason for an action, and perform the action, and yet this reason not be the reason why he did it. Central to the relation between a reason and an action it explains is the idea that the agent performed the action *because* he had the reason. (1963/79: 9)

In a later article, Davidson (1973/80) observes that a lot here depends upon the way in which a reason brings about an act:

> A climber might want to rid himself of the weight and danger of holding another man on a rope, and he might know that by loosening his hold

on the rope he could rid himself of the weight and danger. This belief and want might so unnerve him as to cause him to loosen his hold, and yet it might be the case that he never *chose* to loosen his hold, nor did he do it intentionally. (1973/80: 79)

I leave to premise (4) the question whether the 'because' in the previous quote, and the 'cause' in this one actually involve *physical causation*. The point of the present premise is merely that, however we spell out the ultimate metaphysics, we want to preserve a *quite specific way* in which mental states come about (to put it neutrally) by virtue of other states: otherwise we would seem to have no basis for claiming something was the *real* reason for an act. Similarly, premise (2) could be seen to be based on the insistence of a distinction between *genuine* and only *apparent* thinking: a genuine thinking thing is something that is able to enter into a *process* of *genuine*, and not merely apparent thought, i.e. a process whose results depend in the right way upon the logical properties of the thoughts involved.

Davidson (1973/80: 80) himself despairs of spelling out the appropriate way that would distinguish genuine intentional action from the behavior of the climber. And we might readily agree that there may be no *a priori* way of doing so. But our confidence that there *is* a difference may be justified even though we don't know how to *specify* it. We may, after all, be in the position with respect to the distinction between the intentional and unintentional that Grice (1961/65) urged we were in with regard to perception, and Putnam (1975) argued we were in with regard to other explanatorily interesting distinctions, e.g. between chemical kinds, where we leave "a blank space to be filled in by the specialist" (Grice (1961/65: 463).

Someone could insist, however, that there is a usage of 'believe' and 'desire' that *is* indifferent to any facts about *how* any states come about. This was, of course, the view of analytic behaviorism; but it might also, less dramatically, be the view of a decision theorist, who might be interested in merely the thoughts – the beliefs and preferences – agents have at *specific points in time, irrespective of how they happened to arrive at them*. Predictions about game play or market behavior might be derivable from such an abstract theory, and even be illuminating about many regularities in those domains. Such systems might be said to "have *thoughts*" without actually "*thinking*"; we might call them mere "*thoughters*," not *thinkers*. Now, I don't know whether such creatures are genuinely possible; but it's not hard to see why decision theorists often might not care which they are dealing with.

What is good for behaviorism and decision theory, however, may not be enough for premise (1), which is the claim that there are genuinely *thinking* things.[13] As I've emphasized, that claim (and, I submit, most of our interest in psychology) seems to be committed not merely to individual attitude states, but to the character of the *processes* by which those states can and sometimes do come about.

Premise (3) **First-order logical properties are in part constituted by (semantically valuable) logico-syntactic constituent structure.**

Substantial support for this premise is, of course, provided by the enormous success of so-called "formal" methods in logic.[14] For example, at least a core set of logical truths (e.g. 'P v ~P', 'Fa ⊃ (∃x)Fx', '(∃x)(y)Rxy ⊃ (y)(∃x)Rxy') can be shown to be so by virtue of the way in which their semantically valuable constituents – e.g. predicates, operators – are *syntactically* composed. So far as we know, this kind of account is the *only* adequate *kind* of account of logical thoughts that we have (cf. Maloney 1989: 7).

There is an interesting question about how to characterize precisely the class of formalisms necessary to capture quantificational theory. In addition to the usual Frege/Peano/Russell and Polish notation(s), there is the lambda calculus, Tarski's cylindrical algebras, and the variableless, combinatory logic of Curry and Feys (1958).[15] I venture that what is essential to all such formalisms is that they involve a set of *operators* (such as connectives, quantifiers, abstractors) that *operate in an ordered way on the referential devices of the language* (such as predicates, variables, singular terms): the sentences of such systems involve specific orderings of operators and referential devices; the logical truths are those sentences whose truth does not depend upon the reference of the referential devices. It is these orderings of such constituents that constitute what I have been calling "logico-syntactic structure." The burden of premise (3) is that such structure is not an *accidental* feature of logical properties.

Note that this premise is relying only on *logical* properties of thoughts being constituted by logico-syntactic structure. Though it seems to me a perfectly natural assumption that those properties (though not depending upon the reference of the referential devices) are also *semantic*, the present argument does not require their being so. Certainly premise (1) would be ordinarily understood as entailing that there are things with contentful states. But if one wanted to insist, as does Stich (1983), that syntax is determinate but semantics is not, the whole of argument T could be read as establishing only a *syntactic* LOTH.[16]

There are some (e.g. Stalnaker 1984) who might claim that it is really *propositions* that have entailments, and that it is the inclusion relations among *them*, not logico-syntactic form that is relevant. Now, if propositions are construed as sets of possible worlds, as Lewis and Stalnaker propose, then such an account will not distinguish *logical* truths and entailments from other necessary truths and (strictly speaking) valid arguments, as might arise in mathematics or (given necessary constitutions) even chemistry. In any case, we would still be owed an account of how it is possible for thoughts to give rise to other states *by virtue of* their logical structure, if that logical structure were confined to patterns among possible worlds alone (I will consider a more sentential account of propositions in defending premise (4)).

A possibility that many find attractive is that thought might have no *logical syntax* at all: images, maps, diagrams would suffice. Thus, David Lewis (1994) argues that our ordinary talk of thought is not committed to being seriously language-like, involving logico-syntactic constituents, but could be merely maplike:

> A serious issue, and one on which I take folk psychology to be agnostic, concerns the relation between the whole and the parts of a representation. Suppose I have a piece of paper according to which, *inter alia*, Collingwood is east of Fitzroy. Can I tear the paper up so that I get one snippet that has exactly the content that Collingwood is east of Fitzroy, nothing more and nothing less? If the paper is covered with writing maybe I can; for maybe 'Collingwood is east of Fitzroy' is one of the sentences written there. But if the paper is a map, any snippet according to which Collingwood is east of Fitzroy will be a snippet according to which more is true besides. . . . If our beliefs are 'a map . . . by which we steer', as Ramsey said . . . then they are to that extent not language-like. (1994: 422)

But surely Ramsey's remark was only intended as a useful metaphor; just how thoughts about non-spatial matters could literally be *maps* is left entirely unclear. Indeed, it is revealing that Lewis considers here only a case of a *logically simple 2-place spatial predication*, such as 'Collingwood is east of Fitzroy.' He is certainly right that in such a case a map might suffice as a representation instead of a sentence with a logico-syntactic structure, and that one indication of that fact would be the lack of a specific propositional content to assign a specific representation. Indeed, such maps might well afford a way of capturing certain systematicities: they can represent Collingwood as east of Fitzroy iff they can represent Fitzroy as east of Collingwood. And perhaps many thoughts that people have are representable by maps and other sorts of imagistic representations in this way. But premises (1) and (2) include *quantificational* thoughts, and transitions between them by virtue of their *logical structure*: how are we to exploit maps or images for such a purpose unless we can *also* represent those thoughts as possessing logico-syntactic structure? How are maps alone to represent *negations, conditionals, nested quantifications, modals*, and the combinations of them that are required for the logical transitions demanded by premises (1) and (2)? In any case, until someone provides an *imagistic* system of logic as *expressively powerful* as a logico-syntactic one, I submit we are entitled to suppose that premise (3) captures a deep fact about the nature of logical properties.

Premise (4) **For transitions between thoughts to occur by virtue of logico-syntactic constituent structure, those constituents must be *causally available* features of the thinker.**

So far as premises (1)–(3) are concerned, we could be talking about the thinking capacities of angels. The further question arises as to how *ordinary mortals, creatures in space and time,* can make such transitions between states by virtue of logical structure. Descartes, of course, was skeptical that any material object could make such transitions:

> it is morally impossible that a machine should contain so many varied arrangements as to act in all the events of life in the way that reason enables us to act. (1637/1954: 42).

But his skepticism was begun to be met by Alan Turing, when he supplemented Frege's and Russell's work with his account of *mechanical* computation of, *inter alia,* logical functions.

But while Turing might be regarded as having shown how a spatio-temporal device might *possibly* manage to think, he can't be taken to have shown how something *must* think. And I don't intend to offer any such apodeictic argument here. But I do think, continuing with the reasoning I've advanced so far, that there is the following not "merely empirical" thing to be said.

For the question arises as to how, given the kind of physical/causal world in which we live, we are to make sense of premise (2): how can one thing happen "by virtue of" something else, if not as a result of physical causation? In particular, insofar as it must be possible for states to arise *by virtue of the logical structure* of thought, and, by premise (3), that structure involves semantically valuable syntactic constituents, it would certainly seem as if *those constituents had better be causally efficacious.*

In the very passages of Davidson (1963/79, 1973/80) that we already cited on behalf of premise (2), it is clear that Davidson presumes that the only way to e.g. distinguish a real from a rationalized reason is by relying on *physical* causation. But, ironically enough, those and other later writings might suggest to someone that one could understand the "by virtue of" (and "because") claims of premise (2) not as involving *causal* relations between states, but simply a *conceptually constitutive* relation imposed by the demands of intentional interpretation. After all, Davidson insists:

> If we cannot find a way to interpret the utterances and other behavior of a creature as revealing a set of beliefs largely consistent and true by our own standards, we have no reason to count that creature as rational, as having beliefs, or as saying anything. (1973/84: 137)

Depending upon precisely how one spells out "largely consistent and true by our own standards," someone's being prepared to make logical transitions might be regarded as simply constitutive of their having any thoughts at all.[17]

But such a *constitutive* "by virtue of" claim has the agent *already* believing the logical consequences of any belief merely by virtue of *having* it: the agent doesn't have to *do*, or be disposed to *engage* in any sort of *process* of thought. But it was precisely the possibility of a particular *process* of thought to which I have argued premise (2) commits us. Of course, if the constitutive claim is

135

to be understood as also involving just such a possibility, then it is simply another way of expressing premise (2) – a *far stronger* way, one should note, than argument T or the LOTH requires. If it doesn't commit us to a process, then, I submit, we are back to a form of Dennett's instrumentalism, or, again, merely to *thoughters*, not *thinkers*.[18]

But *thoughts* could be causally efficacious without their *constituents* being so. The objects of thoughts could be identified with merely *abstract objects* that have syntactic structure – indeed, merely *type* sentences, say, in some preferred language of the theorist, who then simply pairs states of people onto them: a person's thought that a is F is to be paired to the structure type [Fa]; her thought that something is F, with [(∃x)Fx]. The (interpreted) sentence with which the person's state is associated could be regarded as providing the *content* of that state. And the theorist might claim that for there to be "a logical transition between these states in virtue of form" is for there simply to be a *law* relating the paired states by reference to those structured entities: e.g. whenever someone is in a state paired to [Fa], she makes a transition to a state paired to [(∃x)Fx]. And so, for her to be a thinking thing, it is enough that it is psychologically possible for her transitions to be governed by such a law. On this view, it would appear that there is no need for the logico-syntactic constituents of those thoughts to be causally available.[19]

This view would seem, however, to fail to capture the kind of "by virtue of" claim that is reasonably intended in premise (2). Consider again Davidson's "climber" case: it might be a *law* about the climber that whenever he finds he wants to loosen his hold this so unnerves him that he does so; but that still presumably wouldn't make the loosening *deliberate*. Similarly, in the case of reasoning, not only do we want to rule out *accidental* transitions in thought, we want to rule out even non-accidental transitions that occur *in the wrong way*. Merely some nomological *association* between one thought and another that happens to be a consequence of it doesn't constitute genuine logical thinking: a student who merely *memorizes* some of the consequences of a claim may well make transitions in thought capturable by a law relating sentences; but he isn't engaged thereby in genuine logical thought. Or imagine that we condition a young child to think and say "Two" whenever he sees that his cat, Alice, is purring, to say "Three" whenever he sees that *anything* is purring, and, where both are to be said, to attend first to Alice, and say "Two." Suppose, indeed, such a pattern of conditioning were applied across a wide variety of cases (dogs, people, teddy bears). If it were successful, there would be a *law* relating the child's thought states that would refer to the syntactic structure of the sentences that express the contents of the child's states: for a wide range of values of 'P' and 'a', whenever the child thinks [Pa] he then thinks [(∃x)Px]. But the transitions here would not occur *by virtue of* the logico-syntactic properties of these thoughts. The child might never notice that Alice's purring *entails* that *something* is purring. We can even suppose that the child's inferential ability is too poor even to unself-reflectively sustain the inference (imagine the child is quite retarded, though still conditionable). So merely satisfying the law would not seem to be a way of satisfying the transition condition of premise (2). In this sort of case it is extremely difficult to see how to capture the requisite *right way by virtue of which* an event is brought about without appealing to *the right sort of causal chains*: such causal details would seem to supply precisely the very fine-grained distinctions needed to distinguish both Davidson's climber from someone more culpable, and our conditioned child from someone more genuinely thoughtful. If premise (3) is correct, these causal details will quite plausibly include logico-syntactic properties.[20]

Someone might reply that, for such a child, the proposed pairing to predicative sentences isn't the right one; rather, it ought to be something more holophrastic like "Alice-purrs" and "It-purreth" (like "It-raineth," cf. Quine 1960: ch 2). But note that (1) there would still *be* a law relating the child's states that *did* advert to sentences paired with those states; and (2) in order to insist on the *right* pairing, distinguishing among necessarily equivalent sentences, one would presumably need to ascertain just which inferences the child *was* disposed to make; which is just to concede that there merely being a law relating states characterizable by sentences isn't sufficient for the transitions between those states to count as genuine inference, i.e. genuine thinking, indeed, not even for having the genuine *thought* at all! What is required for *that*? Well, it would certainly seem that the only way to motivate a *structured* vs. merely *holophrastic* content would be for the constituents of the structure to be causally available to the agent. So premise (4) is established merely with a detour through a theory of content.

Aficionados of the literature in this area will recognize in the example of the child a thinly disguised version of Smolensky's (1991: 212ff.) proposed codings of mental states as tensor product sums.[21] As he points out (p. 225fn7), such a coding is like Gödel numbering of logical formulae, but with the possible advantage that the transitions between the states that realize the code needn't depend upon any of the coded state's logical constituents being causally efficacious.[22] However, what the above examples strongly suggest is that, insofar as such codings are possible, the transitions that would occur on their basis would not count as *logical* transitions in the sense of premise (2): they wouldn't occur by *virtue of logical structure*. Of course, along the lines of the previous paragraph, a genuine thinker might *exploit* such a procedure as a perhaps economical heuristic, much as a medieval monk might recall the *Barbara Celarent* mnemonic in deciding whether a syllogism was valid, or someone might report the cosine of an angle by looking it up in a book. But if a creature could *only* make transitions between thoughts in this way and couldn't also do it by exploiting logical properties (i.e., by premise (3), constituent structure), then it would no more be a thinking thing than would a student who could *only* do logic by the mnemonics be capable of logic, or someone who could only look up cosines in a table be competent at trigonometry.

Note that premise (4) does not require that the logico-syntactic constituents be constituents of the *very* thought state *itself*: someone might think that Alice

137

is purring merely by using an image of a smiling cat, or a Gödel number or a sum of tensor products. What is required is that, insofar as this state is capable of entering into logical transitions, there be *available* to the agent the requisite constituents.[23] The agent would have to be able to move from the image of the smiling cat to representations with the logico-syntactic structure required for logical thought (or from the Gödel numbers or tensor products to their factors).

In any event, a defender of the complete dispensibility [*sic*] of causally efficacious constituents owes us some account of how, without them, *genuine thought* is to be distinguished from merely a behavioristic simulation. What constraint, if any, is being placed on internal processing? Need there be *no* connection between *thought* and *reasoning*, between *reasoning* and *the thinking of reasons*, or between the thinking of *reasons* and *logical properties*? Again, we would seem to be left with no distinction between *thinkers* and mere "thoughters."

The conclusions

The above premises entail:

5   A thinking thing is a thing some of whose states have (semantically valuable) logical syntactic constituents that are causally available to the thinker.

which, in conjunction with premise (1), that there are thinking things, entails:

6   There are things (e.g. oneself) some of whose states have (semantically valuable) logico-syntactic constituents that are causally available to it, i.e. there are things whose states entoken sentences in a LOT.

For example, my thought that I think is capable of giving rise to the thought that something thinks by virtue of the fact that 'I think' has a certain structure, the constituents of which, 'I' and 'think', are both semantically valuable and causally efficacious. The LOTH is in this way very nearly as plausible as Descartes' *cogito*, or, at any rate, *that* claim, and the claim that thinking involves logical transitions that are essentially capturable by logico-syntactic structure.

III   What argument T doesn't show

It is important to see what Argument T does *not* establish.

(1) Argument T is not committed to the usual claims about systematicity, productivity and generality of thought that other authors – e.g. Fodor and Pylyshyn (1988), Davies (1991), Lycan (1993) – have emphasized on behalf of the LOTH. That is, my argument does not require that, for any thought someone can think, she can think it iff she can think all logical permutations

of it (systematicity), or all logical combinations of it and other thoughts, no matter how long and complex (productivity, generality). Although I think there is in fact quite a sufficiency of instances to warrant the LOTH on these grounds, I suspect there are limits: we're notoriously dreadful at understanding certain sorts of iterated nestings of especially the *same* operator (negations, modals, propositional attitudes), and it's by no means clear that everyone can really understand arbitrary combinations of concepts that they understand separately (e.g.[Space–time is curved]; [The world is 11-dimensional], [The reddish thing is greenish]).[24] In any case, if argument T is sound, a defender of the LOTH need not be committed to a stand on these questions.

(2) T does not entail that we are Turing Machines (i.e. that our psychology is best regarded as a realization of one). In arguing for premise (3), I relied on Turing's work to establish that logical features are mechanically computable, and that, given my other premises, anything that could think must have causal *access* to logical constituents. But a person could be a lot *less* than a Turing machine for that to be true (for example, there might be nomologically deter-mined limitations on her memory); and, of course, she conceivably might even have access to a great deal *more*: perhaps some methods of computation of which such people as Penrose (1989: ch 4) dream, when they dream that Gödel's theorem shows we aren't Turing machines. In any case, T is certainly not committed to supposing that our mental architecture remotely resembles that of a Turing Machine, or a von Neumann architecture, or any determin-istic or serial automaton. LOTH presents only a quite weak *constraint* on possible architectures, viz. that logico-syntactic properties be causally effica-cious; and this is compatible with an indefinitely rich variety of architectures, for example, ones that might implement those properties in connectionist and/or massively parallel processors.

(3) T does not establish that *all* or even *most* ordinary mental activities involve an LOTH. The above argument rests upon premises about the *capac-ities* or, in Chomsky's phrase, *competencies* of a creature, not its *actual* activities or *performance*. For all that T establishes, everyone might in reality use short-cut heuristics that save them the effort of genuine thought, just as most of us use simple mnemonic algorithms, not careful deductive reasoning, in doing our daily sums.

The word 'process' that I have used to describe thinking might of course mislead in this connection: it might appear as though I *am* committing the LOTH to claims about actual processing and performance. However, my claim is not that *all*, or even most, or, come to think of it, even *any* of our *actual* mental processes of thought involve logical transitions; only that, insofar as they are processes of thought, that they involve states for which it is at least *psychologically possible* that they are capable of entering into logical transitions. Someone's being a thinking thing requires that she be *capable* of undergoing certain processes of thought, not that she ever actually has or ever will (most people, after all, may well "live lives of quiet desperation" performing mindless connectionist tasks).[25]

This point – a Chomskyean insistence on competence instead of perform-ance – seems to me to get missed so often in the connectionist debate that it is worth pounding the table a bit about it. Van Gelder and Niklasson (1994), for example, recently attack systematicity, claiming that the well-known "selection task" data of Wason (1966) belie Fodor and Pylyshyn's (1988) claim that minds are systematic: people seem to understand "All Fs are Gs," but not to infer from it that "All not Gs are not Fs."

Put aside the question of whether this latter failure has actually anything to do with systematicity.[26] Van Gelder and Niklasson do consider interpreting Fodor and Pylyshyn's systematicity claims as making a claim about an agent's competence, but make the startling claim that

> Fodor and Pylyshyn *explicitly declined* to rely on competence/perform-ance distinctions, acknowledging that the hypothesis of ideal competence was held in suspicion in the opposing camp (connectionists). (1994: 908)

But this misreads Fodor and Pylyshyn's concession. They claim that system-aticity "doesn't require the idealization to *unbounded* competence" (Fodor and Pylyshyn 1988, p. 37, italics mine), not that it doesn't require idealiza-tion to any sort of competence at all! Of course, it does; as does any interesting claim about the mind's abilities.

(4) Given then that the LOTH, and certainly the premises of T, are claims only about a certain competence, they are compatible with proposals that:

(a) People often exploit the resources of "images, prototypes, schemata, semantic frames, metaphors and metonymy" (Johnson 1993: 152; see also Kosslyn 1980). They may – indeed they should – use whatever works. The only constraint demanded by (T) is that, insofar as the agent is a genuine thinker, she had better have available to her the constituents required for logical transitions;

(b) In particular, people may well often reason according to "models," and not by employing the predicate calculus. Thus, Johnson-Laird claims:

> The models that people use to reason are more likely to resemble percep-tion or conception of the events (from a God's-eye view) than a string of symbols directly corresponding to the linguistic form of the premises and then applying rules of inference to them in order to derive a conclu-sion. (1983: 53–4)

Now, it's not altogether clear what contrast Johnson-Laird means to be drawing here: even if people don't ordinarily use the Frege/Russell predicate calculus in reasoning syllogistically, they presumably have to use *some* mechan-ical, representational medium when they "perceive or conceive" events. But it may well be that people often reason far more efficiently by mapping state-ments in some logico-syntactic formalism to some imagistic system, perhaps a spatial-reasoning module that happens to be especially efficient in human beings and other navigating animals. The only commitment of argument T and the LOTH is that such heuristics do not *exhaust* people's reasoning abilities: in order to be *thinking* things they must also be *capable* of making the transitions by virtue of logico-syntactic structures as well;

(c) Much pattern recognition and other mental processes may be due to a connectionist – even "dynamical" – architecture. As many have pointed out, connectionism could afford an implementation of an LOT; but even where it didn't, such processes might well co-exist and interact with LOT states. Indeed, for rapid statistical analyses, connectionist systems seem quite plausible.[27]

IV Resisting the lure of superficialism

I have been concerned to show in this paper how the LOTH can be regarded as a consequence of quite weak and plausible assumptions about what it is to be a thinking thing. But, against all of these assumptions, it might be felt that there is an even weaker and more plausible idea, that there mustn't be anything "hidden" about the mind: the application of folk mental concepts should be exhausted by the evidence of introspection and/or overt behavior. I call this view "superficialism," in contrast to the kind of "internalist" account I have been urging here, and fear it is endemic to much 20th Century thought about the mind.[28] One finds it not only in introspectivist and behaviorist approaches to the mind, but even, as we saw in discussing premise (4), lurking in recent connectionist proposals.

Superficialism can be motivated in a number of ways: an extreme verificationist theory of meaning; a philosophical reluctance to speculate about the structure of the brain or, indeed, to make any substantive, possibly false claims about the world.[29] But it can also be motivated by a quite tenacious intuition emphasized by many philosophers concerning the ordinary irrelevance of any facts about the brain, given our ordinary ignorance about it, and what would appear to be our liberality in what we might count as thinking things. Imagine a person who behaved in a way genuinely indistinguishable from a normal person, but whose skull turned out to be empty or full of oatmeal, or whose processing were very different from ours: would we really claim that such a creature had no mental life? In a recent article, Jackson and Pettit (1993: 304), for example, have argued that our ordinary psychological idiom couldn't be committed to "a distinctive style of information processing," since

> it would be unduly chauvinistic, to insist that in order to count as a believer a creature must solve the informational processing problems a world sets its inhabitants in the same general way that we do, or in anything like the way we do . . . but any science-fiction buff knows that our concept of belief does not thereby preclude [differently constructed] Vesuvians from having beliefs, say, about the location of objects around them. (1993: 304–5)

141

Leaving aside for a moment, the vagaries of the phrase "information processing," it's instructive to become clear about what precisely "any science-fiction buffs knows." Why should we suppose that it makes no difference to our mental concepts what goes on at any psychological level that might be hidden in the brain? As I noted earlier in citing Davidson (1973/80) and Grice (1961/65) in defense of premise (2), distinctions between *genuine* and *merely apparent* intentional action and perception, seem to depend upon speculations about hidden causal connections in the brain. Other examples abound: spontaneous vs. feigned feelings, insincerity vs. self-deception, strong wills vs. weak appetites, courage vs. foolishness, distraction vs. inconsideration:[30] these distinctions plausibly can occur duly in systems organized in a certain way, and would seem to depend upon distinctions among very specific sorts of causal processes. This was, of course, the claim of premises (2) and (4) with regard to *thinking*.

But what then about people (or Vesuvians) whose behavior is indistinguishable from ours but whose skulls are empty or full of oatmeal? It's open to the internalist simply to claim that those structures must be hidden elsewhere than in the usual place: maybe it's in their toes, or in some yet unexamined special ghost stuff. In *some* cases, of course, such as beings remotely controlled from Mars or Block's (1990) "Blockhead," it is in fact perfectly open to the internalist to claim that such beings don't really have any minds at all.

So is argument T an *a priori* argument after all? There is this reason to think it isn't: if it really were to turn out that *none* of even what we take to be the *best examples* of logical thought in human beings actually involved an LOT, then that would be some reason to begin to doubt the LOTH.[31] We would be in something like the position of ancients learning that fire just wasn't *any* sort of "substance," nor stars any sorts of holes. Thus, if it were to turn out that it really was oatmeal in *all* our heads that was responsible for (what appeared to be) our thoughtful ways, or that we were in fact "Blockheads" or radical connectionist machines, then it would perhaps be overly reactionary to hold onto premises (2)–(4) and insist that no one has ever engaged in any thought at all. But it is important to appreciate just how extraordinary such a discovery would be. It would involve not only giving up some of premises (2)–(4), but a massive reconsideration of the distinctions between e.g. thinking and mere memorization, between cogent reasoning and mere association, and the role of these distinctions in our understanding of people. It would be a little like finding out that there is no basis for the distinction between deliberate and unintentional action; between intending and wanting; between real and rationalized reasons for action; or between the experiences of sight and smell (indeed, one wonders how a radical connectionist proposes to capture *these* distinctions as well). It therefore may not be *logically impossible* that these distinctions are groundless, or grounded other than by inner causal structures. So it may not be *a priori* that our brains have a certain structure. But it does seem improbable in the extreme that they don't, about as improbable as finding out, to return to examples with which I began, that animals really haven't evolved, or that there are no genes. In this way, the postulation of inner causal structure seems to me not "merely empirical" either.

Given that superficialism seems generally unwarranted with regard to our mental concepts, there can be no objection to the LOTH, or to my argument on its behalf, that it involves folk speculations about mental processes not open to ordinary folk inspection. The folk know that. They defer to experts and/or the nature of things in the case of the mind as in the case of any other explanatorily interesting region of the world. Indeed, if argument T is correct, they ought to be quite friendly to the suggestion of an LOTH whose details will be revealed by psychology. For if that argument is correct, the LOTH is as natural as the hypothesis that there are genuine thinking things, for example, themselves.[32]

Notes

1 What counts as "logico-syntactic" will be discussed in due course. I prefer the term "semantically *valuable*" to the more common "semantically evaluable" in order to avoid the conventionalist and instrumentalist suggestions of the latter. However, as the parentheses here are meant to indicate, in order to keep the premises of the argument of the present paper as weak as possible, I will try to remain neutral on the issue of semantic realism: I will understand a "LOT" to be a set of logico-syntactic structures available to a thinker, with or without semantic values.

2 I have been influenced here by discussions with Karen Neander of her (forthcoming); see also Lycan's (1993: 412) discussion of "inferences to the *only* explanation". Note that I am not committing myself here to any particular *explanation* of the status of these hypotheses: indeed, one needn't subscribe to a distinction between the philosophical and empirical, much less the analytic and the synthetic, to regard some claims as not "merely empirical": a Quinian could regard the kinds of deep claims I have in mind as simply being more deeply enmeshed in the continuous web of our beliefs.

3 Maloney's (1989) rich discussion is closest to my own (see esp. his §§1.2, 1.4 and 3.1). I contrast my account with these others at various points (see fns. 16, 19 and 20, as well as the beginning of §III).

4 In keeping with my general reluctance to claim my argument is *a priori*, I don't intend, however, to be basing any premises of my argument on any "analytic" claims about (the ordinary use of) the word 'thinking' or its various forms. I use the word only because its traditional associations are closer to my modest intentions than the more formidable 'reason' and its forms.

5 Not that all representations in the predicate calculus represent some thought: some are too long to do so, and some are quite unintuitive (e.g. '$(\exists y)(Fx \supset Gx)$').

6 Dennett's views over the years actually present a number of exegetical difficulties that need not detain us here; see my (1996).

7 For discussion of non-tendentious empirical reasons far believing in a mind (and in a LOT), see my (1991).

8 For present purposes, I will take what is psychologically possible to be what is compatible with an explanatorily adequate description of a thinker's system of

thought under suitable idealization. Spelling out this idealization adequately would require a more complete psychology than is presently available.

9 Let me stress that I do not take myself in what follows to be providing *sufficient* conditions.

10 Or, more generally, "superficialist" ones of the sort address in §IV below.

11 It's not at all unlikely that there were medieval monks who actually relied for much of their logic on the "*Barbara Celarent*" mnemonic method of traditional syllogistic. Presumably they were not genuinely engaged in (the corresponding) logical thought when they did so, any more than would something that passed the Turing Test merely by coordinating conversational moves by means of a lookup table, as in the case of what has come to be called "The Blockhead," cf. Block (1990).

12 Cf. Fodor and Pylyshyn's (1988: p. 50) and Fodor and McLaughlin's (1991) insistence that systematicity be *no accident* of the architecture of the brain; and Davies' (1991: 236) insistence on the presence of a "common mechanism." In view of the kinds of case that will emerge in my defense of premise (4), I don't think these claims are sufficient.

13 Thus, another way that premise (1) could turn out to be false is if it turned out that no one was *capable* of logical transitions in thought. It strikes me as an interesting question whether Descartes would have been unnerved by this, and whether he's entitled to as much certitude about his being a thinker as a thoughter (cf. Lichtenberg's quip that Descartes is only entitled to claim not, "I think," but only "there is a thought").

14 As Michael Devitt (1991) has rightly stressed, partly because of the effect of the combined work of Frege, Russell and Turing, the word "formal" is exasperatingly ambiguous in the modern literature between "logico-syntactic" and "physical" (as in "shape"). I suspect it has come to mean something like "physical feature implementing a logico-syntactic one." So as to help distinguish premise (3) and 4), I shall try to avoid the term.

15 See Quine (1966) for a short, lucid discussion of combinatory logic, and his (1970/76) for a review of such systems more generally.

16 Similarly, although my argument here is certainly cousin to the argument of Davies (1991: 243–7), it doesn't depend in the way Davies' does on the assumption that possession of a concept depends upon either "appreciating" certain *analytic* transitions, like that between 'bachelor' and 'unmarried' (p. 244), much less upon finding them "primitively compelling" (pp. 246–7). I doubt that this approach to conceptual possession conditions in general is promising, and, *pace* p. 236, am skeptical that even if it worked, that there would be a notion of "form" on which it could rely (cf. Rey (1993) and (1996a)). The only "form" on which the present argument is relying is strictly *logico-syntactic* structure (cf. fns. 19 and 20 below).

17 John O'Leary-Hawthorne pressed this argument on me. Clark (1991: 202–5) makes a similar argument against Fodor and Pylyshn's (1988) causal understanding of systematicity. I won't attempt to address whether these later views of Davidson's are compatible with the earlier ones we quoted; see Antony (1989) for an excellent discussion.

18 Indeed, I suspect that the kind of "interpretative" views one finds in Davidson may well arise from the kind of interest he has always had, not in psychology *per se*, but in a fairly abstract decision theory. Thus he writes that, when he found

that subjects in experiments didn't make decisions in accordance with Ramsey's theory, he "gave up [his] career as an experimental psychologist" (1974/80: 236).

19 I am indebted to Jerry Fodor for defending this view (against his own – better? – inclinations). Note that Davies' (1991: 236) right insistence that "to each [semantically coherent] pattern there should be a common mechanism whose presence explains the aspect of input–output transitions that is captured in that pattern" is open to this possibility, particularly since the patterns he cites seem to be *essentially* semantic (and not also logico-syntactic, cf. fns. 16 and 20).

20 Putting aside "primitive compulsions," and limiting "form" to logical syntax (fn. 14 above), this is perhaps a way of spelling out Davies' (1991: 246) suggestion that "mirroring the commonality in the inferences that are primitively compelling – namely their form – there should be a commonality in the causal processes that explain their being so." Indeed, it provides a basis otherwise unavailable to Davies (see fns. 16 and 19 above) for insisting as he does that the "common mechanism" responsible for inference be one that does indeed *mirror* the logico-syntactic structure: merely *arithmetic* or other *domain specific* inferences *don't* seem "formal"; it would seem enough merely that one's reasoning *respect* certain truths, no matter *how* that respect is realized. Maloney (1989: [7, §3.1) quite rightly stresses the importance of *how* e.g. beliefs cause action, but relies only on inferences being sensitive to *content*, which, again, could arise without causally available logico-syntactic structure (without "inference" being "computation" (p. 18)).

21 See also Smolensky (1991 and 1995) for further development of this suggestion. I am indebted to Smolensky for fruitful discussions of this issue, despite (but also because of) our differences with regard to it.

22 It would be miraculous were there to be a machine that operated on Gödel numbers to realize logical relations without the factoring into prime constituents on which Gödel's proof depends. However, I emphasize that, as things presently stand, it is only (epistemically) *possible* that tensor ending is any better off, since it's by no means yet clear that that coding *doesn't* in fact involve causally efficacious constituents.

23 For the need of this hedge, I am indebted to Mark Greenberg.

24 That is, there may be limits to what Evans (1982: 85) calls the "Russell Principle" on which Davies (1991: 240) relies, the principle that to have the concept of being an F, a thinker must know what it is for an arbitrary object (that can be F) to *be* F. The interesting example of "the red thing is green" is raised by an experiment of Crane and Piantanida (1983; cited by Hardin 1988: 124–5) in which, as a result of an unusually stable image on their retinas, *some* subjects report having a color experience they are (nearly enough) inclined to describe in this way. All such possibilities seem to me to undermine Clark's (1991: 205) claim that such properties as systematicity in thought are *conceptual* requirements on any thought ascriptions at all.

25 Lest I be thought a "mere competence" extremist on this issue, I should say that I do think people actually do think, quite often logically, and that LOTH seems to me an excellent hypothesis about how they manage to do so; see §IV for more discussion.

26 Note that all the systematicity needed to establish LOTH is of a "*can* think form: there is no need to claim anything about what a subject "*will* infer". Note also

145

that the Wason selection task involves a question about *confirmation*, which, as Hempel 's "raven paradox" shows, is immensely sensitive to form, notoriously to contraposition!

27 Although it's interesting to note in this regard that the alleged superiority of connectionist over classical architectures has evidently been exaggerated. McLaughlin and Warfield (forthcoming) show that, for a large selection of well-known tasks, there is a classical machine comparable in efficiency to any connectionist one.

28 In Rey (1993) I criticize its role in Russell's and Quine's theories of meaning, in Rey (1994), its role in Wittgenstein's thought, and in Rey (forthcoming-b) in the work of Dennett.

29 In his own "deductive" argument for the LOTH, Lycan (1993) seems to me to present a nice antidote to such superficialist temptations, comparing our mentalistic ways of thinking with the way someone (perhaps a Martian) might think about automobiles whose interiors she thinks she can't inspect: from her observation of the details of a car's motion, he points out, she might be able to formulate fairly rich and accurate hypotheses about its inner structure. Essentially, I want to defend this way of thinking about the matter against an objection Lycan didn't consider.

30 In Rey (1996) I discuss a particularly striking example in reply to Dennett's (1991: 395–6) superficialist discounting of the puzzle many of us have in the case of the taste of beer: we wonder whether in coming to like it since childhood, it's our experiences or our preferences that have changed. Suppose that there is in fact no behavioral or introspective way to tell; but that it turns out that children have more taste buds than adults. One might have independent evidence that both children and adults have the same *preferences* for bitter titillation, but that consequently children reach a painful threshold sooner with the same quantity of a bitter substance. It *tastes* differently, since, arguably, more intense sensation is caused by their tongues.

31 I am indebted to Ramon Das for pressing me on this issue.

32 Argument T emerged in my mind partly in response to discussions with Murat Aydede of his dissertation (1993), which examines the systematicity arguments of Fodor and Pylyshyn (1988), and partly in response to defenses of superficialism by David Braddon-Mitchell, Frank Jackson and Philip Pettit at the Australian National University (for whose warm hospitality I want to express my appreciation). I am also grateful to James Tomberlin for the invitation to write the argument up (and for his patience while I did so), as well as to Ned Block, Michael Devitt, Mark Greenberg, Karen Neander, and the students of my cognitive science seminar at the University of Maryland for comments on drafts.

References

Antony, L. (1989) "Anomalous Monism and the Problem of Explanatory Force," *Philosophical Review*, pp. 153–87.

Aydede, M. (1993) *Syntax, Functionalism, Connectionism, and the Language of Thought*, Ph.D. dissertation, Dept of Philosophy, University of Maryland.

Block, N. (1990) "Computer Model of the Mind," in *An Invitation to Cognitive Science*, ed. by D. Osherson & E. Smith, Vol. 3, pp. 247–89.

Clark, A. (1991) "Systematicity, Structured Representations and Cognitive Architecture: a Reply to Fodor and Pylyshyn," in T. Horgan and G. Graham, *Philosophy and Connectionism*, Dordrecht: Kluwer, pp. 198–218.

Crane, H. and Piantanida, T. (1983) "On Seeing Reddish Green and Yellowish Blue," *Science*, 221: 1078–80.

Curry, H. and Feys, R. (1958) *Combinatory Logic*, Amsterdam: North Holland.

Davidson, D. (1963/79) "Actions, Reasons and Causes," in *Essays on Actions and Events*, Oxford: Clarendon Press, pp. 3–20.

—— (1970/79) "Mental Events," in *Essays on Actions and Events*, Oxford: Clarendon Press, pp. 207–25.

—— (1973/79) "Freedom to Act," in *Essays on Actions and Events*, Oxford: Clarendon Press, pp. 63–81.

—— (1973/84) "Radical Interpretation," in *Inquiries into Truth and Interpretation*, Oxford: Clarendon Press, pp. 125–40.

—— (1974/80) "Philosophy as Psychology," in *Essays on Actions and Events*, Oxford: Clarendon Press, pp. 229–39.

Davies, M. (1991) "Concepts, Connectionism, and the Language of Thought," in *Philosophy and Connectionist Theory*, ed. by W. Ramsey, S. Stick, and W. Rumelhart; Hillsdale, N.J.: Erlbaum, pp. 229–56.

Dennett, D. (1978) *Brainstorms*, Cambridge, Mass.: Bradford (MIT).

—— (1991) *Consciousness Explained*, New York: Little Brown.

Descartes, R. (1637/1954). *Descartes: Philosophical Writings*, tr. & ed. E. Anscombe and P.T. Geach, Norwich: Nelson's University Paperbacks.

Devitt, M. (1991) "Why Fodor Can't Have It Both Ways," *Meaning in Mind: Fodor and his Critics*, B. Loewer and G. Rey, eds., Oxford: Basil Blackwell, pp. 95–118.

Evans, G. (1982) *The Varieties of Reference*. Oxford: Oxford University Press.

Fodor, J. and McLaughlin, B. (1991) "Connectionism and the Problem of Systematicity: Why Smolensky's Solution Won't Work," *Cognition*, 35(2): 183–204.

Fodor, J. and Pylyshyn, Z. (1988) "Connectionism and Cognitive Architecture," in *Connectionism and Symbols*, Cambridge, Mass.: MIT Press, pp. 3–72.

Grice, H.P. (1961/65) "The Causal Theory of Perception," in *Perceiving, Sensing, and Knowing*, ed. by R. Swartz, New York: Doubleday.

Hardin, C. (1988) *Color for Philosophers*, Indianapolis: Hackett.

Jackson, F. and Pettit, P. (1993) "Folk belief and commonplace belief". *Mind and Language* 8: 298–305.

Johnson, Mark (1993) *Moral Imagination*, Chicago: Univ. of Chicago Press.

Johnson-Laird, P.N. (1983) *Mental Models: Towards a Cognitive Science of Language, Inference, and Consciousness*. Cambridge, Mass.: Harvard University Press.

Kosslyn, S. (1980) *Images and Mind*, Cambridge: Harvard Univ. Press.

Lewis, D. (1994) "David Lewis," in Guttenplan, S. (ed.), *A Companion to the Philosophy of Mind*, Oxford: Blackwell.

Lycan, W. (1993) "A Deductive Argument for the Representational Theory of Thought," *Mind and Language*, 8(3): 404–22.

McLaughlin, B. and Warfield, T. (forthcoming) "The Allure of Connectionism Re-Examined," *Synthese* (forthcoming).

Maloney, J. (1989) *The Mundane Matter of the Mental Language*, Cambridge: Cambridge University Press.

Neander, K. (forthcoming) "Swampman Meets Swampcow".

Peacocke, C. (1992) *A Study of Concepts*, Cambridge, Mass.: MIT Press.

Penrose, R. (1989) *The Emperor's New Mind*, Oxford: Oxford Univ. Press.

Putnam, H. (1975) "The Meaning of 'Meaning'," *Philosophical Papers*, vol. II. Cambridge: Cambridge University Press.

Quine, W. (1960) *Word and Object*, Cambridge, Mass.: MIT Press.

—— (1966) "Variables Explained Away," in his *Selected Logical Papers*, New York: Random House, pp. 227–35.

—— (1970/76) "Algebraic Logic and Predicate Functors," in his *The Ways of Paradox and Other Essays*, revised and enlarged edition, Cambridge, Mass.: Harvard Univ. Press pp. 283–307.

Rey, G. (1991) "An Explanatory Budget for Connectionism and Eliminativism," in T. Horgan and G. Graham, *Philosophy and Connectionism*, Dordrecht: Kluwer, pp. 219–40.

—— (1993) "The Unavailability of What We Mean: a Reply to Quine, Fodor and LePore," *Grazer Philosophiphe Studien*, 46: 61–101.

—— (1994) "Wittgenstein, Computationalism and Qualia," in *Philosophy and the Cognitive Sciences*, ed. by R. Casati and G. White.

—— (1996a) "Resisting Primitive Compulsions," contribution to symposium on C. Peacocke, *A Study of Concepts, Philosophy and Phenomenological Research*.

—— (1996) "Dennett's Unrealistic Psychology," *Philosophical Topics*, 22: 259–89.

Smolensky, P. (1991) "Connectionism, Constituency and the Language of Thought," in *Meaning in Mind: Fodor and His Critics*, Oxford: Blackwell.

—— (1995) "Constituent Structure and Explanation in an Integrated Connectionist/ Symbolic Cognitive Architecture," in C. Macdonald and G. Macdonald, eds, *The Philosophy of Psychology: Debates On Psychological Explanation*, Oxford: Basil Blackwell.

Stalnaker, Robert (1984) *Inquiry*. Cambridge, Mass.: Bradford Books/MIT Press.

Van Gelder, T. and Niklasson, L. (1994) "Classicism and Cognitive Architecture," in *Proceedings of the Sixteenth Annual Conference of the Cognitive Science Society*, Hillsdale, N.J.: Lawrence Erlbaum and Associates, pp. 905–9.

Wason, P.C. (1966) "Reasoning". In B.M. Foss (ed.), *New Horizons in Psychology*. Harmondsworth: Penguin.

ID

THE
NEUROCOMPUTATIONAL
MIND

9

P.S. Churchland and T.J. Sejnowski, "Neural Representation and Neural Computation"

The types of representation and the styles of computation in the brain appear to be very different from the symbolic expressions and logical inferences that are used in sentence-logic models of cognition. In this paper we explore the consequences that brain-style processing may have on theories of cognition. Connectionist models are used as examples to illustrate neural representation and computation in the pronouncing of English text and in the extracting of shape parameters from shaded images. Levels of analysis are not independent in connectionist models, and the dependencies between levels provide an opportunity to co-evolve theories at all levels. This is a radical departure from the a priori, introspection-based strategy that has characterized most previous work in epistemology.

1 How do we represent the world?

The central epistemological question, from Plato on, is this: *How is representation of a world by a self possible?* So far as we can tell, there is a reality existing external to ourselves, and it appears that we do come to represent that reality, and sometimes even to know how its initial appearance to our senses differs from how it actually is. How is this accomplished, and how is knowledge possible? How is science itself possible?

The dominant philosophical tradition has been to try to resolve the epistemological puzzles by invoking mainly intuition and logic to figure out such things as the organization of knowledge, the nature of the "mirroring" of the outer world by the inner world, and the roles of reason and inference in the generation of internal models of reality. Epistemology thus pursued was the product of "pure reason," not of empirical investigation, and thus epistemological theories were believed to delimit the necessary conditions, the absolute foundations, and the incontrovertible presuppositions of human knowledge. For this a priori task – a task of reflective understanding and pure reason – empirical observations by psychologists and neurobiologists are

151

typically considered irrelevant, or at least incapable of effecting any significant correction of the a priori conclusions. Plato, Descartes, and Kant are some of the major historical figures in that tradition; some contemporary figures are Chisholm (1966), Strawson (1966), Davidson (1974), and McGinn (1982). It is safe to say that most philosophers still espouse the a priori strategy to some nontrivial extent.

In a recent departure from this venerable tradition of a priori philosophy, some philosophers have argued that epistemology itself must be informed by the psychological and neurobiological data that bear upon how in fact we represent and model the world. First articulated in a systematic and powerful way by Quine (1960),[1] this new "naturalism" has begun to seem more in keeping with evolutionary and biological science and to promise more testable and less speculative answers.

If, as it seems, acquiring knowledge is an essentially biological phenomenon, in the straightforward sense that it is something our brains do, then there is no reason to expect that brains should have evolved to have a priori knowledge of the true nature of things: not of fire, not of light, not of the heart and the blood, and certainly not of knowledge or of its own microstructure and microfunction. There are, undoubtedly, innate dispositions to behave in certain ways, to believe certain things, and to organize data in certain ways, but innateness is no guarantee of truth, and it is the truth that a priori reflections are presumed to reveal. Innate beliefs and cognitive structure cannot be assumed to be either optimal or true, because all evolution "cares" about is that the internal models enable the species to survive. Satisficing is good enough. It is left for science to care about the truth (or perhaps empirical adequacy), and the theories science generates may well show the inadequacies of our innately specified models of external reality. Even more dramatically, they may show the inadequacy of our model of our internal reality – of the nature of our selves.

The a priori insights of the Great Philosophers should be understood, therefore, not as The Absolute Truth about how the mind–brain must be, but as articulations of the *assumptions* that live deep in our collective *conception* of ourselves. As assumptions, however, they may be misconceived and empirically unsound, or at least they may be open to revision in the light of scientific progress. The possibility of such revision does not entail that the assumptions are ludicrous or useless. On the contrary, they may well be very important elements in the theoretical scaffolding as neurobiology and psychology inch their way toward empirically adequate theories of mind–brain function. The methodological point is that in science we cannot proceed with no theoretical framework, so even intuitive folk theory is better than nothing as the scientific enterprise gets underway.

In addition to asking how the self can know about the external reality, Kant asked: How is representation of a *self* by a knowing self possible? One of his important ideas was that the nature of the internal world of the self is no more unmediated or *given* than is knowledge of the external world of physical objects in space and time. A modern version of this insight says: Just as the inner thoughts and experiences may represent but not *resemble* the outer reality, so the inner thoughts may represent but not resemble the inner reality of which they are the representation. This idea, taken with Quine's naturalism, implies that if we want to know how we represent the world – the external world of colored, moving objects, and the internal world of thoughts, consciousness, motives, and dreams – the scientific approach is likely to be the most rewarding. Inner knowledge, like outer knowledge, is conceptually and theoretically mediated – it is the result of complex information processing. Whether our intuitive understanding of the nature of our inner world is at all adequate is an empirical question, not an a priori one.

If empirical results are relevant to our understanding of how the mind–brain represents, it is also entirely possible that scientific progress on this frontier will be as revolutionary as it has been in astronomy, physics, chemistry, biology, and geology. With this observation comes the recognition that it may reconfigure our current assumptions about knowledge, consciousness, representations, and the self at least as much as Copernicus and Darwin reconfigured our dearest assumptions about the nature of the universe and our place in it. Our intuitive assumptions, and even what seems phenomenologically obvious, may be misconceived and may thus undergo reconfiguration as new theory emerges from psychology and neurobiology.

Philosophers – and sometimes psychologists, and occasionally even neuro-scientists – generally make one of two responses to the naturalists' conception of the status of our self-understanding:

1 Philosophy is an a priori discipline, and the fundamental conceptual truths about the nature of the mind, of knowledge, of reason, etc. will come only from a priori investigations. In this way, philosophy sets the bounds for science – indeed, the bounds of sense, as Strawson (1966) would put it. In a more extreme vein, some existentialist philosophers would claim that the naturalistic approach is itself symptomatic of a civilizational neurosis: the infatuation with science. On this view, the scientific approach to human nature is deeply irrational. Mandt (1986: 274) describes the existentialist criticism as follows: "That scientific modes of thought have become paradigmatic indicates the degree to which traditional modes of human life and experience have disintegrated, plunging civilization into a nihilistic abyss."

2 Even if a naturalistic approach is useful for some aspects of the nature of knowledge and representation, the neurosciences in particular are largely irrelevant to the enterprise. Neuroscience may be fascinating enough in its own right, but for a variety of reasons it is irrelevant to answering the questions we care about concerning cognition, representation, intelligent behavior, learning, consciousness, and so forth. Psychology and linguistics

might actually be useful in informing us about such matters, but neuro-biology is just off the book.

2 Why is neurobiology dismissed as irrelevant to understanding how the mind works?

2.1 The traditional problem

In its traditional guise, the mind–body problem can be stated thus: Are mental phenomena (experiences, beliefs, desires, etc.) actually phenomena of the phys-ical brain? Dualists have answered No to this question. On the dualist's view, mental phenomena inhere in a special, nonphysical substance: the mind (also referred to as the soul or the spirit). The mind, on the dualist's theory, is the ghost in the machine; it is composed not of physical material obeying phys-ical laws but of soul-stuff, or "spooky" stuff, and it operates according to principles unique to spooky stuff.

The most renowned of the substance dualists are Plato and Descartes, and, more recently, J. C. Eccles (1977) and Richard Swinburne (1986). Because dualists believe the mind to be a wholly separate kind of stuff or entity, they expect that it can be understood only in its own terms. At most, neuroscience can shed light on the *interaction* between mind and body, but not on the nature of the mind itself. Dualists consequently see psychology as essentially inde-pendent of neurobiology, which, after all, is devoted to finding out how the *physical* stuff of the nervous system works. It might be thought a bonus of dualism that it implies that to understand the mind we do not have to know much about the brain.

Materialism answers the mind–body question (Are mental states actually states of the physical brain?) in the affirmative. The predominant arguments for materialism draw upon the spectacular failure of dualism to cohere with the rest of ongoing science. And as physics, molecular biology, evolutionary biology, and neuroscience have progressed, this failure has become more rather than less marked. In short, the weight of empirical evidence is against the exist-ence of special soul-stuff (spooky stuff). (For a more thorough discussion of the failures of substance dualism, see P. S. Churchland 1986.) Proponents of materialism include Hobbes (in the seventeenth century), B. F. Skinner (1957, 1976), J. J. C. Smart (1959), W. V. O. Quine (1960), D. C. Dennett (1978), and P. M. Churchland (1988).

Despite the general commitment to materialism, there are significant differ-ences among materialists in addressing the central question of how best to explain psychological states. Strict behaviorists, such as Skinner, thought that explanations would take the form of stimulus–response profiles *exclusively*. Supporting this empirical hypothesis with a philosophical theory, philosoph-ical behaviorists claimed that the mental terminology itself could be analyzed into sheerly physicalistic language about dispositions to behave. (For discussion, see P. M. Churchland 1988). Curiously, perhaps, the behaviorists (both empirical and philosophical) share with the dualists the conviction that it is not necessary to understand the workings of the brain in order to explain intelligent behavior. On the behaviorists' research ideology, again we have a bonus: In order to explain behavior, *we do not have to know anything about the brain.*

In contrast to behaviorism, identity theorists (Smart 1959; Enc 1983) claimed that mental states, such as visual perceptions, pains, beliefs, and drives, were in fact identical to states of the brain, though it would of course be up to neuroscience to discover precisely what brain states were in fact identical to what mental states. On the research ideology advocated by these materialists, explanation of behavior will have to refer to inner representations and hence to what the brain is doing.

2.2   *The contemporary problem: theory dualism*

Many philosophers who are materialists to the extent that they doubt the existence of soul-stuff nonetheless believe that psychology ought to be essentially autonomous from neuroscience, and that neuroscience will not contribute significantly to our understanding of perception, language use, thinking, problem solving, and (more generally) cognition. Thus, the mind–body problem in its contemporary guise is this: Can we get a *unified* science of the mind–brain? Will psychological theory reduce to neuroscience?

A widespread view (which we call theory dualism) answers No to the above question. Typically, three sorts of reasons are offered:

(a) *Neuroscience is too hard.* The brain is too complex; there are too many neurons and too many connections, and it is a hopeless task to suppose we can ever understand complex higher functions in terms of the dynamics and organization of neurons.

(b) *The argument from multiple instantiability.* Psychological states are functional states and, as such, can be implemented (instantiated) in diverse machines (Putnam 1967; Fodor 1975; Pylyshyn 1984). Therefore, no particular psychological state, such as believing that the earth is round or that 2 + 2 = 4, can be identified with exactly this or that machine state. So no functional (cognitive) process can be reduced to the behavior of particular neuronal systems.

(c) *Psychological states have intentionality.* That is, they are identified in terms of their semantic content; they are "about" other things; they represent things; they have logical relations to one another. We can think about objects in their absence, and even of nonexistent objects. For example, if someone has the belief that Mars is warmer than Venus, then that psychological state is specified as the state it is in terms of the sentence "Mars is warmer than Venus", which has a specific meaning (its content) and which

155

is logically related to other sentences. It is a belief *about* Mars and Venus, but it is not caused by Mars or Venus. Someone might have this belief because he was told, or because he deduced it from other things he knew. In cognitive generalizations states are related semantically and logically, whereas in neurobiological generalizations states can only be causally related. Neurobiological explanations cannot be sensitive to the logical relations between the contents of cognitive states, or to meaning or "aboutness." They respond only to *causal* properties. Neurobiology, therefore, cannot do justice to cognition, and thus no reduction is possible.

2.3 *What is wrong with theory dualism?*

In opposition to theory dualists, reductionists think we ought to strive for an integration of psychological and neurobiological theory. Obviously, a crucial element in the discussion concerns what is meant by "reduction"; hence, part of what must first be achieved is a proper account of what sort of business inter-theoretic reduction is.

Roughly, the account is this: Reductions are *explanations* of phenomena described by one theory in terms of the phenomena described by a more basic theory. Reductions typically involve the co-evolution of theories over time, and as they co-evolve one theory is normally revised, corrected, and modified by its co-evolutionary cohort theory at the other level. This revisionary interaction can, and usually does, go both ways from the more basic to the less basic theory and vice versa. It is important to emphasize the modification to theories as they co-evolve, because sometimes the modification is radical and entails massive reconfiguration of the very categories used to describe the phenomena. In such an event, the very data to be explained may come to be redescribed under pressure from the evolving theories. Examples of categories that have undergone varying degrees of revision, from the minor to the radical, include impetus, caloric, gene, neuron, electricity, instinct, life, and very recently, excitability (in neurons) (Schaffner 1976; P. M. Churchland 1979; Hooker 1981).

Because reductionism is frequently misunderstood, it is necessary to be explicit about what is *not* meant. First, seeking reductions of macro-level theory to micro level does not imply that one must first know everything about the elements of the micro theory before research at the macro level can be usefully undertaken. Quite the reverse is advocated – research should proceed at all levels of the system, and co-evolution of theory may enhance progress at all levels. Data from one level *constrain* theorizing at that level and at other levels. Additionally, the reduction of theories does *not* mean that the reduced phenomena somehow disappear or are discredited. The theory of optics was reduced to the theory of electromagnetic radiation, but light itself did not disappear, nor did it become disreputable to study light at the macro level. Nor was the reduced theory cast out as useless or discredited; on the contrary, it was and continues to be useful for addressing phenomena at a higher level of description. As for the phenomenon, it is what it is, and it continues to be whatever it is as theories are reduced or abandoned. Whether a category is ultimately rejected or revised depends on its scientific integrity, and that is, of course, determined empirically. (For more detail on inter-theoretic reduction, see P. S. Churchland 1986.)

Given this brief account of reduction as a backdrop, an outline of how the reductionist answers the theory dualist goes as follows:

(a) Neuroscience *is* hard, but with many new techniques now available, an impressive body of data is available to constrain our theories, and a lot of data are very suggestive as to how neural networks function. (See Sejnowski and Churchland, in press.) We have begun to see the shape of neurobiological answers to functional questions, such as how information is stored, how networks learn, and how networks of neurons represent.

(b) High-level states are multiply instantiable. So what? If, in any given species, we can show that particular functional states are identical to specific neuronal configurations (for example, that being in REM sleep is having a specified neuronal state, or that one type of learning involves changing synaptic weights according to a Hebb rule), that will be suffi-cient to declare a reduction relative to that domain (Richardson 1979; Enc 1983; P. S. Churchland 1986; section 3 below). Very pure philosophers who cannot bring themselves to call these perfectly respectable domain-relative explanations "reductions" are really just digging in on who gets to use the word. Moreover, it should be emphasized that the explanation of high-level cognitive phenomena will not be achieved directly in terms of phenomena at the lowest level of nervous-system organization, such as synapses and individual neurons. Rather, the explanation will refer to properties at higher structural levels, such as networks or systems. Functional properties of networks and systems will be explained by refer-ence to properties at the next level down, and so on. What we envision is a chain of explanations linking higher to next-lower levels, and so on down the ladder of structural levels. (See Sejnowski and Churchland, in press.) Aspects of individual variation at the synaptic and cellular levels are probably invisible at the systems level, where similarity of larger-scale emergent properties, such as position in a high-dimensional parameter space, is critical in identifying similarity of information-processing func-tion (Sejnowski et al. 1988).

(c) A theory of how states in a nervous system represent or model the world will need to be set in the context of the evolution and development of ner-vous systems, and will try to explain the interactive role of neural states in the ongoing neuro-cognitive economy of the system. Nervous systems do not represent all aspects of the physical environment; they selectively rep-resent information a species needs, given its environmental niche and its way of life. Nervous systems are programmed to respond to certain selected features, and within limits they learn other features through experience by

157

encountering examples and generalizing. Cognitive neuroscience is now beginning to understand how this is done (Livingstone 1988; Goldman-Rakic 1987; Kelso et al. 1986). Although the task is difficult, it now seems reasonable to assume that the "aboutness" or "meaningfulness" of representational states is not a spooky relation but a neurobiological relation. As we come to understand more about the dynamical properties of networks, we may ultimately be able to generate a theory of how human language is learned and represented by our sort of nervous system, and thence to explain language-dependent kinds of meaning. Because this answer is highly cryptic and because intentionality has often seemed forever beyond the reach of neurobiology, the next section will focus on intentionality: the theory dualist's motivation, and the reductionist's strategy.

3   Levels, intentionality, and the sentence-logic model of the mind

3.1   Sentential attitudes and the computer metaphor

Two deep and interrelated assumptions concerning the nature of cognition drive the third anti-reductionist argument:

1   Cognition essentially involves representations and computations. Representations are, in general, symbolic structures, and computations are, in general, rules (such as rules of logic) for manipulating those symbolic structures.
2   A good model for understanding mind-brain functions is the computer – that is, a machine based on the same logical foundations as a Turing machine and on the von Neumann architecture for a digital computer. Such machines are ideally suited for the manipulation of symbols according to rules. The computer metaphor suggests that the mind–brain, at the information-processing level, can be understood as a kind of digital computer, the problem for cognitive psychology is to determine the program that our brains run.

The motivating vision here is that cognition is to be modeled largely on language and logical reasoning; having a thought is, functionally speaking, having a sentence in the bead, and thinking is, functionally speaking, doing logic, or at least running on procedures very like logic. Put thus baldly, it may seem faintly ridiculous, but the theory is supported quite plausibly by the observation that beliefs, thoughts, hopes, desires, and so forth are essential in the explanation of cognition, and that such states are irreducibly semantic because they are identified in virtue of their content sentences. That is, such states are always and essentially beliefs that p, thoughts that p, or desires that p, where for "p" we substitute the appropriate sentence, such as "Nixon was a Russian spy" or "Custard is made with milk". Such cognitive states – the so-called sentential attitudes – are the states they are in virtue of the sentences that specify what they are about. Moreover, a content sentence stands in specific logical and semantic relations to other sentences. The state transitions are determined by semantic and logical relations between the content sentences, not by casual relations among states neurobiologically described. Thus, cognitive states have *meaning* (that is, content, or intentionality), and it might be argued that it is precisely in virtue of their meaningfulness that they play the role in cognition that they do.

The fundamental conception is, accordingly, well and truly rooted in folk psychology, the body of concepts and everyday lore by means of which we routinely explain one another's behavior by invoking sentential attitudes (Stich 1983; P. M. Churchland 1988) – for example, Smith paid for the vase because he believed that his son had dropped it and he feared that the store owner would be angry. In these sorts of intentional explanations, the basic unit of representation is the sentence, and state transitions arc accomplished through the following of rules: deductive inference, inductive inference, and assorted other rules.

Extending the framework of folk psychology to get an encompassing account of cognition in general, this approach takes it that thinking, problem solving, language use, perception, and so forth will be understood as we determine the sequence of sentences corresponding to the steps in a given information-processing task; that is, as we understand the mechanics of sentence crunching. According to this research paradigm, known as sententialism, it is the task of cognitive science to figure out what programs the brain runs, and neuroscience can then check these top-down hypotheses against the wetware to see if they are generally possible. (See especially Fodor 1975, 1981; Pylyshyn 1984.)

3.2   Is cognition mainly symbol manipulation in the language of thought?

Although this view concerning the nature of cognition and the research strategy for studying cognition may be appealing (where much of the appeal is derived from the comfortable place found for folk psychology), it suffers from major defects. Many of these defects have been discussed in detail by Anderson and Hinton (1981) by P. S. Churchland (1986), and in various chapters of McClelland and Rumelhart (1986). A summary will call them to mind:

1   Many cognitive tasks, such as visual recognition and answering simple true-or-false questions, can be accomplished in about half a second. Given what we know about conduction velocities and synaptic delays in neurons, this allows about 5 milliseconds per computational step, which means that there is time for only about 100 steps. For a sequential program run on a conventional computer, 100 steps is not going to get us remotely close

to task completion. Feldman and Ballard (1982) call this the hundred-step rule.

2 Anatomically and physiologically, the brain is a parallel system, not a sequential von Neumann machine. The neural architecture is highly interconnected. Neurons such as Purkinje cells may have upwards of 80,000 input connections, and neurons in cerebral cortex can have upwards of 10,000 output connections (Anderson and Hinton 1981; Pellionisz and Llinas 1982; Sejnowski 1986).

3 However information is stored in nervous systems, it appears to be radically unlike information storage in a digital computer, where storage and processing are separated and items are stored in memory according to addressable *locations*. In nervous systems, information seems to be stored in the connections between the same neurons that process the information. There does not appear to be a distinct storage location for each piece of stored information, and information is content addressable rather than location addressable. Information storage is probably at least somewhat distributed rather than punctate, since memories tend to be degraded with damage to the system rather than selectively wiped out one by one.

4 A task may fall gracefully to one architecture and not to another. Certain kinds of tasks, such as numerical calculation, fall gracefully to a von Neumann architecture, but others, such as learning or associative memory, do not. Things we humans find effortless (such as facial recognition and visual perception) are tasks which artificial intelligence has great difficulty simulating on a von Neumann architecture, whereas things we find "effortful" (such as simple proofs in the propositional calculus or mathematic calculations) are straightforward for a digital computer (Anderson and Hinton 1981; Rumelhart, Hinton and McClelland 1986). This suggests that the computational style of nervous systems may be very unlike that suited to von Neumann architectures.

5 The hardware/software analogy fails for many reasons, the most prominent of which are that nervous systems are plastic and that neurons continually change as we grow and learn. Related, perhaps, is the observation that nervous systems degrade gracefully and are relatively fault tolerant. A von Neumann machine is rigid and fault intolerant, and a breakdown of one tiny component disrupts the machine's performance.

6 The analogy between levels of description in a conventional computer (such as the hardware/software distinction) and levels of explanation in nervous systems may well be profoundly misleading. Exactly how many levels of organization we need to postulate in order to understand nervous-system function is an empirical question, and it may turn out that there are many levels between the molecular and the behavioral. In nervous systems we may already discern as distinct descriptive levels the molecule, the membrane, the cell, the circuit, networks, maps, brain systems, and several levels of behavior (from the reflexive to the highest levels of cognition). Other levels may come to be described as more is discovered about

the nature of nervous systems. As is discussed below, the properties at one level may constrain the kind of properties realizable at another level.

7 Nonverbal animals and infraverbal humans present a major problem for the sentence-logic theory of cognition: How is their cognition accomplished? On the sentence-logic theory of cognition, either their cognition resembles the human variety (and hence involves symbol manipulation according to rules, and a language of thought replete with a substantial conceptual repertoire) or their cognitive processes are entirely different from the usual human ones. Neither alternative is remotely credible. The first lacks any evidence. At best, its defense is circular; it helps to save the theory. The second alternative entails a radical discontinuity in evolution – sufficiently radical that language-of-thought cognition is a bolt from the blue. This implies that evolutionary biology and developmental neurobiology are mistaken in some fundamental respects. Since neither alternative can be taken seriously, the hypothesis itself has diminished credibility.

If cognition, then, is *not*, in general, to be understood on the sentence-logical model, the pressing questions then are these: How *does* the brain represent? How do nervous systems model the external world of objects in motion and the internal world of the nervous system itself? And when representations do stand in semantic and logical relations to one another, how is this achieved by neural networks? How is the semantic and logical structure of language – as we both comprehend and speak – represented in the brain? According to the rejected model, we postulate an internal organization – a language of thought – with the very same structure and organization as language. But if that model is rejected, what do we replace it with?

These are, of course, *the* central questions, and getting answers will not be easy. But the difficulty should not make the language-of-thought hypothesis more appealing. In certain respects, the current scientific state of a general theory of representation is analogous to the science of embryology in the nineteenth century. The development of highly structured, complex, fully formed organisms from eggs and sperm is a profoundly amazing thing. Faced with this mystery, some scientists concluded that the only way to explain the emergence of a fully structured organism at birth was to join the ancients in assuming that the structure was already there. Hence the homuncular theory of reproduction, which claimed that a miniature but complete human already exists in the sperm and merely expands during its tenure in the womb.

We now know that there *is* structure in the sperm (and the egg) – not in the form of a miniature, fully structured organism, but mainly in the form of DNA – a molecule that looks not at *all* like a fully formed human. Thus, the structure of the cause does not resemble the structure of the effect. Accordingly, the homuncular theorists were right in supposing that the highly structured neonate does not come from *nothing*, but they were wrong in looking for a structural resemblance between cause and effect. It was, of course, terribly hard to imagine the nature of the structural organization that

161

enables development yet in no way resembles the final product. Only through molecular biology and detailed work in embryology have we begun to understand how one kind of structure can, through intermediate mechanisms, yield another, very different kind of structure.

The parallel with cognitive neurobiology is this: The neuronal processes underlying cognition have a structure of some kind, but almost certainly it will not, in general, look anything like the semantic/logic structure visible in overt language. The organizational principles of nervous systems are what permit highly complex, structured patterns of behavior, for it is certain that the behavioral structure does not emerge magically from neuronal chaos. As things stand, it is very hard to imagine what those organizational principles could look like, and, just as in genetics and embryology, we can find answers only by framing hypotheses and doing experiments.

Instead of starting from the old sentence-logic model, we model information processing in terms of *the trajectory of a complex nonlinear dynamical system in a very high-dimensional space*. This structure does not resemble sentences arrayed in logical sequences, but it is potentially rich enough and complex enough to yield behavior capable of supporting semantic and logical relationships. We shall now explore what representing looks like in a particular class of nonlinear dynamical systems called connectionist models.

4 Representation in connectionist models

As the name implies, a connectionist model is characterized by connections and differential strengths of connections between processing units. Processing units are meant to be rather like neurons, and communicate with one another by signals (such as firing rate) that are numerical rather than symbolic. Connectionist models are designed to perform a task by specifying the architecture: the number of units, their arrangement in layers and columns, the patterns of connectivity, and the weight or strength of each connection (figures 9.1 and 9.2). These models have close ties with the computational level on which the task is specified, and with the implementation level on which the task is physically instantiated (Marr 1982). This species of network models should properly be considered a class of algorithms specified at various levels of organization – in some cases at the small-circuit level, in other cases at the system level. Both the task description and the neural embodiment are, however, crucially important in constraining the class of networks that will be explored. On the one hand the networks have to be powerful enough to match human performance of the computational tasks, and on the other hand they have to be built from the available materials. In the case of the brain, that means neurons and synapses; in the ease of network models, that means neuron-like processing units and synapse-like weights.

Digital computers are used to simulate neural networks, and the network models that can be simulated on current machines are tiny in comparison with the number of synapses and neurons in the mammalian brain. The networks

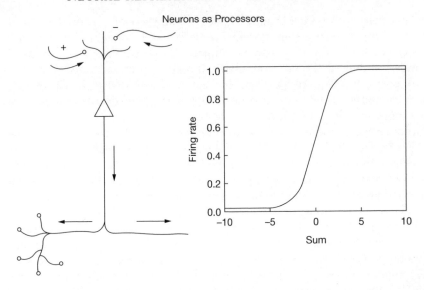

Figure 9.1 Left: Schematic model of a neuron-like processing unit that receives synapse-like inputs from other processing units. Right: Nonlinear sigmoid-shaped transformation between summed inputs and the output "firing rate" of a processing unit. The output is a continuous value between 0 and 1.

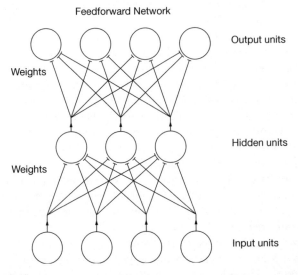

Figure 9.2 Schematic model of a three-layered network. Each input unit makes connections with each of the hidden units on the middle layer, which in turn projects to each of the output units. This is feedforward architecture in which information provided as an input vector flows through the network, one layer at a time, to produce an output vector. More complex architectures allow feedback connections from an upper to a lower layer and lateral interactions between units within a layer.

that have been constructed should be understood, therefore, as small parts of a more complex processing system whose general configuration has not yet been worked out, rather than as simulations of a whole system. To avoid misunderstanding, it should be emphasized that connectionist models cannot yet support a full cognitive system. To begin to reach that goal will require both a computing technology capable of supporting more detailed simulations and a more complete specification of the nervous system.

Granting these limitations, we may none the less be able to catch a glimpse of what representations might look like within the parallel-style architecture of the brain by taking a look inside a connectionist network. The place to look is in the dynamics of the system; that is, in the patterns of activity generated by the system of interconnected units. This approach has its roots in the work of previous generations of researchers – primarily the Gestalt school of psychology and D. O. Hebb (1949), who developed many ideas about learning and representation in neural assemblies. Only recently, however, has sufficient computer power been available to explore the consequences of these ideas by direct simulation, since the dynamics of massively parallel nonlinear networks is highly computation intensive. Parallel-network models are now being used to explore many different aspects of perception and cognition (McClelland and Rumelhart 1986; Feldman and Ballard 1982; *Cognitive Science*, special issue, vol. 9, 1985) but in this chapter we shall focus on two representative examples. The first is NETtalk, perhaps the most complex network model yet constructed, which learns to convert English text to speech sounds (Sejnowski and Rosenberg 1987, 1988). The second is a network model that computes surface curvatures of an object from its gray-level input image. NETtalk will be used primarily to illustrate two things: how a network can learn to perform a very complex task without symbols and without rules to manipulate symbols, and the differences between local and distributed representations.

Connectionist models can be applied on a large scale to model whole brain systems or, on a smaller scale, to model particular brain circuits. NETtalk is on a large scale, since the problem of pronunciation is constrained mainly by the abstract cognitive considerations and since its solution in the brain must involve a number of systems, including the visual system, the motor-articulatory system, and the language areas. The second example is more directly related to smaller brain circuits used in visual processing, the representational organization achieved by the network model can be related to the known representational organization in visual cortex.

In the models reviewed here, the processing units sum the inputs from connections with other processing units, each input weighted by the strength of the connection. The output of each processing unit is a real number that is a nonlinear function of the linearly summed inputs. The output is small when the inputs are below threshold, and it increases rapidly as the total input becomes more positive. Roughly, the activity level can be considered the sum of the postsynaptic potentials in a neuron, and the output can be considered its firing rate (figure 9.1).

4.1 Speech processing: text to speech

In the simplest NETtalk system[2] there are three layers of processing units. The first level receives as input letters in a word: the final layer yields the elementary sounds, or phonemes (table 9.1); and an intervening layer of "hidden units," which is fully connected with the input and output layers, performs the transformation of letters to sounds (figure 9.3). On the input layer, there is *local representation* with respect to letters because single units are used to represent single letters of the alphabet. Notice, however, that the representation could be construed as *distributed* with respect to *words*, inasmuch as each word is represented as a pattern of activity among the input units. Similarly, each phoneme is represented by a pattern of activity among the output units, and phonemic representation is therefore distributed. But each output unit is coded for a particular *distinctive feature* of the speech sound, such as whether the phoneme was voiced, and consequently each unit is local with respect to distinctive features.

Table 9.1 Symbols for phonemes used in NETtalk

Symbol	Phoneme	Symbol	Phoneme
/a/	father	/D/	this
/b/	bet	/E/	bet
/c/	bought	/G/	sing
/d/	debt	/I/	bit
/e/	bake	/J/	gin
/f/	fin	/K/	sexual
/g/	guess	/L/	bottle
/h/	head	/M/	abysm
/i/	Pete	/N/	button
/k/	Ken	/O/	boy
/l/	let	/Q/	quest
/m/	met	/R/	bird
/n/	net	/S/	shin
/o/	boat	/T/	thin
/p/	pet	/U/	book
/r/	red	/W/	bout
/s/	sit	/X/	excess
/t/	test	/Y/	cute
/u/	lute	/Z/	leisure
/v/	vest	/@/	bat
/w/	wet	/!/	Nazi
/x/	about	/#/	examine
/y/	yet	/*/	one
/z/	zoo	/I/	logic
/A/	bite	/^/	but
/C/	chin		

NETtalk has 309 processing units and 18 629 connection strengths (weights) that must be specified. The network does not have any initial or built-in organization for processing the input or (more exactly) mapping letters on to sounds. All the structure emerges during the training period. The values of the weights are determined by using the "back-propagation" learning algorithm developed by Rumelhart, Hinton and Williams (1986). (For a review of network learning algorithms, see Hinton 1988 and Sejnowski 1988.) The strategy exploits the calculated error between the *actual* values of the processing units in the output layer and the *desired* values, which is provided by a training signal. The resulting error signal is propagated from the output

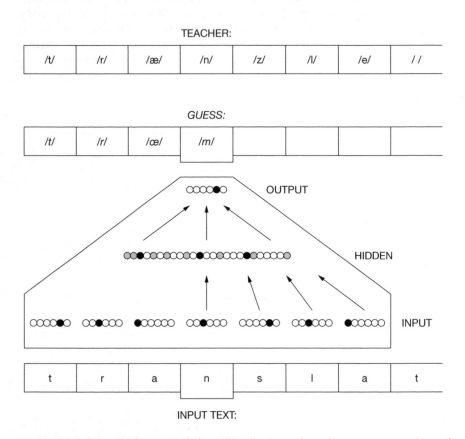

Figure 9.3 Schematic drawing of the NETtalk network architecture. A window of letters in an English text is fed to an array of 203 input units arranged in 7 groups of 29 units each. Information from these units is transformed by an intermediate layer of 80 hidden units to produce a pattern of activity in 26 output units. The connections in the network are specified by a total of 18 629 weight parameters (including a variable threshold for each unit). During the training, information about the desired output provided by the Teacher is compared with the actual output of the network, and the weights in the network are changed slightly so as to reduce the error.

layer backward to the input layer and used to adjust each weight in the network. The network learns, as the weights are changed, to minimize the mean squared error over the training set of words. Thus, the system can be characterized as following a path in weight space (the space of all possible weights) until it finds a minimum (figure 9.4). The important point to be illustrated, therefore, is this: The network processes information by nonlinear dynamics, not by manipulating symbols and accessing rules. It learns by gradient descent in a complex interactive system, not by generating new rules (Hinton and Sejnowski 1986).

The issue that we want to focus on next is the structural organization that is "discovered" by the network, in virtue of which it succeeds in converting letters to phonemes and manages to pronounce, with few errors, the many irregularities of English. If there are no rules in the network, how is the transformation accomplished? Since a trained network can generalize quite well to new words, some knowledge about the pattern of English pronunciation must be contained inside the network. Although a representational organization was imposed on the input and output layers, the network had to create new,

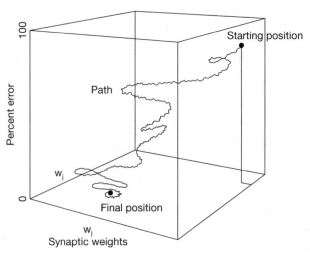

Figure 9.4 Schematic drawing of a path followed in weight space as the network finds a minimum of the average error over the set of training patterns. Only two weights out of many thousands are shown. The learning algorithm only ensures convergence to a local minimum, which is often a good solution. Typically, many sets of weights are good solutions, so the network is likely to find one of them from a random starting position in weight space. The learning time can be reduced by starting the network near a good solution; for example, the pattern of connections can be limited to a geometry that reduces the number of variable weights that must be searched by gradient descent.

internal representations in the hidden layer of processing units. How did the network organize its "knowledge"? To be more accurate: How did the equivalence class of networks organize its knowledge? (Each time the network was started from a random set of weights, a different network was generated.)

The answers were not immediately available, because a network does not leave an explanation of its travels through weight space, nor does it provide a decoding scheme when it reaches a resting place. Even so, some progress was made by measuring the activity pattern among the hidden units for specific inputs. In a sense, this test mimics at the modeling level what neurophysiologists do at the cellular level when they record the activity of a single neuron to try to find the effective stimulus that makes it respond. NETtalk is a fortunate "preparation," inasmuch as the number of processing units is relatively small, and it is possible to determine the activity patterns of all the units for all possible input patterns. These measurements, despite the relatively small network, did create a staggering amount of data, and then the puzzle was this: How does one find the order in all these data?

For each set of input letters, there is a pattern of activity among the hidden units (figure 9.5). The first step in the analysis of the activity of the hidden units was to compute the average level of activity for each letter-to-sound correspondence. For example, all words with the letter c in the middle position yielding the hard-c sound /k/ were presented to the network, and the average level of activity was calculated. Typically, about 15 of the 80 hidden units were very highly activated, and the rest of the hidden units had little or no activity. This procedure was repeated for each of the 79 letter-to-sound correspondences. The result was 79 vectors, each vector pointing in a different direction in the 80-dimensional space of average hidden-unit activities. The next step was to explore the relationship among the vectors in this space by cluster analysis. It is useful to conceive of each vector as the internal code that is used to represent a specific letter-to-sound correspondence; consequently, those vectors that clustered close together would have similar codes.

Remarkably, all the vectors for vowel sounds clustered together, indicating that they were represented in the network by patterns of activity in units that were distinct from those representing the consonants (which were themselves clustered together). (See figure 9.6.) Within the vowels, all the letter-to-sound correspondences that used the letter a were clustered together, as were the vectors of e, i, o, and u and the relevant instances of y. This was a very robust organizational scheme that occurred in all the networks that were analyzed, differences in starting weights notwithstanding. The coding scheme for consonants was more variable from network to network, but as a general rule the clustering was based more on similarities in sounds than on letters. Thus, the labial stops /p/ and /b/ were very close together in the space of hidden-unit activities, as were all the letter-to-sound correspondences that result in the hard-c sound /k/.

Other statistical techniques, such as factor analysis and multidimensional scaling, are also being applied to the network, and activity patterns from

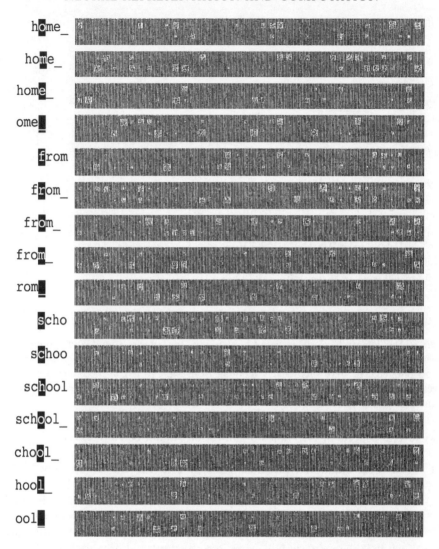

Figure 9.5 Levels of activation in the layer of hidden units for a variety of words. The input string in the window of seven letters is shown to the left, with the target letter emphasized. The output from the network is the phoneme that corresponds to the target letter. The transformation is accomplished by 80 hidden units, whose activity levels are shown to the right in two rows of 40 units each. The area of each white square is proportional to the activity level. Most units have little or no activity for a given input, but a few are highly activated.

individual inputs, rather than averages over classes, are also being studied (Rosenberg 1988). These statistical techniques are providing us with a detailed description of the representation for single inputs as well as classes or input–output pairs.

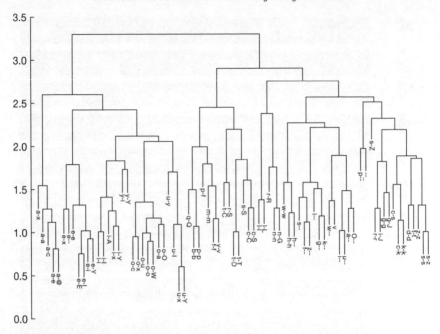

Figure 9.6 Hierarchical clustering of hidden units for letter-to-sound correspondences. The vectors of average hidden unit activity for each correspondence ('l-p' for letter l and phoneme p) were successively merging from right to left in the binary tree. The scale at the top indicates the Euclidean distance between the clusters. (From Sejnowski and Rosenberg 1987.)

Several aspects of NETtalk's organization should be emphasized:

1   The representational organization visible in the trained-up network is not programmed or coded into the network; it is found by the network. In a sense it "programs" itself, by virtue of being connected in the manner described and having weights changed by experience according to the learning algorithm. The dynamical properties of this sort of system are such that the network will settle into the displayed organization.

2   The network's representation for letter-to-sound correspondences is neither local nor completely distributed; it is somewhere in between. The point is, each unit participates in more than one correspondence, and so the representation is not local, but since it does not participate in all correspondences, the representation is not completely distributed either.

3   The representation is a property of the collection of hidden units, and does not resemble sentence-logic organization.

4   The organization is structured, which suggests that emergent subordinate and superordinate relations might be a general principle of network organization that could be used as input for other networks assigned other tasks if NETtalk were embedded in a larger system of networks.

170

5   General properties of the hierarchical organization of letter-to-sound
     correspondences emerged only at the level of groups of units. This organ-
     ization was invariant across all the networks created from the same sample
     of English words, even where the processing units in distinct networks had
     specialized for a different aspect of the problem.
6   Different networks created by starting from different initial conditions
     all achieved about the same level of performance, but the detailed response
     properties of the individual units in the networks differed greatly.
     Nonetheless, all the networks had similar functional clusterings for letter-
     to-sound correspondence (figure 9.6). This suggests that single neurons
     code information relative to other neurons in small groups or assemblies
     (Hebb 1949).

The representational organization in NETtalk may illustrate important
principles concerning network computation and representation, but what do
they tell us about neural representations? Some of the principles uncovered
might be generally applicable to a wide class of tasks, but it would be
surprising if the details of the model bore any significant resemblance to the
way reading skills are represented in the human nervous system. NETtalk is
more of a demonstration of certain network capacities and properties than
a faithful model of some subsystem of the brain, and it may be a long time
before data concerning the human neurobiology of reading become available.
Nevertheless, the same network techniques that were used to explore the
language domain can be applied to problems in other domains, such as vision,
where much more is known about the anatomy and the physiology.

4.2   Visual processing: computing surface curvature
from shaded images

The general constraints from brain architecture touched on in section 3 should
be supplemented, wherever possible, by more detailed constraints from brain
physiology and anatomy. Building models of real neural networks is a difficult task, however, because essential knowledge about the style of computation in the brain is not yet available (Sejnowski 1986). Not only is the fine
detail (such as the connectivity patterns in neurons in cerebral cortex) not
known, but even global-level knowledge specifying the flow of information
through different parts of the brain during normal function is limited. Even if
more neurophysiological and neuroanatomical detail were available, current
computing technology would put rather severe limits on how much detail
could be captured in a simulation. Nevertheless, the same type of network
model used in NETtalk could be useful in understanding how information is
coded within small networks confined to cortical columns. The processing
units in this model will be identified with neurons in the visual cortex.

Ever since Hubel and Wiesel (1962) first reported that single neurons in the
cat visual cortex respond better to oriented bars of light and to dark/light edges

171

than to spots of light, it has been generally assumed, or at least widely hoped, that the function of these neurons is to detect boundaries of objects in the world. In general, the inference from a cell's response profile to is function in the wider information-processing economy is intuitively very plausible, and if we are to have any hope of understanding neural representations we need to start in an area such as visual cortex – where it is possible to build on an impressive body of existing data. The trouble is, however, that many functions are consistent with the particular response properties of a neuronal population. That a cell responds optimally to an oriented bar of light is compatible with its having lots of functions other than detecting object boundaries, though the hypothesis that it serves to detect boundaries does tend to remain intuitively compelling. To see that our intuitions might really mislead us as we try to infer function from response profiles, it would be useful if we could demonstrate this point concretely. In what follows we shall show how the same response properties could in fact serve in the processing of visual information about the regions of a surface between boundaries rather than about the boundaries themselves.

Boundaries of objects are relatively rare in images, yet the preponderance of cells in visual cortex respond preferentially to oriented bars and slits. If we assume that all those cells are detecting boundaries, then it is puzzling that there should be so many cells whose sole function is to detect boundaries when there are not many boundaries to detect. It would, therefore, seem wasteful if, of all the neurons with oriented fields, only a small fraction carried useful information about a particular image. Within their boundaries, most objects have shaded or textured surfaces that will partially activate these neurons. The problem, accordingly, is this: Can the information contained in a population of partially activated cortical neurons be used to compute useful information about the three-dimensional surfaces between the boundaries of objects in the image?

One of the primary properties of a surface is its curvature. Some surfaces, such as the top of a table, are flat, and have no intrinsic curvature. Other surfaces, such as cylinders and spheres, are curved, and around each point on a surface the degree of curvature can be characterized by the direction along the surface of maximum and minimum curvature. It can be shown that these directions are always at right angles to each other, and the values are called the *principal curvatures* (Hilbert and Cohn-Vossen 1952). The principal curvatures and the orientation of the axes provide a complete description of the local curvature.

One problem with extracting the principal curvatures from an image is that the gray-level shading depends on many factors, such as the direction of illumination, the reflectance of the surface, and the orientation of the surface relative to the viewer. Somehow our visual system is able to separate these variables and to extract information about the shape of an object independent of these other variables. Pentland (1984) has shown that a significant amount of information about the curvature of a surface is available locally.

Can a network model be constructed that can extract this information from shaded images?

Until recently it was not obvious how to begin to construct such a network, but network learning algorithms (see above) provide us with a powerful method for creating a network by giving it examples of the task at hand. The learning algorithm is being used in this instance simply as a design tool to see whether some network can be found that performs the task. Many examples of simple surfaces (elliptic paraboloids) were generated and presented to the network. A set of weights was indeed found with this procedure that, independent of the direction of illumination, extracted the principal curvatures of three-dimensional surfaces and the direction of maximum curvature from shaded images (Lehky and Sejnowski 1987).

The input to the network is from an array of on-center and off-center receptive fields similar to those of cells in the lateral geniculate nucleus. The output layer is a population of units that conjointly represent the curvatures and the broadly tuned direction of maximum curvature. The units of the intermediate layer, which are needed to perform the transformation, have oriented receptive fields, similar to those of simple cells in the visual cortex of cats and monkeys that respond optimally to oriented bars and edges (figure 9.7). It is important to emphasize that these properties of the hidden units were not put into the network directly but emerged during training. The system "chose" these properties because they are useful in performing a particular task. Interestingly, time output units, which were required to code information about the principal curvatures and principal orientations of surfaces, had properties, when probed with bars of light, that were similar to those of a class of complex cells that are end-stopped (Lehky and Sejnowski 1988). The surprising thing, given the plausible receptive-field-to-function inference rule, is that the function of the units in the network is not to detect boundary contours, but to extract curvature information from shaded images.

What the shape-from-shading network demonstrates is that we cannot directly infer function from receptive field properties. In the trained-up network, the hidden units represent an intermediate transformation for a computational task quite different from the one that has been customarily ascribed to simple cells in visual cortex – they are used to determine shape from shading, not to detect boundaries. It turns out, however, that the hidden units have *receptive fields similar to those of simple cells in visual cortex*. Therefore, bars and edges as receptive-field properties do not necessarily mean that the cell's function is to detect bars and edges in objects; it might be to detect curvature and shape, as it is in the network model, or perhaps some other surface property such as texture. The general implication is that there is no way of determining the function of each hidden unit in the network simply by "recording" the receptive-field properties of the unit. This, in turn, implies that, despite its intuitive plausibility, the receptive-field-to-function inference rule is untenable.

173

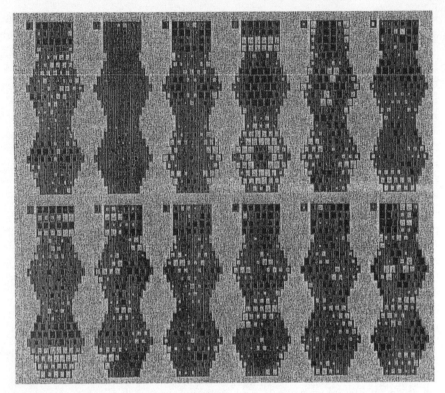

Figure 9.7 Hinton diagram showing the connection strengths in a network that computes the principal curvatures and direction of minimum curvature from shaded images in a small patch of the visual field corresponding roughly to the area represented in a cortical column. There are 12 hidden units which receive connections from the 122 inputs and project to each of the 23 output units. The diagram shows each of the connection strengths to and from the hidden units. Each weight is represented by one square, the area of which is proportional to the magnitude of the weight. The color is white if the weight is excitatory and black if it is inhibitory. The inputs are two hexagonal arrays of 61 processing units each. Each input unit has a concentric on-center (top) or off-surround (bottom) receptive field similar to those of principal cells in the lateral geniculate nucleus. The output consists of 24 units that conjointly represent the direction of maximum curvature (six columns) and principal curvature (four rows: two for each principal curvature). Each of the 12 hidden units is represented in the diagram in a way that reveals all the connections to and from the unit. Within each of the 12 gray background regions, the weights from the inputs are shown on the bottom and the weights to the output layer are shown above. To the left of each hidden unit, the lone square gives the threshold of the unit, which was also allowed to vary. Note that there emerged two different types of hidden units as revealed by the "projective field." The six units in the bottom row and the fourth and fifth from the left in the top row were mainly responsible for providing information about the direction of minimum curvature, while others were responsible for computing the signs and magnitudes of the two principal curvatures The curvature-selective units could be further classified as convexity detectors (top row, thud from left) or elongation filters (top row, second and sixth from left).

174

The function of a unit is revealed only when its *outputs* – its "projective field" (Lehky and Sejnowski 1988) – are also examined. It is the projective field of a unit that provides the additional information needed to interpret the unit's computational role in the network. In the network model the projective field could be examined directly, but in real neural networks it can only be inferred indirectly by examining the next stage of processing. Whether or not curvature is directly represented in visual cortex, for example, can be tested by designing experiments with images of curved surfaces.

4.3   Next-generation networks

NETtalk and time shape-from-shading network are important examples because they yield clues to how the nervous system can embody models of various domains of the world. Parallel-network modeling is still in a pioneering stage of development. There are bound to be many snags and hitches, and many problems yet undreamt of will have to be solved. At this stage, the representational structure of networks has not yet been explored in detail, nor is it known how well the performance of network models will scale with the number of neurons and the difficulty of the task. (That is, will representations and computations in a cortical column with 200 000 neurons be similar to those in a model network comprising only a few hundred processing units?)

Moreover, taken literally as a model of functioning neurons, back-propagation is biologically implausible, inasmuch as error signals cannot literally be propagated back down the very same axon the signal came up. Taken as a *systems-level* algorithm, however, back-propagation may have a realization using feedback projections that do map on to neural hardware. Even squarely facing these cautionary considerations, the important thing is that something with this sort of character at least lets us see what representational structure – good, meaty, usable structure – could *look* like in a neuronal network.

Temporal chaining of sequences of representations is probably a prominent feature of many kinds of behavior, and it may turn out to be particularly important for language acquisition and use. It is conceivable that structured sequences – long, temporally extended sequences – are the elements of an abstract sort of neural state space that enable humans to use language. Sereno (1986) has suggested something along these lines, pointing out that DNA, as a spatially extended sequence of nucleotides, allows for encoding; by analogy, one may envision that the development of mechanisms for generating temporally extended sequences of neuronal (abstract) structures may allow for a kind of structured behavior (that is, language) that short sequences do not allow for. (See also MacKay 1987; Dehaene et al. l987.)

One promising strategy will be to try first to unscramble the more fundamental kinds of representing accomplished by nervous systems, shelving until later the problem of complex representations such as linguistic representations. To solve such problems, the solutions discovered for simpler representations may be crucial. At the most basic level, there appears to be an isomorphism between cell responses and external events (for example, cells in visual cortex responding to bars of light moving in a specific direction). At higher levels the receptive-field properties change (Allman et al. 1985; Andersen 1987), and it may be that the lower-level isomorphism gives way to more complicated and dynamic network effects. Motivation, planning, and other factors may, at this level, have roles in how a representation is generated. At still higher levels, still other principles may be operative. Once we understand the nature of representing in early sensory processing, as we have indeed begun to do, and go on to address the nature of representations at more and more abstract levels, we may finally be able to address how learning a language yields another kind of representation, and how symbols can be represented in neural networks. Whatever the basic principles of language representation, they are not likely to be utterly unrelated to the way or ways that the nervous system generates visual representations or auditory representations, or represents spatial maps and motor planning. (On semantic relations in connectionist models, see Hinton 1981, 1986.)

5   Dogmas and dreams: George Boole, Ramon y Cajal, David Marr

The connectionist models discussed are valuable for the glimpse of representational and computational space that they provide, for it is exactly such glimpses that free us from the bonds of the intuitive conceptions of representations as language-like and computation as logic-like. They thus free us from what Hofstadter (1982) called the *Boolean Dream*, where all cognition is symbol-manipulation according to the rules of logic.

Equally important, they also free us from what we call the *Neurobiologists' Dream* (perhaps, with all due respect, it might be called Cajal's Dream), which is really the faith that the answers we seek will be manifest once the fine-grain details of each neuron (its morphology, physiology, and connections) are revealed – these models also teach the tremendously important lesson that *system properties are not accessible at the single-unit level*. In a system, what we need to know is how the elements in large sets of elements interact over time. Until we have new physiological techniques for supplying data of that sort, building network models is a method of first resort.

To be really useful, a model must be biologically constrained. However, exactly which biological properties are crucial to a model's utility and which can be safely ignored until later are matters that can be decided only by hunches until a mature theory is in place. Such "bottom-up" constraints are crucial, since computational space is immensely vast – too vast for us to be lucky enough to light on the correct theory simply from the engineering bench. Moreover, the brain's solutions to the problems of vision, motor control, and so forth may be far more powerful, more beautiful, and even more simple than what we engineer into existence. This is the point of Orgel's Second Rule:

Nature is more ingenious than we are. And we stand to miss all that power and ingenuity unless we attend to neurobiological plausibility. The point is, *evolution has already done it*, so why not learn how that stupendous machine, our brain, actually works?

This observation allows us to awake from *Marr's Dream* of three levels of explanation: the computational level of abstract problem analysis, the level of the algorithm, and the level of physical implementation of the computation. In Marr's view, a higher level was independent of the levels below it, and hence computational problems could be analyzed independent of an understanding of the algorithm that executes the computation, and the algorithmic problem could be solved independent of an understanding of the physical implementation. Marr's assessment of the relations between levels has been re-evaluated, and the dependence of higher levels on lower levels has come to be recognized.

The matter of the interdependence of levels marks a major conceptual difference between Marr and the current generation of connectionists. Network models are not independent of either the computational level or the implementational level; they depend in important ways on constraints from all levels of analysis. Network models show how knowledge of brain architecture can contribute to the devising of likely and powerful algorithms that can be efficiently implemented in the architecture of the nervous system and may alter even how we construe the computational problems.

On the heels of the insight that the use of constraints from higher up and lower down matters tremendously, the notion that there are basically *three* levels of analysis also begins to look questionable. If we examine more closely how the three levels of analysis are meant to map on to the organization of the nervous system, the answer is far from straightforward.

To begin with, the idea that there is essentially one single implementational level is an oversimplification. Depending on the fineness of grain, research techniques reveal structural organization at many strata: the biochemical level; then the levels of the membrane, the single cell, and the circuit; and perhaps yet other levels, such as brain subsystems, brain systems, brain maps, and the whole central nervous system. But notice that at each structurally specified stratum we can raise the functional question: What does it contribute to the wider, functional business of the brain?

This range of structural organization implies, therefore, that the oversimplification with respect to implementation has a companion oversimplification with respect to computational descriptions. And indeed, on reflection it does seem most unlikely that a single type of computational description can do justice to the computational niche of diverse structural organization. On the contrary, one would expect distinct task descriptions corresponding to distinct structural levels. But if there is a ramifying of task specifications to match the ramified structural organization, this diversity will probably be reflected in the ramification of the *algorithms* that characterize how a task is accomplished. And this, in turn, means that the notion of *the* algorithmic levels is as oversimplified as the notion of the implementation level.

177

Similar algorithms were used to specify the network models in NETtalk and the shape-from-shading network, but they have a quite different status in these two examples. On this perspective of the levels of organization, NETtalk is a network relevant to the *systems* level, whereas the shape-from-shading network is relevant to the *circuit* level. Since the networks are meant to reflect principles at entirely different levels of organization, their implementations will also be at different scales in the nervous system. Other computational principles may be found to apply to the single cell or to neural maps.

Once we look at them closely, Marr's three *levels of analysis* and the brain's *levels of organization* do not appear to mesh in a very useful or satisfying manner. So poor is the fit that it may be doubted whether levels of analysis, as *conceived by Marr*, have much methodological significance. Accordingly, in light of the flaws with the notion of *independence*, and in light of the flaws with the *tripartite* character of the conception of levels, it seems that Marr's dream, inspiring though it was for a time, must be left behind.

The vision that inspires network modeling is essentially and inescapably interdisciplinary. Unless we explicitly theorize above the level of the single cell we will never find the key to the order and the systematicity hidden in the blinding minutiae of the neuropil. Unless our theorizing is geared to mesh with the neurobiological data, we risk wasting our time exploring some impossibly remote, if temporarily fashionable, corner of computational space. Additionally, without the constraints from psychology, ethology, and linguistics to specify more exactly the parameters of the large-scale capacities of nervous systems, our conception of the functions for which we need explanation will be so woolly and tangled as to effectively smother progress.

Consequently, cross-disciplinary research, combining constraints from psychology, neurology, neurophysiology, linguistics, and computer modeling, is the best hope for the co-evolution that could ultimately yield a unified, integrated science of the mind–brain. It has to be admitted, however, that this vision is itself a dream. From within the dream, we cannot yet reliably discern what are the flaws that will impede progress, what crucial elements are missing, or at which points the vague if tantalizing hunches might be replaced by palpable results.

Notes

1 An earlier exploration of these ideas is to be found in Kenneth Craik's book *The Nature of Explanation* (Cambridge University Press, 1943).
2 NETtalk networks can differ in how input letters and output phonemes are represented, and in the number and arrangement of hidden units.

References

Allman, J., Miezin, F., and McGuinness E. (1985) "Stimulus specific responses from beyond the classic receptive field." *Annual Review of Neuroscience* 8: 407–30.

Andersen, R. A. (1987) "The role of posterior parietal cortex in spatial perception and visual-motor integration." In *Handbook of Physiology – The Nervous System V*, ed. V. B. Mountcastle, F. Plum and S. R. Geiger.

Anderson, J. A. and Hinton, G. E. (1981) "Models of information processing in the brain." In Hinton and Anderson 1981.

Chisholm, R. M. (1966) *Theory of Knowledge*. Englewood Cliffs, N.J.: Prentice-Hall.

Churchland, P. M. (1979) *Scientific Realism and the Plasticity of Mind*. Cambridge University Press.

Churchland, P. M. (1988) *Matter and Consciousness* (revised edition). Cambridge, Mass.: MIT Press.

Churchland, P. S. (1986) *Neurophilosophy: Toward a Unified Science of the Mind–Brain*. Cambridge, Mass.: MIT Press.

Davidson, D. (1974) "On the very idea of a conceptual scheme." *Proceedings and Addresses of the American Philosophical Association* 47: 5–20.

Dehaene, S., Changeux, J.-P., and Nadal, J.-P. (1987) "Neural networks that learn temporal sequences by selection." *Proceedings of the National Academy of Sciences* 84: 2727–31.

Dennett, D. C. (1978) *Brainstorms: Philosophical Essays on Mind and Psychology*. Cambridge, Mass.: MIT Press.

Eccles, J. C. (1977) Part II of K. Popper, *The Self and Its Brain*. Berlin: Springer-Verlag.

Enc, B. (1983) "In defense of the identity theory." *Journal of Philosophy* 80: 279–98.

Feldman, J. A., and Ballard, F. H. (1982) "Connectionist models and their properties." *Cognitive Science* 6: 205–54.

Fodor, J. A. (1975) *The Language of Thought*. New York: Crowell. (Paperback edition: Cambridge, Mass.: MIT Press, 1979.)

Fodor, J. A. (1981) *Representations*. Cambridge, Mass.: MIT Press.

Goldman-Rakic, P. S. (1987) "Circuitry of primate prefrontal cortex and regulation of behavior by representational memory." In *Handbook of Physiology – The Nervous System V*, ed. V. B. Mountcastle, F. Plum and S. R. Geiger.

Hebb D. O. (1949) *The Organization of Behavior*. New York: Wiley.

Hilbert, J. and Cohn-Vossen, S. (1952) *Geometry and the Imagination*. New York: Chelsea.

Hinton, G. E. (1981) "Implementing semantic networks in parallel hardware." In Hinton and Anderson 1981.

Hinton, G. E. (1986) "Learning distributed representations of concepts." In *Proceedings of the Eighth Annual Conference of the Cognitive Science Society*. Hillsdale, N.J.: Erlbaum.

Hinton, G. E. (1988) "Connectionist learning procedures." *Artificial Intelligence*, in press.

Hinton, E. E. and Anderson, J. A. (eds) (1981) *Parallel Models of Associative Memory*. Hillsdale, N.J.: Erlbaum.

Hinton, G. E. and Sejnowski, T. J. (1986) "Learning and relearning in Boltzmann machines." In McClelland and Rumelhart 1986.

Hofstadter, D. R. (1982) "Artificial intelligence: Subcognition as computation." *Technical Report No. 132*, Computer Science Department, Indiana University.

Hooker, C. A. (1981) "Toward a general theory of reduction. Part I: Historical and scientific setting. Part II: Identity in reduction. Part III: Cross-categorical reduction." *Dialogue* 20: 38–59, 201–36, 496–529.

Hubel, D. H. and Wiesel, T. N. (1962) "Receptive fields, binocular interaction and functional architecture in the cat's visual cortex." *Journal of Physiology* 160: 106–54.

Kelso, S. R., Ganong, A. H. and Brown, T. H. (1986) 'Hebbian synapses in hippocampus." *Proceedings of National Academy of Sciences* 83: 5326–30.

Lehky, S. and Sejnowski, T. J. (1987) "Extracting 3-D curvatures from images using a neural model." *Society for Neuroscience Abstracts* 13: 1451.

Lehky, S. and Sejnowski, T. J. (1988) "Neural network model for the representation of surface curvature from images of shaded surfaces." In *Organizing Principles of Sensory Processing*, ed. J. Lund, Oxford University Press.

Livingstone, M. S. (1988) "Art, illusion, and the visual system." *Scientific American* 258: 78–85.

McClelland, J. L. and Rumelhart, D. E. (1986) *Parallel Distributed Processing: Explorations in the Microstructure of Cognition*. Cambridge, Mass.: MIT Press.

McGinn, C. (1982) *The Character of Mind*. Oxford University Press.

MacKay, D. (1987) *The Organization and Perception of Action*. Berlin: Springer-Verlag.

Mandt, A. J. (1986) "The triumph of philosophical pluralism? Notes on the transformation of academic philosophy." *Proceedings and Addresses of the American Philosophical Association* 60: 265–77.

Marr, D. (1982) *Vision*. San Francisco: Freeman.

Pellionisz, A. and Llinas, R. (1982) "Space–time representation in the brain. The cerebellum as a predictive space–time metric tensor." *Neuroscience* 7: 2249–70.

Pentland, A. P. (1984) "Local shading analysis." *IEEE Transactions: Pattern Analysis and Machine Intelligence* 6: 170–87.

Putnam, H. (1967) "The nature of mental states." In *Arts, Mind and Religion*, ed. W. H. Capitan and D. D. Merrill (University of Pittsburgh Press). Reprinted in H. Putnam, *Mind, Language, and Reality: Philosophical Papers*, vol. 2 (Cambridge University Press, 1975).

Pylyshyn, Z. (1984) *Computation and Cognition*. Cambridge, Mass.: MIT Press.

Quine, W. V. O. (1960) *Word and Object*. Cambridge, Mass.: MIT Press.

Richardson, R. (1979) "Functionalism and reductionism." *Philosophy of Science* 46: 533–58.

Rosenberg, C. R. (1988) PhD. thesis, Princeton University.

Rumelhart, D. E., Hinton, G. E. and McClelland, J. L. (1986) "A general framework for parallel distributed processing." In McClelland and Rumelhart 1986.

Rumelhart, D. E., Hinton, G. E. and Williams, R. J. (1986) "Learning internal representations by error propagation." In McClelland and Rumelhart 1986.

Schaffner, K. F. (1976) "Reductionism in biology: Prospects and problems." In *PSA Proceedings 1974*, ed. R. S. Cohen, C. A. Hooker, A. C. Michalos and J. W. Van Evra. Dordrecht: Reidel.

Sejnowski, T. J. (1986) "Open questions about computation in cerebral cortex." In McClelland and Rumelhart 1986.

Sejnowski, T.J. (1988) "Neural network learning algorithms" In *Neural Computers*, ed. R. Eckmiller and C. von der Malsberg, Berlin: Springer-Verlag.

Sejnowski, T. J. and Churchland, P. S. In press. "Brain and cognition." In *Foundations of Cognitive Science*, ed. M. I. Posner, Cambridge, Mass.: MIT Press.

Sejnowski, T. J. and Rosenberg, C. R. (1987) "Parallel networks that learn to pronounce English text." *Complex Systems* I: 145–68.

Sejnowski, T. J. and Rosenberg, C. R. (1988) "Learning and representation in connectionist models." In *Perspective in Memory Research and Training*, ed. M. Gazzaniga, Cambridge, Mass.: MIT Press.

Sejnowski, T. J., Koch. C. and Churchland, P. S. (1988) "Computational neuroscience." *Science*, 241: 1299–1306.

Sereno, M. (1986) "A program for the neurobiology of mind." *Inquiry* 29: 217–40.

Skinner, B. F. (1957) *Verbal Behavior*. New York: Appleton-Century-Crofts.

Skinner, B. F. (1976) *About Behaviorism*. New York: Knopf.

Smart, J. J. C. (1959) "Sensations and brain processes." *Philosophical Review* 68: 141–56.

Stich, S. P. (1983) *From Folk Psychology to Cognitive Science: The Case Against Belief.* Cambridge, Mass.: MIT Press.

Strawson P. F. (1966) *The Bounds of Sense: An Essay on Kant Critique of Pure Reason.* London: Methuen.

Swinburne, R. (1986) *The Evolution of the Soul.* Oxford University Press.

10

P. McLeod, K. Plunkett, and E.T. Rolls, "The Attraction of Parallel Distributed Processing for Modelling Cognition"

The representation and processing of information in connectionist networks is distributed. Decisions are reached by consensus of a large number of simple computations taking place in parallel as stimulus information interacts with stored knowledge. In consequence, connectionist memories display many human characteristics: They are relatively immune to damaged components within the system or to noisy input; they allow retrieval by content; they are likely to retrieve typical instances from categories.

The last decade has seen an explosive growth in the connectionist modelling of cognitive processes, with simulation of most of the classical experimental paradigms of cognitive psychology. One reason for this enthusiasm is that, independent of their success at modelling human performance at any particular cognitive task, all connectionist models exhibit some general characteristics which are shown by human cognitive processes and distinguish them from non-biological computational systems such as computer programs: They still perform reasonably well after minor damage to components of the system; they still perform reasonably well if their input is noisy or inaccurate; they allow memory retrieval by content.

In this chapter we will look at two aspects of connectionist systems which are responsible for these characteristics. These are based on general observations of brain structure. First, knowledge representation is *distributed* across many processing units. Second, computations take place in *parallel* across these distributed representations. The result is that conclusions are reached on the basis of a consensus of many calculations rather than depending on any particular one.

These principles put connectionist models in direct contrast to many traditional models in cognitive psychology or artificial intelligence where knowledge representation is local and computation is serial. In general, such models are not immune to damage or resistant to noisy input. So a traditional model of, say, syllogistic reasoning, might give as good a fit to the experimental data as a connectionist model, but it would do so without exhibiting the full range of human characteristics as it performed the task.

The representation of knowledge in connectionist networks is distributed

Traditional models of cognitive processing usually assume a local representation of knowledge. That is, knowledge about different things is stored in different, independent locations. In a traditional model of reading aloud, for example, information about how to pronounce the letter string DOG is stored in one place and information about how to pronounce the string CAT in another. What could be more natural? The two pieces of information are independent and would be required at different times. So storing them independently makes obvious sense. The information storage systems we are familiar with in everyday life – dictionaries, telephone directories, computer discs – use local representation. Each discrete piece of information is stored separately. How else could it be done?

In connectionist models information storage is not local, it is *distributed*. There is no one place where a particular piece of knowledge can be located. Consider a network which is learning to read aloud. Any input, such as the letter string DOG, would excite units and connections all over the network. Learning takes place by changing the weights of the connections leading to all output units which have an incorrect level of activity. The knowledge of how to pronounce the input DOG is distributed across many different connections in different parts of the system. It is the sum total effect of all these connections which produces the pronunciation, not any single one of them.

The concept of distributed storage may be difficult to grasp at first because it is counter to our everyday experience of information storage systems. The connections which contain the system's knowledge about how to pronounce DOG are the same as those with the knowledge about how to pronounce any other letter string. All the knowledge that the network contains is superimposed on the *same* set of connections. Intuitively this may seem entirely implausible. How can the same set of weights store independent and even contradictory pieces of information? As we will see, it can be done, and some of the emergent properties of such systems are intriguingly similar to properties of human cognitive processes. But for the moment this will have to be taken on trust. There are no familiar information storage systems which use distributed coding, so analogy to a familiar system is not possible.

Distributed representations are damage resistant and fault tolerant

When one considers the structure of the brain it is remarkable that it ever manages to come to the correct conclusion about anything. By any

conventional standards neurons are an entirely unsuitable medium for computation: they die throughout the brain's life, causing random loss of stored
information; they have a finite probability of firing even when they are not
engaged in signal processing; the response of a neuron to any particular input
is probabilistic, not fixed.

If we look at the firing pattern of a single neuron the problem that probabilistic responses cause for the system will become clear. The upper part of
figure 10.1 shows the average response of a single neuron in the visual cortex
to a stimulus presented to the eye. The stimulus is presented at time 0. Time
after the presentation of the stimulus is shown on the horizontal axis. The
vertical axis shows the neuron's firing rate. It has an average background firing
rate of a few spikes per second. When the stimulus is presented a signal is
superimposed on this. About 50 ms after the stimulus appears the neuron fires
strongly for about 30 ms. 100 ms later it fires again, rather less intensely, for
about 50 ms. This is the signal that the neuron transmits to the other neurons
to which it is connected, indicating what pattern of stimulation it has received.

This seems fairly straightforward. But the histogram was obtained by
summing the spike patterns over a number of presentations of the stimulus.
The lower part of the figure shows 12 different occasions on which the same
stimulus was presented. Each time the neuron fires there is a vertical spike. If
we look at these individual trials the pattern which emerges is much less clear
than that suggested by the overall average at the top. On trial 5 the initial
burst was missing. On trial 10 the second burst was missing. On trial 11 the
neuron did not respond at all. It is clear that the 'signal' which the histogram
at the top shows is an idealised average. On any given trial the output will
only approximate this, sometimes quite closely, sometimes not at all. How can
the system produce a reliable response on every trial when the individual
components only produce their signal on average across trials?

If the processing components in a conventional digital computer produced
random spontaneous output, a different response to the same stimulus on
different occasions and suffered from random component drop-out, the system
would be totally unpredictable! Sometimes it would work correctly, but if a
computation required access to the contents of a missing memory unit, or a
burst of noise obliterated a signal, the result would be garbage. Although the
components in the brain can fire and die at random, the computations
performed by the brain are not unpredictable. With minor damage it becomes
a little slower and less accurate, but it still produces roughly the same answer.
It has to suffer serious damage before it produces nonsense.

The brain escapes the consequences of the unpredictable behaviour of
individual neurons because its computations are performed in parallel on
representations which are distributed over many neurons. No one neuron
plays a crucial role in processing. The overall result is the outcome of
many distributed sub-computations. Even if individual components of the
calculation are not accurate, the ensemble averaging can nevertheless give an
answer which is accurate enough. When the memory location required for a

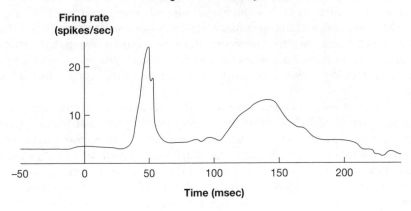

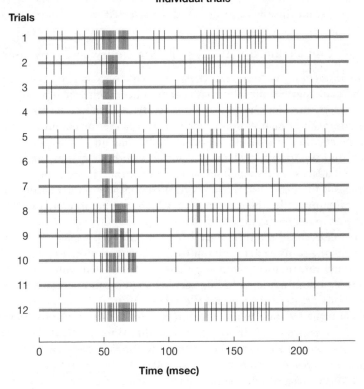

Figure 10.1 The response of a neuron in the visual cortex for 250 ms after stimulus presentation. Upper: The firing rate of the neuron summed over a number of presentations of the stimulus. Lower: The pattern on 12 of the trials which contributed to the average response shown at the top. Each vertical line represents the time at which the neuron fired. (Based on Morrell 1972.)

calculation in a localist information storage system is damaged, the result is disaster. If the first page of a dictionary is missing, there is no way of checking whether *aardvark* is really spelt like that. But, in a connectionist system, there is no such thing as 'the memory location required for a calculation'. Information and calculation are spread across the network. If one unit or connection in the network is damaged, others can make up for the missing part.

The system will, of course, be slightly less accurate if a connection is lost. But the pattern of loss is quite different in localist and distributed systems. Damage to a localist system causes some information to be lost totally while other information is unaffected. In a distributed system any damage causes partial loss of a range of information. As damage increases, the performance of the system inevitably begins to drop. But a small amount of damage may have no noticeable effect on the output of the system. The ability of brains and connectionist models to continue to produce a reasonable approximation to the correct answer following damage, rather than undergoing catastrophic failure, is an example of fault tolerance referred to as *graceful degradation*.

Connectionist networks allow memory access by content

Human memory is content-addressable. That is, you can access a memory by using some part of the information contained in the memory (the *content*) as a retrieval cue. This is unlike retrieval from familiar forms of information storage, such as dictionaries, telephone directories or computer discs. In these, the place where the information is stored has an *address*. The only way to access information for retrieval is with the address. For example, in a diction- ary the address is the spelling of the word; the information stored with this address is the definition of the word. In a computer system a typical address is the name of a file; the information which can be accessed with this address is the contents of the file.

To understand the difference between accessing a memory by address and by content, contrast retrieving information from a dictionary with obtaining the same information from a person. Imagine that you want to know the name of a man-made wall, built across a valley, to contain water to build up a head of pressure to generate electricity. With a dictionary, there is no way to access the location where this information is stored and extract the missing piece, the word 'dam'. If you start with the address (DAM) you can access all the information stored at the address. Without it you can access nothing. In contrast, a person given part of the information would probably be able to retrieve the rest. Unlike a dictionary, human memory allows access via any part of the information that forms the memory. One of the reasons why connectionist models of human memory are attractive is that content address- ability follows as a natural consequence of their distributed structure. Content addressability can be built into localist storage but only by adding a complex cross-referencing system.

Any information processing system which works in the brain must be fault tolerant because the signals it has to work with are seldom perfect. There is a random component to neuronal firing; speech is usually heard against a background of other noises; objects rarely present the same image on different occasions. An attractive aspect of content-addressable memory is that it is inherently fault tolerant. Imagine someone asked you to guess who they were thinking of: 'This man was a British Conservative politician. He became Prime Minister in 1978 and was Prime Minister during the Falklands War. He was ousted from office by his own party, being held responsible for the fiasco of the Poll Tax. He was eventually replaced as Prime Minister by John Major.' You could probably suggest 'Margaret Thatcher' as an answer despite the fact that some of the information is incorrect. Mrs Thatcher did not become Prime Minister until 1979, of course. With content-addressable memory the weight of evidence pointing to one answer can overcome other evidence that is incon- sistent. A best fit solution can be chosen even if it is not perfect. This is unlike memory systems in which access by address is the only possibility. Any error in the address will lead to failure. A search of Who's Who using the address 'Margaret Patcher' would discover nothing, despite the fact that most of the search term fits an existing entry.

Retrieving information from a distributed database

To see how a distributed system with parallel processing works in practice we will look at retrieval from a simple connectionist memory described by McClelland (1981).[1] This memory demonstrates content addressability and fault tolerance, It also shows typicality effects in retrieval – if asked to retrieve a random member of a category it will produce a typical member. Considering the simplicity of the simulation it demonstrates a remarkable range of human characteristics in memory retrieval.

Imagine that you live in a neighbourhood where many of your male acquaintances belong to one of the two rival local gangs, the Jets or the Sharks. Your knowledge about these characters will come from a succession of inde- pendent episodes. One night Fred emerges from behind a bush and offers you some white powder. You hear Dave and his wife trading insults as she drives off with a car full of suitcases. Everyone in the bar is laughing because Don has been admitted to college on the basis of forged examination results. Nick hangs out with Karl whom you know to be a Shark. All these pieces of information about your neighbours are gradually assembled over the years. Fred is a pusher; Dave is divorced; Don went to college; Nick is a Shark.

Table 10.1 shows how this information might be stored in a conventional information storage system. The system has a set of storage locations, corre- sponding to a set of cards in an index file or a set of files on disc in a computer, for example, each headed by an address. The address is the name of the person. Each new piece of information relating to him is stored at the location headed by this address. In this simple simulation we imagine that we have

Table 10.1

Address	Contents				
	Gang	Age	Education	Marital Status	Occupation
Alan	Jets	30s	JH	Married	Burglar
Art	Jets	40s	JH	Single	Pusher
Clyde	Jets	40s	JH	Single	Bookie
Dave	Sharks	30s	HS	Divorced	Pusher
Don	Sharks	30s	Col	Married	Burglar
Doug	Jets	30s	HS	Single	Bookie
Earl	Sharks	40s	HS	Married	Burglar
Fred	Jets	20s	HS	Single	Pusher
Gene	Jets	20s	Col	Single	Pusher
George	Jets	20s	JH	Divorced	Burglar
Greg	Jets	20s	HS	Married	Pusher
Ike	Sharks	30s	JH	Single	Bookie
Jim	Jets	20s	JH	Divorced	Burglar
John	Jets	20s	JH	Married	Burglar
Karl	Sharks	40s	HS	Married	Bookie
Ken	Sharks	20s	HS	Single	Burglar
Lance	Jets	20s	JH	Married	Burglar
Mike	Jets	30s	JH	Single	Bookie
Neal	Sharks	30s	HS	Single	Bookie
Ned	Sharks	30s	Col	Married	Bookie
Nick	Sharks	30s	HS	Single	Pusher
Oliver	Sharks	30s	Col	Married	Pusher
Pete	Jets	20s	HS	Single	Bookie
Phil	Sharks	30s	Col	Married	Pusher
Ralph	Jets	30s	JH	Single	Pusher
Rick	Sharks	30s	HS	Divorced	Burglar
Sam	Jets	20s	Col	Married	Bookie

(Based on McClelland 1981.)

information about the **Gang** each person belongs to (*Jets* or *Sharks*), a rough idea of his **Age** (*20s, 30s* or *40s*), the extent of his **Education** (*Junior High, High School* or *College*), his **Marital Status** (*Married, Single* or *Divorced*), and his **Occupation** (*Bookie, Burglar* or *Pusher*) The format used in table 10.1, address + contents, is a logical way of storing the information since the name *Alan* is the key which binds one set of information together, *Clyde* connects another set, and so on.

This form of storage is efficient for retrieving information in response to questions like 'Is Fred a pusher?' The question contains the address, and the address leads directly to the place where the information which provides the answer is stored. But it is not so good for answering other enquiries. If you are asked 'Do you know the name of a pusher?', the only way is to search through the list of addresses until you find one where the information *Pusher* is stored under **Occupation**. Although the information *Pusher* is stored at many locations, it does not form part of the address. So an answer to this question cannot be extracted directly from the memory.

Admittedly, with this particular database it would not take long to find a pusher if you searched addresses at random. But a more realistic representation of knowledge of these people would include many unique pieces of information, such as the fact that Fred's grandparents came from Ballylickey. The only way to store this in a system like that shown in table 10.1 is as the fact 'grandparents came from Ballylickey' at the storage location with the address *Fred*. The question 'Whose grandparents came from Ballylickey?' could only be answered by random search of the addresses until the one containing that information was found. This might take a long time although you would get there in the end. But a human memory would not respond like that. If you could remember the information at all you would usually produce the answer reasonably quickly. This is because human memory can be accessed by *content* – any part of the knowledge base can be used to access any other part. 'Ballylickey' can be used as a cue, and will lead to *Fred*. The information storage system shown in table 10.1 is perfectly logical. Indeed, it is probably the sort of system you would use if you were asked to store the information about the Jets and Sharks. But human memory cannot be organised like this. A memory organised like table 10.1 does not allow content-addressable retrieval; human memory does.

Another way of seeing why human memory cannot be organised so that access is only possible by address is to consider how you would answer the question 'What are the Jets like?'. Table 10.1 allows easy access to information about individual Jets, But it offers no simple way to answer questions requiring generalisations across a number of entries. Human memory does allow generalisations across areas of memory. A person who knew these two gangs could probably tell you that the Jets were younger than the Sharks without having to think very hard. Although the method of information storage shown in table 10.1 seems natural, it cannot be the way that human memory is organised.

(1) *Setting up a distributed database for the Jets and Sharks base*. McClelland explored the consequences of storing the information about the Jets and Sharks in a distributed system The architecture of his system is shown in the upper part of figure 10.2. To store the information in table 10.1 we need to represent facts about **Name, Gang Membership Age, Education, Marital Status** and **Occupation**. Within each of these areas of knowledge there is a node corresponding to the possible values that someone could have. So in the **Age** area there are nodes for *20s, 30s* and *40s*, in **Occupation** for *Burglar, Bookie* and *Pusher*, in **Gang** for *Jet* and *Shark*, and so on. This model might seem to be localist rather than distributed because there are individual nodes to represent specific concepts. But, as we shall see, the underlying dynamics

of the model are parallel and distributed. The result of any input is determined by interaction across the entire database. The localist coding of concepts is used to make it easy to see what the model is doing in the examples which follow.

A memory is formed by setting up a link between two nodes. If we discover that Sam is a bookie we set up a positive connection between the *Sam* node in the **Name** area and the *Bookie* node in the **Occupation** area. If we then discover that he is married we set up a positive connection between *Sam* in the **Name** area and *Married* in **Marital Status**, and between *Bookie* and *Married* (since we now know of a bookie who is married). To store all the information we know about Sam we would set up positive links between all the possible pairwise combinations of *Sam* in **Name**, *Jet* in **Gang**, *20s* in **Age**, *College* in **Education**, *Married* in **Marital Status** and *Bookie* in **Occupation**. The way that McClelland did this is shown in the middle of figure 10.2. He set up a Person node in the central region of the model and then made a positive connection between this and each fact that was related to that person. The result is similar to setting up all 15 links necessary to represent these facts individually, but requires fewer links. Person nodes were then set up for each of the people in table 10.1 and the necessary links formed to represent everything that is known about them.[2]

The bottom part of figure 10.2 shows the connections between the various nodes building up as information about five of the people is added to the system. This also shows a second element of the model. There are mutually inhibitory connections between each of the exemplar nodes within a knowledge area, There must be some inhibitory links in a network like this where everything is interconnected or the result of activating any node would be that everything in the network would eventually reach its maximum activity level and no differential response to different inputs would be possible. These connections represent the fact that, for example, if someone is in his 20s, he cannot be in either his 30s or his 40s. This fact could have been implemented by making negative connections from each person node to all the things he is not. Building mutually inhibitory links between alternative instance nodes within an area has a similar effect on the performance of the net but greatly reduces the number of connections required. As we shall see, the way that inhibition is built into this network has an important role to play in the way the model runs.

Figure 10.2 The architecture of McClelland's system for storing the information about the Jets and Sharks shown in table 10.1. (a) Each cloud represents an area of knowledge about the members of the two gangs, with the nodes within a cloud representing possible instances. (b) The information about Sam is represented by setting up excitatory connections between the facts that are known about him, This is done by setting up a Person node (the black node in the central circle) and linking this to all the instance nodes which represent his properties. If any one of these nodes becomes active these

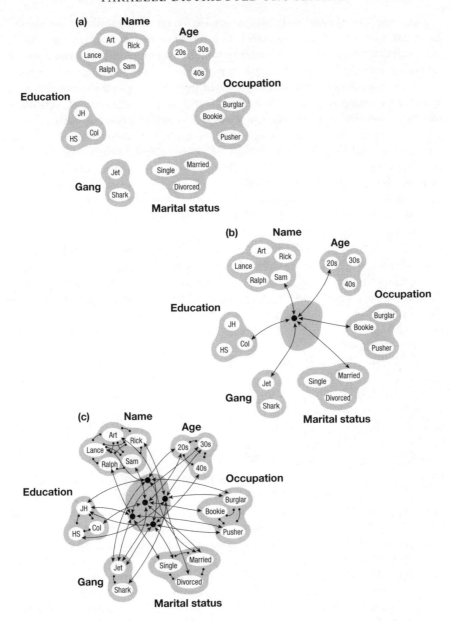

links will ensure that the nodes representing his other characteristics will be activated. (c) The excitatory connections necessary to represent all the information about five members of the gang have been entered. Inhibitory connections (links with filled circles on their ends) have been set up between competing instances nodes within each area of knowledge. When the model runs, any node which has a positive activity level will inhibit any other node to which it is connected by one of these links. (Based on McClelland 1981.)

191

(2) *Running the network*. The nodes are the processing units of the model. Each has an activity level associated with it. When the model runs, each node passes activity to all the other nodes to which it is connected. The input to the receiving node is the product of the activity level of the sending node and the weight of the connection between them. In this simple model the weight of all positive connections between nodes is +1 and that of negative connections is −1.[3] So, when the model runs, every node which has a positive activity level tries to increase the activity level of every node to which it has a positive connection, and to reduce the activity of every node to which it has a negative connection. The net input of each node is determined by summing these negative and positive inputs. The net input is then converted by an activation function to an activity level. The activation function used by McClelland had the same effect as a sigmoid function, namely, limiting the maximum value which the activity level could reach, and slowing the change in activity level with changes in net input as the unit's activity level approached its maximum value. In a single processing cycle the activity level of each unit is computed by summing its inputs and converting these to an activity level with the activation function. On the next cycle these new activity levels are used to compute the new net inputs to each unit, and thus their new activity level. This is continued until the net reaches a steady state. That is, until each node in the network reaches a constant activity level.

(3) *Retrieval from the database*. To test the memory performance of this system we ask it a question such as 'Can you remember the name of a pusher?' This is done by activating the *Pusher* node in **Occupation** and waiting to see which unit becomes active in the **Name** area as activity passes round the network. The activity of all nodes starts at a level of −0.1. Activity of the *Pusher* node increases the activity level of all nodes to which it has a positive connection and decreases the activity of all those to which it has a negative connection. Once the activity level of a node rises above 0 it excites all the nodes to which it has a positive connection and inhibits all those to which it has a negative connection. Eventually the system reaches a steady state in which the activity level of each node is constant, either because it has reached its maximum or minimum permitted value, or because its negative and positive inputs are exactly balanced.[4] The **Name** node which is most strongly activated when steady state is reached is the system's answer to the question.

Does such a system behave like human memory? Apart from being able to retrieve the information it had been given directly, by answering such questions as 'What does Fred do?', anyone who knew these people would find it easy to answer questions like 'Do you know the name of a pusher?' or 'What are the Jets like?' These are the sort of questions which it is difficult to answer with a localist memory store organised like table 10.1. Will this distributed, connectionist memory system find them any easier?

With the aid of the bottom part of figure 10.2 it is possible to get some idea of what happens when the system runs. To see what answer the system will retrieve when it is asked: 'Can you remember the name of a pusher?' the *Pusher* node is activated. This activity passes along all the connections from the *Pusher* node. So the *Ralph* and *Art* **Person** nodes become excited because there is a positive connection to them from *Pusher*. (In the real model all the **Person** nodes of pushers would be excited. For simplicity we will just follow two of them.) The *Bookie* and *Burglar* nodes become inhibited because there are negative connections to them from *Pusher*. In the next processing cycle the *Ralph* **Name**, *Jet*, *30s*, *JH*, *Single* and *Pusher* nodes are excited by the *Ralph* **Person** node, and the *Art* **Name**, *Jet*, *40s*, *JH*, *Single* and *Pusher* nodes become excited by the *Art* **Person** node. At each succeeding cycle every node which is active influences every node to which it is connected by an amount which depends on its activity level and in a direction which depends on whether the connection between them is excitatory or inhibitory. So, for example, the fact that the *30s* node is excited by the *Ralph* **Person** node will in turn cause excitation of all the **Person** nodes connected to *30s*, and inhibition of the *20s* and *40s* **Age** nodes. At the same time the excitation of the *40s* **Age** node by the *Art* **Person** node may be sufficient to overcome this and cause excitation of all **Person** nodes connected to *40s* and the inhibition of the *30s* and *20s* **Age** nodes. After several processing cycles the activity level of every node in the system is being influenced by a mixture of positive and negative inputs. Obviously it soon becomes impossible to keep track of the patterns of excitation and inhibition and predict whether the system will reach a stable state, and if so, what will be excited and what depressed. The only way to find out what the system will do in response to stimulation of any of its nodes is to run a computer simulation of the whole system.

It should now be clear that a connectionist memory system is totally unlike a conventional memory such as a computer filing system. In a conventional system independent pieces of information are stored separately. When a specific piece of information is accessed, it and it alone is retrieved. But in a distributed connectionist system, an attempt to extract any information from the system leads to a flow of excitation and inhibition throughout the system to everything which has any relation to this information. This results in many different nodes becoming active. What is retrieved is the information which corresponds to the most active node(s) once this flow has stabilised. If one is accustomed to information retrieval from a conventional, non-connectionist system such as a telephone directory, this might seem very odd. If you looked up Tom Brown's number in a connectionist telephone directory the number retrieved would be influenced by the entries of everyone with a similar name or a similar number to Tom's. This would not be useful. You do not want the number retrieved to be influenced by the fact that there happens to be someone called Tim Brown who has a telephone number quite unlike Tom's. You want the information stored at the location with the address 'Tom Brown' and nothing else. But the interference which a connectionist system allows during retrieval between related items of stored information turns out to have some interesting and useful properties.

(4) *Content-addressable memory in Jets and Sharks.* To see whether this memory system allows access by content, we can ask it the question 'Do you know the name of a pusher?' To do this we activate the *Pusher* node, leave it on, and see which **Name** nodes become activated. Figure 10.3 shows the activity level of three of the **Name** nodes as a function of the number of processing cycles for which the system has been allowed to run. All the pushers names initially become activated. Most of them, like *Oliver*, quickly return to their resting level. But *Fred* and *Nick* both become increasingly activated. After about 50 cycles *Fred* starts to dominate and soon the system enters a stable state with *Fred* activated and all the other names back at their resting level. The system answers the question with the reply: 'Err . . . Fred.' So, unlike the storage system of table 10.1, this system does allow information to be retrieved when it has been accessed by content rather than address.

The relative activity of the name *Fred* compared to the name *Nick* over the last 50 cycles demonstrates an important characteristic of models with mutual inhibition between competing responses. When alternatives are equally activated they inhibit each other equally and everything is balanced. But once one gets ahead it inhibits the others more than they inhibit it. This reduces their

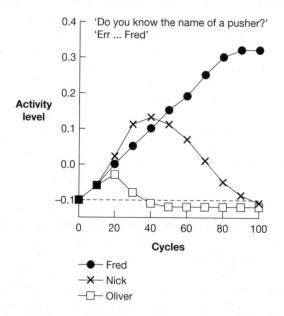

Figure 10.3 To see how the system responds to the question, the *Pusher* node in the **Occupation** area is held On and activity flows from here through the system. The initial activity level of all nodes is set to –0.1. The activity level of three of the nodes in the Name area is plotted as a function of the number of cycles of activity passing around the system.

activity and thus the extent to which they inhibit the one which is ahead. So it becomes more active and inhibits the others yet more. This rapidly results in the one that is a little more active consolidating its position in the lead and completely inhibiting the alternatives. The effect is sometimes referred to as 'the rich get richer' or 'winner takes all'.

Building positive feedback into the system in this way makes it likely that the system will quickly come to a definite conclusion, even if the difference between the evidence favouring one alternative rather than the other is small. But it makes the decision process vulnerable to noise. A random disturbance may be magnified and treated as a signal. This would generally be considered a drawback in a decision making system but it has one useful consequence. Figure 10.3 suggests that the system would always answer the question 'Do you know a pusher?' with the reply 'Fred'. If so, it would be an indifferent model of human memory. People would give a different answer to this question on different occasions, or if asked for an alternative answer, could provide the names of other pushers. It is straightforward to achieve this response variability with the model. If random noise is added to the starting activity levels the system will produce a different answer. Positive feedback ensures that a node that gets ahead is likely to consolidate its advantage. So a small change in starting conditions, or during processing, can make a radical difference to the outcome. Figure 10.4 shows the result of setting the initial activity level of Nick's **Person** node to −0.07 rather than −0.1 before activating the *Pusher*

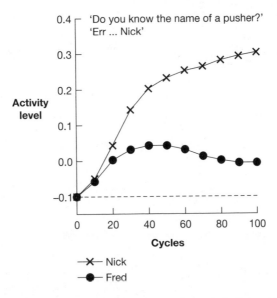

Figure 10.4 The effect of adding noise to the activity levels before asking the question. The initial activity of Nick's **Person** node is set to −0.07 rather than −0.1.

node. Now the system answers the question 'Do you know a pusher?' with the reply 'Err . . . Nick'. Given that we know the brain is a noisy system, it is appropriate to model it with an inherently noisy network. The result is the human characteristic of variability in response to the same input.

(5) *Typicality effects in memory retrieval.* If the information about the Jets and Sharks was stored in the manner of table 10.1 it would not be possible to retrieve the names of pushers directly, because 'pusher' is not part of the address. But the information could be extracted by sampling addresses at random and giving the names of ones that turned out to contain the information *Pusher* under **Occupation**. In that case any pusher would have an equal chance of being produced as an example. But this is not how the network behaves when asked to name pushers. As figure 10.3 shows, it is more likely to retrieve the names of some pushers than others. It might retrieve Fred or Nick, but it is unlikely to produce Oliver's name.

Human memory retrieval has the same characteristic (see, for example, Rosch 1975). If you ask people to produce a list of birds (the equivalent of asking the network 'Tell me the names of all the pushers you know') most people will include Robin in their list but fewer will include Chicken. Some information is more easily available for retrieval from memory than other information from the same category. Since the answers which are most likely to be given to this question are the names of birds which would be rated as *typical* examples of the category, this result is called, unsurprisingly, a typicality effect.

The reason why the network is likely to retrieve Fred rather than Oliver in reply to the request for the name of a pusher can be seen in table 10.2. Pushers are more likely to be a Jet than a Shark, they tend to be in their 30s, to have been educated to High School level and to be single. So the **Person** nodes which get excited when *Pusher* is activated send more activity to the *Jet, 30s, HS* and *Single* nodes than to other nodes.

Table 10.2 The pushers

Gang	*Jets* 5	*Sharks* 4		
Age	*20s* 3	*30s* 5	*40s* 1	
Education	*JH* 2	*HS* 4	*College* 3	
Marital status	*Single* 5	*Married* 3	*Divorced* 1	
The prototypical pusher:	*Jet*	*30s*	*HS*	*Single*
Fred	Jet	20s	HS	Single
Nick	Shark	30s	HS	Single
Oliver	Shark	30s	Col	Married

The mutual inhibition between alternative instance nodes with an area means that *Single*, *HS* and *Jet* become more activated, and *Married*, *College* and *Shark* become less activated. This in turn means that the **Person** nodes connected to *Single*, *HS* and *Jet* get supported, and the **Name** nodes connected to these become activated but the **Person** nodes and hence the **Name** nodes connected to *Married*, *College* and *Shark* do not. Fred is a single, High School educated, Jet; Oliver is a married, College educated, Shark. So, as a result of Fred's similarity to a *prototypical* pusher, his **Person** and **Name** nodes become more and more active as processing continues. Oliver's dissimilarity to the prototypical pusher means that his become less and less active. The result is that when the system is asked to think of a pusher, Fred's name is retrieved but Oliver's is not. If asked to generate instances from a category, distributed connectionist nets automatically generate typical instances, just like people.

Constraint satisfaction in connectionist networks

When activity flows through a connectionist network in response to an input, each unit influences the state of all the units to which it is connected. If the connection weight is positive the sending unit tries to put the receiving unit into the same state of activity as itself; if the connection weight is negative it tries to put it into the opposite state. Since all activity changes are determined by these influences, each input can be seen as setting constraints on the final state (i.e. set of unit activities) which the system can settle into. When the system runs, the activities of individual units will change in a way which increases the number of these constraints which are satisfied. Thus connectionist networks are said to work by *constraint satisfaction*.

The ideal final state would be a set of activities for the individual units where all the constraints were satisfied. The network would then be stable because no unit would be trying to change the state of any of the units to which it was connected. This ideal solution is unlikely to exist because most units are connected to some units which are trying to increase its activity and others which are trying to reduce it. There is no way of satisfying both. But if the system can find a state in which any change in the activity levels of the units reduces the overall number of satisfied constraints, it will stop changing activities. That is, it will have found a stable state. For most networks there will be many possible stable states with a different pattern of activity, each one of which will be reached from a different pattern of input activity. The realisation that these stable states could be viewed as the network's memories – that is, the set of possible states that it could reach in response to different inputs – was an important step in the history of connectionism.

In a conventional connectionist network where knowledge is distributed across many units, it is difficult to follow constraint satisfaction at work because it is difficult to see what role any particular unit is playing. In Jets and Sharks it is easy, because the concept coding is localist rather than distributed. Each node stands for an identifiable concept. The constraints on the system are the various facts in table 10.1, each one of which is represented by one of the links in the network. The fact that Clyde is a Jet in his 40s means that if either of the nodes representing these concepts is activated it will try to activate the other, and inhibit the *Shark, 30s* and *20s* nodes. The fact that there are also both Jets and Sharks in their 30s and 20s means that a whole set of other, mutually contradictory constraints are influencing the way that the system changes the activity level of the units in response to any particular pattern of input. The key point is that the changes in activity on each cycle will increase the number of constraints which are satisfied.

A system which works by constraint satisfaction has a number of desirable characteristics for modelling human cognition. The main one is that it allows a decision to be reached by a consensus of evidence, a reasonable fit between input and memory, rather than requiring an exact match. We have already seen this as a virtue in any model of human cognition because the nature of the nervous system requires a degree of fault tolerance in the information processing system (remember figure 10.1). It is also desirable because of the nature of the input which the cognitive system has to work with in the real world. Consider what happens when you listen to one particular speaker in a crowded room. The signals arriving at your ear contain the sounds made by the person you are listening to, but superimposed on these are a jumble of sounds from different speakers, the whole thing obliterated from time to time by bursts of laughter and other noises. And yet, most of the time, what you perceive is words. The signal you receive bears *some* relationship to a proto-typical representation of the word that you perceive but will be far from an exact match. The fact that you *perceive* words shows that the word recognition system must be looking for a *best fit* to the word patterns it has stored rather than for an exact match. This effect has been studied in the laboratory with an experimental paradigm called 'phoneme restoration'. In the original study by Warren (1970) the sound /s/ was removed from the word *'legislature'* and replaced with a cough. People then listened to a sentence containing the word *'legi<cough>lature'* and were asked what they heard. People reported the sentence correctly, adding that there was a cough before or after the word 'legislature'. In other words, the perceptual system does not necessarily give a veridical account of the stimulus, it gives a plausible *interpretation* of the input, given its knowledge of English words.

The same effect can be seen in the Jets and Sharks system. Figure 10.5 shows what happens when the system is probed with a variety of retrieval cues. The filled circles show what happens when the net is asked: 'Do you know a Shark, in his 20s, who went to High School, who is single and a burglar?' (i.e. the *Shark, 20s, HS, Single* and *Burglar* nodes are all switched On). The circles joined by solid lines show the activity of Ken's **Name** node and the circles joined by dashed lines the activity of the next most activated **Name** node. Not surprisingly, the net answers 'Ken' quickly.

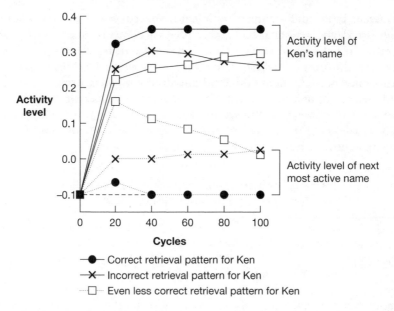

Figure 10.5 Constraint satisfaction in operation. Given a correct description of Ken as a retrieval cue, the system retrieves Ken's name. Given progressively less accurate retrieval cues, which are, nevertheless, closer to a description of him than to anyone else in the database, it still produces his name. Input activity levels:

(●) *Shark* = 1; *20s* = 1; *HS* = 1; *Single* = 1; *Burglar* = 1.
(✖) *Shark* = 1; *20s* = 1; *JH* = 1; *Single* = 1; *Burglar* = 1.
(□) *Shark* = 1; *20s* = 1; *JH* = 1; *Single* = 1; *Burglar* = 0.5; *Pusher*=0.25; *Bookie*=0.25.

This is the equivalent of presenting a listener with a clear and unambiguous example of the word 'legislature' and asking her what word she heard. The crosses show what happens when *High School* is changed to *Junior High* in the input activity pattern. This input is no longer an accurate description of anyone in the database (the equivalent of presenting a listener with 'legi<cough>lature'). A system which tried to find an exact match to the input would fail. There is no person who matches that input pattern in the database. But the network has no problem. It takes slightly longer to respond (i.e. Ken's name takes more time to become activated, and does not reach such a high level) but *Ken* still comes out as the clearly preferred item retrieved from memory. The squares show what happens with an even more ambiguous input. In this the *Bookie* and *Pusher* nodes have all been activated as well as *Burglar*. As long as the input pattern is closer to a description of Ken than to any alternative, the system makes a clear decision in favour of the response 'Ken'.[5]

The fact that connectionist systems work by constraint satisfaction is the reason why they exhibit fault tolerance. No part of the input uniquely determines the outcome. The network's response is the best fit it can make between the current input and information it has acquired in the past. It would be possible to devise a system, based on address + contents information storage like table 10.1, which, if given an input that failed to match any stored information, could compute a best fit. However, this would be a time consuming process once possible inputs achieved any degree of complexity. The parallel distributed computation in the Jets and Sharks database automatically computes a best fit between input and stored information. It would continue to do so whatever the degree of complexity of the patterns describing the individual entries without taking any more time.

There is no distinction between 'memory' and 'processing' in connectionist models

One general point to note about distributed representations is that they blur the distinction between memory and processing. Traditional models of cognitive processes often distinguish between 'memory', a store of learnt information, and 'processing', operations which enable the system to interpret incoming information. The processing operations may use information from memory, but the conceptual distinction is clear. Indeed, in many models this is made explicit with separate parts of the model labelled 'memory' and 'processor'. Such models exploit the analogy to conventional digital computers where there are independent systems for storing information and for processing it.

There is no such distinction in connectionist models. All the information which the network has – its memory – is stored in the weights of the connections between units. All the processing that the net can do is determined by the same set of weights.

Problems for distributed representations

We have emphasised the advantage of distributed representations over localist representations in allowing the system some degree of resistance to damage and tolerance of noisy inputs. Given the unreliable nature of the matter which the brain uses for computation, it seems inevitable that it would use distributed representations. However, there are two properties of human memory which would not seem to be easy to account for with connectionist models but which would be expected with localist information storage: First, the addition of new information does not necessarily cause the loss of old. Second, learning can be immediate.

In a distributed system, any new information has to be added to the connections which already carry the system's current store of knowledge. To add the new information the strength of connections must be changed. If this is done in a single trial, addition of new information is likely to lead to some loss of old information. In a localist system, in contrast, the addition of new information is no problem. It is simply added to new storage locations and does not affect old information. At this point, however, we will just suggest that at an intuitive level there are different sorts of human learning.

At one extreme it seems clear that some sorts of knowledge can be acquired immediately, without interfering with other information. All young chess players are shown the smothered mate sequence with a queen sacrificed to a rook on g1 followed by mate of the king on h1 by a knight moving from h3 to f2. If you understand chess you only have to see this sequence once to remember it for ever, despite the fact that you may never have an opportunity to use it in a game. Similarly, if you knew anything about the British ex-Prime Minister Mrs Thatcher, and were told that her nickname at school was 'Bossy Roberts', you would be unlikely to forget it. A novel piece of information which you find interesting or amusing, in a domain where you already have sufficient knowledge to understand its significance, is likely to be remembered after a single presentation. And it can be retrieved as a specific item of information in future, independent of any other facts in the database. It is difficult to believe that such acquisition is accompanied by the loss of any other information. Quick, cost-free, addition of new information to existing databases characterises certain sorts of human knowledge acquisition. It is natural with localist representation of knowledge – you just add another entry to the database. But it is difficult to see how it can happen with a distributed system.

At the other extreme there are many areas of knowledge acquisition, such learning to play tennis or learning to talk, where acquisition of new knowledge is gradual, and accompanied by the modification or loss of previous patterns. As your tennis serve improves or you learn to pronounce the language correctly you *want* to lose some aspects of your old response patterns because they were inaccurate. Later it is difficult to recall when a specific piece of information was added to the database. Such a pattern, where new information is inextricably interwoven with old, occurs naturally with a distributed system, but not with a localist one. Distinctions between different sorts of knowledge representation occur in many models of the cognitive system. Most of the connectionist learning algorithms we will look at are more appropriate for modelling the latter sort of acquisition and representation than the former.

Notes

1 The Jets and Sharks memory system is not implemented in **tlearn** but its properties and examples described in the text can be explored using the **iac** program in McClelland and Rumelhart (1988).

2 It might seem that the Person node corresponds to the address for the information just as the name Sam does in table 10.1. When information is retrieved from the net the Person node cannot be accessed, so it cannot be used as a retrieval address. It is just a convenience which reduces the number of connections required to set up the model and makes the operation of the model easier to follow.

3　There is no gradual learning phase in Jets and Sharks. Facts are given to the model complete. Therefore the weights do not develop as knowledge is acquired as they would in a conventional connectionist model. The way that information is entered into this system is an example of Hebbian learning. If two things are mutually consistent (e.g. being in your 20s and being a burglar) a positive connection (via the appropriate Person node) is made between them. If two things are mutually inconsistent (e.g. being in your 20s and 30s) a negative connection is made between them.

4　In McClelland's model the activity of each unit also decays on each cycle by an amount proportional to its activity level. This affects the dynamic behaviour of the net but to understand why the net reaches a steady state it can be considered as another negative input contributing to the balance between positive and negative inputs to each unit.

5　The interaction of information in the Jets and Sharks system produces some strange and unpredictable results which can only be appreciated by playing with the **iac** model. For example, figure 10.5 shows that if you wait long enough the *less* accurate description of Ken produces a stronger preference for his name than the more accurate description.

References

McClelland, J. (1981) 'Retrieving general and specific information from stored knowledge of specifics', *Proceedings of the Third Annual Meeting of the Cognitive Science Society* 170–2.

McClelland, J.L. and Rumelhart, D.E. (1985) 'Distributed memory and the representation of general and specific information', *Journal of Experimental Psychology: General* 114: 159–97.

—— (1988) *Explorations in Parallel Distributed Processing*. Cambridge, Mass.: MIT Press.

Morrell, F. (1972) 'Integrative properties of parastriate neurons', in A. Karczmar and J. Eccles (eds), *Brain and Human Behavior*. Berlin: Springer–Verlag.

Rosch, E. (1975) 'Cognitive representations of semantic categories', *Journal of Experimental Psychology: General* 104: 192–223.

Warren, R. (1970) 'Perceptual restoration of missing speech sounds', *Science* 167: 392–3.

PART II

COMMONSENSE
PSYCHOLOGY

INTRODUCTION

Each of the four pictures of the mind explored in Part I offers different answers to the interface problem (the problem of explaining how the ways we make sense of each other by using the basic categories and generalizations of commonsense psychology interface with the type of explanations offered lower down in the hierarchy of explanation). The differences between the four pictures of the mind are at least in part a function of differences in how they view commonsense psychology and the constraints that its success (or otherwise) imposes upon a general account of the mind. The papers in Part II all focus on how to understand commonsense psychology and the practices of explanation and prediction that make use of it.

The papers in IIA present two very different perspectives on the relation between belief–desire psychology and the explanation of behavior. Whereas Jerry Fodor argues that the concepts of commonsense psychology are indispensable for psychological explanation, and uses this as an argument for the representational theory of mind (see also IC above), Stephen Stich finds a fundamental incompatibility between belief–desire psychology and what he takes to be the guiding principle of psychological explanation (the principle of the autonomy of the psychological). In IIB the papers explore the relation between commonsense psychology and mental representation. The principal issue here is whether the explanatory and predictive power of commonsense psychology stands or falls with propositional attitudes being realized in discrete physical states that can enter into causal interactions. The papers in IIC are concerned primarily with how we understand the nature of commonsense psychological explanation. Should we take it to be essentially theory-like, as assumed by most of the papers in IIA and IIB? Or is psychological explanation and prediction more a matter of simulation and empathetic understanding than of subsuming behavior and mental states under lawlike generalizations.

IIA Commonsense psychology and explaining behavior

What role does commonsense psychology play in explaining behavior? This question can be taken in a number of different ways. It might be interpreted as a question about our ordinary, everyday practices of making sense of other people.

On this interpretation, one would be asking how deeply the propositional attitudes are implicated in our ordinary, everyday explanatory and predictive practices. It is a widely held view among philosophers that propositional attitudes concepts play a very fundamental role in social understanding and social coordination (understood as activities at the personal level), and this view is shared by both of the authors in this subsection. But we can ask about the role of commonsense psychology in a very different way. We can ask about the role that propositional attitude psychology will play in a *scientific* understanding of behavior. How likely is it that a complete scientific theory of behavior will make appeal to beliefs and desires?

In "The Persistence of the Attitudes", the first chapter his book *Psycho-semantics*, **Jerry Fodor** makes an eloquent case for the ineliminability of propositional attitude psychology. Fodor suggests that commonsense belief–desire psychology is a powerful implicit theory on which we continually rely and that rarely lets us down. He notes that the generalizations of commonsense psychology have built into them riders to the effect that they apply only *ceteris paribus* (all other things being equal), but claims that this is typical of generalizations in the special sciences (such as geology or economics) and does not in any way limit their explanatory power. According to Fodor, the centrality of propositional attitude psychology in our lives, and our inability to imagine an alternative to it, means that any scientific psychology will have to be, as he puts it, commonsensical about the attitudes. Any satisfactory scientific psychology will have to postulate states that have three basic features that are defining features of the propositional attitudes. First, those states must be *semantically evaluable* (that is, they must be the sort of thing that can be true or false). Second, they must have *causal powers*, and in particular they must be the sort of thing that can stand as causal antecedents of behavior. Third, the implicit generalizations of commonsense psychology must be largely true of them.

Fodor argues that these three requirements can be jointly satisfied only by the *representational theory of mind.* The basic states in the representational theory of mind are symbol structures that can be thought of as sentences in the language of thought (Mentalese). These symbol structures can be thought of both syntactically and semantically. From a semantic point of view sentences in the language of thought are entities that have representational content (they represent states of affairs in the world, and of course states of affairs that do not actually hold). From a syntactic point of view, sentences in the language of thought are physical entities that have a certain structure corresponding to the structure of what they represent. By the same token, transitions between sentences in the language of thought can be viewed either syntactically or semantically. Viewed syntactically, these transitions are causal sequences of symbol structures, while viewed semantically they are, in effect, processes of reasoning. Since Fodor takes the language of thought to be a formal language much like the first-order predicate calculus, he appeals to metalogical results to argue that the semantics of the language of thought will track the syntax, so that causal sequences of symbol structures at the level of syntax turn out to implement processes of reasoning that respects the semantic relations between the contents of the relevant symbol structures. According to Fodor, the representational theory of mind provides a vindication of commonsense psychology by showing how semantically evaluable states can have causal powers in ways that are consistent with the generalizations of commonsense psychology (which tend to rest upon the semantic relations between the propositional attitude contents).

Stephen Stich's "Autonomous Psychology and the Belief–Desire Thesis" is much more pessimistic than Fodor about the prospects for what he terms the *belief–desire thesis*, which is the thesis that the concepts of belief and desire will play a central role in a complete psychological theory of human behavior. The principal difficulty that Stich identifies for the belief–desire thesis is that it seems to come into conflict with what he takes to be a basic principle governing psychological theorizing. This is the *principle of psychological autonomy*, which holds that any two organisms that are physically identical are *ipso facto* identical with respect to the properties that will be invoked in psychological explanation. Stich claims that this principle plays a regulative role in psychology. It is, he suggests, a methodological principle that guides research and constrains theorizing, rather than being a substantive thesis that might be disproved or rejected in the future.[1] The principle of psychological autonomy (also known as the principle of *methodological solipsism*) needs to be distinguished from the familiar claim that psychological properties supervene upon physical properties, since Stich's whole argument rests upon there being psychological properties (in one sense of "psychological") that do not supervene upon physical properties. What he wants to do is to deny that *those* psychological properties (such as the property of being in a particular belief-state) can have any role to play in scientific psychology.

Stich argues that the principle of psychological autonomy creates difficulties for the belief–desire thesis because the contents of propositional attitudes do not supervene upon physical properties in the way that the principle requires. He gives a number of examples of what he takes to be subjects who are identical with respect to all the properties that might be relevant to psychological explanation but who have different beliefs. All four examples that he discusses exploit the following principle for individuating belief contents: If two belief tokens differ in truth value then they cannot be tokens of the same type (where we can think of two belief tokens counting as tokens of the same type just when they have the same content). Put another way, if two subjects have beliefs with the same content, then their beliefs will always match in truth value. Stich's argument rests upon finding cases where it seems plausible to say that two subjects are type-identical with respect to the properties relevant to psychological explanation, but where the truth-value principle entails that they have different beliefs.

IIB   Commonsense psychology and mental representation

The debate explored in IIA is a debate about the place of commonsense psychology within scientific psychology and cognitive science. It is a debate in which the direction of argument is fundamentally top-down. Arguments about explanation in scientific psychology (such as Fodor's argument that commonsense psychology is ineliminable from scientific psychology, or Stich's argument that scientific psychology individuates states in a fundamentally different way from commonsense psychology) have consequences for how we think about the architecture of cognition. If Fodor is right, for example, then the architecture of cognition is essentially linguistic. But it is also possible to argue in the opposite direction, from claims about cognitive architecture to conclusions about the status of commonsense psychology. The principal issue in this area is the implications of connectionism and neural network models for how we think about propositional attitude psychology – an issue particularly relevant to the neurocomputational picture of the mind (see ID above).

William Ramsey, Stephen Stich, and **Joseph Garon**'s "Connectionism, Eliminativism and the Future of Folk Psychology" makes a conditional claim to the effect that *if* connectionist networks turn out to be accurate models of cognition, *then* we will have to adopt some version of *eliminativism* about the propositional attitudes. As they conceive of it, eliminativism about the propositional attitudes is the claim that there are no such things as beliefs, desires, hopes and fears, and so on. (Note that this is stronger than Stich's claim in "Autonomous Psychology and the Belief–desire Thesis" that propositional attitudes cannot feature in scientific psychology.) Eliminativism about the attitudes is opposed to realism, which Ramsey, Stich, and Garon interpret in a manner much like that proposed by Fodor in "The Persistence of the Attitudes". Realism about the propositional attitudes requires them to be *functionally discrete*, *semantically evaluable*, and *causally efficacious* (i.e. standing in causal relations to other propositional attitudes, to sensory input, and to behavior). Ramsey, Stich, and Garon term this bundle of claims the requirement of *propositional modularity*, which they take to be deeply implicated both in commonsense psychology and in influential paradigms in scientific psychology. In their view, if scientific psychology rejects propositional modularity, then we have no choice but to be eliminativists about the propositional attitudes.

Ramsey, Stich, and Garon see propositional modularity as seriously threatened by a particular class of connectionist networks. These are connectionist networks that are proposed as *models* of cognitive processes (as opposed to hypotheses at the implementational level – see ID above and IIIA below) and that take representations to be *distributed* across a large number of connection weights. In connectionist networks of this type there is no distinct and identifiable symbolic expression that can be identified with a particular propositional attitude. Not only are representations distributed, but individual units within the network cannot be given a symbolic interpretation that would allow them to be mapped onto constituents of a proposition. There is, quite simply, no way of locating propositional attitudes within connectionist networks of the specified type and hence no way in which the requirements of propositional modularity can be met. Ramsey, Stich, and Garon argue that within such networks there are no functionally discrete representations of which one can even ask whether they play a causal role in generating outputs or what their truth-value is. They illustrate this claim with reference to two connectionist models of memory. Their conclusion is that, although the jury remains out on whether cognition is indeed best modeled on connectionist lines, if mental representation does turn out to be distributed in the manner of connectionist networks, then eliminativism about the propositional attitudes is an inescapable consequence.

The force of Ramsey, Stich, and Garon's argument that connectionist models of mental processes are incompatible with realism about the propositional attitudes depends, of course, on the crucial premise that realism requires propositional modularity. **Daniel Dennett** has consistently resisted the inference from the usefulness and accuracy of psychological explanation to the existence of *causally efficacious* internal items corresponding to the beliefs and desires cited in those explanations. What makes a psychological explanation useful and accurate, so the argument for propositional modularity goes, is its truth and that truth consists in correctly identifying the beliefs and desires responsible for generating the behavior in question. Responsibility here is to be understood in causal terms. So we are led to the demand for causally efficacious internal items, generally understood to be neurophysiological states of one kind or another. Dennett's initial resistance to this line of argument focused on the first stage – on the claim that we need to understand the predictive utility of psychological explanations in terms of their truth. At various points in his earlier writings (e.g. Dennett 1981) he developed a position that has struck many as a form of instrumentalism about psychological explanations. This instrumentalism effectively turns the standard argument on its head, maintaining that there is nothing more to the truth of psychological explanations than their predictive utility. Dennett once suggested that all there is to being a believer is behaving in ways that are usefully explicable according to what he called the intentional stance – that is to say, within the personal level framework of commonsense psychology.

More recently Dennett himself has moved away from instrumentalism towards what he calls a "mild realism", which is explored in "Real Patterns". The difference between instrumentalism and mild realism is, in essence, a view about the *truth-aptness* of commonsense psychological explanations. Mild realism permits a more robust sense in which psychological explanations can be evaluated for truth or falsity. Dennett thinks that the truth of belief–desire explanations consists in their tracking genuinely existing patterns in the behavior of the organisms and systems to which those explanations are applied. These patterns, which Dennett calls "real patterns", are not observer-dependent (in the way that ascriptions of propositional attitudes seemed to be on Dennett's earlier instrumentalism). There is a genuine fact of the matter as to whether they hold or not. These independently existing real patterns provide the truth-makers for psychological explanations – they are the beliefs and desires cited in the explanation. And the existence of those patterns is, of course, what makes commonsense psychological explanation and prediction effective. Dennett's real patterns hold over *emergent* properties of intentional agents and cognitive systems. They are patterns in the behavior of the agent or system as a whole and cannot be reduced to, or understood in terms of, the operation of parts of the agent or system. This conception of emergent properties (which Dennett illustrates through an intriguing example inspired by the mathematics of *cellular automata*) is part of what makes Dennett an autonomy theorist and allows him to deny that personal level facts about the behavior of the system as a whole can be understood in terms of facts about inner states or modules at the subpersonal level.

IIC   The machinery of commonsense psychology: Theory or simulation?

The problems explored in IIA and IIB can be spelled out on a very generic under-standing of commonsense psychology. The discussion up to now has understood commonsense psychology simply in terms of a commitment to practices of expla-nation and prediction that invoke propositional attitudes. But there is a number of different ways of understanding those practices of explanation and prediction. In particular, there is an extensive debate about whether making commonsense psychological predictions and explanations involves deploying a primitive psycho-logical theory, or whether it should be understood more as an exercise in simulation and empathetic understanding ("putting oneself in someone else's shoes").

Paul Churchland's "Folk Psychology and the Explanation of Human Behavior" is a robust presentation of the theoretical interpretation of commonsense psych-ology. Churchland argues that commonsense psychology is a theory in the sense that it (a) consists of laws, (b) supports causal explanations, and (c) is used to explain, predict and manipulate a certain domain of phenomena (i.e. human social interactions). He responds to a number of objections that have been raised to the theoretical view of commonsense psychology, arguing that commonsense psychology is no more subject to *ceteris paribus* clauses than any other "folk" theory (such as folk mechanics or folk biology) and that processes of simulation and empathetic understanding are not really alternatives to the theory theory but rather themselves depend upon a theoretical understanding of one's own psychology.

The position that Churchland defends, however, differs in a number of important respects from standard presentations of what has come to be known as the *theory theory*. The theory theory is often presented in conjunction with a *deductive-nomological* model of explanation, so that commonsense psychological explanations and predictions are taken to be deductive inferences from univer-sally quantified general sentences that state laws (in conjunction, of course, with a statement of the particular circumstances of the case in question, making clear why it falls under the law). Churchland rejects this conception of commonsense psychological laws as universal generalizations that might be represented in the brain, for example, as sentences in a language of thought. This rejection is part and parcel of his rejection of the deductive-nomological model of scientific expla-nation, and the model of knowledge-representation on which it rests, in favor of a different model, one inspired by connectionist models of cognitive processes. Churchland suggests that we replace the idea that a law, whether a scientific law or a folk-theoretic law, is represented in the form of a universal generalization about things or events of a particular type with the idea that it is represented through prototypical examples of the relevant thing or event. Instead of a generalization to the effect that all Fs are G, we have a representation of a prototypical F that is G in the context of a similarity metric that explains what is to count as relevant similarity to the prototype. As Churchland points out in the final section of the paper, the idea that theoretical understanding is represented in this way goes hand in hand with the idea that information is represented in the brain in much the same way as it is in a connectionist network.

Supporters of the simulationist approach to commonsense psychology challenge the theoretical understanding of how our knowledge of commonsense psychology is represented and applied. Simulationists think that we explain and predict the behavior of other agents by projecting ourselves into the situation of the person whose behavior is to be explained/predicted and then using our own mind as a model of theirs. Suppose that we have a reasonable sense of the beliefs and desires that it would be appropriate to attribute to someone else in a particular situation, so that we understand both how they view the situation and what they want to achieve in it. And suppose that we want to find out how they will behave. Instead of using generalizations about how mental states typically feed into behavior to predict how that person will behave, the simulationist thinks that we use our own decision-making processes to run a simulation of what would happen if we ourselves had those beliefs and desires. We do this by running our decision-making processes *off-line*, so that instead of generating an action directly they generate a description of an action or an intention to act in a certain way. We then use this description to predict the behavior of the person in question.

Alvin Goldman's "Interpretation Psychologized" suggests that there are two dominant philosophical models of social understanding and interpretation. The first, which he terms the rationality approach and identifies with Donald Davidson and Daniel Dennett, is governed by a principle of charity to the effect that one should attribute psychological states to an agent in a way that will maximize the rationality of his behavior. Goldman's objection to the rationality approach is that the notion of rationality is poorly specified and in most of the obvious ways of specifying it (as determined, for example, by the basic principles of deductive logic and probability theory), it often makes sense to attribute irrational combinations of attitudes to other people. The second dominant model is the theory theory, which he sees as closely allied with philosophical functionalism (see IB above). Goldman objects to the theory theory on the grounds that it is irremediably vague (he particularly objects to *ceteris paribus* clauses); that the laws that tend to be cited as examples of commonsense psychological laws are at best highly inaccurate; and that there is no reason to think that there is a single set of psychological laws deployed by all who participate successfully in social interactions.

In opposition to these two models, Goldman offers a version of the simulation approach and argues that his version of the simulation approach to social understanding is free of the problems that arise for both of the dominant models. In the case of common probabilistic fallacies (such as the gambler's fallacy, where someone judges that a fair coin is more likely to come down tails after a long series of heads), for example, the fact that I am as likely to be prey to this fallacy as the person whose behavior I am predicting means that I am likely to correctly attribute the fallacious belief in just the circumstances in which the person really has it. Goldman suggests also that the simulation approach is supported by research into children with autism – in particular by studies identifying strong correlations between impairments in social understanding and poverty in pretend play (which he sees as involving the same mechanisms that are deployed in simulation).

The version of simulationism espoused by Goldman still requires the *explicit* attribution of beliefs and desires to the person being simulated. On this view, in order to simulate someone, I need to form explicit judgments about how they represent the relevant situation and what they want to achieve in that situation. These judgments serve as the input to the simulation process and I reach them by thinking introspectively about the beliefs and desires I myself would have in a particular situation and then making an analogical inference about what the person being simulated will do. According to the *radical simulationism* proposed by **Robert Gordon** in "Simulation Without Introspection or Inference from Me to You", the process of simulation does not require either introspection or analogical inference. In fact, simulation does not even require the simulator to possess concepts of the propositional attitudes. According to Gordon, instead of coming explicitly to the view that the person whose behavior I am trying to predict has a certain belief (say, the belief that *p*), what I need to do is to imagine how the world would appear from his or her point of view. The distinction is between, on the one hand, forming a belief about how another person represents the world (a belief with the content that the person believes that *p*) and, on the other, holding a belief about the world in one's imagination (a belief with the content simply that *p*). The simulator is thinking about the world *from the perspective of the person being simulated*, rather than thinking about their beliefs, desires, and other psychological states.

In response to the question of where the simulator obtains the inputs for the process of simulation, Gordon offers an account based upon what he calls *ascent routines*. Gordon denies that we identify our own beliefs by inward-directed processes of introspection. Instead, he suggests, we establish whether or not we believe that *p* by asking whether it is the case that *p*. This basic method is, he thinks, just as suited to finding out about another person's beliefs as it is to finding out about one's own. If I am simulating someone else, then I have *recentered* my own perspective on the world onto theirs, and from that recentered perspective I can ask the question of whether or not it is the case that *p*. This gives me what is in effect information about what that person believes, but I obtain that information without deploying the concept of belief.

Notes

1   Note that the principle of psychological autonomy stresses a different type of autonomy from that pressed by proponents of the autonomous mind. Autonomy theorists frequently reject psychological autonomy, and vice versa.

FURTHER READING

Useful collections/anthologies

Carruthers, P. and Smith, P.K. (eds) (1996) *Theories of Theories of Mind*, Cambridge: Cambridge University Press.

Davies, M.K. and Stone, T. (eds) (1995a) *Folk Psychology: The Theory of Mind Debate*, Oxford: Blackwell.

Davies, M.K. and Stone, T. (eds) (1995b) *Mental Simulation*, Oxford: Blackwell.

Greenwood, J. (ed.) (1991) *The Future of Folk Psychology*, Cambridge: Cambridge University Press.

IIA   Commonsense psychology and explaining behavior

Baker, L.R. (1988) *Saving Belief*, Princeton, N.J.: Princeton University Press.

Churchland, P.M. (1981) "Eliminative materialism and the propositional attitudes", *Journal of Philosophy* 78(2) 67–90. Reprinted in W. Lycan (ed.), *Mind and Cognition: A Reader*, Oxford: Blackwell, 2nd edition 1999.

Horgan, T. and Woodward, J. (1985) "Folk psychology is here to stay", *Philosophical Review* 94: 197–226. Reprinted in W. Lycan (ed.), *Mind and Cognition: A Reader*, Oxford: Blackwell, 2nd edition 1999.

Kitcher, P. (1984) "In defense of intentional psychology", *Journal of Philosophy* 81: 89–106.

Stich, S. (1983) *From Folk Psychology to Cognitive Science*, Cambridge, Mass.: MIT Press.

IIB   Commonsense psychology and mental representation

Baker, L.R. (1995) *Explaining Attitudes*, Cambridge: Cambridge University Press. Particularly Ch. 6.

Clark, A. (1996) "Dealing in futures: Folk psychology and the role of representations in cognitive science", in R.N. McCauley (ed.), *The Churchlands and their Critics*, Oxford: Blackwell.

Dennett, D. (1981) "True believers: The intentional strategy and why it works", in A.F. Heath (ed.), *Scientific Explanation*, Oxford: Oxford University Press. Reprinted in W. Lycan (ed.), *Mind and Cognition: A Reader*, Oxford: Blackwell, 2nd edition 1999.

Haugeland, J. (1993) "Pattern and being", in B. Dahlbom (ed.) *Dennett and His Critics*, Oxford: Blackwell. Reprinted in *Having Thought: Essays in the Metaphysics of Mind*, Cambridge, Mass.: Harvard University Press (1998).

Heil, J. 1990. "Being Indiscrete", in Greenwood (1991).

Smolensky, P. (1995a) "On the projectable predicates of connectionist psychology: A case for belief", in C. MacDonald and G. MacDonald (eds), *Connectionism: Debates on Psychological Explanation*, Oxford: Blackwell.

IIC   The machinery of commonsense psychology:
theory or simulation?

Currie, G. (1996) "Simulation, theory-theory, and the evidence from autism", in Carruthers and Smith (1996).

Heal, J. (1986) "Replication and functionalism", in J. Butterfield (ed.), *Language, Mind and Logic*, Cambridge: Cambridge University Press, 135–50. Reprinted in Davies and Stone (1995a).

Nichols, S., Stich, S., and Leslie, A. (1995) "Choice effects and the ineffectiveness of simulation", *Mind & Language* 10(4): 437–45.

Morton, A. (2003) *The Importance of Being Understood: Folk Psychology as Ethics*, London: Routledge.

Stich, S.P. and Nichols, S. (1992) "Folk psychology: Simulation or tacit theory?", *Mind & Language* 7(1): 35–71. Reprinted in Davies and Stone (1995a).

IIA

COMMONSENSE PSYCHOLOGY AND EXPLAINING BEHAVIOR

11

J. Fodor, "The Persistence of the Attitudes"

A Midsummer Night's Dream, act 3, scene 2.
Enter Demetrius and Hermia.

Dem. O, why rebuke you him that loves you so?
Lay breath so bitter on your bitter foe.

Herm. Now I but chide, but I should use thee worse;
For thou, I fear, hast given me cause to curse.
If thou hast slain Lysander in his sleep,
Being o'er shoes in blood, plunge in the deep,
And kill me too.
The sun was not so true unto the day
As he to me: would he have stol'n away
From sleeping Hermia? I'll believe as soon
This whole earth may be bor'd; and that the moon
May through the centre creep, and so displease
Her brother's noontide with the antipodes.
It cannot be but thou hast murder'd him;
So should a murderer look; so dead, so grim.

Very nice. And also very *plausible*; a convincing (though informal) piece of implicit, nondemonstrative, theoretical inference.

Here, leaving out a lot of lemmas, is how the inference must have gone: Hermia has reason to believe herself beloved of Lysander. (Lysander has told her that he loves her – repeatedly and in elegant iambics – and inferences from how people say they feel to how they do feel are reliable, *ceteris paribus*.) But if Lysander does indeed love Hermia, then, *a fortiori*, Lysander wishes Hermia well. But if Lysander wishes Hermia well, then Lysander does not voluntarily desert Hermia at night in a darkling wood. (There may be lions. 'There is not a more fearful wild-fowl than your lion living.') But Hermia was, in fact, so deserted by Lysander. Therefore not voluntarily. Therefore *in*voluntarily. Therefore it is plausible that Lysander has come to harm. At whose hands? Plausibly at Demetrius' hands. For Demetrius is Lysander's rival for the love of Hermia, and the presumption is that rivals in love do *not* wish one another well. Specifically, Hermia believes that Demetrius believes that a live Lysander is an impediment to the success of his (Demetrius') wooing of her (Hermia). Moreover, Hermia believes (correctly) that if x wants that P, and x believes that not-P unless Q, and x believes that x can bring it about that Q, then (*ceteris paribus*) x tries to bring it about that Q. Moreover, Hermia believes (again correctly) that, by and large, people succeed in bringing about what they try to bring about. *So*: Knowing and believing all this, Hermia infers that perhaps Demetrius has killed Lysander. And we, the audience, who know what Hermia knows and believes and who share, more or less, her views about the psychology of lovers and rivals, understand how she has come to draw this inference. We sympathize.

In fact, Hermia has it all wrong. Demetrius is innocent and Lysander lives. The intricate theory that connects beliefs, desires, and actions – the implicit theory that Hermia relies on to make sense of what Lysander did and what Demetrius may have done; and that *we* rely on to make sense of Hermia's inferring what she does; and that Shakespeare relies on to predict and manipulate our sympathies ('*deconstruction*' *my foot*, by the way) – this theory makes no provision for nocturnal interventions by mischievous fairies. Unbeknownst to Hermia, a peripatetic sprite has sprung the *ceteris paribus* clause and made her plausible inference go awry. 'Reason and love keep little company together now-a-days: the more the pity that some honest neighbours will not make them friends.'

Granting, however, that the theory fails from time to time – and not just when fairies intervene – I nevertheless want to emphasize *(1) how often it goes right, (2) how deep it is, and (3) how much we do depend upon it.* Commonsense belief/desire psychology has recently come under a lot of philosophical pressure, and it's possible to doubt whether it can be saved in face of the sorts of problems that its critics have raised. There is, however, a prior question: whether it's worth the effort of trying to save it. That's the issue I propose to start with.

How often it works

Hermia got it wrong; her lover was less constant than she had supposed. Applications of commonsense psychology mediate our relations with one another, and when its predictions fail these relations break down. The resulting disarray is likely to happen in public and to be highly noticeable.

> *Herm.* Since night you lov'd me; yet since night you left me;
> Why, then, you left me, – O, the gods forbid! –
> In earnest, shall I say?
>
> *Lys.* Ay, by my life,
> And never did desire to see thee more.
> Therefore be out of hope ...

This sort of thing makes excellent theater; the *successes* of common-sense psychology, by contrast, are ubiquitous and – for that very reason – practically invisible.

Commonsense psychology works so well it disappears. It's like those mythical Rolls-Royce cars whose engines are sealed when they leave the factory; only it's better because it isn't mythical. Someone I don't know phones me at my office in New York from – as it might be – Arizona. 'Would you like to lecture here next Tuesday?' are the words that he utters. 'Yes, thank you. I'll be at your airport on the 3 p.m. flight' are the words that I reply. That's *all* that happens, but it's more than enough; the rest of the burden of predicting behavior – of bridging the gap between utterances and actions – is routinely taken up by theory. And the theory works so well that several days later (or weeks later, or months later, or years later; you can vary the example to taste) and several thousand miles away, there I am at the airport, and there he is to meet me. Or if I *don't* turn up, it's less likely that the theory has failed than that something went wrong with the airline. It's not possible to say, in quantitative terms, just how successfully commonsense psychology allows us to coordinate our behaviors. But I have the impression that we manage pretty well with one another; often rather better than we cope with less complex machines.

The point – to repeat – is that the theory from which we get this extraordinary predictive power is just good old commonsense belief/desire psychology. That's what tells us, for example, how to infer people's intentions from the sounds they make (if someone utters the form of words 'I'll be at your airport on the 3 p.m. flight,' then, *ceteris paribus*, he intends to be at your airport on the 3 p.m. flight) and how to infer people's behavior from their intentions (if someone intends to be at your airport on the 3 p.m. flight, then, *ceteris paribus*, he will produce behavior of a sort which will eventuate in his arriving at that place at that time, barring mechanical failures and acts of God). And all this works not just with people whose psychology you know intimately: your closest friends, say, or the spouse of your bosom. It works with *absolute strangers*; people you wouldn't know if you bumped into them. And it works not just in laboratory conditions – where you can control the interacting variables – but also, indeed preeminently, in field conditions where all you know about the sources of variance is what commonsense psychology tells you about them. Remarkable. If we could do that well with predicting the weather, no one would ever get his feet wet; and yet the etiology of the weather must surely be child's play compared with the causes of behavior.

Yes, but what about all those *ceteris paribuses*? I commence to digress: Philosophers sometimes argue that the appearance of predictive adequacy that accrues to the generalizations of commonsense psychology is spurious. For, they say, as soon as you try to make these generalizations explicit, you see that they have to be hedged about with *ceteris paribus* clauses; hedged about in ways that make them *trivially* incapable of disconfirmation. 'False or vacuous' is the charge.

Consider the defeasibility of 'if someone utters the form of words "I'll be at your airport on the 3 p.m. flight," then he intends to be at your airport on the 3 p.m. flight.' This generalization does *not* hold if, for example, the speaker is lying; or if the speaker is using the utterance as an example (of a false sentence, say); or if he is a monolingual speaker of Urdu who happens to have uttered the sentence by accident; or if the speaker is talking in his sleep; or ... whatever. You can, of course, defend the generalization in the usual way; you can say that '*all else being equal*, if someone utters the form of words "I'll be at your airport on the 3 p.m. flight," then he intends to be at your airport on the 3 p.m. flight.' But perhaps this last means nothing more than: 'if someone says that he intends to be there, then he does intend to be there – unless he doesn't.' That, of course, is predictively adequate for sure; nothing that happens will disconfirm it; nothing that happens could.

A lot of philosophers seem to be moved by this sort of argument; yet, even at first blush, it would be surprising if it were any good. After all, we do use commonsense psychological generalizations to predict one another's behavior; and the predictions do – very often – come out true. But how could that be so if the generalizations that we base the predictions on are *empty*?

I'm inclined to think that what is alleged about the implicit reliance of commonsense psychology on uncashed *ceteris paribus* clauses is in fact a perfectly general property of the *explicit* generalizations in *all* the special sciences; in all empirical explanatory schemes, that is to say, other than basic physics. Consider the following modest truth of geology: A meandering river erodes its outside bank. 'False or vacuous'; so a philosopher might argue. 'Take it straight – as a strictly universal generalization – and it is surely false. Think of the case where the weather changes and the river freezes; or the world comes to an end; or somebody builds a dam; or somebody builds a concrete wall on the outside bank; or the rains stops and the river dries up ... or whatever. You can, of course, defend. the generalization in the usual way – by appending a ceteris paribus clause: '*All else being equal*, a meandering river erodes its outside bank.' But perhaps this last means nothing more than: 'A meandering river erodes its outside bank – unless it doesn't.' That, of course, is predictively adequate for sure. Nothing that happens will disconfirm it; nothing that happens could.

Patently, something has gone wrong. For 'All else being equal, a meandering river erodes its outside bank' is neither false nor vacuous and it doesn't mean 'A meandering river erodes its outside bank – unless it doesn't.' It is, I expect, a long story how the generalizations of the special sciences manage to be both hedged and informative (or, if you like, how they manage to support counterfactuals even though they have exceptions). Telling that story is part of making clear why we have special sciences at all; why we don't just have basic physics. It is also part of making clear how idealization works in science. For surely '*Ceteris paribus*, a meandering river erodes its outside bank' means something like 'A meandering river erodes its outside bank in any nomologically possible world where the operative idealizations of geology are satisfied.'

That this is, in general, stronger than 'P in any world where not not-P' is certain. So if, as it would appear, commonsense psychology relies upon its *ceteris paribus* clauses, so too does geology.

There is, then, a face similarity between the way implicit generalizations work in commonsense psychology and the way explicit generalizations work in the special sciences. But maybe this similarity is *merely* superficial. Donald Davidson is famous for having argued that the generalizations of real science, unlike those that underlie commonsense belief/desire explanations, are 'perfectible'. In the real, but not the intentional, sciences we can (in principle, anyhow) get rid of the *ceteris paribus* clauses by actually enumerating the conditions under which the generalizations are supposed to hold.

By this criterion, however, the only real science is basic physics. For it simply isn't true that we can, even in principle, specify the conditions under which – say – geological generalizations hold *so long as we stick to the vocabulary of geology*. Or, to put it less in the formal mode, the causes of exceptions to geological generalizations are, quite typically, not themselves *geological* events. Try it and see: 'A meandering river erodes its outer banks unless, for example, the weather changes and the river dries up.' But 'weather' isn't a term in *geology*; nor are 'the world comes to an end', 'somebody builds a dam', and indefinitely many other descriptors required to specify the sorts of things that can go wrong. All you can say that's any use is: If the generalization failed to hold, then the operative idealizations must somehow have failed to be satisfied. But so, too, in commonsense psychology: If he didn't turn up when he intended to, then something must have gone wrong.

Exceptions to the generalizations of a special science are typically *inexplicable* from the point of view of (that is, in the vocabulary of) that science. That's one of the things that makes it a *special* science. But, of course, it may nevertheless be perfectly possible to explain the exceptions *in the vocabulary of some other science*. In the most familiar case, you go 'down' one or more levels and use the vocabulary of a more 'basic' science. (The current failed to run through the circuit because the terminals were oxidized; he no longer recognizes familiar objects because of a cerebral accident. And so forth.) The availability of this strategy is one of the things that the hierarchical arrangement of our sciences buys for us. Anyhow, to put the point succinctly, the same pattern that holds for the special sciences seems to hold for commonsense psychology as well. On the one hand, its *ceteris paribus* clauses are ineliminable from the point of view of its proprietary conceptual resources. But, on the other hand, we have – so far at least – no reason to doubt that they can be discharged in the vocabulary of some lower-level science (neurology, say, or biochemistry; at worst, physics).

If the world is describable as a closed causal system at all, it is so only in the vocabulary of our most basic science. From this nothing follows that a psychologist (or a geologist) needs to worry about.

I cease to digress. The moral so far is that the predictive adequacy of commonsense psychology is beyond rational dispute; nor is there any reason to suppose that it's obtained by cheating. If you want to know where my physical body will be next Thursday, mechanics – our best science of middle-sized objects after all, and reputed to be pretty good in its field – is *no use to you at all*. Far the best way to find out (usually, in practice, the *only* way to find out) is: ask me!

The depth of the theory

It's tempting to think of commonsense psychology as merely a budget of such truisms as one learns at Granny's knee: that the burnt child fears the fire, that all the world loves a lover, that money can't buy happiness, that reinforcement affects response rate, and that the way to a man's heart is through his stomach. None of these, I agree, is worth saving. However, as even the simple example sketched above serves to make clear, subsumption under platitudes is *not* the typical form of commonsense psychological explanation. Rather, when such explanations are made explicit, they are frequently seen to exhibit the 'deductive structure' that is so characteristic of explanation in real science. There are two parts to this: the theory's underlying generalizations are defined over unobservables, and they lead to its predictions by iterating and interacting rather than by being directly instantiated.

Hermia, for example, is no fool and no behaviorist; she is perfectly aware both that Demetrius' behavior is caused, by his mental states and that the pattern of such causation is typically intricate. There are, in particular, no plausible and counterfactual-supporting generalizations of the form $(x)(y)(x$ is a rival of $y) \rightarrow (x$ kills $y)$. Nothing like that is remotely true; not even *ceteris paribus*. Rather, the generalization Hermia takes to be operative – the one that *is* true and counterfactual-supporting – must be something like *If x is y's rival, then x prefers y's discomfiture, all else being equal*. This principle, however, doesn't so much as mention behavior; it leads to behavioral predictions, but only via a lot of further assumptions about how people's preferences may affect their actions in given situations. Or rather, since there probably are no generalizations which connect preferences to actions irrespective of beliefs, what Hermia must be relying on is an implicit theory of how beliefs, preferences, and behaviors interact; an implicit decision theory, no less.

It is a deep fact about the world that the most powerful etiological generalizations hold of unobservable causes. Such facts shape our science (they'd better!). It is thus a test of the depth of a theory that many of its generalizations subsume interactions among unobservables. By this test, our implicit, commonsense *meteorology* is presumably *not* a deep theory, since it consists largely of rule-of-thumb generalizations of the 'red at night, sailor's delight' variety. Correspondingly, the reasoning that mediates applications of commonsense meteorology probably involves not a lot more than instantiation and *modus ponens*. (All this being so, it is perhaps not surprising that commonsense meteorology doesn't work very well.) Commonsense psychology, by contrast, passes the test. It takes for granted that overt behavior comes at the

222

end of a causal chain whose links are mental events – hence unobservable – and which may be arbitrarily long (and arbitrarily kinky). Like Hermia, we are all – quite literally, I expect – born mentalists and Realists; and we stay that way until common sense is driven out by bad philosophy.

Its indispensability

We have, in practice, no alternative to the vocabulary of commonsense psychological explanation; we have no other way of describing our behaviors and their causes if we want our behaviors and their causes to be subsumed by any counterfactual-supporting generalizations that we know about. This is, again, hard to see because it's so close.

For example, a few paragraphs back, I spoke of the commonsense psychological generalization *people generally do what they say that they will do* as bridging the gap between an exchange of utterances ('Will you come and lecture . . .', 'I'll be at your airport on Thursday . . .') and the consequent behaviors of the speakers (my arriving at the airport, his being there to meet me). But this understates the case for the indispensability of commonsense psychology, since without it we can't even describe the utterances as forms of words (to say nothing of describing the ensuing behaviors as kinds of acts). *Word* is a *psychological* category. (It is, indeed, *irreducibly* psychological, so far as anybody knows; there are, for example, no acoustic properties that all and only tokens of the same word type must share. In fact, surprisingly, there are no acoustic properties that all and only *fully intelligible* tokens of the same word type must share. Which is why our best technology is currently unable to build a typewriter that you can dictate to.)

As things now stand – to spell it out – we have *no* vocabulary for specifying event types that meets the following four conditions:

1   My behavior in uttering 'I'll be there on Thursday . . .' counts as an event of type T_i
2   My arriving there on Thursday counts as an event of Type T_j.
3   'Events of type T_j are consequent upon events of type T_i' is even roughly true and counterfactual supporting.
4   Categories T_i and T_j are other than irreducibly psychological.

For the only known taxonomies that meet conditions 1–3 acknowledge such event types as uttering the *form of words* 'I'll be there on Thursday' or *saying that* one will be there on Thursday, or *performing the act* of meeting someone at the airport; so they fail condition 4.

Philosophers and psychologists used to dream of an alternative conceptual apparatus, one in which the commonsense inventory of types of *behavior* is replaced by an inventory of types of *movements*; the counterfactual-supporting generalizations of psychology would then exhibit the contingency of these movements upon environmental and/or organic variables. That behavior is indeed contingent upon environmental and organic variables is, I suppose, not to be denied; yet the generalizations were not forthcoming. Why? There's a standard answer: It's because behavior consists of actions, and actions cross-classify movements. The generalization is that the burnt child avoids the fire; but what movement constitutes avoidance depends on where the child is, where the fire is . . . and so, drearily, forth. If you want to know what generalizations subsume a behavioral event, you have to know what *action type* it belongs to; knowing what *motion type* it belongs to usually doesn't buy anything. I take all that to be Gospel.

Yet is is generally assumed that this situation *must* be remediable, at least in principle. After all, the generalizations of a completed physics would presumably subsume every motion of every thing, hence the motions of organisms *inter alia*. So, if we wait long enough, we will after all have counterfactual-supporting generalizations that subsume the motions of organisms *under that description*. Presumably, God has them already.

This is, however, a little misleading. For, the (putative) generalizations of the (putative) completed physics would apply to the motions of organisms *qua* motions, but not *qua* organismic. Physics presumably has as little use for the categories of macrobiology as it does for the categories of commonsense psychology; it dissolves the behav*er* as well as the behav*ior*. What's left is atoms in the void. The subsumption of motions of organisms – and of every-thing else – by the counterfactual-supporting generalizations of physics does not therefore guarantee that there is any science whose ontology recognizes organisms and their motions. That is: The subsumption of the motions of organisms – and of everything else – by the laws of physics does not guarantee that there are any laws about the motions of organisms *qua* motions or organisms. So far as anybody knows – barring, perhaps, a little bit of the psychology of classical reflexes – there are no such laws; and there is no metaphysical reason to expect any.[1]

Anyhow, this is all poppycock. Even if psychology were dispensable *in principle*, that would be no argument for dispensing with it. (Perhaps geology is dispensable in principle; every river is a physical object after all. Would that be a reason for supposing that rivers aren't a natural kind? Or that 'mean-dering rivers erode their outside banks' is untrue?) What's relevant to whether commonsense psychology is worth defending is its dispensability *in fact*. And here the situation is absolutely clear. We have no idea of how to explain ourselves to ourselves except in a vocabulary which is *saturated* with belief/desire psychology. One is tempted to transcendental argument: What Kant said to Hume about physical objects holds, *mutatis mutandis*, for the propositional attitudes; we can't give them up *because we don't know how to*.[2]

So maybe we had better try to hold onto them. Holding onto the attitudes – vindicating commonsense psychology – means showing how you could have (or, at a minimum, showing that you could have) a respectable science whose ontology explicitly acknowledges states that exhibit the sorts of properties that common sense attributes to the attitudes. This undertaking presupposes, however, some consensus about what sorts of properties common sense does attribute to the attitudes. That is what the next bit of this chapter is about.

The essence of the attitudes

How do we tell whether a psychology *is* a belief/desire psychology? How, in general, do we know if propositional attitudes are among the entities that the ontology of a theory acknowledges? These sorts of questions raise familiar and perplexing issues of intertheoretic identification. How do you distinguish elimination from reduction and reconstruction? Is the right story that there's no such thing as dephlogistinated matter, or is 'dephlogistinizing' just a word for oxidizing? Even behaviorists had trouble deciding whether they wanted to deny the existence of the mental or to assert its identity with the behavioral. (Sometimes they did both, in successive sentences. Ah, they really knew about insouciance in those days.)

I propose to stipulate. I will view a psychology as being common-sensical about the attitudes – in fact, as endorsing them – just in case it postulates states (entities, events, whatever) satisfying the following conditions:

(i) They are semantically evaluable.
(ii) They have causal powers.
(iii) The implicit generalizations of commonsense belief/desire psychology are largely true of them.

In effect, I'm assuming that *(i)-(iii)* are the essential properties of the attitudes. This seems to me intuitively plausible; if it doesn't seem intuitively plausible to you, so be it. Squabbling about intuitions strikes me as vulgar.

A word about each of these conditions.

(i) Semantic evaluation

Beliefs are the kinds of things that are true or false; desires are the kinds of things that get frustrated or fulfilled; hunches are the kinds of things that turn out to be right or wrong; so it goes. I will assume that what makes a belief true (/false) is something about its relation to the nonpsychological world (and not – e.g. – something about its relation to other beliefs; unless it happens to be a belief about beliefs). Hence, to say of a belief that it is true (/false) is to evaluate that belief in terms of its relation to the world. I will call such evaluations 'semantic'. Similarly, *mutatis mutandis*, with desires, hunches, and so forth.

It is, as I remarked in the preface, a puzzle about beliefs, desires, and the like that they are semantically evaluable; almost nothing else is. (Trees aren't; numbers aren't; people aren't. Propositions *are* [assuming that there are such things], but that's hardly surprising; propositions exist to be what beliefs and desires are attitudes *toward*.) We will see, later in this book, that it is primarily the semantic evaluability of beliefs and desires that gets them into philosophical trouble – and that a defense of belief/desire psychology needs to be a defense of it.

Sometimes I'll talk of the *content* of a psychological state rather than its semantic evaluability. These two ideas are intimately interconnected. Consider – for a change of plays – Hamlet's belief that his uncle killed his father. That belief has a certain semantic value; in particular, it's a *true* belief. Why true? Well, because it corresponds to a certain fact. Which fact? Well, the fact that Hamlet's uncle killed Hamlet's father. But why is it *that* fact that determines the semantic evaluation of Hamlet's belief? Why not the fact that 2 is a prime number, or the fact that Demetrius didn't kill Lysander? Well, because the *content* of Hamlet's belief is *that* his uncle killed his father. (If you like, the belief 'expresses the proposition' that Hamlet's uncle killed his father.) *If you know what the content of a belief is, then you know what it is about the world that determines the semantic evaluation of the belief*; that, at a minimum, is how the notions of content and semantic evaluation connect.

I propose to say almost nothing more about content at this stage; its time will come. Suffice it just to add that propositional attitudes have their contents essentially: the canonical way of picking out an attitude is to say (a) what sort of attitude it is (a belief, a desire, a hunch, or whatever); and (b) what the content of the attitude is (that Hamlet's uncle killed his father; that 2 is a prime number; that Hermia believes that Demetrius dislikes Lysander; or whatever). In what follows, nothing will count as a propositional-attitude psychology – as a reduction or reconstruction or vindication of commonsense belief/desire explanation – that does not acknowledge states that can be individuated in this sort of way.

(ii) Causal powers

Commonsense psychological explanation is deeply committed to mental causation of at least three sorts: the causation of behavior by mental states; the causation of mental states by impinging environmental events (by 'proximal stimulation' as psychologists sometimes say); and – in some ways the most interesting commonsense psychological etiologies – the causation of mental states by one another. As an example of the last sort, common sense acknowledges *chains of thought* as species of complex mental events. A chain of thought is presumably a *causal* chain in which one semantically evaluable mental state gives rise to another; a process that often terminates in the fixation of belief. (That, as you will remember, was the sort of thing Sherlock Holmes was supposed to be very good at.)

Every psychology that is Realist about the mental *ipso facto* acknowledges its causal powers.[3] Philosophers of 'functionalist' persuasion even hold that the causal powers of a mental state determine its identity (that for a mental state to be, as it might be, the state of believing that Demetrius killed Lysander is just for it to have a characteristic galaxy of potential and actual causal relations). This is a position of some interest to us, since if it is true – and if it is also true that propositional attitudes have their contents essentially – it follows that the causal powers of a mental state somehow determine its content. I do not, however, believe that it is true. More of this later.

What's important for now is this: It is characteristic of commonsense belief/desire psychology – and hence of any explicit theory that I'm prepared to view as vindicating commonsense belief/desire psychology – that it attributes contents and causal powers *to the very same mental things that it takes to be semantically evaluable*. It is Hamlet's belief that Claudius killed his father – the very same belief which is true or false in virtue of the facts about his father's death – that causes him to behave in such a beastly way to Gertrude.[4]

In fact, there's a deeper point to make. It's not just that, in a psychology of propositional attitudes, content and causal powers are attributed to the same things. It's also that causal relations among propositional attitudes somehow typically contrive to respect their relations of content, and belief/desire explanations often turn on this. Hamlet believed that somebody had killed his father because he believed that Claudius had killed his father. His having the second belief explains his having the first. How? Well, presumably via some such causal generalization as 'if someone believes Fa, then *ceteris paribus* he believes $\exists x(Fx)$'. This generalization specifies a causal relation between two kinds of mental states picked out by reference to (the logical form of) the propositions they express; so we have the usual pattern of a simultaneous attribution of content and causal powers. The present point, however, is that the contents of the mental states that the causal generalization subsumes are themselves semantically related; Fa entails $\exists x(Fx)$, so, of course, the semantic value of the latter belief is not independent of the semantic value of the former.

Or, compare the pattern of implicit reasoning attributed to Hermia at the beginning of this chapter. I suggested that she must be relying crucially on some such causal generalization as: 'If x wants that P, and x believes that $-P$ unless Q, and x believes that it is within his power to bring it about that Q, then *ceteris paribus* x tries to bring it about that Q.' Common sense seems pretty clearly to hold that something like that is true and counterfactual supporting; hence that one has explained x's attempt to bring it about that Q if one shows that x had beliefs and desires of the sort that the generalization specifies. What is absolutely typical is (a) the appeal to causal relations among semantically evaluable mental states as part and parcel of the explanation; and (b) the existence of content relations among the mental states thus appealed to.

Witness the recurrent schematic letters; they function precisely to constrain the content relations among the mental states that the generalization subsumes. Thus, unless, in a given case, what x wants is the same as what x believes that he can't have without Q, and unless what x believes to be required for P is the same as what he tries to bring about, the generalization isn't satisfied and the explanation fails. It is self-evident that the explanatory principles of commonsense psychology achieve generality by quantifying over agents (the 'practical syllogism' purports to apply, *ceteris paribus*, to all the *x*'s). But it bears emphasis that they also achieve generality by abstracting over *contents* ('if you want *P* and you believe not-*P* unless *Q* . . . you try to bring it about that *Q*,' whatever the *P* and *Q* may be). The latter strategy works only because, very often, the same *P*'s and *Q*'s – the same contents – recur in causally related mental states; viz., only because causal relations very often respect semantic ones.

This parallelism between causal powers and contents engenders what is, surely, one of the most striking facts about the cognitive mind as common-sense belief/desire psychology conceives it: the frequent similarity between trains of thought and *arguments*. Here for example, is Sherlock Holmes doing his thing at the end of 'The Speckled Band':

> I instantly reconsidered my position . . . it became clear to me that what-ever danger threatened an occupant of the room couldn't come either from the window or the door. My attention was speedily drawn, as I have already remarked to you, to this ventilator, and to the bell-rope which hung down to the bed. The discovery that this was a dummy, and that the bed was clamped to the floor, instantly gave rise to the suspi-cion that the rope was there as a bridge for something passing through the hole, and coming to the bed. The idea of a snake instantly occurred to me, and when I coupled it with my knowledge that the Doctor was furnished with a supply of the creatures from India I felt that I was prob-ably on the right track.

The passage purports to be a bit of reconstructive psychology: a capsule his-tory of the sequence of mental states which brought Holmes first to suspect, then to believe, that the doctor did it with his pet snake. What is therefore interesting, for our purposes, is that Holmes's story isn't *just* reconstructive psychology. It does double duty, since it also serves to assemble *premises* for a plausible inference to the *conclusion* that the doctor did it with the snake. Because his train of thought is like an argument, Holmes expects Watson to be *convinced* by the considerations which, when they occurred to Holmes, caused his own conviction. What connects the causal-history aspect of Holmes's story with its plausible-inference aspect is the fact that the thoughts that fix the belief that *P* provide, often enough, reasonable *grounds* for believing that *P*. Were this not the case – were there not this general harmony between the semanti-cal and the causal properties of thoughts, so that, as Holmes puts it in another story, 'one true inference invariably suggests others' – there wouldn't after all, be much profit in thinking.

All this raises a budget of philosophical issues; just *what sorts* of content relations are preserved in the generalizations that subsume typical cases of belief/desire causation? And – in many ways a harder question – how could the mind be so constructed that such generalizations are true of it? What sort of mechanism could have states that are both semantically and causally connected, and such that the causal connections respect the semantic ones? It is the intractability of such questions that causes many philosophers to despair of commonsense psychology. But, of course, the argument cuts both ways: if the parallelism between content and causal relations is, as it seems to be, a deep fact about the cognitive mind, then unless we can save the notion of content, there is a deep fact about the cognitive mind that our psychology is going to miss.

(iii) Generalizations preserved

What I've said so far amounts largely to this; An explicit psychology that vindicates commonsense belief/desire explanations must permit the assignment of content to causally efficacious mental states and must recognize behavioral explanations in which covering generalizations refer to (or quantify over) the contents of the mental states that they subsume. I now add that the generalizations that are recognized by vindicating theory mustn't be *crazy* from the point of view of common sense; the causal powers of the attitudes must be, more or less, what common sense supposes that they are. After all, commonsense psychology won't be vindicated unless it turns out to be at least approximately true.

I don't, however, have a shopping list of commonsense generalizations that must be honored by a theory if it wants to be ontologically committed to bona fide propositional attitudes. A lot of what common sense believes about the attitudes must surely be false (a lot of what common sense believes about *anything* must surely be false). Indeed, one rather hopes that there will prove to be many more – and much odder – things in mind than common sense had dreamed of; or else what's the fun of doing psychology? The indications are, and have been since Freud, that this hope will be abundantly gratified. For example, contrary to common sense, it looks as though much of what's in the mind is unconscious. and, contrary to common sense, it looks as though much of what's in the mind is unlearned. I retain my countenance, I remain self-possessed.

On the other hand, there is a lot of commonsense psychology that we have – so far at least – no reason to doubt, and that friends of the attitudes would hate to abandon. So, it's hard to imagine a psychology of action that is committed to the attitudes but doesn't acknowledge some such causal relations among beliefs, desires, and behavioral intentions (the 'maxims' of acts) as decision theories explicate. Similarly, it's hard to imagine a psycholinguistics (for English) which attributes beliefs, desires, communicative intentions, and such to speaker/hearers but fails to entail an infinity of theorems recognizably similar to these:

- 'Demetrius killed Lysander' is the form of words standardly used to communicate the belief that Demetrius killed Lysander.

229

- 'The cat is on the mat' is the form of words standardly used to communicate the belief that the cat is on the mat.
- 'Demetrius killed Lysander or the cat is on the mat' is the form of words standardly used to communicate the belief that Demetrius killed Lysander or the cat is on the mat.

And so on indefinitely. Indeed, it's hard to imagine a psycholinguistics that appeals to the propositional attitudes of speakers/hearers of English to explain their verbal behavior but that doesn't entail that they *know* at least one such theorem for each sentence of their language. So there's an infinite amount of common sense for psychology to vindicate already.

Self-confident essentialism is philosophically fashionable this week. There are people around who have Very Strong Views ('modal intuitions', these views are called) about whether there could be cats in a world in which all the domestic felines are Martian robots, and whether there could be Homer in a world where nobody wrote the *Odyssey* or the *Iliad*. Ducky for them; their epistemic condition is enviable, but I don't myself aspire to it. I just don't know how much commonsense psychology would have to be true for there to be beliefs and desires. Let's say, some of it at a minimum; lots of it by preference. Since I have no doubt at all but that lots of it *is* true, this is an issue about which I do not stay up nights worrying.

RTM

The main thesis of this book can now be put as follows: *We have no reason to doubt – indeed, we have substantial reason to believe – that it is possible to have a scientific psychology that vindicates commonsense belief/desire explanation.* But though that is my thesis, I don't propose to argue the case in quite so abstract a form. For there is already in the field a (more or less) empirical theory that is, in my view, reasonably construed as ontologically committed to the attitudes and that – again, in my view – is quite probably approximately true. If I'm right about this theory, it *is* a vindication of the attitudes. Since, moreover, it's the only thing of its kind around (it's the *only* proposal for a scientific belief/desire psychology that's in the field), defending the commonsense assumptions about the attitudes and defending this theory turn out to be much the same enterprise; extensionally, as one might say.

That, in any event, is the strategy that I'll pursue: I'll argue that the sorts of objections philosophers have recently raised against belief/desire explanation are (to put it mildly) not conclusive against the best vindicating theory currently available. The rest of this chapter is therefore devoted to a sketch of how this theory treats the attitudes and why its treatment of the attitudes seems so promising. Since this story is now pretty well known in both philosophical and psychological circles, I propose to be quick.

What I'm selling is the Representational Theory of Mind (hence RTM). At the heart of the theory is the postulation of a language of thought: an infinite set of 'mental representations' which function both as the immediate objects of propositional attitudes and as the domains of mental processes. More precisely, RTM is the conjunction of the following two claims:

Claim 1 (the nature of propositional attitudes):

For any organism *O*, and any attitude *A* toward the proposition *P*, there is a ('computational'/'functional') relation *R* and a mental representation *MP* such that

MP means that *P*, and
O has *A* iff [if and only if] *O* bears *R* to *MP*.

(We'll see presently that the biconditional needs to be watered down a little; but not in a way that much affects the spirit of the proposal.)

It's a thin line between clarity and pomposity. A cruder but more intelligible way of putting claim 1 would be this: To believe that such and such is to have a mental symbol that means that such and such tokened in your head in a certain way; it's to have such a token 'in your belief box', as I'll sometimes say. Correspondingly, to hope that such and such is to have a token of that same mental symbol tokened in your head, but in a rather different way; it's to have it tokened 'in your hope box'. (The difference between having the token in one box or the other corresponds to the difference between the causal roles of beliefs and desires. Talking about belief boxes and such as a shorthand for representing the attitudes as *functional* states is an idea due to Steve Schiffer.) And so on for every attitude that you can bear toward a proposition; and so on for every proposition toward which you can bear an attitude.

Claim 2 (the nature of mental processes):

Mental processes are causal sequences of tokenings of mental representations.

A train of thoughts, for example, is a causal sequence of tokenings of mental representations which express the propositions that are the objects of the thoughts. To a first approximation, to think 'It's going to rain; so I'll go indoors' is to have a tokening of a mental representation that means *I'll go indoors* caused, in a certain way, by a tokening of a mental representation that means *It's going to rain*.

So much for formulating RTM.

There are, I think, a number of reasons for believing that RTM may be more or less true. The best reason is that some version or other of RTM underlies practically all current psychological research on mentation, and our best science is *ipso facto* our best estimate of what there is and what it's made of. There are those of my colleagues in philosophy who do not find this sort of argument persuasive. I blush for them. (For a lengthy discussion of how RTM shapes current work on cognition, see Fodor, 1975, especially chapter 1. For a discussion of the connection between RTM and commonsense Intentional Realism – and some arguments that, given the latter, the former is practically mandatory – see the Appendix, Fodor, 1987.)

But we have a reason for suspecting that RTM may be true even aside from the details of its empirical success. I remarked above that there is a striking parallelism between the causal relations among mental states, on the one hand, and the semantic relations that hold among their propositional objects, on the other; and that very deep properties of the mental – as, for example, that trains of thought are largely truth preserving – turn on this symmetry. RTM suggests a plausible mechanism for this relation, and that is something that no previous account of mentation has been able to do. I propose to spell this out a bit; it helps make clear just *why* RTM has such a central place in the way that psychologists now think about the mind.

The trick is to combine the postulation of mental representations with the 'computer metaphor'. Computers show us how to connect semantical with causal properties for *symbols*. So, if having a propositional attitude involves tokening a symbol, then we can get some leverage on connecting semantical properties with causal ones for *thoughts*. In this respect, I think there really has been something like an intellectual breakthrough. Technical details to one side, this is – in my view – the only aspect of contemporary cognitive science that represents a major advance over the versions of mentalism that were its eighteenth- and nineteenth-century predecessors. Exactly what was wrong with Associationism, for example, was that there proved to be no way to get a *rational* mental life to emerge from the sorts of causal relations among thoughts that the 'laws of association' recognized. (See the concluding pages of Joyce's *Ulysses* for a – presumably inadvertent – parody of the contrary view.)

Here, in barest outline, is how the new story is supposed to go: You connect the causal properties of a symbol with its semantic properties *via its syntax*. The syntax of a symbol is one of its higher-order physical properties. To a metaphorical first approximation, we can think of the syntactic structure of a symbol as an abstract feature of its shape.[5] Because, to all intents and purposes, syntax reduces to shape, and because the shape of a symbol is a potential determinant of its causal role, it is fairly easy to see how there could be environments in which the causal role of a symbol correlates with its syntax. It's easy, that is to say, to imagine symbol tokens interacting causally *in virtue of* their syntactic structures. The syntax of a symbol might determine the causes and effects of its tokenings in much the way that the geometry of a key determines which locks it will open.

But, now, we know from modern logic that certain of the semantic relations among symbols can be, as it were, 'mimicked' by their syntactic relations; that, when seen from a very great distance, is what proof-theory is about. So, within certain famous limits, the semantic relation that holds between two symbols when the proposition expressed by the one is entailed by the proposition expressed by the other can be mimicked by syntactic relations in virtue of which one of the symbols is derivable from the other. We can therefore build machines which have, again within famous limits, the following property:

The operations of the machine consist entirely of transformations of symbols;

in the course of performing these operations, the machine is sensitive solely to syntactic properties of the symbols;

and the operations that the machine performs on the symbols are entirely confined to altering their shapes.

Yet the machine is so devised that it will transform one symbol into another if and only if the propositions expressed by the symbols that are so transformed stand in certain *semantic* relations – e.g., the relation that the premises bear to the conclusion in a valid argument. Such machines – computers, of course – just *are* environments in which the syntax of a symbol determines its causal role in a way that respects its content. This is, I think, a perfectly terrific idea; not least because it works.

I expect it's clear how this is supposed to connect with RTM and ontological commitment to mental representations. Computers are a solution to the problem of mediating between the causal properties of symbols and their semantic properties. So *if* the mind is a sort of computer, we begin to see how you can have a theory of mental processes that succeeds where – literally – all previous attempts had abjectly failed; a theory which explains how there could be nonarbitrary content relations among causally related thoughts. But, patently, there are going to have to be mental representations if this proposal is going to work. In computer design, causal role is brought into phase with content by exploiting parallelisms between the syntax of a symbol and its semantics. But that idea won't do the theory of *mind* any good unless there are *mental* symbols: mental particulars possessed of both semantical and syntactic properties. There must be mental symbols because, in a nutshell, only symbols have syntax, and our best available theory of mental processes – indeed, the *only* available theory of mental processes that isn't *known* to be false – needs the picture of the mind as a syntax-driven machine.

It is sometimes alleged against commonsense belief/desire psychology, by those who admire it less than I do, that it is a 'sterile' theory; one that arguably hasn't progressed much since Homer and hasn't progressed at all since Jane Austen. There is, no doubt, a sense in which this charge is warranted; commonsense psychology may be implicit science, but it isn't, on anybody's story, implicit *research* science. (What novelists and poets do doesn't count as research by the present austere criteria.) If, in short, you want to evaluate progress, you need to look not at the implicit commonsense theory but at the best candidate for its explicit vindication. And here the progress has been enormous. It's not just that we now know a little about memory and perception (*qua* means to the fixation of belief), and a little about language (*qua* means to the communication of belief); see any standard psychology text. The real achievement is that we are (maybe) on the verge of solving a great mystery about the mind: *How could its causal processes be semantically coherent? Or,* if you like yours with drums and trumpets: *How is rationality mechanically possible?*[6] Notice that this sort of problem can't even be stated, let alone solved, unless we suppose – just as commonsense belief/desire psychology wants us to – that there are mental states with both semantic contents and causal roles. A good theory is one that leads you to ask questions that have answers. And vice versa, *ceteris paribus*.

Still, RTM won't do in quite the raw form set forth above. I propose to end this chapter with a little polishing.

According to claim 1, RTM requires both the following:

For each tokening of a propositional attitude, there is a tokening of a corresponding relation between an organism and a mental representation;

and

For each tokening of that relation, there is a corresponding tokening of a propositional attitude.[7]

This is, however, much too strong; the equivalence fails in both directions.

As, indeed, we should expect it to, given our experience in other cases where explicit science co-opts the conceptual apparatus of common sense. For example, as everybody points out, it is simply not true that chemistry identifies each sample of water with a sample of H_2O; not, at least, if the operative notion of water is the commonsense one according to which what we drink, sail on, and fill our bathtubs with all qualifies. What chemistry does is reconstruct the commonsense categories *in what the theory itself identifies as core cases; chemically pure* water is H_2O. The ecological infrequency of such core cases is, of course, no argument against the claim that chemical science vindicates the commonsense taxonomy: Common sense was right about there being such stuff as water, right about there being water in the Charles River, and right again that it's the water in what we drink that quenches our thirst. It never said that the water in the Charles is chemically pure; 'chemically pure' isn't a phrase in the commonsense vocabulary.

Exactly similarly, RTM vindicates commonsense psychology for what RTM identifies as the core cases; in those cases, what common sense takes to be tokenings of propositional attitudes are indeed tokenings of a relation between an organism and a mental representation. The other cases – where you get either attitude tokenings without the relation or relation tokenings without the attitudes – the theory treats as derivative. This is all, I repeat, *exactly* what you'd expect from scientific precedent. Nevertheless, philosophers have made an awful fuss about it in discussing the vindication of the attitudes (see the controversy over the 'explicit representation' – or otherwise – of grammars recently conducted by, among others, Stabler in Stabler 1983 and Demopoulos and Matthews 1983. So let's consider the details awhile. Doing so will lead to a sharpening of claim 1, which is all to the good.

Case 1. Attitudes without mental representations

Here's a case from Dennett:

> In a recent conversation with the designer of a chess-playing program I heard the following criticism of a rival program: 'It thinks it should get its queen out early.' This ascribes a propositional attitude to the program in a very useful and predictive way, for as the designer went on to say, one can usually count on chasing that queen around the board. But for all the many levels of explicit representation to be found in that program, nowhere is anything roughly synonymous with 'I should get my queen out early' explicitly tokened. The level of analysis to which the designer's remark belongs describes features of the program that are, in an entirely innocent way, emergent properties of the computational processes that have 'engineering reality'. I see no reason to believe that the relation between belief/talk and psychological-process talk will be any more direct (Dennett 1981: 107; see also Matthews 1984).

Notice that the problem Dennett raises isn't just that some of what common sense takes to be one's propositional attitudes are *dispositional*. It's not like the worry that I might now be said to believe some abstruse consequence of number theory – one that I have, commonsensically speaking, never even thought of – because I *would* accept the proof of the theorem *if* I were shown it. It's true, of course, that merely dispositional beliefs couldn't correspond to *occurrent* tokenings of relations to mental representations, and claim 1 must therefore be reformulated. But the problem is superficial, since the relevant revision of claim 1 would be pretty obvious; viz., that for each *occurrent* belief there is a corresponding *occurrent* tokening of a mental representation; and for each *dispositional* belief there is a corresponding *disposition* to token a mental representation.

This would leave open a question that arises independent of one's views about RTM: viz., when are attributions of dispositional beliefs *true*? I suppose that one's dispositional beliefs could reasonably be identified with the closure of one's occurrent beliefs under principles of inference that one explicitly accepts. And, if it's a little vague just what beliefs belong to such a closure, RTM could live with that. *Qua dispositional*, attitudes play no causal role in *actual* mental processes; only occurrent attitudes – for that matter, only occurrent *anythings* – are actual causes. So RTM can afford to be a little operationalist about merely dispositional beliefs (see Lycan 1986: 61–82) so long as it takes a hard line about occurrent ones.

However, to repeat, the problem raised in Dennett's text is not of this sort. It's not that the program believes 'get your queen out early' *potentially*. Dennett's point is that the program actually operates on this principle; but not in virtue of any tokening of any symbol that expresses it. And chess isn't, of course, the only sort of case. Behavioral commitment to *modus ponens*, or to the syntactic rule of 'wh'-movement *might* betoken that these are inscribed in brain writing. But it needn't, since these rules might be – as philosophers sometimes say – complied with but not literally followed.

In Dennett's example, you have an attitude being, as it were, an emergent out of its own implementation. This way of putting it might seem to suggest a way of saving claim 1: The machine doesn't explicitly represent 'get your queen out early', but at least we may suppose that it *does* represent, explicitly, some more detailed rules of play (the ones that Dennett says have 'engineering reality'). For these rules, at least, a strong form of claim 1 would thus be satisfied. But that suggestion won't work either. *None* of the principles in accordance with which a computational system operates need be explicitly represented by a formula tokened in the device; there is no guarantee that the program of a machine will be explicitly represented in the machine whose program it is. (See Cummins 1982; roughly, the point is that for any machine that computes a function by executing an explicit algorithm, there exists another machine – one that's 'hard-wired' – that computes the same function but *not* by executing an explicit algorithm.) So what, you might wonder, does the 'computer metaphor' buy for RTM after all?

There is even a point of principle here – one that is sometimes read in (or into) Lewis Carroll's dialogue between Achilles and the Tortoise: Not all the rules of inference that a computational system runs on *can* be represented *just* explicitly in the system; some of them have to be, as one says, 'realized in the hardware'. Otherwise the machine won't run at all. A computer in which the principles of operation are *only* explicitly represented is just like a blackboard on which the principles have been written down. It has Hamlet's problem: When you turn the thing on, nothing happens.

Since this is all clearly correct and arguably important, the question arises how to state RTM so that these cases where programs are hardwired don't count as disconfirmations of claim 1. We'll return to this momentarily; first let's consider:

Case 2. Mental representations without attitudes

What RTM borrows from computers is, in the first instance, the recipe for mechanizing rationality: Use a syntactically driven machine to exploit parallelisms between the syntactic and semantic properties of symbols. Some – but not all – versions of RTM borrow more than this; not just a theory of rationality but a theory of intelligence too. According to this story, intelligent behavior typically exploits a 'cognitive architecture' constituted of *hierarchies* of symbol processors. At the top of such a hierarchy might be a quite complex capacity: solving a problem, making a plan, uttering a sentence. At the bottom, however, are only the sorts of unintelligent operations that Turing machines can perform: deleting symbols, storing symbols, copying symbols, and the rest. Filling in the middle levels is tantamount to reducing – analyzing – an intelligent capacity into a complex of dumb ones; hence to a kind of explanation of the former.

Here's a typical example of a kind of representational theory that runs along these lines:

> This is the way we tie our shoes. There is a little man who lives in one's head. The little man keeps a library. When one acts upon the intention to tie one's shoes, the little man fetches down a volume entitled *Tying One's Shoes*. The volume says such things as: 'Take the left free end of the shoelace in the left hand. Cross the left free end of the shoelace over the right free end of the shoelace . . .,' etc. . . . When the little man reads 'take the left free end of the shoelace in the left hand', we imagine him ringing up the shop foreman in charge of grasping shoelaces. The shop foreman goes about supervising that activity in a way that is, in essence, a microcosm of tying one's shoe. Indeed, the shop foreman might be imagined to superintend a detail of wage slaves, whose functions include: searching representations of visual inputs for traces of shoelace, dispatching orders to flex and contract fingers on the left hand, etc. (Fodor 1981: 63–4).

At the very top are states which may well correspond to the propositional attitudes that common sense is prepared to acknowledge (knowing how to tie one's shoes, thinking about shoe tying). But at the bottom and middle levels there are bound to be lots of symbol-processing operations that correspond to nothing that *people* – as opposed to their nervous systems – ever do. These are the operations of what Dennett has called 'subpersonal' computational systems; and though they satisfy the present formulation of claim 1 (in that they involve causally efficacious tokenings of mental representations), yet it's unclear that they correspond to anything that common sense would count as the tokening of an attitude. But then how are we to formulate claim 1 so as to avoid disconfirmation by subpersonal information processes?

Vindication vindicated

There is a sense in which these sorts of objections to claim 1 strike me as not very serious. As I remarked above, the vindication of belief/desire explanation by RTM does *not* require that every case common sense counts as the tokening of an attitude should correspond to the tokening of a mental representation, or vice versa. All that's required is that such correspondences should obtain in what the vindicating theory itself takes to be the core cases. On the other hand, RTM had better be able to say which cases it does count as core. Chemistry is allowed to hold the Charles River largely irrelevant to the confirmation of 'water is H_2O', but only because it provides independent grounds for denying that what's in the Charles is a chemically pure sample. Of anything!

So, what are the core cases for RTM? The answer should be clear from claim 2. According to claim 2, mental processes are causal sequences of transformations of mental representations. It follows that tokenings of attitudes *must* correspond to tokenings of mental representations when they – the attitude tokenings – are episodes in mental processes. If the intentional objects of such causally efficacious attitude tokenings are *not* explicitly represented, then RTM is simply false. I repeat for emphasis: If the occurrence of a thought is an episode in a mental process, then RTM is committed to the explicit representation of its content. The motto is therefore No Intentional Causation without Explicit Representation.

Notice that this way of choosing core cases squares us with the alleged counterexamples. RTM says that the contents of a sequence of attitudes that constitutes a mental process must be expressed by explicit tokenings of mental representations. But the rules that determine the course of the transformation of these representations – *modus ponens*, 'wh'-movement, 'get the queen out early', or whatever – need not themselves ever be' explicit. They can be emergents out of explicitly represented procedures of implementation, or out of hardware structures, or both. Roughly: According to RTM, programs – corresponding to the 'laws of thought' – *may* be explicitly represented; but 'data structures' – corresponding to the contents of thoughts – *have to be*.

Thus, in Dennett's chess case, the rule 'get it out early' may or may not be expressed by a 'mental' (/program language) symbol. That depends on just how the machine works; specifically, on whether *consulting* the rule is a step in the machine's operations. I take it that in the machine that Dennett has in mind, it isn't; *entertaining the thought 'Better get the queen out early' never constitutes an episode in the mental life of that machine.*[8] But then, the intentional content of this thought need *not* be explicitly represented consonant with 'no intentional causation without explicit representation' being true. By contrast, the representations of the board – of actual or possible states of play – over which the machine's computations are defined *must* be explicit, precisely *because* the machine's computations *are* defined over them. These computations constitute the machine's 'mental processes', so either they are causal sequences of explicit representations, or the representational theory of chess playing is simply false of the machine. To put the matter in a nutshell: Restricting one's attention to the status of rules and programs can make it seem that the computer metaphor is neutral with respect to RTM. But when one thinks about the constitution of mental processes, the connection between the idea that they are computational and the idea that there is a language of thought becomes immediately apparent.[9]

What about the subpersonal examples, where you have mental representation tokenings without attitude tokenings? Commonsense belief/desire explanations are vindicated if scientific psychology is ontologically committed to beliefs and desires. But it's *not* also required that the folk-psychological inventory of propositional attitudes should turn out to exhaust a natural kind. It would be astounding if it did; how could common sense know all that? What's important about RTM – what makes RTM a vindication of intuitive belief/desire psychology – isn't that it picks out a kind that is precisely co-extensive with the propositional attitudes. It's that RTM shows how intentional states could have causal powers; precisely the aspect of common-sense intentional realism that seemed most perplexing from the metaphysical point of view.

Molecular physics vindicates the intuitive taxonomy of middle-sized objects into liquids and solids. But the nearest kind to the liquids that molecular physics acknowledges includes some of what common sense would not; glass, for example. So what?

So much for RTM; so much for this chapter, too. There is a strong prima facie case for commonsense belief/desire explanation. Common sense would be vindicated if some good theory of the mind proved to be committed to entities which – like the attitudes – are both semantically evaluable and etio-logically involved. RTM looks like being a good theory of the mind that is so committed; so if RTM is true, common sense is vindicated. It goes without saying that RTM needs to make an empirical case; we need good accounts, independently confirmed, of mental processes as causal sequences of trans-formations of mental representations. Modern cognitive psychology is devoted, practically in its entirety, to devising and confirming such accounts. For present purposes, I shall take all that as read.

Notes

1 Perhaps there are laws that relate the *brain states* of organisms to their motions. But then again, perhaps there aren't, since it seems entirely possible that the lawful connections should hold between brain states and *actions* where, as usual, actions cross-classify movements. This is, perhaps, what you would predict upon reflection. Would you really expect the same brain state that causes the utter-ances of 'dog' in tokens of 'dog' to be the one that causes it in tokens of 'dogmatic'? How about utterances of (the phonetic sequence) [empedokliz liptl] when you're talking English and when you're talking German?

2 The trouble with transcendental arguments being, however, that it's not obvious why a theory couldn't be both indispensable and *false*. I wouldn't want to buy a transcendental deduction of the attitudes if operationalism were the price I had to pay for it.

3 Denying the etiological involvement of mental states was really what behaviorism was about; it's what 'logical' behaviorists and 'eliminativists' had in common. Thus, for example, to hold – as Ryle did, more or less – that mental states are species of dispositions is to refuse to certify as literally causal such psycholog-ical explanations as 'He did it with the intention of pleasing her,' or, for that matter, 'His headache made him groan,' to say nothing of 'The mere thought of giving a lecture makes him ill.' (For discussion, see Fodor 1981, 'Something on the State of the Art', Introduction to *Representations*.)

4   Some philosophers feel very strongly about enforcing an object/state (or maybe object/event) distinction here, so that what have *causal powers* are tokenings of mental state types (e.g., Hamlet's *believing* that Claudius killed his father), but what have *semantic values* are *propositions* (e.g., the proposition that Claudius killed Hamlet's father). The point is that it sounds odd to say that Hamlet's *believing* that *P* is true but all right to say that Hamlet's *belief* that *P* is.

I'm not convinced that this distinction is one that I will care about in the long run, since sounding odd is the least of my problems and in the long run I expect I want to do without propositions altogether. However, if you are squeamish about ontology, that's all right with me. In that case, the point in the text should be: Belief/desire psychology attributes causal properties to the very same things (viz., tokenings of certain mental state types) to which it attributes propositional objects. It is thus true of Hamlet's believing that Claudius killed his father both that it is implicated in the etiology of his behavior Gertrudeward and that it has as its object a certain belief, viz., the proposition that Claudius killed his father. If we then speak of Hamlet's *state* of believing that Claudius killed his father (or of the event which consists of the tokening of that state) as semantically evaluable, we can take that as an abbreviation for a more precise way of talking. The state *S* has the semantic value *V* if *S* has as its object a proposition whose value is *V*.

It goes without saying that none of this ontological fooling around makes the slightest progress toward removing the puzzles about intentionality. If (on my way of talking) it's metaphysically worrying that beliefs and desires are semantically evaluable though trees, rocks, and prime numbers aren't, it's equally metaphysically worrying (on the orthodox way of talking) that believings have propositional objects though trees, rocks and prime numbers don't.

5   *Any* nomic property of symbol tokens, however – any property in virtue of the posession of which they satisfy causal laws – would, in principle, do just as well. (So, for example, syntactic structure could be realized by relations among electromagnetic states rather than relations among shapes; as, indeed, it is in real computers.) This is the point of the Functionalist doctrine that, in principle, you can make a mind out of almost anything.

6   Which is not to deny that there are (ahem!) certain residual technical difficulties. (See, for example, part 4 of Fodor 1983.) A theory of rationality (i.e., a theory of *our* rationality) has to account not merely for the 'semantic coherence' of thought processes in the abstract but for our ability to pull off the very sorts of rational inferences that we do. (It has to account for our ability to make science, for example.) No such theory will be available by this time next week.

7   Because I don't want to worry about the ontology of mind, I've avoided stating RTM as an identity thesis. But you could do if you were so inclined.

8   Like Dennett, I'm assuming for purposes of argument that the machine *has* thoughts and mental processes; nothing hangs on this, since we could, of course, have had the same discussion about people.

9   We can now see what to say about the philosophical chestnut about Kepler's Law. The allegation is that intentionalist methodology permits the inference from '*x*'s behavior complies with rule *R*' to '*R* is a rule that *x* explicitly represents.' The embarrassment is supposed to be that this allows the inference from 'The movements of the planets comply with Kepler's Law' to some astronomical version of LOT.

240

But in fact no such principle of inference is assumed. What warrants the hypothesis that *R* is explicitly represented is not mere behavior in compliance with *R*; it's an etiology according to which *R* figures as the content of one of the intentional states whose tokenings are causally responsible for *x*'s behavior. And, of course, it's *not* part of the etiological story about the motions of the planets that Kepler's Law occurs to them as they proceed upon their occasions.

References

Cummins, R. (1982) 'The internal manual model of psychological explanation', *Cognition and Brain Theory*, 5(3): 257–68.

Demopoulos, N. and Matthews, R. (1983) 'On the hypothesis that grammars are mentally represented', *Behavioral and Brain Sciences* 3: 405–06.

Dennett, D. (1981) 'A cure for the common code'. In *Brainstorms*. Cambridge, Mass.: MIT Press.

Fodor, J. (1981) *Representations*. Cambridge, Mass.: MIT Press.

—— (1983) *The Modularity of Mind: An Essay on Faculty Psychology*. Cambridge, Mass.: MIT Press.

—— (1987) *Psychosemantics*. Cambridge, Mass.: MIT Press.

Lycan, W.G. (1986) 'Tacit belief'. In Bogdan, R. (ed.) *Belief: Form, Content and Function*, Oxford: Clarendon Press.

Matthews, R. (1984) 'Troubles with representationalism', *Social Research*, 51(4): 1065–97.

Stabler, E. (1983) 'How are grammars represented?' *Behavioral and Brain Sciences* 3: 391–402.

12

S.P. Stich, "Autonomous Psychology and the Belief–Desire Thesis"

A venerable view, still very much alive, holds that human action is to be explained at least in part in terms of beliefs and desires. Those who advocate the view expect that the psychological theory which explains human behavior will invoke the concepts of belief and desire in a substantive way, I will call this expectation the *belief–desire thesis*. Though there would surely be a quibble or a caveat here and there, the thesis would be endorsed by an exceptionally heterogeneous collection of psychologists and philosophers ranging from Freud and Hume, to Thomas Szasz and Richard Brandt. Indeed, a number of philosophers have contended that the thesis, or something like it, is embedded in our ordinary, workaday concept of action.[1] If they are right, and I think they are, then insofar as we use the concept of action we are *all* committed to the belief–desire thesis. My purpose in this essay is to explore the tension between the belief–desire thesis and a widely held assumption about the nature of explanatory psychological theories, an assumption that serves as a fundamental regulative principle for much of contemporary psychological theorizing. This assumption, which for want of a better term I will call the *principle of psychological autonomy*, will be the focus of the first of the sections below. In the second section I will elaborate a bit on how the belief–desire thesis is to be interpreted, and try to extract from it a principle that will serve as a premise in the argument to follow. In the third section I will set out an argument to the effect that large numbers of belief–desire explanations of action, indeed perhaps the bulk of such explanations, are incompatible with the principle of autonomy. Finally, in the last section, I will fend off a possible objection to my argument. In the process, I will try to make clear just why the argument works and what price we should have to pay if we were resolved to avoid its consequences.

1   The principle of psychological autonomy

Perhaps the most vivid way of explaining the principle I have in mind is by invoking a type of science fiction example that has cropped up with some frequency in recent philosophical literature. Imagine that technology were available which would enable us to duplicate people. That is, we can build living human beings who are atom for atom and molecule for molecule replicas of some given human being.[2] Now suppose that we have before us a human being (or, for that matter, any sort of animal) and his exact replica. What the principle of autonomy claims is that these two humans will be psychologically identical, that any psychological property instantiated by one of these subjects will also be instantiated by the other.

Actually, a bit of hedging is needed to mark the boundaries of this claim to psychological identity. First, let me note that the organisms claimed to be psychologically identical include any pair of organisms, existing at the same time or at different times, who happen to be atom for atom replicas of each other. Moreover, it is inessential that one organism should have been built to be a replica of the other. Even if the replication is entirely accidental, the two organisms will still be psychologically identical.

A caveat of another sort is needed to clarify just what I mean by calling two organisms "psychologically identical." For consider the following objection: "The original organism and his replica do not share *all* of their psychological properties. The original may, for example, remember seeing the Watergate hearings on television, but the replica remembers no such thing. He may think he remembers it, or have an identical "memory trace," but if he was not created until long after the Watergate hearings, then he did not see the hearings on television, and thus he could not remember seeing them." The point being urged by my imagined critic is a reasonable one. There are many sorts of properties plausibly labeled "psychological" that might be instantiated by a person and not by his replica. Remembering that p is one example, knowing that p and seeing that p are others. These properties have a sort of "hybrid" character. They seem to be analyzable into a "purely psychological" property (like seeming to remember that p, or believing that p) along with one or more nonpsychological properties and relations (like p being true, or the memory trace being caused in a certain way by the fact that p). But to insist that "hybrid" psychological properties are not psychological properties at all would be at best a rather high handed attempt at stipulative definition. Still, there is something a bit odd about these hybrid psychological properties, a fact which reflects itself in the intuitive distinction between "hybrids" and their underlying "purely psychological" components. What is odd about the hybrids, I think, is that we do not expect them to play any role in an explanatory psychological theory. Rather, we expect a psychological theory which aims at explaining behavior to invoke only the "purely psychological" properties which are shared by a subject and its replicas. Thus, for example, we are inclined to insist it is Jones's *belief* that there is no greatest prime number that plays a role in the explanation of his answering the exam question. He may, in fact, have *known* that there is no greatest prime number. But even if he did not know it, if, for example, the source of his information had himself only been guessing, Jones's behavior would have been unaffected. What knowledge adds to belief is psychologically irrelevant. Similarly the difference between really remembering that p and merely seeming to remember that p

makes no difference to the subject's behavior. In claiming that physical replicas are psychologically identical, the principle of psychological autonomy is to be understood as restricting itself to the properties that can play a role in explanatory psychological theory. Indeed, the principle is best viewed as a claim about what sorts of properties and relations may play a role in explanatory psychological theory. If the principle is to be observed, then the only properties and relations that may legitimately play a role in explanatory psychological theories are the properties and relations that a subject and its replica will share.

There is another way to explain the principle of psychological autonomy that does not appeal to the fanciful idea of a replica. Jaegwon Kim has explicated and explored the notion of one class of properties *supervening* upon another class of properties.[3] Suppose S and W are two classes of properties, and that S# and W# are the sets of all properties constructible from the properties in S and W respectively. Then, following Kim, we will say that the family S of properties supervenes on the family W of properties (with respect to a domain D of objects) just in case, necessarily, any two objects in D which share all properties in W# will also share all properties in S#. A bit less formally, one class of properties supervenes on another if the presence or absence of properties in the former class is completely determined by the presence or absence of properties in the latter.[4] Now the principle of psychological autonomy states that the properties and relations to be invoked in an explanatory psychological theory must be supervenient upon the *current, internal physical* properties and relations of organisms (i.e., just those properties that an organism shares with all of its replicas).

Perhaps the best way to focus more sharply on what the autonomy principle states is to look at what it rules out. First, of course, if explanatory psychological properties and relations must supervene on *physical* properties, then at least some forms of dualism are false. The dualist who claims that there are psychological (or mental) properties which are not nomologically correlated with physical properties, but which nonetheless must be invoked in an explanation of the organism's behavior, is denying that explanatory psychological states supervene upon physical states. However, the autonomy principle is not inimical to all forms of dualism. Those dualists, for example, who hold that mental and physical properties are nomologically correlated need have no quarrel with the doctrine of autonomy. However, the principle of autonomy is significantly stronger than the mere insistence that psychological states supervene on physical states.[5] For autonomy requires in addition that certain physical properties and relations are psychologically irrelevant in the sense that organisms which differ *only* with respect to those properties and relations are psychologically identical.[6] In specifying that only "current" physical properties are psychologically relevant, the autonomy principle decrees irrelevant all those properties that deal with the history of the organism, both past and future. It is entirely possible, for example, for two organisms to have quite different physical histories and yet, at a specific pair of moments, to be replicas

244

of one another. But this sort of difference, according to the autonomy principle, can make no difference from the point of view of explanatory psychology. Thus remembering that p (as contrasted with having a memory trace that p) cannot be an explanatory psychological state. For the difference between a person who remembers that p and a person who only seems to remember that p is not dependent on their current physical state, but only on the history of these states. Similarly, in specifying that only *internal* properties and relations are relevant to explanatory psychological properties, the autonomy principle decrees that relations between an organism and its external environment are irrelevant to its current (explanatory) psychological state. The restriction also entails that properties and relations of external objects cannot be relevant to the organism's current (explanatory) psychological state. Thus neither my seeing that Jones is falling nor my knowing that Ouagadougou is the capital of Upper Volta can play a role in an explanatory psychological theory, since the former depends in part on my relation to Jones, and the latter depends in part on the relation between Ouagadougou and Upper Volta.

Before we leave our discussion of the principle of psychological autonomy, let us reflect briefly on the status of the principle. On Kim's view, the belief that one set of properties supervenes on another "is largely, and often, a combination of metaphysical convictions and methodological considerations."[7] The description seems particularly apt for the principle of psychological autonomy. The autonomy principle serves a sort of regulative role in modern psychology, directing us to restrict the concepts we invoke in our explanatory theories in a very special way. When we act in accordance with the regulative stipulation of the principle we are giving witness to the tacit conviction that the best explanation of behavior will include a theory invoking properties supervenient upon the organism's current, internal physical state.[8] As Kim urges, this conviction is supported in part by the past success of theories which cleave to the principle's restrictions, and in part by some very fundamental metaphysical convictions. I think there is much to be learned in trying to pick apart the various metaphysical views that support the autonomy principle, for some of them have implications in areas quite removed from psychology. But that is a project for a different paper.

2 The belief–desire thesis

The belief–desire thesis maintains that human action is to be explained, at least in part, in terms of beliefs and desires. To sharpen the thesis we need to say more about the intended sense of *explain*, and more about what it would be to explain action *in terms of beliefs and desires*. But before trying to pin down either of these notions, it will be useful to set out an example of the sort of informal belief–desire explanations that we commonly offer for our own actions and the actions of others.

Jones is watching television; from time to time he looks nervously at a lottery ticket grasped firmly in his hand. Suddenly he jumps up and rushes toward the phone. Why? It was because the TV announcer has just announced the winning lottery number, and it is the number on Jones's ticket. Jones believes that he has won the lottery. He also believes that to collect his winnings he must contact the lottery commission promptly. And, needless to say, he very much wants to collect his winnings.

Many theorists acknowledge that explanations like the one offered of Jones rushing toward the phone are often true (albeit incomplete) explanations of action. But this concession alone does not commit the theorist to the belief–desire thesis as I will interpret it here. There is considerable controversy over how we are to understand the "because" in "Jones rushed for the phone because he believed he had won the lottery and he wanted . . ." Some writers are inclined to read the "because" literally, as claiming that Jones's belief and his desire were the *causes* (or among the causes) of his action. Others offer a variety of non-causal accounts of the relation between beliefs and desires on the one hand and actions on the other'.[9] However, it is the former, "literal," reading that is required by the belief–desire thesis as I am construing it.

To say that Jones's belief that he had won the lottery was among the causes of his rushing toward the phone is to say of one specific event that it had among its causes one specific state. There is much debate over how such "singular causal statements" are to be analyzed. Some philosophers hold that for a state or event S to be among the causes of an event E, there must be a law which somehow relates S and E. Other philosophers propose other accounts. Even among those who agree that singular causal statements must be subsumed by a law, there is debate over how this notion of subsumption is to be understood. At the heart of this controversy is the issue of how much difference there can be between the properties invoked in the law and those invoked in the description of the event if the event is to be an instance of the law.[10] Given our current purposes, there is no need to take a stand on this quite general metaphysical issue. But we will have to take a stand on a special case of the relation between beliefs, desires, and the psychological laws that subsume them. The belief–desire thesis, as I am viewing it, takes seriously the idea of developing a psychological theory couched in terms of beliefs and desires. Thus, in addition to holding that Jones's action was caused by his belief that he had won the lottery and his desire to collect his winnings, it also holds that this singular causal statement is true in virtue of being subsumed by laws which specify nomological relations among beliefs, desires, and action.[11]

There is one further point that needs to be made about my construal of the belief–desire thesis. If the thesis is right, then action is to be explained at least in part by appeal to laws detailing how beliefs, desires, and other psychological states effect action. But how are we to recognize such laws? It is, after all, plainly not enough for a theory simply to invoke the terms "belief" and "desire" in its laws. If it were, then it would be possible to convert any theory into a belief–desire theory by the simple expedient of replacing a pair of its theoretical terms with the terms "belief" and "desire." The point I am laboring is that the belief–desire thesis must be construed as the claim that psychological theory will be couched in terms of beliefs and desires *as we ordinarily conceive of them*. Thus to spell out the belief–desire thesis in detail would require that we explicate our intuitive concepts of belief and desire. Fortunately, we need not embark on that project here.[12] To fuel the arguments I will develop in the following section, I will need only a single, intuitively plausible, premise about beliefs.

As a backdrop for the premise that I need, let me introduce some handy terminology. I believe that Ouagadougou is the capital of Upper Volta, and if you share my interest in atlases then it is likely that you have the same belief. Of course, there is also a perfectly coherent sense in which your belief is not the same as mine, since you could come to believe that Bobo Dioulasso is the capital of Upper Volta, while my belief remains unchanged. The point here is the obvious one that beliefs, like sentences, admit of a type–token distinction. I am inclined to view belief tokens as states of a person. And I take a state to be the instantiation of a property by an object during a time interval. Two belief states (or belief tokens) are of the same type if they are instantiations of the same property and they are of different types if they are instantiations of different properties.[13] In the example at hand, the property that both you and I instantiate is *believing that Ouagadougou is the capital of Upper Volta*.

Now the premise I need for my argument concerns the identity conditions for belief properties. Cast in its most intuitive form, the premise is simply that if a particular belief of yours is true and a particular belief of mine is false, then they are not the same belief. A bit more precisely: If a belief token of one subject differs in truth value from a belief token of another subject, then the tokens are not of the same type. Given our recent account of belief states, this is equivalent to a sufficient condition for the non-identity of belief properties: If an instantiation of belief property p_1 differs in truth value from an instantiation of belief property p_2 then p_1 and p_2 are different properties. This premise hardly constitutes an analysis of our notion of sameness of belief, since we surely do not hold belief tokens to be of the same type if they merely have the same truth value. But no matter. There is no need here to explicate our intuitive notion of belief identity in any detail. What the premise does provide is a necessary condition on any state counting as a belief. If a pair of states can be type identical (i.e., can be instantiations of the same property) while differing in truth value, then the states are not beliefs as we ordinarily conceive of them.

Before putting my premise to work, it might be helpful to note how the premise can be derived from a quite traditional philosophical account of the nature of beliefs. According to this account, belief is a relation between a person and a proposition. Two persons have the same belief (instantiate the same belief property) if they are belief-related to the same proposition. And, finally, propositions are taken to be the vehicles of truth, so propositions with different truth values cannot be identical. Given this account of belief, it follows straightforwardly that belief tokens differing in truth value differ in type. But the entailment is not mutual, so those who, like me, have some suspicions about the account of belief as a relation between a person and a proposition are free to explore other accounts of belief without abandoning the intuitively sanctioned premise that differences in truth value entail difference in belief.

3 The tension between autonomy and the belief–desire thesis

In this section I want to argue that a certain tension exists between the principle of psychological autonomy and the belief–desire thesis. The tension is not, strictly speaking, a logical incompatibility, Rather, there is an incompatibility between the autonomy principle and some assumptions that are naturally and all but universally shared by advocates of the belief–desire thesis. The additional assumptions are that singular causal statements like the ones extractable from our little story about Jones and the lottery ticket are often true. Moreover, they are true because they are subsumed by laws which invoke the very properties which are invoked in the characterization of the beliefs and desires. A bit less abstractly, what I am assuming is that statements like "Jones's belief that he had won the lottery was among the causes of his rushing toward the phone" are often true; and that they are true in virtue of being subsumed by laws invoking properties like *believing that he had just won the lottery*. The burden of my argument is that if we accept the principle of autonomy, then these assumptions must be rejected. More specifically, I will argue that if the autonomy principle is accepted then there are large numbers of belief properties that cannot play a role in an explanatory psychological theory. My strategy will be to examine four different cases, each representative of a large class. In each case we will consider a pair of subjects who, according to the autonomy principle, instantiate all the same explanatory psychological properties, but who have different beliefs. So if we accept the principle of psychological autonomy, then it follows that the belief properties our subjects instantiate cannot be explanatory psychological properties. After running through the examples, I will reflect briefly on the implications of the argument for the belief–desire thesis.

Case 1: Self-referential beliefs[14]

Suppose, as we did earlier, that we have the technology for creating atom for atom replicas of people. Suppose, further, that a replica for me has just been created. I believe that I have tasted a bottle of Chateau d'Yquem, 1962. Were you to ask me whether I had ever tasted a d'Yquem, 1962, I would likely reply,

"Yes, I have." An advocate of the belief–desire thesis would urge, plausibly enough, that my belief is among the causes of my utterance. Now if you were to ask my replica whether he had ever tasted a d'Yquem, 1962, he would likely also reply, "Yes, I have." And surely a belief–desire theorist will also count my replica's belief among the causes of his utterance. But the belief which is a cause of my replica's utterance must be of a different type from the one which is a cause of my utterance. For his belief is false; he has just been created and has never tasted a d'Yquem, nor any other wine. So by the premise we set out in section 2, the belief property he instantiates is different from the one I instantiate. Yet since we are replicas, the autonomy principle entails that we share all our explanatory psychological properties. It follows that the property of believing that I have tasted a Chateau d'Yquem, 1962, cannot be one which plays a role in an explanatory psychological theory. In an obvious way, the example can be generalized to almost all beliefs about oneself. If we adhere to the principle of autonomy, then beliefs about ourselves can play no role in the explanation of our behavior.

Case 2:   Beliefs about one's spatial and temporal location

Imagine, to vary the science fiction example, that cryogenics, the art of freezing people, has been perfected to the point at which a person can be frozen, stored, then defrosted, and at the end of the ordeal be atom for atom identical with the way he was at the beginning of the freezing process. Now suppose that I submit myself to cryogenic preservation this afternoon, and, after being frozen, I am transported to Iceland where I am stored for a century or two, then defrosted. I now believe that it is the twentieth century and that there are many strawberry farms nearby. It would be easy enough to tell stories which would incline the belief–desire theorists to say that each of these beliefs is serving as a cause of my actions. I will leave the details to the reader's imagination. On being defrosted, however, I would presumably still believe that it is the twentieth century and that there are many strawberry farms nearby. Since my current beliefs are both true and my future beliefs both false, they are not belief tokens of the same type, and do not instantiate the same belief property. But by hypothesis, I am, on defrosting, a replica of my current self. Thus the explanatory psychological properties that I instantiate cannot have changed. So the belief property I instantiate when I now believe that it is the twentieth century cannot play any role in an explanatory psychological theory. As in the previous case, the example generalizes to a large number of other beliefs involving a subject's temporal and spatial location.

Case 3:   Beliefs about other people

In several papers Hilary Putnam has made interesting use of the following fanciful hypothesis.[15] Suppose that in some distant corner of the universe there is a planet very much like our own. Indeed, it is so much like our own that there is a person there who is my doppelganger. He is atom for atom identical with me and has led an entirely parallel life history. Like me, my doppelganger teaches in a philosophy department, and like me has heard a number of lectures on the subject of proper names delivered by a man called "Saul Kripke." However, his planet is not a complete physical replica of mine. For the philosopher called "Saul Kripke" on that planet, though strikingly similar to the one called by the same name on our planet, was actually born in a state they call "South Dakota," which is to the north of a state they call "Nebraska." By contrast, our Saul Kripke was born in Nebraska – our Nebraska, of course, not theirs. But for reasons which need not be gone into here, many people on this distant planet, including my doppelganger, hold a belief which they express by saying "Saul Kripke was born in Nebraska." Now I also hold a belief which I express by saying "Saul Kripke was born in Nebraska." However, the belief I express with those words is very different from the belief my doppelganger expresses using the same words, so different, in fact, that his belief is false while mine is true. Yet since we are doppelgangers the autonomy principle dictates that we instantiate all the same explanatory psychological properties. Thus the belief property I instantiate in virtue of believing that Saul Kripke was born in Nebraska cannot be a property invoked in an explanatory psychological theory.

Case 4: *Natural kind predicates*

In Putnam's doppelganger planet stories, a crucial difference between our planet and the distant one is that on our planet the substance which we call "water," which fills our lakes, etc. is in fact H_2O, while on the other planet the substance they call "water" which fills their lakes, etc. is in fact some complex chemical whose chemical formula we may abbreviate XYZ. Now imagine that we are in the year 1700, and that some ancestor of mine hears a story from a source he takes to be beyond reproach to the effect that when lizards are dipped in water, they dissolve. The story, let us further suppose, is false, a fact which my ancestor might discover to his dismay when attempting to dissolve a lizard. For the belief–desire theorist, the unsuccessful attempt has as one of its causes the belief that lizards dissolve in water. Now suppose that my ancestor has a doppelganger on the far-off planet who is told an identical sounding story by an equally trustworthy raconteur. However, as it happens that story is true, for there are lizards that do dissolve in XYZ, though none will dissolve in H_2O. The pattern should by now be familiar. My ancestor's belief is false, his doppelganger's is true. Thus the belief tokens instantiate different belief properties. But since *ex hypothesis* the people holding the beliefs are physically identical, the belief properties they instantiate cannot function in an explanatory psychological theory.[16]

This completes my presentation of cases. Obviously, the sorts of examples we have looked at are not the only ones susceptible to the sort of arguments

I have been using. But let us now reflect for a moment on just what these arguments show. To begin, we should note that they do *not* show the belief–desire thesis is false. The thesis, as I have construed it here, holds that there are psychological laws which invoke various belief and desire properties and which have a substantive role to play in the explanation of behavior. Nothing we have said here would suffice to show that there are no such laws. At best, what we have shown is that, if we accept the principle of psychological autonomy, then a large class of belief properties cannot be invoked in an explanatory psychological theory. This, in turn, entails that many intuitively sanctioned singular causal statements which specify a belief as a cause of an action cannot be straightforwardly subsumed by a law. And it is just here, I think, that our argument may serve to undermine the belief–desire thesis. For the plausibility of the thesis rests, in large measure, on the plausibility of these singular causal statements. Indeed, I think the belief–desire thesis can be profitably viewed as the speculation that these intuitively sanctioned singular causal statements can be cashed out in a serious psychological theory couched in terms of beliefs and desires. In showing that large numbers of these singular causal statements cannot be cashed out in this way, we make the speculation embodied in the belief–desire thesis appear idle and unmotivated. In the section that follows, I will consider a way in which an advocate of the belief–desire thesis might try to deflect the impact of our arguments, and indicate the burden that this escape route imposes on the belief–desire theorist.

4   A way out and its costs

Perhaps the most tempting way to contain the damage done by the arguments of the previous section is to grant the conclusions while denying their relevance to the belief–desire thesis. I imagine a critic's objection going something like this: "Granted, if we accept the autonomy principle, then certain belief properties cannot be used in explanatory theories. But this does nothing to diminish the plausibility of the belief–desire thesis, because the properties you have shown incompatible with autonomy are the *wrong kind* of belief properties. All of the examples you consider are cases of *de re* beliefs, none of them are *de dicto* beliefs. But those theorists who take seriously the idea of constructing a belief–desire psychological theory have in mind a theory invoking *de dicto* beliefs and desires. *De re* beliefs are a sort of hybrid; a person has a *de re* belief if he has a suitable underlying *de dicto* belief, *and* if he is related to specific objects in a certain way. But it is only the underlying *de dicto* belief that will play a role in psychological explanation. Thus your arguments do not cast any serious doubt on the belief–desire thesis.[17]

Before assessing this attempt to protect the belief–desire thesis, a few remarks on the *de dicto/de re* distinction are in order. In the recent philosophical discussion of *de re* and *de dicto* beliefs, the focus has been on the logical relations among various sorts of belief attributions. Writers concerned with the issue have generally invoked a substitution criterion to mark the boundary between *de dicto* and *de re* belief attributions. Roughly, a belief attribution of the form.

 S believes that *p*

is *de re* if any name or other referring expression within *p* can be replaced with a co-designating term without risk of change of truth value, otherwise the attribution is *de dicto*.[18]

But now given this way of drawing the *de re/de dicto* distinction, my imagined critic is simply wrong in suggesting that all of the examples used in my arguments are cases of *de re* belief. Indeed, just the opposite is true; I intend all of the belief attribution in my examples to be understood in the *de dicto* sense, and all my arguments work quite as well when they are read in this way. Thus, for example, in Case 3 I attribute to myself the belief that Saul Kripke was born in Nebraska. But I intend this to be understood in such a way that

 Stich believes φ was born in Nebraska

might well be false if φ were replaced by a term which, quite unbeknownst to me, in fact denotes Saul Kripke.

There is, however, another way the critic could press his attack that sidesteps my rejoinder. Recently, a number of writers have challenged the substitutional account of the *de dicto/de re* distinction. The basic idea underlying their challenge is that the term "*de re*" should be used for all belief attributions which intend to ascribe a "real" relation of some sort between the believer and the object of his belief. The notion of a real relation is contrasted with the sort of relation that obtains between a person and an object when the object happens to satisfy some description that the person has in mind.[19] Burge, for example, holds that "a *de dicto* belief is a belief in which the believer is related only to a completely expressed proposition (*dictum*)," in contrast to a *de re* belief which is "a belief whose correct ascription places the believer in an appropriate, *nonconceptual*, *contextual* relation to the objects the belief is about."[20] Thus, if Brown believes that the most prosperous Oriental rug dealer in Los Angeles is an Armenian, and if he believes it simply because he believes all prosperous Oriental rug dealers are Armenian, but has no idea who the man may be, then his belief is *de dicto*. By contrast, if Brown is an intimate of the gentleman, he may have the *de re* belief that the most prosperous Oriental rug dealer in Los Angeles is an Armenian. The sentence

 Brown believes that the must prosperous Oriental rug dealer in Los Angeles is an Armenian.

is thus ambiguous, since it may be used either in the *de re* sense to assert that Brown and the rug dealer stand in some "appropriate, nonconceptual, contextual relation" or in the *de dicto* sense which asserts merely that Brown endorses the proposition that the most prosperous rug dealer in Los Angeles (whoever he may be) is an Armenian.

The problem with the substitutional account of the *de dicto/de re* distinction is that it classifies as *de dicto* many belief attributions which impute a "real" relation between the believer and the object of his belief. In many belief attributions the names or definite descriptions that occur in the content sentence do a sort of double duty. First, they serve the function commonly served by names and descriptions; they indicate (or refer to) an object, in this case the object to which the believer is said to be related. The names or descriptions in the content sentence *also* may serve to indicate how the believer conceives of the object, or how he might characterize it. When a name or description serving both roles is replaced by a codesignating expression which does *not* indicate how the believer conceives of the object, then the altered attribution (interpreted in the "double duty" sense) will be false. Thus the substitutional account classifies the original attribution as *de dicto*, despite its imputation of a "real" relation between believer and object?[21]

Now if the *de dicto/de re* distinction is drawn by classifying as *de re* all those belief attributions which impute a "real" relation between believer and object, then the critic conjured in the first paragraph of this section is likely right in his contention that all of my arguments invoke examples of *de re* beliefs. Indeed, the strategy of my arguments is to cite an example of a *de re* (i.e., "real relation") belief, then construct a second example in which the second believer is a physical replica of the first, but has no "real relation" to the object of the first believer's belief. However, to grant this much is not to grant that the critic has succeeded in blunting the point of my arguments.

Let me begin my rejoinder with a fussy point. The critic's contentions were two: first, that my examples all invoked *de re* belief properties; second, that *de re* belief properties are hybrids and are analyzable into *de dicto* belief properties. The fussy point is that even if both the critic's contentions are granted, the critic would not quite have met my arguments head on. The missing premise is that *de dicto* belief properties (construed now according to the "real relation" criterion) are in fact compatible with the principle of psychological autonomy. This premise may be true, but the notion of a "real" relation, on which the current account of *de dicto* belief properties depends, is sufficiently obscure that it is hard to tell. Fortunately, there is a simple way to finesse the problem. Let us introduce the term *autonomous beliefs* for those beliefs that a subject must share with all his replicas; and let us use the term *non-autonomous* for those beliefs which a subject need not share with his replica.[22] More generally, we can call any property which an organism must share with its replicas an *autonomous property*. We can now reconstrue the critic's claims as follows:

1   All the examples considered in section 3 invoke non-autonomous belief properties.

2 Non-autonomous belief properties are hybrids, analyzable into an underlying autonomous belief property (which can play a role in psychological explanation) plus some further relation(s) between the believer and the object of his belief.

On the first point I naturally have no quarrel, since a principal purpose of this essay is to show that a large class of belief properties are non-autonomous. On the second claim, however, I would balk, for I am skeptical that the proposed analysis can in fact be carried off. I must hasten to add that I know of *no argument* sufficient to show that the analysis is impossible. But, of course, my critic has no argument either. Behind my skepticism is the fact that no such analysis has ever been carried off. Moreover, the required analysis is considerably more demanding than the analysis of *de re* belief in terms of *de dicto* belief, when the distinction between the two is drawn by the substitutional criterion. For the class of autonomous beliefs is significantly smaller than the class of *de dicto* beliefs (characterized substitutionally).[23] And the most impressive attempts to reduce *de re* beliefs to *de dicto* plainly will not be of much help for the analysis my critic proposes.[24] But enough, I have already conceded that I cannot prove my critic's project is impossible. What I do hope to have established is that the critic's burden is the burden of the belief–desire theorist. If the reduction of non-autonomous beliefs to autonomous beliefs cannot be carried off, then there is small prospect that a psychological theory couched in terms of beliefs and desires will succeed in explaining any substantial part of human behavior.

A final point. It might be argued that, however difficult the analysis of non-autonomous beliefs to autonomous ones may be, it must be possible to carry it off. For, the argument continues, a subject's non-autonomous beliefs are determined in part by the autonomous psychological properties he instantiates and in part by his various relations to the objects of the world. Were either of these components suitably altered, the subject's non-autonomous beliefs would be altered as well. And since non-autonomous beliefs are jointly determined by autonomous psychological properties and by other relations, there must be some analysis, however complex, which specifies how this joint determination works. Now this last claim is not one I would want to challenge. I am quite prepared to grant that non-autonomous beliefs admit of some analysis in terms of autonomous psychological properties plus other relations. But what seems much more doubtful to me is that the autonomous properties invoked in the analysis would be *belief properties*. To see the reasons for my doubt, let us reflect on the picture suggested by the examples in section 3. In each case we had a pair of subjects who shared all their autonomous properties though their non-autonomous beliefs differed in truth value. The difference in truth value, in turn, was rooted in a difference in reference; the beliefs were simply about different persons, places, or times. In short, the beliefs represented different states of affairs. If the non-autonomous belief properties of these examples are to be analyzed into autonomous psychological properties plus various historical or external relations, then it is plausible to suppose that the autonomous psychological properties do not determine a truth value, an appropriate reference, or a represented state of affairs. So the state of exhibiting one (or more) of these autonomous properties itself has no truth value, is not referential, and does not represent anything. And this, I would urge, is more than enough reason to say that it is not a belief at all. None of this amounts to an *argument* that non-autonomous beliefs are not analyzable into autonomous ones. Those who seek such an analysis are still free to maintain that there will be at least one autonomous belief among the autonomous properties in the analysis of each non-autonomous belief property. But in the absence of an argument for this claim, I think few will find it particularly plausible. The ball is in the belief–desire theorist's court.[25, 26]

Appendix

A bit more needs to be said about the premise urged at the end of section 2. The premise, it will be recalled, was this:

> If a belief token of one subject differs in truth value from a belief token of another subject, then the tokens are not of the same type.

A number of helpful critics base pointed out to me that we actually have a variety of intuitively sanctioned ways to decide when two belief tokens are of the same type. Moreover, some of these patently violate my premise. Thus, for example, if Jones and Smith each believes that he will win the next presidential election, there would be no intuitive oddness to the claim that Jones and Smith have the same belief. Though, of course, if Jones's belief is true, Smith's belief is false. It would be equally natural in this case to say that Jones and Smith have different beliefs. So I cannot rest my premise on our intuitive judgments; the intuitions will not bear the weight.

I think the best way of defending the premise is to make clear how it is related to a certain view (actually a category of views) about what beliefs are. The views I have in mind all share two features in common:

(i)   they take belief to be a relation between a believer and a type of abstract object;
(ii) they take the abstract objects to be representational – that is, the abstract objects are taken to picture the world as being a certain way, or to claim that some state of affairs obtains. Thus the object, along with the actual state of the believer's world, determines a truth value.

For example, certain theorists take belief to be a relation between a person and a proposition; a proposition, in turn, determines a truth value for every possible world – truth for those worlds in which it is true and falsity for those worlds in which it is false. A person's belief is true if the proposition is true in his or her world. Rather more old fashioned is the theory which holds belief to be a relation between a person and an image or a mental picture. The belief is true if and only if the mental picture correctly depicts the believer's world.

Now on views such as these which take belief to be a relation between a person and an abstract object, the most natural way of determining when a pair of belief tokens are of the same type is by appeal to the abstract objects. A pair of subjects' belief tokens are of the same type when the subjects are related to the same abstract object. Thus when subjects are in the same possible world, their belief tokens are of the same type only if they are identical in truth value. And this, in effect, was the premise advanced in section 2. The thesis of this essay is best taken to be that the principle of psychological autonomy is in conflict with the belief–desire thesis, *when beliefs are construed as in (i) and (ii)*. Let me add a final observation. A number of theorists have taken belief to be a relation between a person and a sentence or sentence-like object. For example, in *The Language of Thought* (Fodor 1975) Jerry Fodor holds that belief is a relation between a person and a sentence in "the language of thought." It is interesting to ask whether a theory like Fodor's is at odds with the principle of psychological autonomy. The answer, I think, turns on whether the sentences in the language of thought are taken to have truth values, and whether their referring expressions are taken to determine a referent in a given world, independent of the head in which they happen to be inscribed. If sentences in the language of thought are taken to be analogous to Quine's eternal sentences, true or false in a given world regardless of who utters them or where they may be inscribed, then Fodor's view will satisfy (i) and (ii) and will run head on into the principle of psychological autonomy. For Fodor, I suspect, this would be argument enough to show that the sentences in the language of thought are not eternal.

Notes

1 The clearest and most detailed elaboration of this view that I know of is to be found in Goldman (1970). The view is also argued in Brandt and Kim (1963), and in Davidson (1963). However Davidson does not advocate the belief–desire thesis as it will be construed below (cf. n. 11).
2 Cf. Putnam (1973 and 1975).
3 Kim (1978).
4 Kim's account of supervenience is intentionally noncommittal on the sort of necessity invoked in the definition. Different notions of necessity will yield different, though parallel, concepts of supervenience.
5 This weaker principle is discussed at some length in Kim (1977).
6 Note, however, that physical properties that are irrelevant in this sense may nonetheless be *causally* related to those physical properties upon which psychological properties supervene. Thus they may be "psychologically relevant" in the sense that they may play a role in the explanation of how the organism comes to have some psychological property.

7 Kim (1978).

8 It has been my experience that psychologists who agree on little else readily endorse the autonomy principle. Indeed, I have yet to find a psychologist who did not take the principle to be obviously true. Some of these same psychologists also favored the sort of belief–desire explanations of action that I will later argue are at odds with the autonomy principle. None, however, was aware of the incompatibility, and a number of them vigorously resisted the contention that the incompatibility is there.

9 For a critique of these views, cf. Goldman (1970: chapter 3); Alston (1967b).

10 For discussion of these matters, see Kim (1973). Kim defends the view that the property invoked in the description must be identical with the one invoked in the law. For a much more liberal view see Davidson (1967).

11 Thus Davidson is not an advocate of the belief–desire thesis as I am construing it. For on his view, though beliefs and desires may be among the causes of actions, the general laws supporting the causal claims are not themselves couched in terms of beliefs and desires (cf. Davidson 1970). But Davidson's view, though not without interest, is plainly idiosyncratic. Generally, philosophers who hold that beliefs and desires are among the causes of behavior also think that there are psychological laws to be found (most likely probabilistic ones) which are stated in terms of beliefs and desires, Cf., for example, Hempel (1965: 463–87), Alston (1967a and 1967b); Goldman (1970: chapters 3 and 4).

We should also note that much of recent psychology can be viewed as a quest for psychological laws couched in terms of beliefs and/or desires. There is, for example, an enormous and varied literature on problem solving (cf. Newell and Simon 1972) and on informal inference (cf. Nisbett and Ross 1980) which explores the mechanisms and environmental determinants of belief formation. Also, much of the literature on motivation is concerned with uncovering the laws governing the formation and strength of desires (cf. Atkinson 1964).

12 For an attempt to explicate our informal concepts of belief and desire in some detail, see Stich (1983).

13 For more on this way of viewing states and events, cf. Kim (1969 and 1976). I think that most everything I say in this essay can be said as well, though not as briefly, without presupposing this account of states and events.

14 The examples in Case 1 and Case 2, along with my thinking on these matters, have been influenced by a pair of important papers by Castañeda (1966 and 1967).

15 Putnam (1973 and 1975).

16 We should note that this example and others invoking natural kind words work only if the extension of my ancestor's word "water" is different from the extension of the word "water" as used by my ancestor's doppelganger. I am inclined to agree with Putnam that the extensions are different. But the matter is controversial. For some support of Putnam's view, see Kripke (1972) and Teller (1977); for an opposing view cf. Zemach (1976). Incidentally, one critic has expressed doubt that my doppelganger and I could be physically identical if that stuff called "water" on the far-off planet is actually XYZ. Those who find the point troubling are urged to construct a parallel example using kinds of material not generally occurring within people.

17 The idea that de dicto beliefs are psychologically more basic is widespread. For a particularly clear example, see Armstrong (1973: 25–31). Of the various

attempts so analyze *de re* beliefs in terms of *de dicto* beliefs, perhaps the best known are to be found in Kaplan (1968) and Chisholm (1976).

18 The substitutional account of the *de re/de dicto* distinction has a curious consequence that has been little noted. Though most belief sentences of the form

S believes that Fa

can be used to make either *de re* or *de dicto* attributions, the substitutional account entails that some can only be used to make *de re* attributions. Consider, for example.

(i) Quine believes that the Queen of England is a turtle.

The claim of course, is false. Indeed, it is *so* false that it could not be used to make a *de dicto* belief attribution. For in all likelihood, there is *no* name or definite description ϕ denoting Elizabeth II such that

Quine believes that ϕ is a turtle

is true. Thus "Quine believes that the Queen of England is a turtle" is false and cannot be turned into a truth by the replacement of "the Queen of England" by a codesignating expression. So on the substitutional account, this sentence can be used to make only *de re* attributions. A parallel problem besets Quine's well known substitutional account of a *purely referential position* (Quine 1960: 142ff.). In (i) the position occupied by "the Queen of England" can only be regarded as purely referential.

19 For more on the distinction between "real" relations and mere "satisfaction" relations, cf. Kim (1977).

20 Burge (1977: 345 and 346), last emphasis added.

21 For more on this "double duty" view of the role of names and descriptions in content sentences, see Loar (1972).

22 Of course when the notion of a "real relation" has been suitably sharpened it might well turn out that the autonomous/non-autonomous distinction coincides with the "real relation" version of the *de dicto/de re* distinction.

23 For example, when I say, "I believe that Kripke was born in Nebraska," I am attributing to myself a belief which is substitutionally *de dicto*, but not autonomous.

24 Kaplan's strategy, for example, will be of no help, since his analysans are, for the most part, non-autonomous substitutionally *de dicto* belief sentences. Cf. Kaplan (1968) and Burge (1977: 350ff.).

25 I am indebted to Robert Cummins, Jaegwon Kim, William Alston, and John Bennett for their helpful comments on the topics discussed in this essay.

26 After completing this essay, I was delighted to discover a very similar view in Perry (1979). Fodor (1980) defends a version of the principle of psychological autonomy.

References

Alston, W.P. (1967a) "Motives and motivation," *The Encyclopedia of Philosophy*, New York.

—— (1967b) "Wants, actions and causal explanations," in H.N. Castañeda (ed.) *Intentionality, Minds and Perception*, Detroit.

Armstrong, D.M. (1973) *Belief, Truth and Knowledge*, Cambridge.

Atkinson, J.W. (1964) *An Introduction to Motivation*, New York.

Brandt, R.B. and Kim Jaegwon (1963) "Wants as explanations of actions," *Journal of Philosophy* LX, 425–35.

Burge, T. (1977) "Belief de re," *Journal of Philosophy* LXXIV, 338–62.

Castañeda, H.N. (1966) "'He': A study in the logic of self-consciousness," *Ratio* 8, 130–57.

—— (1967) "Indicators and quasi-indicators," *American Philosophical Quarterly* 4, 85–100.

Chisholm, R. (1976) *Person and Object*, LaSalle, Ill.

Davidson, D. (1963) "Actions, reasons and causes," *Journal of Philosophy* LX, 685–700.

—— (1967) "Causal relations," *Journal of Philosophy* LXIV, 691–703.

—— (1970) "Mental events," in L. Foster and J.W. Swanson (eds), *Experience and Theory*, Amherst.

Fodor, J. (1975) *The Language of Thought*. Cambridge, Mass.

—— (1980) "Methodological solipsism considered as a research strategy in cognitive psychology," *Behavioral and Brain Sciences* 3, 63–73.

Goldman, A. (1970) *A Theory of Human Action*, Englewood Cliffs.

Hempel, C.G. (1965) *Aspects of Scientific Explanation*, New York.

Kaplan, D. (1968) "Quantifying in," *Synthese* 19, 178–214.

Kim, J. (1969) "Events and their descriptions: Some considerations," in N. Rescher et al. (eds), *Essays in Honor of C. G. Hempel*, Dordrecht, Holland.

—— (1973) "Causation, nomic subsumption and the concept of event," *Journal of Philosophy*, LXX, 217–36.

—— (1976) "Events as property-exemplifications," in M. Brand and D. Walton (eds), *Action Theory*, Dordrecht, Holland.

—— (1977) "Perception and reference without causality," *Journal of Philosophy* 74, 606–20.

—— (1978) "Supervenience and nomological incommensurables." *American Philosophical Quarterly* 15(2), 149–56.

Kripke, S. (1972) "Naming and necessity," in D. Davidson and G. Harman (eds), *Semantics and Natural Language*, Dordrecht, Holland.

Loar, B. (1972) "Reference and propositional attitudes," *Philosophical Review* LXXX, 43–62.

Newell, A. and Simon, H.A. (1972) *Human Problem Solving*, Englewood Cliffs.

Nisbett, R. and Ross, L. (1980) *Human Inference: Strategies and Shortcomings of Social Judgment*, Prentice-Hall.

Perry, J. (1979) "The problem of the essential indexical," *Noûs* 13, 3–21.

Putnam, H. (1973) "Meaning and reference," *Journal of Philosophy* LXX, 699–711.

—— (1975) "The meaning of 'meaning'," in K. Gunderson (ed.), *Language, Mind and Knowledge*, Minneapolis.

Quine, W.V.O. (1960) *Word and Object*, Cambridge.

Stich, S. (1983) *From Folk Psychology to Cognitive Science*, Cambridge, Mass.

Teller, P. (1977) "Indicative introduction," *Philosophical Studies* 31, 173–95.

Zemach, E. (1976) "Putnam's theory on the reference of substance terms," *Journal of Philosophy* LXXXIII, 116–27.

IIB

COMMONSENSE PSYCHOLOGY AND MENTAL REPRESENTATION

13

W. Ramsey, S. Stich and J. Garon, "Connectionism, Eliminativism and The Future of Folk Psychology"[1]

1 Introduction

In the years since the publication of Thomas Kuhn's *Structure of Scientific Revolutions*, the term "scientific revolution" has been used with increasing frequency in discussions of scientific change, and the magnitude required of an innovation before someone or other is tempted to call it a revolution has diminished alarmingly. Our thesis in this paper is that if a certain family of connectionist hypotheses turn out to be right, they will surely count as revolutionary, even on stringent pre-Kuhnian standards. There is no question that connectionism has already brought about major changes in the way many cognitive scientists conceive of cognition. However, as we see it, what makes certain kinds of connectionist models genuinely revolutionary is the support they lend to a thoroughgoing eliminativism about some of the central posits of common sense (or "folk") psychology. Our focus in this paper will be on beliefs or propositional memories, though the argument generalizes straightforwardly to all the other propositional attitudes. If we are right, the consequences of this kind of connectionism extend well beyond the confines of cognitive science, since these models, if successful, will require a radical reorientation in the way we think about ourselves.

Here is a quick preview of what is to come. Section 2 gives a brief account of what eliminativism claims, and sketches a pair of premises that eliminativist arguments typically require. Section 3 says a bit about how we conceive of common sense psychology, and the propositional attitudes that it posits. It also illustrates one sort of psychological model that exploits and builds upon the posits of folk psychology. Section 4 is devoted to connectionism. Models that have been called "connectionist" form a fuzzy and heterogeneous set whose members often share little more than a vague family resemblance. However, our argument linking connectionism to eliminativism will work only for a restricted domain of connectionist models, interpreted in a particular way; the main job of Section 4 is to say what that domain is and how the models in the domain are to be interpreted. In Section 5 we will illustrate what a connectionist model of belief that comports with our strictures might look like, and

263

go on to argue that if models of this sort are correct, then things look bad for common sense psychology. Section 6 assembles some objections and replies. The final section is a brief conclusion.

Before plunging in we should emphasize that the thesis we propose to defend is a *conditional* claim: *If* connectionist hypotheses of the sort we will sketch turn out to be right, so too will eliminativism about propositional attitudes. Since our goal is only to show how connectionism and eliminativism are related, we will make no effort to argue for the truth or falsity of either doctrine. In particular, we will offer no argument in favor of the version of connectionism required in the antecedent of our conditional. Indeed our view is that it is early days yet – too early to tell with any assurance how well this family of connectionist hypotheses will fare. Those who are more confident of connectionism may, of course, invoke our conditional as part of larger argument for doing away with the propositional attitudes.[2] But, as John Haugeland once remarked, one man's *ponens* is another man's *tollens*. And those who take eliminativism about propositional attitudes to be preposterous or unthinkable may well view our arguments as part of a larger case against connectionism. Thus, we'd not be at all surprised if trenchant critics of connectionism, like Fodor and Pylyshyn, found both our conditional and the argument for it to be quite congenial.[3]

2   Eliminativism and folk psychology

'Eliminativism', as we shall use the term, is a fancy name for a simple thesis. It is the claim that some category of entities, processes or properties exploited in a common sense or scientific account of the world do not exist. So construed, we are all eliminativists about many sorts of things. In the domain of folk theory, witches are the standard example. Once upon a time witches were widely believed to be responsible for various local calamities. But people gradually became convinced that there are better explanations for most of the events in which witches had been implicated. There being no explanatory work for witches to do, sensible people concluded that there were no such things. In the scientific domain, phlogiston, caloric fluid and the luminiferous ether are the parade cases for eliminativism. Each was invoked by serious scientists pursuing sophisticated research programs. But in each case the program ran aground in a major way, and the theories in which the entities were invoked were replaced by successor theories in which the entities played no role. The scientific community gradually came to recognize that phlogiston and the rest do not exist.

As these examples suggest, a central step in an eliminativist argument will typically be the demonstration that the theory in which certain putative entities or processes are invoked should be rejected and replaced by a better theory. And that raises the question of how we go about showing that one theory is better than another. Notoriously, this question is easier to ask than to answer. However, it would be pretty widely agreed that if a new theory provides more accurate predictions and better explanations than an old one, and does so over a broader range of phenomena, and if the new theory comports as well or better with well established theories in neighboring domains, then there is good reason to think that the old theory is inferior, and that the new one is to be preferred. This is hardly a complete account of the conditions under which one theory is to be preferred to another, though for our purposes it will suffice.

But merely showing that a theory in which a class of entities plays a role is inferior to a successor theory plainly is not sufficient to show that the entities do not exist. Often a more appropriate conclusion is that the rejected theory was wrong, perhaps seriously wrong, about some of the properties of the entities in its domain, or about the laws governing those entities, and that the new theory gives us a more accurate account *of those very same entities*. Thus, for example, pre-Copernican astronomy was very wrong about the nature of the planets and the laws governing their movement. But it would be something of a joke to suggest that Copernicus and Galileo showed that the planets Ptolemy spoke of do not exist.[4]

In other cases the right thing to conclude is that the posits of the old theory are reducible to those of the new. Standard examples here include the reduction of temperature to mean molecular kinetic energy, the reduction of sound to wave motion in the medium, and the reduction of genes to sequences of polynucleotide bases.[5] Given our current concerns, the lesson to be learned from these cases is that even if the common sense theory in which propositional attitudes find their home is replaced by a better theory, that would not be enough to show that the posits of the common sense theory do not exist.

What more would be needed? What is it that distinguishes cases like phlogiston and caloric, on the one hand, from cases like genes or the planets on the other? Or, to ask the question in a rather different way, what made phlogiston and caloric candidates for elimination? Why wasn't it concluded that phlogiston is oxygen, that caloric is kinetic energy, and that the earlier theories had just been rather badly mistaken about some of the properties of phlogiston and caloric?

Let us introduce a bit of terminology. We will call theory changes in which the entities and processes of the old theory are retained or reduced to those of the new one *ontologically conservative* theory changes. Theory changes that are not ontologically conservative we will call *ontologically radical*. Given this terminology, the question we are asking is how to distinguish ontologically conservative theory changes from ontologically radical ones.

Once again, this is a question that is easier to ask than to answer. There is, in the philosophy of science literature, nothing that even comes close to a plausible and fully general account of when theory change sustains an eliminativist conclusion and when it does not. In the absence of a principled way of deciding when ontological elimination is in order, the best we can do is to look at the posits of the old theory – the ones that are at risk of elimination – and ask whether there is anything in the new theory that they might be identified with or reduced to. If the posits of the new theory strike us as deeply and funda-mentally different from those of the old theory, in the way that molecular motion seems deeply and fundamentally different from the "exquisitely elastic" fluid posited by caloric theory, then it will be plausible to conclude that the theory change has been a radical one, and that an eliminativist conclu-sion is in order. But since there is no easy measure of how "deeply and fundamentally different" a pair of posits are, the conclusion we reach is bound to be a judgment call.[6]

To argue that certain sorts of connectionist models support eliminativism about the propositional attitudes, we must make it plausible that these models are not ontologically conservative. Our strategy will be to contrast these connectionist models, models like those set out in Section 5, with ontologi-cally conservative models like the one sketched at the end of Section 3, in an effort to underscore just how ontologically radical the connectionist models are. But here we are getting ahead of ourselves. Before trying to persuade you that connectionist models are ontologically radical, we need to take a look at the folk psychological theory that the connectionist models threaten to replace.

3   Propositional attitudes and common sense psychology

For present purposes we will assume that common sense psychology can plau-sibly be regarded as a theory, and that beliefs, desires and the rest of the propositional attitudes are plausibly viewed as posits of that theory. Though this is not an uncontroversial assumption, the case for it has been well argued by others.[7] Once it is granted that common sense psychology is indeed a theory, we expect it will be conceded by almost everyone that the theory is a likely candidate for replacement. In saying this, we do not intend to disparage folk psychology, or to beg any questions about the status of the entities it posits. Our point is simply that folk wisdom on matters psychological is not likely to tell us all there is to know. Common sense psychology, like other folk theo-ries, is bound to be incomplete in many ways, and very likely to be inaccurate in more than a few. If this were not the case, there would be no need for a careful, quantitative, experimental science of psychology. With the possible exception of a few die hard Wittgensteinians, just about everyone is prepared to grant that there are many psychological facts and principles beyond those embedded in common sense. If this is right, then we have the first premise needed in an eliminativist argument aimed at beliefs, propositional memories and the rest of the propositional attitudes. The theory that posits the attitudes is indeed a prime candidate for replacement.

Though common sense psychology contains a wealth of lore about beliefs, memories, desires, hopes, fears and the other propositional attitudes, the crucial folk psychological tenets in forging the link between connectionism and eliminativism are the claims that propositional attitudes are *functionally dis-crete, semantically interpretable*, states that play a *causal role* in the production of other propositional attitudes, and ultimately in the production of behavior. Following the suggestion in Stich (1983), we'll call this cluster of claims *propositional modularity*.[8] (The reader is cautioned not to confuse this notion of propositional modularity with the very different notion of modularity defended in Fodor (1983).)

There is a great deal of evidence that might be cited in support of the thesis that folk psychology is committed to the tenets of propositional modularity. The fact that common sense psychology takes beliefs and other propositional attitudes to have semantic properties deserves special emphasis. According to common sense:

(i) when people see a dog nearby they typically come to believe *that there is a dog nearby*;

(ii) when people believe *that the train will be late if there is snow in the mountains*, and come to believe *that there is snow in the mountains*, they will typically come to believe *that the train will be late*;

(iii) when people who speak English say 'There is a cat in the yard,' they typically believe *that there is a cat in the yard*.

And so on, for indefinitely many further examples. Note that these generalizations of common sense psychology are couched in terms of the *semantic* properties of the attitudes. It is in virtue of being the belief *that p* that a given belief has a given effect or cause. Thus common sense psychology treats the predicates expressing these semantic properties, predicates like 'believes *that the train is late*', as *projectable* predicates – the sort of predicates that are appropriately used in nomological or law-like generalizations.

Perhaps the most obvious way to bring out folk psychology's commitment to the thesis that propositional attitudes are *functionally discrete* states is to note that it typically makes perfectly good sense to claim that a person has acquired (or lost) a single memory or belief. Thus, for example, on a given occasion it might plausibly be claimed that when Henry awoke from his nap he had completely forgotten that the car keys were hidden in the refrigerator, though he had forgotten nothing else. In saying that folk psychology views beliefs as the sorts of things that can be acquired or lost one at a time, we do not mean to be denying that having any particular belief may presuppose a substantial network of related beliefs. The belief that the car keys are in the refrigerator is not one that could be acquired by a primitive tribesman who knew nothing about cars, keys or refrigerators. But once the relevant background is in place, as we may suppose it is for us and for Henry, it seems that folk psychology is entirely comfortable with the possibility that a person may acquire (or lose) the belief that the car keys are in the refrigerator, while the remainder of his beliefs remain unchanged. Propositional modularity does not, of course, deny that acquiring one belief often leads to the acquisition of a cluster of related beliefs. When Henry is told that the keys are in the refrigerator, he may come to believe that they haven't been left in the ignition, or in his jacket pocket. But then again he may not. Indeed, on the folk psychological conception of belief it is perfectly possible for a person to have a long standing belief that the keys are in the refrigerator, and to continue searching for them in the bedroom.[9]

To illustrate the way in which folk psychology takes propositional attitudes to be functionally discrete, *causally active* states let us sketch a pair of more elaborate examples.

(i)   In common sense psychology, behavior is often explained by appeal to certain of the agent's beliefs and desires. Thus, to explain why Alice went to her office, we might note that she wanted to send some e-mail messages (and, of course, she believed she could do so from her office). However, in some cases an agent will have several sets of beliefs and desires each of which *might* lead to the same behavior. Thus we may suppose that Alice also wanted to talk to her research assistant, and that she believed he would be at the office. In such cases, common sense psychology assumes that Alice's going to her office might have been caused by either one of the belief/desire pairs, or by both, and that determining which of these options obtains is an empirical matter. So it is entirely possible that on *this* occasion Alice's desire to send some e-mail played no role in producing her behavior; it was the desire to talk with her research assistant that actually caused her to go to the office. However, had she not wanted to talk with her research assistant, she might have gone to the office anyhow, because the desire to send some e-mail, which was causally inert in her actual decision making, might then have become actively involved. Note that in this case common sense psychology is prepared to recognize a pair of quite distinct semantically characterized states, one of which may be causally active while the other is not.

(ii)   Our second illustration is parallel to the first, but focuses on beliefs and inference, rather than desires and action. On the common sense view, it may sometimes happen that a person has a number of belief clusters, any one of which might lead him to infer some further belief. When he actually does draw the inference, folk psychology assumes that it is an empirical question that he inferred it from, and that this question typically has a determinate answer. Suppose, for example, that Inspector Clouseau believes that the butler said he spent the evening at the village hotel, and that he said he arrived back on the morning train. Suppose Clouseau also believes that the village hotel is closed for the season, and that the morning train has been taken out of service. Given these beliefs, along with some widely shared background beliefs, Clouseau might well infer that the butler is lying. If he does, folk psychology presumes that the inference might be based either on his beliefs about the hotel, or on his beliefs about the train, or both. It is entirely possible, from the perspective of common sense psychology, that although Clouseau has long known that the hotel is closed for the season, this belief played no role in his inference on this particular occasion. Once again we see common sense psychology invoking a pair of distinct propositional attitudes, one of which is causally active on a particular occasion while the other is causally inert.

In the psychological literature there is no shortage of models for human belief or memory which follow the lead of common sense psychology in supposing that propositional modularity is true. Indeed, prior to the emergence of connectionism, just about all psychological models of propositional memory, save for those urged by behaviorists, were comfortably compatible with propositional modularity. Typically, these models view a subject's store of beliefs or memories as an interconnected collection of functionally discrete, semantically interpretable states which interact in systematic ways. Some of these models represent individual beliefs as sentence-like structures – strings of symbols which can be individually activated by transferring them from long term memory to the more limited memory of a central processing unit. Other models represent beliefs as a network of labeled nodes and labeled links through which patterns of activation may spread. Still other models represent beliefs as sets of production rules.[10] In all three sorts of models, it is generally the case that for any given cognitive episode, like performing a particular inference or answering a question, some of the memory states will be actively involved, and others will be dormant.

In Figure 13.1 we have displayed a fragment of a "semantic network" representation of memory, in the style of Collins and Quillian (1972). In this model, each distinct proposition in memory is represented by an oval node along with its labeled links to various concepts. By adding assumptions about the way in which questions or other sorts of memory probes lead to activation spreading through the network, the model enables us to make predictions about speed and accuracy in various experimental studies of memory.

For our purposes there are three facts about this model that are of particular importance. First, since each proposition is encoded in a functionally discrete

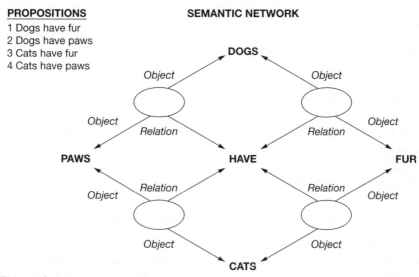

PROPOSITIONS
1 Dogs have fur
2 Dogs have paws
3 Cats have fur
4 Cats have paws

SEMANTIC NETWORK

Figure 13.1

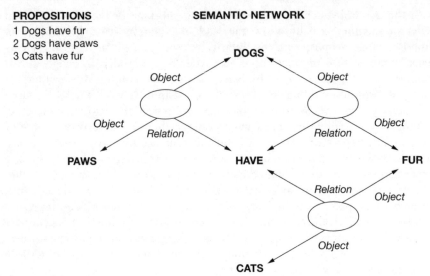

PROPOSITIONS

1 Dogs have fur
2 Dogs have paws
3 Cats have fur

SEMANTIC NETWORK

Figure 13.2

way, it is a straightforward matter to add or subtract a *single* proposition from memory, while leaving the rest of the network unchanged. Thus, for example, Figure 13.2 depicts the result of removing one proposition from the network in Figure 13.1. Second, the model treats predicates expressing the semantic properties of beliefs or memories as *projectable*.[11] They are treated as the sorts of predicates that pick out scientifically genuine *kinds*, rather than mere accidental conglomerates, and thus are suitable for inclusion in the statement of lawlike regularities. To see this, we need only consider the way in which such models are tested against empirical data about memory acquisition and forgetting. Typically, it will be assumed that if a subject is told (for example) that the policeman arrested the hippie, then the subject will (with a certain probability) remember *that the policeman arrested the hippie.*[12] this assumption is taken to express a nomological generalization – it captures something lawlike about the way in which the cognitive system works. So while the class of people who *remember that the policeman arrested the hippie* may differ psychologically in all sorts of ways, the theory treats them as a psychologically natural kind. Third, in any given memory search or inference task exploiting a semantic network model, it makes sense to ask which propositions were activated and which were not. Thus, a search in the network of Figure 13.1 might terminate without ever activating the proposition that cats have paws.

4   A family of connectionist hypotheses

Our theme, in the previous section, was that common sense psychology is committed to propositional modularity, and that many models of memory proposed in the cognitive psychology literature are comfortably compatible with this assumption. In the present section we want to describe a class of connectionist models which, we will argue, are *not* readily compatible with propositional modularity. The connectionist models we have in mind share three properties:

(i) their encoding of information in the connection weights and in the biases on units is *widely distributed*, rather than being *localist*;
(ii) individual hidden units in the network have no comfortable symbolic interpretation; they are *subsymbolic*, to use a term suggested by Paul Smolensky;
(iii) the models are intended as *cognitive models*, not merely as *implementations* of cognitive models.

A bit later in this section we will elaborate further on each of these three features, and in the next section we will describe a simple example of a connectionist model that meets our three criteria. However, we are under no illusion that what we say will be sufficient to give a sharp-edged characterization of the class of connectionist models we have in mind. Nor is such a sharp-edged characterization essential for our argument. It will suffice if we can convince you that there is a significant class of connectionist models which are incompatible with the propositional modularity of folk psychology.

Before saying more about the three features on our list, we would do well to give a more general characterization of the sort of models we are calling "connectionist," and introduce some of the jargon that comes with the territory. To this end, let us quote at some length from Paul Smolensky's lucid overview.

Connectionist models are large networks of simple, parallel computing elements, each of which carries a numerical *activation value* which it computes from neighboring elements in the network, using some simple numerical formula. The network elements or *units* influence each other's values through connections that carry a numerical strength or *weight* . . .

In a typical . . . model, input to the system is provided by imposing activation values on the *input units* of the network; these numerical values represent some encoding or *representation* of the input. The activation on the input units propagates along the connections until some set of activation values emerges on the *output units*; these activation values encode the output the system has computed from the input. In between the input and output units there may be other units, often called *hidden units*, that participate in representing neither the input nor the output.

The computation performed by the network in transforming the input pattern of activity to the output pattern depends on the set of connection strengths; *these weights are usually regarded as encoding the system's knowledge.*[13] In this sense, the connection strengths play the role of the program in a conventional computer. Much of the allure of the connectionist approach is that many connectionist networks *program*

271

themselves, that is, they have autonomous procedures for tuning their weights to eventually perform some specific computation. Such *learning procedures* often depend on training in which the network is presented with sample input/output pairs from the function it is supposed to compute. In learning networks with hidden units, the network itself "decides" what computations the hidden units will perform; because these units represent neither inputs nor outputs, they are never "told" what their values should be, even during training . . . .[14]

One point must be added to Smolensky's portrait. In many connectionist models the hidden units and the output units are assigned a numerical "bias" which is added into the calculation determining the unit's activation level. The learning procedures for such networks typically set both the connection strengths and the biases. Thus in these networks the system's knowledge is usually regarded as encoded in *both* the connection strengths and the biases.

So much for a general overview. Let us now try to explain the three features that characterize those connectionist models we take to be incompatible with propositional modularity.

(i)   In many non-connectionist cognitive models, like the one illustrated at the end of Section 3, it is an easy matter to locate a functionally distinct part of the model encoding each proposition or state of affairs represented in the system. Indeed, according to Fodor and Pylyshyn, "conventional [computational] architecture requires that there be distinct symbolic expressions for each state of affairs that it can represent."[15] In some connectionist models an analogous sort of functional localization is possible, not only for the input and output units but for the hidden units as well. Thus, for example, in certain connectionist models, various individual units or small clusters of units are themselves intended to represent specific properties or features of the environment. When the connection strength from one such unit to another is strongly positive, this might be construed as the system's representation of the proposition that if the first feature is present, so too is the second. However, in many connectionist networks it is not possible to localize propositional representation beyond the input layer. That is, there are no particular features or states of the system which lend themselves to a straightforward semantic evaluation. This can sometimes be a real inconvenience to the connectionist model builder when the system as a whole fails to achieve its goal because it has not represented the world the way it should. When this happens, as Smolensky notes,

> [I]t is not necessarily possible to localize a failure of veridical representation. Any particular state is part of a large causal system of states, and failures of the system to meet goal conditions cannot in general be localized to any particular state or state component."[16]

It is connectionist networks of this sort, in which it is not possible to isolate the representation of particular propositions or states of affairs within the nodes, connection strengths and biases, that we have in mind when we talk about the encoding of information in the biases, weights and hidden nodes being *widely distributed* rather than *localist*.

(ii) As we've just noted, there are some connectionist models in which some or all of the units are intended to represent specific properties or features of the system's environment. These units may be viewed as the model's symbols for the properties or features in question. However, in models where the weights and biases have been tuned by learning algorithms it is often not the case that any single unit or any small collection of units will end up representing a specific feature of the environment in any straightforward way. As we shall see in the next section, it is often plausible to view such networks as collectively or holistically encoding a set of propositions, although none of the hidden units, weights or biases are comfortably viewed as *symbols*. When this is the case we will call the strategy of representation invoked in the model *subsymbolic*. Typically (perhaps always?) networks exploiting subsymbolic strategies of representation will encode information in a widely distributed way.

(iii) The third item on our list is not a feature of connectionist models themselves, but rather a point about how the models are to be interpreted. In making this point we must presuppose a notion of theoretical or explanatory level which, despite much discussion in the recent literature, is far from being a paradigm of clarity.[17] Perhaps the clearest way to introduce the notion of explanatory level is against the background of the familiar functionalist thesis that psychological theories are analogous to programs which can be implemented on a variety of very different sorts of computers.[18] If one accepts this analogy, then it makes sense to ask whether a particular connectionist model is intended as a model at the psychological level or at the level of underlying neural implementation. Because of their obvious, though in many ways very partial, similarity to real neural architectures, it is tempting to view connectionist models as models of the implementation of psychological processes. And some connectionist model builders endorse this view quite explicitly. So viewed, however, connectionist models are not psychological or cognitive models at all, any more than a story of how cognitive processes are implemented at the quantum mechanical level is a psychological story. A very different view that connectionist model builders can and often do take is that their models are at the psychological level, not at the level of implementation. So construed, the models are in competition with other psychological models of the same phenomena. Thus a connectionist model of word recognition would be an alternative to – and not simply a possible implementation of – a non-connectionist model of word recognition; a connectionist theory of memory would be a competitor to a semantic network theory, and so on. Connectionists who hold this view of their theories often illustrate the point by drawing analogies with other sciences. Smolensky, for example, suggests that connectionist models stand to traditional cognitive models (like semantic networks) in much the same way that quantum mechanics stands to classical mechanics. In each case the newer theory is deeper, more general and more accurate over a broader range of phenomena. But in each case the new theory and the old are competing at the same explanatory level. If one is right, the other must be wrong.

In light of our concerns in this paper, there is one respect in which the analogy between connectionist models and quantum mechanics may be thought to beg an important question. For while quantum mechanics is conceded to be a *better* theory than classical mechanics, a plausible case could be made that the shift from classical to quantum mechanics was an ontologically *conservative* theory change. In any event, it is not clear that the change was ontologically *radical*. If our central thesis in this paper is correct, then the relation between connectionist models and more traditional cognitive models is more like the relation between the caloric theory of heat and the kinetic theory. The caloric and kinetic theories are at the same explanatory level, though the shift from one to the other was pretty clearly ontologically radical. In order to make the case that the caloric analogy is the more appropriate one, it will be useful to describe a concrete, though very simple, connectionist model of memory that meets the three criteria we have been trying to explicate.

5   A connectionist model of memory

Our goal in constructing the model was to produce a connectionist network that would do at least some of the tasks done by more traditional cognitive models of memory, and that would perspicuously exhibit the sort of distributed, subsymbolic encoding described in the previous section. We began by constructing a network, we'll call it Network A, that would judge the truth or falsehood of the sixteen propositions displayed above the line in Figure 13.3. The network was a typical three tiered feed-forward network consisting of 16 input units, four hidden units and one output unit, as shown in Figure 13.4. The input coding of each proposition is shown in the center column in Figure 13.3. Outputs close to 1 were interpreted as 'true' and outputs close to zero were interpreted as 'false'. Back propagation, a familiar connectionist learning algorithm, was used to "train up" the network thereby setting the connection weights and biases. Training was terminated when the network consistently gave an output higher than .9 for each true proposition and lower than .1 for each false proposition. Figure 13.5 shows the connection weights between the input units and the leftmost hidden unit in the trained up network, along with the bias on that unit. Figure 13.6 indicates the connection weights and biases further upstream. Figure 13.7 shows the way in which the network computes its response to the proposition *Dogs have fur* when that proposition is encoded in the input units.

There is a clear sense in which the trained up Network A may be said to have stored information about the truth or falsity of propositions (1)–(16), since when any one of these propositions is presented to the network it correctly judges whether the proposition is true or false. In this respect it is similar to various semantic network models which can be constructed to

	Proposition	Input	Output
1	Dogs have fur	11000011 00001111	1 true
2	Dogs have paws	11000011 00110011	1 true
3	Dogs have fleas	11000011 00111111	1 true
4	Dogs have legs	11000011 00111100	1 true
5	Cats have fur	11001100 00001111	1 true
6	Cats have paws	11001100 00110011	1 true
7	Cats have fleas	11001100 00111111	1 true
8	Fish have scales	11110000 00110000	1 true
9	Fish have fins	11110000 00001100	1 true
10	Fish have gills	11110000 00000011	1 true
11	Cats have gills	11001100 00000011	0 false
12	Fish have legs	11110000 00111100	0 false
13	Fish have fleas	11110000 00111111	0 false
14	Dogs have scales	11000011 00110000	0 false
15	Dogs have fins	11000011 00001100	0 false
16	Cats have fins	11001100 00001100	0 false

Added Proposition

17	Fish have eggs	11110000 11001000	1 true

Figure 13.3

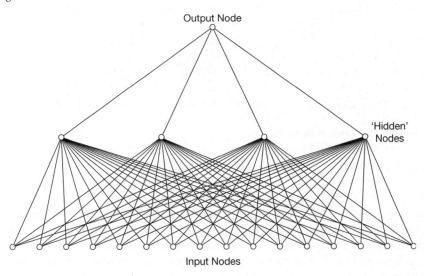

Output Node

'Hidden' Nodes

Input Nodes

Figure 13.4

perform much the same task. However, there is a striking difference between Network A and a semantic network model like the one depicted in Figure 13.1. For, as we noted earlier, in the semantic network there is a functionally distinct sub-part associated with each proposition, and thus it makes perfectly

275

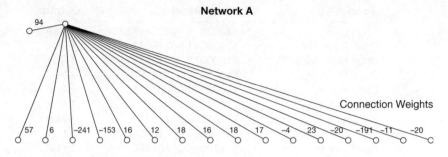

Network A

Connection Weights

Input weights and bias to first hidden node in network with 16 propositions

Figure 13.5

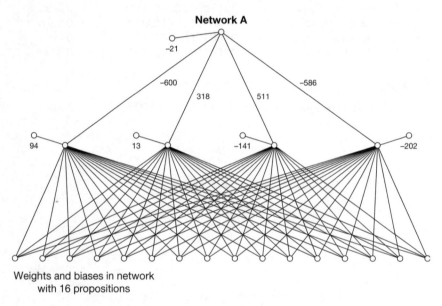

Network A

Weights and biases in network
with 16 propositions

Figure 13.6

good sense to ask, for any probe of the network, whether or not the representation of a specific proposition played a causal role. In the connectionist network, by contrast, there is no distinct state or part of the network that serves to represent any particular proposition. The information encoded in Network A is stored holistically and distributed throughout the network. Whenever information is extracted from Network A, by giving it an input string and seeing whether it computes a high or a low value for the output unit, *many* connection strengths, *many* biases and *many* hidden units play a role in the computation. And any particular weight or unit or bias will help to encode information about *many* different propositions. It simply makes no sense to ask whether or not the representation of a particular proposition plays

276

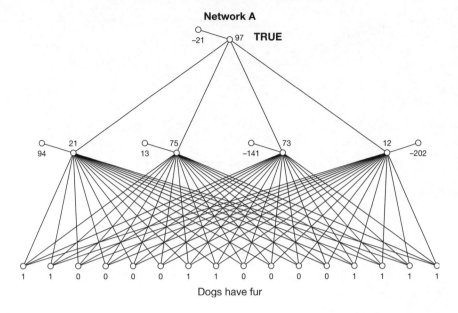

Figure 13.7

a causal role in the network's computation. It is in just this respect that our connectionist model of memory seems radically incongruent with the propositional modularity of common sense psychology. For, as we saw in Section 3, common sense psychology seems to presuppose that there is generally some answer to the question of whether a particular belief or memory played a causal role in a specific cognitive episode. But if belief and memory are subserved by a connectionist network like ours, such questions seem to have no clear meaning.

The incompatibility between propositional modularity and connectionist models like ours can be made even more vivid by contrasting Network A with a second network, we'll call it Network B, depicted in Figures 13.8 and 13.9. Network B was trained up just as the first one was, except that one additional proposition was added to the training set (coded as indicated below the line in Figure 13.3). Thus Network B encodes all the same propositions as Network A plus one more. In semantic network models, and other traditional cognitive models, it would be an easy matter to say which states or features of the system encode the added proposition, and it would be a simple task to determine whether or not the representation of the added proposition played a role in a particular episode modeled by the system. But plainly in the connectionist network those questions are quite senseless. The point is not that there are no differences between the two networks. Quite the opposite is the case; the differences are many and widespread. But these differences do not correlate in any systematic way with the functionally discrete, semantically

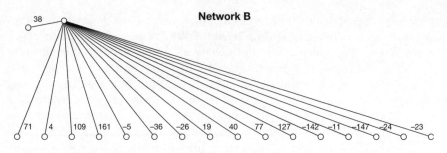

Input weights and bias to first hidden node in network with 17 propositions

Figure 13.8

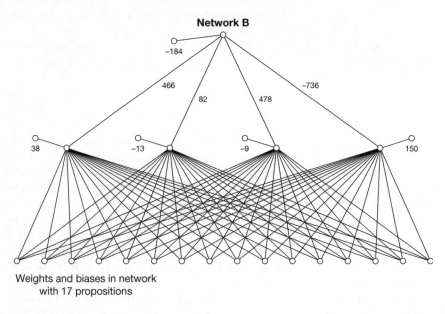

Weights and biases in network
with 17 propositions

Figure 13.9

interpretable states posited by folk psychology and by more traditional cognitive models. Since information is encoded in a highly distributed manner, with each connection weight and bias embodying information salient to many propositions, and information regarding any given proposition scattered throughout the network, the system lacks functionally distinct, identifiable sub-structures that are semantically interpretable as representations of individual propositions.

The contrast between Network A and Network B enables us to make our point about the incompatibility between common sense psychology and these sorts of connectionist models in a rather different way. We noted in Section 3 that common sense psychology treats predicates expressing the semantic properties of propositional attitudes as projectable. Thus 'believes that dogs have fur' or 'remembers that dogs have fur' will be projectable predicates in common sense psychology. Now both Network A and Network B might serve as models for a cognitive agent who believes that dogs have fur; both networks store or represent the information that dogs have fur. Nor are these the only two. If we were to train up a network on the 17 propositions in Figure 13.3 plus a few (or minus a few) we would get yet another system which is as different from Networks A and B as these two are from each other. The moral here is that though there are *indefinitely* many connectionist networks that represent the information that dogs have fur just as well as Network A does, these networks have no projectable features in common that are describable in the language of connectionist theory. From the point of view of the connectionist model builder, the class of networks that might model a cognitive agent who believes that dogs have fur is not a genuine kind at all, but simply a chaotically disjunctive set. Common sense psychology treats the class of people who believe that dogs have fur as a psychologically natural kind; connectionist psychology does not.[19]

6 Objections and replies

The argument we've set out in the previous five sections has encountered no shortage of objections. In this section we will try to reconstruct the most interesting of these, and indicate how we would reply.

> Objection (i): Models like A and B are not serious models for human belief or propositional memory.

Of course, the models we've constructed are tiny toys that were built to illustrate the features set out in Section 4 in a perspicuous way. They were never intended to model any substantial part of human propositional memory. But various reasons have been offered for doubting that *anything like* these models could ever be taken seriously as psychological models of propositional memory. Some critics have claimed that the models simply will not scale up – that while teaching a network to recognize fifteen or twenty propositions may be easy enough, it is just not going to be possible to train up a network that can recognize a few thousand propositions, still less a few hundred thousand.[20] Others have objected that while more traditional models of memory, including those based on sentence-like storage, those using semantic networks, and those based on production systems, all provide some strategy for *inference* or *generalization* which enables the system to answer questions about propositions it was not explicitly taught, models like those we have constructed are incapable of inference and generalization. It has also been urged that these models fail as accounts of human memory because they provide no obvious way to account for the fact that suitably prepared humans can easily acquire propositional information one proposition at a time. Under ordinary circumstances, we can just *tell* Henry that the car keys are in the refrigerator, and he can readily record this fact in memory. He doesn't need anything like the sort of massive retraining that would be required to teach one of our connectionist networks a new proposition.

Reply: If this were a paper aimed at defending connectionist models of propositional memory, we would have to take on each of these putative short-comings in some detail. And in each instance there is at least something to be said on the connectionist side. Thus, for example, it just is not true that networks like A and B don't generalize beyond the propositions on which they've been trained. In Network A, for example, the training set included:

Dogs have fur	Cats have fur.
Dogs have paws	Cats have paws.
Dogs have fleas	Cats have fleas.

It also included

Dogs have legs.

but not

Cats have legs.

When the network was given an encoding of this last proposition, however, it generalized correctly and responded affirmatively. Similarly, the network responded negatively to an encoding of

Cats have scales

though it had not previously been exposed to this proposition.

However, it is important to see that this sort of point by point response to the charge that networks like ours are inadequate models for propositional memory is not really required, given the thesis we are defending in this paper. For what we are trying to establish is a *conditional* thesis: *if* connectionist models of memory of the sort we describe in Section 4 are right, *then* propositional attitude psychology is in serious trouble. Since conditionals with false antecedents are true, we win by default if it turns out that the antecedent of our conditional is false.

Objection (ii): Our models do not really violate the principle of propositional modularity, since the propositions the system has learned are coded in functionally discrete ways, though this may not be obvious.

We've heard this objection elaborated along three quite different lies. The first line – let's call it Objection (iia) – notes that functionally discrete coding may often be very hard to notice, and cannot be expected to be visible on casual inspection. Consider, for example, the way in which sentences are stored in the memory of a typical von Neuman architecture computer – for concreteness we might suppose that the sentences are part of an English text and are being stored while the computer is running a word processing program. Parts of sentences may be stored at physically scattered memory addresses linked together in complex ways, and given an account of the contents of all relevant memory addresses one would be hard put to say where a particular sentence is stored. But nonetheless each sentence is stored in a *functionally discrete* way. Thus if one knew enough about the system it would be possible to erase any particular sentence it is storing by tampering with the contents of the appropriate memory addresses, while leaving the rest of the sentences the system is storing untouched. Similarly, it has been urged, connectionist networks may in fact encode propositions in functionally discrete ways, though this may not be evident from a casual inspection of the trained up network's biases and connection strengths.

Reply (iia) It is a bit difficult to come to grips with this objection, since what the critic is proposing is that in models like those we have constructed there *might* be some covert functionally discrete system of propositional encoding that has yet to be discovered. In response to this we must concede that indeed there might. We certainly have no argument that even comes close to demonstrating that the discovery of such a covert functionally discrete encoding is impossible. Moreover, we concede that if such a covert system were discovered, then our argument would be seriously undermined. However, we're inclined to think that the burden of argument is on the critic to show that such a system is not merely possible but *likely*; in the absence of any serious reason to think that networks like ours do encode propositions in functionally discrete ways, the mere logical possibility that they might is hardly a serious threat.

The second version of Objection (ii) – well call it Objection (iib) – makes a specific proposal about the way in which networks like A and B might be discretely, though covertly, encoding propositions. The encoding, it is urged, is to be found in the pattern of activation of the hidden nodes, when a given proposition is presented to the network. Since there are four hidden nodes in our networks, the activation pattern on presentation of any given input may be represented as an ordered 4-tuple. Thus, for example, when network A is presented with the encoded proposition *Dogs have fur*, the relevant 4-tuple would be (21, 75, 73, 12), as shown in Figure 13.7. Equivalently, we may think of each activation pattern as a point in a four dimensional hyperspace. Since each proposition corresponds to a unique point in the hyperspace, that point may be viewed as the encoding of the proposition. Moreover, that point represents a functionally discrete state of the system.[21]

Reply (iib): What is being proposed is that the pattern of activation of the system on presentation of an encoding of the proposition p be identified with the belief that p. But this proposal is singularly implausible. Perhaps the best

281

way to see this is to note that in common sense psychology beliefs and propositional memories are typically of substantial duration; and they are the sorts of things that cognitive agents generally have lots of even when they are not using them. Consider an example. Are kangaroos marsupials? Surely you've believed for years that they are, though in all likelihood this is the first time today that your belief has been activated or used.[22] An activation pattern, however, is not an enduring state of a network; indeed, it is not a state of the network at all except when the network has had the relevant proposition as input. Moreover, there is an enormous number of other beliefs that you've had for years. But it makes no sense to suppose that a network could have many activation patterns continuously over a long period of time. At any given time a network exhibits at most one pattern of activation. So activation patterns are just not the sorts of things that can plausibly be identified with beliefs or their representations.

Objection (iic): At this juncture, a number of critics have suggested that long standing beliefs might be identified not with activation patterns, which are transient states of networks, but rather with *dispositions to produce activation patterns*. Thus, in network A, the belief that dogs have fur would not be identified with a location in activation hyperspace but with the network's *disposition* to end up at that location when the proposition is presented. This *dispositional state* is an enduring state of the system; it is a state the network can be in no matter what its current state of activation may be, just as a sugar cube may have a disposition to dissolve in water even when there is no water nearby.[23] Some have gone on to suggest that the familiar philosophical distinction between dispositional and occurrent beliefs might be captured, in connectionist models, as the distinction between dispositions to produce activation patterns and activation patterns themselves.

Reply (iic): Our reply to this suggestion is that while dispositions to produce activation patterns are indeed *enduring* states of the system, they are not the right sort of enduring states – they are not the discrete, independently causally active states that folk psychology requires. Recall that on the folk psychological conception of belief and inference, there will often be a variety of quite different underlying causal patterns that may lead to the acquisition and avowal of a given belief. When Clouseau says that the butler did it, he may have just inferred this with the help of his long standing belief that the train is out of service. Or he may have inferred it by using his belief that the hotel is closed. Or both long standing beliefs may have played a role in the inference. Moreover, it is also possible that Clouseau drew this inference some time ago, and is now reporting a relatively long standing belief. But it is hard to see how anything like these distinctions can be captured by the dispositional account in question. In reacting to a given input, say p, a network takes on a specific activation value. It may also have dispositions to take on other activation values on other inputs, say q and r. But there is no obvious way to interpret the claim that these further dispositions play a causal role in the network's reaction to p – or, for that matter, that they do not play a role. Nor can we make any sense of the idea that on one occasion the encoding of q (say, the proposition that the train is out of service) played a role while the encoding of r (say, the proposition that the hotel is closed) did not, and on another occasion, things went the other way around. The propositional modularity presupposed by common sense psychology requires that belief tokens be functionally discrete states capable of causally interacting with one another in some cognitive episodes and of remaining causally inert in other cognitive episodes. However, in a distributed connectionist system like Network A, the dispositional state which produces one activation pattern is functionally inseparable from the dispositional state which produces another. Thus it is impossible to isolate some propositions as causally active in certain cognitive episodes, while others are not. We conclude that reaction pattern dispositions won't do as belief tokens. Nor, so far as we can see, are there any other states of networks like A and B that will fill the bill.

7 Conclusion

The thesis we have been defending in this paper is that connectionist models of a certain sort are incompatible with the propositional modularity embedded in common sense psychology. The connectionist models in question are those which are offered as models at the *cognitive* level, and in which the encoding of information is widely distributed and subsymbolic. In such models, we have argued, there are no *discrete, semantically interpretable* states that play a *causal* role in some cognitive episodes but not others. Thus there is, in these models, nothing with which the propositional attitudes of common sense psychology can plausibly be identified. If these models turn out to offer the best accounts of human belief and memory, we will be confronting an *ontologically radical* theory change – the sort of theory change that will sustain the conclusion that propositional attitudes, like caloric and phlogiston, do not exist.

Notes

1 Thanks are due to Ned Block, Paul Churchland, Gary Cottrell, Adrian Cussins, Jerry Fodor, John Heil, Frank Jackson, David Kirsh, Patricia Kitcher and Philip Kitcher for useful feedback on earlier versions of this paper. Talks based on the paper have been presented at the UCSD Cognitive Science Seminar and at conferences sponsored by the Howard Hughes Medical Foundation and the University of North Carolina at Greensboro. Comments and questions from these audiences have proved helpful in many ways.

2 See, for example, Churchland (1981 and 1986), where explicitly eliminativist conclusions are drawn on the basis of speculations about the success of cognitive models similar to those we shall discuss,

3 Fodor, J. and Pylyshyn, Z. (1988).

4 We are aware that certain philosophers and historians of science have actually entertained ideas similar to the suggestion that the planets spoken of by pre-Copernican astronomers do not exist. See, for example, Kuhn (1970: Ch. 10),

and Feyerabend (1981: Ch. 4). However, we take this suggestion to be singularly implausible. Eliminativist arguments can't be that easy. Just what has gone wrong with the accounts of meaning and reference that lead to such claims is less clear. For further discussion on these matters see Kuhn (1983), and Kitcher (1978 and 1983).

5   For some detailed discussion of scientific reduction, see Nagel (1961); Schaffner (1967); Hooker (1981); and Kitcher (1984). The genetics case is not without controversy. See Kitcher (1982 and 1984).

6   It's worth noting that judgments on this matter can differ quite substantially. At one end of the spectrum are writers like Feyerabend (1981), and perhaps Kuhn (1962), for whom relatively small differences in theory are enough to justify the suspicion that there has been an ontologically radical change. Toward the other end are writers like Lycan, who writes:

> I am at pains to advocate a very liberal view ... I am entirely willing to give up fairly large chunks of our commonsensical or platitudinous theory of belief or of desire (or of almost anything else) and decide that we were just wrong about a lot of things, without drawing the inference that we are no longer talking about belief or desire. ... I think the ordinary word "belief" (*qua* theoretical term of folk psychology) points dimly toward a natural kind that we have not fully grasped and that only mature psychology will reveal. I expect that "belief" will turn out to refer to some kind of information bearing inner state of a sentient being . . ., but the kind of state it refers to may have only a few of the properties usually attributed to beliefs by common sense. (Lycan 1988: 31–2.)

On our view, both extreme positions are implausible. As we noted earlier, the Copernican revolution did not show that the planets studied by Ptolemy do not exist. But Lavoisier's chemical revolution *did* show that phlogiston does not exist, Yet on Lycan's "very liberal view" it is hard to see why we should not conclude that phlogiston really does exist after all – its really oxygen, and prior to Lavoisier "we were just very wrong about a lot of things".

7   For an early and influential statement of the view that common sense psychology is a theory, see Sellars (1956). More recently the view has been defended by Churchland (1970, and 1979: Chs. 1 and 4); and by Fodor (1987: Ch. 1). For the opposite view, see Wilkes (1978); Madell (1986); Sharpe (1987).

8   See Stich (1983: 237ff.).

9   Cherniak (1986: Ch. 3), notes that this sort of absent mindedness is commonplace in literature and in ordinary life, and sometimes leads to disastrous consequences.

10 For sentential models, see John McCarthy (1968, 1980 and 1986); and Kintsch (1974). For semantic networks, see Quillian (1969); Collins and Quillian (1972): Rumelhart, Lindsay and Norman (1972); Anderson and Bower (1973); and Anderson (1976, and 1980: Ch. 4). For production systems, see Newell and Simon (1972); Newell (1973); Anderson (1983); and Holland et. al. (1986).

11 For the classic discussion of the distinction between projectable and non-projectable predicates, see Goodman (1965).

12 See, for example, Anderson and Bower (1973).

13 Emphasis added.

14 Smolensky (1988: 1).

15 Fodor and Pylyshyn (1988: 57).

16 Smolensky (1988: 15).

17 Broadbent, D. (1985); Rumelhart and McClelland (1985 Rumelhart, McClelland and PDP Research Group) (1986: Ch. 4); Smolensky (1988); Fodor and Pylyshyn (1988).

18 The notion of program being invoked here is itself open to a pair of quite different interpretations. For the right reading, see Ramsey (1989).

19 This way of making the point about the incompatibility between connectionist models and common sense psychology was suggested to us by Jerry Fodor.

20 This point has been urged by Daniel Dennett, among others.

21 Quite a number of people have suggested this move, including Gary Cottrell and Adrian Cussins.

22 As Lycan notes, on the common sense notion of belief, people have lots of them "even when they are asleep" (Lycan (1988: 57).

23 Something like this objection was suggested to us by Ned Block and by Frank Jackson.

References

Anderson, J. (1976) *Language, Memory and Thought*, Hillsdale, N.J.: Lawrence Erlbaum Associates.

—— (1980) *Cognitive Psychology and Its Implications*, San Francisco: W.H. Freeman & Co.

—— (1983) *The Architecture of Cognition*, Cambridge, Mass., Harvard University Press.

Anderson, J. and Bower, G. (1973) *Human Associative Memory*, Washington, D.C.: Winston.

Broadbent, D. (1985) "A Question of Levels: Comments on McClelland and Rumelhart," *Journal of Experimental Psychology: General* 114.

Cherniak, C. (1986) *Minimal Rationality*, Cambridge, Mass.: Bradford Books/MIT Press.

Churchland, P.M. (1970) "The Logical Character of Action Explanations," *Philosophical Review* 79.

—— (1979) *Scientific Realism and the Plasticity of Mind*, Cambridge: Cambridge University Press.

—— (1981) "Eliminative Materialism and Propositional Attitudes," *Journal of Philosophy* 78(2).

—— (1986) "Some Reductive Strategies in Cognitive Neurobiology," *Mind* 95.

Collins, A. and Quillian, M. (1972) "Experiments on Semantic Memory and Language Comprehension," in L. Gregg, ed., *Cognition in Learning and Memory*, New York: Wiley.

Feyerabend, P. (1981) *Realism, Rationalism and Scientific Method: Philosophical Papers Vol. 1*, Cambridge, Cambridge University Press.

Fodor, J. (1983) *The Modularity of Mind: An Essay on Faculty Psychology*. Cambridge, Mass.: MIT Press.

—— (1987) *Psychosemantics: The Problem of Meaning in the Philosophy of Mind*, Cambridge, Mass.: Bradford Books/MIT Press.

Fodor, J. and Pylyshyn, Z. (1988) "Connectionism and Cognitive Architecture: A Critical Analysis," *Cognition* 28.

Goodman, N. (1965) *Fact, Fiction and Forecast*, Indianapolis: Bobbs-Merrill.

Holland, J., Holyoak, K., Nisbett, R. and Thagard, P. (1986) *Induction: Processes of Inference, Learning and Discovery*, Cambridge, Mass.:, Bradford Books/MIT Press.

Hooker, C. (1981) "Towards a General Theory of Reduction," Parts I, II and III, *Dialogue* 20.

Kintsch, W. (1974) *The Representation of Meaning in Memory*, Hillsdale, N.J.: Lawrence Erlbaum Associates.

Kitcher, P. (1978) "Theories, Theorists and Theoretical Change," *Philosophical Review* 87.

—— (1982) "Genes," *British Journal for the Philosophy of Science* 33.

—— (1983) "Implications of Incommensurability," *PSA 1982* (Proceedings of the 1982 Biennial Meeting of the Philosophy of Science Association), Vol. 2, ed. by P. Asquith and T. Nickles, East Lansing, Philosophy of Science Association.

—— (1984) "1953 and All That: A Tale of Two Sciences," *Philosophical Review* 93.

Kuhn, T. (1962) *The Structure of Scientific Revolutions*, Chicago: University of Chicago Press, 2nd Edition (1970).

—— (1983) "Commensurability, Comparability, Communicability," *PSA 1982* (Proceedings of the 1982 Biennial Meeting of the Philosophy of Science Association), Vol. 2, ed. by P. Asquith and T. Nickles, East Lansing, Philosophy of Science Association.

Lycan, W. (1988) *Judgement and Justification*, Cambridge: Cambridge University Press.

Madell, G. (1986) "Neurophilosophy: A Principled Skeptic's Response," *Inquiry* 29.

McCarthy, J. (1968) "Programs With Common Sense," in M. Minsky, ed., *Semantic Information Processing*, Cambridge, Mass.:, MIT Press.

—— (1980) "Circumscription: A Form of Non-Monotonic Reasoning" *Artificial Intelligence* 13.

—— (1986) "Applications of Circumscription to Formalizing Common-Sense Knowledge," *Artificial Intelligence* 28.

Nagel, E. (1961) *The Structure of Science*, New York: Harcourt, Brace & World.

Newell, A. (1973) "Production Systems: Models of Control Structures," in W. Chase, ed., *Visual Information Processing*, New York: Academic Press.

Newell, A. and Simon, H. (1972) *Human Problem Solving*, Englewood Cliffs, N.J.: Prentice-Hall.

Quillian, M. (1966) *Semantic Memory*, Cambridge, Mass., Bolt, Branak & Newman.

Ramsey, W. (1989) "Parallelism and Functionalism," *Cognitive Science* 13.

Rumelhart, D. and McClelland, J. (1985) "Level's Indeed! A Response to Broadbent," *Journal of Experimental Psychology: General* 114.

Rumelhart, D., Lindsay, P. and Norman, D. (1972) "A Process Model for Long Term Memory," in E. Tulving and W. Donaldson, eds, *Organization of Memory*, New York: Academic Press.

Rumelhart, D., McClelland, J. and the PDP Research Group (1986) *Parallel Distributed Processing*, Vols I and II, Cambridge, Mass.: Bradford Books/MIT Press.

Schaffner, K. (1967) "Approaches to Reduction," *Philosophy of Science* 34.

Sellars, W. (1956) "Empiricism and the Philosophy of Mind," *Minnesota Studies in the Philosophy of Science*, Vol. I, H. Feigl and M. Scriven, eds, Minneapolis: University of Minnesota Press.

Sharpe, R. (1987) "The Very Idea of Folk Psychology," *Inquiry* 30.

Smolensky, P. (1988) "On the Proper Treatment of Connectionism," *The Behavioral & Brain Sciences* 11.

Stich, S. (1983) *From Folk Psychology to Cognitive Science*, Cambridge, Mass.: Bradford Books/MIT Press.

Wilkes, K. (1978) *Physicalism*, London: Routledge & Kegan Paul.

14

D.C. Dennett "Real Patterns"*

Are there really beliefs? Or are we learning (from neuroscience and psychology, presumably) that, strictly speaking, beliefs are figments of our imagination, items in a superseded ontology? Philosophers generally regard such ontological questions as admitting just two possible answers: either beliefs exist or they do not. There is no such state as quasi existence; there are no stable doctrines of semirealism. Beliefs must either be vindicated along with the viruses or banished along with the banshees. A bracing conviction prevails, then, to the effect that when it comes to beliefs (and other mental items) one must be either a realist or an eliminative materialist.

I Realism about beliefs

This conviction prevails in spite of my best efforts over the years to undermine it with various analogies: are *voices* in your ontology?[1] Are *centers of gravity* in your ontology?[2]

It is amusing to note that my analogizing beliefs to centers of gravity has been attacked from both sides of the ontological dichotomy, by philosophers who think it is simply obvious that centers of gravity are useful fictions, and by philosophers who think it is simply obvious that centers of gravity are perfectly real:

> The trouble with these supposed parallels . . . is that they are all strictly speaking *false*, although they are no doubt useful simplifications for many purposes. It is false, for example, that the gravitational attraction between the Earth and the Moon involves two point masses; but it is a good enough first approximation for many calculations. However, this is not at all what Dennett really wants to say about intentional states.

*Thanks to Kathleen Akins, Akeel Bilgrami, Donald Davidson, Barbara Hannan, Douglas Hofstadter, Norton Nelkin, W. V. O. Quine, Richard Rorty, George Smith, Peter Suber, Stephen White, and the MIT/Tufts philosophy of psychology discussion group for the discussions that provoked and shaped this paper.

For he insists that to adopt the intentional stance and interpret an agent as acting on certain beliefs and desires is to discern a pattern in his actions which is genuinely there (a pattern which is missed if we instead adopt a scientific stance): Dennett certainly does not hold that the role of intentional ascriptions is merely to give us a useful approximation to a truth that can be more accurately expressed in non-intentional terms.[3]

Compare this with Fred Dretske's[4] equally confident assertion of realism:

I am a realist about centers of gravity ... The earth obviously exerts a gravitational attraction on *all* parts of the moon – not just its center of gravity. The *resultant* force, a vector sum, acts through a point, but this is something quite different. One should be very clear about what centers of gravity are *before* deciding whether to be literal about them, *before* deciding whether or not to be a center-of-gravity realist.[5]

Dretske's advice is well-taken. What are centers of gravity? They are mathematical points – abstract objects or what Hans Reichenbach called *abstracta* – definable in terms of physical forces and other properties. The question of whether abstract objects are real – the question of whether or not "one should be a realist about them" – can take two different paths, which we might call the metaphysical and the scientific. The metaphysical path simply concerns the reality or existence of abstract objects generally, and does not distinguish them in terms of their scientific utility. Consider, for instance, the *center of population* of the United States. I define this as the mathematical point at the intersection of the two lines such that there are as many inhabitants north as south of the latitude, and as many inhabitants east as west of the longitude. This point is (or can be) just as precisely defined as the center of gravity or center of mass of an object. (Since these median strips might turn out to be wide, take the midline of each strip as the line; count as inhabitants all those within the territorial waters and up to twenty miles in altitude – orbiting astronauts do not count – and take each inhabitant's navel to be the determining point, etc.) I do not know the center of population's current geographic location, but I am quite sure it is west of where it was ten years ago. It jiggles around constantly, as people move about, taking rides on planes, trains, and automobiles, etc. I doubt that this abstract object is of any value at all in any scientific theory, but just in case it is, here is an even more trivial abstract object: Dennett's lost sock center: the point defined as the center of the smallest sphere that can be inscribed around all the socks I have ever lost in my life.

These abstract objects have the same metaphysical status as centers of gravity. Is Dretske a realist about them all? Should we be? I do not intend to pursue this question, for I suspect that Dretske is – and we should be – more interested in the scientific path to realism: centers of gravity are real because they are (somehow) *good* abstract objects. They deserve to be taken seriously, learned about, used. If we go so far as to distinguish them as *real* (contrasting them, perhaps, with those abstract objects which are *bogus*), that is because we think they serve in perspicuous representations of real forces, "natural" properties, and the like. This path brings us closer, in any case, to the issues running in the debates about the reality of beliefs.

I have claimed that beliefs are best considered to be abstract objects rather like centers of gravity. Smith considers centers of gravity to be useful fictions while Dretske considers them to be useful (and hence?) real abstractions, and each takes his view to constitute a criticism of my position. The optimistic assessment of these opposite criticisms is that they cancel each other out; my analogy must have hit the nail on the head. The pessimistic assessment is that more needs to be said to convince philosophers that a mild and intermediate sort of realism is a positively attractive position, and not just the desperate dodge of ontological responsibility it has sometimes been taken to be. I have just such a case to present, a generalization and extension of my earlier attempts, via the concept of a *pattern*. My aim on this occasion is not so much to prove that my intermediate doctrine about the reality of psychological states is right, but just that it is quite possibly right, because a parallel doctrine is demonstrably right about some simpler cases.

We use folk psychology – interpretation of each other as believers, wanters, intenders, and the like – to predict what people will do next. Prediction is not the only thing we care about, of course. Folk psychology helps us understand and empathize with others, organize our memories, interpret our emotions, and flavor our vision in a thousand ways, but at the heart of all these is the enormous predictive leverage of folk psychology. Without its predictive power, we could have no interpersonal projects or relations at all; human activity would be just so much Brownian motion; we would be baffling ciphers to each other and to ourselves – we could not even conceptualize our own flailings. In what follows, I shall concentrate always on folk-psychological prediction, not because I make the mistake of ignoring all the other interests we have in people aside from making bets on what they will do next, but because I claim that our power to *interpret* the actions of others depends on our power – seldom explicitly exercised – to predict them.[6]

Where utter patternlessness or randomness prevails, nothing is predictable. The success of folk-psychological prediction, like the success of any prediction, depends on there being some order or pattern in the world to exploit. Exactly where in the world does this pattern exist? What is the pattern a pattern *of*?[7] Some have thought, with Fodor, that the pattern of belief must in the end be a pattern of structures in the brain, formulae written in the language of thought. Where else could it be? Gibsonians might say the pattern is "in the light" – and Quinians (such as Donald Davidson and I) could almost agree: the pattern is discernible in agents' (observable) behavior when we subject it to "radical interpretation' (Davidson) "from the intentional stance" (Dennett).

When are the elements of a pattern real and not merely apparent? Answering this question will help us resolve the misconceptions that have led to the proliferation of "ontological positions" about beliefs, the different grades or kinds of realism. I shall concentrate on five salient exemplars arrayed in the space of possibilities: Fodor's industrial-strength Realism (he writes it with a capital 'R'); Davidson's regular strength realism; my mild realism; Richard Rorty's milder-than-mild irrealism, according to which the pattern is only in the eyes of the beholders, and Paul Churchland's eliminative materialism, which denies the reality of beliefs altogether.

In what follows, I shall assume that these disagreements all take place within an arena of common acceptance of what Arthur Fine[8] calls NOA, the natural ontological attitude. That is, I take the interest in these disagreements to lie not in differences of opinion about the ultimate metaphysical status of physical things or abstract things (e.g., electrons or centers of gravity), but in differences of opinion about whether beliefs and other mental states are, shall we say, *as real as* electrons or centers of gravity. I want to show that mild realism is the doctrine that makes the most sense when what we are talking about is real patterns, such as the real patterns discernible from the intentional stance.[9]

In order to make clear the attractions and difficulties of these different positions about patterns, I shall apply them first to a much simpler, more readily visualized, and uncontroversial sort of pattern.

II The reality of patterns

Consider the six objects in Figure 14.1 (which I shall call *frames*):

We can understand a frame to be a finite subset of data, a window on an indefinitely larger world of further data. In one sense A–F all display different patterns; if you look closely you will see that no two frames are exactly alike ("atom-for-atom replicas," if you like). In another sense, A–F all display the same pattern; they were all made by the same basic process, a printing of ten rows of ninety dots, ten black dots followed by ten white dots, etc. The overall effect is to create five equally spaced black squares or bars in the window, I take it that this pattern, which I shall dub *bar code*, is a real pattern if anything

Figure 14.1

is. But some random (actually pseudo-random) "noise" has been allowed to interfere with the actual printing. The noise ratio is as follows:

A: 25%   B: 10%
C: 25%   D: 1%
E: 33%   F: 50%

It is impossible to see that F is not purely (pseudo-) random noise; you will just have to take my word for it that it was actually generated by the same program that generated the other five patterns; all I changed was the noise ratio.

Now, what does it mean to say that a pattern in one of these frames is real, or that it is really there? Given our privileged information about how these frames were generated, we may be tempted to say that there is a single pattern in all six cases – even in F, where it is "indiscernible." But I propose that the self-contradictory air of "indiscernible pattern" should be taken seriously. We may be able to make some extended, or metaphorical, sense of the idea of indiscernible patterns (or invisible pictures or silent symphonies), but in the root case a pattern is "by definition" a candidate for pattern *recognition*. (It is this loose but unbreakable link to observers or perspectives, of course, that makes "pattern" an attractive term to someone perched between instrumentalism and industrial-strength realism.)

Fortunately, there is a standard way of making these intuitions about the discernibility-in-principle of patterns precise. Consider the task of, transmitting information about one of the frames from one place to another. How many bits of information will it take to transmit each frame? The least efficient method is simply to send the "bit map," which identifies each dot *seriatim* ("dot one is black, dot two is white, dot three is white, . . ."). For a black-and-white frame of 900 dots (or pixels, as they are called), the transmission requires 900 bits. Sending the bit map is in effect verbatim quotation, accurate but inefficient. Its most important virtue is that it is equally capable of transmitting any pattern or any particular instance of utter patternlessness.

Gregory Chaitin's[10] valuable definition of mathematical randomness invokes this idea. A series (of dots or numbers or whatever) is random if and only if the information required to describe (transmit) the series accurately is *incompressible*: nothing shorter than the verbatim bit map will preserve the series. Then a series is not random – has a pattern – if and only if there is some more efficient way of describing it.[11] Frame D, for instance, can be described as "ten rows of ninety: ten black followed by ten white, etc., *with the following exceptions*: dots 57, 88, . . ." This expression, suitably encoded, is much shorter than 900 bits long. The comparable expressions for the other frames will be proportionally longer, since they will have to mention, verbatim, more exceptions, and the degeneracy of the "pattern" in F is revealed by the fact that its description in this system will be no improvement over the bit map – in fact, it will tend on average to be trivially longer, since it takes some bits to describe the pattern that is then obliterated by all the exceptions.

Of course, there are bound to be other ways of describing the evident patterns in these frames, and some will be more efficient than others – in the precise sense of being systematically specifiable in fewer bits.[12] Any such description, if an improvement over the bit map, is the description of a real pattern in the data.[13]

Consider bar code, the particular pattern seen in *A–E*, and almost perfectly instantiated in *D*. *That* pattern is quite readily discernible to the naked human eye in these presentations of the data, because of the particular pattern-recognition machinery hard-wired in our visual systems – edge detectors, luminance detectors, and the like. But the very same data (the very same streams of bits) presented in some other format might well yield no hint of pattern to us, especially in the cases where bar code is contaminated by salt and pepper, as in frames *A* through *C*. For instance, if we broke the 900-bit series of frame *B* into 4-bit chunks, and then translated each of these into hexadecimal notation, one would be hard pressed indeed to tell the resulting series of hexadecimal digits from a random series, since the hexadecimal chunking would be seriously out of phase with the decimal pattern – and hence the "noise" would not "stand out" as noise. There are myriad ways of displaying any 900-bit series of data points, and not many of them would inspire us to concoct an efficient description of the series. Other creatures with different sense organs, or different interests, might readily perceive patterns that were imperceptible to us. The patterns would be *there* all along, but just invisible to *us*.

The idiosyncrasy of perceivers' capacities to discern patterns is striking. Visual patterns with axes of vertical symmetry stick out like sore thumbs for us, but if one simply rotates the frame a few degrees, the symmetry is often utterly beyond noticing. And the "perspectives" from which patterns are "perceptible" are not restricted to variations on presentation to the sense modalities. Differences in knowledge yield striking differences in the capacity to pick up patterns. Expert chess players can instantly perceive (and subsequently recall with high accuracy) the total board position in a real game, but are much worse at recall if the same chess pieces are randomly placed on the board, even though to a novice both boards are equally hard to recall.[14] This should not surprise anyone who considers that an expert speaker of English would have much less difficulty perceiving and recalling

The frightened cat struggled to get loose.

than

Te ser.ioghehnde t srugfcalde go tgtt ohle

which contains the same pieces, now somewhat disordered. Expert chess players, unlike novices, not only know how to *play* chess; they know how to *read* chess – how to see the patterns at a glance.

A pattern exists in some data – is real – if *there* is a description of the data that is more efficient than the bit map, whether or not anyone can concoct it. Compression algorithms, as general-purpose pattern describers, are efficient ways of transmitting exact copies of frames, such as *A–F*, from one place to another, but our interests often favor a somewhat different goal: transmitting *inexact* copies that nevertheless preserve "the" pattern that is important to us. For some purposes, we need not list the exceptions to bar code, but only transmit the information that the pattern is bar code with *n*% noise. Following this strategy, frames *A* and *C*, though discernibly different under careful inspection, count *as the same pattern*, since what matters to us is that the pattern is bar code with 25% noise, and we do not care which particular noise occurs, only that it occurs.

Sometimes we are interested in not just ignoring the noise, but eliminating it, improving the pattern in transmission. Copy-editing is a good example. Consider the likely effect thes santince wull hive hod on tha cupy adutor whu preparis thas monescrupt fur prunteng. *My* interest in this particular instance is that the "noise" be transmitted, not removed, though I actually do not care exactly *which* noise is there.

Here then are three different attitudes we take at various times toward patterns. Sometimes we care about exact description or reproduction of detail, at whatever cost. From this perspective, a real pattern in frame *A* is *bar code with the following exceptions*: 7, 8, 11, . . . At other times we care about the noise, but not where in particular it occurs. From this perspective, a real pattern in frame *A* is *bar code with 25% noise*. And sometimes, we simply tolerate or ignore the noise. From this perspective, a real pattern in frame *A* is simply: *bar code*. But is bar code really there in frame *A*? I am tempted to respond: Look! You can see with your own eyes. But there is something more constructive to say as well.

When two individuals confront the same data they may perceive different patterns in them, but since we can have varied interests and perspectives, these differences do not all count as disagreements. Or in any event they should not. If Jones sees pattern α (with n% noise) and Brown sees pattern β (with m% noise) there may be no ground for determining that one of them is right and the other wrong. Suppose they are both using their patterns to bet on the next datum in the series. Jones bets according to the "pure" pattern α, but budgets for n% errors when he looks for odds. Brown does likewise, using pattern β. If both patterns are real, they will both get rich. That is to say, so long as they use their expectation of deviations from the "ideal" to temper their odds policy, they will do better than chance – perhaps very much better.

Now suppose they compare notes. Suppose that α is a simple, easy-to-calculate pattern, but with a high noise rate – for instance, suppose α is bar code as it appears in frame *E*. And suppose that Brown has found some periodicity or progression in the "random" noise that Jones just tolerates, so that β is a much more complicated description of pattern-superimposed-on-pattern. This permits Brown to do better than chance, we may suppose, at predicting when the "noise' will come. As a result, Brown budgets for a lower error rate – say only 5%. "What you call noise, Jones, is actually pattern," Brown might say. "Of course there is still *some* noise in my pattern, but my pattern is better – more real – than yours! Yours is actually just a mere appearance." Jones might well reply that it is all a matter of taste; he notes how hard Brown has to work to calculate predictions, and points to the fact that he is getting just as rich (or maybe richer) by using a simpler, sloppier system and making more bets at good odds than Brown can muster. "My pattern is perfectly real – look how rich I'm getting. If it were an illusion, I'd be broke."

This crass way of putting things – in terms of betting and getting rich – is simply a vivid way of drawing attention to a real, and far from crass, trade-off that is ubiquitous in nature, and hence in folk psychology. Would we prefer an extremely compact pattern description with a high noise ratio or a less compact pattern description with a lower noise ratio? Our decision may depend on how swiftly and reliably we can discern the simple pattern, how dangerous errors are, how much of our resources we can afford to allocate to detection and calculation. These "design decisions" are typically not left to us to make by individual and deliberate choices; they are incorporated into the design of our sense organs by genetic evolution, and into our culture by cultural evolution. The product of this design evolution process is what Wilfrid Sellars[15] calls our *manifest image,* and it is composed of folk physics, folk psychology, and the other pattern-making perspectives we have on the buzzing blooming confusion that bombards us with data. The ontology generated by the manifest image has thus a deeply pragmatic source.[16]

Do these same pragmatic considerations apply to the scientific image, widely regarded as the final arbiter of ontology? Science is supposed to carve nature at the joints – at its *real* joints, of course. Is it permissible in science to adopt a carving system so simple that it makes sense to tolerate occasional misdivisions and consequent mispredictions? It happens all the time. The ubiquitous practice of using idealized models is exactly a matter of trading off reliability and accuracy of prediction against computational tractability. A particularly elegant and handy oversimplification may under some circumstances be irresistible. The use of Newtonian rather than Einsteinian mechanics in most mundane scientific and engineering calculations is an obvious example. A tractable oversimplification may be attractive even in the face of a high error rate; considering inherited traits to be carried by single genes "for" those traits is an example; considering agents in the marketplace to be perfectly rational self-aggrandizers with perfect information is another.

III Patterns in life

The time has come to export these observations about patterns and reality to the controversial arena of belief attribution. The largish leap we must make is nicely expedited by pausing at a stepping-stone example midway between the world of the dot frames and the world of folk psychology: John Horton

Conway's Game of Life. In my opinion, every philosophy student should be held responsible for an intimate acquaintance with the Game of Life. It should be considered an essential tool in every thought-experimenter's kit, a prodigiously versatile generator of philosophically important examples and thought experiments of admirable clarity and vividness. In *The Intentional Stance*, I briefly exploited it to make a point about the costs and benefits of risky prediction from the intentional stance,[17] but I have since learned that I presumed too much familiarity with the underlying ideas. Here, then, is a somewhat expanded basic introduction to Life.[18]

Life is played on a two-dimensional grid, such as a checkerboard or a computer screen; it is not a game one plays to win; if it is a game at all, it is solitaire. The grid divides space into square cells, and each cell is either ON or OFF at each moment. Each cell has eight neighbors: the four adjacent cells north, south, east, and west, and the four diagonals: northeast, southeast, southwest, and northwest. Time in the Life world is also discrete, not continuous; it advances in ticks, and the state of the world changes between each tick according to the following rule:

> Each cell, in order to determine what to do in the next instant, counts how many of its eight neighbors is ON at the present instant. If the answer is exactly two, the cell stays in its present state (ON or OFF) in the next instant. If the answer is exactly three, the cell is ON in the next instant whatever its current state. Under all other conditions the cell is OFF.

The entire physics of the Life world is captured in that single, unexceptioned law. [While this is the fundamental law of the "physics" of the Life world, it helps at first to conceive this curious physics in biological terms: think of cells going ON as births, cells going OFF as deaths, and succeeding instants as generations. Either overcrowding (more than three inhabited neighbors) or isolation (less than two inhabited neighbors) leads to death.] By the scrupulous application of this single law, one can predict with perfect accuracy the next instant of any configuration of ON and OFF cells, and the instant after that, and so forth. In other words, the Life world is a toy world that perfectly instantiates Laplace's vision of determinism: given the state description of this world at an instant, we finite observers can perfectly predict the future instants by the simple application of our one law of physics. Or, in my terms, when we adopt the physical stance toward a configuration in the Life world, our powers of prediction are perfect: there is no noise, no uncertainty, no probability less than one. Moreover, it follows from the two-dimensionality of the Life world that nothing is hidden from view. There is no backstage; there are no hidden variables; the unfolding of the physics of objects in the Life world is directly and completely visible.

There are computer simulations of the Life world in which one can set up configurations on the screen and then watch them evolve according to the single rule. In the best simulations, one can change the scale of both time and space, alternating between close-up and bird's-eye view. A nice touch added to some color versions is that ON cells (often just called pixels) are color-coded by their age; they are born blue, let us say, and then change color each generation, moving through green to yellow to orange to red to brown to black and then staying black unless they die. This permits one to see at a glance how old certain patterns are, which cells are co-generational, where the birth action is, and so forth.[19]

One soon discovers that some simple configurations are more interesting than others. In addition to those configurations which never change – the "still lifes" such as four pixels in a square – and those which evaporate entirely – such as any long diagonal line segment, whose two tail pixels die of isolation each instant until the line disappears entirely – there are configurations with all manner of periodicity. Three pixels in a line make a simple flasher, which becomes three pixels in a column in the next instant, and reverts to three in a line in the next, ad infinitum, unless some other configuration encroaches. Encroachment is what makes Life interesting: among the periodic configura-tions are some that swim, amoeba-like across the plane. The simplest is the *glider*, the five-pixel configuration shown taking a single stroke to the south-east in figure 14.2. Then there are the eaters, the puffer trains and space rakes, and a host of other aptly named denizens of the Life world that emerge in the ontology of a new level, analogous to what I have called the design level. This level has its own language, a transparent foreshortening of the tedious descrip-tions one could give at the physical level. For instance:

> An eater can eat a glider in four generations. Whatever is being con-sumed, the basic process is the same – A bridge forms between the eater and its prey. In the next generation, the bridge region dies from overpopulation, taking a bite out of both eater and prey. The eater then repairs itself. The prey usually cannot. If the remainder of the prey dies out as with the glider, the prey is consumed.[20]

Note that there has been a distinct ontological shift as we move between levels; whereas at the physical level there is no motion, and the only individuals, cells, are defined by their fixed spatial location, at this design level we have the

Glider

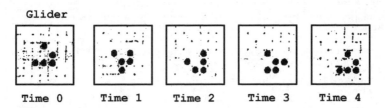

| Time 0 | Time 1 | Time 2 | Time 3 | Time 4 |

Figure 14.2 (from W. Poundstone, *The Recursive Universe: Cosmic Complexity and the Limits of Scientific Knowledge*, New York: Morrow, 1985).

297

motion of persisting objects; it is one and the same glider that has moved southeast in figure 14.2, changing shape as it moves, and there is one less glider in the world after the eater has eaten it in figure 14.3. (Here is a warming-up exercise for what is to follow: should we say that there is *real* motion in the Life world, or only *apparent* motion? The flashing pixels on the computer screen are a paradigm case, after all, of what a psychologist would call apparent motion. Are there *really* gliders that move, or are there just patterns of cell state that move? And if we opt for the latter, should we say at least that these moving patterns are real?)

Notice, too, that at this level one proposes generalizations that require 'usually' or 'provided nothing encroaches' clauses. Stray bits of debris from earlier events can "break" or "kill" one of the objects in the ontology at this level; their *salience as real things* is considerable, but not guaranteed. To say that their salience is considerable is to say that one can, with some small risk, ascend to this design level, adopt its ontology, and proceed to predict – sketchily and riskily – the behavior of larger configurations or systems of configurations, without bothering to compute the physical level. For instance, one can set oneself the task of designing some interesting supersystem out of the "parts" that the design level makes available. Surely the most impressive triumph of this design activity in the Life world is the proof that a working model of a universal Turing machine can in principle be constructed in the Life plane! Von Neumann had already shown that in principle a two-dimensional universal Turing machine could be constructed out of cellular automata, so it was "just" a matter of "engineering" to show how, in principle, it could be constructed out of the simpler cellular automata defined in the Life world. Glider streams can provide the tape, for instance, and the tape reader can be some huge assembly of eaters, gliders, and other bits and pieces. What does

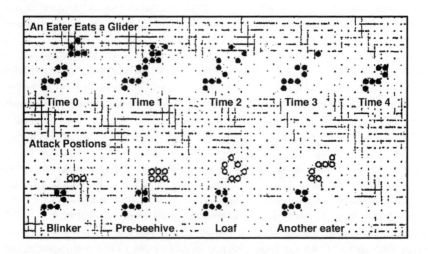

Figure 14.3 (from Poundstone, see figure 14.2).

this huge Turing machine look like? Poundstone calculates that the whole construction, a self-reproducing machine incorporating a universal Turing machine, would be on the order of 10^{13} pixels.

> Displaying a 10^{13}-pixel pattern would require a video screen about 3 million pixels across at least: Assume the pixels are 1 millimeter square (which is very high resolution by the standards of home computers). Then the screen would have to be 3 kilometers (about two miles) across. It would have an area about six times that of Monaco.
>
> Perspective would shrink the pixels of a self-reproducing pattern to invisibility. If you got far enough away from the screen so that the entire pattern was comfortably in view, the pixels (and even the gliders, eaters and guns) would be too tiny to make out. A self-reproducing pattern would be a hazy glow, like a galaxy.[21]

Now, since the universal Turing machine can compute any computable function, it can play chess – simply by mimicking the program of any chess-playing computer you like. Suppose, then, that such an entity occupies the Life plane, playing chess against itself. Looking at the configuration of dots that accomplishes this marvel would almost certainly be unilluminating to anyone who had no clue that a configuration with such powers could exist. But from the perspective of one who had the hypothesis that this huge array of black dots was a chess-playing computer, enormously efficient ways of predicting the future of that configuration are made available. As a first step one can shift from an ontology of gliders and eaters to an ontology of symbols and machine states, and, adopting this higher design stance toward the configuration, predict its future *as* a Turing machine. As a second and still more efficient step, one can shift to an ontology of chessboard positions, possible chess moves, and the grounds for evaluating them; then, adopting the intentional stance toward the configuration, one can predict its future *as* a chess player performing intentional actions – making chess moves and trying to achieve checkmate. Once one fixed on an interpretation scheme, permitting one to say which configurations of pixels count as which symbols (either, at the Turing machine level, the symbols '0' or '1', say, or at the intentional level, '*QxBch*' and the other symbols for chess moves), one can use the interpretation scheme to predict, for instance, that the next configuration to emerge from the galaxy will be such-and-such a glider stream (the symbols for '*RxQ*,', say). There is risk involved in either case, because the chess program being run on the Turing machine may be far from perfectly rational, and, at a different level, debris may wander onto the scene and "break" the Turing machine configuration before it finishes the game.

In other words, real but (potentially) noisy patterns abound in such a configuration of the Life world, there for the picking up if only we are lucky or clever enough to hit on the right perspective. They are not *visual* patterns but, one might say, *intellectual* patterns. Squinting or twisting the page is not apt to help, while posing fanciful interpretations (or what W. V. Quine would call "analytical hypotheses") may uncover a goldmine. The opportunity confronting the observer of such a Life world is analogous to the opportunity confronting the cryptographer staring at a new patch of cipher text, or the opportunity confronting the Martian, peering through a telescope at the Superbowl Game. If the Martian hits on the intentional stance – or folk psychology – as the right level to look for pattern, shapes will readily emerge through the noise.

IV The reality of intentional patterns

The scale of compression when one adopts the intentional stance toward the two-dimensional chess-playing computer galaxy is stupendous: it is the difference between figuring out in your head what white's most likely (best) move is versus calculating the state of a few trillion pixels through a few hundred thousand generations. But the scale of the savings is really no greater in the life world than in our own. Predicting that someone will duck if you throw a brick at him is easy from the folk-psychological stance; it is and will always be intractable if you have to trace the photons from brick to eyeball, the neurotransmitters from optic nerve to motor nerve, and so forth.

For such vast computational leverage one might be prepared to pay quite a steep price in errors, but in fact one belief that is shared by all of the representatives on the spectrum I am discussing is that "folk psychology" provides a description system that permits highly reliable prediction of human (and much nonhuman) behavior.[22] They differ in the explanations they offer of this predictive prowess, and the implications they see in it about "realism."

For Fodor, an industrial-strength Realist, beliefs and their kin would not be real unless the pattern dimly discernible from the perspective of folk psychology could also be discerned (more clearly, with less noise) as a pattern of structures in the brain. The pattern would have to be discernible from the different perspective provided by a properly tuned *syntactoscope* aimed at the purely formal (nonsemantic) features of Mentalese terms written in the brain. For Fodor, the pattern seen through the noise by everyday folk psychologists would tell us nothing about reality, unless it, and the noise, had the following sort of explanation: what we discern from the perspective of folk psychology is the net effect of two processes: an ulterior, hidden process wherein the pattern exists pure, overlaid, and partially obscured by various intervening sources of noise: performance errors, observation errors, and other more or less random obstructions. He might add that the interior belief-producing process was in this respect *just* like the process responsible for the creation of frames *A–F*. If you were permitted to peer behind the scenes at the program I devised to create the frames, you would see, clear as a bell, the perfect bar-code periodicity, with the noise thrown on afterward like so much salt and pepper.

This is often the explanation for the look of a data set in science, and Fodor may think that it is either the only explanation that can ever be given, or at any rate the only one that makes any sense of the success of folk psychology. But the rest of us disagree. As G. E. M. Anscombe put it in her pioneering exploration of intentional explanation, "if Aristotle's account [of reasoning using the practical syllogism] were supposed to describe actual mental processes, it would in general be quite absurd. The interest of the account is that it describes an order which is there whenever actions are done with intentions . . ."[23]

But how *could* the order be there, so visible amidst the noise, if it were not the direct outline of a concrete orderly process in the background? Well, it *could* be there thanks to the statistical effect of very many concrete minutiae producing, as if by a hidden hand, an approximation of the "ideal" order. Philosophers have tended to ignore a variety of regularity intermediate between the regularities of planets and other objects "obeying" the laws of physics and the regularities of rule-following (that is, rule-*consulting*) systems.[24] These intermediate regularities are those which are preserved under selection pressure: the regularities dictated by principles of good design and hence homed in on by self-designing systems. That is, a "rule of thought" may be much more than a mere regularity; it may be a *wise* rule, a rule one would design a system by if one were a system designer, and hence a rule one would expect self-designing systems to "discover" in the course of settling into their patterns of activity. Such rules no more need be explicitly represented than do the principles of aerodynamics that are honored in the design of birds' wings.[25]

The contrast between these different sorts of pattern-generation processes can be illustrated. The frames in figure 14.1 were created by a hard-edged process (ten black, ten white, ten black, . . .) obscured by noise, while the frames in figure 14.4 were created by a process almost the reverse of that: the top frame shows a pattern created by a normal distribution of black dots around means at $x = 10, 30, 50, 70$, and 90 (rather like Mach bands or interference fringes); the middle and bottom frames were created by successive applications of a very simple contrast enhancer applied to the top frame: a vertical slit "window" three pixels high is thrown randomly onto the frame; the pixels in the window vote, and majority rules. This gradually removes the salt from the pepper and the pepper from the salt, creating "artifact" edges such as those discernible in the bottom frame. The effect would be more striking at a finer pixel scale, where the black merges imperceptibly through grays to white but I chose to keep the scale at the ten-pixel period of bar code. I do not mean to suggest that it is impossible to tell the patterns in figure 14.4 from the patterns in figure 14.1. Of course it is possible; for one thing, the process that produced the frames in figure 14.1 will almost always show edges at exactly 10, 20, 30, . . . and almost never at 9, 11, 19, 21, . . . while there is a higher probability of these "displaced" edges being created by the process of figure 14.4 (as a close inspection, of figure 14.4 reveals). Fine tuning could of course reduce these probabilities, but that is not my point. My point is that *even if* the evidence is substantial that the discernible pattern is produced by one process rather than another, it can be rational to ignore those differences and use the simplest pattern description (e.g., *bar code*), as one's way of organizing the data.

Fodor and others have claimed that an interior language of thought is the best explanation of the hard edges visible in "propositional attitude psychology." Churchland and I have offered an alternative explanation of these edges, an explanation for which the process that produced the frames in figure 14.4 is a fine visual metaphor. The process that produces the data of folk psychology, we claim, is one in which the multidimensional complexities of the underlying processes are projected *through linguistic behavior*, which creates an appearance of definiteness and precision, thanks to the discreteness of words.[26] As Churchland puts it, a person's declarative utterance is a "one-dimensional *projection* – through the compound lens of Wernicke's and Broca's areas onto the idiosyncratic surface of the speaker's language – a one-dimensional projection of a four- or five-dimensional 'solid' that is an element in his true kinematic state".[27]

Fodor's industrial-strength Realism takes beliefs to be things in the head – just like cells and blood vessels and viruses. Davidson and I both like Churchland's alternative idea of propositional-attitude statements as indirect "measurements" of a reality diffused in the behavioral dispositions of the brain (and body).[28] We think beliefs are quite real enough to call real just so long as belief talk measures these complex behavior-disposing organs as predictively as it does. What do we disagree about? As John Haugeland[29] has pointed out, Davidson is more of a realist than I am, and I have recently tracked down the source of this disagreement to a difference of opinion we have about the status of Quine's principle of indeterminacy of translation which we both accept.

For Davidson, the principle is not the shocker it is often taken to be; in fact, it is well-nigh trivial – the two different translation manuals between which no fact of the matter decides are like two different scales for measuring temperature.

> We know there is no contradiction between the temperature of the air being 32° fahrenheit and 0° celsius; there is nothing in this 'relativism' to show that the properties being measured are not 'real'. Curiously,

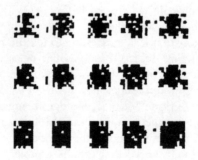

Figure 14.4

though, this conclusion has repeatedly been drawn. . . . Yet in the light of the considerations put forward here, this comes to no more than the recognition that more than one set of one person's utterances might be equally successful in capturing the contents of someone else's thoughts or speech. Just as numbers can capture all the empirically significant relations among weights or temperatures in infinitely many ways, so one person's utterances can capture all the significant features of another person's thoughts and speech in different ways. This fact does not challenge the 'reality' of the attitudes or meanings thus reported.[30]

On Davidson's view, no substantive disagreements emerge from a comparison of the two description schemes, and so they can quite properly be viewed as competing descriptions of the same reality.

I think this is a flawed analogy. A better one is provided by the example of "rival" descriptions of patterns-with-noise. Consider two rival intentional interpretations of a single individual; they agree on the general shape of this individual's collection of beliefs (and desires, etc), but because of their different idealizations of the pattern, they do not agree point-for-point. Recalling a famous analogy of Quine's[31] and extending it beyond radical translation to radical interpretation (as Davidson and I both wish to do), we get the image in Figure 14.5.

To the left we see Brown's intentional interpretation of Ella to the right, Jones's interpretation. Since these are intentional interpretations, the pixels or data points represent beliefs and so forth, not (for instance) bits of bodily motion or organs or cells or atoms, and since these are rival intentional interpretations of a single individual, the patterns discerned are not statistical averages (e.g., "Democrats tend to favor welfare programs") but personal cognitive idiosyncrasies (e.g., "She thinks she should get her queen out early"). Some of the patterns may indeed be simple observed periodicities (e.g., "Ella wants to talk about football on Mondays") but we are to understand the

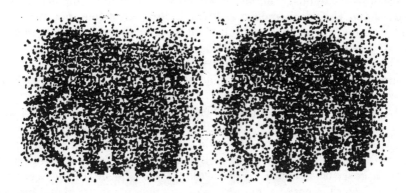

Figure 14.5

pattern to be what Anscombe called the "order which is there" in the rational coherence of a person's set of beliefs desires, and intentions.

Notice that here the disagreements can be substantial – at least before the fact: when Brown and Jones make a series of predictive bets, they will not always make the same bet. They may *often* disagree on what, according to their chosen pattern, will happen next. To take a dramatic case, Brown may predict that Ella will decide to kill herself; Jones may disagree. This is not a trivial disagreement of prediction, and in principle this momentous difference may emerge in spite of the overall consonance of the two interpretations.

Suppose, then, that Brown and Jones make a series of predictions of Ella's behavior, based on their rival interpretations. Consider the different categories that compose their track records. First, there are the occasions where they agree and are right. Both systems look good from the vantage point of these successes. Second, there are the occasions where they agree and are wrong. Both chalk it up to noise, take their budgeted loss and move on to the next case. But there will also be the occasions where they disagree, where their systems make different predictions and in these cases sometimes (but not always) one will win and the other lose. (In the real world, predictions are not always from among binary alternatives, so in many cases they will disagree and both be wrong.) When one wins and the other loses, it will look to the myopic observer as if one "theory" has scored a serious point against the other, but when one recognizes the possibility that both may chalk up such victories, and that there may be no pattern in the victories which permits either one to improve his theory by making adjustments, one sees that local triumphs may be insufficient to provide any ground in reality for declaring one account a closer approximation of the truth.

Now, some might think this situation is *always* unstable; eventually one interpretation is bound to ramify better to new cases, or be deducible from some larger scheme covering other data, etc. That might be true in many cases; but – and this, I think, is the central point of Quine's indeterminacy thesis – it need not be true in all. *If* the strategy of intentional-stance description is, as Quine says, a "dramatic idiom" in which there is ineliminable use of idealization, and if Fodor's industrial-strength Realism is thus not the correct explanation of the reliable "visibility" of the pattern, such radical indeterminacy is a genuine and stable possibility.

This indeterminacy will be most striking in such cases as the imagined disagreement over Ella's suicidal mindset. If Ella does kill herself, is Brown shown to have clearly had the better intentional interpretation? Not necessarily. When Jones chalks up his scheme's failure in this instance to a bit of noise, this is no more ad hoc or unprincipled than the occasions when Brown was wrong about whether Ella would order the steak not the lobster; and chalked those misses up to noise. This is not at all to say that an interpretation can never be shown to be just wrong; there is plenty of leverage within the principles of intentional interpretation to refute particular hypotheses – for instance, by forcing their defense down the path of Pickwickian explosion

("You see, she didn't believe the gun was loaded because she thought that those bullet-shaped things were chocolates wrapped in foil, which was just a fantasy that occurred to her because . . ."). It *is* to say that there could be two interpretation schemes that were reliable and compact predictors over the long run, but that nevertheless disagreed on crucial cases.

It might seem that in a case as momentous as Ella's intention to kill herself, a closer examination of the details just prior to the fatal moment (if not at an earlier stage) would have to provide additional support for Brown's interpretation at the expense of Jones's interpretation. After all, there would be at least a few seconds – or a few hundred milliseconds – during which Ella's decision to pull the trigger got implemented, and during that brief period, at least, the evidence would swing sharply in favor of Brown's interpretation. That is no doubt true, and it is *perhaps* true that had one gone into enough detail earlier, all this last-second detail could have been predicted – but to have gone into *those* details earlier would have been to drop down from the intentional stance to the design or physical stances. From the intentional stance, these determining considerations would have been invisible to both Brown and Jones, who were both prepared to smear over such details as noise in the interests of more practical prediction. Both interpreters concede that they will make false predictions, and moreover, that when they make false predictions there are apt to be harbingers of misprediction in the moments during which the *dénouement* unfolds. Such a brief swing does not constitute refutation of the interpretation, any more than the upcoming misprediction of behavior does.

How, then, does this make me less of a realist than Davidson? I see that there could be two different systems of belief attribution to an individual which differed *substantially* in what they attributed – even in yielding substantially different predictions of the individual's future behavior – and yet where no deeper fact of the matter could establish that one was a description of the individual's *real* beliefs and the other not. In other words, there could be two different, but equally real, patterns discernible in the noisy world. The rival theorists would not even agree on which parts of the world were pattern and which were noise, and yet nothing deeper would settle the issue.[32] The choice of a pattern would indeed be up to the observer, a matter to be decided on idiosyncratic pragmatic grounds. I myself do not see any feature of Davidson's position that would be a serious obstacle to his shifting analogies and agreeing with me. But then he would want to grant that indeterminacy is not such a trivial matter after all.[33]

What then is Rorty's view on these issues? Rorty wants to deny that any brand of "realism" could *explain* the (apparent?) success of the intentional stance. But since we have already joined Fine and set aside the "metaphysical" problem of realism, Rorty's reminding us of this only postpones the issue. Even someone who has transcended the scheme/content distinction and has seen the futility of correspondence theories of truth must accept the fact that *within* the natural ontological attitude we sometimes explain success by correspondence: one does better navigating off the coast of Maine when one uses an up-to-date nautical chart than one does when one uses a road map of Kansas. Why? Because the former accurately represents the hazards, markers, depths, and coastlines of the Maine coast, and the latter does not. Now why does one do better navigating the shoals of interpersonal relations using folk psychology than using astrology? Rorty might hold that the predictive "success" we folk-psychology players relish is itself an artifact, a mutual agreement engendered by the egging-on or consensual support we who play this game provide each other. He would grant that the game has no rivals in popularity, due – in the opinion of the players – to the power it gives them to understand and antici-pate the animate world. But he would refuse to endorse this opinion. How, then, would he distinguish this popularity from the popularity among a smaller coterie of astrology?[34] It is undeniable that astrology provides its adherents with a highly articulated system of patterns that they *think* they see in the events of the world. The difference, however, is that no one has ever been able to get rich by betting on the patterns, but only by selling the patterns to others.

Rorty would have to claim that this is not a significant difference; the rest of us, however, find abundant evidence that our allegiance to folk psychology as a predictive tool can be defended in coldly objective terms. We agree that there is a real pattern being described by the terms of folk psychology. What divides the rest of us is the nature of the pattern, and the ontological impli-cations of that nature.

Let us finally consider Churchland's eliminative materialism from this vantage point. As already pointed out, he is second to none in his apprecia-tion of the power, to date, of the intentional stance as a strategy of prediction. Why does he think that it is nevertheless doomed to the trash heap? Because he anticipates that neuroscience will eventually – perhaps even soon – discover a pattern that is so clearly superior to the noisy pattern of folk psychology that everyone will readily abandon the former for the latter (except, perhaps, in the rough-and-tumble of daily life). This might happen, I suppose. But Churchland here is only playing a hunch, a hunch that should not be seen to gain plausibility from reflections on the irresistible forward march of science. For it is not enough for Churchland to suppose that in principle, neuroscien-tific levels of description will explain more of the variance, predict more of the "noise" that bedevils higher levels. This is, of course, bound to be true in the limit – if we descend all the way to the neurophysiological "bit map." But as we have seen, the trade-off between ease of use and immunity from error for such a cumbersome system may make it profoundly unattractive.[35] If the "pattern" is scarcely an improvement over the bit map, talk of eliminative materialism will fall on deaf ears – just as it does when radical eliminativists urge us to abandon our ontological commitments to tables and chairs. A truly general-purpose, robust system of pattern description more valuable than the intentional stance is not an impossibility, but anyone who wants to bet on it might care to talk to me about the odds they will take.

What does all this show? Not that Fodor's industrial-strength Realism must be false, and not that Churchland's eliminative materialism must be false, but just that both views are gratuitously strong forms of materialism – presumptive theses way out in front of the empirical support they require. Rorty's view errs in the opposite direction, ignoring the impressive empirical track record that distinguishes the intentional stance from the astrological stance. Davidson's intermediate position, like mine, ties reality to the brute existence of pattern, but Davidson has overlooked the possibility of two or more *conflicting* patterns being superimposed on the same data – a more radical indeterminacy of translation than he had supposed possible. Now, once again, is the view I am defending here a sort of instrumentalism or a sort of realism? I think that the view itself is clearer than either of the labels, so I shall leave that question to anyone who stills find illumination in them.

Notes

1 *Content and Consciousness* (Boston: Routledge & Kegan Paul, 1969), ch. 1.
2 "Three Kinds of Intentional Psychology," in R. Healey, ed., *Reduction, Time and Reality* (New York: Cambridge, 1981); and *The Intentional Stance* (Cambridge: MIT, 1987).
3 Peter Smith, "Wit and Chutzpah," review of *The Intentional Stance* and Jerry A. Fodor's *Psychosemantics, Times Higher Education Supplement* (August 7, 1988), p. 22.
4 "The Stance Stance," commentary on *The Intentional Stance*, in *Behavioral and Brain Sciences* XI (1988): 511–12.
5 Ibid., p. 511.
6 R. A. Sharpe, in "Dennett's Journey Towards Panpsychism, *Inquiry* XXXII (1989): 233–40, takes me to task on this point, using examples from Proust to drive home the point that "Proust draws our attention to possible lives and these possible lives are various. But in none of them is prediction of paramount importance" (240). I agree. I also agree that what makes people interesting (in novels and in real life) is precisely their unpredictability. But that unpredictability is only interesting against the backdrop of routine predictability on which all interpretation depends. As I note in *The Intentional Stance* (p. 79) in response to a similar objection of Fodor's, the same is true of chess: the game is interesting only because of the unpredictability of one's opponent, but that is to say: the intentional stance can usually eliminate *only* ninety percent of the legal moves.
7 Norton Nelkin, "Patterns," forthcoming.
8 *The Shaky Game: Einstein, Realism and the Quantum Theory* (Chicago: University Press, 1986); see esp. p. 153n, and his comments there on Rorty, which I take to be consonant with mine here.
9 See *The Intentional Stance*, pp. 38–42, "Real Patterns, Deeper Facts, and Empty Questions."
10 "Randomness and Mathematical Proof," *Scientific American* CCXXXII (1975): 47–52.
11 More precisely: "A series of numbers is random if the smallest algorithm capable of specifying it to a computer has about the same number of bits of information as the series itself" (ibid.: p. 48). This is what explains the fact that the "random number generator" built into most computers is not really properly named, since it is some function describable in a few bits (a little subroutine that is called for

some output whenever a program requires a "random" number or series). If I send you the description of the pseudo-random number generator on my computer, you can use it to generate exactly the same infinite series of random-seeming digits.

12 Such schemes for efficient description, called compression algorithms, are widely used in computer graphics for saving storage space. They break the screen into uniformly colored regions, for instance, and specify region boundaries (rather like the "paint by numbers" line drawings sold in craft shops). The more complicated the picture on the screen, the longer the compressed description will be; in the worst case (a picture of confetti randomly sprinkled over the screen) the compression algorithm will be stumped and can do no better than a verbatim bit map.

13 What about the "system" of pattern description that simply baptizes frames with proper names (*A* through *F*, in this case) and tells the receiver which frame is up by simply sending '*F*'? This looks much shorter than the bit map until we consider that such a description must be part of an entirely general system. How many proper names will we need to name all possible 900-dot frames? Trivially, the 900-bit binary number, 11111111 ... To send the "worst-case" proper name will take exactly as many bits as sending the bit map. This confirms our intuition that proper names are maximally inefficient ways of couching generalizations ("Alf is tall and Bill is tall and . . .").

14 A. D. de Groot, *Thought and Choice in Chess* (The Hague: Mouton, 1965).

15 *Science, Perception and Reality* (Boston: Routledge & Kegan Paul, 1963).

16 In "Randomness and Perceived Randomness In Evolutionary Biology," *Synthese* XLIII (1980): 287–329, William Wimsatt offers a nice example (296): while the insectivorous bird tracks individual insects, the anteater just averages over the ant-infested area; one might say that, while the bird's manifest image quantifies over insects, 'ant' is a mass term for anteaters. See the discussion of this and related examples in my *Elbow Room* (Cambridge, Mass.: MIT, 1984), pp. 108–10.

17 *The Intentional Stance*, pp. 37–9.

18 Martin Gardner introduced the Game of Life to a wide audience in two columns in *Scientific American* in October, 1970, and February, 1971. William Poundstone, *The Recursive Universe: Cosmic Complexity and the Limits of Scientific Knowledge* (New York: Morrow, 1985), is an excellent exploration of the Game and its philosophical implications. Two figures from Poundstone's book are reproduced, with kind permission from the author and publisher, on pp. 297 and 298.

19 Poundstone, *The Recursive Universe*, provides simple BASIC and IBM-PC assembly language simulations you can copy for your own home computer, and describes some of the interesting variations.

20 Ibid., p. 38.

21 Ibid., pp. 227–8.

22 To see that the opposite poles share this view, see Fodor, *Psychosemantics* (Cambridge, Mass.: MIT, 1987), ch. 1, "Introduction: The Persistence of the Attitudes"; and Paul Churchland, *Scientific Realism and the Plasticity of Mind* (New York: Cambridge, 1929), esp. p. 100: "For the P-theory [folk psychology] is in fact a marvelous intellectual achievement. It gives its possessor an explicit and systematic insight into the behaviour, verbal and otherwise, of some of the most complex agents in the environment, and its overall prowess in that respect remains unsurpassed by anything else our considerable theoretical efforts have produced."

23 *Intention* (New York: Blackwell, 1957), p. 80.

24 A notable early exception is Sellars, who discussed the importance of just this sort of regularity in "Some Reflections on Language Games," *Philosophy of Science* XXI (1954), 204–28. See especially the subsection of this classic paper, entitled "Pattern Governed and Rule Obeying Behavior," reprinted in Sellars' *Science, Perception and Reality*, pp. 324–7.

25 Several interpreters of a draft of this article have supposed that the conclusion I am urging here is that beliefs (or their contents) are *epiphenomena* having no causal powers, but this is a misinterpretation traceable to a simplistic notion of causation. If one finds a predictive pattern of the sort just described one has *ipso facto* discovered a causal power – a difference in the world that makes a subsequent difference testable by standard empirical methods of variable manipulation. Consider the crowd-drawing power of a sign reading "Free Lunch" placed in the window of a restaurant, and compare its power in a restaurant in New York to its power in a restaurant in Tokyo. The intentional level is obviously the right level at which to predict and explain such causal powers; the sign more reliably produces a particular belief in one population of perceivers than in the other, and variations in the color of typography of the sign are not as predictive of variations in crowd-drawing power as are variations in (perceivable) meaning. The fact that the regularities on which these successful predictions are based are efficiently capturable (only) in intentional terms and are not derived from "covering laws" does not show that the regularities are not "causal"; it just shows that philosophers have often relied on pinched notions of causality derived from exclusive attention to a few examples drawn from physics and chemistry. Smith has pointed out to me that here I am echoing Aristotle's claim that his predecessors had ignored final causes.

26 See my discussion of the distinction between beliefs and (linguistically infected) *opinions*; in *Brainstorms* (Montgomery, Vt.: Bradford, 1978), ch. 16, and in "The Illusions of Realism," in *The Intentional Stance*, pp. 110–16.

27 "Eliminative Materialism and the Propositional Attitudes,' *The Journal of Philosophy* LXXVLII (2) (February 1981), 67–90, at p. 85.

28 Churchland introduces the idea in *Scientific Realism and the Plasticity of Mind*, pp. 100–17. My adoption of the idea was in "Beyond Belief," in A. Woodfield, ed., *Thought and Object* (New York: Oxford, 1982), repr. as ch. 5 of *The Intentional Stance*. Davidson's guarded approval is expressed in "What is Present to the Mind?" read at the Sociedad Filosófica Ibero Americana meeting in Buenos Aires, 1989.

29 See the discussion of Haugeland's views in the last chapter of *The Intentional Stance*, "Mid-Term Examination: Compare and Contrast," pp 348–9.

30 Davidson, "What is Present to the Mind?" (ms.), p. 10.

31 "Different persons growing up in the same language are like different bushes trimmed and trained to take the shape of identical elephants. The anatomical details of twigs and branches will fulfill the elephantine form differently from bush to bush, but the overall outward results are the same." *Word and Object* (Cambridge, Mass.: MIT, 1960), p. 8.

32 Cf. "The Abilities of Men and Machines," in *Brainstorms*, where I discuss two people who agree exactly on the future behavior of some artifact, but impose different Turing-machine interpretations of it. On both interpretations, the machine occasionally "makes errors" but the two interpreters disagree about

which cases are the errors. (They disagree about which features of the object's behavior count as signal and which as noise.) Which Turing machine is it really? This question has no answer.

33 Andrej Zabludowski seems to me to have overlooked this version of indeterminacy in "On Quine's Indeterminacy Doctrine," *Philosophical Review* XCVIII (1939), 35–64.

34 Cf. my comparison of "the astrological stance" to the intentional stance: *The Intentional Stance*, p. 16.

35 As I have put it, physical-stance predictions trump design-stance predictions, which trump intentional-stance predictions – but one pays for the power with a loss of portability and a (usually unbearable) computational cost.

IIC

THE MACHINERY OF COMMONSENSE PSYCHOLOGY: THEORY OR SIMULATION?

15

P.M. Churchland "Folk Psychology and the Explanation of Human Behavior"

Folk psychology, insist some, is just like folk mechanics, folk thermodynamics, folk meteorology, folk chemistry, and folk biology. It is a framework of concepts, roughly adequate to the demands of everyday life, with which the humble adept comprehends, explains, predicts, and manipulates a certain domain of phenomena. It is, in short, a folk *theory*. As with any theory, it may be evaluated for its virtues or vices in all of the dimensions listed. And as with any theory, it may be rejected in its entirety if it fails the measure of such evaluation. Call this the *theoretical view* of our self understanding.

Folk psychology, insist others, is radically unlike the examples cited. It does not consist of laws. It does not support causal explanations. It does not evolve over time. Its central purpose is normative rather than descriptive, And thus it is not the sort of framework that might be shown to be radically defective by sheerly empirical findings. Its assimilation to theories is just a mistake. It has nothing to fear, therefore, from advances in cognitive theory or the neurosciences. Call this the *anti-theoretical view* of our self understanding.

Somebody here is deeply mistaken. The first burden of this paper is to argue that it is the anti-theoretical view that harbors most, though not all, of those mistakes. In the thirty years since the theoretical view was introduced (see esp. Sellars 1956, Feyerabend 1963, Rorty 1965, Churchland 1970, 1979, 1981), a variety of objections have been levelled against it. The more interesting of those will be addressed shortly. My current view is that these objections motivate no changes whatever in the theoretical view.

The second and more important burden of this paper, however, is to outline and repair a serious failing in the traditional expressions of the theoretical view, my own expressions included. The failing, as I see it, lies in representing one's commonsense understanding of human nature as consisting of *an internally stored set of general sentences*, and in representing one's predictive and explanatory activities as being a matter of *deductive inference* from those sentences plus occasional premises about the case at hand.

This certainly sounds like a major concession to the anti-theoretical view, but in fact it is not. For what motivates this reappraisal of the character of our self-understanding is the gathering conviction that little or *none* of human understanding consists of stored sentences, not even the prototypically

313

scientific understanding embodied in a practicing physicist, chemist, or astronomer. The familiar conception of knowledge as a set of 'propositional attitudes' is itself a central aspect of the framework of folk psychology, according to the reappraisal at hand, and it is an aspect that needs badly to be replaced. Our self-understanding, I continue to maintain, is no different in character from our understanding of any other empirical domain. It is speculative, systematic, corrigible, and in principle replaceable. It is just not so specifically *linguistic* as we have chronically assumed.

The speculative and replaceable character of folk psychology is now somewhat easier to defend than it was in the 60s and 70s, because recent advances in connectionist AI and computational neuroscience have provided us with a fertile new framework with which to understand the perception, cognition, and behavior of intelligent creatures. Whether it will eventually prove adequate to the task of replacing folk psychology remains to be seen, but the mere possibility of systematic alternative conceptions of cognitive activity and intelligent behavior should no longer be a matter of dispute. Alternatives are already abuilding. Later in the paper I shall outline the main features of this novel framework and explore its significance for the issues here at stake. For now, let me acquiesce in the folk psychological conception of knowledge as a system of beliefs or similar propositional attitudes, and try to meet the objections to the theoretical view already outstanding.

I Objections to the theoretical view

As illustrated in Churchland 1970, 1979, and 1984, a thorough perusal of the explanatory factors that typically appear in our commonsense explanations of our internal states and our overt behavior sustains the quick 'reconstruction' of a large number of universally quantified conditional statements, conditionals with the conjunction of the relevant explanatory factors as the antecedent and the relevant explanandum as the consequent. It is these universal statements that are supposed to constitute the 'laws' of folk psychology.

A perennial objection is that these generalizations do not have the character of genuine causal /explanatory laws: rather, they have some other, less empirical, status (e.g., that of normative principles, or rules of language, or analytic truths). Without confronting each of the many alternatives in turn, I think we can make serious difficulties for any objection of this sort.

Note first that the concepts of folk psychology divide into two broad classes. On the one hand there are those fully intentional concepts expressing the various propositional attitudes, such as belief and desire. And on the other hand there are those nonintentional or quasi-intentional concepts expressing all of the other mental states such as grief, fear, pain, hunger, and the full range of emotions and bodily sensations. Where states of the latter kind are concerned, I think it is hardly a matter for dispute that the common homilies in which they figure are causal/explanatory laws. Consider the following.

314

A person who suffers severe bodily damage will feel pain.
A person who suffers a sudden sharp pain will wince.
A person denied food for any length will feel hunger.
A hungry person's mouth will water at the smell of food.
A person who feels overall warmth will tend to relax.
A person who tastes a lemon will have a puckering sensation.
A person who is angry will tend to be impatient.

Clearly these humble generalizations, and thousands more like them, are causal/explanatory in character. They will and regularly do support simple explanations, sustain subjunctive and counterfactual conditionals, and underwrite predictions in the standard fashion. Moreover, concepts of this simple sort carry perhaps the major part of the folk psychological burden. The comparatively complex explanations involving the propositional attitudes are of central importance, but they are surrounded by a quotidian whirl of simple explanations like these, all quite evidently of a causal/explanatory cast.

It won't do then, to insist that the generalizations of folk psychology are on the whole nonempirical or noncausal in character. The bulk of them, and I mean thousands upon thousands of them, are transparently causal or nomological. The best one can hope to argue is that there is a central core of folk-psychological concepts whose explanatory role is somehow *discontinuous* with that of their fellows. The propositional attitudes, especially belief and desire, are the perennial candidates for such a nonempirical role, for explanations in their terms typically display the explanandum event as 'rational'. What shall we say of explanations in terms of beliefs and desires?

We should tell essentially the same causal/explanatory story, and for the following reason. Whatever else humans do with the concepts for the propositional attitudes, they do use them successfully to predict the future behavior of others. This means that, on the basis of presumed information about the current cognitive states of the relevant individuals, one can non-accidentally predict at least some of their future behavior some of the time. But any principle that allows us to do this – that is, to predict one empirical state or event on the basis of another, logically distinct, empirical state or event – has to be empirical in character. And I assume it is clear that the event of my ducking my head is logically distinct both from the event of my perceiving an incoming snowball, and from the states of my desiring to avoid a collision and my belief that ducking is the best way to achieve this.

Indeed, one can do more than merely predict: one can control and manipulate the behavior of others by controlling the information available to them. Here one is bringing about certain behaviors by steering the cognitive states of the subject – by relating opportunities, dangers, or obligations relevant to that subject. How this is possible without an understanding of the objective empirical regularities that connect the internal states and the overt behaviors of normal people is something that the anti-theoretical position needs to explain.

315

The confused temptation to find something special about the case of intentional action derives primarily from the fact that the central element in a full-blooded action explanation is a configuration of propositional attitudes in the light of which the explanandum behavior can be seen as sensible or rational, at least from the agent's narrow point of view. In this rational-in-the-light-of relation we seem to have some sort of super-causal *logical* relation between the explanans and the explanandum, which is an invitation to see a distinct and novel type of explanation at work.

Yet while the premise is true – there is indeed a logical relation between the explanandum and certain elements in the explanans – the conclusion does not begin to follow. Students of the subject are still regularly misled on this point, for they fail to appreciate that a circumstance of this general sort is *typical* of theoretical explanations. Far from being a sign of the nonempirical and hence nontheoretical character of the generalizations and explanations at issue, it is one of the surest signs available that we are here dealing with a high-grade theoretical framework. Let me explain.

The electric current I in a wire or any conductor is causally determined by two factors: it tends to increase with the electromotive force or voltage V that moves the electrons down the wire, and it tends to be reduced according to the resistance R the wire offers against their motion. Briefly, $I = V/R$. Less cryptically and more revealingly.

$(x)(V)(R)[(x$ *is subject to a voltage of* $(V)) \& (x$ *offers a resistance of* $(R)) \supset (\exists I((x$ *has a current of* $(I)) \& (I = V/R))]$

The first point to notice here is that the crucial predicates – *has a resistance of* (R), *is subject to a voltage of* (V) and *has a current of* (I) – are what might be called 'numerical attitudes': they are predicate-forming functors that take singular terms for numbers in the variable position. A complete predicate is formed only when a specific numeral appears in the relevant position. The second point to notice is that this electrodynamical law exploits a relation holding on the domain of numbers in order to express an important empirical regularity. The current I is the *quotient* of the voltage V and the resistance R, whose values will be cited in explanation of the current. And the third point to notice is that this law and the explanations it sustains are typical of laws and explanations throughout science. Most of our scientific predicates express 'numerical attitudes' of the sort displayed, and most of our laws exploit and display relations that hold primarily on the abstract domain of numbers. Nor are they limited to numbers. Other laws exploit the abstract relations holding on the abstract domain of vectors, or on the domain of sets, or groups, or matrices. But none of this means they are nonempirical, or noncausal, or nonnomic.

Action explanations, and intentional explanations in general, follow the same pattern. The only difference is that here the domain of abstract objects being exploited is the domain of propositions, and the relations displayed are logical relations. And like the numerical and vectorial attitudes typical of theo-

316

ries, the expressions for the propositional attitudes are predicate-forming functors. *Believes that P*, for example, forms a complete predicate only when a
specific sentence appears in the variable position *P*. The principles that
comprehend these predicates have the same abstract and highly sophisticated
structure displayed by our most typical theories. They just exploit the relations holding on a different domain of abstract objects in order to express the
important empirical regularities comprehending the states and activities of
cognitive creatures. That makes folk psychology a very interesting theory,
perhaps, but it is hardly a sign of its being *non*theoretical. Quite the reverse
is true. (This matter is discussed at greater length in Churchland 1979, sec.
14, and 1981: 82–4.)

In summary, the simpler parts of folk psychology are transparently causal
or nomic in character, and the more complex parts have the same sophisticated logical structure typical of our most powerful theories.

But we are not yet done with objections. A recurrent complaint is that in
many cases the reconstructed conditionals that purport to be sample 'laws' of
folk psychology are either strictly speaking false, or they border on the trivial
by reason of being qualified by various *ceteris paribus* clauses. A first reply is
to point out that my position does not claim that the laws of folk psychology
are either true or complete. I agree that they are a motley lot. My hope is to
see them replaced entirely, and their ontology of states with them. But this
reply is not wholly responsive, for the point of the objection is that it is implausible to claim the status of an entrenched theoretical framework for a bunch
of 'laws' that are as vague, as loose, and as festooned with *ceteris paribus*
clauses as are the examples typically given.

I will make no attempt here to defend the ultimate integrity of the laws of
folk psychology, for I have little confidence in them myself. But this is not
what is required to meet the objection. What needs pointing out is that the
'laws' of folk theories are *in general* sloppy, vague, and festooned with qualifications and *ceteris paribus* clauses. What the objectors need to do, in order
to remove the relevant system of generalizations from the class of empirical
theories, is to show that folk psychology is significantly *worse* in all of these
respects than are the principles of folk mechanics, or folk thermodynamics, or
folk biology, and so forth. In this they are sure to be disappointed, for these
other folk theories are even worse than folk psychology (see McCloskey 1983).
In all, folk psychology may be a fairly ramshackle theory, but a theory it
remains. Nor is it a point against this that folk psychology has changed little
or none since ancient times. The same is true of other theories near and dear
to us. The folk physics of the 20th century, I regret to say, is essentially the
same as the folk physics of the ancient Greeks (McCloskey 1983). Our conceptual inertia on such matters may be enormous, but a theory remains a theory,
however many centuries it may possess us.

A quite different objection directs our attention to the great many things
beyond explanation and prediction for which we use the vocabulary and
concepts of folk psychology. Their primary function, runs the objection, is not

317

the function served by explanatory theories, but rather the myriad social functions that constitute human culture and commerce. We use the resources of folk psychology to promise, to entreat, to congratulate, to tease, to joke, to intimate, to threaten, and so on. (See Wilkes 1981, 1984.)

The list of functions is clearly both long and genuine. But most of these functions surely come under the heading of control or manipulation, which is just as typical and central a function of theories as is either explanation or prediction, but which is not mentioned in the list of theoretical functions supplied by the objectors. Though the image may be popular, the idle musings of an impotent stargazer provide a poor example of what theories are and what theories do. More typically, theories are the conceptual vehicles with which we literally come to grips with the world. The fact that folk psychology serves a wealth of practical purposes is no evidence of its being non-theoretical. Quite the reverse.

Manipulation aside, we should not underestimate the importance for social commerce of the explanations and predictions that folk psychology makes possible. If one cannot predict or anticipate the behavior of one's fellows at all, then one can engage in no useful commerce with them whatever. And finding the right explanations for their past behavior is often the key to finding the appropriate premises from which to anticipate their future behavior. The objection's attempt to paint the functions of folk psychology in an exclusively non-theoretical light is simply a distortion born of tunnel vision.

In any case, it is irrelevant. For there is no inconsistency in saying that a theoretical framework should also serve a great many non-theoretical purposes. To use an example I have used before (1986), the theory of *witches*, *demonic possession*, *exorcism*, and *trial by ordeal*, was also used for a variety of social purposes beyond strict explanation and prediction. For example, its vocabulary was used to warn, to censure, to abjure, to accuse, to badger, to sentence, and so forth. But none of this meant that demons and witches were anything other than theoretical entities, and none of this saved the ontology of demon theory from elimination when its empirical failings became acute and different conceptions of human pathology arose to replace it. Beliefs, desires, and the rest of the folk psychological ontology all are in the same position. Their integrity, to the extent that they have any, derives from the explanatory, predictive, and manipulative prowess they display.

It is on the topic of explanation and prediction that a further objection finds fault with the theoretical view. Precisely what, begins the objection, is the observable behavior that the ontology of folk psychology is postulated to explain? Is it bodily behavior as *kinematically* described? In some cases perhaps, but not in general, certainly, because many quite different kinematical sequences could count as the same intentional action, and it is generally the *action* that is properly the object of folk psychological explanations of behavior. In general, the descriptions of human behavior that figure in folk-psychological explanations and predictions are descriptions that *already* imply perception, intelligence, and personhood on the part of the agent. Thus it must be wrong to see the relation between one's psychological states and one's behavior on the model of theoretical states postulated to explain the behavior of some conceptually independent domain of phenomena (Haldane 1988).

The premise of this objection is fairly clearly true: a large class of behavior descriptions are not conceptually independent of the concepts of folk psychology. But this affords no grounds for denying theoretical status to the ontology of folk psychology. The assumption that it does reflects a naive view of the relation between theories and the domains they explain and predict. The naive assumption is that the concepts used to describe the domain-to-be-explained must always be conceptually independent of the theory used to explain the phenomena within that domain. That assumption is known to be false, and we need look no farther than the Special Theory of Relativity (STR) for a living counterexample.

The introduction of STR brought with it a systematic reconfiguration of all of the basic observational concepts of mechanics: spatial length, temporal duration, velocity, mass, momentum, etc. These are all one-place predicates within classical mechanics, but they are all replaced by two-place predicates within STR. Each ostensible 'property' has turned out to be a *relation*, and each has a definite value only relative to a chosen reference frame. If STR is true, and since the early years of this century it has seemed to be, then one cannot legitimately describe the observational facts of mechanics save in terms that are drawn from STR itself.

Modern chemistry provides a second example. It is a rare chemist who does not use the taxonomy of the periodic table and the combinatorial lexicon of chemical compounds to describe both the observable facts and their theoretical underpinnings alike. For starters, one can just smell hydrogen sulphide, taste sodium chloride, feel any base, and identify copper, aluminum, iron, and gold by sight.

These cases are not unusual. Our theoretical convictions typically reshape the way we describe the facts-to-be-explained. Sometimes it happens immediately, as with STR, but more often it happens after long familiarity with the successful theory, as is displayed in the idioms casually employed in any working laboratory. The premise of the objection is true. But it is no point at all against the theoretical view. Given the great age of folk psychology, such conceptual invasion of the explanandum domain is only to be expected.

A different critique of the theoretical view proposes an alternative account of our understanding of human behavior. According to this view, one's capacity for anticipating and understanding the behavior of others resides not in a system of nomically-embedded concepts, but rather in the fact that one is a normal person oneself, and can draw on one's own reactions, to real or to imagined circumstances, in order to gain insight into the internal states and the overt behavior of others. The key idea is that of empathy. One uses oneself as a simulation (usually imagined) of the situation of another, and then extrapolates the results of that simulation to the person in question (cf. Gordon 1986; Goldman 1989).

My first response to this line is simply to agree that an enormous amount of one's appreciation of the internal states and overt behavior of other humans derives from one's ability to examine and to extrapolate from the facts of one's own case. All of this is quite consistent with the theoretical view, and there is no reason that one should attempt to deny it. One learns from every example of humanity one encounters, and one encounters oneself on a systematic basis. What we must resist is the suggestion that extrapolating from the particulars of one's own case is the fundamental ground of one's understanding of others, a ground that renders possession of a nomic framework unnecessary. Problems for this stronger position begin to appear immediately.

For one thing, if *all* of one's understanding of others is closed under extrapolation from one's own case, then the modest contents of one's own case must form an absolute limit on what one can expect or explain in the inner life and external behavior of others. But in fact we are not so limited. People who are congenitally deaf, or blind, know quite well that normal people have perceptual capacities beyond what they themselves possess, and they know in some detail what those capacities entail in the way of knowledge and behavior. Moreover, people who have never felt profound grief, say, or love, or rejection, can nonetheless provide appropriate predictions and explanations of the behavior of people so afflicted. And so on. In general, one's immediately available understanding of human psychology and behavior goes substantially beyond what one has experienced in one's own case, either in real life or in pointed simulations. First-person experience or simulation is plainly not *necessary* for understanding the behavior of others.

Nor is it *sufficient*. The problem is that simulations, even if they motivate predictions about others, do not by themselves provide any explanatory understanding of the behavior of others. To see this, consider the following analogy. Suppose I were to possess a marvelous miniature of the physical universe, a miniature I could manipulate in order to simulate real situations and thus predict and retrodict the behavior of the real universe. Even if my miniature unfailingly provided accurate simulations of the outcomes of real physical processes, I would still be no further ahead on the business of *explaining* the behavior of the real world. In fact, I would then have two universes, both in need of explanation.

The lesson is the same for first-person and third-person situations. A simulation itself, even a successful one, provides no explanation. What explanatory understanding requires is an appreciation of the *general patterns* that comprehend the individual events in both cases. And that brings us back to the idea of a moderately general *theory*.

We should have come to that idea directly, since the empathetic account of our understanding of others depends crucially on one's having an initial understanding of oneself. To extrapolate one's own cognitive, affective, and behavioral intricacies to others requires that one be able to conceptualize and spontaneously to recognize those intricacies in oneself. But one's ability to do this is left an unaddressed mystery by the empathetic account.

Self-understanding is not seen as a problem; it is other-understanding that is held up as the problem.

But the former is no less problematic than the latter, If one is to be able to apprehend even the *first*-person intricacies at issue, then one must possess a conceptual framework that draws all of the necessary distinctions, a framework that organizes the relevant categories into the appropriate structure, a framework whose taxonomy reflects at least the more obvious of the rough nomic regularities holding across its elements, even in the first-person case. Such a framework is already a theory.

The fact is, the categories into which any important domain gets divided, by a learning creature emerge jointly with an appreciation of the rough nomic regularities that connect them. A nascent taxonomy that supports the expression of no useful regularities is a taxonomy that is soon replaced by a more insightful one. The divination of useful regularities is the single most dominant force shaping the taxonomies developed by any learning creature in any domain. And it is an essential force, even in perceptual domains, since our observational taxonomies are always radically underdetermined by our untrained perceptual mechanisms. To suppose that one's conception of one's *own* mental life is innocent of a network of systematic expectations is just naive. But such a network is already a theory, even before one addresses the question of others.

This is the cash value, I think, of P.F. Strawson's insightful claim that to be in a position to pose any question about other minds, and to be in a position to try to construct arguments from analogy with one's own case, is already to possess at least the rudiments of what is sought after, namely, a general conception of mental phenomena, of their general connections with each other and with behavior (Strawson, 1958). What Strawson missed was the further insight that such a framework is nothing other than an empirical theory, one justified not by the quasi-logical character of its principles, as he attempted unsuccessfully to show, but by its impersonal success in explaining and predicting human behavior at large. There is no special justificational story to be told here. Folk psychology is justified by what standardly justifies any conceptual framework: namely, its explanatory, predictive, and manipulative success.

This concludes my survey of the outstanding objections to the theoretical view outlined in the opening paragraph of the present paper. But in defending this view there is a major difference between my strategy in earlier writings and that of the present paper. In my 1970 paper, for example, the question was framed as follows: "Are action explanations *deductive-nomological* explanations?' I would now prefer to frame the question thus: "Are action explanations of the same general type as the explanations typically found in the sciences?" I continue to think that the answer to this second question is pretty clearly yes. The reasons are as covered above. But I am no longer confident that the D–N model itself is an adequate account of explanation in the sciences or anywhere else.

The difficulties with the D–N model are detailed elsewhere in the literature, so I shall not pause to summarize them here. My diagnosis of its failings, however, locates the basic problem in its attempt to represent knowledge and understanding by sets of sentences or propositional attitudes. In this, the framers of the D–N model were resting on the basic assumptions of folk psychology. Let me close this paper by briefly exploring how we might conceive of knowledge, and of explanatory understanding, in a systematically different way. This is an important undertaking relative to the concerns of this paper, for there is an objection to the theoretical view, as traditionally expressed, that seems to me to have some real bite. It is as follows.

If one's capacity for understanding and predicting the behavior of others derives from one's internal storage of thousands of laws or nomic generalizations, how is it that one is so poor at enunciating the laws on which one's explanatory and predictive prowess depends? It seems to take a trained philosopher to reconstruct them! How is it that children are so skilled at understanding and anticipating the behavior of humans in advance of ever acquiring the complex linguistic skills necessary to express them? How is it that social hunters such as wolves and lions can comprehend and anticipate each other's behavior in great detail, when they presumably store no internal sentences at all?

We must resist the temptation to see in these questions a renewed motivation for counting folk psychology as special, for the very same problems arise with respect to any other folk theory you might care to mention – folk physics, folk biology, whatever. It even arises for theories in the highly developed sciences, since, as Kuhn has pointed out, very little of a scientist's understanding of a theory consists in his ability to state a list of laws. It consists rather in the ability to apply the conceptual resources of the theory to new cases, and thus to anticipate and perhaps manipulate the behavior of the relevant empirical domain. This means that our problem here concerns the character of knowledge and understanding in general. Let us finally address that problem.

II   An alternative form of knowledge representation

One alternative to the notion of a universal generalization about F is the notion of a *prototype* of F, a central or typical example of F which all other examples of F resemble, more or less closely, in certain relevant respects. Prototypes have certain obvious advantages over universal generalizations. Just as a picture can be worth a thousand words, so a single complex prototype can embody the same breadth of information concerning the organization of co-occurrent features that would be contained in a long list of complex generalizations. Further, prototypes allow us a welcome degree of looseness that is precluded by the strict logic of a universal quantifier: not all Fs need be Gs, but the standard or normal ones are, and the non-standard ones must be related by a relevant similarity relation to those that properly are G.

Various theorists have independently found motive to introduce such a notion in a number of cognitive fields: they have been called *paradigms* and *exemplars* in the philosophy of science (Kuhn 1962), *stereotypes* in semantics (Putnam 1970, 1975), *frames* (Minsky 1981) and *scripts* (Schank and Abelson 1977) in AI research, and finally *prototypes* in psychology (Rosch 1981) and linguistics (Lakoff 1987).

Their advantages aside, prototypes also have certain familiar problems. The first problem is how to determine just what clutch of elements or properties should constitute a given prototype, and the second problem is how to determine the metric of similarity along which 'closeness' to the central prototype is to be measured. Though they pose a problem for notions at all levels, these problems are especially keen in the case of the so-called basic or simple properties, because common sense is there unable even to articulate any 'deeper' constituting elements (for example, what elements 'make up' a purple color, a sour taste, a floral smell, or the phoneme ā?). A final problem concerning prototypes is a familiar one: how might prototypes be effectively represented in a real cognitive creature?

This last question brings me to a possible answer, and to a path that leads to further answers. The relevant research concerns the operations of artificial neural networks, networks that mimic some of the more obvious organizational features of the brain. It concerns how they learn to recognize certain types of complex stimuli, and how they represent what they have learned. Upon repeated presentation of various real examples of the several features to be learned (*F*, *G*, *H*, etc.), and under the steady pressure of a learning algorithm that makes small adjustments in the network's synaptic connections, the network slowly but spontaneously generates a set of internal representations, one for each of the several features it is required to recognize. Collectively, those representations take the form of a set or system of similarity spaces, and the central point or volume of such a space constitutes the network's representation of a *prototypical F*, *G*, or *H*. After learning is completed, the system responds to any *F*-like stimulus with an internal pattern of neuronal activity that is *close* to the prototypical pattern in the relevant similarity space.

The network consists of an initial 'sensory' layer of neurons, which is massively connected to a second layer of neurons. The sizes or 'weights' of the many connections determine how the neurons at the second layer collectively respond to activity across the input layer. The neurons at the second layer are connected in turn to a third layer (and perhaps a fourth, etc., but we will here limit the discussion to three-layer networks). During learning, what the system is searching for is a configuration of weights that will turn the neurons at the second layer into a set of *complex feature detectors*. We then want the neurons at the third or 'output' layer to respond in turn to the second layer, given any *F*-like stimuli at the input layer, with a characteristic pattern of activity. All of this is achieved by presenting the network with diverse examples of *F*s, and slowly adjusting its connection weights in the light of its initially chaotic responses.

Such networks can indeed learn to recognize a wide variety of surprisingly subtle features: phonemes from voiced speech, the shapes of objects from grey-scale photos, the correct pronunciation of printed English text, the presence of metallic mines from sonar returns, and grammatical categories in novel sentences. Given a successfully trained network, if we examine the behavior of the neurons at the second or intermediate layer during the process of recognition, we discover that each neuron has come to represent, by its level of activity, some distinct aspect or dimension of the input stimulus. Taken together, their joint activity constitutes a multi-dimensional analysis of the stimuli at the input layer. The trained network has succeeded in finding a set of dimensions, an abstract *space*, such that all more-or-less typical *F*s produce a characteristic profile of neuronal activity across those particular dimensions, while deviant or degraded *F*s produce profiles that are variously close to that central prototype. The job of the third and final layer is then the relatively simple one of distinguishing that profile-region from other regions in the larger space of possible activation patterns. In this way do artificial neural networks generate and exploit prototypes. It is now more than a suggestion that real neural networks do the same thing. (For a summary of these results and how they bear on the question of theoretical knowledge, see Churchland 1989a. For a parade case of successful learning, see Rosenberg and Sejnowski 1987. For the *locus classicus* concerning the general technique, see Rumelhart *et al.* 1986.)

Notice that this picture contains answers to all three of the problems about prototypes noted earlier. What dimensions go into a prototype of *F*? Those that allow the system to respond to diverse examples of *F* in a distinctive and uniform way, a way that reduces the error messages from the learning algorithm to a minimum. How is similarity to a prototype measured? By geometrical proximity in the relevant parameter space. How are prototypes represented in real cognitive creatures? By canonical activity patterns across an appropriate population of neurons.

Note also that the objective features recognized by the network can also have a temporal component: a network can just as well be trained to recognize typical *sequences* and *processes* as to recognize atemporal patterns. Which brings me to my final suggestion. A normal human's understanding of the springs of human action may reside not in a set of stored generalizations about the hidden elements of mind and how they conspire to produce behavior, but rather in one or more prototypes of the deliberative or purposeful process. To understand or explain someone's behavior may be less a matter of deduction from implicit laws, and more a matter of recognitional subsumption of the case at issue under a relevant prototype. (For a more detailed treatment of this view of explanation – the *prototype activation model* – see Churchland 1989b.)

Such prototypes are no doubt at least modestly complex, and presumably they depict typical configurations of desires, beliefs, preferences, and so forth, roughly the same configurations that I have earlier attempted to express in the form of universally quantified sentences. Beyond this, I am able to say little about them, at least on this occasion. But I hope I have succeeded in making intelligible to you a novel approach to the problem of explanatory under-standing in humans. This is an approach that is grounded at last in what we know about the brain. And it is an approach that ascribes to us neither reams of universally quantified premises, nor deductive activity on a heroic scale. Explanatory understanding turns out to be not quite what we thought it was, because cognition in general gets characterized in a new way. And yet explana-tory understanding remains the same *sort* of process in the case of human behavior as in the case of natural phenomena generally. And the question of the *adequacy* of our commonsense understanding remains as live as ever.

References

Churchland, P.M. (1970) "The Logical Character of Action Explanations", *Philosophical Review* 79(2).

—— (1979) *Scientific Realism and the Plasticity of Mind* (Cambridge: Cambridge University Press).

—— (1981) "Eliminative Materialism and the Propositional Attitudes", *Journal of Philosophy* LXXVIII(2).

—— (1984) *Matter and Consciousness* (Cambridge: MIT Press).

—— (1986) "On the Continuity of Science and Philosophy", *Mind and Language* 1(1).

—— (1989a), "On the Nature of Theories: A Neurocomputational Perspective", in Savage, W., ed., *Scientific Theories: Minnesota Studies in the Philosophy of Science*, Vol. XIV (Minneapolis; University of Minnesota Press).

—— (1989b) "On the Nature of Explanation: A PDP Approach', *A Neurocomputa-tional Perspective* (Cambridge, Mass., MIT Press).

Feyerabend, P.K. (1963) "Materialism and the Mind-Body Problem", *Review of Metaphysics* 17.

Goldman, A. (1989) 'Interpretation psychologized'. *Mind and Language* 4: 161–85.

Gordon, R. (1986) "Folk Psychology as Simulation", *Mind & Language* 1(2).

Haldane, J. (1988) "Understanding Folk", *Proceedings of the Aristotelian Society*, Supplementary Vol. LXII.

Kuhn, T.S. (1962) *The Structure of Scientific Revolutions* (Chicago: University of Chicago Press).

Lakoff, G. (1987) *Women, Fire and Dangerous Things* (Chicago: University of Chicago Press).

McCloskey, M. (1983) "Intuitive Physics", *Scientific American* 248(4).

Minsky, M. (1981) "A Framework for Representing Knowledge", in Haugeland, J., ed., *Mind Design* (Cambridge, Mass.: MIT Press).

Putnam, H. (1970) "Is Semantics Possible?", in Kiefer, H. and Munitz, M. eds, *Languages, Belief, and Metaphysics* (Albany: State University of New York Press). Reprinted in Putnam, H., *Mind, Language and Reality* (Cambridge: Cambridge University Press).

—— (1975) "The Meaning of 'Meaning'", in Gunderson, K., *Language, Mind and Knowledge: Minnesota Studies in the Philosophy of Science*, Vol. VII. Reprinted in Putnam H., *Mind, Language and Reality* (Cambridge: Cambridge University Press).

Rorty, H. (1965) "Mind-Body Identity, Privacy, and Categories", *Review of Metaphysics* 1.

Rosch, E. (1981) "Prototype Classification and Logical Classification: The Two Systems", in Scholnick, E., ed., *New Trends in Cognitive Representation: Challenges to Piaget's Theory* (New Jersey: Lawrence Erlbaum).

Rosenberg, C.R. and Sejnowski, T.J. (1987) "Parallel Networks That Learn To Pronouce English Text", *Complex Systems* 1.

Rumelhart, D.E., Hinton, G.E., and Williams, R.J. (1986) "Learning Internal Representations by Error Propagation", in Rumelhart, D.E. and McClelland, J.L., eds, *Parallel Distributed Processing: Explorations in the Microstructure of Cognition* (Cambridge, Mass.: MIT Press).

Schank, R. and Abelson, H. (1977) *Scripts, Plans, Goals, and Understanding* (New Jersey: John Wiley and Sons).

Sellars, W. (1956) "Empiricism and the Philosophy of Mind", in Feigl, H. and Scriven, M., eds, *Minnesota Studies in the Philosophy of Science*, Vol. I (Minneapolis: University of Minnesota Press). Reprinted in Sellars, W., *Science, Perception and Reality* (London: Routledge and Kegan Paul, 1963).

Strawson, P.F. (1958) "Persons", *Minnesota Studies in the Philosophy of Science*, Vol. II, eds Feigl, H., Scriven, M., and Maxwell, G. (Minneapolis: University of Minnesota Press).

Wilkes, K. (1981) "Functionalism, Psychology, and the Philosophy of Mind", *Philosophical Topics* 12(1).

—— (1984) "Pragmatics in Science and Theory in Common Sense", *Inquiry* 27(4).

16

A.I. Goldman "Interpretation Psychologized"

1 Introduction

A central problem of philosophy of mind is the nature of mental states, or the truth-conditions for the ascription of such states. Especially problematic are the propositional attitudes: beliefs, desires, and so forth. One popular strategy for attacking these problems is to examine the practice of speakers in ascribing these states, especially to others. What principles or procedures guide or underlie the ascriber's activity? In identifying such principles or procedures, one hopes to glean the criteria or satisfaction conditions of the mentalistic predicates (or something like this). Now the ascription of the attitudes involves the assignment of some sort of 'content' or 'meaning' to the mind, which can be seen as a kind of 'interpretation' of the agent or his behavior. (It is also related, on many theories, to the interpretation of the agent's utterances.) Thus, ascription of mental states, especially the attitudes, can be thought of as a matter of interpretation; and the strategy of studying the interpreter, in order to extract the conditions of mentality, or propositional attitudehood, may be called the *interpretation strategy*. I do not assume here that this strategy will or can succeed. Nonetheless, its popularity, if nothing else, makes it worthy of investigation.

The aim of this paper, then, is to study interpretation, specifically, to work toward an account of interpretation that seems descriptively and explanatorily correct. No account of interpretation can be philosophically helpful, I submit, if it is incompatible with a correct account of what people actually do when they interpret others. My question, then, is: how does the (naïve) interpreter arrive at his/her judgments about the mental attitudes of others? Philosophers who have addressed this question have not, in my view, been sufficiently psychological, or cognitivist, even those who are otherwise psychologically inclined. I shall defend some proposals about the activity of interpretation that are, I believe, psychologically more realistic than their chief competitors.

In the very posing of my question – how does the interpreter arrive at attributions of propositional attitudes (and other mental state)? – I assume that the attributor herself has contentful states, at least beliefs. Since I am not trying

327

to prove (to the skeptic) that there is content, this is not circular or question-begging. I assume as background that the interpreter has beliefs, and I inquire into a distinctive subset of them, viz., beliefs concerning mental states. It is conceivable, of course, that a proper theory of interpretation, together with certain ontological assumptions, would undermine the ontological legitimacy of beliefs. This is a prospect to which we should, in principle, stay alert, though it is not one that will actively concern me here. I shall proceed on the premise that the interpreter has beliefs. Indeed, it is hard to see how to investigate the problem without that assumption.

Since I am prepared to explain the interpreter's activity in terms of contentful states, I am obviously not attempting to give a purely 'naturalistic' theory of interpretation, i.e., a theory that makes no appeal to semantical notions. Interpretation theorists standardly hope to extract naturalistic truth-conditions for the presence of content. I take it to be an open question, however, whether the interpretation strategy can yield such fruit.

I structure the discussion in terms of three types of interpretation theories. Two of these have tended to dominate the field: (1) rationality, or charity, theories, and (2) folk-theory theories. According to the first approach, an attributor A operates on the assumption that the agent in question, S, is rational, i.e. conforms to an ideal or normative model of proper inference and choice. The attributor seeks to assign to S a set of contentful states that fits such a normative model. According to the second approach, the attributor somehow acquires a common-sense or folk-psychological theory of the mental, containing nomological generalizations that relate stimulus inputs to certain mental states, mental states to other mental states, and some mental states to behavioral outputs. She then uses this theory to infer, from stimulus inputs and behavioral outputs, what states S is in. The related doctrine of analytical functionalism asserts that our common-sense mentalistic predicates are implicitly *defined* in terms of this common-sense psychological theory.[1] The third approach, which I shall defend, is the simulation theory. This approach has been placed in the field but has not received sustained development, and is not yet sufficiently appreciated.[2]

2   The rationality approach

The most widely discussed version of the charity approach is that of Donald Davidson (1980, 1984). Actually, Davidson's approach to interpretation involves three strands. First, there is a compositional postulate for assigning meanings to the agent's whole utterances as a function of the meanings of their parts. Second, there is a charity principle that enjoins the interpreter (*ceteris paribus*) to assign belief states to the agent so as to maximize (or optimize) the proportion of truths in the agent's belief set. Third, there is the rationality principle that enjoins the interpreter (*ceteris paribus*) to assign beliefs and desires so as to maximize the agent's rationality. Another prominent specimen of the rationality approach is that of Daniel Dennett (1971, 1987a). Dennett's

'intentional stance' is a method of attributing intentional states by first postulating ideal rationality on the part of the target system, and then trying to
predict and/or explain the system's behavior in terms of such rationality.

I shall say nothing here about Davidson's compositional postulate. But a
brief comment on his truthfulness principle is in order before turning to more
extended discussion of rationality. Davidson holds that one constraint on interpretation precludes the possibility of ascribing 'massive' or 'preponderant'
error (by the interpreter's lights) to the interpretee. In an early essay he writes:
'A theory of interpretation cannot be correct that makes a man assent to very
many false sentences: it must generally be the case that a sentence is true when
a speaker holds it to be' (Davidson 1984: 168). And in a more recent essay
he says: 'Once we agree to the general method of interpretation I have
sketched, it becomes impossible correctly to hold that anyone could be mostly
wrong about how things are' (Davidson 1986: 317). These contentions,
however, are dubious. Along with Colin McGinn (1977) I have presented
examples of possible cases in which it seems natural to ascribe to an agent
a set of beliefs that are largely, in fact predominantly, false (Goldman 1986:
175–6). Furthermore, if Davidson were right in this matter, one could dismiss
the intelligibility of radical skepticism out of hand; but it seems implausible
that principles of interpretation should have this result (see McGinn 1986).
There are at least two sorts of context in which an attributor, A, will assign
beliefs to an agent, S, which are false by A's lights: first, where S is exposed
to misleading evidence, and second, where S uses poor inductive methods such
as hasty generalization, or inferential maxims such as 'Believe whatever your
cult leader tells you'. These points are stressed by David Lewis in his own
theory of interpretation (Lewis 1983a).

Let us turn to the rationality component of Davidson's charity approach, a
component common to many writers. For the rationality principle to have
substance, there must be some specification of the norms of rationality. While
few writers say precisely how these norms are to be chosen or fixed, there
seems to be wide agreement that they are derived from a priori models of ideal
rationality, models inspired by formal logic, by the calculus of probability,
and/or by Bayesian decision theory (or its ilk). Even so, there is room for
stronger and weaker norms. Dennett often imputes to the intentional stance
the component of deductive closure. Davidson usually illustrates rationality
with the weaker norm of logical consistency. Let us test the rationality
approach by reference to logical consistency and probabilistic coherence. Do
interpreters impose these norms in making interpretations? I shall argue in
the negative.

Consider a paradox-of-the-preface example. My friend Hannah has just
completed a book manuscript. She says that although she is fully confident of
each sentence in her book, taken singly, she is also convinced of her own
fallibility, and so believes that at least one of her claims is false. At least this
is how she *reports* her beliefs to me. But if these were indeed Hannah's
beliefs, she would be guilty of believing each of a logically inconsistent set of

propositions. Now if the consistency norm were part of our ordinary interpretation procedure, an interpreter would try, other things equal, to avoid ascribing to Hannah all the beliefs she ostensibly avows. Understood as a description of interpretive practice, the rationality approach 'predicts' that interpreters confronted with Hannah's avowals will try to find a way to assign a slightly different set of beliefs than Hannah seems to endorse. Interpreters will feel some 'pressure', some prima facie reason, to revise their belief imputation to be charitable to Hannah. Of course, as Davidson admits, other constraints on interpretation, e.g., the compositional meaning constraint, might make a revision too costly. So an interpreter might settle for imputing inconsistency after all. But some vector will be exerted to avoid the imputation.

Does this approach accord with the facts? Speaking as one interpreter, I would feel no temptation to avoid ascribing the inconsistent belief set to Hannah. And I submit that other everyday interpreters would similarly feel no such temptation. Admittedly, if Hannah said that she recognized she was being inconsistent, but still believed all these things anyway, many people might feel something is amiss. Recognition of inconsistency can be expected to breed caution. But let us suppose that Hannah shows no sign of recognizing the inconsistency. Surely, an ordinary interpreter would have no qualms in attributing an inconsistent belief set to her.

An analogous example is readily produced for the norm of probabilistic coherence. Suppose my friend Jeremy has just been the subject of a probability experiment by the psychologists Amos Tversky and Daniel Kahneman (1983). In this experiment, Jeremy is given a thumbnail sketch of someone called 'Linda', who is described as having majored in philosophy in college, as having been concerned with issues of social justice, and having participated in an antinuclear demonstration. Subjects are then asked to rate the probabilities that Linda is now involved in certain vocations or avocations. Like so many other subjects, Jeremy rates the probability of Linda being both a bank teller and a feminist higher than he rates the probability of Linda being a bank teller. But these comparative probability judgments violate the probability calculus: it is impossible for any conjunctive event A and B to be more probable than either of its conjuncts. So if I accept the coherent probabilities norm of interpretation, my duty is to try to reassign contents so as to avoid the indicated imputations to Jeremy.[3]

Again, as one interpreter, I report feeling no such duty. There seems nothing even prima facie wrong about attributing to Jeremy this set of probability assignments, despite their incoherence. I feel no reason to seek a revised interpretation. So this norm must not in fact play its alleged role in interpretation.[4]

Perhaps the rationality approach should be weakened, so that it no longer imposes ideal rationality as the norm for attitude attribution. Christopher Cherniak (1986: 10) suggests that a better rationality condition is that an agent must display minimal deductive ability; he must make *some*, but not necessarily all, of the sound inferences from his belief set. As a condition for attitude attribution, this is certainly an improvement over an ideal deductive requirement. But Cherniak's purely existential requirement is too vague. It cannot yield any definite predictive or explanatory inferences that an interpreter would make about an agent's beliefs.

Another variant of the rationality approach might say that interpreters expect agents to make 'obvious' inferences. But obvious to whom? To the interpreter? What is obvious to one interpreter is not necessarily obvious to another. So the rationality approach could no longer maintain that a single set of rationality principles constrain the ascription of the attitudes. Alternatively, there might be an attempt to derive obviousness from pure logic. But this is unpromising; obviousness is a psychological, not a logical, notion. Perhaps the rationality theorist should abandon any attempt to distill norms of rationality from logic, probability theory, decision theory, and the like. Perhaps the norms should be distilled from actual human practices of inference and choice (see Cohen 1981; Pollock 1986).

There are two problems with this approach. Experimental findings strongly suggest that human agents think in ways that contravene widely accepted norms. They often commit the so-called gambler's fallacy; in making choices, they commonly flout the 'sure-thing' principle (as Allais's paradox shows); and when it comes to deductive inference, they display a number of failings.[5] It is doubtful, therefore, whether actual practice can establish norms of rationality. Secondly, it is dubious that the naïve interpreter has an accurate reflective grasp of actual practice. But it is precisely the interpretive practice of naïve agents that we seek to illuminate.

Assuming that correct norms of rationality can somehow be identified, is it psychologically plausible to suppose that ordinary interpreters appeal to such norms in making (or constraining) their interpretations? Untrained adults are not generally acquainted with abstract principles like maximizing expected utility, or the sure-thing principle, or probabilistic coherence. Furthermore, we should bear in mind that children display interpretive skills quite early, at least by age four, five, or six. It stretches credulity to suppose that such children employ any of the abstract precepts that rationality theorists commonly adduce. Thus, if we seek to extract principles of interpretation from the psychological determinants of ordinary interpretive practice, norms of rationality do not look promising.

It may be replied that although children lack any explicitly formulated concept of rationality, or any articulated principles of reasoning, they do have *de facto* patterns of reasoning that govern their own cognitive behavior. Perhaps they simply apply those same tacit patterns in interpreting others. This indeed strikes me as a plausible hypothesis. But it is, in effect, a statement of the simulation approach that I shall be advocating shortly

3   The folk-theory approach

I turn next to the folk-theory approach to interpretation. Here again one must wonder whether naïve interpreters, including children, really possess the sorts of principles or common-sense nomological generalizations that this approach postulates, and whether such principles are indeed applied in (all) their interpretive practice.

At least three sorts of problems face the theory theory: vagueness, inaccuracy, and non-universality. When philosophers try to formulate the laws, their examples are typically larded with *ceteris paribus* clauses. This vagueness is a problem because it is hard to see how an interpreter could draw any reasonably definite interpretive conclusion using laws so vague. How could they tell when the *ceteris paribus* clauses are satisfied? Yet interpreters frequently do manage to make quite definite assignments of desires and beliefs. The second problem, the problem of accuracy, arises as follows. It is important for analytical functionalism that the laws be reasonably accurate. If the names of mental states work like theoretical terms, especially in the Ramsey-sentence account of theoretical terms, they do not name anything unless the theory (the cluster of laws) in which they appear is more or less *true* (see Lewis 1983b and 1972). It is doubtful, however, that ordinary interpreters do possess laws that are true. Third, the standard version of this approach assumes that a single set of laws or platitudes is shared by all competent users of mentalistic vocabulary. But this universality assumption is very dubious.

As Stephen Schiffer (1987: ch. 2) argues, perceptual input conditions may be in the worst shape on these scores. If people really possess laws that relate perceptual input conditions to perceptual beliefs, there must be some way of filling out a schema like 'If there is a red block in front of *x* and . . . , then *x* will believe that there is a red block in front of *x*'; and it must be filled out so that it is true and really possessed by all competent speakers. But it is unlikely that this requirement is satisfied. Can *any* ordinary speaker complete this schema so that it yields a truth? (Notice that the gap has to be filled with conditions entailing that *x* is 'well enough' sighted, is not colorblind, is sober and undrugged, etc.) It is doubtful, moreover, that *all* speakers who possess the concept of belief share the *same* perceptual input laws. A blind person, for example, may grasp the concept of belief perfectly well, but not possess the same laws of visual input as sighted people.

The accuracy problem also looms large for internal functional laws, including laws that putatively link certain desires and beliefs with further desires. One of the favorite sorts of platitudes offered by philosophers is something like 'If *x* believes "*p* only if *q*" and *x* desires *p*, then *x* desires *q*'. But the relationship formulated by this 'platitude' simply does not systematically obtain. It ignores the fact that merely dispositional, unactivated desires and beliefs do not have the same inference-inducing powers as activated desires and beliefs (see Goldman 1986: section 10.1, and Goldman 1970: ch. 4). If *x*'s belief in '*p* only if *q*' is stored in memory and fails to get retrieved or activated, it does not influence *x*'s practical reasoning. The problem, of course, is not merely that philosophers neglect these differences, but that it is unlikely that common folk have any firm grasp of these relationships, at least in any 'theoretical' fashion.

Perhaps the functionalist will reply that although the 'folk' do have (more or less) true laws in their possession, philosophers have simply failed to articulate those laws correctly. But why, one wonders, should it be so difficult to articulate laws if we appeal to them all the time in our interpretive practice? Admittedly, they may be merely tacit generalizations, and tacit representations are characteristically difficult to reconstruct. A skeptic is entitled to suspect, however, that what goes on when philosophers proffer mentalistic platitudes is not the extraction of pre-existing representations in the minds of the 'folk', but the fresh creation of laws designed to accommodate philosophical preconceptions about the character of 'theoretical' terms.[6]

Still more grounds for doubt center on the problem of acquisition. Recall the point that children seem to display interpretive skills by the age of four, five, or six. If interpretation is indeed guided by laws of folk psychology, the latter must be known (or believed) by this age. Are such children sophisticated enough to represent such principles? And how, exactly, would they acquire them? One possible mode of acquisition is cultural transmission (e.g. being taught them explicitly by their elders). This is clearly out of the question, though, since only philosophers have ever tried to articulate the laws, and most children have no exposure to philosophers. Another possible mode of acquisition is private construction. Each child constructs the generalizations for herself, perhaps taking clues from verbal explanations of behavior that she hears. But if this construction is supposed to occur along the lines of familiar modes of scientific theory construction, some anomalous things must take place. For one thing, all children miraculously construct the same nomological principles. This is what the (folk-) theory theory ostensibly implies, since it imputes a single folk psychology to everyone. In normal cases of hypothesis construction, however, different scientists come up with different theories. This is especially natural if they do not communicate their hypotheses, which is what obtains in the present case where the hypotheses are presumed to be tacit and unformulated. It is also surprising that the theory should stay fixed in each cognizer once it is acquired, as functionalism apparently assumes. This too contrasts with normal scientific practice, where theories are commonly amended at least to some degree with the accumulation of new data.

Jerry Fodor, a staunch defender of the theory theory, endorses the hypothesis that the folk theory is *innate* (Fodor 1987: 132–3). He cites three pieces of 'evidence' for this: (1) intentional explanation appears to be a cultural universal; (2) a rudimentary awareness of the mental world is present in toddlers and preschoolers; and (3) there are no (plausible) suggestions about how a child might acquire the apparatus of intentional explanation 'from experience'. I agree with Fodor on these points. Indeed, I have just been stressing how hard it is to swallow the supposition that toddlers and preschoolers acquire functional laws by induction or theory construction. Thus, *if* a grasp of the mental world and intentional explanation involves laws, there is credibility in the hypothesis that these laws are possessed innately. But why accept the antecedent? Fodor simply ignores the possibility that the apparatus of intentional explanation may involve no theory at all. By contrast, I submit that intentional explanation and prediction can be accounted for without positing any large-scale theory or set of functional generalizations. This is what I now proceed to argue, apropos of the attribution of intentional states (and mental states generally) to others. The full story may well feature innate components: perhaps an innate propensity to identify mental categories within oneself (analogous to some innate propensities for individuating material bodies), and an innate propensity to project such categories on others. But it need not feature innate possession of *laws*.

4 The simulation approach

The account I favor may be introduced by reference to a proposal of Richard Grandy (1973). Grandy proposes to replace charity principles with what he calls the 'humanity principle'. This is the constraint imposed on translations that the imputed pattern of relations among beliefs, desires, and the world be as similar to our own as possible. This conforms, says Grandy, with our actual practice of predicting people's behavior based on our attitudinal attributions. We do not use mathematical decision theory (i.e. expected utility theory) to make predictions; rather, we consider what *we* should do if we had the relevant beliefs and desires. Now I do not think that naïve interpreters advert to Grandy's humanity principle as an abstract precept. Rather, they ascribe mental states to others by pretending or imagining themselves to be in the other's shoes, constructing or generating the (further) state that they would then be in, and ascribing that state to the other. In short, we *simulate* the situation of others, and interpret them accordingly. This idea has been explicitly put forward by Robert Gordon (1986, and 1987: ch. 7), and something like it has been endorsed by Adam Morton (1980). The idea has been a dominant motif in the *Verstehen* and hermeneutic traditions, and earlier precursors include the eighteenth-century Scottish philosophers.[7]

Several writers on interpretation put forward somewhat analogous views in discussing belief ascriptions. W. V. Quine explains indirect quotation in terms of an 'essentially dramatic act' in which we project ourselves into the speaker's mind (Quine 1960: 219). Similarly, drawing on Davidson's paratactic account of indirect discourse, Stephen Stich proposes that when I say 'Andrea believes that lead floats on mercury', I am performing a little skit: I am saying that Andrea is in a belief state content-identical to one that would lead me to assert the sentence which follows the 'that'-clause (Stich 1983: 84). However, these writers do not explicitly develop the simulation approach; nor do I mean to endorse the proposed paraphrase of belief-state ascriptions.

The simulation idea has obvious initial attractions. Introspectively, it seems as if we often try to predict others' behavior – or predict their (mental) choices – by imagining ourselves in their shoes and determining what we would choose to do. To use one of Gordon's examples, if we are playing chess, I may try to anticipate your next move by imagining myself in your situation and deciding what I would choose to do. Similarly, if we agree to meet for lunch tomorrow, I (mentally) 'predict' that you will expect me at roughly the appointed time and place. I ascribe this expectation to you because this is the expectation I would form if I were in your (presumed) situation. The simulation procedure can also be used for explanatory, or 'retrodictive', assignment of mental states. (Indeed, this is the more central type of case for the theme of 'interpretation'.) If you make a surprising chess move, I may infer a new strategy on your part, one that might have led me, if I were in your situation, to the observed move. To assure the plausibility of this being your strategy, I would see whether I could simulate both (a) arriving at this strategy from your presumed antecedent states, and (b) choosing the observed move given this strategy. Ascriptions of intent that lie behind observed behavior would, on the simulation theory, commonly take this second, explanatory form.

In all of these examples, my inference to a new state of yours draws on assumptions about your prior mental states. Does this not threaten a regress? How do I get any initial entrée into your mental world? Can that be explained by simulation?[8] Yes. The regress presumably stops at perceptual cases, and at basic likings or cravings. From your perceptual situation, I infer that you have certain perceptual experiences or beliefs, the same ones I would have in your situation. I may also assume (pending information to the contrary) that you have the same basic likings that I have: for food, love, warmth, and so on.

Simulation is also relevant in inferring *actions* from mental states, not just mental states from other mental states. For ordinary 'basic' actions, I expect your 'choice' of an action to issue in its production because my own choice would so issue. In more problematic cases, such as uttering a tongue-twister, simulation might lead me to doubt that you will succeed. Morton (1980) points out that 'analysis-by-synthesis' accounts of speech perception invoke a (tacit) simulation of motor activity. According to this approach, in trying to categorize a speaker's acoustic sequence as one or another phonemic string, the perceiver constrains the choice of interpretation by 'running a model' of how his own vocal apparatus might articulate those sounds.

It would be a mistake, of course, to use the simulation procedure too simplistically, without adequate attention to individual differences. If I am a chess novice and you are a master, or vice versa, it would be foolish to assume that your analysis would match mine. To optimize use of the simulation procedure, I must not only imagine myself in possession of your goals and beliefs about the board configuration, but also in possession of your level of chess sophistication. People may not always take such factors into account; and frequently they lack information to make such adjustments accurately. In any case, there is no assumption here that people are always successful or optimal simulators. What I do conjecture is that simulation – whether explicit or implicit – is the fundamental method used for arriving at mental ascriptions to others. (A more complex variant of the simulation theme will be briefly sketched in section 5.)

I am not saying, it should be emphasized, that simulation is the *only* method used for interpersonal mental ascriptions, or for the prediction of behavior. Clearly, there are regularities about behavior and individual differences that can be learned purely inductively. If Jones always greets people with a smile whereas Brown greets them with a grunt, their acquaintances can form appropriate expectations without deploying simulation. If people who enter a car in the driver's seat regularly proceed to start it, this is the basis for future expectations that need not appeal to simulation. The suggestion, then, is that simulation is an intensively used heuristic, and one on which interpretation fundamentally rests. Inductive or nomological information is not wholly absent, but it is sparser than the folk-theory approach alleges.

Does the simulation approach accommodate the problems confronting the rational norms approach? Very straightforwardly. The mere fact that the 'preface' belief ('at least one of my claims is false') produces inconsistency does not tempt me to withhold attribution of this belief to Hannah. This is just the belief I too would form, especially if I were unaware of the inconsistency (a similar point is made by Stich, 1985). Similarly, the mere fact that Jeremy's probability assignments violate the probability calculus does not make me shrink from attributing them; for I too can feel their intuitive pull.

The merits of the simulation approach are further demonstrated by seeing how easily it handles a number of cases that the rival approaches cannot handle, or can handle only with difficulty. In an experiment by Daniel Kahneman and Amos Tversky (1982), subjects were given the following example:

> Mr. Crane and Mr. Tees were scheduled to leave the airport on different flights, at the same time. They traveled from town in the same limousine, were caught in a traffic jam, and arrived at the airport 30 minutes after the scheduled departure time of their flights. Mr. Crane is told that his flight left on time. Mr. Tees is told that his was delayed, and just left five minutes ago. Who is more upset?

Surely people do not possess a tacit folk-psychological *theory* that warrants any particular answer to this question. But 96 percent of the subjects in the experiment said that Mr Tees would be more upset. How did they severally arrive at the same answer? Clearly, by simulation. They imagined how *they* would feel in Mr Crane's and Mr Tees's shoes, and responded accordingly.

More evidence in a similar vein comes from the domain of verbal communication. Verbal communicators commonly make assumptions – often correct – about the contextual information accessible to their audience and likely to be used in the comprehension process. For example, inspired by the landscape, Mary says to Peter, 'It's the sort of scene that would have made Marianne Dashwood swoon.' This allusion to Austen's *Sense and Sensibility* is based on Mary's expectation that this utterance will act as a prompt, making Peter recall parts of the book that he had previously forgotten, and construct the assumptions needed to understand the allusion. My question is: How does a communicator proceed to estimate what pieces of information will be marshalled, or made salient, in the mind of the audience, in short, which pieces of information are 'calculable'?

Dan Sperber and Deirdre Wilson (1986), from whom the preceding example was borrowed, have an interesting theory of the hearer, which postulates a variety of pertinent cognitive traits. For example, they postulate that cognizers have a number of rules of deductive inference, but these are all *elimination* rules (e.g. from '*P* and *Q*' you may infer '*Q*') and not *introduction* rules (e.g. from '*P*' you may infer '*P* or *Q*'). Now assume that this piece of cognitive psychology is correct. Clearly, it is not known or believed by the naïve speaker. The speaker cannot appeal to any such *theoretical* knowledge to make predictions of what is likely to be derived or calculated by the hearer. Nonetheless, speakers are evidently pretty good at making such predictions; more precisely, at predicting what kinds of 'implicatures' will be appreciated by an audience. How do they do that? Again, I suggest, by simulation. They can simulate in themselves the states that result from the inference rules, without knowing what those rules are. Hence, they can project, with fairly substantial reliability, what hearers will be able to infer and understand.

A related point concerns people's intuitive grasp of what others will find *funny*.[9] Again it seems far-fetched to suppose that my ability to gauge what will amuse you is based on a theory of humor (of what amuses people). I do not possess any general theory of this sort. More plausibly, I gauge *your* probable reaction to a joke by projecting my own. (There can be adjustments here for factual information about interpersonal differences, but this is just a corrective to the basic tactic of simulation.) There are (arguably) two states of yours that I judge or anticipate through simulation. I estimate by simulation that you will grasp the intended point of the joke: a cognitive state. I also judge by simulation that you will be amused by it: not a purely cognitive state.

Apropos of non-cognitive states, it is worth stressing that a virtue of the simulation theory is its capacity to provide a uniform account of all mental state attributions, not only of propositional attitudes but of non-propositional mental states like pains and tickles. This contrasts with the rationality approach, which has no resources for explaining the latter. No principle of *rationality* dictates when a person should feel pain, or what one should do when in pain. Similarly for tickles. Thus, a rationality (or charity) approach to propositional attitude interpretation would have to be supplemented by an entirely different element to account for attributions of sensations, and perhaps emotions as well. Such bifurcation has less appeal than the unified account offered by the simulation approach.

In a brief discussion of the simulation idea, Dennett (1987b) finds it very puzzling. How can it work, he asks, without being a kind of theorizing? If I make believe I am a suspension bridge and wonder what I will do when the wind blows, what comes to mind depends on how sophisticated my *knowledge* is of the physics and engineering of suspension bridges. Why should making believe that I have your beliefs be any different? Why should it too not require theoretical knowledge?

To answer this question, we need to say more about the general idea of simulation. For a device to simulate a system is for the former to behave in a way that 'models', or maintains some relevant isomorphism to, the behavior of the latter. This is the sense in which a computer might simulate a weather system or an economy. Now if a person seeks to simulate the weather or the economy, in the sense of mentally constructing or anticipating an actual (or genuinely feasible) sequence of its states, she is very unlikely to be accurate unless she has a good theory of the system. A successful simulation of this kind must be *theory-driven*, let us say. This is Dennett's point. But must all mental simulations be theory-driven in order to succeed? I think not. A simulation of some target systems might be accurate even if the agent lacks such a theory. This can happen if (1) the *process* that drives the simulation is the same as (or relevantly similar to) the process that drives the system, and (2) the initial states of the simulating agent are the same as, or relevantly similar to, those of the target system. Thus, if one person simulates a sequence of mental states of another, they will wind up in the same (or isomorphic) final states as long as (A) they begin in the same (or isomorphic) initial states, and (B) both sequences are driven by the same cognitive process or routine, it is not necessary that the simulating agent have a theory of what the routine is, or how it works. In short, successful simulation can be *process-driven*.

Now, in central cases of interpretation, the interpreter is not actually in the very same initial states as the interpretee. While there may be overlap in beliefs and goals, there are typically relevant differences as well. So how can the interpreter succeed via simulation? The critical move, of course, is that the interpreter tries to imagine, or 'feign', the same initial states as the interpretee. She 'pretends' or 'makes believe' she has the relevant initial states, and then performs reasoning operations (or other cognitive operations) to generate successive states in herself. But are these 'pretend' states – the pseudo-beliefs, pseudo-desires, and so forth – relevantly similar to the genuine beliefs and desires that they model? Is it plausible that imagined beliefs and actual beliefs would yield the same, or analogous, outputs when operated upon by the same cognitive operations?[10]

It *is* plausible, I submit. Consider hypothetical, or subjunctive, reasoning. I ask myself, 'Suppose I did action A – what would be the result?' How do I proceed to answer this question? It seems that what I do is imagine myself believing the proposition 'I do A', and then draw causal inferences from that pseudo-belief together with (certain) antecedent genuine beliefs. Furthermore, it seems that I use the very same inference processes as those I would use on a set of wholly genuine belief inputs. (The output, though, is only a belief in the same hypothetical mood, not a genuine belief.) Similarly, I make contingency plans by executing practical reasoning operations on feigned beliefs in certain contingencies; and these are the same planning operations that I would apply to genuine beliefs in those contingencies. So it seems that 'pretend' belief states *are* relevantly similar to belief states; there are significant isomorphisms. The possibility of isomorphisms between 'genuine' states and imaginatively, or artificially, generated 'copies' is further illustrated in the imagery domain. Roger Shepard, Stephen Kosslyn, and their respective colleagues have produced striking evidence to support the claim that visual images are similar in important respects to genuine visual perceptions (Shepard and Cooper 1982; Kosslyn 1980). To determine the congruence or non-congruence of two shapes, forming a mental image of one being rotated into alignment with the other can be almost as reliable as actually seeing the results of this rotation. This would hardly be possible if imagery were not relevantly similar to genuine perception.[11]

5 Simulation and psychology

Let us explore the psychological defensibility of the simulation approach in more detail. We may first note that several cognitive scientists have recently endorsed the idea of mental simulation as one cognitive heuristic, although these researchers stress its use for knowledge in general, not specifically knowledge of others' mental states. Kahneman and Tversky (1982) propose that people often try to answer questions about the world by an operation that resembles the running of a simulation model. The starting conditions for a 'run', they say, can either be left at realistic default values or modified to assume some special contingency. Similarly, Rumelhart, Smolensky, McClelland and Hinton (1986) describe the importance of 'mental models' of the world, in particular, models that simulate how the world would respond to one's hypothetical actions. They first apply this idea to actual and imagined conversations, and later describe a PDP (parallel distributed processing) network for playing tic-tac-toe, a network that embodies 'simulations' of the world's (i.e. the opponent's) response to the agent's possible moves.

Since part of my argument rests on the superior plausibility of the simulation approach in accounting for children's interpretational ability, let us next look at recent work by developmental psychologists that bears on this point. The most striking findings are those by Heinz Wimmer and Josef Perner, conjoined with a follow-up study by Simon Baron-Cohen, Alan Leslie, and Uta Frith. Various experimental studies had previously shown that as early as two and a half years, children use a substantial vocabulary about perception, volition, major emotions, and knowledge. But experiments by Wimmer and Perner (1983) strongly indicate that around the ages of four to six, an ability to clearly distinguish between someone else's belief state and reality becomes firmly established. In their study, children between three and nine years of age observed a sketch in which a protagonist put an object into a location X. The children then witnessed that, in the absence of the protagonist, the object was transferred from X to location Y. Since this transfer came as a surprise, they should assume that the protagonist still believed that the object was in X. Subjects were then required to indicate where the protagonist will look for the object on his return. None of the three- to four-year-olds, 57 percent of the four- to six-year-olds, and 86 percent of the six- to nine-year-olds pointed correctly to location X. In their related study, Baron-Cohen, Leslie and Frith (1985) studied the ability of autistic children to perform this sort of task. Of critical relevance here are two facts about autistic children. First, the main symptom of autism is impairment in verbal and non-verbal communication. Second, autistic children show a striking poverty of pretend play. Baron-Cohen et al.'s experiment showed that when the tested children were asked where the doll protagonist would look for her marble, 85 percent of the normal children answered correctly, but only 20 percent of the autistic children (with a mean age close to 12 and a relatively high mean IQ of 82) answered correctly. Especially striking was the fact that the test also included a pool of Down's syndrome children, 86 percent of whom answered the crucial question correctly. This suggests that the failure of the autistic children is not due to general mental retardation, a trait shared by Down's syndrome children. Rather it is a specific cognitive deficit. Baron-Cohen et al. hypothesize that autistic children as a group fail to acquire a 'theory of mind', i.e. an ability to impute beliefs to others and therefore predict their behavior correctly. This would account for their social and communicational impairment. It might also be related to their lack of pretend play. Perhaps, as Gordon (1995) suggests, all this points to a prepackaged 'module' for simulation directed at other human beings, a module that is impaired in autism.

One of the co-authors of the autism study, Alan Leslie, has sketched a theory that interrelates pretend play and the representation of mental states (Leslie 1987). He points out that pretending is in some ways an odd practice. From an evolutionary point of view, one might expect a high premium on maintaining an accurate and objective view of the world. A child who acts as if dolls have genuine feelings is scarcely acting upon a veridical picture of the world. Yet pretend play emerges at an early age, and becomes more elaborate during development. It is not implausible to conjecture that pretend play is a preliminary exercise of a mechanism the primary function of which is the simulation of real people's mental states. Roughly this theme is articulated both by Leslie and by Paul Harris (1989). Such a mechanism, on the present theory, underlies interpersonal interpretation, prediction, and perhaps communication as well.

Whatever the force of these findings and speculations, there is a straightforward challenge to the psychological plausibility of the simulation approach. It is far from obvious, introspectively, that we regularly place ourselves in another person's shoes and vividly envision what we would do in his circumstances. This is a natural thing to do while watching a tennis match, perhaps, or while listening to someone relating their tragic life story. But the simulation approach ostensibly makes this empathic attitude the standard mode of interpretation. Is that not difficult to accept?

Two replies should be made. First, simulation need not be an introspectively vivid affair. The approach can certainly insist that most simulation is semi-automatic, with relatively little salient phenomenology. It is a psychological commonplace that highly developed skills become automatized, and there is no reason why interpersonal simulation should not share this characteristic. (On the issue of conscious awareness, the simulation theory is no worse off than its competitors. Neither the rationality approach nor the folk-theory theory is at all credible if it claims that appeals to its putative principles are introspectively prominent aspects of interpretation.)

A second point might be that many cases of rapid, effortless interpretation may be devoid of even automatized simulation. When a mature cognizer has constructed, by simulation, many similar instances of certain action-interpretation patterns, she may develop generalizations or other inductively formed representations (schemas, scripts, and so forth) that can trigger analogous interpretations by application of those 'knowledge structures' alone, *sans* simulation. I have, of course, already acknowledged the role of inductively based predictions of behavior and the need for standard empirical information to make adjustments for individual differences. The present point is a slightly larger concession. It agrees that in many cases the interpreter relies solely (at the time of interpretation) on inductively acquired information. But this information, it suggests, is historically derived from earlier simulations. If this story is right, then simulation remains the fundamental source of interpretation, though not the essence of every act (or even most acts) of interpretation. We might call this the complex variant of the simulation approach. It converges somewhat toward the folk-theory theory (though the exact degree of convergence depends on the nature of the inductively based knowledge structures it posits). It still remains distinct, however, (A) because the folk-theory theory makes no allowance for simulation, and (B) because the complex variant postulates simulation as the originating source of (most) interpretation.

Commenting in part on an earlier version of this paper, Paul Churchland (1989) poses two difficulties for the simulation theory. First, he says, simulation is not necessary for understanding others. People who are congenitally deaf, or blind, are quite capable of understanding normal people, and people who have never themselves felt profound grief or rejection, can nevertheless provide appropriate interpretations of others who are so afflicted. In general, understanding goes beyond what one has personally experienced. I have already granted, however, that straightforwardly empirical information is required to accommodate individual differences, and these examples are just more extreme illustrations of the point. We must certainly allow for the human capacity to extrapolate from one's own case, to project types of sensory or emotional sensibility that one does not oneself instantiate. This concession does not undermine the point that interpretation primarily starts from the home base of one's own experience.

Churchland further objects that while simulation may account for the prediction of others' behavior, it does not provide for *explanation*. The simulation theory makes the understanding of others depend crucially on having an initial understanding of oneself. But it leaves mysterious, he says, the nature of first-person understanding. More specifically, *explanatory* understanding requires appreciation of the *general patterns* that comprehend individual events in both cases. This requires a *theory*, which the simulation approach spurns. In my opinion, however, explanation can consist of telling a story that eliminates various alternative hypotheses about how the event in question came about, or could have come about. This can effectively answer a 'Why'-question, which is the essence of explanation (see van Fraassen 1980: ch. 5). In the case of interpretive explanation this is done by citing a specific set of goals and beliefs, which implicitly rules out the indefinitely many alternative desire-and-belief sets that might have led to the action.

Churchland rejects the deductive nomological theory of explanation on the grounds that it presupposes a sentential, or propositional-attitude, account of knowledge representation. He proposes to replace this picture of cognition with a prototype-based picture, especially one that is elaborated within a connectionist framework. He still wishes to count human cognition as significantly *theoretical*, but theory possession is apparently no longer associated with nomologicality. Churchland is welcome to use the term 'theory' in this neological fashion; but it cannot resuscitate the standard version of the folk-theory approach to interpretation. It is only in the usual, nomological construal of theories that I am addressing (and rejecting) that approach. I am pleased to see Churchland also reject that approach, but it seems to have ramifications for his other views that I shall mention below.

6   Simulation and similarity

Considering the complexity of the human organism, it may well be considered remarkable that we are able to predict human behavior as well as we do. Is this impressive success fully accounted for by the simulation theory? Only, I think, with an added assumption, viz., that the other people, whose behavior we predict, are psychologically very similar to ourselves. Just as the child readily learns a grammar of a natural language because its native grammar-learning structures mirror those of its language-creating mates, so a person can successfully simulate the internal operations of others because they are largely homologous to her own. The fuller picture, then, has strong affinities to Noam Chomsky's emphasis on the role of species-specific traits in mental activity.

Although I view this theme as Chomskyesque, it is also similar to one made by Quine (1969). Quine asks how the language learner manages to learn the law of English verbal behavior connected with 'yellow'. The answer, he says, is that the learner's quality spacing is enough like his neighbor's that such learning is almost a foregone conclusion: he is making his induction in a 'friendly world'. He is playing a game of chance with favorably loaded dice. Similarly, I am suggesting, people's predictions of other people's behavior, based heavily on attributions of content, are so successful because people operate with the same set of fundamental cognitive constraints. (Notice, I need not say that people are successful at assigning correct contents to people's mental states; that would assume that there is an independent fact of the matter about content, prior to the activity of interpretation. Since some interpretation theorists would reject this thesis, I can confine my claim to successful prediction of *behavior*.)

The constraints I have in mind must be constraints on the specific contents assigned to an agent's propositional attitudes. Without positing such constraints, it is hard to account for the definiteness and interpersonal uniformity in content attributions. There would seem to be too much 'play', too much looseness, in the sorts of abstract constraints that a theorist like Davidson, for example, imposes. Assuming the interpretations of the interpreter to be given, we need to explain why she makes those rather than the innumerable other conceivable interpretations.

In a similar (though not identical) context, Lewis (1983c) worries whether enough constraints on content are imposed by his theory to exclude preposterous and perverse misinterpretations. To exclude perverse interpretations, Lewis says we need a priori presumptions about just what sorts of things are apt to be believed or desired. These presumptions should be thought of as built into our interpretation procedures. Adopting a suggestion of Gary Merrill, Lewis proposes that natural kinds are more eligible for content attributions than non-natural kinds. Taking naturalness to be a graded affair, more natural kinds have greater eligibility for content inclusion than less natural kinds. Principles of content possession should therefore impute a bias toward believing that things are green rather than grue, toward having a basic desire for long life rather than for long-life-unless-one-was-born-on-Monday-and-in-that-case-life-for-an-even-number-of-weeks.

I agree with Lewis that to get things right, i.e. to conform to our actual content attributions, account must be taken of what is 'natural' and 'unnatural'. But only if this means 'natural for us': congenial to human psychology. This is not what Lewis means. By 'natural' Lewis means properties Nature herself deems natural, those categories that are objectively, independently, non-anthropocentrically natural. This is not very plausible. Granted that the kind 'a mass of molecules' is more of a natural kind than, say, 'table', it is still less plausible to attribute beliefs about masses of molecules to scientifically untutored people than beliefs about tables. Or take the hue yellow. From an objective, non-anthropocentric viewpoint, yellow is less natural than other possible spectral or reflectancy categorizations. Nonetheless, it is more plausible to attribute contents involving yellow than more objective categorizations of light frequency. Clearly, it is concepts that are humanly more natural, i.e. psychologically congenial, that are more eligible for content.[12]

What I am suggesting, then, is that uniformity in cross-personal interpretations should be partly explained by psychological preferences for certain modes of categorization and 'entification', or more basically, by operations that generate categorial and entificational preferences. The precise nature of these operations and/or preferences remains to be spelled out by cognitive science. But let me give some examples of what I mean.

Our entification practices include propensities to group together, or unify, certain sets of elements rather than others in a perceptual display. The Gestalt principles of similarity, proximity, closedness, and good continuation are attempts to systematize the mental operations that underpin these unificational practices. The Gestalt principles apply not only in the visual domain, but in the temporal domain as well. Thus, presented with the opening passage of Mozart's fortieth symphony, principles of temporal proximity (and so forth) make it natural to segment the passage into three distinct phrases (I oversimplify here). Other conceivable segmentations are highly unnatural. It is plausible to conjecture that the same Gestalt principles are at work in fixing our conceptual (as opposed to perceptual) intuitions of identity, or unity, of objects through time (see Goldman 1987).

Another set of categorial preferences feature what Eleanor Rosch calls the 'basic level' of categories (Rosch 1975, 1978). Language (and presumably thought) is full of category hierarchies such as *poodle, dog, mammal, animal, physical object*. Experiments show that the categories in the middle of such hierarchies, in the present case *dog* rather than *poodle* or *physical object,* have a definite psychological primacy.

How do entitative and categorial preferences of the interpreter get deployed in the interpretation process? Two slightly different hypotheses are possible. First, the preferences may be registered directly; that is, the interpreter uses her own categorial preferences to assign content to the interpretee. Second, they might be used in conjunction with the simulation heuristic. In assigning reference and meaning, the interpreter imagines what the agent's concept-forming or proposition-forming devices might generate in the present context, and this imaginative act is structured by the interpreter's own concept-forming and judgment-forming operations.

In either case, the hypotheses I am advancing would account for a substantial degree of uniformity in specific content attributions. It would also mesh with Davidson's theme of belief similarity among interpreters and interpretees, but only subject to important qualifications. The simulation hypothesis assumes that the interpreter tends to impute to the interpretee the same fundamental categories as her own, or at least the same basic category-forming (and proposition-forming) operations. She also tends to project the same basic belief-forming processes. But these practices still leave room for wide divergence in belief content. The simulation procedure can take account of differences in the agent's evidential exposures, and in the special inferential habits, algorithms, and heuristics that he has learned or acquired.[13] Differences along these dimensions can ramify into substantial differences in belief sets.

My emphasis on conspecific psychological traits may suggest the possibility that only other *people* are interpretable by us. That is not a claim I endorse. On the contrary, we certainly think of ourselves as interpreting other animals; and although we may partly deceive ourselves with misplaced anthropomorphism, we do have moderate predictive success. Of course, the use of straightforward inductively gathered information is prominent here. But, as indicated earlier, we also use our own psychology as a home base, and make conservative revisions from that starting point. Perhaps this is why it is more difficult to construct right-seeming interpretations of heterospecifics than conspecifics. Dolphins seem to be highly intelligent and to communicate among themselves, yet no human has constructed a plausible interpretation of their language.

Although my discussion centers on the psychological dimensions involved in content attributions, it by no means precludes an important role for the external world, especially causal relations with the external world, in the choice of semantic assignments to thoughts. In deciding what is the referent of an imputed thought, in particular, it seems clear that the interpreter takes into account the thought's causal history. Similarly, it is plausible to suppose that imputation of other semantic dimensions of thought involves mind–world connections. These are plausibly part of the conceptual background with which the interpreter operates. Although I am not addressing these issues, which lie at the heart of much current debate, they are complementary to the themes I am pursuing.

7   Philosophical ramifications

In this final section I briefly address several possible philosophical ramifications of the simulation approach, including the interpretation strategy with which I began.

Does the simulation approach imply a sharp divide between explanations of the mental and the physical? If so, it would vindicate the claim of the hermeneutic tradition, which contrasts understanding of human action with understanding of physical phenomena. No sharp contrast necessarily follows from the simulation theory. For one thing, we have already noted that simulation or mental modeling is sometimes postulated as a cognitive heuristic for representing physical phenomena as well as mental states. Admittedly, this realization of the simulation heuristic would presumably be theory-driven rather than process-driven. Still, this already admits an important parallel. Furthermore, proponents of interpretational simulation need not maintain that nomological explanation of human phenomena is impossible. They just maintain that *common-sense* explanations and predictions of the mental do not (in the main) invoke laws.

A second philosophical issue raised by the simulation theory is the epistemology of other minds. Ostensibly, the theory is a version of the 'analogical' theory of mental state ascription. It seems to impute to interpreters inferences of roughly the following form: 'If he is psychologically like me, he must be in mental state M; he is psychologically like me; therefore, he is in mental state M.' But there is a long-standing suspicion of such arguments from analogy, centering on the second premise. How can the interpreter know (or believe justifiably) that the agent is psychologically like her? Can physical and behavioral similarity support this premise? Is not an analogy based on a single case a thin reed on which to rest?

The best line of reply, I think, is to deny that interpreters must believe the second premise. Many beliefs are formed by mechanisms, or routines, that are built into the cognitive architecture. Although these mechanisms might be described in terms of 'rules' or 'principles', it would be misleading to say that the cognizers believe those rules or principles. For example, it is plausible to say that people form perceptual beliefs (or representations) in accord with Gestalt rules, but implausible to say that they literally believe those rules. They represent certain partly occluded figures as being single, unitary objects when there is sufficient 'continuity' between their perceived parts, but they do not believe the continuity principle itself. In our case, cognizers make interpretations in accordance with a routine that could be formulated by the principle, 'Other people are psychologically like me'. But this is not really a believed 'premise' on which they inferentially base their interpretations.

Could a belief that is produced by such a routine qualify as justified, or as a piece of knowledge, if the rule is not believed? Reliabilism is one species of epistemology that would be congenial to this result. If the routine, or process, is a generally reliable one, then reliabilism (in certain forms) may be prepared to count its output beliefs as justified (see Goldman 1986). So there is at least one type of epistemology that promises to resolve the epistemic challenge to the simulation theory.[14]

A third noteworthy philosophical point concerns the ramification of abandoning the folk-theory theory. This theory has been a salient premise in the argument for eliminativism about propositional attitudes. Eliminativists standardly begin by emphasizing that the attitudes – and all our commonsense mentalistic notions – are part of a folk-psychological theory. They then point to the bleak history of past folk scientific theories, suggesting that the same scenario is in store for folk psychology (see Churchland 1981). Since folk psychology will ultimately prove to have poorer predictive value than scientific psychology, its constructs will need to be replaced or eliminated, just like the constructs of, say, alchemy. However, if it turns out that there is no folk theory, in the sense of a set of commonsense generalizations that define the mental terms, then an important premise for eliminativism is no longer available. (This point has been made by Gordon.)

Let me turn now to what is probably the most pressing philosophical issue posed by the simulation theory. What is the relation, it maybe asked, between the simulation approach and what it is for mental ascriptions to be *correct*? The simulation theory purports to give an account of the procedure used in ascribing mental states to others. What light does this shed, however, on the conditions that are *constitutive* of mental state possession (especially possession of the attitudes)? The interpretation strategist hopes to extract from the interpretation procedure some criteria of correctness for mentalistic ascriptions. Certainly the rationality and functionalist theories would generate answers to this question. (Whether or not the answers they generate are correct is another matter. Functionalist definitions, for example, have many familiar problems.) But the simulation theory looks distinctly unpromising on this score. Since simulation is such a fallible procedure, there is little hope of treating 'M is ascribed (or ascribable) to S on the basis of simulation' as constitutive of 'S is in M'. Furthermore, simulation assumes a prior understanding of what state it is that the interpreter ascribes to S. This just re-raises the same question: what state is it that the interpreter is imputing to the agent when she ascribes state M? What does her understanding of the M-concept consist in?

As far as the interpretation strategy is concerned, it indeed appears that if the simulation theory is correct, the interpretation strategy is fruitless. One cannot extract criteria of mentalistic ascription from the practice of interpersonal interpretation if that practice rests on a prior and independent understanding of mentalistic notions. As far as the interpretation strategy goes, then, the moral of the simulation theory is essentially a negative one. It should be recalled, however, that I warned from the outset that the hope of the interpretation strategy may not be well founded.

Since the simulation theory is only a theory of interpretation, a theory of how people apply mental terms to others, it is officially neutral about the *meaning* of these terms. It is even compatible with, say, a functionalist account of their meaning! It is conceivable that what people mean by mental terms is given by functionalism, yet they use simulation as a heuristic procedure for ascertaining or inferring the mental states of others. Although this is compatible with the simulation theory, we have already given independent reasons for concluding that the central presupposition of (commonsense) functionalism, viz., the existence of a folk theory, is not satisfied. Furthermore, other well-known difficulties with functionalism, such as absent qualia problems and (other) threats of liberalism and chauvinism, render its prospects quite bleak (see Block 1980). The time is ripe to reconsider the prospects of the first-person approach to the understanding of mental concepts. It has always seemed plausible, prior to philosophical theorizing, that our naïve understanding of mental concepts should prominently involve introspective and not merely causal /relational elements. Some such approach to the concept of the mental would nicely complement the simulation theory of interpretation. However, this topic cannot be pursued here.[15]

Whether or not I have mounted a successful defense of the simulation theory, I hope I have at least persuaded the reader of the importance of getting the descriptive story of interpretive activity right. Although I think that the evidence in favor of the simulation account is substantial, I am even more convinced of the thesis that philosophers (as well as cognitive scientists) must pay closer attention to the psychology of the interpreter. Making that point has been the principal aim of this paper.

347

Notes

Earlier versions of this paper were presented to the philosophy of mind seminar of the Centre National de la Recherche Scientifique in Paris, a conference on the Chomskyan turn in Jerusalem, the Oxford Philosophical Society, the Society for Philosophy and Psychology, and the philosophy departments at King's College, London and Rutgers University. Commentator and audience comments on all of these occasions were most helpful. I am particularly indebted to Michael Ayers, Michael Bratman, Pascal Engel, Jerry Fodor, Elizabeth Fricker, Samuel Guttenplan, J. Christopher Maloney, Christopher Peacocke, Stephen Schiffer, and Robert van Gulick. Special thanks are due to Holly Smith, who read and commented on several previous drafts.

1   Functionalism, or the folk-theory theory, has not usually been presented under the 'interpretation' label. Nonetheless, I believe it causes no distortion, and indeed provides illumination, to view it in this guise.

2   Not all theories of content are discussed here. Many of these theories are not conveniently formulated as theories of interpretation, i.e. as accounts of the interpreter. For example, the causal, covariational, or information-theoretic approach (Fodor 1987; Dretske 1981) is normally stated directly as a theory of content, not in terms of the methods or constraints employed by an interpreter. The same holds of the evolutionary, 'selectionist', or learning historical, approaches to content (Millikan 1984; Dennett 1987c; Dretske 1988). Furthermore, some of these approaches (especially in their pure forms) do not seem promising as full theories of content ascription unless they are supplemented by one of the three approaches I discuss. The covariational approach seems best suited to handle only beliefs, and indeed only that fraction of beliefs under 'direct' causal control of their referents. To handle all types of beliefs, and the other attitudes, the approach probably needs to be incorporated into a larger, functional framework (or another such framework). Even Fodor, for example, who defends a covariational theory of content, also endorses a functional account of the attitude types (Fodor 1987: 69–70); and he acknowledges that the content of certain mental representations, viz., the logical vocabulary, should be handled in terms of their functional roles (Fodor 1990: 110–11), Furthermore, many of the foregoing theories would be extremely dubious accounts of how we ordinarily understand and ascribe contentful states, which is our present topic. A person can grasp and apply the concept of belief, for example, without any knowledge of, or any commitment to, either evolutionary theory or operant conditioning.

3   Hartry Field (1977) appeals to probabilistic coherence in the context of a theory of content.

4   It may be argued that Jeremy's judgments are not expressions of 'probability' judgments, but merely degrees of inductive support, which need not obey the probability calculus (see Levi 1985). However, even if the Linda-style case does not make the point at hand, other cases involving genuine probabilities could do so.

5   A convenient set of readings on the sure-thing principle appears in Gärdenfors and Sahlin (1988: part III). For a survey of deductive failings, see Anderson (1985: ch. 10). For empirically based misgivings about the charity approach, similar to those expressed here, see Thagard and Nisbett (1983).

6   Putnam (1988) contains some new difficulties for functionalism. But this critique does not challenge the use of functional-style generalizations by interpreters.

7 A classical statement of the *Verstehen* approach is Collingwood (1946). Other recent writers who find the simulation approach congenial include Heal (1986), Ripstein (1987), Putnam (1978: lecture VI), Nozick (1981: 637–8), Montgomery (1987), and Johnson (1988). Heal and Ripstein, in particular, anticipate a number of points made here. Unfortunately, those papers came to my attention only after this one was complete.

8 The threat of a regress was pointed out by Stephen Schiffer.

9 Here I am indebted to Michael Ayers.

10 This question is raised by Dennett (1987b), and its importance was impressed upon me by J. Christopher Maloney. For helpful discussion, see Ripstein (1987).

11 I am indebted here to Christopher Peacocke. Notice that I am not assuming any sort of 'pictorial' theory of imagery, only the 'perception-similitude' thesis about imagery (see Goldman 1986: ch. 12).

12 This answer would admittedly not serve Lewis's purposes, since he wants (roughly) purely 'physicalistic' constraints. This is implied by his own formulation of the problem of radical interpretation (in his paper of that title), as well as by the fact that he is trying to meet Hilary Putnam's challenge to resolve problems of content indeterminacy from an 'externalist' perspective. Although my answer would not serve Lewis's purposes, the crucial point of my argument is that his own answer just is not satisfactory.

13 Here I place significant weight on my distinction between basic 'processes' and acquired 'methods' (see Goldman 1986). It is assumed that the interpreter spontaneously uses the same *processes* as the interpretee, but may differ in the *methods* she deploys.

14 Another variant of the problem of other minds is presented by Wittgenstein and reconstructed by Kripke (1982). According to this problem, if the primary concept of a mental state is derived from my own case, I cannot coherently form even a conception of another person's being in that state. For a good reply to this problem, see Loar (1990).

15 For a first-person, or subjective, rendering of mental content, see Loar (1987). Interestingly, Loar couples his internalist account of content with a 'projective', or simulational, account of understanding others.

References

Anderson, J. (1985) *Cognitive Psychology and Its Implications*, 2nd edn. New York: W. H. Freeman.

Baron-Cohen, S., Leslie, A. and Frith, U. (1985) "Does the autistic child have a 'theory of mind'?" *Cognition* 21: 37–46.

Block, N. (1980) "Troubles with functionalism." In N. Block (ed.), *Readings in Philosophy of Psychology*, vol. 1. Cambridge, Mass.: Harvard University Press.

Cherniak, C. (1986) *Minimal Rationality*. Cambridge, Mass.: MIT Press.

Churchland, P. (1981) "Eliminative materialism and the propositional attitudes." *Journal of Philosophy* 78: 67–90.

—— (1989) "Folk psychology and the explanation of human behavior." In *The Neuro-computational Perspective*. Cambridge, Mass.: MIT Press.

Cohen, L.J. (1981) "Can human irrationality be experimentally demonstrated?" *Behavioral and Brain Sciences* 4: 317–31.

Collingwood, R. (1946) *The Idea of History*. Oxford: Clarendon Press.

Davidson, D. (1980) *Essays on Actions and Events*. Oxford: Oxford University Press.

—— (1984) *Inquiries into Truth and Interpretation*. Oxford: Oxford University Press.

—— (1986) "A coherence theory of truth and knowledge." In E. LePore (ed.), *Truth Interpretation*. Oxford: Blackwell.

Dennett, D. (1971) "Intentional systems." *Journal of Philosophy* 68: 87–106.

—— (1987a) "True believers." In *The Intentional Stance*. Cambridge, Mass.: MIT Press.

—— (1987b) "Making sense of ourselves." In *The Intentional Stance*. Cambridge, Mass.: MIT Press.

—— (1987c) "Evolution, error, and intentionality." In *The Intentional Stance*. Cambridge, Mass.: MIT Press

Dretske, F.(1981) *Knowledge and the Flow of Information*. Cambridge, Mass.: MIT Press.

—— (1988) *Explaining Behavior*. Cambridge, Mass.: MIT Press.

Field, H. (1977) "Logic, meaning, and conceptual role." *Journal of Philosophy* 74: 379–409.

Fodor, J, (1987) *Psychosemantics*. Cambridge, Mass.: MIT Press.

—— (1990) *A Theory of Content and Other Essays*. Cambridge, Mass.: MIT Press.

Gärdenfors, P. and Sahlin, N.E. (eds) (1988) *Decision, Probability, and Utility*. Cambridge: Cambridge University Press.

Goldman, A. (1970) *A Theory of Human Action*. Englewood Cliffs, N.J.: Prentice-Hall.

—— (1986) *Epistemology and Cognition*. Cambridge, Mass.: Harvard University Press.

—— (1987) "Cognitive science and metaphysics." *Journal of Philosophy* 84: 537–44.

Gordon, R. (1986) "Folk psychology as simulation." *Mind and Language* 1: 158–71.

—— (1987) *The Structure of Emotions*. Cambridge: Cambridge University Press.

—— (1995) "Folk psychology as simulation." In M. Davies and T. Stone (eds), *Folk Psychology: The Theory of Mind Debate*. Oxford: Blackwell.

Grandy, R. (1973) "Reference, meaning, and belief." *Journal of Philosophy* 70: 439–52.

Harris, P. (1989) *Children and Emotion: The Development of Psychological Understanding*. Oxford: Blackwell.

Heal, J. (1986) "Replication and functionalism." In J. Butterfield (ed.), *Language, Mind and Logic*. Cambridge: Cambridge University Press.

Johnson, C.N. (1988) "Theory of mind and the structure of conscious experience." In J. Astington, P. Harris, and D. Olson (eds), *Developing Theories of Mind*. Cambridge: Cambridge University Press.

Kahneman, D. and Tversky, A. (1982) "The simulation heuristic." In D. Kahneman, P. Slovic, and A. Tversky (eds), *Judgment under Uncertainty*. Cambridge: Cambridge University Press.

Kosslyn, S. (1980) *Image and Mind*. Cambridge, Mass.: Harvard University Press.

Kripke, S. (1982) *Wittgenstein on Rules and Private Language*. Cambridge, Mass.: Harvard University Press.

LePore, E. (ed.) (1986) *Truth and Interpretation*. Oxford: Blackwell.

Leslie, A. (1987) Pretense and representation: The origins of 'theory of mind'. *Psychological Review* 94: 412–26.

Levi, I. (1985) "Illusions about uncertainty." *British Journal for the Philosophy of Science* 36: 331–40.

Lewis, D. (1972) "Psychophysical and theoretical identifications." *Australasian Journal of Philosophy* 61: 249–58.

—— (1983a) "Radical interpretation." In *Philosophical Papers*, vol. 1. New York: Oxford University Press.

—— (1983b) "How to define theoretical terms." In *Philosophical Papers*, vol. 1. New York: Oxford University Press.

—— (1983c) "New work for a theory of universals." *Australasian Journal of Philosophy* 50: 343–77.

Loar, B. (1987) Subjective intentionality. *Philosophical Topics* 15: 89–124.

—— (1990) "Phenomenal state." In J.E. Tomberlin (ed.), *Philosophical Perspectives*, 4: *Action Theory and Philosophy of Mind*. Atascadero, Calif.: Ridgeview.

McGinn, C. (1977) "Charity, interpretation, and belief." *Journal of Philosophy* 74: 521–35.

—— (1986) "Radical interpretation and epistemology." In LePore (1986).

Millikan, R. (1984) *Language, Thought, and Other Biological Categories*. Cambridge, Mass.: MIT Press.

Montgomery, R. (1987) "Psychologism, folk psychology and one's own case." *Journal for the Theory of Social Behavior* 17: 195–218.

Morton, A. (1980) *Frames of Mind*. Oxford: Oxford University Press.

Nozick, R. (1981) *Philosophical Explanations*. Cambridge, Mass.: Harvard University Press.

Pollock, J. (1986) *Contemporary Theories of Knowledge*. Totowa, N.J.: Rowman & Littlefield.

Putnam, H. (1978) *Meaning and the Moral Sciences*. London: Routledge and Kegan Paul.

—— (1988) *Representation and Reality*. Cambridge, Mass.: MIT Press.

Quine, W.V. (1960) *Word and Object*. Cambridge, Mass.: MIT Press.

—— (1969) "Natural kinds." In *Ontological Relativity and Other Essays*. New York: Columbia University Press.

Ripstein, A. (1987) "Explanation and empathy." *Review of Metaphysics* 40: 465–82.

Rosch, E. (1975) "Cognitive representations of semantic categories." *Journal of Experimental Psychology: General* 104: 192–233.

—— (1978) "Principles of categorization." In B. Rosch and B. Lloyd (eds), *Cognition and Categorization*. Hillsdale, N.J.: Lawrence Erlbaum.

Rumelhart, D., Smolensky, P., McClelland, J., and Hinton, G. (1986) "Schemata and sequential thought processes in PDP models." In J. McClelland, D. Rumelhart, and the PDP Research Group, *Parallel Distributed Processing*, vol. 2. Cambridge, Mass.: MIT Press.

Schiffer. S. (1987) *Remnants of Meaning*. Cambridge Mass.: MIT Press.

Shepard, R. and Cooper, L. (1982) *Mental Images and Their Transformations*. Cambridge, Mass.: MIT Press.

Sperber, D. and Wilson, D. (1986) *Relevance*. Oxford: Blackwell.

Stich, S. (1983) *From Folk Psychology to Cognitive Science: The Case Against Belief*. Cambridge, Mass. MIT Press.

—— (1985) "Could man be an irrational animal?" In H. Kornblith (ed.), *Naturalizing Epistemology*. Cambridge, Mass.: MIT Press.

Thagard, P. and Nisbett, R. (1983) "Rationality and charity." *Philosophy of Science*, 50: 250–67.

Tversky, A. and Kahneman, D. (1983) "Extensional versus intuitive reasoning: The conjunction fallacy in probability judgment." *Psychological Review* 90: 293–315.

Van Fraassen, B. (1980) *The Scientific Image*. New York: Oxford University Press.

Wimmer, H. and Perner, J. (1983) "Beliefs about beliefs: Representation and constraining function of wrong beliefs in young children's understanding of deception." *Cognition* 13: 103–28.

17

R.M. Gordon, "Simulation Without Introspection or Inference from Me to You"

Many philosophers and psychologists would agree that people often predict what another will do in a given situation by imagining being in such a situation and then *deciding* what to do. In deciding what to do they call on their own motivational and emotional resources and their own capacity for practical reasoning. But like actors, they modify these resources as needed, on the basis of evidence, especially the other's past and present behavior. A similar story holds for attributing mental states to others and explaining their actions. That people do sometimes resort to such simulation is not in serious dispute. What is in dispute is the claim that simulation is fundamental to folk psychology or at least is of deep psychological and philosophical significance. In this essay I address some narrower issues that I believe have a considerable bearing on the question of psychological and philosophical significance. They chiefly concern what may be called the *epistemology* of simulation.

Most proponents as well as most critics of the simulation theory have supposed simulation to be founded on an implicit inference from oneself to others. The form of inference is essentially the old argument from analogy (Mill 1869), which requires that one first recognize one's own mental states under actual or imagined conditions and then infer that the other is in similar state.[1] This is usually linked to an introspectionist account of *how* one recognizes and ascribes one's own mental states (Harris 1995; Perner and Howes 1995; Gopnik and Wellman 1995; Goldman 1993a). It is further assumed that, to recognize and ascribe one's own mental states and to mentally transfer these states over to the other, one would need to be equipped with the *concepts* of the various mental states (Fuller 1995; Heal 1995). According to this account, in short, simulation is

1 an analogical inference from oneself to others
2 premised on introspectively based ascriptions of mental states to oneself,
3 requiring prior possession of the concepts of the mental states ascribed.

Most friends of simulation, such as Gary Fuller, Alvin Goldman, Paul Harris, and Jane Heal, accept all three of these components in their accounts of simulation. I reject all three. I have several reasons for doing so. I believe these components – the argument from analogy, introspective self-knowledge, and the solipsistic possession of mental concepts – would add greatly to the burden of establishing the simulation theory. They are targets of well-known objections by Wittgenstein, Ryle, Strawson, Dennett, and other philosophers. No philosopher of the late twentieth century should make use of these notions without confronting the objections. In short, a conception of simulation that incorporates the three components listed above is initially problematic.

Further, even if the objections can be answered, such a conception of simulation would appear to be prejudicial against the simulation *theory*. Various critics have argued that a background theory would be needed to warrant the (supposedly implicit) argument from analogy, and that this background theory would have to be at least in part a *psychological* theory. If they are right about this, then the inference component threatens to collapse the simulation theory into a form of theory theory. In addition, most of the *empirical* arguments against the simulation theory, especially those presented in Gopnik and Wellman (1995) and Perner and Howes (1995), crucially depend on the assumption that in simulating another one recognizes one's own mental states by introspection and then infers that the other is in similar states. That is why Gopnik and Wellman say that if the simulation theory were true, then children would initially develop the capacity to make *first person* attributions of belief, and only later, after mastering the inferential step, develop the capacity for *third-person* attributions. And they cite studies showing that both capacities emerge at about the same time.[2]

Philosophers and psychologists gravitate toward a conception of simulation founded on the above three components mainly for the same reason many philosophers and psychologists have held onto the theory theory: because they see no clear alternative. I have had all along an alternative conception of simulation. In this essay I will try to make it more explicit than in my earlier writings on the topic.

I have argued at some length (1995a) that simulation should not be viewed as having the logical structure of an analogical inference from one's own mental states to the mental states of others (component 1 above). Resuming the discussion, I will respond in section 1 to Fuller and Heal, who argue that if simulation is to yield attributions of mental states to others, then it cannot avoid an analogical leap from one's own states to the other's states – a leap that is possible, they further argue, only if one already possesses the concepts of the relevant states (component 3). In section 2 I will reject the common view that *introspection* plays an important, even an essential role, in simulation (component 2).

1 Not a transfer but a transformation

Fuller (1995) and Heal (1995) each present as a major objection to my position what I believe is essentially the same argument. Both note that for a simulator S to ascribe a mental state of type M to O, it is not enough that

S merely *be* in a state of type M, in pretend mode or off-line. For example, it is not enough, as Heal points out, that S merely "catch" O's mental state by some sort of contagion.

I agree that merely to be in a state M, even to be in M in off-line pretend mode, is not sufficient for attributing M to some particular other person (or even to oneself). But what else is needed? According to Fuller and Heal, what is needed is for S to assign or mentally transfer to O the state S is in. Such a transfer, they both suggest, requires that S believe the following: O is in a state *similar to this state I myself am in now*, in pretend mode, as I simulate O. As in Stich's account of belief ascription (1983: 83–4), S picks out a state of S and assigns to O a similar state. Fuller and Heal do not concern themselves, as they certainly should if they accept this Stich-like account of belief ascription, with Stich's well-founded worries about "similarity *in what respect?*" They simply suppose S to have the capacity to pick out a state of a particular mental-state type M and then to assign to O a state of *the same type*. And to have this capacity, they properly note, S must already have the concept of a state of type M. This line of reasoning leads both Fuller and Heal to agree with Goldman's view that "simulation assumes a prior understanding of what state it is that the interpreter ascribes to [the other]" (1989: 94).

Fuller and Heal seem here to overlook the crucial difference between simulating *oneself* in O's situation and simulating O in O's situation. An additional inferential step of roughly the sort Fuller and Heal describe would indeed be required when I simulate *myself* in O's situation, asking, "What would I (*RMG*) do, think, want, and feel in O's situation?" For an answer to this question leaves open the question, "What about O: what does O do, think, want, or feel in O's situation?" But it is also possible to simulate O in O's situation. Following Goldman and Fuller, I will use the Kahneman and Tversky example of the man who misses his flight by just five minutes. Suppose Mr Tees is an acquaintance of mine.[3] I have the option of imagining in the first person *Mr Tees* barely missing his flight, rather than imagining *myself*, a particular individual distinct from Mr Tees, in such a situation and then extrapolating to Mr Tees. (See Williams 1966; Gordon 1986, 1995a.)

To simulate *Mr Tees* in his situation requires an egocentric shift, a recentering of my egocentric map on Mr Tees (Gordon 1986). He becomes in my imagination the referent of the first person pronoun "I," and the time and place of his missing the plane become the referents of "now" and "here." And I, RMG, *cease* to be the referent of the first person pronoun: what is imagined is not the truth of the counter-identical, "RMG is Mr Tees". Such recentering is the prelude to transforming myself in imagination into Mr Tees much as actors become the characters they play. Although some actors ("method" actors, for example) occasionally step back from the role they are playing and ask, "What would I *myself* do, think, and feel in this situation?" and then transfer their answer (with or without adjustments) to the character, the typical stance of modern actors is that of being, not actors pretending to be characters in a play, but the characters themselves.[4]

The point I am making is that once a personal *transformation* has been accomplished, there is no remaining task of mentally *transferring* a state from one person to another, no question of *comparing* Mr Tees to myself. For insofar as I have recentered my egocentric map on Mr Tees, I am not considering what *RMG* would do, think, want, and feel in the situation. Within the context of the simulation, RMG is out of the picture altogether. In short, when I simulate Mr Tees missing his flight, I am already representing him as having been in a certain state of mind.

Of course, there remains the possibility that my representation is incorrect: that Tees' state of mind after he learned of the barely missed flight was in fact not as my simulation depicts it. But from this possibility it does not follow that I am implicitly making an assumption that Mr Tees' state of mind was in fact what I am representing it to be in my simulation. In general, from the possibility of my being wrong in believing, depicting, or otherwise representing things to be a certain way, it does not follow that in addition to representing things to be that way I am assuming that *I am not wrong* in representing them to be that way.

A dogmatic theory theorist might react as follows to my assertion that in simulating Mr Tees missing his flight, I am already representing him as having been in a certain state of mind:

> But in simulating him you are *not* representing him as being or as having been in a certain state of mind. To represent someone as in a state of mind is to represent him as in *an inner state or states of a sort postulated by belief–desire theory* – for that is what states of mind are. Unless simulation implicitly refers to such theoretical states – for example, implying that Mr Tees was is in belief–desire theoretical states similar to one's own current off-line belief–desire theoretical states – it makes no commitment as to states of mind. It is obvious, therefore, that to represent Mr Tees as being in a particular state of mind, indeed as having mental states of any stripe, you have to step outside your simulation and regard him, not from his own first-person point of view but "from the outside," as an object of a certain kind, namely, a "black box" possessing theoretical states of the sort postulated by belief–desire psychology.

The only response I will offer here to this possible reaction is to counterbalance it with what may appear to be another bit of dogmatism:

> It is obvious that, if I wish to represent to myself a thinking being, I must put myself in his place, and thus substitute, as it were, my own subject for the object I am seeking to consider (which does not occur in any other kind of investigation). (Kant 1781/1953: 336)

In Kant's opinion, it is *only* by performing an egocentric shift and taking the point of view of *x* ("the object I am seeking to consider") that one represents x as a thinking being, and thus as having mental states. Thus there is no option of stepping outside one's simulation in order to check and see "objectively" what state of mind a person actually is in.[5] Whether or not Kant is right in this matter, it does appear counter-intuitive to deny that *a* way of representing what is going on in someone's mind is to imagine it in the first person. And Kant's position may become very credible if I am right in speculating that other minds, that is, the mental attributes of other people, are represented in our brains as sets of transformational operations, with information about a particular individual coded as the set of changes or adjustments required to transform oneself mentally into that individual, rather than as an inventory of the individual's theoretical states, processes, and tendencies (Gordon 1995b).

2   Self-ascription of belief and desire[6]

There is one more reason why it might be thought that simulation must be supplemented by an inference from the simulator's mental states to those of the individual simulated. This is the widely held assumption that simulation is or is part of an introspection-based methodology. As the term "introspection" is commonly understood, one can introspect only one's own mental states. So if an introspection-based methodology is to provide information about another's mental states, then it *must* do so by inference from one's own. Although Fuller and Heal do not explicitly link simulation to introspection, an assumption that there is such a link may be guiding their thinking. Making the assumption explicit, they could mount the following argument against my position.

Let it be granted that, transforming ourselves much as actors do, we can simulate *Mr Tees* in his situation, as opposed to merely simulating ourselves in his situation. We would still have to decide what mental states he is in. We would still have to determine, for example, whether he was *extremely upset*, whether he *thought it was the driver's fault*, and so forth. Assuming that we do not in general decide these matters by applying a theory, how can we decide them? The answer is that we seem to have a fairly reliable (if far from perfect) means of accessing our *own* states: a special quasi-perceptual capacity to monitor or "introspect" them. Unfortunately, the capacity for introspection extends exclusively to our own mental states: no matter what imaginative adjustments we make in simulating another, we cannot strictly speaking introspect the other's mental states. The only way to exploit introspection in the detection of another's states would be to introspect our *own states* and then to attribute the same or similar states to the other.

The argument continues: Our own actual mental states often fail to match the states another is in. That is precisely why we must transform ourselves in imagination, imagining not only being in Mr Tees' situation, but being Mr Tees in his situation. In making this transformation we modify our regular stock of mental states with a complement of artificially induced pretend states, keeping the resulting *adjusted* stock of mental states off-line. Then we introspectively read off this adjusted stock of mental states, in the hope that they will now match Mr Tees' states. The important point is that, even when we imagine being Mr Tees in his situation, *it is only our own (adjusted) states we are capable of reading by introspection*. So an inference from ourselves to Mr Tees is unavoidable.

Although I have not seen this argument put forward by Fuller, Heal, or any other proponent of the analogical-inference interpretation of simulation, I think it is the best argument for that interpretation. It assumes, of course, that the method we ordinarily use to identify our own mental states is exclusively a *one-person* procedure, suited *only* to our own states, as introspection is supposed to be. My own view, as I shall explain shortly, is that the method we ordinarily use is limited to identifying states in the *first person*, but, thanks to our capacity for imaginatively transforming ourselves into *other* "first persons," it is not exclusively a *one-person* method. It is just as well suited to labeling another's states as it is to labeling our own, provided we represent these states in the first person, that is, by an egocentric shift. At least this is the method used to identify those mental states that figure most centrally in the explanation of behavior, namely belief and desire. These are the states I shall be concerned with here.

On the question of how we identify our own beliefs and desires, many philosophers and psychologists evidently reason as follows. If our self-ascriptions are to be generally reliable, then they must be the product of a decision procedure that gives us some (internal, or subjective) justification or basis for thinking we are in the states ascribed. In short, we must ascribe on the basis of evidence of one sort or another. But the only sorts of evidence we have generally available to us are behavioral and situational evidence assessed in the light of a theory, and phenomenological or qualitative evidence. So either it is by applying a theory that we ascertain what our present beliefs and desires are, as many theory theorists would have it; or, as Goldman (1993a) and Harris (1989) maintain, we decide on the basis of *direct non-inferential introspective access*, recognizing our own beliefs and desires by their (alleged) phenomenological or qualitative marks.

Goldman (1993a) briefly considers an alternative view that does not involve a justificatory decision procedure. This is the "classical" functionalist account, which holds that

> Classification of a present state does not involve the comparison of present information with anything stored in long term memory. Just *being* in a mental state *automatically* triggers a classification of yourself as being in that state. (1993a: 22)

But he dismisses this "nonrecognitional" account as useless for cognitive science, because it tells us nothing about the process by which the system makes these "automatic" classifications. Because cognitive science must account for the *reliability* of the process, it would have to explain how the *system* "knows" what classification to make.

I will briefly sketch a nonrecognitional account that readily accounts for the reliability of the process. Here is an illustration. We commonly train children to preface nouns like "banana" and "chocolate milk" with "[I] want ..." under the appropriate circumstances: for example, when they look longingly at a banana. Then we treat their utterance, "[I] want banana," as a *request* or demand for a (or the) banana. Whatever may be the case for adults, young children, at least – two-year-olds, say – request or demand a ϕ only when they actually *want* a ϕ. So well-trained children will say, "[I] want banana," only when they *want* a (or the) banana. (Indeed, young children probably say this virtually *whenever* they want a banana, given the right audience: they haven't learned yet to show restraint in the face of *conflicting* desires.)

Such training obviously won't give children mastery of the concept of wanting or desiring, and it won't even teach them that "I" refers to the speaker. So it isn't sufficient for training children to make genuine ascriptions to themselves. But it gives them a remarkable headstart on self-ascription.[7] Given the right audience (and perhaps within certain other constraints), they're already employing the *linguistic form* of a self-ascription of desire when and only when they have the corresponding desire. They already have the reliability: now all they need are the concepts! If this account is right, then *reliability*, at least in the self-ascription of particular desires, does not demand that we or our "system" somehow *know* when we are in the state ascribed. It doesn't require either theoretical knowledge or introspective access.

Goldman (1993b) objects that the child who learns to say, "I want a banana" only when it wants a banana must have learned "some sort of (internal) cue by which it identifies its present state as a wanting." But he gives no grounds for saying this. Nor is it clear whether he thinks it is just the "*I want*" device for getting a banana that demands introspective recognition of wanting something, or that introspective recognition is a general requirement, a precondition of acting to get what one wants, even of plaintively uttering, "Banana!" or just reaching out and grabbing a banana. Neither option looks very plausible, absent a compelling argument.

I turn from desire to belief. Here is a question I invite you take a moment to answer before reading further:

Do you believe the planet Neptune has rings?

I doubt that in answering the question you examined your recent behavior in the light of a theory. And I doubt that you introspectively searched for a telltale feeling or other experiential mark of belief. You probably just reinterpreted the question as, "Does Neptune have rings?" If your answer to this outer-directed question was affirmative, then you were prepared to say, "Yes, I do believe that Neptune has rings." If your answer was negative, then you were prepared to say, "No, I don't believe that Neptune has rings," or more strongly, "No, I believe that Neptune does not have rings." If you had *no* answer to the lower-order question, then you might have said, "No, I don't believe one way or the other." (There appear to be constraints that rule out, among other things, taking excessive time to retrieve or derive the answer and relying on external sources of information.) Because this procedure answers a metacognitive question by answering a question at the next lower semantic level, I will call it an *ascent routine*.[8]

A point that needs emphasis is that, unlike introspection, an ascent routine for identifying beliefs would be as well suited to identifying another's beliefs as it is to identifying one's own. Whether in my own person or within simulation of O, I can settle the question, "Do I believe that *p*?" by asking, within the constraints indicated earlier, whether it is the case that *p*. But in a simulation of O, remember, "I" refers exclusively to O, the individual on whom my egocentric map has been recentered. So I settle the question of whether O believes that *p* simply by asking, within the context of a simulation of O, whether it is the case that *p*. That is, I simply concern myself with *the world* – O's world, the world from O's perspective (metaphors we can now moor securely to a particular operation or procedure) – and, reporting what is there, I am reporting O's beliefs. That is, reporting O's beliefs *is* just reporting what is there. That is why I held (in Gordon 1986) that to ascribe to O a belief that *p* is to assert that *p* within the context of a simulation of O.

Heal is right, however, to note (1995: 43) that I introduced a problematic element in the "sketchy proposal" (which indeed it was) presented in Gordon (1986). For I suggested that to ascribe to Smith a belief that Dewey won the election could be understood as saying the same as,

Let's do a Smith simulation. Ready? *Dewey won the election.*

But "Let's do a Smith simulation" is an invitation or request to simulate Smith, and this may suggest the view that ascriptions of belief are speech acts quite distinct from assertions or descriptive claims. And as Heal remarks, this would make the account problematic in some of the ways ascriptivist or speech-act accounts of moral discourse are problematic.[9] For example, in the antecedent of a conditional ("If Smith believes that Dewey won the election then . . ."), how do we embed an invitation to simulate?

The difficulty is avoidable, as Heal says, if I drop the prefatory speech act and explain belief attribution in terms of simulation alone. To develop the point, note that there is no problem embedding a supposition or off-line belief within the antecedent of a conditional – not, at least, if we regard the antecedent of a conditional as itself a supposition or off-line belief (as protrayed in the Ramsey test, for example.) To answer the question, "If I believed that *p*, would I do *x*?" I simply suppose or pretend that *p*, using my motivational and other resources to "decide," or at least to form an off-line intention, whether or not to do *x* (Gordon 1986). Where I am supposing another person, Mary, to believe that *p*, I embed the supposition that *p* within a simulation of Mary

359

and, using my *adjusted* motivational and other resources, "decide" whether or not to do *x*. There are complications, of course. An example that calls for thinking on two different semantic levels is this: "If I now believed I was about to inherit a million dollars, I would be a fool."[10] For although I am supposing or pretending that I am about to inherit a million dollars, I am also holding on to the facts as I *actually* see them when I deem myself a fool. A different sort of "split-level" conditional is the following: "If I were about to inherit a million dollars, then I would believe I were about to inherit a million dollars (that is, I would know about it)." I will take up these complications and also discuss propositional attitudes other than belief in a more detailed presentation (Gordon, forthcoming).

Earlier I described a way in which children can be trained to use the linguistic form of a self-ascription of desire only when they have the corresponding desire. There is a parallel way of training children to use the form of a self-ascription of belief. It would be possible to take a child – say, a two-year-old – who can make just a few simple assertions, like, "It's raining," and in one easy step train her to sound *very* sophisticated. Just get her to preface her assertions, optionally, with "I believe." She'll then say, for example, "I believe it's raining."[11] What anomalous precocity: The child is barely able to express simple first-order beliefs, and yet *here she is expressing metabeliefs!* Not only that, they appear to be remarkably *reliable* metabeliefs! That is, we would usually find such self-ascriptions borne out by situational and behavioral evidence. And, as in the case of desire, such reliability would not demand theoretical knowledge or introspective access.

As in the case of desire, such training would not give children mastery of the concept of belief. Merely to train children to preface assertions with the formula, "I believe," would not enable them to distinguish self-ascription of belief from assertion of fact. They would not learn that the *belief* that *p*, unlike the *fact* that *p*, may be false, or at variance with fact. Nor would they learn that someone may fail to believe that *p* even if *p*. And they would not learn that what one individual believes may differ from what another believes. In short, they are not being trained to make genuine ascriptions to themselves. They will not have learned that they believe it is raining, or even that they have beliefs. As far as they are concerned, they are just parroting a formula before saying what they *really* mean to say, namely, that it's raining.

But suppose that in simulating another (or herself at a time other than the present) – in describing "the world" as it is within the context of the simulation – she sometimes makes assertions that contradict assertions of her own, that is, those she makes from her "home" perspective. In other words, she allows "the facts" within a simulation to deviate from the actual facts. And suppose further that she introduces these deviations, not in an arbitrary way, but in response to situational and behavioral evidence, in a way that reduces errors in explanation and prediction. All she has to do then is to preface these deviant assertions with "I believe . . ." – or to follow the slightly more sophisticated ascent routine, answering the question, "Do I believe that *p*?" by answering the lower-level question, "Is it the case that p?" – and she will be making *motivated attributions of false belief*.[12] Whether she "passes" a particular false belief test will depend, of course, on how sophisticated she is in making these adjustments.

Although a capacity to pass a stringent false belief test maybe sufficient for routine proficiency in using the concept of belief, a sophisticated understanding would require much more. For one thing, the child is not yet in a position to understand that *her own present beliefs* may themselves deviate from the facts. She will not come to understand this as long as she ascertains what her own present beliefs are simply by asking what the facts are. To see her own present beliefs as distinguishable from the facts she will have to simulate another for whom the facts are different – or, more broadly, adopt a perspective from which the facts are different, whether this perspective is occupied by a real person or not – and then, from the alien perspective, *simulate herself*. Or at least she will have to realize abstractly that from a perspective distinct from her own present perspective what she now counts as fact may be, not fact, but nothing more than fact-from-her-particular-perspective.

Strictly speaking, this realization does not require a capacity to simulate others. It can arise with development of the capacity to demote some of one's own *memories* to off-line status. For example, suppose the child saw on a table what appeared to be a rock but later proved to be a sponge that looked like a rock. Now she no longer remembers *that there was a rock on the table*, for that "fact" is no longer available as a basis for action, emotion, desire, or factual inference. It attains that status only off-line, for example, when she tries to reconstruct a coherent explanatory narrative for her past actions, emotions, expectations, and inferences. What she learns to report is that she remembers *believing* that there was a rock on the table. The point here is that by simulating a possible later perspective of her own the child may come to conceptualize in a more sophisticated way what she now counts naïvely as fact pure and simple. She comes to think of it instead as fact relative to her present perspective.

Now consider some developmental consequences. If an introspectionist version of the simulation theory, such as that of Goldman or Harris, is right, then we should expect children to be able to identify their own present beliefs with at least fair reliability before they can ascribe beliefs to others or to themselves in the past. For according to that version of the simulation theory, as we have seen, ascriptions to others or to oneself in the past would depend on the capacity to introspectively identify one's own present beliefs.

But if my view is right, and we ordinarily identify our own present beliefs by using an ascent routine, then there is an important distinction to be made between *comprehending* and *uncomprehending* ascriptions: that is, ascriptions made with and ascriptions made without the understanding that the beliefs ascribed may be false. On the one hand, a capacity for reliable *uncomprehending* identification of one's own present beliefs should emerge before one can ascribe beliefs to others or to oneself in the past. It emerges extremely quickly, if my view is right, and *does not even await development of a capacity to introspect*, much less a capacity to recognize a belief by its introspected phenomenological marks. For as I said earlier, a child who makes only the simplest assertions is already in a position to use the linguistic form of a present-tense self-ascription of belief in a highly reliable way. And with just a little more sophistication a child can learn to answer questions of the form, "Do I believe that *p*?" by answering, "Is it the case that *p*?" If on the other hand we are speaking of *genuine, comprehending* ascriptions of belief, ascriptions made with the understanding that the beliefs ascribed may be false, then *present-tense self-ascriptions ought to come last of all*. For these require conceptually prising one's own present beliefs apart from the facts, so that, like the beliefs of another, they may be false or at variance with the facts. This difficult feat requires taking a vantage point outside one's present perspective, whether by simulating another or by memory demotion, and then reflecting back from that vantage point on what one now counts as fact pure and simple and relegating it to a perspectival status.

My coupling of simulation with an ascent routine for self-attribution of belief has further important consequences concerning the attribution of belief. Because an ascent routine is, unlike introspection, as well suited to labeling another's states (after an egocentric shift) as it is to labeling one's own, it may yield conflicting attributions.[13] For example, consider the question, "Should fathers devote as much time to child care as mothers?" Suppose that when I ask myself this question, I answer, "Yes." But you, simulating me on the basis of behavioral evidence, answer for me, within the simulation, "No." So, using an ascent routine, I say, "I believe that fathers should devote as much time as mothers." But using the same routine within your simulation of me, you say, "No, I believe fathers should not devote as much time as mothers" – with "I" of course referring to me, RMG. (You would also be entitled to say, "I do not believe fathers should devote as much time . . .") Even if you think I believe I am being sincere in asserting that fathers should devote as much time, you might still deny that I believe it – that is, really believe it, as opposed to merely believing that I believe it. Here, it would seem, is the opening for unconscious belief. I am thinking not only of Freudian unconscious belief but also unconscious belief of the sort often posited in cognitive science – arising, say, from a decoupling of speech from other systems that control motor behavior.

Finally, the conflict need not be between attributions made by me and attributions made by someone else. Both attributions may be made by the same individual. Just as you might simulate me on the basis of behavioral evidence, so I might simulate myself on that basis, as if I were another person (but with the benefit of behavioral evidence that may be unavailable to others). Speaking for that "other" character I am simulating, I might say or think, "No, fathers should not devote as much time as mothers." I might play myself best, in other words, if I *pretend* that fathers should not devote as much time. Thus I may find myself giving contradictory belief reports. Speaking for myself, RMG, my ascent routine yields, "I believe fathers *should* devote as much time." But, speaking for this fellow RMG that I am simulating, my ascent routine yields, "I believe fathers *should not* devote as much time."

At the beginning of this chapter I suggested that the assumption that simulation involves an implicit inference from oneself to others is propped up by the assumption that simulation is, or is part of, an introspection-based methodology. Rather than rehearse the well-known objections to introspection, I have argued that ascent routines, coupled with our capacity for recentering our egocentric maps, enable us directly, rather than by inference from our own case, to identify the mental states of others.[14]

Notes

1 "I am conscious in myself of a series of facts connected by an uniform sequence, of which the beginning is modifications of my body, the middle is feelings, the end is outward demeanour. In the case of other human beings I have the evidence of my senses for the first and last links of the series, but not for the intermediate link . . . by supposing the link to be of the same nature as in the case of which I have experience, . . . I bring other human beings, as phenomena, under the same generalizations which I know by experience to be the true theory of my own existence" (Mill 1869).

2 These findings are contested by Harris (1995) and also by Goldman (1993a). But if my alternative to the introspection-plus-inference conception of simulation is right, the *significance* of these findings for the simulation-versus-theory debate changes dramatically.

3 If (as in the actual example from Kahneman and Tversky) "Mr Tees" is just a placeholder designating no particular individual – any "typical" person – then there is nothing at issue here. *You* fill the bill just as well as anyone else, unless you have characteristics that might make your answer to the question an atypical one. But if we are talking about a real person or a person referred to in some existing body of fiction, then there is a difference.

4 One very perceptive actor, the late Ray McAnally of the Abbey Theatre in Dublin, described his thoughts while filming a scene in which he played a future British Prime Minister:

> I had a very interesting moment in 10 Downing Street, surrounded by pictures of all the previous Prime Ministers *and me in the middle of it*. And I realized it was true, I was the Prime Minister. It's not that I'm *pretending* to be the Prime Minister . . . I *am* the Prime Minister. (*New York Times*, "A Living Definition of Acting," Jan. 15, 1989)

Of course, McAnally was in fact pretending to be the Prime Minister, only he was doing it so well that he was oblivious to that fact.

5 Kant's larger aim in this passage, it should emphatically be noted, is to combat metaphysical dogma: to criticize the tradition of Cartesian "rational" psychology, which he regards as fallaciously drawing *ontological*, e.g. dualistic or idealistic, conclusions from this "obvious" truth about the mere *form* of our representation of thinking beings *qua* thinking beings. Thus it would be consistent with this merely formal truth to assert that mental predicates are true *only of bodies* and

(although Kant does not address the topic) that mental states are token- or even type-identical with physical states. *Scholarly note*: The passage quoted appears only in the First Edition of the *Critique of Pure Reason*, under the "Second Paralogism of Pure Reason." But in both editions we find the following:

> Now I cannot have any representation whatsoever of a thinking being, through any outer experience, but only through self-consciousness. Objects of this kind are, therefore, nothing more than the transference of this consciousness of mine to other things, which in this way alone can be represented as thinking beings. (Kant 1781/1953: 347/332)

(The term *objects* as used here should be interpreted as "objects *of thought*.")

6 The major portion of this section is adapted from my commentary on target articles by Goldman and Gopnik in *The Behavioral and Brain Sciences* (Gordon 1993).

7 Goldman (1993b) comments that if, as I admit, such training is not sufficient to give children the concept of wanting, "then the training story sheds no light on what it is to grasp the concept of wanting." This doesn't seem to follow. Such training, although not sufficient for acquisition of the concept, may be the most important step in the acquisition of the concept. (To be specific, it links the name of a propositional attitude with the verbal expression of that attitude; and the child who can also expressively use "I want" *when speaking for another* (that is, in the context of a simulation) comes close, in my view, to having grasped the general concept of wanting.)

8 Compare Gareth Evans: "I get myself in position to answer the question whether I believe that *p* by putting into operation whatever procedure I have for answering the question whether *p*" (Evans 1982: 225). Also compare the "answer check procedure" described in Wimmer, Hogrefe, and Sodian (1988): If asked whether you know the answer to a question *q* (for example, about the location of something), simply check to see if *you have* an answer to *q*.

   Descartes says,

> Whatever enables us to know anything else cannot but lead us to a much surer knowledge of our own mind. . . . For it may perhaps be the case that I judge that I am touching the earth even though the earth does not exist at all; but it cannot be that when I make this judgment, my mind which is making this judgment does not exist. (*Principles of Philosophy* I: 11)

Descartes is right in thinking he can peel off an "I believe" from all his assertions about the world. But this requires no reliance on the assumption that minds have a capacity for introspection, much less on the further assumption that introspection yields indubitable knowledge. Becoming aware of something as going on "in himself" when judging that the Earth exists isn't a matter of becoming aware (much less indubitably aware) of something other than the Earth. (On this, see Collins, 1987. But as I note at the end of this paper, Collins fails to see that the ascent routine may be used to make attributions, to others or to oneself, on the basis of evidence.) I believe a similar case can be made with regard to desire, emotions, and even pleasure and pain, but I postpone the details.

9 Brian Loar and Andrew Melnyk made a similar point in conversation.

10 An example like this was provided by Piers Rawling.

11 Although it is common practice to train children to use the form of a self-ascription in order to "express a desire for something," it is neither a common nor in general a useful practice to train young children to use the form "I believe that *p*" as a way of "expressing a belief," that is, as a way of asserting that *p*. (*Adults* often employ the linguistic form of a self-ascription of belief as a way of making an assertion, though they typically do so in order to qualify the assertion, that is, to add a Gricean, "implicature.")

12 If within her "home" perspective there is an answer to the lower-level question but from the other's perspective there is no answer at all – one draws a blank – she attributes ignorance of fact (failure to believe what is true) to the other. Where the asymmetry is reversed, the matter gets more complex.

13 This is the important point that Collins (1987) overlooks.

14 Although this may appear to be a new way to look at simulation, it underlies and makes plausible the comments on belief ascription I made in Gordon (1986). But I was certainly not clear, when I wrote that paper, that my intuitions about simulation were colored by a belief in self-ascription by ascent routines. And I probably would not have become clear, but for some very articulate defenders of a different conception of simulation.

References

The papers marked * are reprinted in M. Davies and T. Stone (eds), *Folk Psychology: The Theory of Mind Debate* (Oxford: Blackwell, 1995).

Collins, A.W. (1987) *Nature of Mental Things*. Notre Dame, Ind.: University of Notre Dame Press.

Davies, M. and Stone, T. (eds) (1995) *Folk Psychology: The Theory of Mind Debate*. Oxford: Blackwell.

Evans, G. (1982) *The Varieties of Reference*. Oxford: Oxford University Press.

Fuller, G. (1995) "Simulation and psychological concepts." In M. Davies and T. Stone (eds), *Mental Simulation*. Oxford: Blackwell.

*Goldman, A. (1989) "Interpretation psychologized." *Mind and Language* 4: 161–85.

—— (1993a) "The psychology of folk psychology." *The Behavioral and Brain Sciences* 16: 15–28.

—— (1993b) "Functionalism, the theory theory, and phenomenology." *The Behavioral and Brain Sciences* 16: 101–8.

Gopnik, A. and Wellman, H. (1995) "Why the child's theory of mind really *is* a theory." In Davies and Stone (1995).

*Gordon, R.M. (1986) "Folk psychology as simulation." *Mind and Language* 1: 158–71.

—— (1993) "Self-ascription of belief and desire." *The Behavioral and Brain Sciences* 16.

—— (1995a) "The simulation theory: Objections and misconceptions." In Davies and Stone (1995).

—— (1995b) Reply to Stich and Nichols. In Davies and Stone (1995).

—— (forthcoming) *Representing Minds*. Cambridge, Mass.: MIT Press.

Harris, P. (1989) *Children and Emotion: The Development of Psychological Understanding*. Oxford: Blackwell.

—— (1995) "From simulation to folk psychology: The case for development." In Davies and Stone (1995).

*Heal, J. (1986) "Replication and functionalism." In J. Butterfield (ed.), *Language, Mind and Logic*. Cambridge: Cambridge University Press.

—— (1995) "How to think about thinking." In M. Davies and T. Stone (eds), *Mental Simulation*. Oxford: Blackwell.

Kant, I. (1781/1953) *Critique of Pure Reason*. First edn. Tr. Norman Kemp Smith. London: Macmillan.

Mill, J.S. (1869) *An Examination of Sir William Hamilton's Philosophy*. Sixth edn. London.

Perner, J. and Howes, D. (1995) "'He thinks he knows': And more developmental evidence against the simulation (role-taking) theory". In Davies and Stone (1995).

Stich, S. (1983) *From Folk Psychology to Cognitive Science: The Case Against Belief*. Cambridge, Mass. MIT Press.

Williams, B.A.O. (1966) "Imagination and the self." Proceedings of the British Academy. Reprinted in P.F. Strawson (ed.), *Studies in Thought and Action*. Oxford: Oxford University Press, 1968.

Wimmer, H., Hogrefe, J., and Sodian, B. (1988) "A second state in children's conception of mental life: Understanding informational access as origins of knowledge and belief." In J.W. Astington, P.L. Harris, and D.R. Olson (eds), *Developing Theories of Mind*. Cambridge: Cambridge University Press.

PART III

REPRESENTATION AND
COGNITIVE ARCHITECTURE

INTRODUCTION

It is almost a commonplace among philosophers and cognitive scientists that cognition is in some sense a form of information-processing (although some philosophers, particularly those adopting what I have termed the picture of the autonomous mind, make a sharp distinction between personal-level thought and the subpersonal information-processing that makes it possible). Unsurprisingly, however, there is no agreement on how information is represented in the mind/brain, or on how those representations are processed (what is often called the architecture of cognition). Each of the five subsections that follow deals with a different dimension of the general problem of how best to understand representation and cognitive architecture.

Part IIIA presents three different perspectives on the basic idea that cognition is a form of computation. The discussion here focuses on what is often called the classical approach to cognitive architecture. In Part IIIB, in contrast, we consider the non-classical approach to computation, which favors models of information-processing in which representations are distributed across patterns of neural activation. One of the key questions in thinking about how information is processed in the mind-brain is the extent to which information-processing is modular – that is, the extent to which specific processing tasks are carried out by dedicated and specialized cognitive systems. The papers in Part IIIC present three different perspectives on modularity. In Part IIID we move to a pressing issue that arises when one starts to think about the relation between subpersonal-level information-processing and personal-level cognition: How are the representations postulated at the subpersonal level related to personal-level beliefs and capacities? Finally, Part IIIE offers three different perspectives on the relation between thought and language.

IIIA   Cognition as computation

The two guiding ideas of what has come to be known as the "cognitive revolution" in psychology and other cognitive sciences are, first, the idea that the mind-brain is an information-processing device and, second, the idea that cognition is a form of computation. The information-processing approach to the mind-brain can be developed in a number of different ways, depending upon how computation is understood. The papers in this section explore what is often called the classical approach to computation, which treats the mind-brain as a symbol-processing device analogous to a digital computer and draws its inspiration from mathematical logic and theoretical computer science (as sketched out in the paper by Newell and Simon). Within the artificial intelligence literature (discussed in the papers by Newell and Simon and by Dennett) the classical approach is often termed *good old-fashioned artificial intelligence* (GOFAI), in contrast with the non-classical approach drawing upon dynamical systems theory and models of parallel distributed processing (see ID and IIB above, and IIIB below).

One fundamental tenet of the information-processing approach to cognition is that an information-processing task must be studied and modeled at different levels. The canonical exposition of the multi-level approach is to be found in **David Marr**'s book *A Theory of Vision*, from which we have reprinted selections. According to Marr, any information-processing analysis of a given cognitive system (such as Marr's own example, the visual system) has to begin with a *computational theory* of the task carried out by the system. Analysis at the computational level provides a detailed specification of the task being carried out and the function that performing that task plays in the organism as a whole. We can understand this *task analysis* as a specification of how the system transforms a given form of input into a given form of output. With this specification in hand, the next level of analysis is the *representational level*, where the job is to specify a process for carrying out the input-output transformation identified at the computational level. Marr thinks that providing such a specification involves, first, specifying how the input information is represented in the system and, second, giving an *algorithm* (i.e. a series of simple computational steps, such as those that take one from one line to the next in a proof in the predicate calculus) that can actually transform that input into the required output. The final level of analysis is the *implementational level*, which provides an account of how the representations and algorithm identified at the representational level are physically realized. Marr illustrates the tri-level analysis by sketching out how he applies it to the visual system, with particular reference to analysis at the computation and representational levels.

In thinking about how to carry forward the project of information-processing analysis outlined by Marr, perhaps the most pressing question is how the representational level is to be understood – what is the format of the representations, and how should we understand the algorithms that operate on them? **Allen Newell and Herbert Simon**'s "Computer Science as Empirical Inquiry: Symbols and Search" offers an influential answer that clearly states the main principles of the classical approach to computation. Newell and Simon are interested primarily in the artificial intelligence end of computer science, which they see as primarily the study of intelligent action. Just as biology is guided by the principle that cells are the basic building blocks of living organisms and plate tectonics by the principle that the surface of the earth is made up of a small number of moving plates, they take computer science to be guided by two basic principles. The first basic principle is the *physical-symbol system hypothesis*, according to which any

370

sufficiently complex physical system capable of storing and processing symbols is capable of intelligent action and any system capable of intelligent action will turn out on analysis to be a physical-symbol system. Newell and Simon show how the physical symbol hypothesis has its origins in the formalization of mathematical logic in the 1920s and 1930s and the genesis of the theory of computability in the work of Alan Turing and others. As they note, the physical-symbol is an empirical hypothesis that stands or falls with its success in modeling intelligent action. In constructing such models, Newell and Simon propose that computer scientists are guided by a second basic principle, the *heuristic search hypothesis*, which is a hypothesis about how physical-symbol systems solve problems. It states that problems are solved by generating and modifying symbol structures until a suitable solution structure is reached. Newell and Simon see the enterprise of artificial intelligence as driven by these two hypotheses. Recent developments in non-classical models have challenged this view, but this paper remains the canonical statement of the central claims of good old-fashioned AI.

Daniel Dennett's "Cognitive Wheels: The Frame Problem of AI" explores some of the difficulties associated with the *frame problem* in artificial intelligence – difficulties that arise for anyone pursuing Newell and Simon's heuristic search hypothesis, for example. The frame problem is essentially the problem of determining which of the indefinitely many deductive consequences of a piece of information are relevant in a given situation. As the amusing vignette with which Dennett opens the paper makes clear, any intelligent system needs to be able to store, access, and process real-world "knowledge" efficiently, and, in particular, it needs to be able to ignore most of what it knows. Dennett reviews some of the proposals that workers in artificial intelligence have proposed for tackling the frame problem, such as the *scripts* and *frames* proposed by Marvin Minsky and Roger Schank. According to Dennett, what all these approaches have in common is that they are attempts to formalize the essentially *non-monotonic* nature of ordinary commonsense reasoning (where reasoning is non-monotonic only if, as is emphatically *not* the case in ordinary predicate logic for example, conclusions can be defeated by the addition of new information). As he notes, there is a danger that the proposed solutions to the frame problem will all turn out to be "cognitive wheels", by which he means theoretical entities that solve theoretical problems but have no biological plausibility. Nonetheless (very much in the spirit of Marr's injunction to careful task analysis) he suggests that constructing artificial models is a necessary first step in understanding the information-processing tasks that the biological brain carries out.

IIIB   Non-classical cognitive architecture

Issues to do with representation and cognitive architecture have been prominent in a number of the articles in Parts I and II. So, for example, whereas the picture of the representational mind is closely bound up with the idea of the mind as an information-processing device that works in much the same way as a digital computer, the picture of the neurocomputational mind favors a fundamentally different, sub-symbolic conception of information-processing. Correspondingly, these two pictures of the mind understand representation in very different ways. Proponents of the representational mind think that information is represented in discrete and causally efficacious symbol structures, whereas neurocomputational theorists typically see representations as distributed across patterns of neural activation. The distinction here is often put as the distinction between classical and non-classical cognitive architectures. Whereas the classical approach was primarily the focus of Part IIIA, the two papers in this section explore the non-classical approach.

Terence Horgan and **John Tienson**'s "Levels of Description in Non-classical Cognitive Science" is a careful discussion of the relation between connectionist information-processing models and Marr's account of levels of description in cognitive science (as expounded in the extract from Marr's *Theory of Vision* reprinted in Part IIIA). As they and others have noted, it is possible to subsume connectionist models within classical cognitive science by locating them at Marr's implementational level – that is, by viewing them as proposals about how classi-cally specifiable algorithms are implemented in the brain. Horgan and Tienson argue, however, that the mathematics of connectionist models makes possible, and indeed plausible, ways of interpreting them as genuine alternatives to clas-sical approaches to cognitive architecture. One of the guiding assumptions of classical cognitive science is that transitions between cognitive states are effected by functions that are algorithmic, in the sense that an algorithm exists that will compute the function in a finite number of computationally simple, single steps (as in the machine table of a Turing machine). Connectionist networks, however, are dynamical systems and the transitions between complete states of dynamical systems do not always fit the algorithmic model. According to Horgan and Tienson, Gordon Berg's connectionist model of natural language sentence parsing is an example of a non-algorithmic dynamical system, and hence one that cannot be subsumed within the classical approach. Horgan and Tienson end with the radical non-classical proposal that functions governing transitions between cognitive states might not even be what they term "computationally tractable". If cogni-tive transitions are subserved by dynamical systems then it might well be the case that there are no general laws *over cognitive states* that will fix the relevant transi-tions, even though at a lower level of description the mathematical transi-tions between the states of the dynamical system are themselves computationally tractable.

One of the key issues in dispute between classical and non-classical approaches to cognitive architecture is whether representations are *composition-ally* structured. Proponents of classicism such as Fodor and Pylyshyn (1988) argue that, since cognition requires compositionally structured representations and the representations in connectionist models are not compositionally struc-tured, connectionist networks can only at best be implementations of classical models. Similar issues arise in debates about the implications of connectionist networks for how we think about propositional attitudes (see the article by Ramsey, Stich, and Garon in Part IIB). **Tim van Gelder**'s "Compositionality:

Connectionist Variations on a Classical Theme" distinguishes two types of compositionality – *concatenative compositionality* and *functional compositionality*. A representational system is compositional in the concatenative sense when its representations mirror the structure of what they represent, in the way that an assertoric sentence contains elements corresponding to the constituents of the fact that it reports. Concatenatively compositional systems of representation include natural languages and the various formal languages employed in mathematics, computer science, and so on. A representational system is functionally compositional, on the other hand, just if it can represent structured objects in such a way that there are effective and reliable processes for producing such an expression given its constituents and decomposing the expression back into its constituents. All concatenative compositional systems are functionally compositional, but the converse does not hold. Van Gelder argues with examples that, although connectionist networks are not concatenatively compositional, many of them are functionally compositional and suggests that functionally compositional representations are structured in a sufficiently robust sense to meet the concerns raised by Fodor and Pylyshyn.

IIIC   Conceptions of modularity

It has become common among psychologists and cognitive scientists to draw a distinction between modular and non-modular cognitive processes. This is, in essence, the distinction between high-level cognitive processes that are open-ended and involve bringing a wide range of information to bear upon very general problems, and lower-level cognitive processes that work quickly to provide rapid solutions to highly determinate problems. The distinction is also often drawn at the level of cognitive architecture, where it has become common for cognitive scientists to identify different cognitive systems (*modules*) responsible for different types of modular processing. Although the basic idea of modularity is well-established in psychology and cognitive science, it can be understood in a range of different ways. Three of these are represented in this section.

The canonical exposition of the hypothesis of modularity at the level of cognitive architecture is **Jerry Fodor**'s 1975 book *The Modularity of Mind*. A summary of the book is reprinted here. Fodor offers his conception of modularity as a way of trying to do justice to elements of two very different ways of thinking about perception. According to the behaviorist paradigm that was dominant in psychology until the "cognitive revolution" of the 1960s, perception can be understood as a complex form of reflex behavior. Identifying an object perceptually is, in the behaviorist view, simply a matter of being able to discriminate it and discriminative responding can be understood purely in terms of conditioned responses that are, to all intents and purposes, completely non-cognitive. In reacting against behaviorism, the cognitivist movement in psychology went to the other extreme, essentially assimilating perception to high-level cognition by arguing (on the basis of *poverty of the stimulus* arguments) that perception involves complex forms of computation and inference. Fodor argues that the straightforward opposition between cognitivism and behaviorism is mistaken. Some perceptual processes (the *modular* ones) are reflex-like in the sense that they are *informationally encapsulated*. That is, they operate independently of the organism's beliefs, desires, and so on. (Fodor takes this to be shown by the fact that visual illusions persists even when one knows them to be illusory.) Nonetheless, they are unlike reflexes in the sense that they involve information-processing. The fact that modular processes are encapsulated allows them to involve information-processing and inference without thereby being assimilated to high-level cognitive processes.

According to Fodor, modules are computational systems that take as inputs a narrow range of the information available to the organism (typically, specifications of what is impinging on the sensory periphery); that have access only to a limited database of proprietary information; that are largely innately specified; that are characteristically associated with specific neuroanatomical areas; and for which it is often possible to identify highly specific pathologies resulting from damage to the module. These characteristics ensure that modular processes and systems can be given standard information-processing analyses on the model set out by Marr (see IIIA above) – and in fact, Marr's analysis of the early visual system can be seen as a paradigm of modular analysis. This positive thesis goes hand in hand with a deeply pessimistic one, however. Fodor argues that non-modular processes are profoundly resistant to psychological analysis. Ultimately, for Fodor, cognitive science and scientific psychology can aspire to understand the modular aspect of cognition, but none of the techniques that will work for modular systems can be applied to non-modular cognition, and we have no idea of what other techniques could be used.

Many cognitive scientists have tried to resist Fodor's pessimistic conclusion by extending the concept of modularity beyond the very circumscribed domain to which Fodor confined it (essentially the early stages of perceptual and linguistic processing). Whereas Fodor is emphatic that beliefs, desires, and other common-sense psychological states are fundamentally non-modular, it has become common for cognitive scientists to postulate modules corresponding to bodies of personal-level knowledge, such as the social intelligence module (responsible for social understanding and social coordination), or the naïve physics module (responsible for our basic understanding of the physical world). In "How to Think About the Modularity of Mind-reading" **Gregory Currie** and **Kim Sterelny** assess the plausibility of thinking of social intelligence as modular. As they note, it is very implausible to think of social intelligence as informationally encapsulated in the manner required for a Fodorean module. Social intelligence as a whole cannot be modular, since just about any type of information can be potentially relevant to, and is frequently deployed in, social understanding. It would be more plausible, they suggest, to think of social intelligence as modular in the modest sense that processes of social understanding take inputs from encapsulated modules that lie between input perceptual processing and "central" belief fixation and that serve the function of attaching social "markers" to representations of people (who might be marked as friendly, for example) and social situations (which might be marked as dangerous). These second-order encapsulated modules are not themselves Fodorean, since their inputs are not from transducers. Currie and Sterelny suggest that postulating second-order modules can do justice to many of the motivations for taking social intelligence as a whole to be modular, from the existence of social illusions to understanding breakdowns in social skills such as autism.

Evolutionary psychology provides a very different and much more radical perspective on modularity. In "Origins of Domain Specificity: The Evolution of Functional Organization" the evolutionary psychologists **Leda Cosmides** and **John Tooby** make the case for what has come to be known as the *massive modularity hypothesis*. They argue that there is no such thing as central processing understood in the way that Fodor understands it. All cognition is domain-specific and we should view the mind as made up of a large number of specialized modules that evolved to deal with highly specific problems confronted by our hominid and pre-hominid ancestors. Evolutionary psychologists postulate the existence of *Darwinian modules* governing different types of social interaction; our everyday understanding of number; our naïve physics (viz. our understanding of the dynamic and kinematic properties of ordinary objects); our naïve biology (viz. our understanding of the basic properties of living things); and so on. According to the massive modularity hypothesis, the mind is a complex structure of superimposed Darwinian modules.

Evolutionary psychologists start from the assumption that, since the mind is a product of evolution, the best way to understand it is as a set of cognitive mechanisms that evolved to deal with specific problems that arose in human evolutionary history. Cosmides and Tooby maintain that these cognitive mechanisms must be *domain-specific* in form (i.e. specialized for dealing with highly specific information-processing problems). They argue for this by arguing that *domain-general* processes of the sort that Fodor and others have taken to govern central processing and belief fixation cannot guide behavior in fitness-preserving ways (and hence cannot be the product of evolution). They draw attention, for example, to the fact that there can be no domain-general criterion of success or failure that correlates with fitness. What promotes fitness varies from domain to domain. It is fitness-promoting to refrain from sexual intercourse with close relatives, but not to withhold assistance from them. It is the job of evolutionary biology, they argue, to construct computational theories of adaptive information-processing problems (which will, in effect, be evolutionary versions of Marr-style task analysis) that will guide the analysis of the mechanisms that solve those problems.

IIID   Tacit knowledge

One question that frequently arises in thinking about representation and cognitive architecture is how we should think about the relation between the personal-level states of commonsense psychology and the subpersonal representational states postulated in, for example, computational theories of vision or syntactic understanding. Many psychologists and cognitive scientists effectively treat the two types of representational state interchangeably, describing language-users for example as *knowing* the rules of generative grammar that are claimed to govern the modular parsing of syntactic information in the early stages of language-processing. From a philosophical point of view, however, it is natural to ask whether this usage is well grounded. Is there a principled distinction to be drawn between two different types of representational state?

Stephen Stich's "Beliefs and Subdoxastic States" answers this question affirmatively. He identifies two basic defining features of beliefs (and other propositional attitudes) that are not shared by the sub-doxastic states appealed to in subpersonal, information-processing models of particular cognitive abilities and capacities. The first defining feature of beliefs is that they are *inferentially integrated* with each other and with the propositional attitudes in general, whereas sub-doxastic states are *inferentially insulated* from the propositional attitude system. (Note the similarities with Fodor's discussion of the informational encapsulation of modular systems as opposed to non-modular central processing.) I may, for example, perhaps as a consequence of my studies in linguistics, come to believe a certain principle about the syntactic structure of sentences in English at the same time as having hard-wired in me a different and incompatible principle that is actually put to work every time I understand an English sentence. Nonetheless, this tension may never become apparent to me, since the information stored in the databases of subpersonal modules is insulated from my personal-level beliefs. Relatedly (and this is the second defining feature) beliefs are consciously accessible. There is (according to Stich) a distinctive conscious experience of being aware that *p* associated with believing that *p* (at least in the occurrent rather than dispositional sense of "believing"), but nothing like this occurs for sub-doxastic states. Stich proposes the doxastic/sub-doxastic distinction both as a corrective to the practices of psychologists and cognitive scientists and as a vindication of the practice of epistemologists of not taking into account the mechanisms that underlie belief formation in reflecting on how beliefs are (inferentially) justified.

Even if we grant that there is a sharp distinction to be drawn between propositional attitudes and sub-doxastic states there is a number of important questions about the relation between them. One such question arises because linguists and philosophers have appealed to conceptions of *tacit knowledge* to explain our understanding of syntax and semantics. We have a syntactic/semantic theory (either hard-wired or learnt) at the subpersonal level and our general capacity to understand language is explained in terms of our tacit or implicit knowledge of the principles of that theory. The best-known appeal to conceptions of tacit knowledge is in Chomskyan syntactic theory, but the first serious philosophical discussion came in **Gareth Evans**'s "Semantic Theory and Tacit Knowledge". Evans's principal interest is in what it is to know a theory of meaning, as opposed to a Chomskyan syntactic theory, but roughly similar theoretical issues arise in both cases. Evans starts from an objection that has been raised to the basic idea that appeals to tacit knowledge of a theory can be explanatory and informative. Philosophers such as Willard Quine have argued that no account of tacit knowledge can be anything other than a redescription of a speaker's competence (Quine 1972). The argument is that the meaning theorist has no way of identifying which of a number of extensionally equivalent theories of meaning a speaker can properly be described as tacitly knowing (where two theories are extensionally equivalent if they deliver the same set of theorems, even though they use different axioms). In responding to this objection, Evans begins from the thought that tacit knowledge of a theory of meaning involves having a disposition corresponding to each axiom of the theory (the disposition being a disposition to react to sentences in a certain way). These dispositions, he argues, should be interpreted in a full-blooded sense, as having categorical bases that causally explain their manifestations. Ascriptions of tacit knowledge do not simply redescribe regularities in the subject's verbal behavior, but also claim that there is a single state of the subject (typically, a sub-doxastic representational state) that causally explains why she behaves in this regular manner. This way of thinking about the causal basis of comprehension offers a way of distinguishing between extensionally equivalent meaning theories, and hence of responding to the skeptical challenge. It also explains how a hearer can understand a previously unencountered sentence S. The hearer understands S in virtue of a complex set of dispositions corresponding to the constituents of S and derived from exposure to those constituents in different sentences and different contexts.

IIIE Thinking and language

Debates about representation and cognitive architecture often turn on issues to do with the relation between thought and language. The language of thought hypothesis, which is the cornerstone of the picture of the representational mind (see the chapters in IC), is essentially the claim that thinking requires a language-like representational vehicle. Arguments for the language of thought hypothesis frequently turn on claims about the systematicity and compositionality of thought, claims that themselves have implications for how we think about propositional attitudes (see IIB above) and about the possibility of non-classical cognitive architectures (see IIIB above). The three papers in this section all tackle the relation between thought and language directly.

In "Language, Thought, and Communication" **Gilbert Harman** contrasts two views about how we use natural language. Each view rests upon a very different conception of the relation between language and thought. According to the view that language is used primarily in thought, the majority of thinking (if not most thinking) is carried out in some natural language. Propositional attitudes, although they are not attitudes *to* natural language sentences, are best seen as attitudes *involving* natural language sentences. When we communicate we do so using the same language that we use in thought. This means that linguistic understanding does not pose any major theoretical or practical problems. The words we utter when we communicate a thought are the same words that we use in thinking that thought in the first place. As Harman puts it, our translation scheme is the identity relation. According to the communicative conception of language, in contrast, language is fundamentally a tool for communicating thoughts, and thought needs to be analyzed completely independently of language in such a way that we can use our account of thought to explain the meanings of natural language sentences. The communicative conception of language is a natural companion to the language of thought hypothesis. In this view, communication involves the speaker encoding a Mentalese thought in a natural language sentence, which is then decoded by the hearer back into Mentalese.

Harman discusses a number of different arguments put forward in support of the communicative conception. Some of these arguments derive from the claim that theories of meaning must be compositional (i.e. they must explain how the meanings of sentences are derived in a rule-governed way from the meanings of their constituent words). Others derive from linguistic phenomena such as ambiguity and synonymy. It might be argued, for example, that we can only identify and disambiguate ambiguous sentences by assigning different Mentalese meanings to them. Conversely, we can only recognize that two expressions are synonymous by assigning the same Mentalese sentence to them. Harman identifies weaknesses in all these arguments. Arguments from compositionality are flawed, he suggests, because they either presuppose the communicative conception of language or merely shift the problem from our understanding of natural languages to our understanding of Mentalese. He objects to arguments from ambiguity and synonymy on the grounds that people distinguish different understandings of ambiguous words not by assigning different "meanings" to them, but by using the expressions in different ways. In the case of synonymous expressions, what matters is that people use the expressions in the same way.

Peter Carruthers's "The Cognitive Functions of Language" is focused more directly on issues of cognitive architecture and representational format than Harman's paper, but he too begins with the basic distinction between the communicative conception of language and what he calls the cognitive conception. Carruthers distinguishes a number of different ways of formulating the cognitive conception, rejecting some and endorsing others. The formulations he rejects include the very general thesis that language is necessarily required for thought (which he takes to be incompatible with what is known about animal cognition) and the thesis, associated with Daniel Dennett among others, that language serves as a "Joycean machine" imposing a serial and compositionally structured cognitive architecture on what (in non-human animals and prelinguistic infants) is essentially a bundle of competing, specialized parallel distributed networks. Carruthers's own positive proposal needs to be seen against the background of the idea that the mind is essentially modular in organization. Unlike Fodor, however, Carruthers assumes a version of *central-process modularism*, allowing for modules (such as the putative social intelligence module) that operate on high-level conceptual inputs). Language is not required for modules to operate successfully, but it is required, Carruthers claims, for thinking that compares, evaluates, and coordinates the outputs of these modules. According to Carruthers, natural language is the medium of inter-modular communication.

Carruthers draws upon some of Chomsky's ideas about linguistic processing to flesh out this basic idea. Chomsky postulates a level at which linguistic items are represented that he calls the level of logical form (LF). These representations have no imagistic/phonological features, but they consist of natural language lexical items organized into syntactic structures. Carruthers's suggestion is that the language module (for Carruthers is committed to there being such a thing) constructs LF representations that draw upon and integrate the outputs of central-process modules. These thoughts can become conscious when they are built up into a fully fledged phonological representation (an "imaged sentence") that is consciously accessible to the thinker. Carruthers's account is, as he recognizes, a somewhat speculative empirical hypothesis about the representational format for certain types of subpersonal information-processing, but it is consistent with both a wide range of empirical data and a number of deep-rooted assumptions in contemporary cognitive science.

In "Language and Thinking about Thoughts", drawn from his book *Thinking without Words*, **José Luis Bermúdez** addresses the question (very relevant to the issues explored by Harman and Carruthers) of whether there are any types of thinking that are in principle unavailable to creatures lacking a public language. He begins by discussing some of the different ways in which Andy Clark has suggested that language can function as a cognitive tool, arguing that none of them marks a fundamental difference in type between linguistic and non-linguistic thinking. Nonetheless, Bermúdez claims that there are certain thoughts that are not available to non-linguistic creatures. These thoughts all involve thinking about thinking (what is often termed *metarepresentation*). Examples of these types of thinking include thinking about other people's mental states and the sort of higher-order reflection that one engages in when one assesses the plausibility of one's beliefs, or the suitability of one's aims and goals. Bermúdez argues that *intentional ascent* (i.e. the move from thinking thoughts to thinking *about* thoughts) requires *semantic ascent* (i.e. thinking about the sentences that express thoughts).

Bermúdez's argument turns on considerations of representational format. Suppose we distinguish first-order *target thoughts* from the higher-order thoughts that are directed at them. It is clear, he claims, that target thoughts must have a representational format (a *vehicle*) that will allow them to be the objects of higher-order thoughts. We can only think about thoughts if they are suitably represented. For the types of thinking that he is discussing (all of which typically involve direct, conscious reflection), it is plausible to think that the vehicles of target thoughts must be at the personal rather than the subpersonal level. This rules out sentences in the language of thought (and, for that matter, sentences in LF) and, Bermúdez argues, leaves only two possibilities. On the one hand, representation might be secured symbolically through the complex symbols of a natural language (complex symbols being required since what are being represented are thoughts about states of affairs). A thought would be represented, therefore, through its linguistic expression and would appear as a potential object of thought *qua* linguistic entity. On the other hand, representation might be secured in an analog manner, through some kind of pictorial model. Of the two, only natural language sentences, Bermúdez claims, can reveal the structure of a target thought in a way that allows the thinker to appreciate its inferential connections with other thoughts. The identity of a thought (what makes it the thought that it is) is a function of its structure, and hence that structure must be perspicuous in the vehicle of a target thought.

FURTHER READING

Useful collections/anthologies

Haugeland, J. (1997) *Mind Design 2*, Cambridge, MA: MIT Press.
Macdonald, C. and Macdonald, G. (eds) (1995a) *Philosophy of Psychology: Debates on Psychological Explanation*, Oxford: Blackwell.
—— (1995b) *Connectionism: Debates on Psychological Explanation*, Oxford: Blackwell.

IIIA   Cognition as computation

Crane, T. (2003) *The Mechanical Mind: A Philosophical Introduction to Minds, Machines and Mental Representation*, London. Routledge.
Kitcher, P. (1988) "Marr's computational theory of vision", *Philosophy of Science* 55: 1–24.
Pylyshyn, Z.W. (1980) "Cognition and computation: Issues in the foundations of cognitive science", *Behavioral & Brain Sciences* 3: 154–69.
Searle, J. (1980) "Minds, brains, and programs", *Behavioral and Brain Sciences* 1: 417–24. Reprinted in Haugeland (1997).
Van Gelder, T. (1995) "What might cognition be if not computation?", *Journal of Philosophy* 92: 345–81.

IIIB   Non-classical cognitive architecture

Churchland, P.M. (1998) "Conceptual similarity across sensory and neural diversity: The Fodor/Lepore challenge answered", *Journal of Philosophy* 95: 5–32.
Cummins, R. (1996) "Systematicity", *Journal of Philosophy* 93: 591–614.
Fodor, J.A., and Pylyshyn, Z. (1981) "Connectionism and cognitive architecture: A critical analysis", *Cognition* 28: 3–71. Reprinted in Macdonald and Macdonald (1995b).
Hadley, R. (1994) "Systematicity in connectionist language learning", *Mind and Language*, 9: 247–71.
Smolensky, P. (1988) "On the proper treatment of connectionism", *Behavioral and Brain Sciences* 11: 1–74. Reprinted in Macdonald and Macdonald (1995b).

IIIC   Conceptions of modularity

Carruthers, P. (2003) "Moderately massive modularity", in A. O'Hear (ed.), *Mind and Persons*, Cambridge: Cambridge University Press.
Carruthers, P. and Chamberlain, A. (eds) (2000) *Evolution and the Human Mind: Modularity, Language, and Meta-Cognition*, Cambridge: Cambridge University Press.

Karmiloff-Smith A. (1994) "Précis of *Beyond Modularity: A Developmental Perspective on Cognitive Science*". *Behavioral and Brain Sciences* 17: 693–706.

Segal, G. (1996) "The modularity of theory of mind", in P. Carruthers and P.K. Smith, *Theories of Theories of Mind*, Cambridge: Cambridge University Press.

Shannon, B. (1988) "Remarks on the modularity of mind", *British Journal for the Philosophy of Science* 39: 331–52.

IIID   Tacit knowledge

Davies, M. (1989) "Tacit knowledge and subdoxastic states", in A. George (ed.), *Reflections on Chomsky*, Oxford: Blackwell.

Dummett, M. (1993) "What do I know when I know a language?", in *The Seas of Language*, Oxford: Oxford University Press.

Peacocke, C. (1989) "When is a grammar psychologically real?", in A. George (ed.), *Reflections on Chomsky*, Oxford: Blackwell.

Quine, W.V. (1972) "Methodological reflections in current linguistic theory", in D. Davidson and G. Harman (eds), *Semantics of Natural Language*, Dordrecht: Reidel.

Searle, J. (1990) "Consciousness, explanatory inversion, and cognitive science", *Behavioral and Brain Sciences* 13: 585–96. Reprinted in Macdonald and Macdonald (1995a).

Wright, C. (1986) "Theories of meaning and speakers' knowledge", in *Realism, Meaning, and Truth*, Oxford: Blackwell.

IIIE   Thinking and language

Budd, M. (1989) *Wittgenstein's Philosophy of Psychology*, London: Routledge. Particularly Chs 5 and 6.

Clark, A. (1998) "Magic words: How language augments cognition", in P. Carruthers and J. Boucher (eds), *Language and Thought: Interdisciplinary Themes*, Cambridge: Cambridge University Press.

Davidson, D. (1975) "Thought and talk", in S. Guttenplan (ed.), *Mind and Language*, Oxford: Oxford University Press. Reprinted in D. Davidson, *Essays on Truth and Interpretation*, Oxford: Oxford University Press (1980).

Harman, G. (1970) "Language learning", *Nous* 4: 33–43. Reprinted in his *Reasoning, Meaning, and Mind*, Oxford. Oxford University Press (1999).

Peacocke, C. (1997) "Concepts without Words", in R. Heck (ed.), *Language, Thought, and Logic*, Oxford: Oxford University Press.

IIIA

COGNITION AS
COMPUTATION

18

D. Marr, "Vision"

Understanding complex information-processing systems

[. . .] Almost never can a complex system of any kind be understood as a simple extrapolation from the properties of its elementary components. Consider, for example, some gas in a bottle. A description of thermodynamic effects – temperature, pressure, density, and the relationships among these factors – is not formulated by using a large set of equations, one for each of the particles involved. Such effects are described at their own level, that of an enormous collection of particles, the effort is to show that in principle the microscopic and macroscopic descriptions are consistent with one another. If one hopes to achieve a full understanding of a system as complicated as a nervous system, a developing embryo, a set of metabolic pathways, a bottle of gas, or even a large computer program, then one must be prepared to contemplate different kinds of explanation at different levels of description that are linked, at least in principle, into a cohesive whole, even if linking the levels in complete detail is impractical. For the specific case of a system that solves an information-processing problem, there are in addition the twin strands of process and representation, and both these ideas need some discussion.

Representation and description

A *representation* is a formal system for making explicit certain entities or types of information, together with a specification of how the system does this. And I shall call the result of using a representation to describe a given entity a *description* of the entity in that representation (Marr and Nishihara 1978).

For example, the Arabic, Roman, and binary numeral systems are all formal systems for representing numbers. The Arabic representation consists of a string of symbols drawn from the set (0, 1, 2, 3, 4, 5, 6, 7, 8, 9), and the rule for constructing the description of a particular integer n is that one decomposes n into a sum of multiples of powers of 10 and unites these multiples into a string with the largest powers on the left and the smallest on the right. Thus, thirty-seven equals $3 \times 10^1 + 7 \times 10^0$, which becomes 37, the Arabic numeral system's description of the number. What this description makes explicit is the number's decomposition into powers of 10. The binary numeral system's description of the number thirty-seven is 100101, and this description makes explicit the number's decomposition into powers of 2. In the Roman numeral system, thirty-seven is represented as XXXVII.

This definition of a representation is quite general. For example, a representation for shape would be a formal scheme for describing some aspects of shape, together with rules that specify how the scheme is applied to any particular shape. A musical score provides a way of representing a symphony; the alphabet allows the construction of a written representation of words; and so forth. The phrase "formal scheme" is critical to the definition, but the reader should not be frightened by it. The reason is simply that we are dealing with information-processing machines, and the way such machines work is by using symbols to stand for things – to represent things, in our terminology. To say that something is a formal scheme means only that it is a set of symbols with rules for putting them together – no more and no less.

A representation, therefore, is not a foreign idea at all – we all use representations all the time. However, the notion that one can capture some aspect of reality by making a description of it using a symbol and that to do so can be useful seems to me a fascinating and powerful idea. But even the simple examples we have discussed introduce some rather general and important issues that arise whenever one chooses to use one particular representation. For example, if one chooses the Arabic numeral representation, it is easy to discover whether a number is a power of 10 but difficult to discover whether it is a power of 2. If one chooses the binary representation, the situation is reversed. Thus, there is a trade-off; any particular representation makes certain information explicit at the expense of information that is pushed into the background and may be quite hard to recover.

This issue is important, because how information is represented can greatly affect how easy it is to do different things with it. This is evident even from our numbers example: It is easy to add, to subtract, and even to multiply if the Arabic or binary representations are used, but it is not at all easy to do these things – especially multiplication – with Roman numerals. This is a key reason why the Roman culture failed to develop mathematics in the way the earlier Arabic cultures had.

An analogous problem faces computer engineers today. Electronic technology is much more suited to a binary number system than to the conventional base 10 system, yet humans supply their data and require the results in base 10. The design decision facing the engineer, therefore, is: Should one pay the cost of conversion into base 2, carry out the arithmetic in a binary representation, and then convert back into decimal numbers on output; or should one sacrifice efficiency of circuitry to carry out operations directly in a decimal representation entation? On the whole, business computers and pocket calculators take the second approach, and general purpose computers take the first. But even though one is not restricted to using just one representation system for a given type of information, the choice of which to use is important and cannot be taken lightly. It determines what information is made explicit and hence what is pushed further into the background, and it has a far-reaching effect on the ease and difficulty with which operations may subsequently be carried out on that information.

Process

The term process is very broad. For example, addition is a process, and so is taking a Fourier transform. But so is making a cup of tea, or going shopping. For the purposes of this book, I want to restrict our attention to the meanings associated with machines that are carrying out information-processing tasks. So let us examine in depth the notions behind one simple such device, a cash register at the checkout counter of a supermarket.

There are several levels at which one needs to understand such a device, and it is perhaps most useful to think in terms of three of them. The most abstract is the level of *what* the device does and *why*. What it does is arithmetic, so our first task is to master the theory of addition. Addition is a mapping, usually denoted by +, from pairs of numbers into single numbers, for example, + maps the pair (3, 4) to 7, and I shall write this in the form $(3 + 4) \rightarrow 7$. Addition has a number of abstract properties, however. It is commutative: both (3 + 4) and (4 + 3) are equal to 7; and associative: the sum of 3 + (4 + 5) is the same as the sum of (3 + 4) + 5. Then there is the unique distinguished element, zero, the adding of which has no effect: $(4 + 0) \rightarrow 4$. Also, for every number there is a unique "inverse," written (–4) in the case of 4, which when added to the number gives zero: $[4 + (–4)] \rightarrow 0$.

Notice that these properties are part of the fundamental *theory* of addition. They are true no matter how the numbers are written – whether in binary, Arabic, or Roman representation – and no matter how the addition is executed. Thus part of this first level is something that might be characterized as *what* is being computed.

The other half of this level of explanation has to do with the question of why the cash register performs addition and not for instance multiplication when combining the prices of the purchased items to arrive at a final bill. The reason is that the rules we intuitively feel to be appropriate for combining the individual prices in fact define the mathematical operation of addition. These can be formulated as *constraints* in the following way:

1 if you buy nothing, it should cost you nothing; and buying nothing and something should cost the same as buying just the something. (The rules for zero.)
2 The order in which goods are presented to the cashier should not affect the total. (Commutativity.)

3   Arranging the goods into two piles and paying for each pile separately should not affect the total amount you pay. (Associativity: the basic operation for combining prices.)
4   If you buy an item and then return it for a refund, your total expenditure should be zero. (Inverses.)

It is a mathematical theorem that these conditions define the operation of addition, which is therefore the appropriate computation to use.

This whole argument is what I call the *computational theory* of the cash register. Its important features are (1) that it contains separate arguments about what is computed and why and (2) that the resulting operation is defined uniquely by the constraints it has to satisfy. In the theory of visual processes, the underlying task is to reliably derive properties of the world from images of it; the business of isolating constraints that are both powerful enough to allow a process to be defined and generally true of the world is a central theme of our inquiry.

In order that a process shall actually run, however, one has to realize it in some way and therefore choose a representation for the entities that the process manipulates. The second level of the analysis of a process, therefore, involves choosing two things: (1) a *representation* for the input and for the output of the process and (2) an *algorithm* by which the transformation may actually be accomplished. For addition, of course, the input and output representations can both be the same, because they both consist of numbers. However this is not true in general. In the case of a Fourier transform, for example, the input representation may be the time domain, and the output, the frequency domain. If the first of our levels specifies what and why this second level specifies *how*. For addition, we might choose Arabic numerals for the representations, and for the algorithm we could follow the usual rules about adding the least significant digits first and "carrying" if the sum exceeds 9. Cash registers, whether mechanical or electronic, usually use this type of representation and algorithm.

There are three important points here. First, there is usually a wide choice of representation. Second, the choice of algorithm often depends rather critically on the particular representation that is employed. And third, even for a given fixed representation, there are often several possible algorithms for carrying out the same process. Which one is chosen will usually depend on any particularly desirable or undesirable characteristics that the algorithms may have; for example, one algorithm may be much more efficient than another, or another may be slightly less efficient but more robust (that is, less sensitive to slight inaccuracies in the data on which it must run). Or again, one algorithm may be parallel, and another, serial. The choice, then, may depend on the type of hardware or machinery in which the algorithm is to be embodied physically.

This brings us to the third level, that of the device in which the process is to be realized physically. The important point here is that, once again, the

388

same algorithm may be implemented in quite different technologies. The child who methodically adds two numbers from right to left, carrying a digit when necessary, may be using the same algorithm that is implemented by the wires and transistors of the cash register in the neighborhood supermarket, but the physical realization of the algorithm is quite different in these two cases. Another example: Many people have written computer programs to play tic-tac-toe, and there is a more or less standard algorithm that cannot lose. This algorithm has in fact been implemented by W.D. Hillis and B. Silverman in a quite different technology, in a computer made out of Tinkertoys, a children's wooden building set. The whole monstrously ungainly engine, which actually works, currently resides in a museum at the University of Missouri in St. Louis.

Some styles of algorithm will suit some physical substrates better than others. For example, in conventional digital computers, the number of connections is comparable to the number of gates, while in a brain the number of connections is much larger ($\times 10^4$) than the number of nerve cells. The underlying reason is that wires are rather cheap in biological architecture, because they can grow individually and in three dimensions. In conventional technology, wire laying is more or less restricted to two dimensions, which quite severely restricts the scope for using parallel techniques and algorithms; the same operations are often better carried out serially.

The three levels

We can summarize our discussion in something like the manner shown in table 18.1, which illustrates the different levels at which an information-processing device must be understood before one can be said to have understood it completely. At one extreme, the top level, is the abstract computational theory of the device, in which the performance of the device is characterized as a mapping from one kind of information to another, the abstract properties of this mapping are defined precisely, and its appropriateness and adequacy for the task at hand are demonstrated. In the center is the choice of representation

Table 18.1 The three levels at which any machine carrying out an information-processing task must be understood

Computational theory	Representation and algorithm	Hardware implementation
What is the goal of the computation, why is it appropriate, and what is the logic of the strategy by which it can be carried out?	How can this computational theory be implemented? In particular, what is the representation for the input and output, and what is the algorithm for the transformation?	How can the representation and algorithm be realized physically?

for the input and output and the algorithm to be used to transform one into the other. And at the other extreme are the details of how the algorithm and representation are realized physically – the detailed computer architecture, so to speak. These three levels are coupled, but only loosely. The choice of an algorithm is influenced for example, by what it has to do and by the hardware in which it must run. But there is a wide choice available at each level, and the explication of each level involves issues that are rather independent of the other two.

Each of the three levels of description will have its place in the eventual understanding of perceptual information processing, and of course they are logically and causally related. But an important point to note is that since the three levels are only rather loosely related, some phenomena may be explained at only one or two of them. This means, for example, that a correct explanation of some psychophysical observation must be formulated at the appropriate level. In attempts to relate psychophysical problems to physiology, too often there is conflation about the level at which problems should be addressed. For instance, some are related mainly to the physical mechanisms of vision – such as afterimages (for example, the one you see after staring at a light bulb) or such as the fact that any color can be matched by a suitable mixture of the three primaries (a consequence principally of the fact that we humans have three types of cones). On the other hand, the ambiguity of the Necker cube (figure 18.1) seems to demand a different kind of explanation. To be sure, part of the explanation of its perceptual reversal must have to do with a bistable neural network (that is, one with two distinct stable states) somewhere inside the brain, but few would feel satisfied by an account that failed to mention the existence of two different but perfectly plausible three-dimensional interpretations of this two-dimensional image.

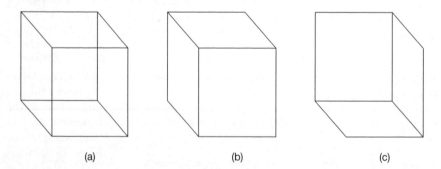

(a) (b) (c)

Figure 18.1 The so-called Necker illusion, named after L.A. Necker, the Swiss naturalist who developed it in 1832. The essence of the matter is that the two-dimensional representation (a) has collapsed the depth out of a cube and that a certain aspect of human vision is to recover this missing third dimension. The depth of the cube can indeed be perceived, but two interpretations are possible, (b) and (c). A person's perception characteristically flips from one to the other.

For some phenomena, the type of explanation required is fairly obvious. Neuroanatomy, for example, is clearly tied principally to the third level, the physical realization of the computation. The same holds for synaptic mechanisms, action potentials, inhibitory interactions, and so forth. Neurophysiology, too, is related mostly to this level, but it can also help us to understand the type of representations being used, particularly if one accepts something along the lines of Barlow's views that I quoted earlier.[1] But one has to exercise extreme caution in making inferences from neurophysiological findings about the algorithms and representations being used, particularly until one has a clear idea about what information needs to be represented and what processes need to be implemented.

Psychophysics, on the other hand, is related more directly to the level of algorithm and representation. Different algorithms tend to fail in radically different ways as they are pushed to the limits of their performance or are deprived of critical information. As we shall see, primarily psychophysical evidence proved to Poggio and myself that our first stereo-matching algorithm (Marr and Poggio 1976) was not the one that is used by the brain, and the best evidence that our second algorithm (Marr and Poggio 1979) is roughly the one that is used also comes from psychophysics. Of course, the underlying computational theory remained the same in both cases, only the algorithms were different.

Psychophysics can also help to determine the nature of a representation. The work of Roger Shepard (1975), Eleanor Rosch (1978), or Elizabeth Warrington (1975) provides some interesting hints in this direction. More specifically, Stevens (1979) argued from psychophysical experiments that surface orientation is represented by the coordinates of slant and tilt, rather than (for example) the more traditional (p, q) of gradient space. He also deduced from the uniformity of the size of errors made by subjects judging surface orientation over a wide range of orientations that the representational quantities used for slant and tilt are pure angles and not, for example, their cosines, sines, or tangents.

More generally, if the idea that different phenomena need to be explained at different levels is kept clearly in mind, it often helps in the assessment of the validity of the different kinds of objections that are raised from time to time. For example, one favorite is that the brain is quite different from a computer because one is parallel and the other serial. The answer to this, of course, is that the distinction between serial and parallel is a distinction at the level of algorithm; it is not fundamental at all – anything programmed in parallel can be rewritten serially (though not necessarily vice versa). The distinction, therefore, provides no grounds for arguing that the brain operates so differently from a computer that a computer could not be programmed to perform the same tasks.

Importance of computational theory

Although algorithms and mechanisms are empirically more accessible, it is the top level, the level of computational theory, which is critically important from an information-processing point of view. The reason for this is that the nature of the computations that underlie perception depends more upon the computational problems that have to be solved than upon the particular hardware in which their solutions are implemented. To phrase the matter another way, an algorithm is likely to be understood more readily by understanding the nature of the problem being solved than by examining the mechanism (and the hardware) in which it is embodied.

In a similar vein, trying to understand perception by studying only neurons is like trying to understand bird flight by studying only feathers: It just cannot be done. In order to understand bird flight, we have to understand aerodynamics; only then do the structure of feathers and the different shapes of birds' wings make sense. More to the point, as we shall see, we cannot understand why retinal ganglion cells and lateral geniculate neurons have the receptive fields they do just by studying their anatomy and physiology. We can understand how these cells and neurons behave as they do by studying their wiring and interactions, but in order to understand *why* the receptive fields are as they are – why they are circularly symmetrical and why their excitatory and inhibitory regions have characteristic shapes and distributions – we have to know a little of the theory of differential operators, band-pass channels, and the mathematics of the uncertainty principle.

Perhaps it is not surprising that the very specialized empirical disciplines of the neurosciences failed to appreciate fully the absence of computational theory, but it is surprising that this level of approach did not play a more forceful role in the early development of artificial intelligence. For far too long, a heuristic program for carrying out some task was held to be a theory of that task, and the distinction between what a program did and how it did it was not taken seriously. As a result, (1) a style of explanation evolved that invoked the use of special mechanisms to solve particular problems, (2) particular data structures, such as the lists of attribute value pairs called property lists in the LISP programming language, were held to amount to theories of the representation of knowledge, and (3) there was frequently no way to determine whether a program would deal with a particular case other than by running the program.

Failure to recognize this theoretical distinction between *what* and *how* also greatly hampered communication between the fields of artificial intelligence and linguistics. Chomsky's (1965) theory of transformational grammar is a true computational theory in the sense defined earlier. It is concerned solely with specifying what the syntactic decomposition of an English sentence should be, and not at all with how that decomposition should be achieved. Chomsky himself was very clear about this – it is roughly his distinction between competence and performance, though his idea of performance did include other factors, like stopping in midutterance – but the fact that his theory was defined by transformations, which look like computations, seems to have confused many people. Winograd (1972), for example, felt able to criticize Chomsky's theory on the grounds that it cannot be inverted and so cannot be made to run on a computer; I had heard reflections of the same argument made by Chomsky's colleagues in linguistics as they turn their attention to how grammatical structure might actually be computed from a real English sentence.

The explanation is simply that finding algorithms by which Chomsky's theory may be implemented is a completely different endeavor from formulating the theory itself. In our terms, it is a study at a different level, and both tasks have to be done. This point was appreciated by Marcus (1980), who was concerned precisely with how Chomsky's theory can be realized and with the kinds of constraints on the power of the human grammatical processor that might give rise to the structural constraints in syntax that Chomsky found. It even appears that the emerging "trace" theory of grammar (Chomsky and Lasnik 1977) may provide a way of synthesizing the two approaches – showing that, for example, some of the rather ad hoc restrictions that form part of the computational theory may be consequences of weaknesses in the computational power that is available for implementing syntactical decoding.

The approach of J.J. Gibson

In perception, perhaps the nearest anyone came to the level of computational theory was Gibson (1966). However, although some aspects of his thinking were on the right lines, he did not understand properly what information processing was, which led him to seriously underestimate the complexity of the information-processing problems involved in vision and the consequent subtlety that is necessary in approaching them.

Gibson's important contribution was to take the debate away from the philosophical considerations of sense-data and the affective qualities of sensation and to note instead that the important thing about the senses is that they are channels for perception of the real world outside or, in the case of vision, of the visible surfaces. He therefore asked the critically important question, How does one obtain constant perceptions in everyday life on the basis of continually changing sensations? This is exactly the right question, showing that Gibson correctly regarded the problem of perception as that of recovering from sensory information "valid" properties of the external world. His problem was that he had a much oversimplified view of how this should be done. His approach led him to consider higher-order variables – stimulus energy, ratios, proportions, and so on – as "invariants" of the movement of an observer and of changes in stimulation intensity.

"These invariants," he wrote, "correspond to permanent properties of the environment. They constitute, therefore, information about the permanent environment." This led him to a view in which the function of the brain was to "detect invariants" despite changes in "sensations" of light, pressure, or loudness of sound. Thus, he says that the "function of the brain, when looped with its perceptual organs, is not to decode signals, nor to interpret messages, nor to accept images, nor to *organize* the sensory input or to *process* the data,

393

in modern terminology. It is to seek and extract information about the environment from the flowing array of ambient energy," and he thought of the nervous system as in some way "resonating" to these invariants. He then embarked on a broad study of animals in their environments, looking for invariants to which they might resonate. This was the basic idea behind the notion of ecological optics (Gibson 1966: 1979).

Although one can criticize certain shortcomings in the quality of Gibson's analysis, its major and, in my view, fatal shortcoming lies at a deeper level and results from a failure to realize two things. First, the detection of physical invariants, like image surfaces, is exactly and precisely an information-processing problem, in modern terminology. And second, he vastly underrated the sheer difficulty of such detection. In discussing the recovery of three-dimensional information from the movement of an observer, he says that "in motion, perspective information alone can be used" (Gibson 1966: 202). And perhaps the key to Gibson is the following:

The detection of non-change when an object moves in the world is not as difficult as it might appear. It is only made to seem difficult when we assume that the perception of constant dimensions of the object must depend on the correcting of sensations of inconstant form and size. The information for the constant dimension of an object is normally carried by invariant relations in an optic array Rigidity is *specified*. (emphasis added)

Yes, to be sure, but *how*? Detecting physical invariants is just as difficult as Gibson feared, but nevertheless we can do it. And the only way to understand how is to treat it as an information-processing problem.

The underlying point is that visual information processing is actually very complicated, and Gibson was not the only thinker who was misled by the apparent simplicity of the act of seeing. The whole tradition of philosophical inquiry into the nature of perception seems not to have taken seriously enough the complexity of the information processing involved. For example, Austin's (1962) *Sense and Sensibilia* entertainingly demolishes the argument, apparently favored by earlier philosophers, that since we are sometimes deluded by illusions (for example, a straight stick appears bent if it is partly submerged in water), we see sense-data rather than material things. The answer is simply that usually our perceptual processing does run correctly (it delivers a true description of what is there), but although evolution has seen to it that our processing allows for many changes (like inconstant illumination), the perturbation due to the refraction of light by water is not one of them. And incidentally, although the example of the bent stick has been discussed since Aristotle, I have seen no philosophical inquiry into the nature of the perceptions of, for instance, a heron, which is a bird that feeds by pecking up fish first seen from above the water surface. For such birds the visual correction might be present.

Anyway, my main point here is another one. Austin (1962) spends much time on the idea that perception tells one about real properties of the external world, and one thing he considers is "real shape" (p. 66), a notion which had cropped up earlier in his discussion of a coin that "looked elliptical" from some points of view. Even so,

it had a real shape which remained unchanged. But coins in fact are rather special cases. For one thing their outlines are well defined and very highly stable, and for another they have a known and a nameable shape. But there are plenty of things of which this is not true. What is the real shape of a cloud? . . . or of a cat? Does its real shape change whenever it moves? If not, in what posture is its real shape on display? Furthermore, is its real shape such as to be fairly smooth outlines, or must it be finely enough serrated to take account of each hair? *It is pretty obvious that there is no answer to these questions – no rules according to which, no procedure by which, answers are to be determined.* (emphasis added) (p. 67)

But there *are* answers to these questions. There are ways of describing the shape of a cat to an arbitrary level of precision, and there are rules and procedures for arriving at such descriptions. That is exactly what vision is about, and precisely what makes it complicated.

A representational framework for vision

Vision is a process that produces from images of the external world a description that is useful to the viewer and not cluttered with irrelevant information (Marr 1976; Marr and Nishihara 1978). We have already seen that a process may be thought of as a mapping from one representation to another, and in the case of human vision, the initial representation is in no doubt – it consists of arrays of image intensity values as detected by the photoreceptors in the retina.

It is quite proper to think of an image as a representation; the items that are made explicit are the image intensity values at each point in the array, which we can conveniently denote by $I(x,y)$ at coordinate (x,y). In order to simplify our discussion, we shall neglect for the moment the fact that there are several different types of receptor, and imagine instead that there is just one, so that the image is black-and-white. Each value of $I(x,y)$ thus specifies a particular level of gray; we shall refer to each detector as a picture element or *pixel* and to the whole array I as an image.

But what of the output of the process of vision? We have already agreed that it must consist of a useful description of the world, but that requirement is rather nebulous. Can we not do better? Well, it is perfectly true that, unlike the input, the result of vision is much harder to discern, let alone specify precisely, and an important aspect of this new approach is that it makes quite concrete proposals about what that end is. But before we begin that discussion, let us step back a little and spend a little time formulating the more general issues that are raised by these questions.

The purpose of vision

The usefulness of a representation depends upon how well suited it is to the purpose for which it is used. A pigeon uses vision to help it navigate, fly, and seek out food. Many types of jumping spider use vision to tell the difference between a potential meal and a potential mate. One type, for example, has a curious retina formed of two diagonal strips arranged in a V. If it detects a red V on the back of an object lying in front of it, the spider has found a mate. Otherwise, maybe a meal. The frog detects bugs with its retina; and the rabbit retina is full of special gadgets, including what is apparently a hawk detector, since it responds well to the pattern made by a preying hawk hovering overhead. Human vision, on the other hand, seems to be very much more general, although it clearly contains a variety of special-purpose mechanisms that can, for example, direct the eye toward an unexpected movement in the visual field or cause one to blink or otherwise avoid something that approaches one's head too quickly.

Vision, in short, is used in such a bewildering variety of ways that the visual systems of different animals must differ significantly from one another. Can the type of formulation that I have been advocating, in terms of representations and processes, possibly prove adequate for them all? I think so. The general point here is that because vision is used by different animals for such a wide variety of purposes, it is inconceivable that all seeing animals use the same representations; each can confidently be expected to use one or more representations that are nicely tailored to the owner's purposes.

As an example, let us consider briefly a primitive but highly efficient visual system that has the added virtue of being well understood. Werner Reichardt's group in Tübingen has spent the last 14 years patiently unraveling the visual flight-control system of the housefly, and in a famous collaboration, Reichardt and Tomaso Poggio have gone far toward solving the problem (Reichardt and Poggio 1976, 1979; Poggio and Reichardt 1976). Roughly speaking, the fly's visual apparatus controls its flight through a collection of about five independent, rigidly inflexible, very fast responding systems (the time from visual stimulus to change of torque is only 21 ms). For example, one of these systems is the landing system; if the visual field "explodes" fast enough (because a surface looms nearby), the fly automatically "lands" toward its center. If this center is above the fly, the fly automatically inverts to land upside down. When the feet touch, power to the wings is cut off. Conversely, to take off, the fly jumps; when the feet no longer touch the ground, power is restored to the wings, and the insect flies again.

In-flight control is achieved by independent systems controlling the fly's vertical velocity (through control of the lift generated by the wings) and horizontal direction (determined by the torque produced by the asymmetry of the horizontal thrust from the left and right wings). The visual input to the horizontal control system, for example, is completely described by the two terms

$$r(\psi)\dot{\psi} + D(\psi)$$

where r and D have the form illustrated in figure 18.2. This input describes how the fly tracks an object that is present at angle ψ in the visual field and has angular velocity $\dot{\psi}$. This system is triggered to track objects of a certain angular dimension in the visual field, and the motor strategy is such that if the visible object was another fly a few inches away, then it would be intercepted successfully. If the target was an elephant 100 yd away, interception would fail because the fly's built-in parameters are for another fly nearby, not an elephant far away.

Thus, fly vision delivers a representation in which at least these three things are specified: (1) whether the visual field is looming sufficiently fast that the fly should contemplate landing; (2) whether there is a small patch – it could be a black speck or, it turns out, a textured figure in front of a textured ground – having some kind of motion relative to its background; and if there is such a patch, (3) ψ and $\dot{\psi}$ for this patch are delivered to the motor system. And that

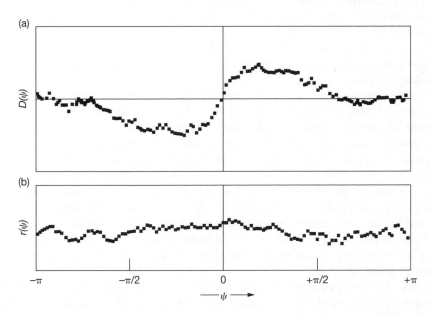

Figure 18.2 The horizontal component of the visual input R to the fly's flight system is described by the formula $R = D(\psi) - r(\psi)\dot{\psi}$, where ψ is the direction of the stimulus and $\dot{\psi}$ is its angular velocity in the fly's visual field. $D(\psi)$ is an odd function, as shown in (a), which has the effect of keeping the target centered in the fly's visual field; $r(\psi)$ is essentially constant as shown in (b).

is probably about 60% of fly vision. In particular, it is extremely unlikely that the fly has any explicit representation of the visual world around him – no true conception of a surface, for example, but just a few triggers and some specifically fly-centered parameters like ψ and $\dot{\psi}$.

It is clear that human vision is much more complex than this, although it may well incorporate subsystems not unlike the fly's to help with specific and rather low-level tasks like the control of pursuit eye movements. Nevertheless, as Poggio and Reichardt have shown, even these simple systems can be understood in the same sort of way, as information-processing tasks. And one of the fascinating aspects of their work is how they have managed not only to formulate the differential equations that accurately describe the visual control system of the fly but also to express these equations, using the Volterra series expansion, in a way that gives direct information about the minimum possible complexity of connections of the underlying neuronal networks.

Advanced vision

Visual systems like the fly's serve adequately and with speed and precision the needs of their owners, but they are not very complicated; very little objective information about the world is obtained. The information is all very much subjective – the angular size of the stimulus as the fly sees it rather than the objective size of the object out there, the angle that the object has in the fly's visual field rather than its position relative to the fly or to some external reference, and the object's angular velocity, again in the fly's visual field, rather than any assessment of its true velocity relative to the fly or to some stationary reference point.

One reason for this simplicity must be that these facts provide the fly with sufficient information for it to survive. Of course, the information is not optimal and from time to time the fly will fritter away its energy chasing a falling leaf a medium distance away or an elephant a long way away as a direct consequence of the inadequacies of its perceptual system. But this apparently does not matter very much – the fly has sufficient excess energy for it to be able to absorb these extra costs. Another reason is certainly that translating these rather subjective measurements into more objective qualities involves much more computation. How, then, should one think about more advanced visual systems – human vision, for example. What are the issues? What kind of information is vision really delivering, and what are the representational issues involved?

My approach to these problems was very much influenced by the fascinating accounts of clinical neurology, such as Critchley (1953) and Warrington and Taylor (1973). Particularly important was a lecture that Elizabeth Warrington gave at MIT in October 1973, in which she described the capacities and limitations of patients who had suffered left or right parietal lesions. For me, the most important thing that she did was to draw a distinction between the two classes of patient (see Warrington and Taylor 1978). For those with lesions on the right side, recognition of a common object was possible *provided* that the patient's view of it was in some sense straightforward. She used the words *conventional* and *unconventional* – a water pail or a clarinet seen from the side gave "conventional" views but seen end-on gave "unconventional" views. If these patients recognized the object at all, they knew its name and its semantics – that is, its use and purpose, how big it was, how much it weighed, what it was made of, and so forth. If their view was unconventional – a pail seen from above, for example – not only would the patients fail to recognize it, but they would vehemently deny that it *could* be a view of a pail. Patients with left parietal lesions behaved completely differently. Often these patients had no language, so they were unable to name the viewed object or state its purpose and semantics. But they could convey that they correctly perceived its geometry – that is, its shape – even from the unconventional view.

Warrington's talk suggested two things. First, the representation of the shape of an object is stored in a different place and is therefore a quite different kind of thing from the representation of its use and purpose. And second, vision alone can deliver an internal description of the shape of a viewed object, even when the object was not recognized in the conventional sense of understanding its use and purpose.

This was an important moment for me for two reasons. The general trend in the computer vision community was to believe that recognition was so difficult that it required every possible kind of information. The results of this point of view duly appeared a few years later in programs like Freuder's (1974) and Tenenbaum and Barrow's (1976). In the latter program, knowledge about offices – for example, that desks have telephones on them and that telephones are black – was used to help "segment" out a black blob halfway up an image and "recognize" it as a telephone. Freuder's program used a similar approach to "segment" and "recognize" a hammer in a scene. Clearly, we do use such knowledge in real life; I once saw a brown blob quivering amongst the lettuce in my garden and correctly identified it as a rabbit, even though the visual information alone was inadequate. And yet here was this young woman calmly telling us not only that her patients could convey to her that they had grasped the shapes of things that she had shown them, even though they could not name the objects or say how they were used, but also that they could happily continue to do so even if she made the task extremely difficult visually by showing them peculiar views or by illuminating the objects in peculiar ways. It seemed clear that the intuitions of the computer vision people were completely wrong and that even in difficult circumstances shapes could be determined by vision alone.

The second important thing, I thought, was that Elizabeth Warrington had put her finger on what was somehow the quintessential fact of human vision – that it tells about shape and space and spatial arrangement. Here lay a way to formulate its purpose – building a description of the shapes and positions of things from images. Of course, that is by no means all that vision can do; it also tells about the illumination and about the reflectances of the surfaces that make the shapes – their brightnesses and colors and visual textures – and about their motion. But these things seemed secondary; they could be hung off a theory in which the main job of vision was to derive a representation of shape.

To the desirable via the possible

Finally, one has to come to terms with cold reality. Desirable as it may be to have vision deliver a completely invariant shape description from an image (whatever that may mean in detail), it is almost certainly impossible in only one step. We can only do what is possible and proceed from there toward what is desirable. Thus we arrived at the idea of a sequence of representations, starting with descriptions that could be obtained straight from an image but that are carefully designed to facilitate the subsequent recovery of gradually more objective, physical properties about an object's shape. The main stepping stone toward this goal is describing the geometry of the visible surfaces, since the information encoded in images, for example by stereopsis, shading, texture, contours, or visual motion, is due to a shape's local surface properties. The objective of many early visual computations is to extract this information.

However, this description of the visible surfaces turns out to be unsuitable for recognition tasks. There are several reasons why, perhaps the most prominent being that like all early visual processes, it depends critically on the vantage point. The final step therefore consists of transforming the viewer-centered surface description into a representation of the three-dimensional shape and spatial arrangement of an object that does not depend upon the direction from which the object is being viewed. This final description is object centered rather than viewer centered.

The overall framework described here therefore divides the derivation of shape information from images into three representational stages (table 18.2): (1) the representation of properties of the two-dimensional image, such as intensity changes and local two-dimensional geometry; (2) the representation of properties of the visible surfaces in a viewer-centered coordinate system, such as surface orientation, distance from the viewer, and discontinuities in these quantities; surface reflectance; and some coarse description of the prevailing illumination; and (3) an object-centered representation of the three-dimensional structure and of the organization of the viewed shape, together with some description of its surface properties.

This framework is summarized in table 18.2.

Synopsis

Our survey of this new, computational approach to vision is now complete. Although there are many gaps in the account, I hope that it is solid enough to establish a firm point of view about the subject and to prompt the reader

Table 18.2 Representational framework for deriving shape information from images

Name	Purpose	Primitives
Image(s)	Represents intensity	Intensity value at each point in the image
Primal sketch	Makes explicit important information about the two-dimensional image, primarily the intensity changes there and their geometrical distribution and organization	Zero-crossings Blobs Terminations and discontinuities Edge segments Virtual lines Groups Curvilinear organization
2½-D sketch	Makes explicit the orientation and rough depth of the visible surfaces, and contours of discontinuities in these quantities in a viewer-centered coordinate frame	Local surface orientation (the "needles" primitives) Distance from viewer Discontinuities in depth Discontinuities in surface orientation
3-D model representation	Describes shapes and their spatial organization in an object-centered coordinate frame, using a modular hierarchical representation that includes volumetric primitives (i.e., primitives that represent the volume of space that a shape occupies) as well as surface primitives	3-D models arranged hierarchically, each one based on a spatial configuration of a few sticks or axes, to which volumetric or surface shape primitives are attached

to begin to judge its value. In this brief chapter, I shall take a very broad view of the whole approach, inquiring into its most important general features and how they relate to one another, and trying to say something about the style of research that this approach implies. It is convenient to divide the discussion into four main points.

The first point is one that we have met throughout the account – the notion of different levels of explanation. The central tenet of the approach is that to understand what vision is and how it works, an understanding at only one level is insufficient. It is not enough to be able to describe the responses of single cells, nor is it enough to be able to predict locally the results of psychophysical experiments. Nor is it enough even to be able to write computer programs that perform approximately in the desired way. One has to do all these things at once and also be very aware of the additional level of explanation that I have called the level of computational theory. The recognition of the existence and importance of this level is one of the most important aspects of this approach. Having recognized this, one can formulate the three levels of explanation explicitly (computational theory, algorithm, and implementation), and it then becomes clear how these different levels are related to the different types of empirical observation and theoretical analysis that can be conducted. I have laid particular stress on the level of computational theory, not because I regard it as inherently more important than the other two levels – the real power of the approach lies in the integration of all three levels of attack – but because it is a level of explanation that has not previously been recognized and acted upon. It is therefore probably one of the most difficult ideas for newcomers to the field to grasp, and for this reason alone its importance should not be understated. [. . .]

The second main point is that by taking an information-processing point of view we have been able to formulate a rather clear overall framework for the process of vision. This framework is based on the idea that the critical issues in vision revolve around the nature of the representations used – that is, the particular characteristics of the world that are made explicit during vision – and the nature of the processes that recover these characteristics, create and maintain the representations, and eventually read them. By analyzing the spatial aspects of the problem of vision, we arrived at an overall framework for visual information processing that hinges on three principal representations: (1) the primal sketch, which is concerned with making explicit properties of the two-dimensional image, ranging from the amount and disposition of the intensity changes there to primitive representations of the local image geometry, and including at the more sophisticated end a hierarchical description of any higher-order structure present in the underlying reflectance distributions; (2) the 2½-D sketch, which is a viewer-centered representation of the depth and orientation of the visible surfaces and includes contours of discontinuities in these quantities; and (3) the 3-D model representation, whose important features are that its coordinate system is object centered, that it includes volumetric primitives (which make explicit the organization of the space occupied by an object and not just its visible surfaces), and that primitives of various size are included, arranged in a modular, hierarchical organization.

The third main point concerns the study of processes for recovering the various aspects of the physical characteristics of a scene from images of it. The critical act in formulating computational theories for such processes is the discovery of valid constraints on the way the world behaves that provide sufficient additional information to allow recovery of the desired characteristic. The power of this type of analysis resides in the fact that the discovery of valid, sufficiently universal constraints leads to conclusions about vision that have the same permanence as conclusions in other branches of science.

Furthermore, once a computational theory for a process has been formulated, algorithms for implementing it may be designed, and their performance compared with that of the human visual processor. This allows two kinds of results. First, if performance is essentially identical, we have good evidence that the constraints of the underlying computational theory are valid and may be implicit in the human processor; second, if a process matches human performance, it is probably sufficiently powerful to form part of a general purpose vision machine.

The final point concerns the methodology or style of this type of approach, and it involves two main observations. First, the duality between representations and processes, which is set out explicitly in figure 18.3, often provides a useful aid to thinking how best to proceed when studying a particular problem. In the study both of representations and of processes, general problems are often suggested by everyday experience or by psychophysical or even neurophysiological findings of a quite general nature. Such general observations can often lead to the formulation of a particular process or representational theory, specific examples of which can be programmed or subjected to detailed psychophysical testing. Once we have sufficient confidence in the correctness of the process or representation at this level, we can inquire about its detailed implementation, which involves the ultimate and very difficult problems of neurophysiology and neuroanatomy.

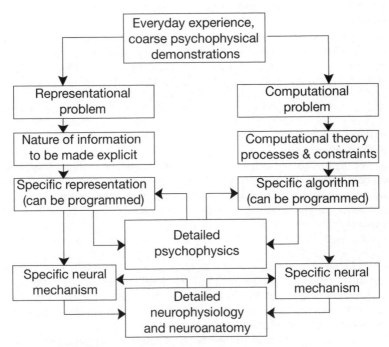

Figure 18.3 Relationships between representations and processes

The second observation is that there is no real recipe for this type of research – even though I have sometimes suggested that there is – any more than there is a straightforward procedure for discovering things in any other branch of science. Indeed, part of the fun is that we never really know where the next key is going to come from – a piece of daily experience, the report of a neurological deficit, a theorem about three-dimensional geometry, a psychophysical finding in hyperacuity, a neurophysiological observation, or the careful analysis of a representational problem. All these kinds of information have played important roles in establishing the framework that I have described, and they will presumably continue to contribute to its advancement in an interesting and unpredictable way. I hope only that these observations may persuade some of my readers to join in the adventures we have had and to help in the long but rewarding task of unraveling the mysteries of human visual perception.

Notes

1 Editor's note: the passages to which Marr here refers are as follows (from pp. 12–13 of *Vision*).

If one explores the responsiveness of single ganglion cells in the frog's retina using handheld targets, one finds that one particular type of ganglion cell is most effectively driven by something like a black disc subtending a degree or so moved rapidly to and fro within the unit's receptive field. This causes a vigorous discharge which can be maintained without much decrement as long as the movement is continued. Now, if the stimulus which is optimal for this class of cells is presented to intact frogs, the behavioral response is often dramatic; they turn towards the target and make repeated feeding responses consisting of a jump and snap. The selectivity of the retinal neurons and the frog's reaction when they are selectively stimulated, suggest that they are "bug detectors" (Barlow 1953) performing a primitive but vitally important form of recognition. The result makes one suddenly realize that a large part of the sensory machinery involved in a frog's feeding responses may actually reside in the retina rather than in mysterious "centers" that would be too difficult to understand by physiological methods. The essential lock-like property resides in each member of a whole class of neurons and allows the cell to discharge only to the appropriate key pattern of sensory stimulation. Lettvin et al. (1959) suggested that there were five different classes of cell in the frog, and Barlow, Hill, and Levick (1964) found an even larger number of categories in the rabbit. [Barlow et al.] called these key patterns "trigger features," and Maturana et al. (1960) emphasized another important aspect of the behavior of these ganglion cells; a cell continues to respond to the same trigger feature in spite of changes in light intensity over many decades. The properties of the retina are such that a ganglion cell can, figuratively speaking, reach out and determine that something specific is happening in front of the eye. Light is the agent by which it does this, but it is the detailed pattern of the light that carries the information, and the overall level of illumination prevailing at the time is almost totally disregarded (Barlow 1972: 373).

The cumulative effect of all the changes I have tried to outline above has been to make us realize that each *single neuron can perform a much more complex and subtle task than had previously been thought* [emphasis added]. Neurons do not loosely and unreliably remap the luminous intensities of the visual image onto our sensorium, but instead they detect pattern elements, discriminate the depth of objects, ignore irrelevant causes of variation and are arranged in an intriguing hierarchy. Furthermore, there is evidence that they give prominence to what is informationally important, can respond with great reliability, and can have their pattern selectivity permanently modified by early visual experience. This amounts to a revolution in our outlook. It is now quite inappropriate to regard unit activity as a noisy indication of more basic and reliable processes involved in mental operations: instead, we must regard single neurons as the prime movers of these mechanisms. Thinking is brought about by neurons and we should not use phrases like "unit activity reflects, reveals or monitors thought processes," because the activities of neurons, quite simply, are thought processes.

This revolution stemmed from physiological work and makes us realize that the activity of each single neuron may play a significant role in perception (ibid.: 380).

References

Austin, J.L. (1962) *Sense and Sensibilia*. Oxford: Clarendon Press.

Barlow, H. (1953) "Summation and inhibition in the frog's retina." *J. Physiol.* (Lond.) 119: 69–88.

—— (1972) "Single units and sensation: A neuron doctrine for perceptual psychology?" *Perception* 1: 371–94.

Barlow, H., Hill, R., and Levick, W. (1964) "Retinal ganglion cells responding selectively to direction and speed of image motion in the rabbit." *J. Physiol.* (Lond.) 173: 377–407.

Chomsky, N. (1965) *Aspects of the Theory of Syntax*. Cambridge, MA: MIT Press.

Chomsky, N. and Lasnik, H. (1977) "Filters and control." *Linguistic Inquiry* 8: 425–504.

Critchley, M. (1953) *The Parietal Lobes*. London: Edward Arnold.

Freuder, E.C. (1974) "A computer vision system for visual recognition using active knowledge." MIT Artificial Intelligence Laboratory Technical Report 345.

Gibson, J.J. (1966) *The Senses Considered as Perceptual Systems*. Boston: Houghton-Mifflin.

—— (1979) *The Ecological Approach to Visual Perception*. Boston: Houghton-Mifflin.

Lettvin, J., Maturana, H., McCulloch, W., and Pitts, W. (1959) "What the frog's eye tells the frog's brain." *Proc. Inst. Rad. Eng.* 47: 1940–51.

Marcus, M.P. (1980) *A Theory of Syntactic Recognition for Natural Language*. Cambridge, MA: MIT Press.

Marr, D. (1976) "Early processing of visual information." *Phil. Transactions of the Royal Society* (Lond. B) 275: 483–524.

Marr, D. and Nishihara, H.K. (1978) "Representatian and recognition of the spatial organization of three-dimensional shapes." *Proceedings of the Royal Society* (Lond. B) 200: 269–94.

Marr, D. and Poggio, T. (1976) "Cooperative computation of stereo disparity." *Science* 194: 283–7.

—— (1979) "A computational theory of human stereo vision." *Proceedings of the Royal Society* 204: 301–28.

Maturana, H., Lettvin, J., McCulloch, W., and Pitts, W. (1960) "Anatomy and physiology of vision in the frog (Rana pipiens)." *Gen. Physiol.* 43 (suppl. no. 2, Mechanisms of Vision): 129–71.

Poggio, T. and Reichardt, W. (1976) "Visual control of orientation behavior in the fly. Part II: Towards the underlying neural interactions." *Quarterly Review of Biophys.* 9: 377–438.

Reichardt, W. and Poggio, T. (1976) "Visual control of orientation behavior in the fly. Part I: A quantitative analysis." *Quarterly Review of Biophys.* 9: 311–75.

—— (1979) "Visual control of flight in flies." In W.E. Reichardt, V. B. Mountcastle, and T. Poggio (eds), *Recent Theoretical Developments in Neurobiology*. New York: Springer.

Rosch, E. (1978) "Principles of categorization." In E. Rosch and B. Lloyd (eds), *Cognition and Categorization* (pp. 27–48). Hillsdale, NJ: Erlbaum.

Shepard, R.N. (1975) "Form formation, and transformation of internal representations." In R. Solso (ed.), *Information Processing and Cognition: The Loyola Symposium* (pp. 87–122). Hillsdale, NJ; Erlbaum.

Stevens, K.A. (1979) "Surface Perception from Local Analysis of Texture and Contour." PhD dissertation, MIT. (Available as: "The information content of texture gradients." *Biological Cybernetics* 42: 95–105; also, "The visual interpretation of surface contours." *Artificial Intelligence* 17 (1981): 47–74.)

Tenenbaum, J.M. and Barrow, H.G. (1976) "Experiments in interpretation-guided segmentation." Stanford Research Institute Technical Note 123.

Warrington. E.K. (1975) "The selective impairment of semantic memory." *Quarterly Journal of Experimental Psychology*, 27, 635–57.

Warrington, E.K. and Taylor, A.M. (1973) "The contribution of the right parietal lobe to object recognition, *Cortex* 9: 152–64.

—— (1978) "Two categorical stages of object recognition." *Perception* 7: 695–705.

Winograd, T. (1972) *Understanding Natural Language*. New York: Academic Press.

19

A. Newell and H.A. Simon,
"Computer Science as Empirical Enquiry:
Symbols and Search"

Computer science is the study of the phenomena surrounding computers. The founders of this society understood this very well when they called themselves the Association for Computing Machinery. The machine – not just the hardware, but the programmed living machine – is the organism we study.

This is the tenth Turing Lecture. The nine persons who preceded us on this platform have presented nine different views of computer science. For our organism, the machine, can be studied at many levels and from many sides. We are deeply honoured to appear here today and to present yet another view, the one that has permeated the scientific work for which we have been cited. We wish to speak of computer science as empirical enquiry.

Our view is only one of many; the previous lectures make that clear. However, even taken together the lectures fail to cover the whole scope of our science. Many fundamental aspects of it have not been represented in these ten awards. And if the time ever arrives, surely not soon, when the compass has been boxed, when computer science has been discussed from every side, it will be time to start the cycle again. For the hare as lecturer will have to make an annual sprint to overtake the cumulation of small, incremental gains that the tortoise of scientific and technical development has achieved in his steady march. Each year will create a new gap and call for a new sprint, for in science there is no final word.

Computer science is an empirical discipline. We would have called it an experimental science, but like astronomy, economics, and geology, some of its unique forms of observation and experience do not fit a narrow stereotype of the experimental method. Nonetheless, they are experiments. Each new machine that is built is an experiment. Actually constructing the machine poses a question to nature; and we listen for the answer by observing the machine in operation and analysing it by all analytical and measurement means available. Each new program that is built is an experiment. It poses a question to nature, and its behaviour offers clues to an answer. Neither machines nor programs are black boxes; they are artefacts that have been designed, both

407

hardware and software, and we can open them up and look inside. We can relate their structure to their behaviour and draw many lessons from a single experiment. We don't have to build 100 copies of, say, a theorem prover, to demonstrate statistically that it has not overcome the combinatorial explosion of search in the way hoped for. Inspection of the program in the light of a few runs reveals the flaw and lets us proceed to the next attempt.

We build computers and programs for many reasons. We build them to serve society and as tools for carrying out the economic tasks of society. But as basic scientists we build machines and programs as a way of discovering new phenomena and analysing phenomena we already know about. Society often becomes confused about this, believing that computers and programs are to be constructed only for the economic use that can be made of them (or as intermediate items in a developmental sequence leading to such use). It needs to understand that the phenomena surrounding computers are deep and obscure, requiring much experimentation to assess their nature. It needs to understand that, as in any science, the gains that accrue from such experimentation and understanding pay off in the permanent acquisition of new techniques; and that it is these techniques that will create the instruments to help society in achieving its goals.

Our purpose here, however, is not to plead for understanding from an outside world. It is to examine one aspect of our science, the development of new basic understanding by empirical enquiry. This is best done by illustrations. We will be pardoned if, presuming upon the occasion, we choose our examples from the area of our own research. As will become apparent, these examples involve the whole development of artificial intelligence, especially in its early years. They rest on much more than our own personal contributions. And even where we have made direct contributions, this has been done in co-operation with others. Our collaborators have included especially Cliff Shaw, with whom we formed a team of three through the exciting period of the late fifties. But we have also worked with a great many colleagues and students at Carnegie Mellon University.

Time permits taking up just two examples. The first is the development of the notion of a symbolic system. The second is the development of the notion of heuristic search. Both conceptions have deep significance for understanding how information is processed and how intelligence is achieved. However, they do not come close to exhausting the full scope of artificial intelligence, though they seem to us to be useful for exhibiting the nature of fundamental knowledge in this part of computer science.

1 Symbols and physical-symbol systems

One of the fundamental contributions to knowledge of computer science has been to explain, at a rather basic level, what symbols are. This explanation is a scientific proposition about Nature. It is empirically derived, with a long and gradual development.

Symbols lie at the root of intelligent action, which is, of course, the primary topic of artificial intelligence. For that matter, it is a primary question for all of computer science. For all information is processed by computers in the service of ends, and we measure the intelligence of a system by its ability to achieve stated ends in the face of variations, difficulties, and complexities posed by the task environment. This general investment of computer science in attaining intelligence is obscured when the tasks being accomplished are limited in scope, for then the full variations in the environment can be accurately foreseen. It becomes more obvious as we extend computers to more global, complex, and knowledge-intensive tasks – as we attempt to make them our agents, capable of handling on their own the full contingencies of the natural world.

Our understanding of the system's requirements for intelligent action emerges slowly. It is composite, for no single elementary thing accounts for intelligence in all its manifestations. There is no 'intelligence principle', just as there is no 'vital principle' that conveys by its very nature the essence of life. But the lack of a simple *deus ex machina* does not imply that there are no structural requirements for intelligence. One such requirement is the ability to store and manipulate symbols. To put the scientific question, we may paraphrase the title of a famous paper by Warren McCulloch (1961): What is a symbol, that intelligence may use it, and intelligence, that it may use a symbol?

Laws of qualitative structure

All sciences characterize the essential nature of the systems they study. These characterizations are invariably qualitative in nature, for they set the terms within which more detailed knowledge can be developed. Their essence can often be captured in very short, very general statements. One might judge these general laws, because of their limited specificity, as making relatively little contribution to the sum of a science, were it not for the historical evidence that shows them to be results of the greatest importance.

The cell doctrine in biology

A good example of a law of qualitative structure is the cell doctrine in biology, which states that the basic building block of all living organisms is the cell. Cells come in a large variety of forms, though they all have a nucleus surrounded by protoplasm, the whole encased by a membrane. But this internal structure was not, historically, part of the specification of the cell doctrine; it was subsequent specificity developed by intensive investigation. The cell doctrine can be conveyed almost entirely by the statement we gave above, along with some vague notions about what size a cell can be. The impact of this law on biology, however, has been tremendous, and the lost motion in the field prior to its gradual acceptance was considerable.

409

Plate tectonics in geology

Geology provides an interesting example of a qualitative structure law, interesting because it has gained acceptance in the last decade and so its rise in status is still fresh in our memory. The theory of plate tectonics asserts that the surface of the globe is a collection of huge plates – a few dozen in all – which move (at geological speeds) against, over, and under each other into the centre of the earth, where they lose their identity. The movements of the plates account for the shapes and relative locations of the continents and oceans, for the areas of volcanic and earthquake activity, for the deep sea ridges, and so on. With a few additional particulars as to speed and size, the essential theory has been specified. It was of course not accepted until it succeeded in explaining a number of details, all of which hung together (e.g. accounting for flora, fauna, and stratification agreements between West Africa and Northeast South America). The plate tectonics theory is highly qualitative. Now that it is accepted, the whole earth seems to offer evidence for it everywhere, for we see the world in its terms.

The germ theory of disease

It is little more than a century since Pasteur enunciated the germ theory of disease, a law of qualitative structure that produced a revolution in medicine. The theory proposes that most diseases are caused by the presence and multiplication in the body of tiny single-celled living organisms, and that contagion consists in the transmission of these organisms from one host to another. A large part of the elaboration of the theory consisted in identifying the organisms associated with specific diseases, describing them, and tracing their life histories. The fact that the law has many exceptions – that many diseases are not produced by germs – does not detract from its importance. The law tells us to look for a particular kind of cause; it does not insist that we will always find it.

The doctrine of atomism

The doctrine of atomism offers an interesting contrast to the three laws of qualitative structure we have just described. As it emerged from the work of Dalton and his demonstrations that the chemicals combined in fixed proportions, the law provided a typical example of qualitative structure: the elements are composed of small, uniform particles, differing from one element to another. But because the underlying species of atoms are so simple and limited in their variety, quantitative theories were soon formulated which assimilated all the general structure in the original qualitative hypothesis. With cells, tectonic plates, and germs, the variety of structure is so great that the underlying qualitative principle remains distinct, and its contribution to the total theory clearly discernible.

410

Conclusion

Laws of qualitative structure are seen everywhere in science. Some of our greatest scientific discoveries are to be found among them. As the examples illustrate, they often set the terms on which a whole science operates.

Physical-symbol systems

Let us return to the topic of symbols, and define a *physical-symbol system*. The adjective 'physical' denotes two important features:

1   Such systems clearly obey the laws of physics – they are realizable by engineered systems made of engineered components;
2   although our use of the term 'symbol' prefigures our intended interpretation, it is not restricted to human symbol systems.

A physical-symbol system consists of a set of entities, called symbols, which are physical patterns that can occur as components of another type of entity called an expression (or symbol structure). Thus a symbol structure is composed of a number of instances (or tokens) of symbols related in some physical way (such as one token being next to another). At any instant of time the system will contain a collection of these symbol structures. Besides these structures, the system also contains a collection of processes that operate on expressions to produce other expressions: processes of creation, modification, reproduction, and destruction. A physical-symbol system is a machine that produces through time an evolving collection of symbol structures. Such a system exists in a world of objects wider than just these symbolic expressions themselves.

Two notions are central to this structure of expressions, symbols, and objects: designation and interpretation.

Designation. An expression designates an object if, given the expression, the system can either affect the object itself or behave in ways depending on the object.

In either case, access to the object via the expression has been obtained, which is the essence of designation.

Interpretation. The system can interpret an expression if the expression designates a process and if, given the expression, the system can carry out the process.

Interpretation implies a special form of dependent action: given an expression, the system can perform the indicated process, which is to say, it can evoke and execute its own processes from expressions that designate them.

411

A system capable of designation and interpretation, in the sense just indicated, must also meet a number of additional requirements, of completeness and closure. We will have space only to mention these briefly; all of them are important and have far-reaching consequences.

1   A symbol may be used to designate any expression whatsoever. That is, given a symbol, it is not prescribed a priori what expressions it can designate. This arbitrariness pertains only to symbols: the symbol tokens and their mutual relations determine what object is designated by a complex expression.
2   There exist expressions that designate every process of which the machine is capable.
3   There exist processes for creating any expression and for modifying any expression in arbitrary ways.
4   Expressions are stable; once created, they will continue to exist until explicitly modified or deleted.
5   The number of expressions that the system can hold is essentially unbounded.

The type of system we have just defined is not unfamiliar to computer scientists. It bears a strong family resemblance to all general-purpose computers. If a symbol-manipulation language, such as LISP, is taken as defining a machine, then the kinship becomes truly brotherly. Our intent in laying out such a system is not to propose something new. Just the opposite: it is to show what is now known and hypothesized about systems that satisfy such a characterization.

We can now state a general scientific hypothesis – a law of qualitative structure for symbol systems:

The Physical-Symbol System Hypothesis. A physical-symbol system has the necessary and sufficient means for general intelligent action.

By 'necessary' we mean that any system that exhibits general intelligence will prove upon analysis to be a physical-symbol system. By 'sufficient' we mean that any physical-symbol system of sufficient size can be organized further to exhibit general intelligence. By 'general intelligent action' we wish to indicate the same scope of intelligence as we see in human action: that in any real situation behaviour appropriate to the ends of the system and adaptive to the demands of the environment can occur, within some limits of speed and complexity.

The Physical-Symbol System Hypothesis clearly is a law of qualitative structure. It specifies a general class of systems within which one will find those capable of intelligent action.

This is an empirical hypothesis. We have defined a class of systems; we wish to ask whether that class accounts for a set of phenomena we find in the real world. Intelligent action is everywhere around us in the biological world, mostly in human behaviour. It is a form of behaviour we can recognize by its effects whether it is performed by humans or not. The hypothesis could indeed be false. Intelligent behaviour is not so easy to produce that any system will exhibit it willy-nilly. Indeed, there are people whose analyses lead them to conclude either on philosophical or on scientific grounds that the hypothesis *is* false. Scientifically, one can attack or defend it only by bringing forth empirical evidence about the natural world.

We now need to trace the development of this hypothesis and look at the evidence for it.

Development of the symbol-system hypothesis

A physical-symbol system is an instance of a universal machine. Thus the symbol-system hypothesis implies that intelligence will be realized by a universal computer. However, the hypothesis goes far beyond the argument, often made on general grounds of physical determinism, that any computation that is realizable can be realized by a universal machine, provided that it is specified. For it asserts specifically that the intelligent machine is a symbol system, thus making a specific architectural assertion about the nature of intelligent systems. It is important to understand how this additional specificity arose.

Formal logic

The roots of the hypothesis go back to the program of Frege and of Whitehead and Russell for formalizing logic: capturing the basic conceptual notions of mathematics in logic and putting the notions of proof and deduction on a secure footing. This effort culminated in mathematical logic – our familiar propositional, first-order, and higher-order logics. It developed a characteristic view, often referred to as the 'symbol game'. Logic, and by incorporation all of mathematics, was a game played with meaningless tokens according to certain purely syntactic rules. All meaning had been purged. One had a mechanical, though permissive (we would now say non-deterministic), system about which various things could be proved. Thus progress was first made by walking away from all that seemed relevant to meaning and human symbols. We could call this the stage of formal symbol-manipulation.

This general attitude is well reflected in the development of information theory. It was pointed out time and again that Shannon had defined a system that was useful only for communication and selection, and which had nothing to do with meaning. Regrets were expressed that such a general name as 'information theory' had been given to the field, and attempts were made to rechristen it as 'the theory of selective information' – to no avail, of course.

Turing machines and the digital computer

The development of the first digital computers and of automata theory, starting with Turing's own work in the thirties, can be treated together. They agree in their view of what is essential. Let us use Turing's own model, for it shows the features well.

A Turing machine consists of two memories: an unbounded tape and a finite-state control. The tape holds data, i.e. the famous zeros and ones. The machine has a very small set of proper operations – read, write, and scan operations – on the tape. The read operation is not a data operation, but provides conditional branching to a control state as a function of the data under the read head. As we all know, this model contains the essentials of all computers, in terms of what they can do, though other computers with different memories and operations might carry out the same computations with different requirements of space and time. In particular, the model of a Turing machine contains within it the notions both of what cannot be computed and of universal machines – computers that can do anything that can be done by any machine.

We should marvel that two of our deepest insights into information processing were achieved in the thirties, before modern computers came into being. It is a tribute to the genius of Alan Turing. It is also a tribute to the development of mathematical logic at the time, and testimony to the depth of computer science's obligation to it. Concurrently with Turing's work appeared the work of the logicians Emil Post and (independently) Alonzo Church. Starting from independent notions of logistic systems (Post productions and recursive functions, respectively), they arrived at analogous results on undecidability and universality – results that were soon shown to imply that all three systems were equivalent. Indeed, the convergence of all these attempts to define the most general class of information-processing systems provides some of the force of our conviction that we have captured the essentials of information-processing in these models.

In none of these systems is there, on the surface, a concept of the symbol as something that *designates*. The data are regarded as just strings of zeros and ones – indeed that data be inert is essential to the reduction of computation to physical process. The finite-state control system was always viewed as a small controller, and logical games were played to see how small a state system could be used without destroying the universality of the machine. No games, as far as we can tell, were ever played to add new states dynamically to the finite control – to think of the control memory as holding the bulk of the system's knowledge. What was accomplished at this stage was half the principle of interpretation – showing that a machine could be run from a description. Thus this is the stage of automatic formal symbol-manipulation.

The stored program concept

With the development of the second generation of electronic machines in the mid-forties (after the Eniac) came the stored program concept. This was rightfully hailed as a milestone, both conceptually and practically. Programs now can be data, and can be operated on as data. This capability is, of course, already implicit in the model of Turing: the descriptions are on the very same tape as the data. Yet the idea was realized only when machines acquired enough memory to make it practicable to locate actual programs in some internal place. After all, the Eniac had only twenty registers.

The stored program concept embodies the second half of the interpretation principle, the part that says that the system's own data can be interpreted. But it does not yet contain the notion of designation – of the physical relation that underlies meaning.

List-processing

The next step, taken in 1956, was list-processing The contents of the data-structures were now symbols, in the sense of our physical-symbol system: patterns that designated, that had referents. Lists held addresses which permitted access to other lists – thus the notion of list-structures. That this was a new view was demonstrated to us many times in the early days of list-processing when colleagues would ask where the data were – that is, which list finally held the collection of bits that were the content of the system. They found it strange that there were no such bits, there were only symbols that designated yet other symbol structures.

List-processing is simultaneously three things in the development of computer science.

1   It is the creation of a genuine dynamic memory structure in a machine that had heretofore been perceived as having fixed structure. It added to our ensemble of operations those that built and modified structure in addition to those that replaced and changed content.
2   It was an early demonstration of the basic abstraction that a computer consists of a set of data types and a set of operations proper to these data types, so that a computational system should employ whatever data types are appropriate to the application, independent of the underlying machine.
3   List-processing produced a model of designation, thus defining symbol-manipulation in the sense in which we use this concept in computer science today.

As often occurs, the practice of the time already anticipated all the elements of list-processing: addresses are obviously used to gain access, the drum machines used linked programs (so-called one-plus-one addressing), and so on. But the conception of list-processing as an abstraction created a new world in which designation and dynamic symbolic structure were defining characteristics. The embedding of the early list-processing systems in languages (the IPLs, LISP) is often decried as having been a barrier to the diffusion of list-processing techniques throughout programming practice; but it was the vehicle that held the abstraction together.

LISP

One more step is worth noting: McCarthy's creation of LISP in 1959–60 (McCarthy 1960). It completed the act of abstraction, lifting list-structures out of their embedding in concrete machines, creating a new formal system with S-expressions, which could be shown to be equivalent to the other universal schemes of computation.

Conclusion

That the concept of the designating symbol and symbol-manipulation does not emerge until the mid-fifties does not mean that the earlier steps were either inessential or less important. The total concept is the join of computability, physical realizability (and by multiple technologies), universality, the symbolic representation of processes (i.e. interpretability), and, finally, symbolic structure and designation. Each of the steps provided an essential part of the whole.

The first step in this chain, authored by Turing, is theoretically motivated, but the others all have deep empirical roots. We have been led by the evolution of the computer itself. The stored program principle arose out of the experience with Eniac. List-processing arose out of the attempt to construct intelligent programs. It took its cue from the emergence of random access memories, which provided a clear physical realization of a designating symbol in the address. LISP arose out of the evolving experience with list-processing.

The evidence

We come now to the evidence for the hypothesis that physical-symbol systems are capable of intelligent action, and that general intelligent action calls for a physical-symbol system. The hypothesis is an empirical generalization and not a theorem. We know of no way of demonstrating the connection between symbol systems and intelligence on purely logical grounds. Lacking such a demonstration, we must look at the facts. Our central aim, however, is not to review the evidence in detail, but to use the example before us to illustrate the proposition that computer science is a field of empirical enquiry. Hence, we will only indicate what kinds of evidence there are, and the general nature of the testing process.

The notion of physical-symbol system had taken essentially its present form by the middle of the 1950s, and one can date from that time the growth of artificial intelligence as a coherent subfield of computer science. The twenty years of work since then has seen a continuous accumulation of empirical evidence of two main varieties. The first addresses itself to the *sufficiency* of physical-symbol systems for producing intelligence, attempting to construct and test specific systems that have such a capability. The second kind of evidence addresses itself to the *necessity* of having a physical-symbol system wherever intelligence is exhibited. It starts with Man, the intelligent system best known to us, and attempts to discover whether his cognitive activity can be explained as the working of a physical-symbol system. There are other forms of evidence, which we will comment upon briefly later, but these two are the important ones. We will consider them in turn. The first is generally called artificial intelligence, the second, research in cognitive psychology.

Constructing intelligent systems

The basic paradigm for the initial testing of the germ theory of disease was: identify a disease, then look for the germ. An analogous paradigm has inspired much of the research in artificial intelligence: identify a task-domain calling for intelligence, then construct a program for a digital computer that can handle tasks in that domain. The easy and well structured tasks were looked at first: puzzles and games, operations-research problems of scheduling and allocating resources, simple induction tasks. Scores, if not hundreds, of programs of these kinds have by now been constructed, each capable of some measure of intelligent action in the appropriate domain.

Of course intelligence is not an all-or-none matter, and there has been steady progress towards higher levels of performance in specific domains, as well as towards widening the range of those domains. Early chess programs, for example, were deemed successful if they could play the game legally and with some indication of purpose; a little later, they reached the level of human beginners; within ten or fifteen years, they began to compete with serious amateurs. Progress has been slow (and the total programming effort invested small) but continuous, and the paradigm of construct-and-test proceeds in a regular cycle – the whole research activity mimicking at a macroscopic level the basic generate-and-test cycle of many of the AI programs.

There is a steadily widening area within which intelligent action is attainable. From the original tasks, research has extended to building systems that handle and understand natural language in a variety of ways, systems for interpreting visual scenes, systems for hand–eye co-ordination, systems that design, systems that write computer programs, systems for speech understanding – the list is, if not endless, at least very long. If there are limits beyond which the hypothesis will not carry us, they have not yet become apparent. Up to the present, the rate of progress has been governed mainly by the rather modest quantity of scientific resources that have been applied and the inevitable requirement of a substantial system-building effort for each new major undertaking.

Much more has been going on, of course, than simply a piling up of examples of intelligent systems adapted to specific task-domains. It would be surprising and unappealing if it turned out that the AI programs performing these diverse tasks had nothing in common beyond their being instances of physical-symbol systems. Hence, there has been great interest in searching for mechanisms possessed of generality, and for common components among programs performing a variety of tasks. This search carries the theory beyond the initial symbol-system hypothesis to a more complete characterization of

417

the particular kinds of symbol systems that are effective in artificial intelligence. In the second section of this paper, we will discuss one example of a hypothesis at this second level of specificity: the heuristic-search hypothesis.

The search for generality spawned a series of programs designed to separate out general problem-solving mechanisms from the requirements of particular task-domains. The General Problem Solver (GPS) was perhaps the first of these; while among its descendants are such contemporary systems as PLANNER and CONNIVER. The search for common components has led to generalized schemes of representation for goals and plans, methods for constructing discrimination nets, procedures for the control of tree search, pattern-matching mechanisms, and language-parsing systems. Experiments are at present under way to find convenient devices for representing sequences of time and tense, movement, causality, and the like. More and more, it becomes possible to assemble large intelligent systems in a modular way from such basic components.

We can gain some perspective on what is going on by turning, again, to the analogy of the germ theory. If the first burst of research stimulated by that theory consisted largely in finding the germ to go with each disease, subsequent effort turned to learning what a germ was – to building on the basic qualitative law a new level of structure. In artificial intelligence, an initial burst of activity aimed at building intelligent programs for a wide variety of almost randomly selected tasks is giving way to more sharply targeted research aimed at understanding the common mechanisms of such systems.

The modelling of human symbolic behaviour

The symbol-system hypothesis implies that the symbolic behaviour of man arises because he has the characteristics of a physical-symbol system. Hence, the results of efforts to model human behaviour with symbol systems become an important part of the evidence for the hypothesis, and research in artificial intelligence goes on in close collaboration with research in information-processing psychology, as it is usually called.

The search for explanations of man's intelligent behaviour in terms of symbol systems has had a large measure of success over the past twenty years; to the point where information-processing theory is the leading contemporary point of view in cognitive psychology. Especially in the areas of problem-solving, concept attainment, and long-term memory, symbol-manipulation models now dominate the scene.

Research in information-processing psychology involves two main kinds of empirical activity. The first is the conduct of observations and experiments on human behaviour in tasks requiring intelligence. The second, very similar to the parallel activity in artificial intelligence, is the programming of symbol systems to model the observed human behaviour. The psychological observations and experiments lead to the formulation of hypotheses about the symbolic processes the subjects are using, and these are an important source of the ideas that go into the construction of the programs. Thus many of the ideas for the basic mechanisms of GPS were derived from careful analysis of the protocols that human subjects produced while thinking aloud during the performance of a problem-solving task.

The empirical character of computer science is nowhere more evident than in this alliance with psychology. Not only are psychological experiments required to test the veridicality of the simulation models as explanations of the human behaviour, but out of the experiments come new ideas for the design and construction of physical-symbol systems.

Other evidence

The principal body of evidence for the symbol-system hypothesis that we have now considered is negative evidence: the absence of specific competing hypotheses as to how intelligent activity might be accomplished – whether by man or by machine. Most attempts to build such hypotheses have taken place within the field of psychology. Here we have had a continuum of theories from the points of view usually labelled 'behaviourism' to those usually labelled 'Gestalt theory'. Neither of these points of view stands as a real competitor to the symbol-system hypothesis, and for two reasons. First, neither behaviourism nor Gestalt theory has demonstrated, or even shown how to demonstrate, that the explanatory mechanisms it postulates are sufficient to account for intelligent behaviour in complex tasks. Second, neither theory has been formulated with anything like the specificity of artificial programs. As a matter of fact, the alternative theories are so vague that it is not terribly difficult to give them information-processing interpretations, and thereby assimilate them to the symbol-system hypothesis.

Conclusion

We have tried to use the example of the Physical-Symbol System Hypothesis to illustrate concretely that computer science is a scientific enterprise in the usual meaning of that term: it develops scientific hypotheses which it then seeks to verify by empirical enquiry. We had a second reason, however, for choosing this particular example to illustrate our point. The Physical-Symbol System Hypothesis is itself a substantial scientific hypothesis of the kind that we earlier dubbed 'laws of qualitative structure'. It represents an important discovery of computer science, which if borne out by the empirical evidence, as in fact appears to be occurring, will have major continuing impact on the field.

We turn now to a second example, the role of search in intelligence. This topic, and the particular hypothesis about it that we shall examine, has also played a central role in computer science in general and in artificial intelligence in particular.

2   Heuristic search

Knowing that physical-symbol systems provide the matrix for intelligent action does not tell us how they accomplish this. Our second example of a law of qualitative structure in computer science addresses this latter question, asserting that symbol systems solve problems by using the processes of heuristic search. This generalization, like the previous one, rests on empirical evidence, and has not been derived formally from other premises. We shall see in a moment, however, that it does have some logical connection with the symbol-system hypothesis, and perhaps we can expect to formalize the connection at some time in the future. Until that time arrives, our story must again be one of empirical enquiry. We will describe what is known about heuristic search and review the empirical findings that show how it enables action to be intelligent. We begin by stating this law of qualitative structure, the Heuristic Search Hypothesis.

> *Heuristic Search Hypothesis.* The solutions to problems are represented as symbol structures. A physical-symbol system exercises its intelligence in problem-solving by search – that is, by generating and progressively modifying symbol structures until it produces a solution structure.

Physical-symbol systems must use heuristic search to solve problems because such systems have limited processing resources; in a finite number of steps, and over a finite interval of time, they can execute only a finite number of processes. Of course that is not a very strong limitation, for all universal Turing machines suffer from it. We intend the limitation, however, in a stronger sense: we mean *practically* limited. We can conceive of systems that are not limited in a practical way but are capable, for example, of searching in parallel the nodes of an exponentially expanding tree at a constant rate for each unit advance in depth. We will not be concerned here with such systems, but with systems whose computing resources are scarce relative to the complexity of the situations with which they are confronted. The restriction will not exclude any real symbol systems, in computer or man, in the context of real tasks. The fact of limited resources allows us, for most purposes, to view a symbol system as though it were a serial, one-process-at-a-time device. If it can accomplish only a small amount of processing in any short time interval, then we might as well regard it as doing things one at a time. Thus 'limited resource symbol system' and 'serial symbol system' are practically synonymous. The problem of allocating a scarce resource from moment to moment can usually be treated, if the moment is short enough, as a problem of scheduling a serial machine.

Problem-solving

Since ability to solve problems is generally taken as a prime indicator that a system has intelligence, it is natural that much of the history of artificial intelligence is taken up with attempts to build and understand problem-solving systems. Problem-solving has been discussed by philosophers and psychologists for two millennia, in discourses dense with a feeling of mystery. If you think there is nothing problematic or mysterious about a symbol system solving problems, you are a child of today, whose views have been formed since mid-century. Plato (and, by his account, Socrates) found difficulty understanding even how problems could be *entertained*, much less how they could be solved. Let me remind you of how he posed the conundrum in the *Meno*:

> MENO: And how will you inquire, Socrates, into that which you know not? What will you put forth as the subject of inquiry? And if you find what you want, how will you ever know that this is what you did not know?

To deal with this puzzle, Plato invented his famous theory of recollection: when you think you are discovering or learning something, you are really just recalling what you already knew in a previous existence. If you find this explanation preposterous, there is a much simpler one available today, based upon our understanding of symbol systems. An approximate statement of it is:

> To state a problem is to designate (1) a *test* for a class of symbol structures (solutions of the problem), and (2) a *generator* of symbol structures (potential solutions). To solve a problem is to generate a structure, using (2), that satisfies the test of (1).

We have a problem if we know what we want to do (the test), and if we don't know immediately how to do it (our generator does not immediately produce a symbol structure satisfying the test). A symbol system can state and solve problems (sometimes) because it can generate and test.

If that is all there is to problem-solving, why not simply generate at once an expression that satisfies the test? This is, in fact, what we do when we wish and dream. 'If wishes were horses, beggars might ride.' But outside the world of dreams, it isn't possible. To know how we would test something, once constructed, does not mean that we know how to construct it – that we have any generator for doing so.

For example, it is well known what it means to 'solve' the problem of playing winning chess. A simple test exists for noticing winning positions, the test for checkmate of the enemy king. In the world of dreams one simply generates a strategy that leads to checkmate for all counter strategies of the opponent. Alas, no generator that will do this is known to existing symbol systems (man or machine). Instead, good moves in chess are sought by generating various alternatives, and painstakingly evaluating them with the use of approximate, and often erroneous, measures that are supposed to indicate the likelihood that a particular line of play is on the route to a winning position. Move generators there are; winning-move generators there are not.

Before there can be a move generator for a problem, there must be a problem space: a space of symbol structures in which problem situations, including the initial and goal situations, can be represented. Move generators are processes for modifying one situation in the problem space into another. The basic characteristics of physical-symbol systems guarantee that they can represent problem spaces and that they possess move generators. How, in any concrete situation they synthesize a problem space and move generators appropriate to that situation is a question that is still very much on the frontier of artificial intelligence research.

The task that a symbol system is faced with, then, when it is presented with a problem and a problem space, is to use its limited processing resources to generate possible solutions, one after another, until it finds one that satisfies the problem-defining test. If the system had some control over the order in which potential solutions were generated, then it would be desirable to arrange this order of generation so that actual solutions would have a high likelihood of appearing early. A symbol system would exhibit intelligence to the extent that it succeeded in doing this. Intelligence for a system with limited processing resources consists in making wise choices of what to do next.

Search in problem-solving

During the first decade or so of artificial intelligence research, the study of problem-solving was almost synonymous with the study of search processes. From our characterization of problems and problem-solving, it is easy to see why this was so. In fact, it might be asked whether it could be otherwise. But before we try to answer that question, we must explore further the nature of search processes as it revealed itself during that decade of activity.

Extracting information from the problem space

Consider a set of symbol structures, some small subset of which are solutions to a given problem. Suppose, further, that the solutions are distributed randomly through the entire set. By this we mean that no information exists that would enable any search generator to perform better than a random search. Then no symbol system could exhibit more intelligence (or less intelligence) than any other in solving the problem, although one might experience better luck than another.

A condition, then, for the appearance of intelligence is that the distribution of solutions be not entirely random, that the space of symbol structures exhibit at least some degree of order and pattern. A second condition is that pattern in the space of symbol structures be more or less detectable. A third condition is that the generator of potential solutions be able to behave differentially, depending on what pattern it detected. There must be information in the problem space, and the symbol system must be capable of extracting and using it. Let us look first at a very simple example, where the intelligence is easy to come by.

Consider the problem of solving a simple algebraic equation:

$$AX + B = CX + D$$

The test defines a solution as any expression of the form, $X = E$, such that $AE + B = CE + D$. Now one could use as generator any process that would produce numbers which could then be tested by substituting in the latter equation. We would not call this an intelligent generator.

Alternatively, one could use generators that would make use of the fact that the original equation can be modified – by adding or subtracting equal quantities from both sides, or multiplying or dividing both sides by the same quantity – without changing its solutions. But, of course, we can obtain even more information to guide the generator by comparing the original expression with the form of the solution, and making precisely those changes in the equation that leave its solution unchanged, while at the same time bringing it into the desired form. Such a generator could notice that there was an unwanted CX on the right-hand side of the original equation, subtract it from both sides, and collect terms again. It could then notice that there was an unwanted B on the left-hand side and subtract that. Finally, it could get rid of the unwanted coefficient $(A - C)$ on the left-hand side by dividing.

Thus by this procedure, which now exhibits considerable intelligence, the generator produces successive symbol structures, each obtained by modifying the previous one; and the modifications are aimed at reducing the differences between the form of the input structure and the form of the test expression, while maintaining the other conditions for a solution.

This simple example already illustrates many of the main mechanisms that are used by symbol systems for intelligent problem-solving. First, each successive expression is not generated independently, but is produced by modifying one produced previously. Second, the modifications are not haphazard, but depend upon two kinds of information. They depend on information that is constant over this whole class of algebra problems, and that is built into the structure of the generator itself: all modifications of expressions must leave the equation's solution unchanged. They also depend on information that changes at each step: detection of the differences in form that remain between the current expression and the desired expression. In effect, the generator incorporates some of the tests the solution must satisfy, so that expressions that don't meet these tests will never be generated. Using the first kind of information guarantees that only a tiny subset of all possible expressions is actually generated, but without losing the solution expression from this subset. Using the second kind of information arrives at the desired solution by a succession of approximations, employing a simple form of means-ends analysis to give direction to the search.

There is no mystery where the information that guided the search came from. We need not follow Plato in endowing the symbol system with a previous existence in which it already knew the solution. A moderately sophisticated generator-test system did the trick without invoking reincarnation.

Search trees

The simple algebra problem may seem an unusual, even pathological, example of search. It is certainly not trial-and-error search, for though there were a few trials, there was no error. We are more accustomed to thinking of problem-solving search as generating lushly branching trees of partial solution possibilities which may grow to thousands, or even millions, of branches, before they yield a solution. Thus, if from each expression it produces, the generator creates B new branches, then the tree will grow as B^D, where D is its depth. The tree grown for the algebra problem had the peculiarity that its branchiness, B, equalled unity.

Programs that play chess typically grow broad search trees, amounting in some cases to a million branches or more. Although this example will serve to illustrate our points about tree search, we should note that the purpose of search in chess is not to generate proposed solutions, but to evaluate (test) them. One line of research into game-playing programs has been centrally concerned with improving the representation of the chess board, and the processes for making moves on it, so as to speed up search and make it possible to search larger trees. The rationale for this direction, of course, is that the deeper the dynamic search, the more accurate should be the evaluations at the end of it. On the other hand, there is good empirical evidence that the strongest human players, grand masters, seldom explore trees of more than one hundred branches. This economy is achieved not so much by searching less deeply than do chess-playing programs, but by branching very sparsely and selectively at each node. This is only possible, without causing a deterioration of the evaluations, by having more of the selectivity built into the generator itself, so that it is able to select for generation only those branches which are very likely to yield important relevant information about the position.

The somewhat paradoxical-sounding conclusion to which this discussion leads is that search – successive generation of potential solution structures – is a fundamental aspect of a symbol system's exercise of intelligence in problem-solving but that amount of search is not a measure of the amount of intelligence being exhibited. What makes a problem a problem is not that a large amount of search is required for its solution, but that a large amount *would* be required if a requisite level of intelligence were not applied. When the symbolic system that is endeavouring to solve a problem knows enough about what to do, it simply proceeds directly towards its goal; but whenever its knowledge becomes inadequate, when it enters *terra incognita*, it is faced with the threat of going through large amounts of search before it finds its way again.

The potential for the exponential explosion of the search tree that is present in every scheme for generating problem solutions warns us against depending on the brute force of computers – even the biggest and fastest computers – as a compensation for the ignorance and unselectivity of their generators. The hope is still periodically ignited in some human breasts that a computer can be found that is fast enough, and that can be programmed cleverly enough, to play good chess by brute-force search. There is nothing known in theory about the game of chess that rules out this possibility. But empirical studies on the management of search in sizable trees with only modest results make this a much less promising direction than it was when chess was first chosen as an appropriate task for artificial intelligence. We must regard this as one of the important empirical findings of research with chess programs.

The forms of intelligence

The task of intelligence, then, is to avert the ever-present threat of the exponential explosion of search. How can this be accomplished? The first route, already illustrated by the algebra example and by chess programs that only generate 'plausible' moves for further analysis, is to build selectivity into the generator: to generate only structures that show promise of being solutions or of being along the path towards solutions. The usual consequence of doing this is to decrease the rate of branching, not to prevent it entirely. Ultimate exponential explosion is not avoided – save in exceptionally highly structured situations like the algebra example – but only postponed. Hence, an intelligent system generally needs to supplement the selectivity of its solution generator with other information-using techniques to guide search.

Twenty years of experience with managing tree search in a variety of task environments has produced a small kit of general techniques which is part of the equipment of every researcher in artificial intelligence today. Since these techniques have been described in general works like that of Nilsson (1971), they can be summarized very briefly here.

In serial heuristic search, the basic question always is: What shall be done next? In tree search, that question, in turn, has two components: (1) from what node in the tree shall we search next, and (2) what direction shall we take from that node? Information helpful in answering the first question may be interpreted as measuring the relative distance of different nodes from the goal. Best-first search calls for searching next from the node that appears closest to the goal. Information helpful in answering the second question – in what direction to search – is often obtained, as in the algebra example, by detecting specific differences between the current nodal structure and the goal structure described by the test of a solution, and selecting actions that are relevant to reducing these particular kinds of differences. This is the technique known as means-ends analysis, which plays a central role in the structure of the General Problem Solver.

The importance of empirical studies as a source of general ideas in AI research can be demonstrated clearly by tracing the history, through large numbers of problem-solving programs, of these two central ideas: best-first search and means-ends analysis. Rudiments of best-first search were already present, though unnamed, in the Logic Theorist in 1955. The General Problem Solver, embodying means-ends analysis, appeared about 1957 – but combined it with modified depth-first search rather than best-first search. Chess programs were generally wedded, for reasons of economy of memory, to depth-first search, supplemented after about 1958 by the powerful alpha-beta pruning procedure. Each of these techniques appears to have been reinvented a number of times, and it is hard to find general, task-independent, theoretical discussions of problem-solving in terms of these concepts until the middle or late 1960s. The amount of formal buttressing they have received from mathematical theory is still minuscule: some theorems about the reduction in search that can be secured from using the alpha-beta heuristic, a couple of theorems (reviewed by Nilsson 1971) about shortest-path search, and some very recent theorems on best-first search with a probabilistic evaluation function.

'Weak' and 'strong' methods

The techniques we have been discussing are dedicated to the control of exponential expansion rather than its prevention. For this reason, they have been properly called 'weak methods' – methods to be used when the symbol system's knowledge or the amount of structure actually contained in the problem space are inadequate to permit search to be avoided entirely. It is instructive to contrast a highly structured situation, which can be formulated, say, as a linear-programming problem, with the less structured situations of combinatorial problems like the travelling salesman problem or scheduling problems. ('Less structured' here refers to the insufficiency or nonexistence of relevant theory about the structure of the problem space.)

In solving linear-programming problems, a substantial amount of computation may be required, but the search does not branch. Every step is a step along the way to a solution. In solving combinatorial problems or in proving theorems, tree search can seldom be avoided, and success depends on heuristic search methods of the sort we have been describing.

Not all streams of AI problem-solving research have followed the path we have been outlining. An example of a somewhat different point is provided by the work on theorem-proving systems. Here, ideas imported from mathematics and logic have had a strong influence on the direction of enquiry. For example, the use of heuristics was resisted when properties of completeness could not be proved (a bit ironic, since most interesting mathematical systems are known to be undecidable). Since completeness can seldom be proved for best-first search heuristics, or for many kinds of selective generators, the effect of this requirement was rather inhibiting. When theorem-proving programs were continually incapacitated by the combinatorial explosion of their search trees, thought began to be given to selective heuristics, which in many cases proved to be analogues of heuristics used in general problem-solving programs. The set-of-support heuristic, for example, is a form of working backward, adapted to the resolution theorem-proving environment.

A summary of the experience

We have now described the workings of our second law of qualitative structure, which asserts that physical-symbol systems solve problems by means of heuristic search. Beyond that, we have examined some subsidiary characteristics of heuristic search, in particular the threat that it always faces of exponential explosion of the search tree, and some of the means it uses to avert that threat. Opinions differ as to how effective heuristic search has been as a problem-solving mechanism – the opinions depending on what task domains are considered and what criterion of adequacy is adopted. Success can be guaranteed by setting aspiration levels low – or failure by setting them high. The evidence might be summed up about as follows: few programs are solving problems at 'expert' professional levels. Samuel's checker program and Feigenbaum and Lederberg's DENDRAL are perhaps the best-known exceptions, but one could point also to a number of heuristic search programs for such operations-research problem domains as scheduling and integer programming. In a number of domains, programs perform at the level of competent amateurs: chess, some theorem-proving domains, many kinds of games and puzzles. Human levels have not yet been nearly reached by programs that have a complex perceptual 'front end': visual scene recognizers, speech understanders, robots that have to manoeuvre in real space and time Nevertheless, impressive progress has been made, and a large body of experience assembled about these difficult tasks.

We do not have deep theoretical explanations for the particular pattern of performance that has emerged. On empirical grounds, however, we might draw two conclusions. First, from what has been learned about human expert performance in tasks like chess, it is likely that any system capable of matching that performance will have to have access, in its memories, to very large stores of semantic information. Second, some part of the human superiority in tasks with a large perceptual component can be attributed to the special-purpose built-in parallel-processing structure of the human eye and ear.

In any case, the quality of performance must necessarily depend on the characteristics both of the problem domains and of the symbol systems used to tackle them. For most real-life domains in which we are interested, the domain structure has so far not proved sufficiently simple to yield theorems about complexity, or to tell us, other than empirically, how large real-world problems are in relation to the abilities of our symbol systems to solve them. That situation may change, but until it does, we must rely upon empirical explorations, using the best problem solvers we know how to build, as a principal source of knowledge about the magnitude and characteristics of problem difficulty. Even in highly structured areas like linear programming, theory has been much more useful in strengthening the heuristics that underlie the most powerful solution algorithms than in providing a deep analysis of complexity.

Intelligence without much search

Our analysis of intelligence equated it with the ability to extract and use information about the structure of the problem space, so as to enable a problem solution to be generated as quickly and directly as possible. New directions for improving the problem-solving capabilities of symbol systems can be equated, then, with new ways of extracting and using information. At least three such ways can be identified.

Non-local use of information

First, it has been noted by several investigators that information gathered in the course of tree search is usually only used *locally*, to help make decisions at the specific node where the information was generated. Information about a chess position, obtained by dynamic analysis of a subtree of continuations, is usually used to evaluate just that position, not to evaluate other positions that may contain many of the same features. Hence, the same facts have to be rediscovered repeatedly at different nodes of the search tree. Simply to take the information out of the context in which it arose and use it generally does not solve the problem, for the information may be valid only in a limited range of contexts. In recent years, a few exploratory efforts have been made to transport information from its context of origin to other appropriate contexts. While it is still too early to evaluate the power of this idea, or even exactly how it is to be achieved, it shows considerable promise. An important line of investigation that Berliner (1975) has been pursuing is to use causal analysis to determine the range over which a particular piece of information is valid. Thus if a weakness in a chess position can be traced back to the move that made it, then the same weakness can be expected in other positions descendant from the same move.

The HEARSAY speech-understanding system has taken another approach to making information globally available. That system seeks to recognize speech strings by pursuing a parallel search at a number of different levels: phonemic, lexical, syntactic, and semantic. As each of these searches provides and evaluates hypotheses, it supplies the information it has gained to a common 'blackboard' that can be read by all the sources. This shared information can be used, for example, to eliminate hypotheses, or even whole classes of hypotheses, that would otherwise have to be searched by one of the processes. Thus increasing our ability to use tree-search information non-locally offers promise for raising the intelligence of problem-solving systems.

Semantic recognition systems

A second active possibility for raising intelligence is to supply the symbol system with a rich body of semantic information about the task-domain it is dealing with. For example, empirical research on the skill of chess masters shows that a major source of the master's skill is stored information that enables him to recognize a large number of specific features and patterns of features on a chess board, and information that uses this recognition to propose actions appropriate to the features recognized. This general idea has, of course, been incorporated in chess programs almost from the beginning.

428

What is new is the realization of the number of such patterns and associated information that may have to be stored for master-level play: something on the order of 50,000,

The possibility of substituting recognition for search arises because a particular, and especially a rare, pattern can contain an enormous amount of information, provided that it is closely linked to the structure of the problem space. When that structure is 'irregular', and not subject to simple mathematical description, then knowledge of a large number of relevant patterns may be the key to intelligent behaviour. Whether this is so in any particular task-domain is a question more easily settled by empirical investigation than by theory. Our experience with symbol systems richly endowed with semantic information and pattern-recognizing capabilities for accessing it is still extremely limited.

The discussion above refers specifically to semantic information associated with a recognition system. Of course, there is also a whole large area of AI research on semantic information processing and the organization of semantic memories that falls outside the scope of the topics we are discussing in this paper.

Selecting appropriate representations

A third line of enquiry is concerned with the possibility that search can be reduced or avoided by selecting an appropriate problem space. A standard example that illustrates this possibility dramatically is the mutilated chequer-board problem. A standard 64-square chequer-board can be covered exactly with 32 tiles, each a 1 x 2 rectangle covering exactly two squares. Suppose, now, that we cut off squares at two diagonally opposite corners of the chequer-board, leaving a total of 62 squares. Can this mutilated board be covered exactly with 31 tiles? With (literally) heavenly patience, the impossibility of achieving such a covering can be demonstrated by trying all possible arrangements. The alternative, for those with less patience and more intelligence, is to observe that the two diagonally opposite corners of a chequer-board are of the same colour. Hence, the mutilated chequer-board has two fewer squares of one colour than of the other. But each tile covers one square of one colour and one square of the other, and any set of tiles must cover the same number of squares of each colour. Hence, there is no solution. How can a symbol system discover this simple inductive argument as an alternative to a hopeless attempt to solve the problem by search among all possible coverings? We would award a system that found a solution high marks for intelligence.

Perhaps, however, in posing these problems we are not escaping from search processes. We have simply displaced the search from a space of possible problem solutions to a space of possible representations. In any event, the whole process of moving from one representation to another, and of discovering and evaluating representations, is largely unexplored territory in the domain of problem-solving research. The laws of qualitative structure governing representations remain to be discovered. The search for them is almost sure to receive considerable attention in the coming decade.

Conclusion

That is our account of symbol systems and intelligence. It has been a long road from Plato's *Meno* to the present, but it is perhaps encouraging that most of the progress along that road has been made since the turn of the twentieth century, and a large fraction of it since the mid-point of the century. Thought was still wholly intangible and ineffable until modern formal logic interpreted it as the manipulation of formal tokens. And it seemed still to inhabit mainly the heaven of Platonic ideals, or the equally obscure spaces of the human mind, until computers taught us how symbols could be processed by machines. A. M. Turing made his great contributions at the mid-century crossroads of these developments that led from modern logic to the computer.

Physical-symbol systems

The study of logic and computers has revealed to us that intelligence resides in physical-symbol systems. This is computer science's most basic law of qualitative structure.

Symbol systems are collections of patterns and processes, the latter being capable of producing, destroying, and modifying the former. The most important properties of patterns are that they can designate objects, processes, or other patterns, and that when they designate processes, they can be interpreted. Interpretation means carrying out the designated process. The two most significant classes of symbol systems with which we are acquainted are human beings and computers.

Our present understanding of symbol systems grew, as indicated earlier, through a sequence of stages. Formal logic familiarized us with symbols, treated syntactically, as the raw material of thought, and with the idea of manipulating them according to carefully defined formal processes. The Turing machine made the syntactic processing of symbols truly machinelike, and affirmed the potential universality of strictly defined symbol systems. The stored-program concept for computers reaffirmed the interpretability of symbols, already implicit in the Turing machine. List-processing brought to the forefront the denotational capacities of symbols, and defined symbol-processing in ways that allowed independence from the fixed structure of the underlying physical machine. By 1956 all of these concepts were available, together with hardware for implementing them. The study of the intelligence of symbol systems, the subject of artificial intelligence, could begin.

Heuristic search

A second law of qualitative structure for AI is that symbol systems solve problems by generating potential solutions and testing them – that is, by searching.

Solutions are usually sought by creating symbolic expressions and modifying them sequentially until they satisfy the conditions for a solution. Hence, symbol systems solve problems by searching. Since they have finite resources, the search cannot be carried out all at once, but must be sequential. It leaves behind it either a single path from starting-point to goal or, if correction and backup are necessary, a whole tree of such paths.

Symbol systems cannot appear intelligent when they are surrounded by pure chaos. They exercise intelligence by extracting information from a problem domain and using that information to guide their search, avoiding wrong turns and circuitous bypaths. The problem domain must contain information – that is, some degree of order and structure – for the method to work. The paradox of the *Meno* is solved by the observation that information may be remembered, but new information may also be extracted from the domain that the symbols designate. In both cases, the ultimate source of the information is the task-domain.

The empirical base

Research on artificial intelligence is concerned with how symbol systems must be organized in order to behave intelligently. Twenty years of work in the area has accumulated a considerable body of knowledge, enough to fill several books (it already has), and most of it in the form of rather concrete experience about the behaviour of specific classes of symbol systems in specific task-domains. Out of this experience, however, there have also emerged some generalizations, cutting across task-domains and systems, about the general characteristics of intelligence and its methods of implementation.

We have tried to state some of these generalizations here. They are mostly qualitative rather than mathematical. They have more the flavour of geology or evolutionary biology than the flavour of theoretical physics. They are sufficiently strong to enable us today to design and build moderately intelligent systems for a considerable range of task domains, as well as to gain a rather deep understanding of how human intelligence works in many situations.

What next?

In our account we have mentioned open questions as well as settled ones; there are many of both. We see no abatement of the excitement of exploration that has surrounded this field over the past quarter century. Two resource limits will determine the rate of progress over the next such period. One is the amount of computing power that will be available. The second, and probably the more important, is the number of talented young computer scientists who will be attracted to this area of research as the most challenging they can tackle.

A. M. Turing concluded his famous paper 'Computing Machinery and Intelligence' with the words: 'We can only see a short distance ahead, but we can see plenty there that needs to be done.'

431

Many of the things Turing saw in 1950 that needed to be done have been done, but the agenda is as full as ever. Perhaps we read too much into his simple statement above, but we like to think that in it Turing recognized the fundamental truth that all computer scientists instinctively know. For all physical-symbol systems, condemned as we are to serial search of the problem environment, the critical question is always: What to do next?

References

Berliner, H. (1975) "Chess as problem solving: The development of a tactics analyzer." Unpublished Ph.D. thesis. Carnegie-Mellon University.

McCarthy, J. (1960) "Recursive functions of symbolic expressions and their computation by machine." *Commun. ACM* 3 (Apr.): 184–95.

McCulloch, W.S. (1961) "What is a number, that a man may know it, and a man that he may know a number?" *General Semantics Bulletin* nos. 26–7: 7–18. Repr. in W.S. McCulloch, *Embodiments of Mind*, pp. 1–18. Cambridge, Mass.: MIT Press.

Nilsson, N.J. (1971) *Problem-Solving Methods in Artificial Intelligence*. New York: McGraw-Hill.

20

D.C. Dennett, "Cognitive Wheels: The Frame Problem of AI"

Once upon a time there was a robot, named R_1 by its creators. Its only task was to fend for itself. One day its designers arranged for it to learn that its spare battery, its precious energy supply, was locked in a room with a time bomb set to go off soon. R_1 located the room, and the key to the door, and formulated a plan to rescue its battery. There was a wagon in the room, and the battery was on the wagon, and R_1 hypothesized that a certain action which it called PULLOUT (WAGON, ROOM) would result in the battery being removed from the room. Straightaway it acted, and did succeed in getting the battery out of the room before the bomb went off. Unfortunately, however, the bomb was also on the wagon. R_1 *knew* that the bomb was on the wagon in the room, but didn't realize that pulling the wagon would bring the bomb out along with the battery. Poor R_1 had missed that obvious implication of its planned act.

Back to the drawing board. 'The solution is obvious,' said the designers. 'Our next robot must be made to recognize not just the intended implications of its acts, but also the implications about their side-effects, by deducing these implications from the descriptions it uses in formulating its plans.' They called their next model, the robot-deducer, R_1D_1. They placed R_1D_1 in much the same predicament that R_1 had succumbed to, and as it too hit upon the idea of PULLOUT (WAGON, ROOM), it began, as designed, to consider the implications of such a course of action. It had just finished deducing that pulling the wagon out of the room would not change the colour of the room's walls, and was embarking on a proof of the further implication that pulling the wagon out would cause its wheels to turn more revolutions than there were wheels on the wagon – when the bomb exploded.

Back to the drawing board. 'We must teach it the difference between relevant implications and irrelevant implications,' said the designers, 'and teach it to ignore the irrelevant ones.' So they developed a method of tagging implications as either relevant or irrelevant to the project at hand, and installed the method in their next model, the robot-relevant-deducer, or R_2D_1 for short. When they subjected R_2D_1 to the test that had so unequivocally selected its ancestors for extinction, they were surprised to see it sitting, Hamlet-like, outside the room containing the ticking bomb, the native hue of its resolution sicklied o'er with the pale cast of thought, as Shakespeare (and more recently Fodor) has aptly put it. 'Do something!' they yelled at it. 'I am,' it retorted. 'I'm busily ignoring some thousands of implications I have determined to be irrelevant. Just as soon as I find an irrelevant implication, I put it on the list of those I must ignore, and . . .' the bomb went off.

All these robots suffer from the *frame problem*.[1] If there is ever to be a robot with the fabled perspicacity and real-time adroitness of R_2D_2 robot-designers must solve the frame problem. It appears at first to be at best an annoying technical embarrassment in robotics, or merely a curious puzzle for the bemusement of people working in Artificial Intelligence (AI). I think, on the contrary, that it is a new, deep epistemological problem – accessible in principle but unnoticed by generations of philosophers – brought to light by the novel methods of AI, and still far from being solved. Many people in AI have come to have a similarly high regard for the seriousness of the frame problem. As one researcher has quipped, 'We have given up the goal of designing an intelligent robot, and turned to the task of designing a gun that will destroy any intelligent robot that anyone else designs!'

I will try here to present an elementary, non-technical, philosophical introduction to the frame problem, and show why it is so interesting. I have no solution to offer, or even any original suggestions for where a solution might lie. It is hard enough, I have discovered, just to say clearly what the frame problem is – and is not. In fact, there is less than perfect agreement in usage within the AI research community. McCarthy and Hayes, who coined the term, use it to refer to a particular, narrowly conceived problem about representation that arises only for certain strategies for dealing with a broader problem about real-time planning systems. Others call this broader problem the frame problem – 'the whole pudding,' as Hayes has called it (personal correspondence) – and this may not be mere terminological sloppiness. If 'solutions' to the narrowly conceived problem have the effect of driving a (deeper) difficulty into some other quarter of the broad problem, we might better reserve the title for this hard-to-corner difficulty. With apologies to McCarthy and Hayes for joining those who would appropriate their term, I am going to attempt an introduction to the whole pudding, calling *it* the frame problem. I will try in due course to describe the narrower version of the problem, 'the frame problem proper' if you like, and show something of its relation to the broader problem.

Since the frame problem, whatever it is, is certainly not solved yet and may be, in its current guises, insoluble, the ideological foes of AI such as Hubert Dreyfus and John Searle are tempted to compose obituaries for the field, citing the frame problem as the cause of death. In *What Computers Can't do* (Dreyfus 1972), Dreyfus sought to show that AI was a fundamentally mistaken method for studying the mind, and in fact many of his somewhat impressionistic complaints about AI models and many of his declared insights into their intrinsic limitations can be seen to hover quite systematically in the neighbourhood of the frame problem. Dreyfus never explicitly mentions the frame problem,[2] but is it perhaps the smoking pistol he was looking for but didn't *quite* know how to describe? Yes, I think AI can be seen to be holding a smoking pistol, but at least in its 'whole pudding' guise it is everyone's problem, not just a problem for AI, which, like the good guy in many a mystery story, should be credited with a discovery, not accused of a crime.

One does not have to hope for a robot-filled future to be worried by the frame problem. It apparently arises from some very widely held and innocuous-*seeming* assumptions about the nature of intelligence, the truth of the most undoctrinaire brand of physicalism, and the conviction that it must be possible to explain how we think. (The dualist evades the frame problem – but only because dualism draws the veil of mystery and obfuscation over all the tough how-questions; as we shall see, the problem arises when one takes seriously the task of answering certain how-questions. Dualists inexcusably excuse themselves from the frame problem.)

One utterly central – if not defining – feature of an intelligent being is that it can 'look before it leaps'. Better, it can *think* before it leaps. Intelligence is (at least partly) a matter of using well what you know – but for what? For improving the fidelity of your expectations about what is going to happen next, for planning, for considering courses of action, for framing further hypotheses with the aim of increasing the knowledge you will use in the future, so that you can preserve yourself by letting your hypotheses die in your stead (as Sir Karl Popper once put it). The stupid – as opposed to ignorant – being is the one who lights the match to peer into the fuel tank,[3] who saws off the limb he is sitting on, who locks his keys in his car and then spends the next hour wondering how on earth to get his family out of the car.

But when we think before we leap, *how do we do it*? The answer seems obvious: an intelligent being learns from experience, and then uses what it has learned to guide expectation in the future. Hume explained this in terms of habits of expectation, in effect. *But how do the habits work*? Hume had a hand-waving answer – associationism – to the effect that certain transition paths between ideas grew more likely-to-be-followed as they became well worn, but since it was not *Hume's* job, surely, to explain in more detail the mechanics of these links, problems about how such paths could be put to good use – and not just turned into an impenetrable maze of untraversable alternatives – were not discovered.

Hume, like virtually all other philosophers and 'mentalistic' psychologists, was unable to see the frame problem because he operated at what I call a purely semantic level, or a *phenomenological* level. At the phenomenological level, all the items in view are *individuated by their meanings*. Their meanings are, if you like, 'given' – but this just means that the theorist helps himself to all the meanings he wants. In this way the semantic relation between one item and the next is typically plain to see, and one just assumes that the items behave as items with those meanings *ought* to behave. We can bring this out by concocting a Humean account of a bit of learning.

Suppose that there are two children, both of whom initially tend to grab cookies from the jar without asking. One child is allowed to do this unmolested but the other is spanked each time she tries. What is the result? The second child learns not to go for the cookies. Why? Because she has had experience of cookie-reaching followed swiftly by spanking. What good does that do? Well, the *idea* of cookie-reaching becomes connected by a habit path to the idea of spanking, which in turn is connected to the idea of pain . . . so *of course* the child refrains. Why? Well, that's just the effect of that idea on that sort of circumstance. But why? Well, what else ought the idea of pain to do on such an occasion? Well, it might cause the child to pirouette on her left foot or recite poetry, or blink, or recall her fifth birthday. But given what the idea of pain *means*, any of those effects would be absurd. True; now *how* can ideas be designed so that their effects are what they ought to be, given what they mean? Designing some internal things – an idea, let's call it – so that it behaves *vis-à-vis* its brethren as if it meant *cookie* or *pain* is the only way of endowing that thing with that meaning; it couldn't mean a thing if it didn't have those internal behavioural dispositions.

That is the mechanical question the philosophers left to some dimly imagined future researcher. Such a division of labour might have been all right, but it is turning out that most of the truly difficult and deep puzzles of learning and intelligence get kicked downstairs by this move. It is rather as if philosophers were to proclaim themselves expert explainers of the methods of a stage magician, and then, when we ask them to explain how the magician does the sawing-the-lady-in-half trick, they explain that it is really quite obvious: the magician doesn't really saw her in half; he simply makes it appear that he does. 'But how does he do *that*?' we ask. 'Not our department', say the philosophers – and some of them add, sonorously: 'Explanation has to stop somewhere.'[4]

When one operates at the purely phenomenological or semantic level, where does one get one's data, and how does theorizing proceed? The term 'phenomenology' has traditionally been associated with an introspective method – an *examination* of what is presented or given to consciousness. A person's phenomenology just was by definition the contents of his or her consciousness. Although this has been the ideology all along, it has never been the practice. Locke, for instance, may have thought his 'historical, plain method' was a method of unbiased self-observation, but in fact it was largely a matter of disguised aprioristic reasoning about what ideas and impressions *had to be* to do the jobs they 'obviously' did.[5] The myth that each of us can observe our mental activities has prolonged the illusion that major progress could be made on the theory of thinking by simply reflecting carefully on our own cases. For some time now we have known better: we have conscious access to only the upper surface, as it were, of the multi-level system of information-processing that occurs in us. Nevertheless, the myth still claims its victims.

So the analogy of the stage magician is particularly apt. One is not likely to make much progress in figuring out *how* the tricks are done by simply sitting attentively in the audience and watching like a hawk. Too much is going on out of sight. Better to face the fact that one must either rummage around backstage or in the wings, hoping to disrupt the performance in telling ways; or, from one's armchair, think aprioristically about how the tricks *must* be done, given whatever is manifest about the constraints. The frame problem is then rather like the unsettling but familiar 'discovery' that so far as armchair thought can determine, a certain trick we have just observed is flat impossible.

Here is an example of the trick. Making a midnight snack. How is it that I can get myself a midnight snack? What could be simpler? I suspect there is some leftover sliced turkey and mayonnaise in the fridge, and bread in the breadbox – and a bottle of beer in the fridge as well. I realize I can put these elements together, so I concoct a childishly simple plan: I'll just go and check out the fridge, get out the requisite materials, and make myself a sandwich, to be washed down with a beer. I'll need a knife, a plate, and a glass for the beer. I forthwith put the plan into action and it works! Big deal.

Now of course I couldn't do this without knowing a good deal – about bread, spreading mayonnaise, opening the fridge, the friction and inertia that will keep the turkey between the bread slices and the bread on the plate as I carry the plate over to the table beside my easy chair. I also need to know about how to get the beer out of the bottle into the glass.[6] Thanks to my previous accumulation of experience in the world, fortunately, I am equipped with all this worldly knowledge. Of course some of the knowledge I need *might* be innate. For instance, one trivial thing I have to know is that when the beer gets into the glass it is no longer in the bottle, and that if I'm holding the mayonnaise jar in my left hand I cannot also be spreading the mayonnaise with the knife in my left hand. Perhaps these are straightforward implications – instantiations – of some more fundamental things that I was in effect *born knowing* such as, perhaps, the fact that if something is in one location it isn't also in another, different location; or the fact that two things can't be in the same place at the same time; or the fact that situations change as the result of actions. It is hard to imagine just how one could learn these facts from experience.

Such utterly banal facts escape our notice as we act and plan, and it is not surprising that philosophers, thinking phenomenologically *but introspectively*, should have overlooked them. But if one turns one's back on introspection, and just thinks 'hetero-phenomenologically'[7] about the purely informational demands of the task – what *must* be known by any entity that can perform this task – these banal bits of knowledge rise to our attention. We can easily satisfy ourselves that no agent that did not *in some ways* have the benefit of the information (that beer in the bottle is not in the glass, etc.) could perform such a simple task. It is one of the chief methodological beauties of AI that it makes one be a phenomenologist in this improved way. As a hetero-phenomenologist, one reasons about what the agent must 'know' or figure out *unconsciously or consciously* in order to perform in various ways.

The reason AI forces the banal information to the surface is that the tasks set by AI start at zero: the computer to be programmed to simulate the agent (or the brain of the robot, if we are actually going to operate in the real, non-simulated world), initially knows nothing at all 'about the world'. The computer is the fabled *tabula rasa* on which every required item must somehow be impressed, either by the programmer at the outset or via subsequent 'learning' by the system.

We can all agree, today, that there could be no learning at all by an entity that faced the world at birth as a *tabula rasa*, but the dividing line between what is innate and what develops maturationally and what is actually learned is of less theoretical importance than one might have thought. While some information has to be innate, there is hardly any particular item that must be: an appreciation of *modus ponens*, perhaps, and the law of the excluded middle, and some sense of causality. And while some things we know must be learned – e.g. that Thanksgiving falls on a Thursday, or that refrigerators keep food fresh – many other 'very empirical' things could in principle be innately known – e.g. that smiles mean happiness, or that unsuspended, unsupported things fall. (There is some evidence, in fact, that there is an innate bias in favour of perceiving things to fall with gravitational acceleration.)[8]

Taking advantage of this advance in theoretical understanding (if that is what it is), people in AI can frankly ignore the problem of learning (it seems) and take the shortcut of *installing* all that an agent has to 'know' to solve a problem. After all, if God made Adam as an adult who could presumably solve the midnight snack problem *ab initio*, AI agent-creators can in *principle* make an 'adult' agent who is equipped with worldly knowledge *as if* it had laboriously learned all the things it needs to know. This may of course be a dangerous short cut.

The installation problem is then the problem of installing in one way or another all the information needed by an agent to plan in a changing world. It is a difficult problem because the information must be installed in a usable format. The problem can be broken down initially into the semantic problem and the syntactic problem. The semantic problem – called by Allen Newell the problem at the 'knowledge level' (Newell 1982) – is the problem of just what information (on what topics, to what effect) must be installed. The syntactic problem is what system, format, structure, or mechanism to use to put that information in.[9]

The division is clearly seen in the example of the midnight snack problem. I *listed* a few of the very many humdrum facts one needs to know to solve the snack problem, but I didn't mean to suggest that those facts are stored in me – or in any agent – piecemeal, in the form of a long list of sentences explicitly declaring each of these facts for the benefit of the agent. That is of course one possibility, officially: it is a preposterously extreme version of the 'language of thought' theory of mental representation, with each distinguishable 'proposition' separately inscribed in the system. No one subscribes to such a view; even an encyclopedia achieves important economies of explicit expression via its organization, and a walking encyclopedia – not a bad caricature of the envisaged AI agent – must use different systemic principles to achieve efficient representation and access. We know trillions of things; we know that mayonnaise doesn't dissolve knives on contact, that a slice of bread is smaller than Mount Everest, that opening the refrigerator doesn't cause a nuclear holocaust in the kitchen.

There must be in us – and in any intelligent agent – some highly efficient, partly generative or productive system of representing – storing for use – all the information needed. Somehow, then, we must store many 'facts' at once – where facts are presumed to line up more or less one-to-one with non-synonymous declarative sentences. Moreover, we cannot realistically hope for what one might call a Spinozistic solution – a *small* set of axioms and definitions from which all the rest of our knowledge is deducible on demand – since it is clear that there simply are no entailment relations between vast numbers of these facts. (When we rely, as we must, on experience to tell us how the world is, experience tells us things that do not at all follow from what we have heretofore known.)

The demand for an efficient system of information storage is in part a space limitation, since our brains are not all that large, but more importantly it is a time limitation, for stored information that is not reliably accessible for use in the short real-time spans typically available to agents in the world is of no use at all. A creature that can solve any problem given enough time – say a million years – is not in fact intelligent at all. We live in a time-pressured world and must be able to think quickly before we leap. (One doesn't have to view this as an a priori condition on intelligence. One can simply note that we do in fact think quickly, so there is an empirical question about how we manage to do it.)

The task facing the AI researcher appears to be designing a system that can plan by using well-selected elements from its store of knowledge about the world it operates in. 'Introspection' on how *we* plan yields the following description of a process: one envisages a certain situation (often very sketchily); one then imagines performing a certain act in that situation; one then 'sees' what the likely outcome of that envisaged act in that situation would be, and evaluates it. What happens backstage, as it were, to permit this 'seeing' (and render it as reliable as it is) is utterly inaccessible to introspection.

On relatively rare occasions we all experience such bouts of thought, unfolding in consciousness at the deliberate speed of pondering. These are occasions in which we are faced with some novel and relatively difficult problem, such as: How can I get the piano upstairs? or Is there any way to electrify the chandelier without cutting through the plaster ceiling? It would be quite odd to find that one had to think *that* way (consciously and slowly) in order to solve the midnight snack problem. But the suggestion is that even the trivial problems of planning and bodily guidance that are beneath our notice (though in some sense we 'face' them) are solved by similar processes. Why? I don't *observe* myself planning in such situations. This fact suffices to convince the traditional, introspective phenomenologist that no such planning is going on.[10] The hetero-phenomenologist, on the other hand, reasons that *one way or another* information about the objects in the situation, and about the intended effects and side-effects of the candidate actions, *must* be used (considered, attended to, applied, appreciated). Why? Because otherwise the 'smart' behaviour would be sheer luck or magic. (Do we have any model for how such unconscious information-appreciation might be accomplished? The only model we have *so far* is *conscious*, deliberate information-appreciation. Perhaps, AI suggests, this is a good model. If it isn't, we are all utterly in the dark for the time being.)

We assure ourselves of the intelligence of an agent by considering counter-factuals: if I had been told that the turkey was poisoned, or the beer explosive, or the plate dirty, or the knife too fragile to spread mayonnaise, would I have acted as I did? If I were a stupid 'automaton' – or like the *Sphex* wasp who 'mindlessly' repeats her stereotyped burrow-checking routine till she drops[11] – I might infelicitously 'go through the motions' of making a midnight snack oblivious to the recalcitrant features of the environment.[12] But in fact, my midnight-snack-making behaviour is multifariously sensitive to current and background information about the situation. The only way it could be so sensitive – runs the tacit hetero-phenomenological reasoning – is for it to examine, or test for, the information in question. The information manipulation may be unconscious and swift, and it need not (it *better* not) consist of hundreds or thousands of *seriatim* testing procedures, but it must occur somehow, and its benefits must appear in time to help me as I commit myself to action.

I may of course have a midnight snack routine, developed over the years, in which case I can partly rely on it to pilot my actions. Such a complicated 'habit' would have to be under the control of a mechanism of some complexity, since even a rigid sequence of steps would involve periodic testing to ensure that subgoals had been satisfied. And even if I am an infrequent snacker, I no doubt have routines for mayonnaise-spreading, sandwich-making, and getting-something-out-of-the-fridge, from which I could compose my somewhat novel activity. Would such ensembles of routines, nicely integrated, suffice to solve the frame problem for me, at least in my more 'mindless' endeavours? That is an open question to which I will return below.

It is important in any case to acknowledge at the outset, and remind oneself frequently, that even very intelligent people do make mistakes; we are not only not infallible planners; we are quite prone to overlooking large and retro-spectively obvious flaws in our plans. This foible manifests itself in the familiar case of 'force of habit' errors (in which our stereotypical routines reveal them-selves to be surprisingly insensitive to some portentous environmental changes while surprisingly sensitive to others). The same weakness also appears on occasion in cases where we have consciously deliberated with some care. How often have you embarked on a project of the piano-moving variety – in which you've thought through or even 'walked through' the whole operation in advance – only to discover that you must backtrack or abandon the project when some perfectly foreseeable but unforeseen obstacle or unintended side-effect loomed? If we smart folk seldom actually paint ourselves into corners, it may be not because we plan ahead so well as that we supplement our sloppy planning powers with a combination of recollected lore (about fools who paint themselves into corners, for instance) and frequent progress checks as we proceed. Even so, we must know enough to call up the right lore at the right time, and to recognize impending problems as such. To summarise: we have been led by fairly obvious and compelling considerations to the conclusion that an intelligent agent must engage in swift information-sensitive 'planning' which has the effect of producing reliable but not foolproof expectations of the effects of its actions. That these expectations are normally in force in intel-ligent creatures is testified to by the startled reaction they exhibit when their expectations are thwarted. This suggests a graphic way of characterizing the minimal goal that can spawn the frame problem: we want a midnight-snack-making robot to be 'surprised' by the trick plate, the unspreadable concrete mayonnaise, the fact that we've glued the beer glass to the shelf. To be sur-prised you have to have expected something else, and in order to have expected the right something else, you have to have *and use* a lot of information about the things in the world.[13]

The central role of expectation has led some to conclude that the frame problem is not a new problem at all, and has nothing particularly to do with planning actions. It is, they think, simply the problem of having good expecta-tions about any future events, whether they are one's own actions, the actions of another agent, or the mere happenings of nature. That is the problem of induction – noted by Hume and intensified by Goodman (Goodman 1965), but still not solved to anyone's satisfaction. We know today that the problem of induction is a nasty one indeed. Theories of subjective probability and belief fixation have not stabilized in reflective equilibrium, so it is fair to say that no one has a good, principled answer to the general question: given that I believe all *this* (have all this evidence), what *ought* I to believe as well (about the future, or about unexamined parts of the world)?

The reduction of one unsolved problem to another is some sort of progress, unsatisfying though it may be, but it is not an option in this case. The frame problem is not the problem of induction in disguise. For suppose the problem of induction were solved. Suppose – perhaps miraculously – that our agent has solved all its induction problems or had them solved by fiat; it believes, then, all the right generalizations from its evidence, and associates with all of them the appropriate probabilities and conditional probabilities. This agent, *ex hypothesi*, believes just what it ought to believe about all empirical matters in its ken, including the probabilities of future events. It might still have a bad case of the frame problem, for that problem concerns how to represent (so it can be *used*) all that hard-won empirical information – a problem that arises independently of the truth value, probability, warranted assertability, or subjective certainty of any of it. Even if you have excellent *knowledge* (and not mere belief) about the changing world, how can this knowledge be represented so that it can be efficaciously brought to bear?

Recall poor R_1D_1, and suppose for the sake of argument that it had perfect empirical knowledge of the probabilities of all the effects of all its actions that would be detectable by it. Thus it believes that with probability 0.7864, executing PULLOUT (WAGON, ROOM) will cause the wagon wheels to make an audible noise; and with probability 0.5, the door to the room will open in rather than out; and with probability 0.999996, there will be no live elephants in the room, and with probability 0.997 the bomb will remain on the wagon when it is moved. How is R_1D_1 to find this last, relevant needle in its haystack of empirical knowledge? A walking encyclopedia will walk over a cliff, for all its knowledge of cliffs and the effects of gravity, unless it is designed in such a fashion that it can find the right bits of knowledge at the right times, so it can plan its engagements with the real world.

The earliest work on planning systems in AI took a deductive approach. Inspired by the development of Robinson's methods of resolution theorem proving, designers hoped to represent all the system's 'world knowledge' explicitly as axioms, and use ordinary logic – the predicate calculus – to deduce the effects of actions. Envisaging a certain situation S was modelled by having the system entertain a set of axioms describing the situation. Added to this were background axioms (the so-called 'frame axioms' that give the frame problem its name) which describe general conditions and the general effects of every action type defined for the system. To this set of axioms the system would apply an action – by postulating the occurrence of some action A in situation S – and then deduce the effect of A in S, producing a description of the outcome situation S'. While all this logical deduction looks like nothing at all in our conscious experience, research on the deductive approach could proceed on either or both of two enabling assumptions: the methodological assumption that psychological realism was a gratuitous bonus, not a goal, of 'pure' AI, or the substantive (if still vague) assumption that the deductive processes described would somehow model the backstage processes beyond conscious access. In other words, either we don't do our thinking deductively in the predicate calculus but a robot might; or we do (unconsciously) think deductively in the predicate calculus. Quite aside from doubts about its psychological realism, however, the deductive approach has not been made to work – the proof of the pudding for any robot – except for deliberately trivialized cases.

Consider some typical frame axioms associated with the action-type: *move x onto v.*

1   If $z \neq x$ and I move x onto y, then if z was on w before, then z is on w after.
2   If x is blue before, and I move x onto y, then x is blue after.

Note that (2), about being blue, is just one example of the many boring 'no-change' axioms we have to associate with this action-type. Worse still, note that a cousin of (2), also about being blue, would have to be associated with every other action-type – with *pick up x* and with *give x to y*, for instance. One cannot save this mindless repetition by postulating once and for all something like

3   If anything is blue, it stays blue,

for that is false, and in particular we will want to leave room for the introduction of such action-types as *paint x red*. Since virtually any aspect of a situation can change under some circumstance, this method requires introducing for each aspect (each predication in the description of S) an axiom to handle whether that aspect changes for each action-type.

This representational profligacy quickly gets out of hand, but for some 'toy' problems in AI, the frame problem can be overpowered to some extent by a mixture of the toyness of the environment and brute force. The early version of SHAKEY, the robot at SRI, operated in such a simplified and sterile world, with so few aspects it could worry about that it could get away with an exhaustive consideration of frame axioms.[14]

Attempts to circumvent this explosion of axioms began with the proposal that the system operate on the tacit assumption that nothing changes in a situation but what is explicitly asserted to change in the definition of the applied action (Fikes and Nilsson 1971). The problem here is that, as Garrett Hardin once noted, you don't do just one thing. This was R_1's problem, when it failed to notice that it would pull the bomb out with the wagon. In the explicit representation (a few pages back) of my midnight snack solution, I mentioned carrying the plate over to the table. On this proposal, my model of S' would leave the turkey back in the kitchen, for I didn't explicitly say the turkey would come along with the plate. One can of course patch up the definition of 'bring' or 'plate' to handle this problem, but only at the cost of creating others. (Will a few more patches tame the problem? At what point should one abandon patches and seek an altogether new approach? Such are the methodological uncertainties regularly encountered in this field, and of course no one can responsibly claim in advance to have a good rule for dealing with them. Premature counsels of despair or calls for revolution are as clearly to be shunned as the dogged pursuit of hopeless avenues; small wonder the field is contentious.)

While one cannot get away with the tactic of supposing that one can do just one thing, it remains true that very little of what could (logically) happen in any situation does happen. Is there some way of fallibly marking the likely area of important side-effects, and assuming the rest of the situation to stay unchanged? Here is where relevance tests seem like a good idea, and they may well be, but not within the deductive approach. As Minsky notes:

443

Even if we formulate relevancy restrictions, logistic systems have a problem using them. In any logistic system, all the axioms are necessarily 'permissive' – they all help to permit new inferences to be drawn. Each added axiom means more theorems; none can disappear. There simply is no direct way to add information to tell such a system about kinds of conclusions that should *not* be drawn! ... If we try to change this by adding axioms about relevancy, we still produce all the unwanted theorems, plus annoying statements about their irrelevancy (Minsky 1981: 125).

What is needed is a system that genuinely *ignores* most of what it knows, and operates with a well-chosen portion of its knowledge at any moment. Well-chosen, but not chosen by exhaustive consideration. How, though, can you give a system *rules* for ignoring – or better, since explicit rule-following is not the problem, how can you design a system that reliably ignores what it ought to ignore under a wide variety of different circumstances in a complex action environment?

John McCarthy calls this the qualification problem, and vividly illustrates it via the famous puzzle of the missionaries and the cannibals.

Three missionaries and three cannibals come to a river. A rowboat that seats two is available, if the cannibals ever outnumber the missionaries on either bank of the river, the missionaries will be eaten. How shall they cross the river?

Obviously the puzzler is expected to devise a strategy of rowing the boat back and forth that gets them all across and avoids disaster ...

Imagine giving someone the problem, and after he puzzles for a while, he suggests going upstream half a mile and crossing on a bridge. 'What bridge?' you say. 'No bridge is mentioned in the statement of the problem.' And this dunce replies, 'Well, they don't say there isn't a bridge.' You look at the English and even at the translation of the English into first order logic, and you must admit that 'they don't say' there is no bridge. So you modify the problem to exclude bridges and pose it again, and the dunce proposes a helicopter, and after you exclude that, he proposes a winged horse or that the others hang onto the outside of the boat while two row.

You now see that while a dunce, he is an inventive dunce. Despairing of getting him to accept the problem in the proper puzzler's spirit, you tell him the solution. To your further annoyance, he attacks your solution on the grounds that the boat might have a leak or lack oars. After you rectify that omission from the statement of the problem, he suggests that a sea monster may swim up the river and may swallow the boat. Again you are frustrated, and you took for a mode of reasoning that will settle his hash once and for all (McCarthy 1980: 29–30).

What a normal, intelligent human being does in such a situation is to engage in some form of *non-monotonic inference*. In a classical, monotonic logical system, *adding* premises never *diminishes* what can be proved from the premises. As Minsky noted, the axioms are essentially permissive, and once a theorem is permitted, adding more axioms will never invalidate the proofs of earlier theorems. But when we think about a puzzle or a real-life problem, we can achieve a solution (and even prove that it is a solution, or even the only solution to *that* problem), and then discover our solution invalidated by the addition of a new element to the posing of the problem; e. g. 'I forgot to tell you – there are no oars' or 'By the way, there's a perfectly good bridge upstream.'

What such late additions show us is that, contrary to our assumption, other things weren't equal. We had been reasoning with the aid of a *ceteris paribus* assumption, and now our reasoning has just been jeopardized by the discovery that something 'abnormal' is the case. (Note, by the way, that the abnormality in question is a much subtler notion than anything anyone has yet squeezed out of probability theory. As McCarthy notes, 'The whole situation involving cannibals with the postulated properties cannot be regarded as having a probability, so it is hard to take seriously the conditional probability of a bridge given the hypothesis' (ibid.).)

The beauty of a *ceteris paribus* clause in a bit of reasoning is that one does not have to say exactly what it means. 'What do you mean, "other things being equal"? Exactly which arrangements of which other things count as being equal?' If one had to answer such a question, invoking the *ceteris paribus* clause would be pointless, for it is precisely in order to evade that task that one uses it. If one could answer that question, one wouldn't need to invoke the clause in the first place. One way of viewing the frame problem, then, is as the attempt to get a computer to avail itself of this distinctively human style of mental operation. There are several quite different approaches to non-monotonic inference being pursued in AI today. They have in common only the goal of capturing the human talent for *ignoring* what should be ignored, while staying alert to relevant recalcitrance when it occurs.

One family of approaches, typified by the work of Marvin Minsky and Roger Schank (Minsky 1981; Schank and Abelson 1977), gets its ignoring-power from the attention-focusing power of stereotypes. The inspiring insight here is the idea that all of life's experiences, for all their variety, boil down to variations on a manageable number of stereotypic themes, paradigmatic scenarios – 'frames' in Minsky's terms, 'scripts' in Schank's.

An artificial agent with a well-stocked compendium of frames or scripts, appropriately linked to each other and to the impingements of the world via its perceptual organs, would face the world with an elaborate system of what might be called habits of attention and benign tendencies to leap to particular sorts of conclusions in particular sorts of circumstances. It would 'automatically' pay attention to certain features in certain environments and assume that certain unexamined normal features of those environments were present.

Concomitantly, it would be differentially alert to relevant divergences from the stereotypes it would always begin by 'expecting'.

Simulations of fragments of such an agent's encounters with its world reveal that in many situations it behaves quite felicitously and apparently naturally, and it is hard to say, of course, what the limits of this approach are. But there are strong grounds for skepticism. Most obviously, while such systems perform creditably when the world co-operates with their stereotypes, and even with *anticipated* variations on them, when their worlds turn perverse, such systems typically cannot recover gracefully from the misanalyses they are led into. In fact, their behaviour *in extremis* looks for all the world like the preposterously counter-productive activities of insects betrayed by their rigid tropisms and other genetically hard-wired behavioural routines.

When these embarrassing misadventures occur, the system designer can improve the design by adding provisions to deal with the particular cases. It is important to note that in these cases, the system does not redesign itself (or learn) but rather must wait for an external designer to select an improved design. This process of redesign recapitulates the process of natural selection in some regards; it favours minimal, piecemeal, *ad hoc* redesign which is tantamount to a wager on the likelihood of patterns in future events. So in some regards it is faithful to biological themes.[15] Nevertheless, until such a system is given a considerable capacity to learn from its errors without designer intervention, it will continue to respond in insectlike ways, and such behaviour is profoundly unrealistic as a model of human reactivity to daily life. The short cuts and cheap methods provided by a reliance on stereotypes are evident enough in human ways of thought, but it is also evident that we have a deeper understanding to fall back on when our short cuts don't avail, and building some measure of this deeper understanding into a system appears to be a necessary condition of getting it to learn swiftly and gracefully.

In effect, the script or frame approach is an attempt to *pre-solve* the frame problems the particular agent is likely to encounter. While insects do seem saddled with such control systems, people, even when they do appear to be relying on stereotypes, have back-up systems of thought that can deal more powerfully with problems that arise. Moreover, when people do avail themselves of stereotypes, they are at least relying on stereotypes of their own devising, and to date no one has been able to present any workable ideas about how a person's frame-making or scriptwriting machinery might be guided by its previous experience.

Several different sophisticated attempts to provide the representational framework for this deeper understanding have emerged from the deductive tradition in recent years. Drew McDermott and Jon Doyle have developed a 'non-monotonic logic' (1980), Ray Reiter has a 'logic for default reasoning' (1980), and John McCarthy has developed a system of 'circumscription', a formalized 'rule of conjecture that can be used by a person or program for "jumping to conclusions"' (1980). None of these is, or is claimed to be, a complete solution to the problem of *ceteris paribus* reasoning, but they might be components of such a solution. More recently, McDermott has offered a 'temporal logic for reasoning about processes and plans' (McDermott 1982). I will not attempt to assay the formal strengths and weaknesses of these approaches. Instead I will concentrate on another worry. From one point of view, non-monotonic or default logic, circumscription, and temporal logic all appear to be radical improvements to the mindless and clanking deductive approach, but from a slightly different perspective they appear to be more of the same, and at least as unrealistic as frameworks for psychological models.

They appear in the former guise to be a step towards greater psychological realism, for they take seriously, and attempt to represent, the phenomenologically salient phenomenon of common sense *ceteris paribus* 'jumping to conclusions' reasoning. But do they really succeed in offering any plausible suggestions about how the backstage implementation of that conscious thinking is accomplished *in people*? Even if on some glorious future day a robot with debugged circumscription methods manoeuvred well in a non-toy environment, would there be much likelihood that its constituent processes, *described at levels below the phenomeno-logical*, would bear informative relations to the unknown lower-level backstage processes in human beings? To bring out better what my worry is, I want to introduce the concept of a *cognitive wheel*.

We can understand what a cognitive wheel might be by reminding ourselves first about ordinary wheels. Wheels are wonderful, elegant triumphs of technology. The traditional veneration of the mythic inventor of the wheel is entirely justified. But if wheels are so wonderful, why are there no animals with wheels? Why are no wheels to be found (functioning as wheels) in nature? First, the presumption of that question must be qualified. A few years ago the astonishing discovery was made of several microscopic beasties (some bacteria and some unicellular eukaryotes) that have wheels of sorts. Their propulsive tails, long thought to be flexible flagella, turn out to be more or less rigid corkscrews, which rotate continuously, propelled by microscopic motors of sorts, complete with main bearings.[16] Better known, if less interesting for obvious reasons, are the tumbleweeds. So it is not quite true that there are no wheels (or wheeliform designs) in nature.

Still, macroscopic wheels – reptilian or mammalian or avian wheels – are not to be found. Why not? They would seem to be wonderful retractable landing gear for some birds, for instance. Once the question is posed, plausible reasons rush in to explain their absence. Most important, probably, are the considerations about the topological properties of the axle/bearing boundary that make the transmission of material or energy across it particularly difficult. How could the life-support traffic arteries of a living system maintain integrity across this boundary? But once that problem is posed, solutions suggest themselves, suppose the living wheel grows to mature form in a non-rotating, non-functional form, and is then hardened and sloughed off, like antlers or an outgrown shell, but not completely off: it then rotates freely on a lubricated fixed axle. Possible? It's hard to say. Useful? Also hard to say,

447

especially since such a wheel would have to be free-wheeling. This is an inter-esting speculative exercise, but certainly not one that should inspire us to draw categorical, a priori conclusions. It would be foolhardy to declare wheels biologically impossible, but at the same time we can appreciate that they are at least very distant and unlikely solutions to *natural* problems of design.

Now a cognitive wheel is simply any design proposal in cognitive theory (at any level from the purest semantic level to the most concrete level of 'wiring diagrams' of the neurones) that is profoundly unbiological, however wizardly and elegant it is as a bit of technology.

Clearly this is a vaguely defined concept, useful only as a rhetorical abbre-viation, as a gesture in the direction of real difficulties to be spelled out carefully. 'Beware of postulating cognitive wheels' masquerades as good advice to the cognitive scientist, while courting vacuity as a maxim to follow.[17] It occupies the same rhetorical position as the stockbroker's maxim: buy low and sell high. Still, the term is a good theme-fixer for discussion.

Many critics of AI have the conviction that *any* AI system is and must be nothing but a gearbox of cognitive wheels. This could of course turn out to be true, but the usual reason for believing it is based on a misunderstanding of the methodological assumptions of the field. When an AI model of some cognitive phenomenon is proposed, the model is describable at many different levels, from the most global, phenomenological level at which the behaviour is described (with some presumptuousness) in ordinary mentalistic terms, down through various levels of implementation all the way to the level of program code – and even further down, to the level of fundamental hardware operations if anyone cares. No one supposes that the model maps onto the process of psychology and biology *all the way down*. The claim is only that for some high level or levels of description below the phenomenological level (which merely *sets* the problem) there is a mapping of model features onto what is being modelled: the cognitive processes in living creatures, human or otherwise. It is understood that all the implementation details below the level of intended modelling will consist, no doubt, of cognitive wheels – bits of unbiological computer activity mimicking the gross effects of cognitive subcomponents by using methods utterly unlike the methods still to be discov-ered in the brain. Someone who failed to appreciate that a model composed microscopically of cognitive wheels could still achieve a fruitful isomorphism with biological or psychological processes at a higher level of aggregation would suppose there were good a priori reasons for generalized skepticism about AI.

But allowing for the possibility of valuable intermediate levels of modelling is not ensuring their existence. In a particular instance a model might descend directly from a phenomenologically recognizable level of psychological description to a cognitive wheels implementation without shedding any light at all on how we human beings manage to enjoy that phenomenology. I *suspect* that all current proposals in the field for dealing with the frame problem have that shortcoming. Perhaps one should dismiss the previous sentence as mere autobiography. I find it hard to imagine (for what that is worth) that any of the *procedural details* of the mechanization of McCarthy's circumscriptions, for instance, would have suitable counter-parts in the backstage story yet to be told about how human common-sense reasoning is accomplished. If these procedural details lack 'psychological reality' then there is nothing left in the proposal that might model psychological processes except the phenomeno-logical-level description in terms of jumping to conclusions, ignoring, and the like – and we already know we do that.

There is an alternative defence of such theoretical explorations, however, and I think it is to be taken seriously. One can claim (and I take McCarthy to claim) that while formalizing common-sense reasoning in his fashion would not tell us anything *directly* about psychological processes of reasoning, it would clarify, sharpen, systematize the purely semantic-level characterization of the demands on any such implementation, biological or not. Once one has taken the giant step forward of taking information-processing seriously as a real process in space and time, one can then take a small step back and explore the implications of that advance at a very abstract level. Even at this very formal level, the power of circumscription and the other versions of non-monotonic reasoning remains an open but eminently explorable question.[18]

Some have thought that the key to a more realistic solution to the frame problem (and indeed, in all likelihood, to any solution at all) must require a complete rethinking of the semantic-level setting, prior to concern with syntactic-level implementation. The more or less standard array of predicates and relations chosen to fill out the predicate-calculus format when representing the 'propositions believed' may embody a fundamentally inappropriate parsing of nature for this task. Typically, the interpretation of the formulae in these systems breaks the world down along the familiar lines of objects with properties at times and places. Knowledge of situations and events in the world is represented by what might be called sequences of verbal snapshots. State S, constitutively described by a list of sentences true at time t asserting various n-adic predicates true of various particulars, gives way to state S', a similar list of sentences true at t'. Would it perhaps be better to reconceive of the world of planning in terms of histories and processes?[19] Instead of trying to model the capacity to *keep track of things* in terms of principles for passing through temporal cross-sections of knowledge expressed in terms of terms (*names* for *things*, in essence) and predicates, perhaps we could model keeping track of things more directly, and let all the cross-sectional information about what is deemed true moment by moment be merely implicit (and hard to extract – as it is for us) from the format. These are tempting suggestions, but so far as I know they are still in the realm of handwaving.[20]

Another, perhaps related, handwaving theme is that the current difficulties with the frame problem stem from the conceptual scheme engendered by the serial-processing von Neumann architecture of the computers used to date in AI. As large, fast parallel processors are developed, they will bring in their wake huge conceptual innovations which are now of course only dimly imaginable. Since brains are surely massive parallel processors, it is tempting to suppose that the concepts engendered by such new hardware will be more readily adaptable for realistic psychological modelling. But who can say? For the time being, most of the optimistic claims about the powers of the parallel-processing belong in the same camp with the facile observations often encountered in the work of neuroscientists, who postulate marvellous cognitive powers for various portions of the nervous system without a clue how they are realized.[21]

Filling in the details of the gap between the phenomenological magic show and the well-understood powers of small tracts of brain tissue is the immense research task that lies in the future for theorists of every persuasion. But before the problems can be solved they must be encountered, and to encounter the problems one must step resolutely into the gap and ask how-questions. What philosophers (and everyone else) have always known is that people – and no doubt all intelligent agents – can engage in swift, sensitive, risky-but-valuable *ceteris paribus* reasoning. How do we do it? AI may not yet have a good answer, but at least it has encountered the question.[22]

Notes

1 The problem is introduced by John McCarthy and Patrick Hayes in their 1969 paper. The task in which the problem arises was first formulated in McCarthy (1968). I am grateful to John McCarthy, Pat Hayes, Bob Moore, Zenon Pylyshyn, John Haugeland, and Bo Dahlbom for the many hours they have spent trying to make me understand the frame problem. It is not their fault that so much of their instruction has still not taken.

I have also benefited greatly from reading an unpublished paper, 'Modelling change: The frame problem', by Lars-Erik Janlert, Institute of Information Processing, University of Umea, Sweden. It is to be hoped that a subsequent version of that paper will soon find its way into print, since it is an invaluable vade-mecum for any neophyte, in addition to advancing several novel themes.

2 Dreyfus mentions McCarthy (1968: 213–14), but the theme of his discussion there is that McCarthy ignores the difference between a *physical state* description and a *situation* description, a theme that might be succinctly summarized: a house is not a home.

Similarly, he mentions *ceteris paribus* assumptions (in the introduction to the rev. edn, pp. 56ff.), but only in announcing his allegiance to Wittgenstein's idea that 'whenever human behaviour is analyzed in terms of rules, these rules must always contain a *ceteris paribus* condition . . .' But this, even if true, misses the deeper point, the need for something like *ceteris paribus* assumptions confronts Robinson Crusoe just as ineluctably as it confronts any protagonist who finds himself in a situation involving human culture. The point is not, it seems, restricted to *Geisteswissenschaft* (as it is usually conceived); the 'intelligent' robot on an (otherwise?) uninhabited but hostile planet faces the frame problem as soon as it commences to plan its days.

3 The example is from an important discussion of rationality by Christopher Cherniak (1983), in 'Rationality and the structure of memory'.

4   Note that on this unflattering portrayal, the philosophers might still be doing *some* valuable work; think of the wild goose chases one might avert for some investigator who had rashly concluded that the magician really did saw the lady in half and then miraculously reunite her. People have jumped to such silly conclusions, after all; many philosophers have done so, for instance.

5   See my 1982a, a commentary on Goodman (1982).

6   This knowledge of physics is not what one learns in school, but in one's crib. See Hayes (1978, 1979).

7   For elaborations of hetero-phenomenology, see Dennett (1978: ch. 10, 'Two approaches to mental images'), and Dennett (1982b). See also Dennett (1982c).

8   Gunnar Johannsen has shown that animated films of 'falling' objects in which the moving spots drop with the normal acceleration of gravity are unmistakably distinguished by the casual observer from 'artificial' motions. I do not know whether infants have been tested to see if they respond selectively to such displays.

9   McCarthy and Hayes (1969) draw a different distinction between the 'epistemological' and the 'heuristic'. The difference is that they include the question 'In what kind of internal notation is the system's knowledge to be expressed?' in the epistemological problem (see p. 466), dividing off *that* syntactic (and hence somewhat mechanical) question from the procedural questions of the design of 'the mechanism that on the basis of the information solves the problem and decides what to do'.

    One of the prime grounds for controversy about just which problem the frame problem is springs from this attempted division of the issue. For the answer to the syntactical aspects of the epistemological question makes a large difference to the nature of the heuristic problem. After all, if the syntax of the expression of the system's knowledge is sufficiently perverse, then in spite of the *accuracy* of the representation of that knowledge, the heuristic problem will be impossible. And some have suggested that the heuristic problem would virtually disappear if the world knowledge were felicitously couched in the first place.

10 Such observations also convinced Gilbert Ryle, who was, in an important sense, an introspective phenomenologist (and not a 'behaviourist'). See Ryle (1949).

    One can readily imagine Ryle's attack on AI: 'And how many inferences do I perform in the course of performing my sandwich? What syllogisms convince me that the beer will stay in the glass?' For a further discussion of Ryle's skeptical arguments and their relation to cognitive science, see my 'Styles of mental representation' (Dennett 1983).

11 'When the time comes for egg laying the wasp *Sphex* builds a burrow for the purpose and seeks out a cricket which she stings in such a way as to paralyze but not kill it. She drags the cricket into her burrow, lays her eggs alongside, closes the burrow, then flies away, never to return. In due course the eggs hatch and the wasp grubs feed off the paralyzed cricket, which has not decayed, having been kept in the wasp equivalent of deep freeze. To the human mind, such an elaborately organized and seemingly purposeful routine conveys a convincing flavour of logic and thoughtfulness – until more details are examined. For example, the wasp's routine is to bring the paralyzed cricket to the burrow, leave it on the threshold, go inside to see that all is well, emerge, and then drag the cricket in. If, while the wasp is inside making her preliminary inspection the cricket is moved a few inches away, the wasp, on emerging from the burrow, will bring the cricket back to the threshold, but not inside, and will then repeat the

451

preparatory procedure of entering the burrow to see that everything is all right. If again the cricket is removed a few inches while the wasp is inside, once again the wasp will move the cricket up to the threshold and re-enter the burrow for a final check. The wasp never thinks of pulling the cricket straight in. On one occasion, this procedure was repeated forty times, always with the same result' (Wooldridge 1963).

This vivid example of a familiar phenomenon among insects is discussed by me in *Brainstorms*, and in Hofstadter (1982).

12 See my 1982c: 58–9, on 'Robot theater'.

13 Hubert Dreyfus has pointed out that *not expecting x* does not imply *expecting y* (where $x \neq y$), so one can be startled by something one didn't expect without it having to be the case that one (unconsciously) expected something else. But this sense of *not expecting* will not suffice to explain startle. What are the odds against your seeing an Alfa Romeo, a Buick, a Chevrolet, and a Dodge parked in alphabetical order some time or other within the next five hours? Very high, no doubt, all things considered, so I would not expect you to expect this; I also would not expect you to be startled by seeing this unexpected sight – except in the sort of special case where you had reason to expect something else at that time and place.

Startle reactions are powerful indicators of cognitive state – a fact long known by the police (and writers of detective novels). *Only* someone who expected the refrigerator to contain Smith's corpse (say) would be *startled* (as opposed to mildly interested) to find it to contain the rather unlikely trio: a bottle of vintage Chablis, a can of cat food, and a dishrag.

14 This early feature of SHAKEY was drawn to my attention by Pat Hayes. See also Dreyfus (1972: 26). SHAKEY is put to quite different use in Dehnett (1982b).

15 In one important regard, however, it is dramatically unlike the process of natural selection, since the trial, error, and selection of the process is far from blind. But a case can be made that the impatient researcher does nothing more than telescope time by such foresighted interventions in the redesign process.

16 For more details, and further reflections on the issues discussed here, see Diamond (1983).

17 I was interested to discover that at least one researcher in AI mistook the rhetorical intent of my new term on first hearing; he took 'cognitive wheels' to be an accolade. If one thinks of AI, as he does, not as a research method in psychology but as a branch of engineering attempting to extend human cognitive powers, then of course cognitive wheels are breakthroughs. The vast and virtually infallible memories of computers would be prime examples: others would be computers' arithmetical virtuosity and invulnerability to boredom and distraction. See Hofstadter (1982) for an insightful discussion of the relation of boredom to the structure of memory and the conditions of creativity.

18 McDermott (1982, 'A temporal logic for reasoning about processes and plans', §6, 'A sketch of an implementation') shows strikingly how many *new* issues are raised once one turns to the question of implementation, and how indirect (but still useful) the purely formal considerations are.

19 Patrick Hayes has been exploring this theme, and a preliminary account can be found in 'Naïve physics 1: The ontology of liquids' (Hayes 1978).

20 Oliver Selfridge's *Tracking and Trailing* (1992), promises to push back this frontier, I think, but I have not yet been able to assimilate its messages. There

are also suggestive passages on this topic in Ruth Garrett Millikan's *Language, Thought, and Other Biological Categories.*

21 To balance the 'top-down' theorists' foible of postulating cognitive wheels, there is the bottom-up' theorists' penchant for discovering *wonder tissue.* (Wonder tissue appears in many locales. J. J. Gibson's theory of perception, for instance, seems to treat the whole visual system as a hunk of wonder tissue, for instance, resonating with marvellous sensitivity to a host of sophisticated 'affordances'. See e.g. Gibson 1979.)

22 One of the few philosophical articles I have uncovered that seem to contribute to the thinking about the frame problem – though not in those terms – is Ronald de Sousa's 'The rationality of emotions' (de Sousa 1979). In the section entitled 'What are emotions for?' de Sousa suggests, with compelling considerations, that: the function of emotion is to fill gaps left by [mere wanting plus] 'pure reason' in the determination of action and belief. Consider how Iago proceeds to make Othello jealous. His task is essentially to direct Othello's attention, to suggest questions to ask . . . Once attention is thus directed, inferences which, before on the same evidence, would not even have been thought of, are experienced as compelling. In de Sousa's understanding, 'emotions are determinate patterns of salience among objects of attention, lines of inquiry, and inferential strategies' (p. 50) and they are not 'reducible' in any way to 'articulated propositions'. Suggestive as this is, it does not, of course, offer any concrete proposals for how to endow an inner (emotional) state with these interesting powers. Another suggestive – and overlooked – paper is Howard Darmstadter's 'Consistency of Belief' (Darmstadter 1971: 301–10). Darmstadter's exploration of *ceteris paribus* clauses and the relations that might exist between beliefs as psychological states and sentences believers may utter (or have uttered about them) contains a number of claims that deserve further scrutiny.

References

Cherniak, C. (1983) "Rationality and the structure of memory." *Synthese* 57: 163–86.

Darmstadter, H. (1971) "Consistency of belief." *J. Philosophy* 68: 301–10.

Dennett, D.C. (1978) *Brainstorms*, Cambridge, Mass.: MIT Press/Bradford Books.

—— (1982a) "Why do we think what we do about why we think what we do?" *Cognition* 12: 219–27.

—— (1982b) "How to study consciousness empirically: Or nothing comes to mind." *Synthese* 53: 159–80.

—— (1982c) "Beyond belief." In A. Woodfield (ed.), *Thought and Object*, pp. 1–96. Oxford: Clarendon Press.

—— (1983) "Styles of mental representation." *Proc. Aristotelian Soc.* 83: 213–26.

Diamond, J. (1983) "The biology of the wheel." *Nature* 302: 572–3.

Dreyfus, H.L. (1972) *What Computers Can't Do*. New York: Harper & Row.

Fikes, R. and Nilsson, N. (1971) "STRIPS: A new approach to the application of theorem proving to problem solving." *Artificial Intelligence* 2: 189–208.

Gibson, J.J. (1979) *The Ecological Approach to Visual Perception*. Boston, Mass.: Houghton-Mifflin.

Goodman, N. (1965) *Fact, Fiction and Forecast*, 2nd edn. Indianapolis: Bobbs-Merrill.

—— (1982) "Thoughts without words." *Cognition* 12: 211–17.

Hayes, P.J. (1978) "Naïve physics I: The ontology of liquids." Working Paper 35, Institute for Semantic and Cognitive Studies, Geneva.

—— (1979) "The naïve physics manifesto." In D. Michie (ed.), *Expert Systems in the Micro-Electronic Age*, pp. 242–70. Edinburgh: Edinburgh University Press.

Hofstadter, D. (1982) "Can inspiration be mechanized?" *Scientific American* 247: 18–34.

McCarthy, J. (1968) "Programs with common sense." *Proceedings of the Teddington Conference on the Mechanization of Thought Processes*, London. Repr. in M. Minsky (ed.), *Semantic Information Processing*, pp 403–18. Cambridge, Mass.: MIT Press.

—— (1980) "Circumscription – A form of non-monotonic reasoning." *Artificial Intelligence* 13: 27–39.

McCarthy, J. and Hayes, P.J. (1969) "Some philosophical problems from the standpoint of artificial intelligence." In B. Meltzer and D. Michie (eds), *Machine Intelligence 4*, pp. 463–502. Edinburgh: Edinburgh University Press.

McDermott, D. (1982) "A temporal logic for reasoning about processes and plans." *Cognitive Science* 6: 101–55.

McDermott, D. and Doyle, J. (1980) "Non-monotonic logic." *Artifical Intelligence* 13: 41–72.

Millikan, R.G. (1984) *Language, Thought and Other Biological Categories*. Cambridge, Mass.: MIT Press/Bradford Books.

Minsky, M. (1981) "Framework for representing knowledge." Originally published as MIT AI Lab. Memo 3306. Quotation drawn from excerpts repr. in J. Haugeland (ed.), *Mind Design*, pp. 95–128. Cambridge, Mass.: MIT Press/ Bradford Books.

Newell, A. (1982) "The knowledge level." *Artifical Intelligence* 18: 87–127.

Reiter, R. (1980) "A logic for default reasoning." *Artificial Intelligence* 13: 81–132.

Ryle, G. (1949) *The Concept of Mind*. London: Hutchinson.

Schank, R.C. and Abelson, R.P. (1977) *Scripts. Plans, Goals, and Understanding: An Inquiry into Human Knowledge*. Hillsdale, N.J.: Erlbaum.

Selfridge, O. (1992) *Tracking and Trailing: Adaptation in Movement Strategies*. Cambridge, Mass.: MIT Press.

De Sousa, R. (1979) "The rationality of emotions." *Dialogue* 18: 41–63.

Wooldridge, D. (1963) *The Machinery of the Brain*. New York: McGraw-Hill

IIIB

NON-CLASSICAL
COGNITIVE ARCHITECTURE

21

T. Horgan and J. Tienson, "Levels of Description in Nonclassical Cognitive Science"

David Marr (1982) provided an influential account of levels of description in classical cognitive science. In this paper we contrast Marr's treatment with some alternatives that are suggested by the recent emergence of connectionism. Marr's account is interesting and important both because of the levels of description it distinguishes, and because of the way his presentation reflects some of the most basic, foundational, assumptions of classical AI-style cognitive science (*classicism*, as we will call it henceforth). Thus, by focusing on levels of description, one can sharpen foundational differences between classicism and potential non-classical conceptions of mentality that might emerge under the rubric of connectionism.

We say 'potential conceptions' of mentality because at present there is no such thing as 'the connectionist conception of the mind', in the form of a determinate set of foundational assumptions differing in specific, explicit, ways from those of classicism. There may be several, incompatible conceptions of mind that could develop from or be wedded to connectionism. At present, connectionism is primarily an alternative way of *doing things* in cognitive science, rather than an alternative set of doctrines or theses. One constructs network models and trains them up with learning algorithms, rather than writing programs.

We will 'genericize' Marr's three levels of description, yielding a tripartite levels-typology that remains neutral about key foundational assumptions of classicism that are built into Marr's original formulation. With this generic typology as a guide, we will set forth a succession of approaches to mentality which, although they all conform to the generic format, deviate increasingly from classicism.

Each of these approaches could potentially get articulated and defended in the context of connectionist work in cognitive science – although none is necessarily tied to connectionist-style network structures *per se*. The final approach we will describe – the one which differs most radically from classicism – is the one we think probably embodies the truth about human cognition. We will not attempt to argue this here, however; we have done so elsewhere. Our main purposes at present are to propose a map of the intellectual landscape of possible views about mentality, and to *call attention* to several options on that landscape that have been largely overlooked – not only by philosophers, but also by practising cognitive scientists, connectionists included.

1 Marr's three levels

Marr suggests that in order to understand complex information-processing systems, *qua* processors of information, one needs to consider such systems from a tripartite theoretical perspective. He writes:

> At one extreme, the top level, is the abstract computational theory of the device, in which the performance of the device is characterized as a mapping from one kind of information to another, the abstract properties of this mapping are defined precisely, and its appropriateness and adequacy for the task are demonstrated. In the center is the choice of representation for the input and output and the algorithm to transform one into the other. At the other extreme are the details of how the algorithm and representation are realized physically – the detailed computer architecture, so to speak (1982: 24–25).

He labels these three levels, respectively, (1) the theory of the computation; (2) representation and algorithm; and (3) hardware implementation.

The top level involves systematic transitional connections among intentional state types as such. For a cognitive system as a whole, these are *total cognitive states* (TCS's), sometimes comprising several individual cognitive states that are simultaneously co-instantiable (perhaps in various different cognitive subsystems). The theory of computation delineates a *cognitive transition function* (CTF) over TCS's. For all TCS's instantiable by the system, the CTF specifies the appropriate immediate-successor TCS's. The CTF is the function to be computed by the system.

The middle level involves the account of how cognitive transitions are subserved by computation. This level addresses the kinds of structured states that serve as representations, and the computational processes by which these representations are manipulated. These processes conform to programmable rules that are purely formal, i.e., that advert solely to the form or structure of the representations and not to their content. The formal rules over the representations constitute an *algorithm* for computing the CTF; i.e., under the relevant assignment of content to the representations, processing in conformity to the rules is guaranteed to effect the cognitive transitions described by the theory of the computation.

The level of implementation, in turn, involves the account of how the formal/syntactic representations are themselves subserved by physico-chemical states and structures, and how the rule-describable manipulations of these representations are subserved via physico-chemical causal processes.

Within classical cognitive science, theorizing at Marr's top level typically involves a whole vertical hierarchy of sub-levels. In terms of familiar flowchart analyses ('boxology', as Cummins (1983) puts it), one adds another, lower, sub-level by adding more interconnected boxes to one's flow chart, either between existing ones or within them. Each box in a flowchart depicts a specific function that gets computed, within the system. The entire flowchart, for a total cognitive system, depicts the system's CTF; thus the system's TCS, at any moment t, is the full set of inputs and outputs (at t) to and from each box in the overall flowchart. Elaborating the flowchart, by adding additional boxes within or between the current ones, is essentially the boxological counterpart of hypothesizing that the system computes the functions represented by the boxes in the original flow chart by computing compositions of other functions – where the compositions are depicted by the more detailed boxology. (The function f is a composition of the functions g and h if $f(x) = g[h(x)]$.) The system thus computes each CTF in the hierarchy by computing a more fine-grained CTF in which it is embedded. Impressive cognitive transitions are thus ultimately composed of numerous cognitive 'baby steps', many of which are presumed to be rapid and unconscious. Each of these baby steps is simple enough to be subservable by symbol manipulation conforming to rules that advert only to the syntactic structure of the symbols, not to their content. Choice of symbol forms and rules adverting to those forms moves one to Marr's middle level.

For both Marr's top (cognitive-transition) level and his middle (algorithm) level, the downward inter-level relation between (i) state-types at that level, and (ii) state-types at the level just below it, is evidently the relation commonly called *realization*. How best to characterize the realization relation is a metaphysical question beyond our concerns in this article. But two key features of the relation bear emphasis. First, it is transitive: if a state-type S realizes a state-type R, and R in turn realizes a state-type T, then S realizes T. Second, it is a many-one relation: in general, a realizable state-type is *multiply* realizable by a variety of different lower-level state types.[1]

Philosophers and cognitive scientists undoubtedly think of the relation between Marr's middle level and his bottom level as realization, in the sense just characterized. Indeed, Marr's term 'implementation', which he invokes to name the bottom level, is essentially the computer scientist's word for what philosophers call realization. But among philosophers at least, it has not always been appreciated that the relation between Marr's top and middle levels is also best viewed as realization; there has been a tendency to instead construe the latter as *type identity*. Yet the case for realization as the top/middle bridging relation is quite straightforward, and goes as follows. Since a single computable function can generally be computed by a variety of distinct algorithms (some employing different representations than others), there is bound to be a one-many relation between (i) the cognitive transition function at Marr's top level, and (ii) the algorithms (with their associated representations) that compute that function. But middle-level state-types are individuated functionally, in terms of the specific algorithms in which they figure; distinct algorithms yield distinct middle-level state types. Hence, the intentional mental states posited by the theory of the computation are multiply realizable at the middle level, by various different computational state-types.[2]

As he presents it, Marr's tripartite account seems to build in the assumption that human cognitive processing is deterministic at the intentional level of description. For what a computational system computes is a function from TCS's to TCS's; and such a function pairs each TCS with a unique TCS as its successor. (Marr's immediate concern was to provide theoretical underpinnings for his own computational theory of vision, which was deterministic at the cognitive level.) But classical cognitive science can, and often does, allow for non-deterministic cognitive transitions. And it can, and often does, apply the notion of computation to the middle-level processes that subserve such transitions.

It is not difficult to generalize Marr's characterization of the three levels of description in classicism, to explicitly accommodate non-deterministic cognitive transitions and 'non-deterministic computation'. The basic idea is essentially this: the middle-level processes still count as computation because they still conform to programmable rules over representations; it's just that these rules include occasional 'dice throws' (involving, say, the system's consulting a random-number table), with subsequent processing steps depending on the outcome of the dice throws.

2   Foundational assumptions of classicism

The classical view that cognition is mathematically realized by an algorithm, i.e., by rule-governed symbol manipulation, involves three basic assumptions:

1   Intelligent cognition employs structurally complex mental representations.
2   Cognitive processing is sensitive to the structure of these representations, and thereby is sensitive to their content.
3   Cognitive processing conforms to precise, exceptionless rules, statable over the representations themselves and articulable in the format of a computer program.

Claims (2) and (3) are frequently not distinguished at all or are taken to be equivalent. But it is crucial to avoid this conflation; (3) implies (2), but (2) does not imply (3). This becomes important in Sections 7 and 8, below.

We will call the rules mentioned in (3) *programmable, representation level, rules* (for short, PRL rules). It is important that these rules are supposed to be statable at the level of the representations themselves; i.e., they refer solely to those structural aspects of the representations that play representational roles. Although processing in certain systems may also conform with rules statable at one or more lower levels (e.g., the level of machine language in a conventional computer), such lower-level rules are not the kind that count. This is important because there can be (non-classical) systems that conform to programmable rules at lower levels, but do not conform to rules statable only at the level of representations, as we discuss in Section 8, below.

460

Classicism does not assert that the PRL rules of cognitive processing must be represented by (or within) the cognitive system itself. Although programs are explicitly represented as stored data structures in the ubiquitous general purpose computer, stored programs are not an essential feature of the classical point of view. Rather, a classical system can conform with representation-level rules simply because it is hardwired to do so. It is, for example, plausible from the classical point of view to regard some innate processes as hardwired.

Assumptions (1)–(3) are widely recognized. However, to assert that cognitive transitions are subserved by an algorithm that computes those transitions is to presuppose something further, something so basic that its status as an assumption is often not even noticed, viz.,

4   Human cognitive transitions conform to a tractably computable function over total cognitive states (TCS's).[4]

This is hardly a truism; on the contrary, it is a very strong assumption indeed. Even granting that human cognitive transitions conform to a function, there is nothing independent of the assumptions of classicism to indicate that the cognitive transition function must be computable, let alone tractably computable. However, this assumption is never, to the best of our knowledge, argued for on independent grounds.

It is obviously presupposed by classicism, since cognitive transitions couldn't possibly be subserved by computation unless those transitions were themselves tractably computable.

With respect to assumptions (1)–(4), an attitude of 'What Else Could Cognition Be?' has pervaded classicism since its inception. The intended force of the rhetorical question is that there is nothing else it could be. Cognitive states have content-based causal roles, and it is felt that the only way they could have such roles is via computational processes. The question is rhetorical, but taken literally as a question it is fair enough; below we will sketch some answers.

Assumptions (1)–(4) of classicism are built right into Marr's tri-level typology for cognitive science. But classicism makes an additional foundational assumption, which is not officially presupposed in the three levels as characterized:

5   Many mental representations encode propositional information via language-like syntactic structure.

Although classicists can, and sometimes do, allow that *some* computational processes subserving human cognition might operate on representations with some kind of formal structure other than language-like syntactic structure, they also maintain that the systematic semantic coherence of human thought rests largely, and essentially, on computational manipulation of language-like mental representations.

461

3 Genericizing Marr's three levels

Marr's tri-level typology for cognitive science is a species of a more generic tri-level topology. Table 21.1 describes both versions. The generic version will serve as a touchstone below when we describe some potential alternatives to classicism.

Notice, to begin with, that Marr's three levels conform to this more generic characterization. A cognitive function will determine cognitive state-transitions. And the theory of algorithms is, of course, a part of mathematics. An algorithm, or program, is a mathematical beast, a set of rules for manipulating symbols or data-structures purely on the basis of their formal/structural properties, independently of any intentional content they might have; and the symbols and data-structures, so described, are themselves mathematical objects.

Cognitive science, since its inception, has embodied the following central and important idea about cognitive design, an idea reflected both in Marr's own typology and the generic one. What is important about the brain, *vis-à-vis* mentality, is not its specific neurobiological properties, but rather the abstract functional/organizational properties in virtue of which the physical state-transitions are systematically appropriate to the content of the mental states they subserve. These properties involve neither physical states and structures *qua* physical, nor mental states and structures *qua* mental; they are mathematical. The mathematical level of description is the appropriate one for characterizing the abstract system of functional/organizational features that constitutes Nature's engineering design for human cognition. This level mediates between the other two: cognitive states are realized by mathematical states, which in turn are realized by physical states of the cognizer's hardware or wetware.

The seminal idea that a system of mathematical state-transitions is the locus of cognitive design is built into classicism, with its emphasis on the algorithm. The genericization of Marr's three levels retains this key idea, but does so without building in assumptions (1)–(5) of classicism. There is more to mathematics, of course, than those branches of it that have traditionally figured most prominently in computer science. Part of what's important about connectionism is the mathematics that goes most naturally with it. We turn next to that.

Table 21.1

	Marr	*Generic*
Top level	COGNITIVE FUNCTION	COGNITIVE STATE-TRANSITIONS
Middle level	ALGORITHM	MATHEMATICAL STATE-TRANSITIONS
Bottom level	IMPLEMENTATION	IMPLEMENTATION

4 Connectionist networks and dynamical systems[5]

If one focuses on the theoretical and mathematical aspects of the recent connectionist movement in cognitive science, one finds connectionists increasingly invoking a rich mathematical framework with a distinguished history: the mathematical theory of *dynamical systems*. This framework fundamentally involves *continuous* mathematics rather than *discrete* mathematics – even though it can be brought to bear on systems which, at the relevant level of description, are literally discrete (say, because they evolve in discrete time-steps). In classicism, on the other hand, discrete mathematics is the natural mode of description: computation, as investigated in logic and computability theory, is the discrete, stepwise, rule-governed manipulation of symbols and data structures. An algorithm, or a program, is a set of rules for such discrete symbol manipulation.

To treat a system as a dynamical system is to specify in a certain way its temporal evolution, both actual and hypothetical. The set of all possible states of the system – so characterized – is the system's abstract *state space*. Each possible state of the system is a point in its state space, and each magnitude or parameter is a separate dimension of this space. The dynamical system, as such, is essentially the full collection of temporal trajectories the system would follow through state space – with a distinct trajectory emanating from each possible point in state space. A dynamical system can be identified with a set of state space trajectories in roughly the same sense in which a formal system can be identified with the set of its theorems. Just as there are many different axiomatizations of a formal system such as S5 or the classical propositional calculus, so likewise there might be many different mathematical ways of delineating a certain dynamical system or class of dynamical systems. (It is common practice to use the term 'dynamical system' ambiguously for abstract mathematical systems and for physical systems – such as planetary systems and certain networks – whose behaviour can be specified via some associated mathematical dynamical system. In the present paper, we will use the term mainly for mathematical systems.)

In classical mechanics, for instance, the magnitudes determining the state space of a given mechanical system are the instantaneous positions, masses, and velocities of the various bodies in the system. Temporal evolution of such a system, from one point in its state space to another, is determined by Newton's laws, which apply globally to the entire state of the system at an initial time.[6]

An *attractor* in state space is a point, or a set of points, in state space toward which the system will evolve from any of various other points. These others are said to lie within the *basin* of the attractor – the idea being that the attractor itself lies at the 'bottom' of the basin. The *boundary* of an attractor basin separates those points in state space lying within the basin from those lying outside it. A *point* attractor is a single stable point in state space; when a system evolves to a point attractor, it will remain in that state (unless perturbed). A *periodic* attractor is an orbit in state space that repeats back on itself; when a system evolves to a periodic attractor, it will oscillate perpetually through the same sequence of states (unless perturbed). A *quasiperiodic* attractor is an orbit in state space which, although it is not literally periodic, is asymptotic to a periodic trajectory. A *chaotic* (or *strange*) attractor is a nonrepeating orbit in state space that is not quasiperiodic. (Chaotic attractors are probably important in the brain's information processing. See Skarda and Freeman (1987), and Freeman (1991).)

A dynamical system is a geometrical/topological sort of mathematical critter. A useful geometrical metaphor for dynamical systems is the notion of a *landscape*. Consider a system involving just two magnitudes; its associated state space is two dimensional, and thus can be envisioned as a Cartesian plane. Now imagine this plane being topologically molded into a contoured, non-Euclidean, two dimensional surface. Imagine this 'landscape' oriented horizontally, in three dimensional space, in such a way that for each point p in the system's two dimensional state space, the path along the landscape that a ball would follow if positioned at p and then allowed to roll freely is the temporal trajectory that the network itself would follow, through its state space, if it were to evolve (without perturbation) from p. A dynamical system involving n distinct magnitudes can be thought of as a landscape too; it is the n-dimensional analog of such a two dimensional, non-Euclidean, contoured surface: i.e., a topological molding of the n-dimensional state space such that, were this surface oriented 'horizontally' in an (n+l) dimensional space, then a ball would 'roll along the landscape', from any initial point, in a way that corresponds to the way the system itself would evolve through its state space (barring perturbation) from that point.

Connectionist systems are naturally describable, mathematically, as dynamical systems. The magnitudes determining the state space of a given connectionist system are the instantaneous *activation* levels of each of the nodes in the network. Thus the state space of a network is frequently called its 'activation space'. The activation space of a network has as many dimensions as the network has nodes. The rules governing the system's temporal evolution apply locally, at each node of the system; this simultaneous local updating of all nodes determines the system's evolution through time.[7] The topology of a given network's activation landscape will be jointly determined by two factors: (i) the structural features of the network, in particular the pattern of connections between nodes and the weights on these connections; and (ii) the rules by which the individual nodes update their own activations and output signals. In connectionist models, cognitive processing is typically construed as the system's evolution along its activation landscape from one point in activation space to another – where the initial point in the temporal trajectory, and also the final point, and perhaps certain intermediate points, have certain representational contents (whereof more presently). In typical systems a problem is posed to the system by activating a set of nodes which are interpreted as having a certain content. From a dynamical systems perspective, this amounts to positioning the system at some point in its state or activation space. (Which specific point this is will often depend also upon the activation level of nodes other than those involved in posing the problem.) The network eventually settles into a stable state which constitutes its 'solution' to the problem – another point in its activation space. From the dynamical systems perspective, the system has evolved to a point attractor, from an initial point – the posed problem – within the associated attractor basin.

Learning too is typically construed, within connectionism, as temporal evolution of a connectionist network through a state space. When the issue is learning as opposed to processing, however, the weights on the network's connections are viewed as malleable rather than fixed; learning involves incremental changes in the weights. Hence the relevant states of the system are given by total specifications of its weights, at a given moment of time during learning. From the dynamical systems perspective, learning is thus a matter of the network's temporal evolution through its *weight space* (with the weight of each inter-node connection being a dimension of this space). However, a connectionist network as it evolves through weight space is not by itself a full-fledged dynamical system, because weight changes are effected not by the network itself, but by system-external application of a weight change algorithm.

Henceforth in this paper, we will frame our discussion with an eye toward connectionist networks as the sorts of physical devices that are to subserve cognitive processing. For simplicity, our focus will be on cognitive processing in a fixed network, rather than on learning; since the relevant dynamical systems will thus be ones whose dimensions correspond to activation levels of individual nodes, we will frequently refer to such a mathematical system as an 'activation landscape'.

Also for simplicity, we will couch our remarks in terms of *entire* connectionist networks, and the entire activation landscape subserved by a given network. But it should be kept in mind that a total connectionist network can consist of distinct, though interacting, subnetworks; and hence can be mathematically analysed as subserving separate, though coupled, dynamical systems. At the mathematical level of description, in such a case, the component dynamical systems are embedded in a larger, higher-dimensional, total dynamical system – just as the component physical sub-networks are embedded in a larger total network.

Though we focus on connectionism for concreteness, our discussion below is not necessarily limited to connectionist systems *per se*. Human-like cognition might only be subservable by physical systems quite different in nature from current connectionist networks; and in principle, our subsequent discussion would carry over, *mutatis mutandis*, to such alternative systems. Moreover, it is probably a mistake to treat the notion of a connectionist system as determined by the sorts of networks currently being explored under the rubric of connectionism. In a broader sense, a 'connectionist system' might better be construed simply as any dynamical system, physically realized by a network architecture. In this broader sense, there are numerous possible connectionist systems (including human brains, perhaps) that differ substantially from the kinds of networks currently being explored by connectionists.

Several points about connectionist systems as dynamical systems should be borne in mind, with respect to the remarks to follow. First, we again stress that the dynamical system, the activation landscape, is not itself a *physical* system; rather, it is a high-dimensional *mathematical* entity, a topologically complex surface in a high dimensional space. This space is not directly, but indirectly and abstractly, related to the physical space of the network that realizes it.

That is, second, although this abstract entity is indeed physically realized by a network, local regions of the activation landscape will not, in general, correspond to physically local portions of the *network*; quite the contrary. A *point* in activation space is determined by activation values for *every* node in the network; i.e., by the network as a whole. Conversely, a given value for a single node in an n-node network determines an n–1 dimensional region of activation space.

Hence, third, the more physically distributed the scheme of representation – so that representations are physically subserved by activation patterns involving many nodes, rather than by activation in single nodes or small node-pools – the more efficiently the abstract space is used for realizing representational states; i.e., the more physically distributed the representations, the more abstractly local! If representation is relatively local physically, so that relatively few nodes are required to take on certain values in order for a given TCS to be realized, then numerous total activation states of the system will realize that TCS; and each of these total activation states corresponds to a different point in activation space. Conversely, if representation is highly distributed, then in general comparatively fewer points in activation space will count as realizers of the TCS. In the extreme case of distributed representation, a TCS is realizable only by a single total activation pattern over all the nodes of the network; mathematically, the corresponding activation vector specifies a *unique* point in activation space.

Fourth, as dramatic recent developments in the mathematics of dynamical systems have shown, physical systems in nature can realize dynamical systems involving enormously complex, and enormously non-homogeneous, variation in local topography at different local regions of the abstract temporal landscape.[8] (This local topological complexity can involve, among other factors, the nature of the attractors, including chaotic ones; the nature of the basin boundaries, including fractal ones; and highly intricate intertwinings of attractor basins, some of them fractal.) Hence, fifth, the more distributed the scheme of representation, and hence the more localized the representational states are in *abstract* space, the greater are the opportunities for harnessing this local topological complexity, on the abstract activation landscape, to subserve sophisticated cognitive processing.

5 Connectionist systems as implementation architecture

With the discussion in Sections 1–4 as groundwork, we turn now to a succession of potential approaches to mentality that all fall under the generic tri-level typology of Section 3, and yet differ in increasingly radical ways from classicism. We will proceed 'up from the bottom' through the three levels. In this section, without yet calling into question classicism's assumptions about mathematical transitions or about cognitive transitions, we consider connectionist networks as potential implementations of the classical conception of cognition. Then in Section 6 we will turn to the view that the mathematical transitions, although they do involve algorithmic manipulation of representations, employ only representations whose formal/mathematical structure is *non-sentential*. In Section 7 we will consider the possibility that human cognition is mathematically subserved by a (network-realizable) dynamical system that is *non-algorithmic*. Finally, in section 8 we will consider the possibility that human cognitive transitions do not conform to a tractably computable function at all.

The dynamical-systems mathematical framework is quite broad and general, and is not intrinsically incompatible with the classical theory of computation. In principle, a connectionist network might be characterizable both (i) as executing an algorithm over representations, and (ii) as realizing a certain dynamical system. That is, mathematically, the network would subserve *both* an algorithm for computing a cognitive transition function, *and* a dynamical system whose trajectories through its state space subserve that function. If so, then in terms of the three levels of description from Section 3, the algorithmic characterization would belong to the mathematical level, whereas the dynamical-system characterization would belong to the implementation level. For, the latter would specify, albeit mathematically rather than physically, one way among many of implementing the algorithm – a way that is itself physically realizable via a network structure.[9]

So the least radical possibility for connectionism is that it might provide for new ways of implementing computational processes over structurally complex mental representations, including language-like representations. This might lead to interesting new developments at higher levels of description – for instance, to new kinds of algorithms, ones that are more naturally implemented in connectionist architecture than in von Neumann machines. Important as such new developments might be, however, they would not amount to a new conception of cognition, over against classicism's conception. On the contrary, as long as assumptions (1)–(5) from Section 2 remain in force, cognition is still being conceived classically. Implementational connectionism would be no deviation from classicism at all, but merely a species of it.[10]

6 Non-syntactic computationalism

One way to depart from classicism, however, is to reject assumption (5), while still retaining (1)–(4). On this view of the mind, human cognitive transitions do conform to a tractably computable transition function over total cognitive states; and these transitions are still subserved by an algorithm that computes that function – i.e., by PRL rules over mental representations. However, the representations themselves are not sentential, and thus their structure is not *syntactic* structure.

With connectionist networks in mind one might claim, for instance, that mental representations are non-sentential *vectors*, and that the algorithm effects vector-to-vector transformations that are systematically sensitive to vectorial structure, and thereby are systematically sensitive to the content of these non-sentential representations. Connectionist networks, on this view of things, are devices that are naturally suited to perform such non-sentential computation; vectors are realized as activation patterns over sets of nodes. Thus, the claim goes, connectionism can and should evolve toward non-sentential computationalism as an alternative to classicism.[11]

This approach fits naturally, although perhaps not inevitably, with the idea that human cognition, at the top level of description, involves state-transitions that are all essentially *associative* – in the sense that they reflect statistical correlations among items the cognitive system can represent, and can be analysed as the drawing of statistical inferences. Many fans of connectionism evidently see things this way, and tend to regard connectionism as breathing new life into associationism. Prominent foes of connectionism, notably Fodor and Pylyshyn (1988), also see things this way; but they regard the link with associationism as grounds for maintaining that connectionism, in so far as it strives to do more than implement classicism, is bound to founder on the same kinds of problems that plagued traditional associationism. Concerning the non-implementational prospects for connectionist networks in cognitive science, Fodor and Pylyshyn write:

> A good bet is that networks sustain such processes as can be analysed as the drawing of statistical inferences; as far as we can tell, what network models really are is just analog machines for computing such inferences. Since we doubt that much of cognitive processing does consist of analysing statistical relations, this would be quite a modest estimate of the prospects for network theory. (p. 68)

We ourselves share Fodor and Pylyshyn's doubts about the prospects for associationism, given the problems this doctrine faces in accommodating the semantic coherence of thought. On the more general question whether human cognitive transitions conform to a transition function that is tractably computable via computational processes operating entirely over non-sentential representations, we are also pessimistic; again, it is hard to see how rule-based transformations of representations could reflect the systematic semantic coherence of thought, for the vastly many distinct cognitive states that humans are capable of instantiating, unless many of those representations encode propositional information in systematic, productive ways, i.e., syntactically.

More fundamentally, however, we doubt whether cognition in general is subserved by representation-level computation *at all* – i.e., that it is subserved by transformations of representations in accordance with PRL rules.[12] Still more fundamentally, we doubt whether human cognitive transitions even conform to a tractably *computable* transition function, either a deterministic one or a nondeterministic one. Connectionism, we think, might well be wedd-able to non-classical conceptions of mentality that are more radical than non-sentential computationalism, and that have little to do with associationism. It is time to turn to these.

7 Non-algorithmic dynamical systems

Perhaps human cognitive transitions are subserved by a dynamical system that is not also an algorithm for computing those transitions. Even if human cognitive transitions happen to be tractably computable, as classicism assumes, they might not be subserved via representation-level computation – i.e., via manipulation of language-like mental representations, in conformity with PRL rules adverting to the structure of those representations. Instead, the system's transitions from one total cognitive state to another might leap fairly large cognitive gaps in single steps that are not decomposable, via classicist 'boxology', into computationally subservable cognitive baby steps (either serial ones, or simultaneous ones, or both).[13] This possibility, obviously, is quite radically at odds with classicism.

Here is a simple hypothetical example, to illustrate what we mean. Consider standard decision theory, viewed as a putative psychological model of human deliberation and choice, rather than a normative theory. According to this model, a deliberating agent will choose an action with maximum expected utility. The expected utility of an envisioned act is a certain kind of weighted sum: the sum of the respective numerical values the agent assigns to the various envisioned potential outcomes of that act, with each value being weighted by the agent's subjective probability of the given outcome's resulting from the act.

Now, one way that such a decision-making system might work would be computational. For instance, it might actually *calculate* this weighted sum, for each envisioned act; then compare the totals for the acts and *calculate* which act or acts have maximal expected utility; and then pick an act with maximal expected utility. But here is another possibility, without representation-level computation. There are various beliefs and desires at work in the system, with various strengths. They all enter the hopper at once and interact directly – somewhat in the manner of a complex combination of interacting physical forces in a planetary system, with the various bodies exerting mutual gravitational influence on one another. The way they interact is via a kind of 'resolution of forces', where the forces get resolved in such a way that the cognitive system eventually settles on an alternative with maximal expected utility.[14]

Under this second mode of mathematical realization, there would be no separate baby steps (either sequential or simultaneous) of actually calculating weighted sums, of actually comparing them pairwise, and the like. Instead there would be a mathematically more direct route to a decision: viz., the system's *settling*, by evolving quickly and automatically to a point attractor realizing a decision to go with one of the acts that has maximal expected utility. One of the potential acts *wins out*.

It is important to appreciate that this hypothetical scenario would indeed constitute a very important departure from classicism. At the mathematical level of description, we would have not an *algorithm* that subserves cognitive transitions via representation level computational baby-steps (either sequential or simultaneous), but instead a dynamical system that subserves cognitive transitions via non-algorithmic, leaps-and-bounds-ish, state transitions.[15]

It is also important to realize that connectionist networks could, in principle, subserve non-algorithmic cognitive transitions, even though each node in the network updates its own activation, locally, in accordance with an algorithm. For, the local updatings of individual nodes need not be parallel baby-steps in some algorithm *over representations* – some set of programmable rules for manipulating and transforming complex representations on the basis of their representation-level structure. Instead, the node-level computation in the network might be entirely *sub*-representational, and hence implementational. This possibility seems especially salient for connectionist systems in which activation-levels of individual nodes do not have any specific, determinate, representational content – for instance, systems employing a representation scheme in which all representations, even the semantically atomic ones, are *distributed* activation-patterns.

The example of a non-algorithmic decision maker is hypothetical. We turn now to an actual connectionist model which is a good *prima facie* candidate for being a system that performs a sophisticated information-processing task in a non-algorithmic way. It is a model of natural-language sentence parsing, due to George Berg (1992).[16] The system receives, as external input, a temporal sequence of word-representations, each of which represents a successive word in an English sentence. It constructs a representation of the sentence's syntactic structure; and it can recursively decompose this parse-representation, in order to successively represent the sentence's main syntactic constituents, then the main sub-constituents of each of these constituents, and so on – all the way down to the constituent words.

Berg's model adapts and extends an approach for representing recursive structures first developed by Jordan Pollack (1990), called 'recursive auto-associative memory', or RAAM. In Pollack's RAAM networks, the representations all have so-called 'fixed bandwidth'; i.e., for any node-pool in which representations are instantiated, each representation is a fully distributed activation pattern involving every node in the pool. In one part of a RAAM system, fixed-bandwidth representations can be constructed for recursive structures of arbitrary complexity; in the other part, such representations can be recursively decomposed, thereby successively reconstructing the representations of the successive substructures.

The overall structure of Berg's network is depicted in *Figure 21.1*. It has five layers, with recurrent feedback from the hidden layer back to the input layer. Nodes are segmented into specific pools, as shown. The input layer has two pools, one for word-representations and the other which duplicates the current hidden-layer representation. The output layer has four pools, one for

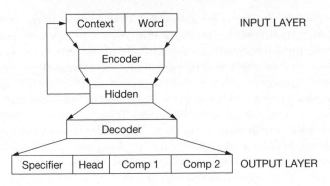

Figure 21.1 The basic structure of Berg's parser network (Berg 1992)

each of the four syntactic roles – specifier, head word, first complement, and second complement – of an 'X-Bar template' of the sort posited in the form of theoretical syntax known as 'government and binding theory' (cf. Chomsky 1981; Sells 1985). Such X-Bar structures can exhibit recursive embedding, because the roles of specifier, first complement, and second complement can be filled by X-Bar structures themselves.

Representations in Berg's model are fixed-bandwidth activation patterns. Words get represented as distributed activation patterns in the word pool of the input layer, and in the head-word pool of the output layer. These two pools have the same number of nodes, this number being the bandwidth of the word-representations. X-Bar structures themselves, including the 'null' structure, get represented as distributed activation patterns in the hidden layer, in the context pool of the input layer, and in the specifier and complement pools of the output layer. Each of these pools has the same number of nodes, this number being the bandwidth of the X-Bar representations.

Construction of parse representations occurs in the first three layers of Berg's network, in the following way. A representation of the first word of an English sentence is activated in the word pool of the input layer, with the context pool initially dormant; activation then passes forward through the encoder layer to the hidden layer, thereby generating in the hidden layer a tentative, partial, parse representation. This tentative representation is then copied back to the 'context' pool in the input layer, at the same time that the next word of the English sentence is being activated in the 'word' pool; activation then passes forward from the context and word pools of the input layer, through the encoder layer to the hidden layer, thereby generating a new tentative parse representation. This process continues, with as many feed-forward passes from input to hidden layer as there are words in the English sentence. The hidden layer ends up containing a fully distributed representation of the sentence's syntactic structure.

Recursive decomposition of the parse representations occurs in the bottom three layers of the network, as follows. When the total parse representation is

471

present in the hidden layer, activation is fed forward through the decoder layer to the output layer; this generates, within the four respective pools in the output layer, fixed-bandwidth representations of the sentence's four primary X-Bar constituents – the specifier, head word, first complement, and second complement respectively. (Some of these constituents might be null.) If the specifier-representation, and/or either complement-representation, is not null, then it can be copied back into the hidden layer, and then decomposed by another forward activation-pass through the decoder layer to the output layer. This process can be conducted recursively; along the way, fixed-bandwidth representations of all the sentence's syntactic constituents and sub-constituents get recovered. (The atomic constituents, i.e., the words, all turn up at one point or another in the head-word (or specifier) pool of the output layer.)

Since the parse representations all have fixed bandwidth, regardless of the complexity of the parse structures they represent, recursive complexity in the representations themselves is obviously not a matter of parse-substructures being represented by activation patterns that are physical components of the activation patterns representing the larger structures. But recursive information is systematically encoded nonetheless, since the representations of X-Bar sub-structures are recursively recoverable from representations of the larger structures.

Berg trains up his network, as did Pollack his original RAAM systems, by means of a sophisticated adaptation of the back-propagation learning algorithm, incorporating what Pollack calls the 'moving target strategy'. Back-propagation is a method which adjusts the weights of the network in the direction of the correct, 'target' output, doing this repeatedly until the network produces the correct output. Pollack divides the training regimen into successive 'epochs'. With the moving target strategy, in each epoch, the 'target' representations, for whole tree structures and for their constituent sub-structures, are the ones the system itself has developed in the preceding epoch. The representations thus change along with the weights from epoch to epoch, in a process of controlled co-evolution.[17] The system, as it learns, gradually *discovers* appropriate representations. With sufficient training, it gradually converges on a combination of weights and representations under which the representations of parsing structures and substructures are recursively recoverable, accurately and systematically.

Berg's connectionist parser works quite well, on a wide range of sentences of varying recursive depth. It also generalizes quite effectively to new sentences that were not part of the training corpus. Berg writes:

> Testing and training are done on separate corpora each containing the patterns for 1000 sentences. The average sentence is between 6.5 to 7 words long ... The corpora contain sequential presentations of randomly generated, syntactically legal sentences. There is no restriction on the length or 'depth' of the generated sentences ... This results in most of the sentences being between 2 and 8 phrases deep, with fewer

sentences of greater depths, typically with a maximum between 14 and 20 ... [These] networks typically converge to 1–8% overall error for both training and testing corpora. (p. 5)

From the successive decoding of the phrases of a sentence, one can read off the X-Bar syntax of that sentence. *Figure 21.2*, for instance, is an 'unrolled network' diagram showing how a series of decodings reveals the overall syntactic structure of a sample sentence.

It seems highly unlikely that this connectionist system does this parsing by executing an algorithm at the level of representations themselves. There are two interrelated reasons to think so. First, the representations are quite thoroughly distributed: activation values of individual nodes are not assigned any specific, determinate, representational content. Since rules for activation-updating apply locally at individual nodes, whereas representation is fully non-local, the node-level computations appear to be purely subrepresentational, rather than being component steps in some set of (highly parallel) representation-level rules. Second, although the structures being represented have varying, arbitrarily deep, recursive complexity, all such structures are represented by activation patterns of the *same* bandwidth, within the *same* pools of nodes; hence, recursive complexity of representational content is quite unrelated to the physical part/whole structure of the representations themselves. Since the activation patterns representing complex structures are not anything like 'physical sums' of smaller activation patterns representing the

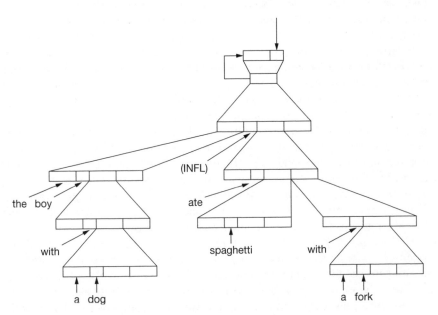

Figure 21.2 The 'unrolled' network for the sentence 'the boy with a dog ate spaghetti with a fork'. Unlabelled phrases at the output level are empty (Berg 1992)

component sub-structures, it is all the more unlikely that the system's manipulation of these patterns can be analysed as conforming to PRL rules involving numerous simultaneous representation-level baby-steps.

But how else, it might be asked, *could* the system be accomplishing its parsing task so successfully, if not by implementing some representation-level algorithm? What other sort of characterization might it have, at the mathematical level of description, that would constitute a successful design for the subserving of systematically content-appropriate transitions over intentional states?

Part of what we find interesting and exciting about Berg's model, and also about Pollack's RAAM's, is that their use of the 'moving target' training strategy suggests a general answer to this question: an alternative, non-classical, approach to mathematical design for information-processing systems. The key ideas are as follows. As the network gets progressively altered at the physical level during learning, via successive changes in the weights on the connections, at higher levels of description what's happening is the progressive co-evolution of two interrelated factors. On one hand, the dynamical system itself is being altered by weight changes; the local topography throughout the high-dimensional activation landscape is being progressively *molded*. On the other hand, because of the moving target strategy, there is also progressive alteration of the position of representations on the activation landscape.[18] This repositioning effects a refinement of the realization relation from intentional states (i.e., representational states *qua* representational) to points on the activation landscape. The realization relation exhibits increasing systematicity, coming to reflect, in the way it positions representation-realizing points relative to one another on the activation landscape, important relations among the intentional states being realized. The realization relation and the landscape topography end up 'made for each other', with respect to the information-processing task the system is being trained to perform: the final weight setting for the network subserves a high-dimensional activation landscape whose overall local topography yields systematically content-appropriate temporal trajectories, under the operative intentional/mathematical realization relation. Thus, the key to the system's design is that the shape of the activation landscape, and the overall positioning of representation-realizing points on that landscape, are jointly just right to subserve the relevant intentional transition function, for a very large class of potential intentional states. Moreover, it's neither an accident nor a miracle that this is so; rather, it's the understandable result of applying a learning algorithm in a way that incorporates the moving target strategy.

There is nothing in this story about cognitive design that requires that a cognitive system even conform to programmable rules over representations, let alone proceed by executing such rules. This story evidently is true of Berg's system. So we have a possible answer to the question: how else, if not by a representation-level algorithm, could the system accomplish its parsing task?

In addition, the story is obviously quite general in its potential scope: it is entirely possible that the abstract 'engineering design' for much of human cognition does not involve any representation-level algorithm, but instead involves a high-dimensional activation landscape and a cognitive/mathematical realization relation that fit together like hand and glove to subserve the system's cognitive transition function. For a human, of course, the CTF involves an *enormous* range of distinct total cognitive states the system can instantiate – vastly more than it ever *will* instantiate in its lifetime. Given this fact, and given that all trajectories on the activation landscape that commence from any TCS-realizing point must yield content-appropriate cognitive transitions, a suitable cognitive/mathematical realization relation would probably have to exhibit a very high degree of systematicity: i.e., it would position all the TCS-realizing points throughout the landscape in such a way that their various relative-position relations reflect many important semantic relations among the TCS's themselves.

The semantic relations reflected in this way would very likely include relations of *semantic constituency* among complex intentional states: for instance, the relation *being about the same individual,* or the relation *predicating the same property.* In so far as (i) such semantic constituency relations get systematically reflected in the positioning in activation space of representation-realizing points, and (ii) this fact is important in the dynamical system's successfully subserving content-appropriate cognitive transitions, these relative-position relations would function as *syntactic* relations. That is, the overall distribution of representation-realizations in high-dimensional activation space would structurally encode the kinds of semantic relations that get encoded in public languages by names, predicates, quantifiers, and so forth; and would do so in a manner that is directly implicated in the design whereby the system subserves cognition – and in particular is directly implicated in the explanation of the systematicity of cognition that Fodor *et al.* have rightly insisted on. This is not what Fodor and McLaughlin (1990) call *classical* syntax, by which they mean a kind of structural constituency in which the constituents of a complex representation are always tokened whenever the representation itself is tokened. It is, however, the kind of syntax that looks natural for an approach to cognitive design in which cognition is subserved, at the mathematical level of description, by a dynamical system rather than an algorithm over representations.[19]

8   Cognition without (tractable) computability

Classicism's most fundamental foundational supposition, the one we listed as assumption (4) in Section 2, is that human cognitive transitions conform to a tractably computable transition function (CTF) over total cognitive states (TCS's) – either a deterministic function or a non-deterministic one. As yet we have not questioned this assumption. The burden of Section 7 was that even if it is true, classicism might be mistaken anyway. For, human cognitive transitions might be subserved not by an algorithm that computes the CTF, but rather by a non-algorithmic dynamical system.

It is very important, however, that the general approach to cognitive engineering just sketched does not *presuppose* that a human CTF is tractably computable. Thus arises an even more radically non-classicist possibility: viz., that a human CTF is not a tractably computable function at all, either deterministic or non-deterministic. A CTF that is not tractably computable might be subservable by a non-algorithmic dynamical system which is itself subservable by a neural network.[20]

What would it mean for a human CTF not to be tractably computable? In addressing this question, it is useful to think about ways the function might, or might not, be specifiable. The CTF itself can be construed as an enormous set of ordered pairs, each of which associates a single TCS with a set of one or more successor TCS's. One way to specify this function would be via a huge (possibly infinite) *list*: each ordered pair in the CTF being specified by a separate entry on the list. Such a list, even if finite, would be truly gargantuan – far too big to itself constitute a tractable set of programmable rules.[21] So to be tractably computable, given the enormous number of distinct cognitive transitions, a CTF would have to be fully specifiable in some way other than via a brute list.

What classicism assumes, of course, is that a human CTF is specifiable via some set of *general* laws over cognitive states; each cognitive transition is just a particular instance of these laws, and the function the laws delineate is itself tractably computable. Conversely, if the CTF is not tractably computable then it will not be thus specifiable. If cognitive transitions are effected by a dynamical system of the sort imagined in the previous section, there is no reason why the CTF would have to be tractably computable.

This would not necessarily mean that there would be no interesting, systematic, psychological laws. For, there remain these two possibilities: either (i) there are psychological laws that fully specify the CTF, but happen to delineate a transition function that is not tractably computable; or (ii) there are laws that only *partially* specify the CTF, because they contain ineliminable *ceteris paribus* clauses adverting to potential psychology-level factors that could prevent *ceteris* from being *paribus*.[22]

In general, the failure of a CTF to be tractably computable could be the result of either or both of the following factors: (i) the dynamical system itself, whose mathematical state-transitions might not be tractably computable; or (ii) the way TCS's are realized as points in the dynamical system's state space. Concerning the first factor, it may well be possible for non-computable dynamical systems to be subserved by neural networks – especially if the networks are made more analog in nature by letting the nodes take on a continuous range of activation values, and/or letting them update themselves continuously, rather than by discrete time steps.

Moreover, even if the mathematical state-transitions of the dynamical system are tractably computable (as they are, for instance, for current connectionist systems – which are usually simulated on standard computers), the CTF subserved by the dynamical system might fail to be tractably computable anyway. Consider the converse of the realization relation between TCS's and points in a dynamical system's state-space. This is a function – call it the *realizes-function* – mapping points in a dynamical system's state space to TCS's. (It is a function because it never pairs a point in state space with more than one TCS.) This function itself might not be tractably computable. If not, then obviously it would not be possible to compute cognitive transitions this way; given the initial mathematical state of the dynamical system, (i) compute the dynamical system's trajectory through state space; and (ii) for each point p on the trajectory, compute the TCS (if any) realized by p. And if the cognitive transitions subserved by the dynamical system are not computable in *this* way, it seems likely that they would turn out not to be tractably computable in any other way either. That is, there might well be a network-subservable dynamical system S, a CTF C, and a realizes-function R, such that

(i) S's mathematical state-transitions are tractably computable;
(ii) C is not tractably computable; and yet
(iii) S subserves C, under R.

Needless to say, therefore, one should not infer from the fact that a system's non-cognitive state transitions are tractably computable that it cannot subserve a CTF which fails to be tractably computable.

The possibility that cognitive transitions are not tractably computable deserves to be taken very seriously. Given what we have said in the last two sections, tractably computable CTF's might well be only a rather small subset of the CTF's that nature could have evolved the hardware to subserve. Thus there is no obvious reason to suppose that nature's CTF's *are* tractably computable.

Moreover, we have elsewhere argued (Horgan and Tienson 1989, 1990, 1993, 1994) that when one reflects carefully on certain problems (like the frame problem) that have persistently arisen in classicism and that largely spawned connectionism, a strong case emerges for the contention that human cognition is just too complex and too subtle to conform to programmable representation-level rules. If so, then the heart of Nature's evolutionary blueprint for human cognition cannot be an algorithm; instead it might well be a non-algorithmic dynamical system, subserving cognitive transitions that are not tractably computable at all

Notes

1 Multiple realizability is no doubt ubiquitous in nature. The case most discussed is higher-level state-types being differently realized in different species or creature-kinds. But the same higher-level state-type might be multiply realizable in different members of the same species; or in a single individual at distinct moments in its own history; or even in a single individual at a single moment in its own history.

2 For further elaboration of this point, see Horgan (1992). Marr himself evidently saw the point quite clearly – as evidenced in the following passage from Marr (1977). The passage sets forth an example to illustrate the distinction between the computational level of description and the algorithm level, in a way that also brings in the hardware/wetware level: '[T]ake the case of Fourier analysis. The (computational) theory of the Fourier transform is well understood, and is expressed independently of the particular way in which it is computed. There are, however, several algorithms for implementing the Fourier transform – the Fast Fourier transform . . ., which is a serial algorithm, and the parallel "spatial" algorithms that are based on the mechanisms of coherent optics. All these algorithms carry out the same computation, and the choice of which one to use depends upon the available hardware. In passing, we also note that the distinction between serial and parallel also resides at the algorithm level and is not a deep property of a computation' (Marr 1977: 37). Note that in this passage he uses the term 'implementation' to characterize the relation between the computational level and the algorithm level. The idea is that computations are implemented via algorithms, which themselves get implemented in hardware (or wetware); multiple modes of implementation are possible between each level and the one immediately below it.

3 In keeping with the classical idea that cognition is computation, this means generalizing the notion of computation in some appropriate way. We suggest one way of doing it in Chapter 2 of Horgan and Tienson (1993). The reader should keep in mind, for the discussion that follows, that classicism allows for the possibility that a human CTF is non-deterministic, and that the notion of 'computing' a TCS should be understood accordingly. (A non-deterministic CTF is a function that takes each CTF to the set of its potential successor TCS's or to a probability distribution over the members of that set.)

4 The commonly heard term 'tractably computable' is vague and perhaps also somewhat context dependent. '*Not* tractably computable' means something stronger, of course, than simply not *easily* computable. 'Not tractably computable' seems sometimes to be used to mean something like: not computable with the computational resources that are available or likely to become available. It also seems to be used with a – not unrelated – sense something like: not computable with roughly the order of computational resources of the human brain, whatever that may be. It does not matter for our present purposes which sense is used. To overcome the vagueness of the term, when we discuss below the possibility that human cognitive transitions do not conform to a tractably computable function, we will mean that they do *not* do so under any reasonable resolution of the vagueness of 'tractably computable'.

5 This section is largely adapted from section 3 of Horgan and Tienson (1992a).

6 Some dynamical systems, including many that have been studied in physics, evolve in accordance with relatively *simple* laws, typically involving global states of the system. Usually such laws are expressed via differential equations, or difference equations if discrete time-steps are involved. But it is very important to appreciate that in general, a dynamical system need not conform to such laws.

7 Thus, connectionist networks need not, in general, conform to simple update-rules expressible over global activation-states, Cf. note 6.

8 This is especially true when the physical systems involve nonlinear dynamical behaviour. Connectionist networks are like this, as they provably must be to avoid

well known limitations in their computational power similar to the limitations of two-layer perceptrons. Each node updates its activation in accordance with a non-linear function.

9 This way of putting the point involves seeing the implementation level as hierarchically stratified, involving one or more mathematically specified sub-levels before 'bottoming out' in physical states and state-transitions in a physical machine. This kind of implementational hierarchy is ubiquitous in conventional computers: there is a mathematically describable 'virtual machine', executing algorithms over sentences that belong to a high-level formal language and whose content is the information the system is supposed to be processing; this mathematical machine is simulated by another mathematically describable machine, executing algorithms over sentences in a different formal language whose sentences have different representational content (typically, some sort of number-crunching content); this simulational embedding of one mathematical virtual machine within another proceeds down to the level of machine language, and then bottoms out in physical realization of the lowest-level mathematical machine.

One could, alternatively, think of the hierarchy as belonging to the middle, design level, and the implementation level as involving only physical realization. However one chooses to put it, the point is that there is typically an implementational hierarchy between the level of cognitive design and bottoming out in physical realization.

10 Cf. Fodor and Pylyshyn (1988). For a more detailed discussion of the matter of 'mere implementation,' see Horgan and Tienson (1992b).

11 Paul Churchland (1989) is a fan of connectionism who appears to see the matter this way.

12 It is the PRL rules we doubt, not the representations; this is why we have elsewhere called our view 'representations without rules.' We also maintain that human cognition requires representations with some form of *syntax*. But if the proper middle level of description in cognitive science involves a dynamical system and not an algorithm, as we believe, then syntactic constituency relations are likely to look very different than in classicism. See the end of Section 7.

13 The metaphor of connectionist systems leaping large cognitive gaps in a single bound is from Lloyd (1991). He there floats, as worth serious consideration, the limit-case view that all mental states are conscious ones – there are no unconscious, intervening mental steps between conscious mental states.

14 The analogy with the interaction of physical forces is not exact, since the cognitive system must settle into *cognitive* states, and in general a relatively small portion of the physical states of the system will realize cognitive states. (Equivalently, only relatively few points in activation space realize cognitive states.) Simple summation of forces in a network would in general not lead to cognitive states. Thus, there must be some sort of 'winner-take-all' feature built into the cognitive system that ensures that it ends up in cognitive states (and by and large, relevant ones).

15 With non-algorithmic dynamical systems, in general one might expect there to be many fewer cognitive transitions than are posited in classicism, because classical models often require numerous sequential cognitive baby-steps (many of which are supposed to occur rapidly and unconsciously); cf. note 13 above. When the temporal trajectory subserving a cognitive transition passes through a number of

479

intermediate points on the activation landscape, it may be that few or none of those points realize *cognitive* states.

16 The task is sophisticated enough that it probably cannot be accomplished by a purely associative/statistical algorithm, one that merely performs statistical inferences involving, for instance, transition-frequencies among words of English. And as we discuss below, the network generalizes substantially beyond the English sentences that constitute its training corpus – which means that it presumably doesn't learn by merely encoding a 'look-up table' correlating each input in its training regimen with the correct output. Thus, Berg's model is a plausible candidate for being a system that performs a non-associative information-processing task in a non-algorithmic way.

17 Berg's training procedure implements the moving target strategy somewhat differently than does Pollack; but the differences need not concern us here.

18 At the physical level of description, intentional states are realized in networks by activation patterns. But mathematically, the activation vector describing a particular physical pattern is also a specification of a set of coordinates in the dynamical system's state-space. Thus, from the dynamical systems perspective, the states realizing a given intentional state are the points on the activation landscape that have the coordinates specified in that vector.

19 Some might object to calling relations of relative position, among points in activation space, syntactic constituency relations, even though they do reflect relations of semantic constituency in a way that figures centrally in the system's design. We ourselves think that this usage is indeed sanctioned by the ordinary, pre-theoretical notion of syntax. But the important question, of course, is whether the relative-position relations *can* play this role – not whether their doing so would suffice to sanction calling them syntactic.

20 Most of what we say in this section applies if a human CTF is not computable at all – which may be the case if there are literally infinitely many distinct cognitive states that a cognizer can instantiate. If there are only finitely many such states, then the cognizer's CTF is computable in the official mathematical sense. We take no stand on whether there are literally infinitely many cognitive states that human cognizers can instantiate, or only a huge finite number. Our view is that if human CTF's are computable at all in the mathematical sense, it is only because they are finite. But *tractable* computability is the important concept in the context of classical cognitive science, so we will focus on this.

21 This is our answer to the main argument of Aizawa (1994). To get a sense of how huge the list would have to he, there are on the order of 10^{20} English sentences of 20 words or less (Miller 1965). For most of these there is a potential corresponding thought, and potential thoughts far outstrip sentences because of our ability to make relevant discriminations that we lack linguistic resources to describe. For comparison, there are 10^{15} or so neurons in the human brain, and there have been around 10^7 seconds in the history of the universe.

22 The second possibility is the one we ourselves think most likely for human cognizers. Cf. Horgan and Tienson (1989, 1990, 1993).

References

Aizawa, K. (1994) "Representations without rules, connectionism, and the syntactic argument." *Synthese* 101: 465–92.

Berg, G. (1992) "A connectionist parser with recursive sentence structure and lexical disambiguation." *Proceedings of the American Association for Artificial Intelligence*, AAAI–92. San José: Calif.

Chomsky, N. (1981) *Lectures on Government and Binding*. Dordrecht: Foris.

Churchland, P.M. (1989) *A Neurocomputational Perspective: The Nature of Mind and the Structure of Science*. Cambridge, Mass.: MIT Press.

Cummins, R. (1983) *The Nature of Psychological Explanation*. Cambridge, Mass.: MIT.

Fodor, J.A. and Pylyshyn, Z. (1988) "Connectionism and cognitive architecture: A critical analysis," in S. Pinker and J. Mehler (eds) *Connections and Symbols*, Cambridge, Mass.: MIT Press.

Fodor, J. and McLaughlin, B. (1990) "Connectionism and the problem of systematicity: Why Smolensky's solution doesn't work." *Cognition* 35: 183–204.

Freeman, W. (1991) "The physiology of perception." *Scientific American* 264(2): 78–85.

Horgan, T. (1992) "From cognitive science to folk psychology: Computation, mental representation, and belief." *Philosophy and Phenomenological Research* 52: 449–84.

Horgan, T. and Tienson, J. (1989) "Representations without rules." *Philosophical Topics* 17: 27–43.

—— (1990) "Soft laws." *Midwest Studies in Philosophy* 15: 256–79.

—— (1992a) "Cognitive systems as dynamical systems." *Topoi* 11: 27–43.

—— (1992b) "Structured representations in connectionist systems." In S. Davis (ed.) *Connectionism: Theory and Practice*. Oxford: Oxford University Press.

—— (1993) *Connectionism and the Philosophy of Psychology: Representational Realism without Rules*. Cambridge, Mass.: MIT Press.

—— (1994) "A nonclassical framework for cognitive science." *Synthese* 101: 305–45.

Lloyd, D. (1991) "Leaping to conclusions: Connectionism, consciousness, and the computational mind." In T. Horgan and J. Tienson (eds), *Connectionism and the Philosophy of Mind*. Dordrecht: Kluwer.

Marr, D. (1982) *Vision*. New York: Freeman.

—— (1977) "Artificial intelligence – a personal view." *Artifical Intelligence* 9, 37–47. Reprinted in J. Haugeland (ed.) *Mind Design*. Cambridge, Mass.: MIT Press.

Miller, G. (1965) "Some preliminaries to psycholinguistics." *American Psychologist* 20: 15–20.

Pollack, J. (1990) "Recursive distributed representations." *Artificial Intelligence* 46: 77–105.

Sells, P. (1985) *Lectures on Contemporary Syntactic Theories*. Stanford, Calif.: Center for the Study of Language and Information.

Skarda, C. and Freeman, W. (1987) "How brains make chaos in order to make sense of the world." *Behavioral and Brain Sciences* 10: 161–95.

481

22

T. van Gelder, "Compositionality: A Connectionist Variation on a Classical Theme"

Connectionism has been attacked on the grounds that it does not employ compositionally structured representations (e.g., Fodor and Pylyshyn 1988). This article develops the response that Connectionist models can, and in fact sometimes do, employ compositionally structured representations without, thereby, simply implementing a Classical "Language of Thought." Focusing on the mode of combination employed in constructing representations, it distinguishes concatenative compositionality, essential to the Classical approach, from a merely functional counterpart increasingly common in Connectionist research. On the basis of this distinction it is possible to demonstrate that Connectionist representations can be compositional without being Classical, and further, that Fodor and Pylyshyn's supposedly conclusive arguments in favor of the Classical approach do not in fact support that approach over the Connectionist alternative (as opposed to an "associationist" straw man).

Must mental representations be structured objects? If so, in what sense? These very general questions, never far below the surface in both the theory and practice of cognitive science, have arisen once again in the guise of a clash between defenders of mainstream symbolic or "Classical" orthodoxy, and advocates of the rival Connectionist approach to the modeling of cognition, Classicalists, such as Fodor and Pylyshyn (1988), have argued that the explanation of cognition requires representations with a combinatorial syntax and semantics; Connectionism is doomed, it is claimed, unless it finds a way to implement such representations. Smolensky, meanwhile, has proposed a formidable defense: Connectionist representations can be compositional without being strictly combinatorial in the Classical sense, and on this basis Connectionism can account for cognition needing to implement a "Language of Thought" (Smolensky 1987b, 1988).

There is at least one basic point of agreement among the various parties: In order to exhibit any reasonably sophisticated cognitive functions, a system must be able to represent complex structured items. To take an obvious example, engaging in conversation requires, at some level, the ability to represent to oneself the sentences being used. The conflict between the two approaches is, in large part, a disagreement over how to do this. What kind of structure (if any) is needed *in the representations themselves* in order to represent such items effectively? And how does such structure interact with mental processes to generate complex cognitive behavior? At the core of this debate is the notion of compositional structure. Both sides agree that representations need to be compositional[1] but disagree over what this entails and how such structure contributes to the explanation of cognition.

This article takes up and develops Smolensky's insight that mental representations can be compositional without being Classical. It begins with an examination of the notion of compositionality, and argues that at least two broad kinds need to be distinguished carefully. One is extremely familiar, and characteristic of the Classical approach; while the other, previously virtually unknown, is increasingly common in Connectionism, for reasons deeply tied to the nature of Connectionist theorizing. The question, then, is which kind is to be preferred for the purpose of modeling cognition? Although any general answer to this question is far beyond the scope of the current article, it is shown in the final section that Fodor and Pylyshyn's supposedly conclusive arguments for a Language of Thought, in fact, fail to rule out the Connectionist alternative. Connectionism is therefore in a position to avoid the apparent dilemma of either implementing a Language of Thought or failing to account for cognition. With its distinctive style of compositionality in hand, it may well do neither.

1   Styles of compositionality

In the most general (and vague) sense, any item is appropriately said to have a compositional structure when it is built up, in a systematic way, out of regular parts drawn from a certain determinate set; those parts are then the *components* or *constituents* of the item.[2] There are, however, a number of ways in which an item can be "built up" out of parts, and a number of corresponding notions of "part" or "constituent." To see this, it is useful to start with a commonplace example of compositionality, generalizing from there to some minimal abstract conditions that a scheme of representation should satisfy to count as compositional. It will then be apparent that there are a variety of ways that a particular scheme might satisfy those conditions.

Consider, then, a paradigm of compositionally structured representation, the expressions of the propositional or sentential logic (PL). Here are some samples:

(1) *P*
(2) *(P&Q)*
(3) *((P&Q)&R)*

It is immediately apparent that each of these expressions has been constructed out of tokens drawn from a restricted set of primitive types; for example, connectives such as & and sentential variables such as P, Q and so on. These are the primitive constituents of the expressions. Some expressions, such as (3), also have *expressions* as constituents; this can be stated, in a general way, as the principle that expressions of Type (3) have expressions of Type (2) as constituents. Generalizing, it would seem that a compositional scheme of representation must satisfy at least the following conditions.

(a) There is a set of primitive types (symbols, words, etc.) P_i; for each type, there is available an unbounded number of instances or tokens
(b) There is a (possibly unbounded) set of expression types[3] R_i; likewise, for each type, there is available an unbounded number of tokens
(c) There is a set of transitive and nonreflexive *constituency* relations over these primitive and expression types. Thus, expressions of type R_j (such as $((P\&Q)\&R)$) might have as constituents expressions of type R_i (such as $(P\&Q)$), in which case the situation can be described more succinctly using the general schema $C(R_i, R_j)$.

Clearly, these are extremely general conditions, and do not themselves amount to a specification of any *particular* scheme. If one wants a real, usable compositional scheme, a scheme one could actually say something with or deploy in cognitive modeling, one has to flesh out the various abstract notions employed in the general conditions. One has to specify, for instance, just what primitives and expressions are to be allowed in the scheme and the constituency relations obtaining among them. How is this to be done?

The first thing to notice is that this specification task has to be carried out at two quite distinct levels, corresponding to the crucial distinction between primitive and expression *types* and their corresponding instances or *tokens* that is stressed in conditions (a) and (b). In general, any compositional scheme, such as, for example, a natural language, can be thought of either in terms of its abstract structure or in terms of the details of its particular, concrete implementation. One important kind of difference between English and German is that these languages begin with different primitives (vocabularies) and they combine those primitives according to their distinctive grammatical rules to obtain quite distinct expression types (sentences). These are differences at the level of abstract structure. Expressions of a particular language such as English, moreover, can be realized or instantiated in a wide variety of different ways: spoken utterances, typescript, electrical signals in a computer memory, Braille script, to name just a few. The crucial point is that in order to specify a compositional scheme of representation fully, the details at *both* these levels must be filled. On the one hand, it must be known what general *types* of primitives and expressions there are; while on the other, it must be known what *kinds of things* (physical items) are to count as instances or tokens of each type.

A second crucial fact is that virtually all compositional schemes of any interest are infinite, in the sense that there is an unbounded number of distinct expression types. (Indeed, one reason compositional schemes are so widely employed is *precisely because* they allow the generating, in a systematic fashion, of an unbounded number of distinct expressions.) For this reason, in specifying a compositional scheme simple lists cannot be relied upon; finite creatures would never have time to complete the list, so the specification task would remain incomplete. The appropriate response, of course, is to use recursive methods, which give recipes for constructing, from a set of primitives which *is* given via a simple list, any expression, as long as one is prepared to invest some finite amount of work.

These are, of course, both familiar points, but when put together they lead to a point that is not so familiar: Namely, that there must be recursive specification at *both* levels of the compositional scheme. On one hand, recursive rules that specify the infinite expression types in the language are needed; a set of rules performing this task is just a grammar for the compositional scheme. (Conveniently, from the order of application of these rules, one can typically read off the abstract constituency relations among expression types.) Grammatical rules, however, do not themselves tell what the primitives or expressions of the language look like; they do not tell what kinds of things are to count as tokens of the language. Indeed, this is a very important feature of an abstract grammar; it is because grammars are not constrained in this way that, for example, one grammar can be used to describe a given language in all its different concrete manifestations. Consequently, in order to specify a particular compositional scheme fully, it is necessary to supplement the grammatical rules with recursive principles telling how expressions of the scheme happen to be instantiated. A systematic recipe for generating tokens of any given expression type is needed. This is typically done by providing *sample* tokens of each of the primitive types, together with a *mode of combination*, which, in accordance with the abstract grammatical rules, takes primitive tokens and combines them to generate instances of compound expressions. The samples of the primitive types provide (generally implicitly, or "ostensively") criteria for the identification of tokens of the primitives (e.g., having a certain shape and size). Then, having identity criteria for primitives and knowing the systematic effects of the mode of combination, criteria for the identification of instances of expressions are automatically provided. In the case of standard PL, for example, the mode of composition is spatial concatenation; consequently, knowing what primitive symbol tokens look like (since sample tokens are provided on the page), and knowing how to write symbols alongside one another according to the grammatical rules, it is automatically known what kinds of inscriptions count as tokens of any of an unbounded number of formulae of PL.

In virtually all descriptions of compositional schemes, both these specification tasks are rolled together into one. Thus, in standard versions of PL, grammatical rules stated in something like the following way are usually found:

If A and B are well-formed formulae, then ⌜(A&B)⌝ is a well-formed formula.

The fact that the symbols or expressions are to be combined by spatial concatenation is not mentioned explicitly, but rather is implicit in the way the rule is written down. It is, nevertheless, very important for the following analysis that the two levels and their respective specification tasks be teased apart, for without doing so it is easy to overlook an important distinction among styles of compositionality. Above, I suggested that essential to a compositional scheme is the requirement that its expressions stand in certain abstract constituency relations. It is through the mode of combination, which relates primitive tokens to compound expression tokens, that these constituency relations are realized in a particular scheme; and it is because there can be important differences between modes of combination that various styles of compositionality can be distinguished.

Since the discussion began with PL, the first general mode of combination to be considered is that of concatenation.[4] As noted, standard versions of PL utilize *spatial* concatenation: Tokens of constituents of an expression are, quite literally, placed alongside each other to generate a token of the compound expression. But of course this kind of spatial juxtaposition is only one particular form of concatenation. Another is temporal juxtaposition: When successively uttering the constituents of a PL formula, one is concatenating tokens no less then when writing them down. Symbolic sequences in a computer memory, moreover, can be concatenated even though they happen to be scattered in complex ways throughout the memory; here, the juxtaposition, if it can be called that, is really an operational variety, implemented via pointers which provide a way of getting from the location of one primitive constituent token to the location of the next. Intuitively, it seems that the essence of a concatenative mode of combination is not really juxtaposition at all; rather, it is that it provides a way of *linking* or *ordering* successive constituents without altering them in any way as it forms the compound expression. Thus, tokens of the symbol "P" are the same whether appearing standing alone, *P*, or in the context of an expression such as (*P&Q*). The crucial difference is that in the latter case, from the fact that it has been placed directly between instances of the "(" and "&" symbols, we can infer the appropriate constituency and grammatical relations.

If this is right, it suggests the following minimal condition: For a mode of combination to be concatenative, it must preserve tokens of an expression's constituents (and the sequential relations among tokens) in the expression itself. More formally, given any expression of type R_j, then for every primitive or expression type α_i such that $C(\alpha_i, R_j)$, it must at least be the case that any R_j token contains a token of each α_i, in the sense that some part of the R_j token satisfies the identity criteria for counting as an instance of type α_i.[5] By extension, a compositional scheme can be described as concatenative if it uses a concatenative mode of composition in generating its compound representations, and a particular representation as concatenative just in case it belongs to such a scheme.

Virtually every standardly familiar compositional scheme is concatenative in this sense; this includes natural languages,[6] the formal languages of mathematics, logic, and computer science, and so on. Given the way concatenation is defined, it is obvious that when describing a representation as having a concatenative structure, one is making more than just the grammatical point that it stands in certain abstract constituency relations, and also more than just the quasi-historical point that it happened to have been built up out of a certain set of (recoverable) constituents. One is also saying that it will have an internal formal structure of a certain kind; that is, such that the abstract constituency relations among expression types find direct, concrete instantiation in the physical structure of the corresponding tokens. An appropriate name for this kind of internal structure is *syntactic* structure.[7] Thus, the syntactic structure of a representation is the kind of formal structure that results when a concatenative mode of combination is used.

Largely because concatenative modes are so common and familiar, it is easy to lose sight of the fact that concatenation, even as generically described here, is not the only way of implementing the combination of tokens in order to obtain expressions. In the general case, all that is required of a mode of combination is to have systematic methods for generating tokens of compound expressions, given their constituents, and for decomposing them back into those constituents again. From the point of view of generating expressions satisfying the abstract constituency relations, there is no inherent necessity that these methods preserve tokens of constituents in the expressions themselves; rather, all that is important is that the expressions exhibit a kind *functional* compositionality. Functional compositionality is obtained when there are general, effective, and reliable processes for (a) producing an expression given its constituents, and (b) decomposing the expression back into those constituents. Such processes are *general* if they can be applied, in principle, in constructing and decomposing arbitrarily complex representations; thus, simple look-up table techniques, for example, are ruled out. To be *effective* they must be mechanistically implementable; that is, it must be possible to build a machine that can carry out these processes. This rules out appeals to oracles and the like. Finally, for these processes to be *reliable*, they must always generate the same answer for the same inputs.

Standardly, of course, concatenative schemes are functionally compositional. Indeed, this is one major reason concatenative schemes are so pervasive: The operation of concatenation is a very straightforward way of implementing the composition processes and facilitating the decomposition processes necessary for functional compositionality. Nevertheless, it is important to realize that it is quite possible to have compositional schemes of representation that are *not* concatenative, that is, that are *merely* functionally compositional. What would such a scheme look like? Below, a number of examples drawn from Connectionist research will be discussed. For the moment, however, a useful illustration is found in the notion of a Gödel numbering scheme for a formal language. The technique of Gödel numbering provides simple, general recipes for assigning a unique natural number to every expression of a given compositional scheme. One such recipe for PL assigns the following numbers:

PL expression	Gödel number
P	32
(P&Q)	51342984000
((P&Q)&R)	388282251281722597800000
etc.	etc.

Imagine, now, that instead of writing down standard tokens of expressions of PL, the corresponding Gödel *numerals* were to be written down in their place. In one sense, this would just be a notational shift. Since there is a unique Gödel number for every expression of PL, one could express – just by writing down Gödel numerals – everything that could have been expressed by writing regular PL formulae. This notational alternative, which might be called "Gödelese," is just a different way of realizing the abstract structure of PL in concrete tokens.

A crucial feature of a Gödel numbering scheme is that it is completely reversible. From the Gödel number of any expression one can (by virtue of the prime decomposition theorem) easily determine the Gödel numbers of the primitive constituents of that expression. For this reason, Gödelese counts as functionally compositional; given Gödel numeral constituents, there are general, effective, and reliable processes for generating "complex" Gödel numeral expressions, and vice versa. Yet, and this is a crucial fact, the Gödel *numeral* for a complex expression does not literally contain the Gödel *numerals* of its constituents, except perhaps entirely fortuitously. You cannot, for example, find an instance of the sign design *32* anywhere in the sign design *51342984000*; it simply does not occur there. This is just a blunt fact about the shapes of the various inscriptions on the page; it is not at all impugned by the obvious truth that, by using a little straightforward mathematics, a *quite distinct* token of *32* can be generated. Whatever reasonable, systematically applicable criteria are used for counting something as a *32* inscription, those criteria are not satisfied by any part of the token *51342984000*.

In principle, then, it is easy enough to imagine a group of eccentric logicians writing down their arguments in Gödelese rather than in standard PL. While they would, strictly speaking, suffer no loss of expressive power, such logicians would be using a language that is compositional *without* being concatenative; which is just to say that there are systematic processes for generating individual Gödelese expressions, and for decomposing them back into their primitive constituents again, but the complex Gödelese expressions themselves do not literally contain tokens of their constituents.

In general, devising a feasible compositional but nonconcatenative system of representation involves overcoming at least one major hurdle: designing and implementing the required combination and decomposition processes. To do this without simply concatenating tokens is, to say the least, a difficult engineering problem. It may appear easy enough to solve in the case of Gödelese – after all, multiplication and prime factorization are not particularly difficult to implement – but Gödelese is, in fact, an immensely impractical proposal, not least because Gödel numerals tend to be so embarrassingly large. For this reason, it is both interesting and encouraging that Connectionists are finding various ways to implement nonconcatenative schemes making use of the massive and distinctive processing capacities of neural networks.

Since representations in a nonconcatenative scheme do not contain tokens of their constituents, they are without syntactic structure in the sense defined above. This gives rise to an important general point: A nontrivial representation of a complex structured item *need not itself have an internal compositional structure*.[8] The absence of strictly syntactic structure, however, does not imply the absence of significant structure of any kind. There simply couldn't be the kinds of reliable and effective processes needed for functional compositionality unless the internal physical constitutions of the tokens involved are such as to be systematically compatible with the composing and decomposing processes. In particular, the internal structure of a "compound" representation must be such as to *constrain* the decomposing process to issue in the correct set of constituent tokens again. Thus, for example, the fact that one could easily construct decomposition processes for expressions of Gödelese, depends crucially on the fact that Gödelese numerals have the internal formal structure that they do. Any mechanistic manipulator that could extract the Gödelese constituents of *51342984000* would be relying on the fact that the expression has a characteristic physical make-up that is systematically distinguishable from that of, say, *51342911111*. Nevertheless, this kind of internal structure does not count as syntactic structure, since its parts do not, in general, satisfy the identity criteria for the various constituents. This distinction between formal structure and strictly syntactic structure will turn out to be of central importance in Section 3.

The basic distinction between concatenative and nonconcatenative compositionality has been defined in terms of the notion of constituent tokens being "literally present" or "contained" in an expression. That notion has in turn been characterized in terms of the applicability of the criteria of identification appropriate to primitive constituents to the expression itself. Before moving on, it is important to make a few points about this characterization. First, if there is a real distinction to be made between the two kinds of compositionality, it must be possible to identify constituent tokens in expressions *independently* of the processes by virtue of which these expressions count as functionally compositional. Another way of putting this is that the identity criteria for constituent tokens have to be independent of the processes that generate and decompose expressions, in the sense that they can be applied, and provide answers, without making use of those processes. If the only handle on the presence of tokens is via the very processes responsible for the attribution of functional compositionality, then concatenative compositionality simply collapses into the wider functional variety.

Second, the criteria used for this independent identification have to be constrained by considerations of explanatory utility in the context of the system or model in which the representations are employed. By this, I mean that the tokens identified by means of these criteria must be capable of figuring in explanations of the various relevant functional properties of the representations themselves. In general, *whenever* there is a scheme of representations possessing systematically interesting causal properties, including of course functional compositionality, there is always an outstanding problem: Namely, explaining how it is that those interactions turn out the way they do. Very often, it will be enormously useful to discern in the representations themselves tokens of their constituents, such that the behavior of the system manipulating these representations can then be explained by reference to the causal effects of such constituent tokens. (Think, for example, of how you might go about explaining to someone the behavior of a pocket calculator.) In order to make such a move, criteria for the identification of tokens are needed, criteria that earn their keep precisely because they make possible such explanations. Conversely, proposed criteria are to be accepted if there is substantial explanatory payoff in employing them. Whether a representation is appropriately said to be concatenative, then, ultimately boils down to a determinate empirical question: Is there a way of identifying constituent tokens such that the various causal interactions of the representation as a whole can be explained in the system in which it is employed, by reference to the causal role of the constituent tokens?

2 Classicalism versus Connectionism: differing styles of compositionality

Having made this distinction between strictly concatenative and merely functional compositionality, it is natural to ask: Which kind is characteristic of mental representations? Are tokens in the head syntactically structured or not? Now, this might at first seem like a rather uninteresting question, since, in one sense, all that is being talked about is the "shape" of the expression tokens themselves; in other respects, concatenative and nonconcatenative schemes appear to be formally equivalent. There is, however, a real issue here. Classical theorists, it turns out, have a deep theoretical commitment to the idea that mental representations are strictly concatenative, while in Connectionist research an increasing tendency can be discerned to reject syntactic structure in the representations themselves in favor of a merely functional compositionality. This has at least one important consequence for the current debate: Namely, it can be seen how Connectionsts can use compositional representations, while at the very same time correctly claim to reject the traditional Language-of-Thought hypothesis. On this way of looking at things, the most pertinent and informative contrast between the Classical approach and Connectionism is not, as Fodor and Pylyshyn (1988) have suggested, between a commitment to structured (Classical) as opposed to unstructured (Connectionist) representations; rather, it is between two very different ways of implementing compositional structure.

2.1   The Classical approach: concatenative compositionality

Although the distinction between concatenative and merely functional compositionality is obvious enough, the issue has not often been explicitly considered. For this reason, when looking back over the various canonical descriptions of the Classical approach, it is often difficult to find succinct statements clearly indicating a preference for one style of compositionality over the other, even though standard *practice* in mainstream symbolic modeling has always been to utilize the stronger style. Fortunately, however, in their recent definitive restatement of the Classical approach, Fodor and Pylyshyn (1988) indicate quite clearly and unambiguously that the Language of Thought is syntactically structured in the sense used here; as they put it, mental representations must have

> a *combinatorial syntax and semantics*, in which (a) there is a distinction between structurally atomic and structurally molecular representations; (b) structurally molecular representations have syntactical constituents that are themselves either structurally molecular or structurally atomic; and (c) the semantic content of a (molecular) representation is a function of the semantic contents of its syntactic parts, together with its constituent structure. (p. 12)

The fact that there must be *structurally molecular* representations that have *syntactical constituents* indicates that they take Classical representations to possess a strictly concatenative compositionality. Nevertheless, so as to guard against the slightest possibility of misinterpretation, they go on at numerous other points to make it abundantly clear that a representation must have tokens of its constituents as literal parts:

> In the Classical machine, the objects to which the content A&B is ascribed (viz., tokens of the expression "A&B") literally contain, as proper parts, objects to which the content A is ascribed (viz., tokens of the expression "A") . . . In short, it is characteristic of Classical systems . . . to exploit arrays of symbols some of which are atomic (e.g., expressions like "A") but indefinitely many of which have other symbols as

syntactic and semantic parts (e.g., expressions like "A&B") (Fodor and Pylyshyn 1988: I6)

The presence of this kind of internal syntactical structure in the representations themselves plays a crucial theoretical role in the whole Classical approach to modeling cognition. The problem, stated in its most general form, is this: It is necessary to be able to explain how a physical system, such as a brain or a computer, can exhibit complex, semantically coherent behavior; how, in other words, its state changes, which are governed by normal physical laws, can at the same time make *sense* in various ways. Virtually any approach to solving this very general problem will involve a crucial role for representations: States of the system, which on the one hand have semantic properties (i.e., are meaningful, can be interpreted as being about something), while on the other play a causal role in the generation of the system's behavior. Representations, thus, mediate between the semantic and the physical constraints on behavior. The Classical approach goes on to offer a particular story about what mental representations (and the corresponding mental processes) must be like in order to be able to play this central mediating role in any reasonably complex system. Briefly, they must have an internal syntactic structure, which can be set up in systematic correspondence with semantic features; in this way, semantic properties of representations come to be reflected in their syntactic (and hence physical) properties. It is then possible to construct physical systems whose state changes are systematically determined, in an appropriate way, by the syntactic structure of its representations. The result is a purely physical system that can respect semantic criteria in its behavior *by virtue of* the causal role in the system of the syntactic structure of its representations; it is a purely "syntactic engine" generating meaningful activity. As Fodor and Pylyshyn (1988) put it,

> If, in principle, syntactic relations can be made to parallel semantic relations, and if, in principle, you can have a mechanism whose operations on formulas are sensitive to their syntax, then it may be possible to construct a *syntactically* driven machine whose state transitions satisfy *semantical* criteria of coherence. Such a machine would be just what's required for a mechanical model of the semantical coherence of thought: Correspondingly, the idea that the brain *is* such a machine is the foundational hypothesis of Classical cognitive science. (p. 30)

Clearly, internal constituent structure plays a critical role here. The presence of tokens of constituents in the representations themselves is the key to both sides of the account. On one hand, the meaning of the representation as a whole is fixed by the meanings assigned to the constituent tokens, and on the other, the presence of these tokens simply is the formal syntactic structure which drives the causal processes in the system. For this reason, no true Classicalist could possibly be satisfied with mental representations exhibiting a merely functional compositionality, since, by definition, such representations are without syntactic structure, and so cannot play anything like the role that representations are required to play in the Classical account of cognitive processes. Without syntactic structure (and, hence, concatenative compositionality) you simply cannot tell the classic Classical story.

Does this description of the Classical approach ascribe to such theorists too strong a position? Classicalists, it is often argued, clearly distinguish the *cognitive* level, the level at which it is crucial that representations be syntactically structured, from the *implementation* level. They are explicit, moreover, that the cognitive level is the level of the *functional* architecture of the system. When they claim that mental representations must be syntactically structured, they mean only that representations must have the right kind of functional properties, which is to say, roughly, that in all causal interactions they must behave as if they did have such structure. How this behavior is in fact achieved is a mere implementation detail; there is no requirement that it result from representations having syntactic structure in the current strong sense. In short, according to this objection, my version of the Classical position errs in failing to see that just because *mental* representations have to be conceived as syntactically structured, it does not follow that their real physical counterparts at the implementation level have to be. To suppose otherwise is to forget the difference between the functional architecture of a cognitive system and its actual implementation.

Now, although this objection carries a certain initial plausibility, it in fact misunderstands the essence of the Classical approach. The mainstream symbolic view purports to be telling a story about *how it is possible* for a physical system to exhibit semantically coherent behaviors. A story about how it is possible for an actual system to realize certain patterns of systematic behaviors must be, at some suitable level, an implementation story; it must describe the underlying physical mechanisms responsible for generating those behaviors. The Classical claim is that the only way a physical system could possibly exhibit such subtle and complex behaviors is by instantiating representations with syntactic structure and utilizing processes sensitive to that very structure. Thus, representations must not merely be syntactically structured at the functional level, there must also be some level at which that structure can actually be found to be instantiated in the hardware itself. Fodor and Pylyshyn (1988) go to great lengths to stress this point:

> ... the symbol structures in a Classical model are assumed to correspond to real physical structures in the brain and the *combinatorial structure* of a representation is supposed to have a counterpart in structural relations among physical properties of the brain. For example, the relation "part of," which holds between a relatively simple symbol and a more complex one, is assumed to correspond to some physical relation among brain states ... This bears emphasis because the classical theory is committed not only to there being a system of physically instantiated

493

symbols, but also to the claim that the physical properties onto which the structure of the symbols is mapped *are the very properties that cause the system to behave as it does.* (pp. 13–14)

They go on to describe, in detail, the nature of the instantiation mapping from the syntactic structure of the (cognitive-level) representations onto features of the brain. There is of course a certain trivial sense in which the Classical theorist would be satisfied if he could be shown a system that exhibits sophisticated cognitive behaviors on the basis of representations that do not have syntactic structure. The trouble is, the orthodox Classicalist believes there never will be such a thing, because he believes that, as a matter of contingent fact, only systems with structured representations and structure-sensitive processes *can* exhibit such behaviors. If you propose to substitute for Classical syntactically structured representations their merely functionally compositional counterparts, you must have somewhere up your sleeve, a quite different story about how that functional compositionality, and the semantic coherence of behavior more generally, is mechanistically implemented. But, according to the Classicalist, you will not be able to provide such a story. It is a contingent, empirical truth about the world that only physical symbol systems can exhibit sophisticated cognitive behaviors.

2.2 The Connectionist approach: functional compositionality

The general theoretical framework surrounding the wide variety of connectionist attempts to model aspects of cognition is, by comparison, relatively undeveloped; consequently, it is rather more difficult to make the corresponding argument that Connectionists have any kind of deep theoretical commitment to nonconcatenative representations. Nevertheless, it is possible to discern in their work an increasing tendency to utilize this style of compositionality. Three examples are briefly discussed in this section: Pollack's Recursive Auto-Associative Memory (RAAM), Hinton's techniques for the representation of hierarchical structures via reduced descriptions, and Smolensky's tensor product framework. In all three cases, the adoption of a merely functional compositionality resulted fairly directly from the attempt to represent complex structured items using the kinds of strictly limited resources available in networks of simple processing units. Insofar as Connectionists are committed to those kinds of limited resources, then, the rejection of concatenation (and hence syntactic structure) does indeed seem to be an essential part of the Connectionist paradigm.

Note that the particular approaches to be described here have been chosen primarily because, at time of writing, they constitute useful illustrations of the central point at issue. Nothing of importance to my argument is staked either on any of their idiosyncratic details, or on future development of the approaches.

2.2.1 Pollack's Recursive Auto-Associative Memory (RAAM)

One of the standard assumptions of Connectionist modeling is that the network of processing units one has to work with is always of a certain fixed size. It is also clear, however, that many of the complex items one might need to represent are quite unpredictable in size. Sentences of natural language, for example, do not come limited to a certain length of, say, 4 or 10 or 20 words. The most convenient way to represent such items is to have a system of dynamic memory allocation, which can always provide just enough by way of memory resources, no matter what size the item happens to be. Conventional digital computers generally work this way, but no such simple solution is available to Connectionists. Pollack (1988) confronted this problem head on, aiming to produce a general method for representing variable sized data structures over strictly limited Connectionist resources. His approach was to train a network to be able to function as a *stack*, and in particular to implement, in network processes, the standard stack operations of *push* and *pop*. In this network, a state of the stack (i.e., having a certain series of elements stored) is just a particular pattern of activity over a fixed set of 10 hidden units. Every possible stack state thus corresponds to a different 10-place vector describing an activity pattern over this central group of units. Pushing a new element onto the current stack means generating the appropriate new pattern, corresponding to the expanded stack, over the hidden units. This new pattern is formed by the network in a process that merges the previous stack state with the new element. Popping an element off the top of the stack is just reversing this process. From a central stack pattern, the network generates two new patterns: one is the topmost element, and the other constitutes the stack minus that element.

Of course, storing a complex structured item, such as a tree, involves more than simply storing the individual basic elements; it is also necessary to record the structural relations among elements. Pollack solved this problem by realizing that whole stack states themselves can be pushed onto and popped off other stacks, just as if they were simple elements. Thus, for example, one branch of a binary tree could be stored in one stack, the other in another stack, and then one stack pushed onto the other. This process can be performed recursively, with the result that any given recursively structured sequence can be stored in an appropriately trained network.

In short, Pollack's RAAM model provides the means to build representations of complex structured items out of representations of their components, and the ability to decompose those representations again reliably. It provides a way of implementing the full range of constituency relations needed in building compositional representations of those complex items. Consequently, the stack states in an appropriately trained network constitute a compositional scheme according to the abstract characterization offered above. The crucial point, however, is that the mode of combination is *not* concatenation. If one carefully dissects the pattern of activity, which is the stack representation of a structured item, it is apparent that nothing in the pattern counts as a token of any of the various constituents, even though those constituents are (given the network) extractable from that pattern. Pollack's RAAM representations are functionally compositional without being concatenative, that is, without having internal syntactic structure.

2.2.2   Representing hierarchies via reduced descriptions

In a classic example of researchers converging on the same problem area and producing alternative solutions embodying some of the same key ideas, Hinton has proposed a solution to the problem of "how to map a part–whole hierarchy into a finite amount of parallel hardware" (Hinton 1988: 52). Suppose one wanted to represent some hierarchically structured situation in which one level of the hierarchy has much in common with the next. In Hinton's example, one of the constituents of "Bill was annoyed that John disliked Mary" bears a strong structural similarity to the overall sentence. While the standard approach using conventional methods would be to assign separate memory resources to each level, with pointers to keep the hierarchical structure intact, this has some drawbacks from a Connectionist standpoint: First, to store an arbitrarily complex structure requires arbitrarily extended resources, and second, such a method fails to capitalize on the fact that there are structural similarities between levels. In his novel approach, Hinton proposes that the fixed network be used as if it were a window looking only onto a certain level in the hierarchy at a given time. For effective representation of the whole hierarchy, it must be possible to move the window up or down levels as necessary, and so Hinton proposes methods doing exactly this. To move from one level down to the next, the network focuses on what is only a constituent at that upper level, and expands it into representation of a whole lower level. So, for example, to move from a representation of *Bill was annoyed that* [?] to *John disliked Mary* the network needs to focus on the [?] constituent and expand it into full-fledged representation, over the whole network, of *John disliked Mary*. This process is only possible if the [?] constituent contains enough information to allow the recovery of the full situation; it must therefore amount, in Hinton's terms, to a "reduced description" of that situation. There is, of course, a structural similarity between the levels to be represented, and so the Connectionist hardware can be designed to take advantage of these similarities in order to facilitate the expansion process.

Like a stack representation in Pollack's (1988) RAAM model, then, a top-level representation of a part–whole hierarchy allows recovery of all the constituents of that hierarchy; in that sense it can be described as a compositionally structured representation. But, like a stack representation, this is not achieved by having first concatenated those constituents. There is no requirement that constituents figure, in the representation of the whole, in anything like the form they appear in when the constituent has been fully expanded; as Hinton (1988) puts the point:

The crucial property of the moveable window scheme is that the pattern of activity that represents the current whole is totally different from the pattern of activity that represents the very same object when it is viewed as being a constituent of some other whole. (p. 52)

In fact, the point can be put even more forcefully: A constituent buried deeply in the hierarchy may have *no* distinct pattern of activity representing it at all when the focus is on the top level. What is true is only that the constituent can eventually be recovered from the top-level pattern. Thus, the contrast with strictly concatenative compositionality, which (by definition) must preserve tokens of the constituents, could not be greater.

2.2.3   Tensor product representations

For a final example of nonconcatenative compositionality emerging from Connectionist research, it is important to consider Smolensky's (1987a) tensor product framework for the representation of structured objects. On one hand, this framework has been the subject of more extensive formal development then any other Connectionist proposal, while on the other, Smolensky himself has given considerable attention to the difference between representation (and indeed the compositionality of representation) in his approach and that characteristic of Classical theorizing.

Again, the basic problem facing Smolensky is that of representing complex structured objects with the kinds of limited resources available in Connectionist networks. Since Connectionist representations are most usefully thought of as vectors (whether describing patterns of activity over processing units or the connections between such units) Smolensky conceives of the problem as that of "finding a mapping from a set of structured objects (e.g., trees) to a vector space" (Smolensky 1987a: 2). This mapping should, moreover, preserve the various constituency relations among representations, such that a representation of a complex item as a combination of the representations of its parts can be generated, and recover those parts as necessary.

Connectionists have always been aware that, under the right circumstances, the operation of vector addition can be used to combine two representations to generate a representation of a more complex object.[10] Smolensky's first insight is to see the extensive applicability, within Connectionist theorizing, of the more complex but also more powerful operation of tensor product formation. The tensor product of an n-place vector $\mathbf{v}$ and an m-place vector $\mathbf{w}$ is the $(n \times m)$-place vector whose values consist in all the pairwise products of the values of $\mathbf{v}$ and $\mathbf{w}$. The tensor product is thus very similar to the more familiar outer product of two vectors, except that the result is considered as a vector rather than a matrix (Smolensky 1988: 12). Since a tensor product is itself a vector, it can enter into vector sums and tensor products just like any other vector.

Smolensky's second insight is the introduction of the notion of "role decomposition," a general framework for reducing complex structured items to sets of pairs. In this framework, the complex item to be represented is analyzed as being made up of a set of distinct roles with each role having a certain filler. For example, the complex concept *cup of coffee* would be analyzed as having two roles: *contains*, and *contained by*. The first role is occupied by *cup*, the second by *coffee* (for more sophisticated examples, see Smolensky 1987a: 15–20). Analysis via role decomposition, on the one hand, and the generation of compound vectors via addition and tensor product formation on the other, then fit together as hand and glove. Each distinct role and filler is assigned a distinctive primitive vector, fillers are "bound" to roles by forming the tensor product of their respective primitive vectors, and the resulting tensor products are added together to obtain a single compound representation of the whole structured item. The remarkable fact is that, within certain limits,[11] the filler for any role can be extracted from the representation of the whole structure by simply multiplying the overall tensor product representation by the vector corresponding to that role (and vice versa). In this way, the whole structure can be effectively recovered from the vectorial representation. Thus, the representation is more than just a representation of a structured object: It is also managing, by virtue of its compositional properties, to capture the *structure* of that object.

Smolensky develops the tensor product framework for representing structured items with considerable imagination and precision. He shows how the framework encompasses a considerable number of previous Connectionist schemes of representation, and he and others are utilizing it in development of further models of various kinds. He is also careful to distinguish vectorial representations in the tensor product framework from the kinds of symbolic representations characteristic of the Classical approach, stressing at least two major differences. First, in the tensor product framework, primitive vector constituents are unlike standard symbolic constituents in that they are typically context-dependent; that is, the vector constituent standing for a given concept can be expected to vary somewhat from one composite representation to the next, with the consequence that there is no single canonical vector for that concept. Rather, a concept will generally be represented via a cluster of vectors related by a kind of "family resemblance." It also has the consequence that the breakdown of a composite is not, in general, "precise and uniquely defined." Second, the mode of combination of these primitive constituents (i.e., vector addition and tensor product formation) is subject to various kinds of imperfections; for example, various kinds of ambiguities and interference effects can also prevent any precise breakdown into the original constituents (for further elaboration, see Smolensky 1988: 14).

For these reasons, Smolensky (1988) takes it that tensor product representations provide "new instantiations of compositionality principles" (p. 16) and hence offer a genuine alternative to the Language of Thought. Now this may be true, but from the current point of view there is an equally important difference, leading to the same conclusion, which Smolensky did not note, namely, that while Classical representations are essentially concatenative, the compositionality of tensor product representations is merely functional. The vectors which result from forming and then adding together successive role/filler bindings are not syntactically structured; they do not contain tokens of the primary constituents (i.e., the primitive vectors assigned to the original roles and fillers) in any sense other than that there are processes that can generate those constituents given the compound representation. Close examination of a tensor product representation of a complex structure fails to reveal the vectors that represent the parts of that structure considered independently; to get those, you first have to apply the various decomposition operations. Thus, even if one carefully constrains the tensor product methods to the point where the constituent vectors are in fact "precise and uniquely defined," there will still always remain an important conceptual gulf between the resulting tensor product representations and their more traditional symbolic counterparts.

Understanding this point is essential in order to be able to characterize properly the compositionality of tensor product representations, and hence, the relation between Connectionist models based on such representations and their Classical counterparts. Smolensky often describes tensor product representations as "compositionally structured" or as having "constituent structure," but these phrases are, to say the least, ambiguous between concatenative and merely functional compositionality. Indeed, to say that a representation has compositional structure generally implies that one is talking about the internal structure of the representation itself (i.e., syntactic structure, in the current sense), rather than just its various functionally implemented constituency relations; but tensor product representations do not have such internal structure.

Failing clearly to distinguish these kinds of compositionality led Smolensky to two different conceptions of the causal role of compositional structure in cognitive processes, conceptions that stand in manifest tension with each other. For example, on the one hand, he claims that it is possible to design "structure sensitive processes" (Smolensky 1988: 1), with the result that "the systematic behavior of the cognitive system is to be explained by appealing to the systematic constituent structure of the representational vectors" (Smolensky 1988: 22). Statements like these imply that the constituent structure of the representations has a direct causal role in the behavior of the system; that, in other words, the explanation of cognitive processes will proceed in basically the same manner as the Classical explanation, although the constituents themselves are perhaps not as precise and unique.

In other places, however, Smolensky (1988) denies any causal role for constituent structure:

> ... the constituency relation among distributed representations is one
> that is important for the analysis of connectionist models, and for

explaining their behavior, but it is *not* a part of the information-processing mechanism within the connectionist model . . . (p. 10)

and he stresses that the behavior of the system cannot be explained precisely at the level at which semantic assignments are made (i.e., at the level of representations and their constituents). Since tensor product representations do not have internal constituent structures, this must be the correct general approach. It does, however, immediately generate a rather difficult problem: Explaining exactly how the functional compositionality of representations can "influence" (in whatever sense it does) mental processes, or, to put it a different way, how one can *explain* the behavior of Connectionist models by reference to constituency relations, even if those relations are not "part of the information-processing mechanism within the model." (In Section 3 some points will be made that should facilitate such explanation.) At any rate, for the moment, the point is this: The distinction between concatenative and merely functional compositionality clarifies the compositionality of tensor product representations; it reveals the inherent awkwardness in describing such representations as "compositionality structured," and it removes the temptation to think of Connectionist explanations of cognitive processes as being closer to the Classical style than they in fact are.

2.2.4   *Concatenation versus distribution*

All three of these researchers have been facing essentially the same problem: that of representing arbitrarily complex structures over finite resources. Their solutions, although different in details, all agree in rejecting any role for simple concatenation of constituent representations. Not surprisingly, there is a broad underlying reason for this. The essence of concatenation is the preservation of constituent tokens, and each token must take up a certain amount of the available representational resources. Thus, in order to represent an arbitrarily complex structure via concatenative methods requires arbitrarily extended resources, something not available in the typical Connectionist framework. In each case, it was found that the resource restrictions entailed that the various parts of a given complex structure had to be represented at once, in what is effectively a superimposed fashion, over the same space; that, in other words, it was necessary to employ *distributed* representations of the complex structures. Distributing transformations, which take various constituents and superimpose them to achieve a new representation of the whole over the same space, inevitably destroys those tokens in the process (although not necessarily their recoverability), and hence are incompatible with any variety of concatenation. In short, the finite resource restrictions characteristic of Connectionism preclude concatenative styles of compositionality in favor of distributed (and so merely functional) styles. The fact that a broad alternative conception of compositionality is emerging in Connectionist research is thus a fairly direct consequence of one of its basic commitments, a commitment that stands in stark contrast with the Classical assumption that resources are always, at least in principle, arbitrarily extendable (as in, e.g., the unbounded tape on a Turing Machine). (For a clear statement of this Classical assumption, and why it is made, see Fodor and Pylyshyn 1988: 33–6.)

3   Styles of compositionality and the explanation of cognition

The fact that classical cognitive architectures are essentially committed to representations with concatenative compositional structure, while Connectionist architectures tend to opt for a merely functional alternative, gives rise to an obvious question: Which is to be preferred? Is there any reason to suppose that a commitment to strict syntactic compositionality is essential to the success of cognitive modeling? It is, of course, impossible in the context of this article to offer any general evaluation of the many and varied considerations that argue either in favor of, or against, the Classical approach. My more modest aim is to show that the supposedly conclusive arguments which Fodor and Pylyshyn (1988) have recently offered in favor of the Classical approach do not, in fact, support that approach over the emerging Connectionist alternative.

In "Connectionism and Cognitive Architecture" Fodor and Pylyshyn (1988) maintain that if we suppose mental representations have a combinatorial syntax, we are in a position to give a straightforward causal explanation of some very general and important aspects of our cognitive lives. The aspects they focus on can be described, generically, as the *systematicity of cognition*. Systematicity consists in such mundane facts as these: that we are capable of having indefinitely many different kinds of thoughts; that the ability to entertain one kind of thought always goes along with the ability to entertain systematically related thoughts;[12] and that the ability to perform one kind of inference always goes along with the ability to perform systematically related inferences.[13] Now, if mental representations have a combinatorial syntax and semantics, these kinds of systematicities will be just what we would expect. The fact that we can have indefinitely many thoughts, for example, is explained by the fact that a combinatorial syntax gives us indefinitely many well-formed expressions with which to represent thoughts. Other kinds of systematicity are explained if the further assumption is made that there are mental processes which are "sensitive to" the combinatorial structure of the representations. (The term "sensitive to," although widely used, is conveniently vague; in this context it can only mean something like "causally influenced by.") Thus, the fact that everybody who can infer P from $(P \& Q)$ can also infer P from $((P \& Q) \& R)$, is explained by reference to the structural similarity of the representations involved and the fact that there are cognitive processes which can pick up on (i.e., are causally influenced by) that structural similarity.

It is essential to be clear about the form of argument involved here. Fodor and Pylyshyn are claiming that *if* mental representations have combinatorial structure, then there is a natural explanation of certain sorts of facts about people's mental lives; from this they infer that mental representations must have combinatorial structure. In the philosophy of science, this kind of argument is generally known as something like an "inference to the best explanation." As a form of argument, it amounts to little more than the old fallacy of affirming the consequent, *unless* those advancing it also take the further step of somehow ruling out alternative explanations of the same empirical phenomena. Fully aware of this, Fodor and Pylyshyn canvass and argue against an alternative, non-Classical strategy for explaining the systematicity of cognition.

On this alternative picture, which they label "associationist," mental representations are (*ex hypothesi*) unstructured, which is to say, they have no significant internal structure at all. Since representations are without internal structure, there cannot be mental processes sensitive to such structure. Therefore, according to Fodor and Pylyshyn, any model based on such representations must employ purely *associationist* mental processes. The hallmark of an associationist process is that it is based not on the content or the internal structure of the representations themselves, but only on the extent of their correlation in previous "experience" (e.g., in the training set). Associationist processes ignore formal or structural features of a representation except insofar as they are relevant in determining its identity, which, in turn, determines its associative connections. Since associationist processes are based only on prior experience, there is no guarantee that mental processes will be systematic; rather, they will be *at most* as systematic as the experience upon which they are based. Consequently, according to Fodor and Pylyshyn, the systematicity of thought, which goes well beyond that contained in experience, is an unexplained mystery if it is assumed that the mind is non-Classical, that is, associationist in character.

It is this argument which they take in order to refute Connectionism as an account of the human cognitive architecture; for, insofar as Connectionist models are truly non-Classical, they must (according to Fodor and Pylyshyn 1988) be simply associationist in the above sense and must fail for the same reason.

As mentioned, this "inference to the Classical explanation" is only legitimate insofar as they rule out alternative explanations of the same phenomena. Consequently, their argument is only as good as their supporting argument that the alternative they considered – the broadly associationist architecture – is the only plausible alternative there is. Nowhere, however, do they provide any such discussion or argument. Rather, that crucial premise is simply implicit in their choice of language: Their favored architectures are "Classical," anything else must be "non-Classical." However, in doing this they are overtly assimilating all "non-Classical" representations with their completely unstructured "associationist" representations, and thereby rather deftly leaving entirely out of consideration the intermediate case: representations that have significant internal structure while nevertheless not counting as *syntactically*

502

structured. A cognitive architecture based on such representations cannot properly be classified as *either* Classical or associationist under the terms of their taxonomy. If the argument in the previous sections is correct, moreover, this is precisely the kind of architecture that Connectionists are in the process of developing. Consequently, in only taking the trouble to rule out the associationist alternative, they are *not* ruling out the position that Connectionists are increasingly taking up. Their diatribes against associationism simply miss the intended target. Associationism is thus serving as a convenient straw man (as is so often its lot in the philosophy of psychology); all Connectionist approaches are first misassimilated to a crude associationism, and then the latter is shot down in flames without further ado

Now, one does not refute an inference to what is currently the best explanation of a certain phenomenon by simply pointing out some bizarre alternative that has not yet been conclusive eliminated. If that were all that were required, I could refute contemporary astronomy, for example, by alluding to the fact that astronomers have failed to rule out conclusively the common hypothesis that celestial events turn out the way they do because the moon is made of green cheese. Likewise, in order to refute the Fodor and Pylyshyn argument fully, it is not sufficient merely to point out that there are other possible architectures out there; it also has to be demonstrated that it is at least *plausible* (to the best of our knowledge at this stage) that such an architecture could be employed in generating explanations (and perhaps even *superior* explanations) of cognitive functioning, and in particular the systematicity of cognition. The most convincing demonstration, of course, would actually be to build Connectionist models of systematic cognitive functioning. But that demands lots of hard empirical work, and the issue here is precisely whether it is worth investing that kind of effort, or whether (as Fodor and Pylyshyn believe) there are principled reasons for supposing that such an enterprise is doomed from the very start. In what follows it will be shown that Connectionist architectures should in fact be regarded as serious candidates, since they offer *exactly the kind of basic resources that, according to Fodor and Pylyshyn themselves, are necessary in order to generate an explanation of systematicity.*

In short, I wish to counter Fodor and Pylyshyn's (1988: 33) ambitious claim to have provided "something close to a demonstration that ... the mind cannot be, in its general structure, a Connectionist network." My strategy directly parallels a response that the Wright brothers might have made to those doubting the value of experimenting with their new and somewhat implausible flying machines. Imagine a balloon enthusiast, for example, arguing the following way:

In order for any object to fly, it must be able to stay up in the air, in which case the total forces pushing it upwards must be at least as great as gravity. The only remotely feasible way for that to happen is for the object itself to be lighter than air. Birds, kites and so forth are all very well, but they are invariably suited only to low-level flight; the principles in play there could never shape up to general kinds of transportation, such as carrying people and cargo. In fact, your machines do little more than exhume the old idea that mere propulsion is sufficient for flight (i.e., Propulsionism), an idea thoroughly discredited many years ago; as far as we can tell, nothing has changed in the meantime.

Now the Wrights, with more faith in aerodynamics than in hot air, would no doubt have agreed that the upward forces must be at least as great as gravity, but would point out that propulsion, when combined with an appropriate wing (and hull?) shape, *can* produce the required upward forces. Consequently, their *kind* of machine has, at least in principle, exactly the sort of feature the balloonist himself believes is necessary for sustainable flight. In responding this way, the Wrights would have effectively discredited the balloonist's argument even if the *Kitty Hawk* had not yet actually flown; and they would be quite justified in continuing their efforts to demonstrate that aeroplanes, in general, *can* fly.

Returning, then, to the main line of argument: Fodor and Pylyshyn (1988) summarize the crucial inference from systematicity to a Classical cognitive architecture as follows:

> It is perhaps obvious by now that all the arguments we've been reviewing – the argument from systematicity, the argument from compositionality, and the argument from inferential coherence – are really much the same: If you hold the kind of theory that acknowledges structured representations, it must perforce acknowledge representations with *similar* or *identical* structure ... So, if your theory also acknowledges mental processes that are structure sensitive, then it will predict that similarly structured representations will generally play similar roles in thought. (p. 48)

So the real key to explaining the systematicity of cognition is to have a scheme of representations that stand in the right kinds of similarity relations; that is, such that representations of similar things can be treated in similar ways by mental processes. That's what having strict syntactic structure in the representations themselves buys for you. If representations are constructed by concatenation according to regular principles, then you are guaranteed to have a scheme in which representations bear structural similarities to each other, which can, in turn, be capitalized on by mental processes. Thus the expression $(P \& Q,)$ bears an obvious structural similarity to the expression $((P \& Q) \& R)$, and it is straightforward enough to design processes for extracting conjuncts that will treat these – and indeed all conjunctions – "similarly."

The crucial question, then, is whether it is possible to have a scheme of presentations that stands in those kinds of structural similarity relations without utilizing Classical compositionality. If the notion of structural similarity is restricted to similarities of *syntactic* structure, then of course the answer will be no. But it was stressed above that representations can have internal structure that is not strictly syntactic; indeed, such structure is the key to the possibility of merely functional compositionality. Consequently, there can also be nonsyntactic structural *similarities* among representations. In fact, if a scheme of representations exhibiting merely functional compositionality is utilized, then useful kinds of formal similarities over the space of representations are exactly what would be expected. Since general, reliable, and effective processes for combination and decomposition are needed, tokens corresponding to (P&Q), for example, are expected to bear certain similarities (which may have to be defined relative to the particular machine carrying out the composition and decomposition processes) to tokens corresponding to (PvQ), even though those similarity relationships will *not* be a matter of having the same constituents literally present.

What kinds of similarities will these be? In general, this will depend very much on the nature of the functionally compositional scheme in question and the details of its implementation. Fortunately, however, in the case of the Connectionist approaches described above, this general point can be cashed out in fairly concrete terms. In these approaches the representations themselves are vectors in a certain high-dimensional space describing the activity levels over a set of units. These vectors stand in similarity relations by virtue of their internal configuration, relations that can be measured using standard vector comparison methods. These similarities are usefully understood as similarities (or indeed dissimilarities) of *location* in the space, and they are of direct causal significance in Connectionist networks, since the behavior of these networks, which are complex dynamical systems, depends crucially on the particular current activity values of the units themselves (i.e., on the precise location of the current representation). Moreover, the requirement that we be able to map systematically an indeterminate number of arbitrarily complex structured items onto points in that space has the consequence that the abstract constituency relations among the representations themselves are mirrored in the similarity relations thus detected (i.e., structurally similar sequences are mapped into "neighboring" points in the space). It is, in fact, these "spatial" similarities, which underlie the general and effective processes, that are used to generate and decompose these representations.

Thus, merely functionally compositional schemes of representations can, in fact, provide the crucial basic resources needed in generating an explanation of the systematicity of cognition; that is, a system of representations standing in systematic structural similarity relationships. The only task that remains in order to put the Fodor and Pylyshyn argument finally to rest is to construct actual models of systematic cognitive processing on the basis of such nonconcatenative representations. Having devised their flying machines, Connectionists now need to show they can actually stay in the air. This means developing processes that are causally sensitive to, and hence constrained by, the systematic structural similarities among the representations themselves, so that the overall system exhibits the right kinds of systematic behaviors. (Classical theorists, of course, face exactly the same kind of challenge. Even given syntactically structured representations, adequate processes over those representations do not come free; if they did, there wouldn't be such a discipline as computer programming, let alone AI.)

It is important to stress that there are, broadly speaking, at least two ways Connectionists might go about meeting the design challenge posed when non-concatenative representations are to be centrally incorporated in a model of cognitive processing. A first and somewhat unsatisfying approach always proceeds by initially utilizing the decomposition processes (by virtue of which their representations count as functionally compositional) in order to extract the basic constituents, and then having the general structure-sensitive processes operate on the constituents in their separated form. In this approach, although storage in the system uses representations that are merely functionally compositional, the processes responsible for generating cognitive activity operate in the straightforwardly concatenative domain. A good example is Touretzky's (1986) BoltzCONS, a variety of distributed connectionist production system. In this model a central working memory stores complex data structures in what is, in fact, a merely functionally compositional form, but the first step in any processing cycle is to use subsidiary networks to *pull out* more basic constituent triples; it is on these that the primary structure-sensitive operations take place.

A second and more radical approach is to devise models in which structure-sensitive processes operate on the compound representations themselves *without* first stopping to extract the basic constituents. These processes must capitalize *directly* on the inherent and systematic structural similarities among the nonconcatenative representations. In such models it is not only storage that takes place in the nonconcatenative domain, but the primary processing responsible for systematic cognitive behavior as well. Thus, if the ability to extract conjuncts is an observed systematic feature of human cognition, then a model of this feature will have to be capable of mapping the nonconcatenative vectorial representation of a conjunction directly to the vectorial representation of one of its conjuncts, without first extracting the constituents, identifying the dominant connective as a conjunction symbol, and so on. Mapping one vector directly to another without intermediate rule-governed processing steps is, of course, exactly what Connectionist networks are good at. The crucial point here is that such a network can be expected to be able to do so *systematically* because (a) in this functionally compositional scheme of representation, all conjunctions will have been systematically grouped in certain regions of the vector space (i.e., they are structurally similar); and (b) it is in the nature of Connectionist networks as dynamical systems that they map all points from a given (more or less widely specified) region onto similar points in the output, in a way that is subtly sensitive to the precise location of that point.

Thus, there are at least two significantly different kinds of cognitive architecture that Connectionists might develop, each of which in some sense incorporates nonconcatenative representations in central processing. Only the second approach, however, presents any real threat to Classical orthodoxy. The first, in performing the primary structure-sensitive processing on the basis of regular Classical representations, really just amounts to a trivial variant on the overall Classical picture. In moving to the concatenative domain whenever real action is called for, it is effectively conceding to the Classicalist that systematic cognitive processing can only take place on the basis of syntactically structured representations. It is the second approach that offers a distinctively Connectionist strategy in the explanation of systematic cognitive functioning, and it is models along these lines that will need to be fully developed in finally meeting the Fodor and Pylyshyn challenge.

At this stage relatively little real progress has been made in this direction. None of the methods discussed in this article, for example, achieve general structure-sensitive processing wholly within the nonconcatenative domain. They are directed only at solving the first stage in developing such capabilities, that of generating the functionally compositional representations themselves. RAAMs are an excellent case in point: They are simply a method for storing structured symbol sequences and retrieving them again, and no other kinds of interesting processing take place on the basis of the representations in their superimposed, nonconcatenative form. However, this lack of progress *cannot* yet be attributed to inherent difficulties in the second approach itself, since, by and large, Connectionists have simply not yet gotten around to taking up the challenge. If the arguments in this article are broadly correct, Connectionism is entering a critical stage in the process of developing an alternative paradigm to supersede the Classical approach. Early indications at least are promising. Pollack (1990), who has probably taken this line of development further than any other Connectionist to date, has reported success in using his RAAM mechanisms to generate representations of short sequences, which then form the basis, in other networks, for *direct* structure-sensitive processing in the nonconcatenative domain. Whether such initial explorations can in fact be developed into comprehensive accounts of systematic cognitive processing is a matter for further investigation (which is just another way of pointing out that the disagreement between the Classicalist and the Connectionist, construed this way, is a straightforwardly empirical one). What the current considerations show is simply that Classical architectures are not the only ones that have access to the raw resources required to generate such accounts. Connectionist architectures that use compositional but nonconcatenative representations in their primary processing will be able to take advantage of systematic structural similarities among representations, and yet it is precisely this feature that Fodor and Pylyshyn assume to be crucial for the explanation of systematicity and (erroneously) take to be uniquely characteristic of Classical architectures. Connectionism therefore constitutes a plausible alternative according to Fodor and Pylyshyn's very own criteria of plausibility, and so their general "inference to the Classical explanation" does not go through.

Obviously, the argument provided here does not give any *positive* reason to prefer Connectionist methods for representing complex objects over their Classical, syntactically structured counterparts. At least superficially, it might even seem somewhat perverse to design models using nonconcatenative representations. After all, one reason concatenation is so common is that having syntactic structure manifest in the representations themselves is extremely *useful* (although, as I have argued, not *necessary*) from the point of view of designing structure-sensitive operations. There are, in short, immensely appealing practical engineering considerations that argue in favor of the Classical view. The Connectionist will counter, however, that there are other, different, but equally compelling considerations that argue in favor of nonconcatenative methods. There is some reason to believe, for example, that by working within their favored high-dimensional vector spaces, Connectionists are able to develop methods of representation, including compositional representation, which are in fact expressively *more* rich (i.e., sensitive to more subtle differences and similarities), than any feasible Classical alternative. Whether that is true or not, it is undoubtedly the case that a Connectionist implementation of a compositional scheme offers certain distinctive computational advantages as compensation for its apparent drawbacks. (See, e.g., Smolensky 1988: 11–15 for a discussion of some computational advantages of tensor product representations.) In general, the commitment to nonconcatenative compositionality will be made as part of a quite *general* commitment to Connectionist architectures over their Classical counterparts, and consequently the choice of nonconcatenative methods will turn out to be vindicated insofar as Connectionist approaches in general prove to be superior (if they do). I have not tried to say anything here that would help decide this latter question, except (a) to draw the lines of battle in a more perspicuous way, and (b) to point out that it would be a serious mistake to suppose that Classical architectures are superior in principle because only they have the basic resources necessary to account for the systematicity of cognition.

4   Conclusion

When paradigms clash, issues and problems that were previously dormant are brought into the open. The dispute between Connectionists and Classicalists over the nature of mental representation has done exactly that for (*inter alia*) the notion of the compositional structure of a representation. The fact that various senses had typically been assimilated in one uncritical notion of compositionality was crucial in allowing Fodor and Pylyshyn to formulate their seemingly powerful attack on Connectionism. Once these senses are pulled apart, however, one is left with a clearer idea of exactly what the Language of Thought hypothesis consists in, and consequently what kinds of representations Connectionists can employ without merely implementing the Classical approach. Since nonconcatenative compositional schemes have at least the raw materials for an explanation of the systematicity of cognition,

Connectionists models employing such representations can, at least for the moment, be taken seriously as candidates for the explanation of cognition while nevertheless remaining quite distinct from the Classical approach.

Notes

1 Fodor and Pylyshyn (1988: 42) use the term "combinatorial" in circumstances where the currently predominant tendency in cognitive science is, for better or for worse, to use "compositional." They then proceed to use "compositional" to refer to the situation where a syntactic constituent makes roughly the same semantic contribution in all places it occurs.

2 From here on I will reserve "constituent" for a part of a representation, and "component' for a part of the represented item.

3 Expression types here are not to be confused with their grammatical category. In the current sense, there can be many different expression types, which are all, for example, conjunctions.

4 Concatenation is a notion that has been given a specific formal treatment by logicians and linguists (see Quine 1960: 283–4). In those contexts, concatenation is taken to be a linear and associative relation intended primarily to pin down, at the level of tokens, the notion of *successor of*. My concern here, by contrast, is to capture a more general and intuitive notion inherent in the academic layman's understanding of the term; apologies to those who feel their terminological toes have been trodden on.

5 Strictly speaking, this condition should be stated in an even stronger fashion: Each token must contain a α_i token for every occurrence of a constituent of type α_i. Here, of course, the notion of an *occurrence* of a constituent must be defined in terms of the application of the grammatical rules in generating expressions.

6 At least, natural languages as they are written. Phonemic distortions in phrases of spoken languages make it awkward to claim that the spoken versions are strictly concatenative.

7 This use of "syntactic structure" is appropriate in the context of the debate over styles of mental representation to which this article is intended as a contribution. In some other contexts, "syntax" is used in a more abstract way; see, for example, Brandom's (1987) very important contribution to the study of linguistic structure.

8 Classical theorists, who (it will be argued below) are committed to concatenative representations, sometimes read this slogan as making a point that is too obvious to be worth mentioning. After all, they point out, the word "Chicago" is syntactically unstructured but it represents a very highly structured object. Note, however, that while "Chicago" represents Chicago, and Chicago is structured, the word "Chicago" is not in any way representing the structure of Chicago. Thus, a stranger in Chicago will not be able to find her way around if all she knows is that the city she is in is called "Chicago." Even the more precise expression "the structure of Chicago" would not be much help. To represent the structure of Chicago in any nontrivial way using Classical representations requires a (quite lengthy) description; that is, complex syntactic structure.

9 Note also: "Real constituency does have to do with parts and wholes; the symbol 'Mary' is literally a part of the symbol 'John loves Mary.' It is because their symbols

509

enter into real-constituency relations that natural languages have both atomic symbols and complex ones . . ." (Fodor and Pylyshyn 1988: 22).

10 The notion of vector addition in play here is the standard one: The sum of two *n*-place vectors, **v** + **w**, is simply the *n*-place vector whose values are the sum of the corresponding values of **v** and **w**.

11 These limits are explored in careful detail in Smolensky (1987a: 22–3); see also Smolensky (1988: 11–15). These limitations are one reason the tensor product framework does not simply amount to a Language of Thought.

12 For example, everyone who can have the thought that John loves the girl can also have the thought that the girl loves John. Although their discussion is not altogether clear on this point, Fodor and Pylyshyn (1988) suggest that these kinds of thoughts are systematically related in two ways: on a structural level, and also "from a semantic point of view" (pp. 31–42). This is the difference between the "systematicity of cognitive representation" and the "compositionality of representations."

13 Thus, for example, if you can infer *P* from *P&Q* then you can also infer *Q* from *P&Q* and *P* from *P&Q&R* (see Fodor and Pylyshyn 1988: 46–8).

References

Brandom, R. (1987) "Singular terms and sentential sign designs." *Philosophical Topics* 15: 125–67.

Fodor, J.A. and Pylyshyn, Z.W. (1988) "Connectionism and cognitive architecture: A critical analysis." *Cognition* 28: 3–71.

Hinton, G.E. (1988) "Representing part–whole hierarchies in connectionist networks." *Proceedings of the Tenth Annual Conference of the Cognitive Science Society* (pp. 48–54). Montreal, Quebec, Canada.

Pollack, J. (1988) "Recursive auto-associative memory: Devising compositional distributed representations." *Proceedings of the Tenth Annual Conference of the Cognitive Science Society*. Montreal, Quebec, Canada.

—— (1990) "Recursive distributed representations." *Artificial Intelligence* 46: 77–105.

Quine, W.V.O. (1960) *Mathematical Logic*. Cambridge, Mass.: Harvard University Press.

Smolensky, P. (1987a). *On Variable Binding and the Representation of Symbolic Structres in Connectionist Systems* (Tech. Rep. No. CU–CS–355–87). Boulder: University of Colorado, Department of Computer Science.

—— (1987b) "The constituent structure of connectionist mental states: A reply to Fodor and Pylyshyn." *Southern Journal of Philosophy* 26: (Suppl.): 137–63.

—— (1988) *Connectionistism, Constituency, and the Language of Thought* (Tech. Rep. No. CU–CS–416–88). Boulder: University of Colorado, Department of Computer Science.

Touretzky, D.S. (1986) "BoltzCONS: Reconciling connectionism with the recursive nature of stacks and trees." *Proceedings of the Eighth Annual Conference of the Cognitive Science Society*. Amherst, Mass.

IIIC

CONCEPTIONS OF
MODULARITY

23

J.A. Fodor, "Précis of *The Modularity of Mind*"

Everybody knows that something is wrong. But it is uniquely the achievement of contemporary philosophy – indeed, it is uniquely the achievement of contemporary *analytical* philosophy – to have figured out just what it is. What is wrong is that not enough distinctions are being made. If only we made all the distinctions that there are, then we should all be as happy as kings. (Kings are notoriously *very* happy.)

The Modularity of Mind (henceforth *Modularity*) is a monograph much in the spirit of that diagnosis. I wanted to argue there (and will likewise argue here) that modern Cognitivism failed, early on, to notice a certain important distinction: roughly, a distinction between two ways in which computational processes can be "smart." Because it missed this distinction, Cognitivism failed to consider some models of mental architecture for which a degree of empirical support can be marshaled, models that may, indeed, turn out to be true. If these models *are* true, then standard accounts of the nature of cognition and perception – and of the relations between them – are seriously misled, with consequences that can be felt all the way from artificial intelligence to epistemology. That was my story, and I am going to stick to it.

"What," you will ask, "was this missed distinction; who missed it; and how did missing it lead to these horrendous consequences?" I offer a historical reconstruction in the form of a fairy tale. None of what follows actually happened, but it makes a good story and has an edifying moral.

So then: Once upon a time, there was a Wicked Behaviorist. He was, alas, a stingy and dogmatic creature of little humor and less poetry; but he did keep a clean attic. Each day, he would climb up to his attic and throw things out, for it was his ambition eventually to have *almost nothing in his attic at all*. (Some people whispered that this was his *only* ambition, that the Wicked Behaviorist was actually just a closet Ontological Purist. For all I know, they were right to whisper this.)

Anyhow, one day when the Wicked Behaviorist was upstairs cleaning out his attic, the following Very Interesting Thought occurred to him. "Look," he said to himself, "*I can do without perceptual processes.*" (Because he had been educated in Vienna, the Wicked Behaviorist usually thought in the formal mode. So what actually occurred to him was that he could do without a theory of perceptual processes. It comes to much the same thing.) "For," it continued to occur to him, "perceptual identification reduces without residue to discriminative responding. And discriminative responding reduces without residue to the manifestation of conditioned (as it might be, operant) reflexes. And the theory of conditioned reflexes reduces without residue to Learning Theory. So, though learning is one of the things that there are, perceptual processes are one of the things there aren't. There also aren't: The True, or The Beautiful, or Santa Claus, or Tinkerbell; and unicorns are metaphysically impossible and George Washington wore false teeth. So there. Grrr!" He really was a *very* Wicked Behaviorist.

Fortunately, however, in the very same possible world in which the WB eked out a meager existence as a value of a bound variable (for who would call that living), there was also a Handsome Cognitivist. And whereas the WB had this preference for clean attics and desert landscapes, the HC's motto was: "The more the merrier, more or less!" It was the HC's view that almost nothing reduces to almost anything else. To say that the world is so full of a number of things was, he thought, putting it mildly; for the HC, every day was like Christmas in Dickens, ontologically speaking. In fact, far from wishing to throw old things out, he was mainly interested in turning new things up "Only collect," the HC was often heard to say. Above all – and this is why I'm telling you this story – the HC wanted mental processes in general, and perceptual processes in particular, to be part of his collection.

Moreover, the HC had an argument. "Perceptual processes," he said, "*can't* be reflexes because, whereas reflexes are paradigmatically dumb, perceptual processes are demonstrably smart. Perception is really a part of cognition; it involves a kind of thinking."[1]

"And what demonstrates that perceptual processes are smart?" grumbled the Wicked Behaviorist.

"I will tell you," answered the Handsome Cognitivist. "What demonstrates that perceptual processes are smart is *Poverty of The Stimulus Arguments*." (A Poverty of The Stimulus Argument alleges that there is typically *more information* in a perceptual response than there is in the proximal stimulus that prompts the response; hence perceptual integration must somehow involve the contribution of information by the perceiving organism. (See Chomsky 1980.)) No one knows how to quantify the relevant notion of information, so it is hard to show conclusively that this sort of argument is sound. On the other hand, such phenomena as the perceptual constancies have persuaded almost everybody – except Gibsonians and Wicked Behaviorists (see Ullman 1980; and Rachlin 1985 – that Poverty of The Stimulus Arguments have to be taken very seriously. I shall assume, in what follows, that that is so.) "Poverty of The Stimulus Arguments," continued the HC, "show that perceptual identifications can't be reflexive responses to proximal stimulus invariants. In fact, Poverty of The Stimulus Arguments strongly suggest that perceptual identifications depend on some sort of *computations*, perhaps on computations of quite considerable complexity. So, once we have understood the force of Poverty of The Stimulus Arguments, we see that there probably are perceptual processes after all." "And," the HC added in a rush, "I believe that there are Truth and Beauty and Santa Claus and Tinkerbell too (only you have to read the existential quantifier leniently). And I believe that for each drop of rain that falls / A flower is born. So *there*." (Some people whispered that the Handsome Cognitivist, though he was *very* handsome, was perhaps just a little wet. For all I know, they were right to whisper that, too.) End of fairy tale.

My point is this: Modern cognitivism starts with the use of Poverty of The Stimulus Arguments to show that perception is smart, hence that perceptual identification can't be reduced to reflexive responding. However – and I think this is good history and not a fairy tale at all – in their enthusiasm for this line of argument, early Cognitivists failed to distinguish between two quite different respects in which perceptual processes might be smarter than reflexes. Or, to put it the other way around, they failed to distinguish between two respects in which perception might be similar to cognition. It's at precisely this point that *Modularity* seeks to insert its wedge.

Reflexes, it is traditionally supposed, are dumb in two sorts of ways: They are *noninferential* and they are *encapsulated*.[2] To say that they are noninferential is just to say that they are supposed to depend on "straight-through" connections. On the simplest account, stimuli elicit reflexive responses directly, without mediating mental processing. It is my view that the HC was right about perceptual processes and reflexive ones being different in *this* respect; Poverty of The Stimulus Arguments do make it seem plausible that a lot of inference typically intervenes between a proximal stimulus and a perceptual identification.

By contrast, to describe reflexes as encapsulated is to say that they go off largely without regard to the beliefs and utilities of the behaving organism; to a first approximation, all that you need do to evoke a reflex is to present the appropriate eliciting stimulus. Here's how *Modularity* put this point:

> Suppose that you and I have known each other for many a long year ... and you have come fully to appreciate the excellence of my character. In particular, you have come to know perfectly well that under no conceivable circumstances would I stick my finger in your eye. Suppose that this belief of yours is both explicit and deeply felt. You would, in fact, go to the wall for it. Still, if I jab my finger near enough to your eyes, and fast enough, you'll blink ... [The blink reflex] has no access to what you know about my character or, for that matter, to any other of your beliefs, utilities [or] expectations. For this reason the blink reflex is often produced when sober reflection would show it to be uncalled for.... (p. 71)

In this respect reflexes are quite unlike a lot of "higher cognitive" behavior, or so it would certainly seem. Chess moves, for example, aren't elicited willy-nilly by presentations of chess problems. Rather, the player's moves are determined by the state of his utilities (is he trying to win? or to lose? or is he, perhaps, just fooling around?) and by his beliefs, including his beliefs about the current state of the game, his beliefs about the structure of chess and the likely consequences of various patterns of play, his beliefs about the beliefs and utilities of his opponent, his beliefs about the beliefs of his opponent about his beliefs and utilities, and so on up through ever so many orders of intentionality.

So, then, cognition is smart in two ways in which reflexes are dumb. Now the question arises: What is *perception* like in these respects? *Modularity* offers several kinds of arguments for what is, really, a main thesis of the book: Although perception is smart like cognition in that it is typically inferential, it is nevertheless dumb like reflexes in that it is typically encapsulated. Perhaps the most persuasive of these arguments – certainly the shortest – is one that adverts to the persistence of perceptual illusions. The apparent difference in length of the Mueller–Lyer figures, for example, doesn't disappear when one learns that the arrows are in fact the same size. It seems to follow that at least *some* perceptual processes are insensitive to at least some of one's beliefs. Very much wanting the Mueller–Lyer illusion to go away doesn't make it disappear either; it seems to follow that at least some perceptual processes are insensitive to at least some of one's utilities. The ecological good sense of this arrangement is surely self-evident. Prejudiced and wishful seeing makes for dead animals.

This sort of point seems pretty obvious; one might wonder how Cognitivist enthusiasm for "top down," "cognitively penetrated" perceptual models managed to survive in face of it. I think we have already seen part of the answer: Cognitivists pervasively confused the question about the encapsulation of perception with the question about its computational complexity. Because they believed – rightly – that Poverty of The Stimulus Arguments settled the second question, they never seriously considered the issues implicit in the first one. You can actually *see* this confusion being perpetrated in some of the early Cognitivist texts. The following passage is from Bruner's "On Perceptual Readiness":

> Let it be plain that no claim is being made for the utter indistinguishability of perceptual and more conceptual inferences. . . . I may know that the Ames distorted room that looks so rectangular is indeed distorted, but unless conflicting cues are put into the situation . . . the room still looks rectangular. So too with such compelling illusions as the Mueller–Lyer: In spite of knowledge to the contrary, the line with the extended arrowheads looks longer than the equal-length line with arrowheads inclined inward. *But these differences, interesting in themselves, must not lead us to overlook the common feature of inference underlying so much of cognitive activity.* (Bruner 1973: 8; emphasis added)

The issue raised by the persistence of illusion is not, however, whether some inferences are "more conceptual" than others – whatever, precisely, that might mean. Still less is it whether perception is in some important sense inferential. Rather, what's at issue is: How rigid is the boundary between the information available to cognitive processes and the information available to perceptual ones? How much of what you know/believe/desire actually does affect the way you see? The persistence of illusion suggests that the answer must be: "at most, less than all of it."

So far, my charge has been that early Cognitivism missed the distinction between the inferential complexity of perception and its cognitive penetrability. But, of course, it's no accident that it was just that distinction that Cognitivists confused. Though they are independent properties of computational systems, inferential complexity and cognitive penetrability are intimately related – so intimately that, unless one is *very* careful, it's easy to convince oneself that the former actually entails the latter. (For discussion see Pylyshyn 1980.)

What connects inferential complexity and cognitive penetrability is the truism that inferences need premises. Here's how the argument might seem to go: Poverty of The Stimulus Arguments show that the organism must contribute information to perceptual integrations; "perceptual inferences" just are the computations that effect such contributions. Now, this information that the organism contributes – the premises, as it were, of its perceptual inferences – must include not just sensory specifications of current proximal inputs but also "background knowledge" drawn from prior experience or innate endowment; for what Poverty of The Stimulus Arguments show is precisely that sensory information alone underdetermines perceptual integrations. But, surely, the availability of background knowledge to processes of perceptual integration *is* the cognitive penetration of perception. So if perception is inferentially elaborated, it *must* be cognitively penetrated. Q.E.D.

What's wrong with this argument is that it depends on what one means by cognitive penetration. One might mean the availability to perceptual integration of some information not given in the proximal array. Because Poverty of The Stimulus Arguments show that some such information must be available to perceptual integration, it follows that to accept Poverty of The Stimulus Arguments is to accept the cognitive penetrability of perception *in this sense*. But one might also mean by the cognitive penetrability of perception that *anything that the organism knows, any information that is accessible to any of its cognitive processes*, is *ipso facto* available as a premise in perceptual inference. This is a much more dramatic claim; it implies the *continuity* of perception with cognition. And, if it is true, it has all sorts of interesting epistemic payoff (see Fodor 1984). Notice, however, that this stronger claim does not follow from the inferential complexity of perception.

Why not? Well, for the following boring reason. We can, in principle, imagine three sorts of architectural arrangements in respect of the relations between cognition and perception: *no* background information is available to perceptual integration; *some but not all* background information is available to perceptual integration; *everything one knows* is available to perceptual integration. Because Poverty of The Stimulus Arguments imply the inferential

517

elaboration of perception, and because inferences need premises, the first of these architectures is closed to the Cognitivist. But the second and third are still open, and the persistence of illusions is prima facie evidence that the second is the better bet.

We arrive, at last, at the notion of a psychological module. A module is (*inter alia*) an informationally encapsulated computational system – an inference-making mechanism whose access to background information is constrained by general features of cognitive architecture, hence relatively rigidly and relatively permanently constrained. One can conceptualize a module as a special-purpose computer with a proprietary database, under the conditions that: (a) the operations that it performs have access *only* to the information in its database (together, of course, with specifications of currently impinging proximal stimulations), and (b) at least some information that is available to at least some cognitive process is *not* available to the module. It is a main thesis of *Modularity* that perceptual integrations are typically performed by computational systems that are informationally encapsulated in this sense.

Modularity has two other main theses, which I might as well tell you about now. The first is that, although informational encapsulation is an essential property of modular systems, they also tend to exhibit other psychologically interesting properties. The notion of a module thus emerges as a sort of "cluster concept," and the claim that perceptual processes are modularized implies that wherever we look at the mechanisms that effect perceptual integration we see that this cluster of properties tends to recur. The third main thesis is that, whereas perceptual processes are typically modularized – hence encapsulated, hence stupid in one of the ways that reflexes are – the really "smart," really "higher" cognitive processes (thinking, for example) are not modular and, in particular, not encapsulated. So *Modularity* advocates a *principled distinction* between perception and cognition in contrast to the usual Cognitivist claims for their continuity.

Since *Modularity* goes into all of this in some detail, I don't propose to do so here; otherwise, why would you buy the book? But I do want to stress the plausibility of the picture that emerges. On the one hand, there are the perceptual processes; these tend to be input driven, very fast, mandatory, superficial, encapsulated from much of the organism's background knowledge, largely organized around bottom-to-top information flow, largely innately specified (hence ontogenetically eccentric), and characteristically associated with specific neuroanatomical mechanisms (sometimes even with specific neuroanatomical loci). They tend also to be domain specific, so that – to cite the classic case – the computational systems that deal with the perception/ production of language appear to have not much in common with those that deal with, for example, the analysis of color or of visual form (or, for that matter, the analysis of nonspeech auditory signals). So strikingly are these systems autonomous that they often rejoice in their proprietary, domain-specific pathologies: compare the aphasias and agnosias. *Modularity* takes the view that it is high time to praise Franz Joseph Gall for having predicted the existence of psychological mechanisms that exhibit this bundle of properties. (Gall was approximately a contemporary of Jane Austen's, so you see how far we have come in cognitive psychology – and in the novel, for that matter.) It is precisely in the investigation of these "vertical faculties" that modern Cognitivism has contributed its most important insights, and *Modularity* suggests that this is no accident. Precisely because the perceptual mechanisms are encapsulated, we can make progress in studying them without having to commit ourselves about the general nature of the cognitive mind.

On the other hand, there are the true higher cognitive faculties. So little is known about them that one is hard put even to say *which* true higher cognitive faculties there are. But "thought" and "problem solving" are surely among the names in the game, and here *Modularity*'s line is that these are everything that perception is not: slow, deep, global rather than local, largely under voluntary (or, as one says, "executive") control, typically associated with diffuse neurological structures, neither bottom-to-top nor top-to-bottom in their modes of processing, but characterized by computations in which information flows every which way. Above all, they are paradigmatically *un*encapsulated; the higher the cognitive process, the more it turns on the integration of information across superficially dissimilar domains. *Modularity* assumes that in this respect the higher cognitive processes are notably similar to processes of scientific discovery – indeed, that the latter are the former writ large. Both, of course, are deeply mysterious; we don't understand non-demonstrative inference in either its macrocosmic or its microcosmic incarnation.

If much of the foregoing is right, then mainstream Cognitive science has managed to get the architecture of the mind *almost exactly backwards*. By emphasizing the continuity of cognition with perception, it missed the computational encapsulation of the latter. By attempting to understand thinking in terms of a baroque proliferation of scripts, plans, frames, schemata, special-purpose heuristics, expert systems, and other species of domain-specific intellectual automatisms – jumped-up habits, to put it in a nutshell – it missed what is most characteristic, and most puzzling, about the higher cognitive mind: its nonencapsulation, its creativity, its holism, and its passion for the analogical. One laughs or weeps according to one's temperament. It was, perhaps, Eeyore who found precisely the right words: "'Pathetic,' he said, 'That's what it is, pathetic.'"

Well, yes, but *is* much of this right? I want at least to emphasize its plausibility from several different points of view. Perception is above all concerned with keeping track of the state of the organism's local spatiotemporal environment. Not the distant past, not the distant future, and not – except for ecological accidents like stars – what is very far away. Perception is built to detect what is right here, right now – what is available, for example, for eating or being eaten by. If this is indeed its teleology, then it is understandable that perception should be performed by fast, mandatory, encapsulated, ... etc. systems that – considered, as it were, detection-theoretically – are prepared to

519

trade false positives for high gain. It is, no doubt, important to attend to the eternally beautiful and to believe the eternally true. But it is more important not to be eaten.

Why, then, isn't perception even stupider, even less inferential than it appears to be? Why doesn't it consist of literally reflexive responses to proximal stimulations? Presumably because there is so much more variability in the proximal projections that an organism's environment offers to its sensory mechanisms than there is in the distal environment itself. This kind of variability is by definition irrelevant if it is the distal environment that you care about – which, of course, it almost always is. So the function of perception, from this vantage point, is to propose to thought a representation of the world from which such irrelevant variability has been effectively filtered. What perceptual systems typically "know about" is how to infer current distal layouts from current proximal stimulations: the visual system, for example, knows how to derive distal form from proximal displacement, and the language system knows how to infer the speaker's communicative intentions from his phonetic productions. Neither mechanism, on the present account, knows a great deal else, and that is entirely typical of perceptual organization. Perceptual systems have access to (implicit or explicit) theories of the mapping between distal causes and proximal effects. But that's all they have.

If the perceptual mechanisms are indeed local, stupid, and extremely nervous, it is teleologically sensible to have the picture of the world that they present tempered, reanalyzed, and – as Kant saw – above all *integrated* by slower, better informed, more conservative, and more holistic cognitive systems. The purposes of survival are, after all, *sometimes* subserved by knowing the truth. The world's deep regularities don't show in a snapshot, so being bullheaded, ignoring the facts that aren't visible on the surface – encapsulation in short – is not the cognitive policy that one wants to pursue *in the long run*. The surface plausibility of the *Modularity* picture thus lies in the idea that Nature has contrived to have it both ways, to get the best out of fast dumb systems and slow contemplative ones, by simply refusing to choose between them. That is, I suppose, the way that Nature likes to operate: "I'll have some of each" – one damned thing piled on top of another, and nothing in moderation, ever.

It will have occurred to you, no doubt, that Cognitivism could quite possibly have hit on the right doctrine, even if it did so for the wrong reasons. Whatever confusions may have spawned the idea that perception and cognition are continuous, and however plausible the encapsulation story may appear to be *a priori*, there is a lot of experimental evidence around that argues for the effects of background knowledge in perception. If the mind really is modular, those data are going to have to be explained away. I want to say just a word about this.

There are, pretty clearly, three conditions that an experiment has to meet if it is to provide a bona fide counter-instance to the modularity of a perceptual system.

1   It must, of course, demonstrate the influence of background information in some computation that the system performs. But, more particularly, the background information whose influence it demonstrates must be exogenous from the point of view of the module concerned. Remember, each module has its proprietary database; whatever information is in its database is *ipso facto* available to its computations. So, for example, it would be no use for purposes of embarrassing modularity theory to show that words are superior to non-words in a speech perception task. Presumably, the language processing system has access to a grammar of the language that it processes, and a grammar must surely contain a lexicon. What words are in the language is thus one of the things that the language module can plausibly be assumed to know consonant with its modularity.

2   The effect of the background must be distinctively perceptual, not post-perceptual and not a criterion shift. For example, it is of no use to demonstrate that utterances of "implausible" sentences are harder to process than utterances of "plausible" ones if it turns out that the mechanism of this effect is the hearer's inability to believe that the speaker could have said what it sounded like he said. No one in his right mind doubts that perception interacts with cognition *somewhere*. What's at issue in the disagreement between modularity theory and "New Look" Cognitivism (e.g., Bruner 1973) is the *locus* of this interaction. In practice, it usually turns out that the issue is whether the recruitment of background information in perception is *predictive*. Modularity theory says almost never; New Look Cognitivism says quite a lot of the time.

3   The cognitively penetrated system must be the one that shoulders the burden of perceptual analysis in normal circumstances, and not, for example, some backup, problem-solving type of mechanism that functions only when the stimulus is too degraded for a module to cope with. Therefore, it is of no use to show that highly redundant lexical items are easier to understand than less redundant ones when the speech signal is very noisy – unless, of course, you can also show that the perception of very noisy speech really is bona fide speech perception.

So far as I know, there is very little in the experimental literature that is alleged to demonstrate the cognitive penetration of perception that meets all three of these conditions (to say nothing of replicability). This isn't to claim that such experiments cannot be devised or that, if devised, they might not prove that New Look Cognitivism is right after all. I claim only that, contrary to the textbook story, the empirical evidence for the continuity of perception with cognition is not overwhelming when contemplated with a jaundiced eye. There is, in any event, something for laboratory psychology to do for the next twenty years or so: namely, try to develop some designs subtle enough to determine who's right about all this.

"But look," you might ask, "why do you care about modules so much? You've got tenure; why don't you take off and go sailing?" This is a perfectly reasonable question and one that I often ask myself. Answering it would require exploring territory that I can't get into here and raising issues that *Modularity* doesn't even broach. But roughly, and by way of striking a closing note: The idea that cognition saturates perception belongs with (and is, indeed, historically connected with) the idea in the philosophy of science that one's observations are comprehensively determined by one's theories; with the idea in anthropology that one's values are comprehensively determined by one's culture; with the idea in sociology that one's epistemic commitments, including especially one's science, are comprehensively determined by one's class affiliations; and with the idea in linguistics that one's metaphysics is comprehensively determined by one's syntax. All these ideas imply a sort of relativistic holism: because perception is saturated by cognition, observation by theory, values by culture, science by class, and metaphysics by language, rational criticism of scientific theories, ethical values, metaphysical world-views, or whatever can take place only *within* the framework of assumptions that – as a matter of geographical, historical, or sociological accident – the interlocutors happen to share. What you can't do is rationally criticize the framework.

The thing is: I *hate* relativism. I hate relativism more than I hate anything else, excepting, maybe, fiberglass powerboats. More to the point, I think that relativism is very probably false. What it overlooks, to put it briefly and crudely, is the fixed structure of human nature. (This is not, of course, a novel insight; on the contrary, the *malleability* of human nature is a doctrine that relativists are invariably much inclined to stress. See, for example, John Dewey in *Human Nature and Conduct* (1922).) Well, in cognitive psychology the claim that there is a fixed structure of human nature traditionally takes the form of an insistence on the heterogeneity of cognitive mechanisms and on the rigidity of the cognitive architecture that effects their encapsulation. If there are faculties and modules, then not everything affects everything else; not everything is plastic. Whatever the All is, at least there is more than One of it.

These are, as you will have gathered, not issues to be decisively argued – or even perspicuously formulated – in the course of a paragraph or two. Suffice it that they seem to be the sorts of issues that our cognitive science ought to bear on. And they are intimately intertwined: surely, *surely*, no one but a relativist would drive a fiberglass powerboat.

Coming in our next installment: "*Restoring Basic Values: Phrenology in an Age of License.*" Try not to miss it!

Notes

1   See, for example, Gregory (1970: 30): "perception involves a kind of problem-solving; a kind of intelligence." For a more recent and comprehensive treatment that runs along the same lines, see Rock (1983).

2   I don't at all care whether these "traditional assumptions" about reflexes are in fact correct, or even whether they were traditionally assumed. What I want is an ideal type with which to compare perception and cognition.

References

Bruner, J. (1973) "On perceptual readiness." In J. Anglin (ed.), *Beyond the Information Given* (pp. 7–42). New York: Norton.

Chomsky, N. (1980) "Rules and representations." *Behavioral and Brain Sciences* 3: 1–62.

Dewey, J. (1922) *Human Nature and Conduct.* New York: Henry Holt.

Fodor, J. (1983) *The Modularity of Mind.* Cambridge, Mass.: MIT Press.

—— (1984) "Observation reconsidered." *Philosophy of Science* 51: 23–43

Gregory, R. (1970) *The Intelligent Eye.* New York: McGraw-Hill,

Pylyshyn, Z. (1980) "Computation and cognition." *Behavioral and Brain Sciences* 3: 111–69.

Rachlin, H. (1985) "Pain and behavior." *Behavioral and Brain Sciences* 8: 43–83.

Rock, I. (1983) *The Logic of Perception.* Cambridge, Mass.: MIT Press.

Ullman, S. (1980) "Against direct perception." *Behavioral and Brain Sciences* 3: 373–415.

24

G. Currie and K. Sterelny,
"How to Think About the Modularity
of Mind-reading"

I Introduction

It is widely accepted that the complexities of hominid social life are responsible for the evolution of distinctively human mental capacities. Certainly one
distinctive feature of human intelligence is social intelligence, and this is often
expressed as the idea that we are 'mind-readers', able to develop an intentional
profile of other agents in the course of explaining and predicting their behaviour.[1] Mind-reading and the capacity to negotiate the social world are not the
same thing, but the former seems to be necessary for the latter: people with
autism are extremely restricted in their comprehension of mental states and
they have comparable difficulties in negotiating the social world. And no
wonder: while not every social fact is a mental fact, and not every social property definable in mentalistic terms, our basic grip on the social world depends
on our being able to see our fellows as motivated by beliefs and desires we
sometimes share and sometimes do not. Social institutions are, then, intelligible as (imperfect) devices for harnessing the agreement and resolving the
conflict. So it is no surprise that in evolutionary and developmental theories
of social intelligence the primary focus has been on our capacity for detecting,
thinking about and responding to the mental states of conspecifics, particularly with a view to co-operating and/or competing with them. Clearly such
social understanding is deeply and almost exclusively mentalistic. It is that
subdomain of social understanding which concerns us here.

Is our mind-reading capacity a modular capacity? The question is interesting for several reasons. One of them is this. Mind-reading is a cognitive
rather than a perceptual ability. It is not controversial that important aspects
of perception are modular; they are subserved by dedicated, specialized and
perhaps even informationally autonomous mechanisms. But the suggestion
that belief fixation might be modular *is* controversial. Developing an intentional profile is further removed from immediate perception than are the
paradigms of modular cognition. So this is a good case for testing the hypothesis that there are *cognitive* modules.

We deny the strong claim that there is a modular central system wherein the fixation of social belief takes place. But our doubts are not based on any general animosity towards the idea of modularity in the design of human beings; we think the mind is probably full of modules. We think a somewhat less ambitious hypothesis about the modularity of social intelligence is plausible. We argue that social intelligence exhibits a mix of modular and non-modular aspects. This hybrid character cannot be explained on a strong, centralist version of the modularity hypothesis, but it falls naturally out of the picture we suggest.

II   Fodorian modularity

It is very common for people who advocate the modularity of social intelligence to represent themselves as revising in some fundamental way Fodor's picture of mental architecture.[2] A common observation is that Fodor 'did not go far enough', because he did not recognize that central belief fixing systems can be modular, and that excellent evidence for this is to be found in the domain of social intelligence. Jackendoff, for example, argues that 'there is a module or group of modules (a faculty) that is specialized for social cognition', and he remarks that this is contrary to Fodor's view: 'Fodor, for instance, specifically denies that modularity applies to thought as well as to perception'.[3] And Gigerenzer says 'I disagree with Fodor's opposition between modular sensory processes (and language) and general-purpose central processes. Social intelligence involves both perceptual processes and mechanisms for reasoning and inductive inference.'[4] In order to see what this commits advocates of the modularity of social intelligence to, we should remind ourselves of Fodor's picture of mental architecture.

In *The Modularity of Mind* Fodor argues that cognitive systems come in two kinds. Systems of the first kind are domain-specific: they answer questions from a restricted area. Such systems are often, Fodor suggests, encapsulated: in dealing with their thus restricted domains they draw on a narrow and proprietary range of information. In certain specific cases there may be information flow between modules. My visual system imports information about my head and eye-movements, and thus discriminates changes in the retinal image caused by these movements from changes produced by external causes. But in their processing they are not susceptible to influence by information from higher levels, levels at or above that at which they deliver outputs. This specific form of encapsulation is sometimes called 'cognitive impenetrability': what we want or believe makes no difference to how the module works.

The actual cognitive systems Fodor identifies as encapsulated are the 'input-systems', those that interpret transduced information and make it available for central processing.[5] And the input systems are, he says, perceptual systems plus language processing. These are Fodor's modules. And they are characterized not just by being domain-specific and encapsulated. They are fast; they are independent of voluntary control; they are relatively inaccessible to central systems not just in their informational encapsulation but also in being opaque to introspection; the representations they compute are relatively shallow; they are innately specified and have a fixed neural architecture; they are subject to specific breakdown.

Fodor emphasized that he was not offering necessary and sufficient conditions for modularity, but merely a list of features one is likely to find together. He also said that encapsulation is the most important of these features (p. 37), and on one occasion that it is the 'essence' of modularity (p. 71). Perhaps the thought was that while other features like speed and inaccessibility are indicative of modularity, they are all features that might be possessed by non-modular systems.[6] But encapsulation, being the essence of modularity, is what really makes a system modular and explains the other features. On this reading, we move from the superficial features of putatively modular systems (speed, inaccessibility, and the like) to their best explanation – encapsulation. Thus a modular system is fast because its encapsulation drastically cuts computational demands on it. Its informational autonomy explains its inaccessibility to introspection, and the possibility of selective loss of just that capacity. Some more recent work on modularity takes domain-specificity rather than encapsulation to be fundamental.[7] The trouble is that domains cannot in general be characterized independently of the modules that deal with them. Whether mate choice is a domain, or an ensemble of distinct domains concerning such things as fidelity, desertion, kin help and punishment, depends on whether we think there is a module for dealing with it, or merely a set of modules, one for each of these other domains. Would anyone think that face recognition is a single domain of problems if there were no evidence that highly selective brain damage can wipe out face recognition and leave other recognition functions intact?

However, encapsulation is not merely a theoretical postulate. Fodor argued that the encapsulation of perceptual systems is evidenced directly by the fact that perception does not change when it conflicts with belief, as in cases of visual illusion. He also argued along similar lines that the processing of the semantics and syntax of language is encapsulated, but not the processing of its pragmatics. So arguments about Fodor-style modules should primarily be arguments about encapsulation, and in particular about whether the system in question imports information from specifically higher cognitive systems. Towards the end of the paper we return to one other feature, proneness to breakdown.

Fodor did not claim that the mind is wholly or even largely modular. He argued that while input systems are modular, central systems – those which serve to fix belief – are not modular. For when it comes to the fixation of belief, everything is potentially relevant to everything else. While the lines in a Müller–Lyer experiment look dissimilar in length, you may conclude that they are in fact the same length. You may believe this for any number of reasons:

because measurement shows them to be the same, because someone you think of as reliable said they were, because you know that when people show you such displays they are generally doing so to illustrate a certain perceptual illusion, and so on.

What is the moral of this tale for us, whose interest is not perception but social understanding? It is that philosophers influenced by Fodor's framework and formulations who claim that social intelligence is modular might be understood in one of two ways. They might be claiming that there really is a social belief fixation module, that the processes we engage in which deliver social beliefs ('This person thinks or wants so and so', 'That person would be a good ally', etc.) are encapsulated, and in particular are cognitively impenetrable, and so are made on the basis of a narrow information base proprietary to the system itself. In contrast, there is a more modest modularity thesis: among the determinants of social judgements are outputs from processes that are encapsulated. We start with the strong claim that social belief fixation is cognitively impenetrable.

III   The modularity of social intelligence: the strong thesis

Of all the areas one might choose, social intelligence looks the least likely candidate for being an encapsulated system of belief fixation. Deciding what other people think or want, whether they constitute a threat or offer an opportunity, are highly complex judgements. In making them, information from all kinds of areas might be and often is seen as relevant. Machiavellian reasoning seems to depend on integrating information from a wide variety of sources. This difficulty for the modularist view of social intelligence might be eased by taking advantage of Fodor's further observation that encapsulation 'comes in degrees'. A system can be more or less encapsulated. But where is the evidence that in making social judgements there is a significant area of knowledge on which we cannot draw? If Max's confederate says he withdrew money from their London bank today there are all sorts of reasons why Max might suspect him: because, it is a public holiday there; because there was a total blackout of the city; because the confederate was spotted in New York at lunchtime. Just where are the bits of information to which we are systematically blind in making our social judgements? The whole *genre* of the detective story depends on our interest and skill in bringing improbable bits of far-away information to bear on the question of someone's credibility. To suggest that we do not have that skill defies belief.

We agree, of course, that there are features of social belief fixation which look a bit like encapsulation. In practice we often do make inferences and decisions in the social area on much less than optimal information, quickly and in ways that seem to be at least close to being automatic and mandatory.[8] But this cannot be the test of encapsulation; otherwise you must say that a system is encapsulated unless all the information the subject possesses is always brought to bear on a problem. Only an inferentially and informationally optimal system would then be non-modular, leaving us with an extremely impoverished and uninteresting sense of 'encapsulated'. The fact that we do not always exploit relevant information is not fixed by architectural features of the mind. Given time, care and inclination we can bring all our knowledge to bear on social questions. To resurrect the terminology of bygone days, this suggests that these limitations on access are limitations of performance, not competence.

It is not surprising, then, that believers in the social modularity thesis rarely argue explicitly that there is a genuinely Fodorian social module, though we have seen that they sometimes advertise their view in this way. We know of only a couple of arguments specifically designed to show that social reasoning is encapsulated – and then only to a degree. One is due to Gabriel Segal,[9] and it is an argument that raises issues that will occupy us throughout this paper. He uses the example of fiction-watching to argue (p. 147) that what he calls 'the psychology faculty' exhibits a 'degree of informational encapsulation':

> Watching a good actor can generate a sort of theory-of-mind illusion; even though one knows that he is really not in pain, or in love, or trying hard to solve a problem, it still seems to one that he is. It appears, then, that relevant information about the actor's real psychological states fails to influence the workings of the psychology faculty.

Of course it does look to us as if the actor is in pain: the actor is, after all, putting on a pained expression. But Segal needs more than this as evidence that 'relevant information about the actor's real psychological states fails to influence the workings of the psychology faculty'. A psychology faculty, if there is one, provides us with psychological beliefs. Segal seems to be suggesting that this faculty, being encapsulated, delivers not merely recognition that the actor's look is a pained one, but the belief that the actor is in pain when we 'know' that he is not. Such an illusion would be cognitive, constituted by a belief that is insulated from much else of what the agent knows.

This kind of case is central to the argument for the modularity of social belief fixation. If social belief fixation is modular, we ought to find cases where social belief is fixed by salient, largely perceptual, cues and in defiance of general knowledge – just the kind of case that the actor feigning pain offers us. But does the case really support modularity? It can seem so, especially if we attend to the affective side of watching or reading fiction. Good actors can make their make-believe threats feel very menacing; their make-believe offers seem heartbreakingly generous. Do we believe these to be real threats or generous offers? No. Despite various attempts to make it credible, the view that we believe in the fictions we encounter, even when we get deeply absorbed in those fictions, remains a nonstarter. We do not rush on stage to Desdemona's defence, or seek to intervene in even the most naturalistically staged aggressions. Since belief is a matter of degree, should we say that we give a limited (very limited) credence to the proposition that the actor is in love, or in pain, or whatever? We should not. Any measurable credence we gave to the proposition that he is would be in conflict with our belief, indeed our knowledge, that he is not. If we say that those engaged by a fiction are limited believers of it, we are bound to say that being engaged by a fiction is an epistemic vice. If we say that those engaged by a murder on stage believe, to some degree, that a murder is about to be committed in front of them, we are bound to say that their unwillingness to intervene is a moral vice. But fictions are not entrapment tools, and responsiveness to fiction is an imaginative virtue, not a vice of any kind. We must find some way of characterizing engagement with fictions that does not depend on claiming that fiction induces belief.

One answer, already hinted at, is to invoke the imagination. Seeing the actor's contorted face, we imagine he is in pain, and imagining this can cause us to have some of the uncomfortable sensations we would have if we really believed that he was in pain. And it seems that none of this is a matter of decision or inference; about the only way to stop imagining what the fiction makes it appropriate to imagine is to turn the TV off. If imagination is mandatory, it is starting to sound as if we have found the modularity of social intelligence in an unexpected place!

A modular theory of the imagination would be little help to advocates of the modularity of social intelligence, whose concern, we take it, is with the formation of social belief and the behaviour to which such beliefs lead. Imagination may be automatic in something like the way a module is. Given the right experience, imaginative engagement kicks in without conscious decision. But it cannot be a Fodorian module, since it is not encapsulated nor domain-specific. Certainly it is not a social module. Responses to fiction are not restricted to imagining just the thoughts and feelings of actors and fictional characters. Science fiction addicts regularly imagine travel through black holes and battles between giant aphids; they do not just imagine, Nagel-style, what it would be like to fight a giant aphid. So what we are capable of imagining goes beyond the realm of the social or the intentional even in the broadest of senses. It is not plausible that imagination is a domain-specific skill.

It might be replied that there is an ambiguity in the idea of domain-specificity, and that our science fiction examples are not decisive against one disambiguation of the idea of a domain-specific imagination machine. Dan Sperber has distinguished between the *actual* and the *proper* domain of a module – the proper domain is the domain for which a cognitive device is designed. He points out that radical changes in the human environment might have generated a quite dramatic disjunction between the domain for which a device is actually currently used and the reasoning tasks for which it is adapted and which explain its evolution. So the proper domain of imagination could be social reasoning, even though we actually imagine things in the non-social domain. But we would, of course, need some independent evidence that this is so. It is easy enough to tell plausible Just So stories about other possibilities. Imagination may exist at least partly to make it possible for us to predict the results of our actions in our physical environment.

If this is right, imagination is not domain-specific in either sense. And it certainly is not encapsulated. The arguments given already for saying that social belief is not encapsulated apply just as well to social imagining. Our responses to fictions are often informationally open, both synchronically and diachronically. For one thing, those responses draw on general knowledge in a potentially unlimited way. We import a great deal of background knowledge into our responses to fictions, tacitly assuming that the world of the fiction deviates only in minimal ways from the way we take the real world to be. And our emotional and evaluative responses to the fiction are driven by and reflect our desires and evaluative beliefs. This is not to suggest that we respond to fictions exactly as we do to life, but merely to point out that no account of our responses to fictions which claimed that they are encapsulated from general belief could succeed. And not only is imagination open to the influence of an unlimited range of beliefs; imaginings themselves combine in unrestricted ways. The actor's contorted face can cause us to imagine that the character he plays is in pain – but not always. It can be part of the story that the character is faking pain, and if we are sensitive to subtle clues available within what we already imagine, we can come to imagine that the pain is phoney.

We note just one other place where someone is tempted to reach for the encapsulation of social belief formation as a solution to a problem. Gigerenzer (p. 270) mentions 'the frame problem in artificial intelligence' as one reason for thinking that social intelligence is modular. The problem, he says, is that an organism which has to take into account all possibly relevant information (he calls this 'the infinite possibilities to combine elements and relations') would be 'paralysed and unable to react in time'. Assuming that distinct domains, including the social domain, are dealt with by systems of interconnected modules solves the problem, since (p. 277) 'modules that are hierarchically organized can act quickly, as only a few of the branches of the combinatorial tree need to be travelled'.

But wait! What exactly is the problem and how is modularity a solution to it? The frame problem is the problem of how to give an artificial system the capacity to take account of all the information we know a human is able to take account of in forming beliefs. That certainly is a problem, but how can thinking that human intelligence is modular help to solve it? Gigerenzer seems to be suggesting that by assuming modular structure, including some degree of encapsulation, we can suppose that the human mind cuts down on relevant information by having fast, dirty heuristics that act on highly restricted information bases. That would be one way for humans to solve problems in the social domain. But we know they do not do it in that way. We know that people often take into account all sorts of information from all over the place in solving social problems, and that is why it is difficult to mimic social intelligence in an artificial system. Indeed, that is why there is a frame problem in the first place. The frame problem is, as Gigerenzer says, a problem for artificial intelligence: how can a machine take into account all that a human believes? Gigerenzer seems to have it backwards: he wants to solve the frame problem by devising a theory of the human mind for which no frame problem would arise.

We conclude that the strong view of social modularity is too strong. Social judgements are not produced by an encapsulated mechanism.

IV   The modest thesis

Retreating from the strong modularity view, a natural-sounding alternative is to treat our hypothetical social intelligence module as analogous to perceptual modules. Perceptual modules, as Fodor often notes, do not fix belief. Seeing is not believing, for we can sometimes realize (or think we realize) that perceptual appearances are misleading. But perceptions make a powerful and functionally distinctive contribution to the fixation of belief. So a second reading of the social modularity hypothesis is that the fixation of social belief takes inputs from encapsulated systems.[10]

However, this second reading needs to be strengthened. Visual perception is probably modular. In that case, since visual perception contributes to the fixation of social belief; social intelligence would come out as modular on the present reading. That is too easy a victory for modularity. Instead we need to say something like this: amongst the systems feeding input to the fixation of social belief are modules that are *specfically adapted for that very role*. Modularized systems for perceptual processing may contribute to the fixation of social belief, but they contribute to the fixation of all sorts of other beliefs as well. Our suggestion is that there is a modularized layer between perception and belief fixation, and this layer adds a specifically social content to what are then the inputs to belief fixation. And the inputs of this module will be the outputs of perceptual modules, not transducer outputs. We shall call a module like this a 'second-order module'.

Why call it a 'module' at all? We earlier decided to treat encapsulation, and in particular encapsulation from higher cognitive systems, as the essence of modularity. The claim that there is a social module is thus the claim that there is a system which tags information from below with social markers, and does so even in the face of the belief that those markers do not literally apply, as when we believe, and indeed, know, that this person is not friendly, that this statue is not an intentional agent, that these are just geometric shapes – examples we discuss immediately below.

V   Saving the phenomena

Can a modularity hypothesis of this kind, one that avoids attributing modularity to belief fixation, explain the phenomena that have been thought of as suggestive of modularity in social cognition? We think it can. First, the thesis

531

of modularity of inputs and the non-modularity of central systems was never meant to suggest that belief fixation is like vote-counting in a democratic election. Someone who believes that belief fixation is non-modular will also believe that the perceptual beliefs we acquire will mostly reflect the contents of the perceptual inputs; as we noted above, one does not search through all the possibly relevant data from memory before forming those beliefs. Thus some perceptual inputs play a privileged role in belief fixation, and their influence can be turned aside only in unusual circumstances. So if there is an input system – a system that provides inputs for belief fixation – which adds socially relevant tags to data from perceptual inputs lower down, we can expect that to be reflected in certain biases in social reasoning and judgement.[11] And we can expect this without supposing that the fixation of social belief is modular, but merely on the supposition that certain inputs to social belief fixation – the shiftiness of a look, the openness of a smile – play a privileged role in belief fixation. That, after all, is what the social module is for. Just as the data from perception push us in the direction of certain perceptual beliefs rather than others, this social-intentional module will serve to push us in the direction of certain social beliefs, without itself being the mechanism that *fixes* belief. Bearing this in mind, we shall look at some relevant features of our response to the social world.

Perceptual illusion is often cited as striking evidence for modularity in perception. We think that there are persistent social illusions, that they add weight to the case for the modularity of social cognition, but that they do not involve the fixation of illusory belief. We have three different types of example in mind.

First and most obvious are cases of anthropomorphism, where there is no on-reflection temptation actually to form social beliefs. Our responses to cartoons and puppets indicate how easy it is to get us to imagine intentionality in something that only vaguely resembles the face of a living creature. And Heider and Simmel's well known experiments with moving abstract shapes show how natural we find it to imagine mental states around which we can then structure a narrative of the shapes' interaction.[12] But, as with the experience of watching an actor, we ought not to take this as evidence for the operation of encapsulated mechanisms which serve to fix our beliefs about mental states – we do not end up *believing* that the shapes have intentionality, any more than we believe that Desdemona has been murdered on stage. Attributions of intentionality where they do not belong do sometimes get to the level of belief, as with people who believe their pets understand English; and such beliefs can certainly be resistant to evidence and reason. But this is too general a phenomenon for it to support the modularity of belief in the social domain. Rather it is evidence for the influence of desire on belief; no one is tempted to suppose that beliefs like 'My children are not taking drugs' are modularized simply because they are irrationally formed and persisted with.

In the second kind of case, we dislike or distrust someone even while acknowledging an entire lack of rational basis for that judgement (there are cases that run the other way – the honest-faced scoundrel we find it difficult to mistrust). And some of the time these attributions do influence our interactions with people. What this suggests is that emotional responses, or some of them, can be triggered in multiple ways. We can experience fear when we know or believe that the man standing there means us harm, but also when a perception, or even a perceptual memory, is tagged with the appropriate intentional marker. In that case we experience the fear contrary to our judgement, and may even be moved to action by it. Perhaps it is this experience of 'being moved to action' against the dictates of reason that provides the most powerful case for the claim we reject, that social belief fixation is modular. If the feeling that this man is dangerous influences our behaviour, though we can find no supporting reason for the aversion, that seems to be a case of a belief to the effect that he is dangerous, but a belief on which our acknowledged lack of evidence makes no impact. Supposing that the deliverance of an input system can trigger emotion, and hence behaviour, provides an alternative way of seeing the matter, and one for which there is independent evidence. Someone may experience fear, and even behave aversively, at the sight of a spider he knows is harmless. Not all human action is routed through belief fixation followed by practical reasoning.

One other thing favours our modest modularism. It offers an evolutionarily plausible compromise between two competing constraints, the need for social intelligence to be *highly* intelligent, and the need for it to solve problems in real time. People do attempt to deceive us, they sometimes smile when they mean us harm; and the costs to us of their success can be very high indeed. So we cannot afford an automatic transition from the perception of a smile to the belief that this is a friend and ally. Encapsulated mechanisms are exploitable. On the other hand, smiles are sufficiently highly correlated with friendly intentions for us not to want the belief system to work through all the possible scenarios for deceptive intent every time we see a smile. For one thing, we would have lost many valuable allies during the time it would take us to come to a conclusion. Tagging the perception with an intentional marker serves to push the belief fixation system in the direction of one conclusion rather than another. Without strong countervailing pressure from other beliefs, we shall conclude quickly and efficiently that this is a friend. But the intentional marker always leaves room for such countervailing pressure, and for the consequent rejection of the friendliness hypothesis.

VI   Ways to make this more complicated

We have been arguing that the modularity of social intelligence is very like the modularity in perception that Fodor and others have advocated, and not at all a radical modularity of belief fixation. The picture we have presented has been kept simple so as not to lose sight of the contrast between these two options. But there are complications to the simple picture which might be forced upon us by the empirical data, as well as some open questions. For example, we have been supposing for the sake of the argument that perception, or at least some very substantial part of it, is modular in Fodor's sense. That might turn out not to be quite right: perhaps there are ways to train people not to be subject to the Müller–Lyer illusion, and other bits of evidence for the influence of top-down processing on input analysis. Perhaps there are also ways in which belief can influence the application of lower-level intentional markers. So it may turn out that neither perception nor social intelligence is strictly modular after all.

We could live with that. Our bottom line is that the evidence, such as it is, for modularity in social intelligence is at best evidence for modularity at a level prior to that of belief fixation. While we believe that perception and social intelligence both exhibit something close to this kind of modularity, it is entirely an empirical question as to how close the relation really is.

Secondly, we have suggested that the intentionality module is 'second order', distinct from and causally posterior to modular perceptual systems. That also might turn out to be a simplification. It might be that social markers get applied at various stages of perceptual processing, and not simply when perception has done its work. Again this would not bother us, for it would not disturb our claim that the adapted mechanisms of social intelligence generate subdoxastic representations rather than beliefs. If those mechanisms exist, their relations to more general perceptual mechanisms will depend on the nature of the outputs from perceptual systems, and the richness and complexity of the social markers that get applied prior to social belief fixation. To those issues we briefly turn.

A question that arises concerning an input module is 'How rich are its computations?' If the concepts deployed in our visual beliefs are also deployed in the outputs of visual perception, the visual perception modules could not be encapsulated diachronically, even if they are synchronically. If 'T-34 ahead!' is amongst the representations a visual module can present to the central processor for acceptance or rejection, the concepts we learn over our lifetime – 'teapot', 'white-crowned babbler', 'T-34', and the like – would have to be made available to the visual modules. Alternatively, one might suppose that the outputs of the module (more precisely, the assembled structure of modules) of visual perception are much more shallow. Perhaps (as Fodor seems to suggest) only something like Marr's 2½-dimensional sketch is computed by encapsulated processes. An analogous issue arises for our social intelligence-module. Social *beliefs* can be extraordinarily complex, as when I believe that you hope that she believes that I want this or that. It seems to us unlikely that social intelligence adds markers that have anything like this sophistication; they are more likely to be concerned with basic intentional-*cum*-emotional indicators like 'means me harm', 'is friendly', 'is angry'. A further possibility is that the outputs use representational categories that are not part of folk psychology at all. It might be objected that it is simply dogma on our part to assume that the markers provided by the social intelligence module are relatively impoverished. But our point is simply that, in line with Fodor's own

views on perceptual modularity, we should assume that the descriptive apparatus available to the module is thin unless the evidence strongly suggests that
it is not. Refinements much beyond this would then be the product of the
unencapsulated belief fixation mechanism.

This claim about the modularity of social intelligence affects the options
for understanding the ways in which a person's capacity to deal with the social
world can break down or fail to develop. It makes a great deal of difference
to our interpretation of these breakdowns whether we locate them at the level
of belief fixation or at the level of what we have been calling a 'second-order
module'. In recent years, for example, a number of psychologists have
suggested that the central features of autism are the result of damage to a
'theory-of-mind module', the purpose of which is to enable the agent to formulate beliefs about the mental states of others.[13] There are a number of reasons
why such a view is probably an oversimplification, but our proposal suggests
a new way of reading it. Up to now the assumption has been that the theory-
of-mind module fixes belief. But our suggestion is that it merely provides
intentional markers to the inputs which help to fix belief. Damage to such a
module would not in itself mean that the agent was unable to formulate
thoughts about thoughts – and indeed there is evidence that people with autism
do not suffer so pervasive a disability as this. But if people with autism were
impaired in their capacity to apply intentional markers to perceptual contents,
it would not be surprising if they were then less than fully competent at
forming beliefs about beliefs. Indeed, the often heard remark that people with
autism are 'mindblind' would be more appropriate on our model, which assimilates social intelligence to perceptual processing, than it is on a model that
pictures autism as a disability of belief fixation.

Indeed, there is some evidence that autistic people's disability with the
social is more like a perceptual disability than it is like a disability in belief
fixation itself. Psychologists have studied people's responses to filmed displays
of points of light, produced by having people in a darkened setting wear reflective patches on their joints and at other places on their bodies. Normal adults
can recognize the resulting display as indicative of a human figure, even with
very brief display times, and infants only three months old respond selectively
to them. And it is clear that this is a matter of the provision of intentional
markers, rather than of a modularized system for belief fixation. Seeing such
displays in the context of, say, a cartoon or mechanized presentation, we are
likely to imagine the pattern as indicative of intentionality, in much the
way that we respond to Heider and Simmel's shape patterns. But we may
very well not *believe* that the movement is that of an intentionally-animated
human body.

Peter Hobson and colleagues studied the responses of autistic subjects to
such patterns. While the autistic subjects in Hobson's experiment had no difficulty recognizing human figures as well as various objects from the displays,
they were much less apt than controls to describe what the human figures were
doing in emotional terms (whereas normal subjects readily described a figure

as, e.g., 'sad'), and were poor at judging the emotional states of the figures when specifically asked to do so.[14] Conceivably this could be because we have a module that fixes our beliefs about people's emotional states, and because people with autism suffer damage to the module. Our argument throughout this paper has been that the existence of such a belief fixing module is unlikely. But if there is a second-order module which adds (among other things) emotional markers, and if the module is damaged in autism, then autistic difficulty with emotion recognition would be explained without making implausible assumptions about the modularity of belief fixation.

Finally, a word on our responses to fiction. We have argued that they are not to be explained in terms of our coming to believe in the reality of the pain or the love that the actor's expression suggests. But the second-order module we postulate would certainly be triggered by the perceptual inputs from such a scene. What, then, of fictions in modes that deny us the relevant kind of perceptual access, such as literature? The words we see and read would not, presumably, trigger those same responses, at least not directly. If second-order modules play a role here it might be via the subject's mental imagery, serving as a kind of intermediary between the linguistically encoded narrative and our emotionally charged imaginings. Whether imagery can really play this role depends on the answers to questions we cannot settle here about how much overlap there is between perceptual and imagistic systems, and in particular whether imagery retains perception-like connections with affect.[15] Literary theorists have disagreed on the role of imagery in our encounters with literature; our suggestion at this point is simply that the question should be treated as partly one of empirical science.

VII   Conclusion

So our responses to fiction, the cognitive illusions generated by our response to the expression of emotion and intention, our anthropomorphizing responses to animals, devices and illustrations, all support the supposition that social intelligence depends on a module that takes its input from perceptual modules and which itself feeds to central belief forming mechanisms. But believers in the modularity of social cognition make an error when they claim that their thesis entails the modularity of central systems. We have suggested that a more modest thesis, involving second-order modules as input systems, is capable of explaining what genuinely needs to be explained. Our beliefs about the social are no more modular than are our beliefs about the shapes, sizes and colours of things.[16]

Notes

1   R. Byrne and A. Whiten (eds), *Machiavellian Intelligence* (Oxford: Oxford UP, 1988), and *Machiavellian Intelligence II: Extensions and Evaluations* (Cambridge: Cambridge UP, 1997).

2   J. Fodor, *The Modularity of Mind: an Essay on Faculty Psychology* (Cambridge, Mass.: Bradford Books, 1983).

3   R. Jackendoff, *Languages of the Mind* (Cambridge, Mass.: MIT Press, 1992), pp. 70, 71. See also J.H. Barkow, L. Cosmides and J. Tooby (eds), *The Adapted Mind: Evolutionary Psychology and the Generation of Culture* (Oxford: Oxford UP, 1992), p. 165; D. Sperber, *Explaining Culture: a Naturalistic Approach* (Oxford: Blackwell, 1996), p. 39. See also T. Shallice, *From Neuropsychology to Mental Structure* (Cambridge: Cambridge UP, 1988), ch. 12, for a different approach to reconsidering Fodor's ban on central modules. Fodor himself has suggested that knowledge of folk psychology is innate, which is a quite different claim from the claim that it is modular: see his *Psychosemantics* (Cambridge, Mass.: MIT Press, 1987), p. 132.

4   G. Gigerenzer, 'The Modularity of Social Intelligence', in Byrne and Whiten (eds), *Machiavellian Intelligence II*, pp. 264–88, at p. 273. We come back to Gigerenzer's view later.

5   But this is a contingent claim. 'Module' and 'input system' are not synonymous, *pace* A. Karmiloff-Smith, *Beyond Modularity* (Cambridge, Mass.: MIT Press, 1997), p. 2.

6   There might, as Martin Davies put it in conversation, be 'fools' modules'.

7   See, e.g., L. Cosmides and J. Tooby, 'The Psychological Foundations of Culture', in J.H. Barkow, L. Cosmides and J. Tooby (eds), *The Adapted Mind*, pp. 19–136.

8   We are indebted to Jay Garfield here.

9   G .Segal, 'The Modularity of Theory of Mind', in P. Carruthers and P.K. Smith (eds), *Theories of Theories of Mind* (Cambridge: Cambridge UP, 1996), pp. 141–57.

10 Curiously, at one point (*Modularity of Mind* p. 73) Fodor appears to argue that encapsulation is infectious downwards. So a process which contributes to an unencapsulated mechanism is thereby itself unencapsulated. But that cannot be right, for otherwise the whole notion of encapsulation would unravel.

11 Such biases appear to be manifested in superior performance on reasoning tasks when they are given a social interpretation. It has been argued that these biases show that social reasoning is modularized: see D. Cummins, 'Evidence for the Innateness of Deontic Reasoning', *Mind and Language* 11 (1996), pp. 160–90; but cf. M. Oakford and N. Chater, 'Deontic Reasoning, Modules and Innateness: a Second Look', *Mind and Language* 11 (1996), pp. 191–202. Our conclusion is that such biases show at most that social reasoning is modular at the level of inputs, not that there is a modularized central system for the fixation of social belief.

12 F. Heider and M. Simmel, 'An Experimental Study of Apparent Behavior', *American Journal of Psychology* 57 (1944), pp. 243–9. Jackendoff cites this example in support of the thesis of a central faculty of social cognition. See Jackendoff, *Languages of the Mind*, p. 74; see also Gigerenzer, 'The Modularity of Social Intelligence', p. 277.

13 See A. Leslie and T. German, 'Knowledge and Ability in "Theory of Mind": One-eyed Overview of Debate', in M. Davies and T. Stone (eds), *Mental Simulation: Evaluations and Applications* (Oxford: Blackwell, 1995), pp. 123–50; S. Baron-Cohen, *Mindblindness: an Essay on Autism and the Theory of Mind* (Cambridge, Mass.: MIT Press, 1995).

14 D. Moore, R.P. Hobson and A. Lee, 'Components of Person Perception: An Investigation with Autistic, Non-autistic, Retarded and Typically Developing Children and Adolescents', *British Journal of Developmental Psychology* 15

(1997), pp. 401–23. Similarly, Sally Rogers and Bruce Pennington argue that 'early social capacities involving imitation, emotion sharing, and theory of mind are primarily and specifically deficient in [infantile autism]', S.J. Rogers and B.F. Pennington, 'A Theoretical Approach to the Deficits in Infantile Autism', *Development and Psychopathology* 3 (1991), pp. 137–62.

15 Cognitive scientists are divided on this question. For a recent defence of the view that there is a substantial overlap see S. Kosslyn, W. Thompson and N. Alpert, 'Neural Systems Shared by Visual Imagery and Visual Perception', *Neuroimage* 6 (1997), pp. 320–34. Another issue that would have to be confronted here is whether the relevant imagery must always be conscious.

16 This paper arose out of discussions at the ARC-funded workshop on modularity, University of Tasmania, December 1998. Versions of it were read at a meeting of the Scots Philosophical Club at the University of Aberdeen, at the University of Glasgow, the Victoria University of Wellington, the University of Auckland, and at the 1999 conference of the Australasian Association of Philosophy. Thanks to all those who contributed to the discussions on these occasions, and especially to Max Coltheart, Martin Davies, Jay Garfield and Timothy Williamson. We also thank an anonymous referee for *The Philosophical Quarterly*.

25

L. Cosmides and J. Tooby, "Origins of Domain Specificity: The Evolution of Functional Organization"

By establishing that domain-specific machinery is necessary to explain human cognitive performance, psychologists who advocate modular or domain-specific approaches have found themselves in an unanticipated situation. Metaphorically speaking, it is as if they had laboriously built a road up one side of a nearly impassable mountain range into unexplored terrain, only to find themselves met at the top by a foreign road construction crew – evolutionary functionalist researchers – who had been building a road upward to the same destination from the far side of the mountains. Quite unexpectedly, cognitive psychologists find their field intimately connected to a whole new intellectual landscape that had previously seemed remote, unfamiliar, and all but irrelevant. Yet the proliferating connections tying together the cognitive and evolutionary communities promise to transform both fields, with each supplying necessary principles, methods, and a species of rigor that the other lacks. Although the sudden conjunction of these two communities has led to the customary level of mutual misunderstanding, the long-run significance of these developments is unmistakable. From this emerging integrated perspective, the domain-specific mechanisms or modules cognitive psychologists have been studying can be readily recognized for what they are – evolved adaptations, produced by the evolutionary process acting on our hunter-gatherer ancestors (Cosmides and Tooby 1987).

Natural selection and ancestral environments

Viewed from a more encompassing scientific framework, the confluence of these two research communities seems inevitable (Tooby and Cosmides 1992). The human brain did not fall out of the sky, an inscrutable artifact of unknown origin, and there is no longer any sensible reason for studying it in ignorance of the causal processes that constructed it. Rather, the reliably developing cognitive mechanisms that collectively constitute the architecture of the human mind acquired their particular functional organization through the process of evolution. The evolutionary history leading to modern humans consisted of a step-by-step succession of designs modified across millions of generations, with two independent forces – chance and natural selection – governing at every point whether each new modification would be incorporated into our species-typical cognitive architecture.

Although chance plays a delimited role in evolution and explains the existence and distribution of many simple and trivial properties, one thing cannot be plausibly explained as the product of chance processes: complex functional design (Williams 1966; Dawkins 1986; Pinker and Bloom 1990; Tooby and Cosmides 1990a, 1990b). Random walks do not systematically build intricate and improbably functional arrangements such as the visual system, the language faculty, or motor control. The only known explanation for the existence of complex functional design in organic systems is natural selection. Therefore, the existence of any complexly functional species-typical cognitive mechanisms must be related to the cumulative operation of selection (Dawkins 1986; Pinker and Bloom 1990), Necessarily, then, the design or functional organization of the mechanisms present in our cognitive architecture reflects the principles and logic of natural selection. Thus, cognitive psychologists, like physiologists, are usually studying adaptations and their effects, and they can find a productive new analytic tool in a carefully reasoned adaptationist approach (e.g., Cosmides 1989; Cosmides and Tooby 1989, 1992; Freyd 1987; Gallistel 1990; Gigerenzer and Hug 1992; Jackendoff 1992; Leslie 1987, 1988; Marr 1982; Pinker and Bloom 1990; Ramachadran 1990; Rozin 1976; Sherry and Schacter 1987; Shepard 1981, 1984, 1987a, 1987b; Shiffrar and Freyd 1990; Staddon 1988).

Natural selection operates through the testing of alternative designs through repeated encounters with evolutionarily recurrent situations (long-enduring adaptive problems). In our evolutionary history, design changes that enhanced their own propagation relative to alternative designs were selected for – that is, they caused their own successive spread until they became universal, species-typical features of our evolved architecture.[1] The systematic contribution of a design to its own propagation was the exclusive criterion, aside from chance, that determined which design changes became incorporated into our psychological architecture and which were excluded. Cognitive psychologists need to recognize that in explaining or exploring the reliably developing organization of a cognitive mechanism, the *function* of a design refers solely to how it contributed to its own propagation in ancestral environments. It does not refer to any of the various intuitive or folk definitions of function such as "contributing to the attainment of the individual's goals," "contributing to one's well-being," or "contributing to society." These other kinds of utility may or may not exist as side-effects of a given evolved design, but they can play no role in explaining how such designs came into existence or why they have the organization that they do. The fact that sexual jealousy, for example, may not contribute to any individual's well-being or to any positive social good is irrelevant in explaining why the cognitive mechanisms that reliably produce it under certain limited conditions became part of our species-typical psychological architecture (Daly, Wilson, and Weghorst 1982; see Tooby and Cosmides 1990a, for a cognitive-functionalist analysis of emotions).

Evolution is a historical process, not a foresightful one. The evolved design of modern organisms was caused by events in the past without regard to the problems of the present. Natural selection is not a teleological process capable of foreseeing the future and planning ahead for it. Our evolved mechanisms were constructed and adjusted in response to the statistical composite of situations actually encountered by our species during its evolutionary history (Symons 1992; Tooby and Cosmides 1990a). These mechanisms were not designed to deal with modern circumstances that are evolutionarily unprecedented. By the same token, they cannot have been designed to solve all potential problems under all possible circumstances either, because our species did not encounter all problems under all circumstances. For humans, the situations our ancestors encountered as Pleistocene hunter-gatherers define the array of adaptive problems our cognitive mechanisms were *designed* to solve, although these do not, of course, exhaust the range of problems they are capable of solving. These mechanisms should be well-engineered for solving this ancestral array of problems – and not necessarily any more inclusive class.

For these reasons, there is no warrant for thinking that selection would have favored cognitive mechanisms that are well-engineered for solving classes of problems beyond those encountered by Pleistocene hunter-gatherers. The widespread prejudice among cognitive psychologists for theories positing evolved architectures that consist of nothing but general-purpose problem-solvers is therefore unjustified. The fact that a mechanism can sometimes solve novel modern problems can play no role in explaining how that mechanism came to have the design it does, because natural selection had no crystal ball. The fact that our evolved mechanisms sometimes operate successfully in changed modem circumstances is a purely secondary consequence of their Pleistocene-forged design. Moreover, well-engineered performance should be evident only under conditions that mimic relevant aspects of the ancestral environments in which these mechanisms were designed to operate.

In short, the statistically recurrent conditions encountered during hominid evolutionary history constituted a series of adaptive problems. These conditions selected for a set of cognitive mechanisms that were capable of solving the associated adaptive problems. An adaptive problem can be defined as an evolutionarily recurrent problem whose solution promoted reproduction, however long or indirect the chain of causation by which it did so. Thus, although enhanced lifetime reproduction of self or kin was the ultimate functional product of adaptations, their proximate functional product need not have been closely associated with reproduction *per se*. A hominid life history of successfully achieved reproduction (including kin reproduction) required accomplishing the entire tributary network of preconditions and facilitations to reproduction in complex ecological and social environments. This entailed, of course, distinct families of specialized information gathering, inference, and decision making for our hominid ancestors. For this reason, humans are equipped with a diverse range of adaptations designed to perform a wide variety of tasks, from solicitation of assistance from one's parents, to language acquisition, to modeling the spatial distribution of local objects, to coalition formation and cooperation, to the deduction of intentions on the basis of facial expressions, to avoiding incest, to allocating effort between activities, to the interpretation of threats, to mate selection, to object recognition.

When abstracted from their ancestral hunter-gatherer contexts, such varied competences may seem (or be) disconnected from modern reproduction, and the operation of our cognitive architectures may appear instead to be a haphazard expression of activities of no particular evolutionary significance or patterning. This is an illusion produced by considering the operation of our psychological designs in isolation from their natural ancestral environments and without having developed task analyses – what Marr called computational theories – of the adaptive problems our mechanisms evolved to solve (Marr 1982). An understanding of the nature of the problems to be solved and a model of the detailed structure of these ancestral contexts makes functional sense of the otherwise puzzling design features of our problem-solving mechanisms (for an example of such functional clarification, see Profet (1992) on pregnancy sickness as an adaptation to the teratogenic effects of toxins present in plant foods in hunter-gatherer diets).

Of course, the design of our mechanisms should reflect the structure of the adaptive problems our ancestors faced only to the extent that natural selection is an effective process. Is it one? Evolutionary biologists since Darwin have been aware that selection does not produce perfect designs (Darwin 1859; Williams 1966; Dawkins 1976, 1982; for a recent convert from the position that organisms are optimally designed to the traditional adaptationist position, see Lewontin 1967 vs. 1978). Still, because natural selection is a hill-climbing process that tends to choose the best of the variant designs that actually appear, and because of the immense numbers of alternatives that appear over the vast expanse of evolutionary time, natural selection tends to cause the accumulation of increasingly and impressively functional designs. The eye and visual system are collections of cognitive adaptations that are well-engineered products of the evolutionary process, and although they may not be "perfect" or "optimal" – however these somewhat vague concepts may be interpreted – they are better at vision than any human-engineered system yet developed.

In consequence, not only is natural selection the only explanation for the functional organization of our cognitive mechanisms, but these mechanisms can be expected to be relatively well-engineered for solving ancestral adaptive problems. Two related questions arise when one assesses particular hypotheses about our cognitive architecture. The first is a learnability (or solvability) ques-

542

tion: What kind of mechanisms are capable of solving the adaptive problems our ancestors are known to have faced and regularly solved – domain-general mechanisms or domain-specific ones? The second is an evolvability question: If there is an adaptive problem that can be solved either by a domain-general or a domain-specific mechanism, which design is the better engineering solution and, therefore, the design more likely to have been selected for?

What's wrong with domain-general mechanisms: an evolutionary perspective

Evolutionary biology provides a series of reasons why it is implausible and unparsimonious to assume that the human mind is an equipotential, general-purpose machine (Cosmides and Tooby 1987; Tooby and Cosmides 1992).

In the first place, the more important the adaptive problem, the more intensely natural selection specializes and improves the performance of the mechanism for solving it. This is because different adaptive problems often require different solutions, and different solutions can, in most cases, be implemented only by different, functionally distinct mechanisms. Speed, reliability, and efficiency can be engineered into specialized mechanisms because there is no need to engineer a compromise between competing task demands. Competing task demands can, however, be handled by separate, specialized systems. This accounts for the pervasive empirical finding that natural selection tends to produce functionally distinct adaptive specializations, such as a heart to pump blood, a liver to detoxify poisons, an immune system to defeat infections. As a rule, when two adaptive problems have solutions that are incompatible or simply different, a single general solution will be inferior to two specialized solutions. In such cases, a jack of all trades is necessarily a master of none because generality can be achieved only by sacrificing effectiveness. Consequently, domain-specific cognitive mechanisms, with design features that exploit the stable structural features of evolutionarily recurring situations, can be expected to systematically outperform (and hence preclude or replace) more general mechanisms that fail to exploit these features.

The alarm calls of vervet monkeys illustrate this point clearly. Vervets have three major predators: leopards, eagles, and snakes. Each of these predators requires different evasive action: climbing a tree (leopard), looking up in the air or diving straight into the bushes (eagle), or standing on hind legs and looking into the grass (snake). Accordingly, vervets have evolved cognitive mechanisms that produce (and respond to) a different alarm call for each of these three predators (Cheney and Seyfarth 1990). A single, general-purpose alarm call (and response system) would be less effective because the recipients of the call would not know which of the three different and incompatible evasive actions to take.

Simply to survive and reproduce, our Pleistocene ancestors had to be good at solving an enormously broad array of adaptive problems – problems that would defeat any modern artificial intelligence system. A small sampling includes foraging for food, navigating, selecting a mate, parenting, engaging in social exchange, dealing with aggressive threat, avoiding pathogenic contamination, avoiding predators, avoiding naturally occurring plant toxins, avoiding incest, and so on. A woman who used the same caste preference mechanisms in choosing a mate that she used to choose nutritious foods would choose a very strange mate indeed, and such a design would rapidly select itself out. These different adaptive problems are frequently incommensurate: They cannot, in principle, be solved by the same mechanism (Sherry and Schacter 1987). Even a restricted consideration of hunter-gatherer tasks suggests that it is unlikely that any single general computational system could solve them all under ancestral conditions. (Indeed, it is difficult to imagine a domain-general computational system that could solve *any* of them.)

For this reason, the human mind can be expected to include a number of functionally distinct cognitive adaptive specializations (for discussion, see Chomsky 1980; Cosmides and Tooby 1987; Rozin 1976; Rozin and Kalat 1971; Sherry and Schacter 1987; Tooby and Cosmides 1992). Both empirically and theoretically, there is no more reason to expect any two cognitive mechanisms to be alike than to expect the eye and the spleen, or the pancreas and the pituitary to be alike. The argument frequently made by advocates of domain-general mechanisms – that a hypothetical and yet-to-be-described general problem-solving design would solve a larger class of unencountered or rarely encountered problems – is irrelevant: What governs the course of evolution and, therefore, the design of the human mind, is the statistical distribution of past situations that our ancestors actually encountered over evolutionary time.

In fact, we think the case can be put even more strongly. It is not simply a matter of plausibility, of efficiency, or of evolution being more likely to have produced a better system. Even simple learnability analyses show that *it is in principle impossible for a human psychology that contained nothing but domain-general mechanisms to have evolved, because such a system cannot consistently behave adaptively: It cannot solve the problems that must have been solved in ancestral environments for us to be here today.* A small number of domain-general mechanisms are inadequate in principle to account for adaptive behavior. We have developed this argument in detail elsewhere (Cosmides and Tooby 1987; Tooby and Cosmides 1992), so we won't belabor it here. Instead, we will summarize a few of the relevant points.

First, the ground rules for the argument.

1 To be a viable hypothesis about human cognitive architecture, the proposed design must in principle be able to solve its target problem. At a minimum, any proposed cognitive architecture had to produce minimally adaptive behavior in ancestral environments – we know this because we are here today. Just as a hypothesized set of cognitive mechanisms underlying language must be able to account for the facts of human linguistic behavior, so too must any hypothetical domain-general cognitive architecture solve all the

problems that were necessary to survival and reproduction in the Pleistocene. If it can be shown that there are essential adaptive problems that humans must have been able to solve in order to have propagated, and that domain-general mechanisms cannot solve them, then the domain-general hypothesis fails. We think there are a number of such problems, including inclusive fitness regulation, nutritional regulation, incest avoidance, sexual jealousy, predator avoidance – at a minimum, any kind of information-processing problem that involves motivation, and many others as well.

2 Because we know that the human mind evolved primarily by natural selection, hypotheses about the design of the mind gain or lose plausibility depending on whether the proposed design would have enhanced function-ality under ancestral conditions – in biological terminology, whether it produced an increase in "fit" behavior. Evolutionary biology suggests that there is no principled reason for parsimony to be a design criterion for the mind, particularly when it conflicts with increased functionality. Enhanced functionality is the only criterion to which natural selection responds. (Equally, there is no reason why chance evolutionary processes would create cognitive architectures that operate according to simple, general, parsimonious princi-ples either.)

A domain-general psychological architecture cannot guide behavior in ways that promote fitness for at least three related reasons:

1   What counts as fit behavior differs from domain to domain, so there is no domain-general criterion of success or failure that correlates with fitness.
2   Adaptive courses of action can be neither deduced nor learned by general criteria, because they depend on statistical relationships between features of the environment, behavior, and fitness that emerge over many genera-tions and are, therefore, not observable during a single lifetime.
3   Combinatorial explosion paralyzes any truly domain-general system when encountering real-world complexity.

Reason 1: The definition of error is domain-dependent. For a domain-general system to learn what to do, it must have some criterion of success and failure; trial-and-error learning requires some definition of error. But there is no domain-independent criterion of success or failure that is correlated with fitness. This is because what counts as fit behavior differs markedly from domain to domain. For example, suppose our hypothetical domain-general learning mechanism guiding an ancestral hunter-gatherer somehow inferred that sexual intercourse is a necessary condition for producing offspring. Should the individual, then, have sex at every opportunity? In fact, such a design would rapidly be selected out. There are large fitness costs associated with incest, to pick only a single kind of sexual error. Given a potential partner with a physique, personality, or resources that would normally elicit sexual desire, the information that the potential partner is a family member must inhibit sexual impulses. Now suppose that this equipotential psyche had somehow learned that avoiding sex with kin had positive fitness consequences. How then should it generalize this knowledge about kin to other domains of human activity? Should one, for instance, avoid any interaction with kin? This would be a mistake; selectively avoiding sex with kin has positive fitness consequences, but selectively avoiding helping kin has negative fitness consequences. With relatives as with so many other things, what counts as adaptive error differs from domain to domain. In the sexual domain, error = sex with kin. In the helping domain, error = not helping kin given the appropriate envelope of circumstances. In cooperative exchanges, error = being cheated, which is paying a cost without receiving the benefit to which this entitles you. When a lion is looking for lunch, error = offering yourself as an appetizer. Because what counts as the wrong thing to do differs from domain to domain, there must be as many domain-specific cognitive mechanisms as there are domains in which the definitions of successful behavioral outcomes are incommensurate. This simple point has been underappreciated because of the traditional emphasis within cognitive psychology on the acquisition of knowledge rather than on the regulation of action. The brain evolved mechanisms to acquire knowledge because knowledge was important in the regulation of successful action.

Reason 2: Many relationships necessary to the successful regulation of action cannot be observed by any individual during his or her lifetime. Asking the question of how a domain-general architecture could acquire all the classes of necessary domain-specific knowledge exposes a fatal weakness in domain-general systems: They are limited to knowing what can be validly derived by general processes from perceptual information. Domain-specific mechanisms are not limited in this way. The world has a statistically recurrent domain-specific structure (e.g., snakes and spiders are often venomous, objects are solid, self-propelled entities are usually animals, the person who nursed you is likely to be your mother, human speech is consistent with Universal Grammar). A domain-general system has to bring the same general procedures to bear on spiders, speech, objects, mothers, and self-propelled entities, and so cannot initially treat any of these categories differently. Its subsequent operation is limited to what can be perceptually derived based on the application of general procedures. In contrast, content-sensitive architectures can come equipped with domain-specific procedures, representations, or representational formats prepared to exploit unobserved and indeed, individually unobservable – sequelae to membership in various domains. The individual need not observe or experience death from a snake bite to manifest a caution around snakes, or run a long-term epidemiological study of the effects of inbreeding to manifest a distaste for sex with siblings. Chomsky's argument from the poverty of the stimuli is of this kind: Perception alone cannot supply infants with a list of constraints on the hypothesis space of potential human grammars (Chomsky 1975; Pinker 1984).

In its most general form, the difficulty of discovering what fitness consequences various actions or choices in knowledge representation have is fatal to any proposed domain-general system. The systematic statistical consequences of many courses of action on fitness are not stably assessable for several generations, and then only by evolutionary biologists, Divine Beings, or – and this is the essential point – natural selection. Because the promotion of fitness means differential representation of genes in subsequent generations, the time at which the consequences of an action can be assessed is remote from the time at which the action must be taken. Adaptive courses of action can be neither deduced nor learned by general criteria alone because they depend on statistical relationships between features of the environment, behavior, and fitness that emerge over many generations and are, therefore, often not observable during a single lifetime.

For example, how would a general-purpose mechanism situated in an ancestral hunter-gatherer ever discover that it should regulate behavior in approximate accordance with Hamilton's kin selection equation – that X should help Y whenever $C_x < r_{xy}$?[2] When an individual sees a relative, there is nothing in the stimulus array that tells her how much she should help that relative. And there is no consequence that she can observe that tells her whether, from a fitness point of view, she helped too much, not enough, or just the right amount. Even worse, there is no one in the situation from whom she could learn, because selection will have created mechanisms in her relatives that cause them to encourage her to behave in ways that violate the above equation. A design feature that causes X to help her brother will spread through the population when it causes her behavior toward her full brother to fall within the bounds dictated by $C_x < \frac{1}{2} B_{brother}$. But selection should also have designed mechanisms that cause her brother to encourage her to help him whenever $\frac{1}{2}C_x < B_{brother}$ as well as mechanisms that cause their mother to encourage her to help her brother whenever $C_x < B_{brother}$. In other words, what counts as adaptively "correct" behavior is individual-specific. Learnability theorists of language have pointed out that a learning theory is inadequate if the information required for induction is absent from the child's environment. In the case of helping kin, the information is not only absent, but other individuals in the situation should be designed to try to socialize the child into behaving in ways that are contrary to the very rule that the child must induce.

In contrast, natural selection can detect these statistical relationships. This is because natural selection does not work by inference or simulation. It takes the real problem, runs the experiment, and retains those design features that lead to the best available outcome. Natural selection "counts up" the results of alternative designs operating in the real world, over millions of individuals, over thousands of generations, and weights alternatives by the statistical distribution of their consequences. In this sense it is omniscient – it is not limited to what could be validly deduced by one individual, based on a short period of experience, it is not limited to what is locally perceivable, and it is not confused by spurious local correlations. It uses the statistical foundation of the actual lives of organisms, in the actual range of environments they encounter, under the statistical regularities they experience and, using alternative developmental programs leading to alternative designs, tests for the best solution. Some statistical regularities may be picked up by some kind of inductive learning system, but many can only be detected by the feedback process of natural selection.

Reason 3: Combinatorial explosion paralyzes any system that is truly domain-general. A domain-general evolved architecture is defined by what it lacks: It lacks any content, either in the form of domain-specific knowledge or domain-specific procedures, that can guide it toward the solution of an adaptive problem. As a result, a domain-general system must evaluate all alternatives it can define. Permutations being what they are, alternatives increase exponentially as the problem complexity increases. By the time you analyze any biological problem of routine complexity, a mechanism that contains no domain-specific rules of relevance, procedural knowledge, or privileged hypotheses could not solve the problem in the amount of time the organism has to solve it (e.g., Carey 1985; Cosmides and Tooby 1987; Gallistel, Brown, Carey, Gelman, and Keil 1991; Keil 1989; Markman 1989; Tooby and Cosmides 1992). Indeed, a great deal of research on domain-specific reasoning in children has been motivated by this concern (see Carey and Gelman 1991; Keil 1989; Markman 1989; and volume 14 of *Cognitive Science*).

In short, although some mechanisms in the cognitive architecture may be domain-general, these could not have produced fit behavior under Pleistocene conditions (and therefore could not have been selected for) unless they were embedded in a constellation of specialized mechanisms that have domain-specific procedures, or operate over domain-specific representations, or both.

Evolutionary biology, computational theories, and learnability

An evolutionary perspective can aid research on domain specificity in cognitive development in two ways. (1) It allows one to pinpoint the important, long-enduring adaptive problems for which humans are most likely to have cognitive adaptive specializations – that is, it suggests what domains it might be fruitful to investigate. (2) Evolutionary biology provides richly contentful theories and relevant data that allow one to construct detailed computational theories or task analyses of these domains. This facilitates both the experimental investigation of the associated cognitive mechanisms and the application of learnability (or, more generally, solvability) criteria.

Why a theory of adaptive function is important

Many psychologists study the mind without asking what it was designed to do. Instead, they hope to uncover its structure by studying things it is *capable* of doing. Playing chess, remembering nonsense syllables or long strings of numbers, programming computers, doing college-level statistics – these are all activities that we *can* do, but they are certainly not activities that our minds were *designed* to do. It is highly unlikely that the cognitive architecture of the human mind includes procedures that are *dedicated* to solving any of these problems: The ability to solve them well would not have enhanced the survival or reproduction of the average Pleistocene hunter-gatherer, and the performance of modern humans on such tasks is generally poor and uneven. In all probability, a wide and somewhat idiosyncratic array of mechanisms and knowledge bases is mobilized when we try to solve this kind of problem, so the study of such problems is unlikely to lead us to carve nature at the joints (Marr and Nishihara 1978).

There is a big difference between studying what a mechanism *can* do, and what it was *designed* to do. Suppose you have to figure out how an appliance works by studying some of the things it can do. I tell you that it can be used as a paperweight, that you can use it to warm your hands on a cold day, and that you can kill someone who is taking a bath by throwing it into the tub with him. By studying each of these uses of the appliance, you will learn a little bit about its structure – it is heavy enough to keep paper from blowing away, it generates heat, it is electrical – but you won't get a very coherent idea of what it is or how it works. It sounds like an electrical, heat-generating paperweight. Where do you go from here? Where is the heuristic value in this research strategy?

Suppose, on the other hand, that I tell you that the appliance is a mechanism that was designed to toast slices of bread – it is a "toaster." Your research strategy for discovering how it works would be completely different. Knowing its function, you would look for mechanisms that were specially designed for fulfilling that function; in this case, you would look for mechanisms that were specially designed for toasting bread. For example, you might hypothesize that the appliance has elements that generate heat; that it has two of these heating elements, one for each side of a slice of bread; that these elements are parallel to each other; that the distance between them is a little wider than the width of the average slice of bread; that it has a mechanism for detecting when the bread is toasted and for turning off the heat, a mechanism that allows you to retrieve the toasted bread without burning your fingers, and so on. It also tells you what features of the toaster are functionally arbitrary; the trait, "heavy enough to use as a paperweight," is not relevant to a toaster's function – it is merely a byproduct of the fact that the toaster's functioning parts are heavier than paper.

Knowing what the appliance was designed to do – what its function is – has enormous heuristic value because it suggests what design features it is likely to have. It allows you to pinpoint the kinds of problems a toaster should be very good at solving. Although it does not tell you the exact structure of the mechanisms that solve these problems (will the toast be delivered by a pop-up mechanism or by opening a door?), it suggests sharply focused hypotheses about the structure of these design features. It allows you to develop a task analysis for that problem, or what David Marr would call a "computational theory" for that problem domain: a theory specifying what functional characteristics a mechanism for solving that problem must have (Marr and Nishihara 1978; Marr 1982).

Evolvability constraints and computational theories

The most important contribution that evolutionary biology can make in the study of domain-specific mechanisms is in the development of computational theories of adaptive information-processing problems. Natural selection theory is a theory of *function*: it allows one to pinpoint adaptive information-processing problems that the human mind was selected to solve and therefore should be good at solving. Because an adaptive problem and its cognitive solution – a mechanism – need to fit together like a lock and a key, understanding adaptive problems tells one a great deal about the associated cognitive mechanisms. Natural selection shapes domain-specific mechanisms so that their structure meshes with the evolutionarily stable features of their particular problem domains. Understanding the evolutionarily stable features of problem domains – and what selection favored as a solution under ancestral conditions – illuminates the design of cognitive specializations. Although a computational theory of an adaptive problem cannot, by itself, tell you the exact structure of the information-processing mechanisms that solve the problem, it does suggest what design features they are likely to have and places important constraints on the family of possible mechanisms.

For example, the evolution of altruism, or helping behavior, was a puzzle for evolutionary theory. How can a new design feature spread through the population until it becomes species-typical if it causes an individual to harm its own reproductive success – the number of offspring it has – in order to increase another individual's reproductive success? The individual who has the new design feature is, by definition, selecting itself out.

In 1964, W.D. Hamilton provided an answer to this question. Using mathematical game theory, he showed that if an organism helps a kin member whenever the cost to itself (in reproductive terms) is less than the benefit to its kin member, discounted by the probability that the kin member shares the same design feature, then that helping design can spread through the population. Any design feature that causes an individual to help more than this – or less than this – would be selected against. This constraint is completely general: It is inherent in the dynamics of natural selection, true of any species on any planet at any time.

This means that the cognitive programs of an organism that confers benefits on kin cannot violate the [Cost to self < (Benefit to kin member) x (coefficient of relatedness to kin member)] constraint of Hamilton's kin selection theory. Cognitive programs that systematically violate this constraint cannot be selected for. Cognitive programs that satisfy this constraint can be selected for. A species may lack the ability to confer benefits on kin, but if it has such an ability, then it has it by virtue of cognitive programs that produce behavior that respects this constraint. One can call theoretical constraints of this kind *evolvability constraints*; they specify the class of mechanisms that can, in principle, evolve (Tooby and Cosmides 1992).

The specification of constraints imposed by the evolutionary process – the specification of an adaptive function – does not, in itself, constitute a complete computational theory. Evolvability constraints merely define what counts as adaptive behavior. Cognitive programs are the means by which behavior – adaptive or otherwise – is produced. The important question a computational theory must address is: What kind of cognitive programs must an organism have if it is to behave adaptively?

Evolutionary biologists do not usually think of their theories as defining information-processing problems, yet this is exactly what they do. For example, Hamilton's kin selection theory raises – and answers – questions such as: How should the information that X is your brother affect your decision to help him? How should your assessment of the cost to you of helping your brother, versus the benefit to your brother of receiving your help, affect your decision? Will the information that Y is your cousin have a different effect on your decision than if you thought Y were your brother? In general, how should information about your relatedness to X, the costs and benefits to you of what X wants you to do for him, and the costs and benefits to X of your coming to his aid, affect your decision to help X?

As these questions show, an organism's behavior cannot fall within the bounds of the constraints imposed by the evolutionary process unless it is guided by cognitive programs that can solve certain information-processing problems that are very specific. To confer benefits on kin in accordance with the evolvability constraints of kin selection theory, the organism must have cognitive programs that allow it to extract certain specific information from its environment: Who are its relatives? Which kin are close and which distant? What are the costs and benefits of an action to itself? To its kin? The organism's behavior will be random with respect to the constraints of kin selection theory unless (1) it has some means of extracting information relevant to these questions from its environment, and (2) it has well-defined decision rules that use this information in ways that instantiate the theory's constraints. We are one of the species that has evolved the ability to help kin. Consequently, we can be expected to have evolved mechanisms that are dedicated to solving such problems, and can therefore solve them quickly, reliably, efficiently, automatically, effortlessly, and unconsciously. Trying to study domain-specific processes without a detailed computational theory that is either derived from, or at least compatible with, evolutionary biology would be like trying to study language acquisition without knowing the grammar of any human language.

The development of detailed computational theories of adaptive problems not only facilitates the experimental investigation of human cognition, but it also lays the groundwork for conducting a learnability (or, more generally, a solvability) analysis (e.g., Pinker 1979, 1984; Tooby and Cosmides 1992; Wexler and Culicover 1980). The fact that many adaptive problems are of a very specialized kind suggests that many cognitive processes will be far more specific than is usually assumed, even by psychologists sympathetic to a domain-specific viewpoint. For example, evolutionary biology identifies a large number of distinct problems posed by social life that learnability analyses indicate must involve very different procedures for their solution. Rules that will cause one to accurately detect cheaters in a situation of social exchange, for example, do not map onto the rules of inference of the propositional calculus (Cosmides 1989; Cosmides and Tooby 1992; Gigerenzer and Hug 1992). Nor do they map onto rules for detecting violations of aggressive threats. For example, a social contract has a different cost–benefit structure from a threat; a social contract is not in effect unless both parties agree to it, whereas a threat is a unilateral speech act; a social contract does not have a biconditional entailment structure whereas a threat does; from the point of view of a single actor, there is only one way of violating a social contract, whereas there are two ways of violating a threat, and so on. Rules of inference for detecting cheaters on social contracts cannot, in principle, detect bluffs and double-crosses in situations of threat. Different rules are required for these different domains: The "grammar" of social contracts is very different from the grammar of threat. If someone were to propose a learning mechanism that accounts for the acquisition of both social contract algorithms *and* threat algorithms, their theory would have to meet stringent learnability criteria: Given the informational environment to which a child is exposed, this same mechanism would have to induce two entirely separate sets of rules that act on very different mental representations, plus metarules for when to apply each set of rules. Developing computational theories of different social problem domains has led us to believe that it is unlikely that "social cognition" will turn out to be a unitary domain (Cosmides and Tooby 1989, 1992).

Notes

1   In certain situations two or more alternative designs can be stably maintained in a population through frequency-dependent selection, as in the case of contagion-retarding protein variation. However, natural selection in interaction with sexual recombination tends to impose a specieswide uniformity in our complex adaptations, providing an explanation for the existence of a universally shared human nature (Tooby and Cosmides 1990b). Nonfunctional traits can vary freely, but the developmental programs underlying our complex adaptations are constrained to be virtually species-typical.

2   In this equation, C_i and B_i refer to costs and benefits to individual i, measured as decreases and increases in i's reproduction caused by the design feature in question. r_{ij} – the coefficient of relatedness between individuals i and j – refers to the probability that i and j share the same design feature by virtue of common descent.

References

Carey, S. (1985) "Constraints on semantic development." In J. Mehler and R. Fox (eds), *Neonate Cognition* (pp. 381–98). Hillsdale, N.J.: Erlbaum.

Carey, S. and Gelman, R. (eds) (1991) *The Epigenesis of Mind*. Hillsdale, N.J.: Erlbaum.

Cheney, D.L. and Seyfarth, R. (1990) *How Monkeys See the World*. Chicago: University of Chicago Press.

Chomsky, N. (1975) *Reflections on Language*. New York: Random House.

—— (1980) *Rules and Representations*. New York: Columbia University Press.

Cognitive Science 14 (1990) Special issue on structural constrains on cognitive development.

Cosmides, L. (1989) "The logic of social exchange: has natural selection shaped how humans reason? Studies with the Wason selection task." *Cognition* 31: 187–276.

Cosmides, L. and Tooby, J. (1987) "From evolution to behavior: evolutionary psychology as the missing link." In J. Dupre (ed.), *The Latest on the Best: Essays on Evolution and Optimality*. Cambridge, Mass.: MIT Press.

—— (1989) "Evolutionary psychology and the generation of culture, Part II. A computational theory of social exchange." *Ethology and Sociobiology* 10: 51–97.

—— (1992) "Cognitive adaptations for social exchange." In J. Barkow, L. Cosmides, and J. Tooby (eds), *The Adapted Mind: Evolutionary Psychology and the Generation of Culture*. New York: Oxford University Press.

Daly, M., Wilson, M., and Weghorst, S.J. (1982) "Male sexual jealousy." *Ethology and Sociobiology* 3: 11–27.

Darwin, C. (1859) *On the Origin of Species*. London: Murray.

Dawkins, R. (1976) *The Selfish Gene*. New York: Oxford University Press.

—— (1982) *The Extended Phenotype*. San Francisco: W.H. Freeman.

—— (1986) *The Blind Watchmaker*. New York: Norton.

Freyd, J.J. (1987) "Dynamic mental representations." *Psychological Review* 94: 427–38.

Gallistel, C.R. (1990) *The Organization of Learning*. Cambridge, Mass.: MIT Press.

Gallistel, C.R., Brown, A.L., Carey, S., Gelman, R. and Keil, F.C. (1991) "Lessons from animal learning for the study of cognitive development." In S. Carey and R. Gelman (eds), *The Epigenesis of Mind*. Hillsdale, N.J.: Erlbaum.

Gigerenzer, G. and Hug, K. (1992) "Domain-specific reasoning: social contracts, cheating and perspective change." *Cognition* 43: 127–71.

Hamilton, W.D. (1964) "The genetical theory of social behavior." *Journal of Theoretical Biology* 7: 1–52.

Jackendoff, R. (1992) *Languages of the Mind*. Cambridge, Mass.: MIT Press.

Keil, F.C. (1989) *Concepts, Kinds, and Cognitive Development*. Cambridge, Mass.: MIT Press.

Leslie, A.M. (1987) "Pretense and representation: the origins of 'theory of mind'." *Psychological Review* 94: 412–26.

—— (1988) "The necessity of illusion: perception and thought in infancy." In L. Weiskrantz (ed.), *Thought without Language* (pp. 185–210). Oxford: Clarendon Press.

Lewontin, R.C. (1967) "Spoken remark." In P.S. Moorhead and M. Kaplan (eds), *Mathematical Challenges to the Neo-Darwinian Interpretation of Evolution. Wistar Institute Symposium Monograph* 5: 79.

—— (1978) "Adaptation." *Scientific American* 239: 156–69.

Markman, E.M. (1989) *Categorization and Naming in Children: Problems of Induction.* Cambridge, Mass.: MIT Press.

Marr, D. (1982) *Vision: A Computational Investigation into the Human Representation and Processing of Visual Information.* San Francisco: Freeman.

Marr, D. and Nishihara, H.K. (1978) "Visual information-processing: artifical intelligence and the sensorium of sight." *Technological Review*, October: 28–49.

Pinker, S. (1979) "Formal models of language learning." *Cognition* 7: 217–83.

—— (1984) *Language Learnability and Language Development.* Cambridge, Mass.: Harvard University Press.

Pinker, S. and Bloom, P. (1990) "Natural language and natural selection." *Behavioral and Brain Sciences* 13: 707–84.

Profet, M. (1992) "Pregnancy sickness as adaptation: a deterrent to maternal ingestion of teratogens." In J. Barkow, L. Cosmides, and J. Tooby (eds), *The Adapted Mind: Evolutionary Psychology and the Generation of Culture.* New York: Oxford University Press.

Ramachadran, V.S. (1990) "Visual perception in people and machines." In A. Blake and T. Troscianko (eds), *AI and the Eye.* New York: Wiley.

Rozin, P. (1976) "The evolution of intelligence and access to the cognitive unconscious." In J.M. Sprague and A.N. Epstein (eds), *Progress in Psychobiology and Physiological Psychology.* New York: Academic Press.

Rozin, P. and Kalat, J.W. (1971) "Specific hungers and poison avoidance as adaptive specialization of learning." *Psychological Review* 78: 459–86.

Shepard, R.N. (1981) "Psychophysical complementarity." In M. Kubovy and J.R. Pomerantz (eds), *Perceptual Organization.* Hillsdale, N.J.: Erlbaum.

—— (1984) "Ecological constraints on internal representations: resonant kinematics of perceiving, imagining, thinking, and dreaming." *Psychological Review* 91: 417–47.

—— (1987a) "Evolution of a mesh between principles of the mind and regularities of the world." In J. Dupre (ed.), *The Latest on the Best: Essays on Evolution and Optimality.* Cambridge, Mass.: MIT Press.

—— (1987b) "Towards a universal law of generalization for psychological science." *Science* 237: 1317–23.

Sherry, D.F. and Schacter, D.L. (1987) "The evolution of multiple memory systems." *Psychological Review* 94: 439–54.

Shiffrar, M. and Freyd, J.J. (1990) "Apparent motion of the human body." *Psychological Science* 1: 257–64.

Staddon, J.E.R. (1988) "Learning as inference." In R.C. Bolles and M.D. Beecher (eds), *Evolution and Learning.* Hillsdale, N.J.: Erlbaum.

Symons, D. (1992) "On the use and misuse of Darwinism in the study of human behavior." In J. Barkow, L. Cosmides, and J. Tooby (eds), *The Adapted Mind: Evolutionary Psychology and the Generation of Culture.* New York: Oxford University Press.

Tooby, J. and Cosmides, L. (1990a) "The past explains the present: emotional adaptations and the structure of ancestral environments." *Ethology and Sociobiology* 11: 375–424.

—— (1990b) "On the universality of human nature and the uniqueness of the individual: the role of genetics and adaptation." *Journal of Personality* 58: 17–67.

—— (1992) "The psychological foundations of culture." In J. Barkow, L. Cosmides, and J. Tooby (eds), *The Adapted Mind: Evolutionary Psychology and the Generation of Culture*. New York: Oxford University Press.

Wexler, K. and Culicover, P. (1980) *Formal Principles of Language Acquisition*. Cambridge, Mass.: MIT Press.

Williams, G.C. (1966) *Adaptation and Natural Selection*. Princeton: Princeton University Press.

IIID

TACIT KNOWLEDGE

26

S.P. Stich*, "Beliefs and Subdoxastic States"

It is argued that the intuitively sanctioned distinction between beliefs and non-belief states that play a role in the proximate causal history of beliefs is a distinction worth preserving in cognitive psychology. The intuitive distinction is argued to rest on a pair of features exhibited by beliefs but not by subdoxastic states. These are access to consciousness and inferential integration. Harman's view, which denies the distinction between beliefs and subdoxastic states, is discussed and criticized.

This is a paper about a distinction, one which is deeply imbedded in our everyday, pre-theoretic thinking about human psychology. It is a distinction which separates beliefs from a heterogeneous collection of psychological states that play a role in the proximate causal history of beliefs, though they are not beliefs themselves. I will call the states in this latter collection *subdoxastic* states. The distinction is an intuitive one, in the sense that when confronted with descriptions of various imaginable states it is intuitively clear that some are to be counted as beliefs while others are not. Part of my project in this paper is to explain these intuitive decisions by noting some of the characteristics that we ordinarily take beliefs to have which are lacking in subdoxastic states. Since these intuitive judgements mark part of the boundary of our pre-theoretic concept of belief, an explanation of the principles underlying the intuitions may also be viewed as part of an analysis of our ordinary concept of belief. It is this analytic project that occupies the early sections of the paper.

The intuitive distinction between beliefs and subdoxastic states is of interest quite apart from the insight it promises into our ordinary notion of belief. For much of the best recent work in cognitive psychology has ignored it. The implication, albeit a tacit one, of this neglect is that the distinction entrenched in intuition does not mark a psychologically interesting boundary. Now there is surely no *a priori* argument for rejecting this view. There is no reason to expect

*I am indebted to Clayton Lewis and Robert Cummins for helpful criticism of the views set forth in this paper.

that every distinction embedded in our intuitive, pre-scientific psychological concepts reflects a distinction worth preserving in an empirically motivated psychological theory. What is unsettling about the neglect of the distinction in recent psychology is that it seems to be largely undefended. The fact that pre-theoretically we recognize the distinction as readily and consistently as we do is surely evidence that there is some basis to the distinction, some property or cluster of properties that we tacitly take account of when we classify a given example as a belief or as a subdoxastic state. The properties which we exploit in drawing the distinction may be psychologically uninteresting. But to be confident of this one would like to know what these properties are and why they can be safely ignored in psychological theorizing. The psychologists who ignore the distinction do not inspire confidence in this way. Such limited philosophical discussion as there has been of the topic is not reassuring. Gilbert Harman (1973) sketches an argument that might be construed as an attack on the psychological significance of the distinction. So construed, the argument is singularly unconvincing. The latter sections of my paper will be devoted to a critique of Harman's view. I will also try to defend the view that the boundary between beliefs and subdoxastic states marks an important psychological distinction which serious cognitive psychology neglects to its peril.

1   Our first job is to focus in on the particular intuitive distinction I have in mind. Let me begin a bit obliquely by noting the shadow the distinction casts in traditional epistemology. It is obvious that many of our beliefs are inferred from other beliefs. But, as epistemologists were quick to note, there must be some beliefs which are not inferred from others, on pain of circularity or infinite regress. Since Descartes, the orthodox position has been to take as non-inferential those beliefs that concern the believer's own cognitive states – beliefs about what she believes, what she seems to be perceiving, what she seems to remember, etc. In recent years, the orthodoxy has been challenged by philosophers who advocate a much more expansive account of non-inferential belief. The expansionists urge that most perceptually-based beliefs about our immediate surroundings are non-inferential. Thus, while agreeing that our beliefs about our current cognitive states are non-inferential, the expansionists would also include among the non-inferential beliefs the belief that there is a pig nearby, if acquired under unexceptional circumstances as the result of a pig coming into view a few meters away. (cf., for example, Austin [1964: 115ff.] and Dretske [1969: 159]). We need not pause here to trace the moves in the debate between the expansionist and the advocate of orthodoxy. For our purposes it is important only to note that despite their differences, both sides in the dispute recognize that some beliefs must be non-inferential. These non-inferential beliefs may serve as the premises for inferences but not as the conclusion. The class of non-inferential beliefs marks the boundary between two different sorts of psychological states. On one side of the boundary are

beliefs, both inferred and non-inferential. On the other side are the psychological states which, though not beliefs, are part of the causal process leading to belief formation. Typically, epistemologists have been silent on the nature and workings of the mechanisms which underlie belief formation. Their silence, no doubt, was rooted in the sensible suspicion that the study of subdoxastic mechanisms is more properly the province of psychology.

2   To sharpen our intuitive feel for the distinction between beliefs and subdoxastic states, let us look at a few examples of the sort of states that fall in the latter category. Consider first the offering of grammatical intuitions. Given a few well-chosen examples of grammatical sentences and a few well-chosen examples of ungrammatical ones, speakers are able to go on to classify new examples as either grammatical or ungrammatical with impressive consistency. This ability seems to be largely independent of previous formal grammatical training. Naive subjects (particularly bright ones) quickly get the point. On the other hand, the ability plainly does depend on some elaborate and little-understood system of psychological states and processes which is gradually built up in the process of language acquisition. Moreover, it seems plausible to speculate that the psychological mechanisms which underlie the offering of grammatical intuitions also play a central role in the much more important business of speech production and comprehension. (For a general discussion of grammatical intuitions see Stich [1971, 1975]; for some critical reaction, see Chomsky and Katz [1974] and Graves et al. [1973].)

Now suppose that a grammatically naive subject has just been taught by example to apply the labels "grammatical" and "ungrammatical." We give the subject a new sentence and ask whether or not it is grammatical. The subject replies – and presumably believes – that it is grammatical. But if we ask him how he made the judgement and came to hold that belief, he will be at a loss to say. On hearing the sentence, he simply comes to believe that it is grammatical. The belief is non-inferential. There is, of course, a mechanism of some complexity mediating between the subject's hearing the sentence and the formation of the belief that it is grammatical. And, while we know little in detail about the workings of this mechanism, it is plausible to speculate that the mechanism exploits a system of psychological states which serve to store information about the grammar of the subject's language.[1] If this speculation proves accurate, then these states which store grammatical information are a prime example of subdoxastic states. They play a role in the proximate causal history of beliefs, though they are not beliefs themselves. I have, of course, given no argument that these states are not beliefs. My claim, rather, is that this is intuitively obvious. After we have seen a few more examples of subdoxastic states, I will try to dissect out those aspects of our concept of belief which are responsible for the intuitions.

3   For a second example of subdoxastic states, let us attend to the complicated matter of depth perception. Our ability to judge the relative distances

of objects in our visual field rests on a bewilderingly complex set of factors. Perspective, size, surface texture, the perception of edges and corners, occlusion, illumination gradients and stereopsis all play a role. (For a survey of this topic, see Haber and Hershenson [1973: chapter 13].) Some of the information available to our depth perception mechanisms would appear to be redundant. We can, for example, make depth judgements with one eye closed, or about the objects in a painting. In both cases stereopsis is irrelevant. Julesz (1970), in an interesting series of experiments, has shown that binocular disparity alone is enough to bring about perception of depth. The experiment employed random patterns of black and white dots in a 100 x 100 cell matrix. The randomness of the patterns served to guarantee that no depth information was conveyed by the patterns themselves. When two identical copies of a random dot pattern are presented to a subject, one to each eye, no depth is perceived. However, if a section of one copy of the pattern is displaced laterally, there is a clear perception of depth, with the moved section appearing either in front of or behind the rest of the pattern, depending on whether it was moved toward the nose or toward the ears. When a subject in Julesz's experiment is presented with a pair of dot patterns one of which has a laterally displaced section, he will report – and presumably believe – that some of the dots seem to be in front of or behind the rest. Asked why he believes this, he will be unable to say. Some dots just do look to be in front of the others, and the belief that they do is non-inferential. Underlying the belief there is, no doubt, a complex psychological mechanism which serves to measure the degree of binocular disparity and to use this information in the production of an appropriate belief about apparent relative depth. If, as seems inevitable, the process leading from retinal stimulation to belief involves various psychological states which represent features of the retinal images, then these states are subdoxastic. Though they are causal antecedents of belief, there is a strong intuitive inclination to insist that they are not beliefs themselves.

4   Let us look now at a final example of subdoxastic states. In a series of experiments, E.H. Hess (1965; see also Hess 1975) presented male subjects with a pair of almost identical photos of a girl. One of the photos had been retouched by enlarging the size of the girl's pupils. The subjects regularly reported (and presumably believed) that the girl in the retouched photo appeared more attractive. However, subjects were quite unable to say why the girl in the retouched photo was more attractive; indeed, they were generally unable to identify any specific differences between the original and retouched photos. Their belief that the girl is more attractive in one photo than in the other is non-inferential. Plainly, there is some cognitive mechanism which detects the enlarged pupil size and which gives rise to the belief that one photo is more attractive than the other. As in the previous examples, we know little about the detailed functioning of this mechanism. However, it is plausible to suppose that there are psychological states which serve to record information about pupil size, and that these states play a role in the process that leads to

belief formation. If so, these states are another example of subdoxastic states. They play a role in the proximate causal history of beliefs, but there is strong intuitive inclination to deny that they are beliefs themselves.

5 Having surveyed some examples of states that fall on the subdoxastic side of the belief-subdoxastic state distinction, let us now consider what the basis may be for our strong intuitive inclination to insist that the sorts of states we have been describing are not beliefs. I think there are two rather different properties that we ordinarily take to be characteristic of belief and which are lacking in the examples of subdoxastic states. The first of these is actually a cluster of properties that revolves around the sort of *access* we ordinarily have to the contents of our beliefs; the second might be characterized as the inferential integration of beliefs. I will consider them in turn.

It is ordinarily the case, for typical or paradigmatic examples of belief, that adult subjects can report the contents of their belief. Thus, if a subject is psychologically (and physiologically) normal, inclined to be cooperative and has no motivation to deceive us, then if she believes that p and is asked whether p is the case, she will generally say that it is. (The subject must, of course, be asked in a language she understands and she must be paying attention. Hereafter I will take this to be built into the notion of asking.) Normal cooperative adult subjects can also tell us whether they *believe* that p, if we ask them. The two abilities are distinct. Toddlers, for example, are able to assent to p if they believe it, but are often not able to answer the question: "Do you believe that?" Nonetheless, the two abilities run in tandem in normal adults, and it is hard to believe that they are not intimately connected.

Both of these abilities are themselves associated with an ability to become aware of or to be conscious of the contents of one's beliefs. Suppose, for example, that a subject believes that p but fails to satisfy one or another of the additional conditions which, conjoined with belief, generally guarantee that a subject will assent to p if asked. The subject may be temporarily paralyzed and thus unable to assent to anything. Or he may have a strong desire to mislead his questioner, or simply wish to say nothing. Still, under these circumstances, if we ask a subject whether p is the case, he will generally have a certain sort of characteristic experience which, as best I can discover, has no standard description in English. Some philosophers have labelled the experience "having the occurrent belief that p." One might also describe the experience as being aware that p or being conscious that p. Often, but perhaps not always, the experience of having an occurrent belief is accompanied by (consists in?) a perceived inclination to respond to the inquirer's question, or perhaps a response which is thought but not spoken. I do not propose to attempt any thoroughgoing phenomenological account of the experience of having an occurrent belief. Nor, in fact, am I much concerned whether it is a single sort of experience or a group of related ones. My point is the (I hope) uncontroversial one that in typical cases of belief a subject will have a certain sort of characteristic conscious experience when his attention is suitably directed to the content of the belief. While little is known about the psychological mechanisms responsible for the experience of having an occurrent belief, it is certainly plausible to speculate that the processes underlying this conscious experience and the processes underlying a subject's assent to a proposition he believes (under normal circumstances) are in important ways interconnected.

I have been claiming that access to the contents of our beliefs is a general characteristic of beliefs. However, there is a *prima facie* exception to this generalization: viz. the unconscious beliefs that figure prominently in psychoanalytic theory. While I admit to some qualms about how seriously psychoanalytic theory ought to be taken, I do not think I need take on all of psychoanalytic theory to defend the claims I want to make about a subject's access to the contents of her beliefs. For all of my claims can be construed as subjunctive conditionals about what would happen (or would be likely to happen) if a subject were normal and otherwise suitably situated. And psychoanalytic theory can be viewed as postulating a psychological mechanism capable of interfering with the ordinary process leading from belief to assent or to conscious awareness. So to protect our generalizations about access, we will have to add to the conditions in the antecedent of our subjunctive condition a clause specifying that there are no psychological mechanisms at work blocking the ordinary process leading from belief to assent or conscious awareness.

Now one of the ways in which our first two examples of subdoxastic states differ from beliefs is just that subjects have no access to them. People do not assent to a statement of a rule of their grammar as they do to a statement of the contents of a belief. Nor do they have any conscious awareness of the rules of their grammar. Indeed, if they did writing a grammar for a language would be a far less arduous business. Similarly, we cannot report, nor are we consciously aware of, any information about binocular disparity. Awareness stops at the level of apparent comparative depth. Of course, it might be the case that these seemingly subdoxastic states are actually analogous to subconscious beliefs in that subjects would have access to them but for the intervention of some presently unsuspected psychological mechanism which blocks the ordinary processes that facilitate access. This possibility reflects something important about our pre-theoretic concept of belief. We might be willing to classify an apparent subdoxastic state as a belief if there were evidence that a subject's access is actively blocked by some mechanism. But we would, I think, be much more reluctant to countenance a special category of beliefs which are by nature not open to conscious awareness or reporting. It is quite central to our concept of belief that subjects under ordinary circumstances have access to their beliefs.

Our third example of a subdoxastic state poses some special problems. In Hess' experiments, subjects were not consciously aware that the pupils in one photo were larger than those in the other. However, at least some of the subjects might have become aware of it if their attention were suitably directed by, say, asking them. In this respect, the state which serves to represent the information that one pupil is larger than another is analogous to quite unexceptional cases of belief. For we are ordinarily quite unaware of most of our beliefs, and the experience of having the belief occurrently is provoked when our attention is directed to the content of the belief. I think this similarity between unproblematic cases of belief and the state that we have hypothesized in the Hess example is reflected in our intuition. For of our three examples, our intuitive inclination to rule that a state is not a belief is weakest in this case. But still, I think there is a strong inclination to resist calling the supposed state a belief. An attractive alternative is to say that, though not a belief itself, the state can give rise to a belief under certain circumstances. And thus the role of drawing a subject's attention to the relative size of the pupils is *not* analogous to what goes on when, for example, we ask a subject (who has been thinking about other things) what her mother's maiden name is. In the latter case, the question serves to make occurrent or bring to consciousness a belief which the subject has had all along. In the former case, however, questioning the subject about relative pupil size serves rather to instigate a process of belief formation in which, perhaps, the pre-existing subdoxastic state plays a role. If I am right that this alternative account of what is going on sits better with our intuition than the account which assimilates the Hess case to standard examples of belief, then we are left with the question of why this should be so. What is it about the state in the Hess example that makes us reluctant to treat it as a belief? I think the answer is that this state shares with our other two examples of subdoxastic states a sort of inferential isolation from the body of our accessible beliefs. This is the topic to which I now will turn.

6   It is characteristic of beliefs that they generate further beliefs via inference. What is more, beliefs are inferentially promiscuous. Provided with a suitable set of supplementary beliefs, almost any belief can play a role in the inference to any other. Thus, for example, if a subject believes that p and comes to believe that if p then q, he may well come to believe that q – and do so as the result of an inferential process. In addition to the well-integrated network of potential deductive inferences, beliefs also generate other beliefs via inductive inference. So there is generally a huge number of inferential paths via which a given belief can lead to most any other. It is in this sense that a person's beliefs are *inferentially integrated*.

Of course, the patterns of valid inference specified in deductive logic and those that would be specified by a theory of inductive logic, if there were such a theory, correspond in no simple way to the inference pattern exhibited among a person's beliefs. We do not, for example, draw all logically possible inferences from our beliefs. Nor are all our inferences logically valid. What is more, there is no reason to suppose *a priori* that each logically permissible inference is in fact psychologically possible. And it is at least possible that there are some beliefs that cannot be acquired by inference at all. The non-inferential beliefs of traditional epistemology would be an example, if indeed there are any such beliefs. However, none of these caveats detracts from our principal point about the inferential integration of beliefs: a person's body of beliefs forms an elaborate and interconnected network with a vast number of potential inference patterns leading from every belief to almost any other.

Now it is my contention that part of the reason we are intuitively inclined to say subdoxastic states are not beliefs is that subdoxastic states, as contrasted with beliefs, *are largely inferentially isolated from the large body of inferential integrated beliefs to which a subject has access.* This is not to say that subdoxastic states do not play any role in inference to and from accessible beliefs, but merely that they are inferentially impoverished, with a comparatively limited range of potential inferential patterns via which they can give rise to beliefs, and a comparatively limited range of potential inferential patterns via which beliefs can give rise to them. This last remark may strike some as paradoxical. For, it might be protested, inference is a relation *among* beliefs. It is (one of) the ways beliefs generate other beliefs. And subdoxastic states are not beliefs, then they cannot be *inferentially* related to anything. The objection is an important one, and its central claim – that inference is a relation exclusively among beliefs – is one that will play a prominent role in the following section. For the moment however, let us grant that at least some of the routes by which subdoxastic states give rise to beliefs or other subdoxastic states can sensibly be taken to be instances of inference. Granting this assumption, the picture I am urging is this. Consciously accessible beliefs are embedded in an elaborate network of potential inferential connections with each other. Each belief is a potential premise in inferences to a vast array of further beliefs. By contrast, the inferential contact between subdoxastic states and beliefs is specialized and limited. When a subdoxastic state can serve as a premise in an inference to beliefs, there is only a narrow range of beliefs to which it may potentially lead. Similarly, when a subdoxastic state can result from an inference with beliefs among the premises, the range of beliefs that can serve in this capacity is restricted and specialized. If we think in terms of a cognitive simulation model, the view I am urging is that beliefs form a consciously accessible, inferentially integrated cognitive subsystem. Subdoxastic states occur in a variety of separate, special purpose cognitive subsystems. And even when the subdoxastic states within a specialized subsystem generate one another via a process of inference, their inferential interactions with the integrated body of accessible beliefs is severely limited. Similarly, in all likelihood, the potential inferential connections among subdoxastic states in different specialized subsystems are extremely limited or non-existent. To get a clearer view of my thesis about the inferential integration of beliefs, let us see how it applies to our examples.

Even on the most generous assumptions about the inferential potential of the states which store grammatical information, these states are largely isolated from the body of a subject's beliefs. These grammar storing states can plausibly be assumed to play a role in the formation of beliefs about what has been said to a person (that is, in the process leading from auditory stimulation to comprehension). They can also, as we have seen, be presumed to play a role in the process leading to formation of beliefs about grammatical properties and relations – the sorts of beliefs expressed when an informant is offering grammatical intuitions. And let us suppose that the processes involved are properly viewed as inferential. Then the states storing grammatical information do have some limited inferential links with beliefs. But let us compare the state storing a grammatical rule with the explicit belief in that rule, say on the part of the linguist.[2] The linguist's explicit belief can enter into an almost endless number of inferences in which the competent speaker's subdoxastic state cannot participate. For example, if a linguist believes a certain generalization to the effect that no transformational rule exhibits a certain characteristic, and if he comes to believe a given transformation which violates the generalization, he may well infer that the generalization is false. But merely having the rule stored (in the way that we are assuming all speakers of the language do) does not enable the linguist to draw the inference. As another example, suppose that, for some putative rule r, you have come to believe that if r then Chomsky is seriously mistaken. Suppose further that, as it happens, r is in fact among the rules stored by your language processing mechanism. That belief along with the subdoxastic state will not lead to the belief that Chomsky is seriously mistaken. By contrast, if you believe (perhaps even mistakenly) that r, then the belief that Chomsky is seriously mistaken is likely to be inferred. It would be easy enough to marshal many more illustrations of the fact that the subdoxastic states which store grammatical information are largely inferentially isolated from beliefs.

The situation is, if anything, clearer for the states which process and store information about binocular disparity. Let us suppose that at a given stage in the process leading to the formation of judgements about apparent comparative depth in Julesz's experiments, a certain subdoxastic state represents the information that a dot on a certain part of the left retina is displaced five seconds further toward the nose then the similarly situated dot on the right retina. It may well be that a fairly complicated process of computation and inference is required for the formation of this subdoxastic state. The process might, for example, utilize and compare information about the distribution of dots on each separate retina in order to locate "corresponding" dots. It may also be the case that the process leading from our hypothesized subdoxastic state to the belief that the displaced dot appears in front of the others is itself inferential. On this assumption, the subdoxastic state does have a potential inferential path to an accessible belief. However, it is a vastly more restrictive path than beliefs have to each other. Contrast, for example, the *subdoxastic state* representing the information that a dot on a certain part of the left retina is displaced five seconds further toward the nose than the similarly situated dot on the right retina, with the *belief* that the dot in that part of the retina is displaced five seconds further toward the nose than the similarly situated dot on the right retina. The subdoxastic state can lead directly only to a restricted class of beliefs about apparent relative depth (and perhaps some other aspects of the visual field). By contrast, the belief, if supplemented by suitable additional beliefs, can lead to just about any belief. There is also a striking contrast in the ways other beliefs can *lead* to either the subdoxastic state or the belief. A subject might inferentially acquire the belief (that a dot on a certain part of the left retina . . . etc.) in numerous and diverse ways. He may be told that the dot is thus displaced by a person he takes to be trust-worthy, and infer that it is on the basis of his belief about what his informant believes. Or he may infer it from beliefs formed by observing the readings on certain test instruments. Indeed, most any other belief, say the belief that *p*, can inferentially give rise to the belief about the relative positions of the retinal dots, provided that the subject also believes a proposition of the form *if p then d*, where *d* is the proposition that a dot on a certain part of the left retina . . . etc. On the other hand, it is most likely the case that there are *no beliefs at all* which can lead inferentially to the subdoxastic state that represents the fact that *d*.

This example illustrates with particular clarity a feature also exhibited by our other examples of subdoxastic states. Part of the reason we are inclined to insist that a subdoxastic state is not a belief is that if it were, we would be unable to say *what* belief it was. That is, if a subdoxastic state were taken to be a belief, there would be no sentence *p* such that inserting *p* in "*S* believes that _____" would express the fact that the subject was in the state. The problem is most noticeable when, as in our current examples, we contrast the belief that *p* with the subdoxastic state which stores or represents the informa-tion that *p*. Since the subdoxastic state differs so markedly from the belief both in its potential inferential connections and in the subject's potential access to it, we are disinclined to identify the subdoxastic state with the belief. But surely if a state representing the information that *p* is a belief at all, then it is the belief that *p*.

These reflections bring us perilously close to a cluster of questions I have been doing my utmost to sidestep. All this glib talk about a state representing information may get one wondering just what it might *mean* to say that a state "represents (the information (or fact) that) *p*." I do not think it would be unreasonable to duck the issue entirely in this paper. For though this talk of states representing facts is difficult to explicate in a philosophically tolerable way, it is surprisingly easy to master intuitively. Even the barest introduction to work in artificial intelligence and cognitive simulation quickly leaves one comfortable with attributions of content or representational status to the states of an information processing theory. And nothing I want to say here presup-poses anything more than the ability to use these locutions as they are customarily used. Still, a hint of how I think such talk is to be analyzed may be welcome. On my view, saying that a state in an information processing system represents (the information (or fact) that) *p* is to say that the state bears some interesting resemblances to the belief that *p*. Generally the resemblances are with respect to the ordinary causes of the state, or some part of the inferential pattern of the state, or some other (non-inferential) effect the state may have (or some combination of the three). On this account, of course, the belief that *p* represents (the information (or fact) that) *p*; indeed, it is the prototype of such representation. Also, on my account, many different states can represent *p*, and can do so to varying degrees. There is no minimum degree of resemblance required for us to say that a state represents *p*. Rather the appropriateness of the content attribution depends on the particular needs and interests of the project at hand. For more on all this, along with a theory about what we are saying when we say a belief is the belief that *p*, see my *From Folk Psychology to Cognitive Science* (1983).

Our third example of a subdoxastic state, the Hess example, is quite parallel to the second. The subdoxastic state which serves to represent the information that the pupils in one photo are larger than those in the other is significantly less inferentially integrated with the body of a subject's beliefs than is the *belief* that the pupils in one photo are larger. As in the previous case, the paths leading to formation of the subdoxastic state are relatively few and involve only a restricted range of beliefs (if any), while almost any belief can play a direct role in an inference to the *belief* that the pupils in one photo are enlarged. Also, the subdoxastic state has a significantly more restricted set of possible inferences in which it may play a role. The belief that the pupils in the retouched photo are larger, along with the belief that, say, the earlobes in that photo are much enlarged, may lead to the belief that several facial features are enlarged. But one of Hess' subjects who has the *second* belief is unlikely to infer the belief that several facial features are enlarged (unless, of course, the subdoxastic state gives rise to the conscious *belief* that the pupils are enlarged). I think it is the inferential isolation of the state Hess' subjects are in that incline us to insist these are not to be counted as beliefs.

It is time to take stock of our discussion so far. I began by noting the distinction between beliefs and subdoxastic states, which is quite fundamental to our ordinary, pre-theoretic thinking about beliefs. With some examples of subdoxastic states on hand, we began to look for the basis of our intuitive distinction. My thesis has been that the distinction is drawn on the basis of two characteristics which beliefs exhibit and subdoxastic states do not: access to consciousness and inferential integration. In the course of our discussion we also noted, if only to then ignore, a further principle embedded in our pre-theoretic notion of belief, which ties together the concepts of belief and inference. The principle holds that inference (at least when viewed as a relation among psychological states) is a relation exclusively among beliefs. This principle, along with the features which divide beliefs from subdoxastic states, accounts for the location in traditional epistemology of non-inferential beliefs. For if the psychological states causally underlying a belief are not themselves beliefs, then, according to the principle, the process leading to the belief cannot be inference.

7 This principle that inference is a relation among beliefs deserves a less cavalier look than has been accorded it so far. For the principle plays a central role in an argument advanced by Gilbert Harman aimed at undermining the belief-subdoxastic distinction. Harman notes that "a person determines how far away a perceived object is by means of cues involving overlapping of surfaces and texture gradients." It is natural, he continues, "to describe this as a matter of inference: given these cues the perceiver infers that objects are in those places. The relevant cues make it reasonable to suppose the objects are where the perceiver infers they are" (1973: 175). Harman anticipates the objection that talk of perceptual inference uses the word "inference" in a peculiar or special sense. He replies as follows:

> Contemporary psychologists tend to view a perceiver as an information processing mechanism, a kind of analogue computer. . . . Now it is natural to describe mechanical information-processing machines – like computers – as if they could calculate, figure something out, and infer conclusions. When the perceiver is conceived as an information processing device, it becomes natural to describe him in the same way. Having extended the application of 'inference' so that computers can be said to infer, it is natural to extend it so that perceivers are also said to infer. (1973: 176–7)

The view that inference is involved in the formation of beliefs about our perceived environment is hardly novel. Descartes would have had no objection. But Descartes would have balked at Harman's view of the premises for such inferences. In the Cartesian tradition, the premises are beliefs about experience, about how things look to the subject. Harman rejects this position. "One problem is that some aspects of the way things appear is determined by inference. For example, reasoning involving overlap, texture gradients, and perspective figures in the apparent location of objects. Inference gets into the story before it is determined how things look" (1973: 180). Nor, on Harman's view, is there any more basic level of visual experience to serve as data. "there does not seem to be any more basic level of visual experience not itself the product of inference, and used itself as data for inference to how things look" (1973: 181). Instead, Harman traces the path of inference all the way back to retinal stimulations, which, he holds, are the basic data for perceptual knowledge.

> I suggested that the data are the sensory stimulations that provide the input to the complex information processing system composed of brain and nervous system. Perceptual knowledge is based on inference from sensory stimulations. (1973: 185)

Finally, Harman claims that retinal stimulations and other sensory stimulations which serve as the basic data for perceptual knowledge are themselves *beliefs*.

> Does he [the perceiver] believe the data? He uses them in the way one uses beliefs in inference. So there is some reason to say that he believes them. (1973: 186)

Now note that if we go along with Harman, then the distinction between beliefs and subdoxastic states seems to vanish. For on Harman's view, both retinal stimulations and all of the various psychological states that may be inferred from them count as *beliefs*. If Harman is right, then our intuitive psychological theory has led us seriously astray; many states which intuition insists are not beliefs turn out to be beliefs nonetheless. Let us take a more careful look at just how Harman reaches this surprising conclusion.

I think the argument is best viewed as proceeding in two stages, the first defending the view that retinal stimulations and various other intuitively subdoxastic states are inferentially related to beliefs and to each other, and the second marshaling the principle that inference is a relation among beliefs. The claim of the first stage, in turn, follows from a pair of contentions: first, that it is appropriate to use the word "inference" in describing the processes leading to beliefs about our perceived surroundings; and second, that it is suitable to describe these processes as inferential "all the way down," to the level of retinal stimulations.

I am largely in agreement with the claim that there are inferential relations among (intuitively) subdoxastic states, and among subdoxastic states and beliefs. However, I think that Harman's defense of this view deflects attention from the important issue involved. In arguing that inference is involved in the process leading to the formation of beliefs about our perceptual environment, Harman stresses the "naturalness" of this use of the word "inference," a naturalness which is allegedly enhanced by the analogous use in talk of computers. It seems to me, however, that the intuitive naturalness of this use of "inference" is largely beside the point. What is important is not whether perceptual psychologists are using "inference" in some natural extension of its ordinary sense, but rather whether the phenomena they are describing are in important ways similar to more standard cases of inference. Similarly, the conjecture that inferential processes extend all the way down the causal chain to the level of retinal stimulations does not turn on the intuitive naturalness of calling these processes "inferential." What is at stake is whether these processes are in fact in fundamental ways similar to the process of inference in standard cases. These are empirical questions, not to be settled by appeal to ordinary usage. What we need to know are the similarities and differences between the process leading from sensory stimulation to belief, and the process (ordinarily called "inference") leading from pre-existing beliefs to the formation of new beliefs. If the processes are sufficiently similar, the proposed extension of "inference" to cover the former is a reasonable one. At present neither perception nor more standard cases of inference are sufficiently well understood in detail to settle the question definitively. But recent efforts at modeling perception and at modeling inference and problem solving make it plausible that the two processes may be essentially congruent.[3] If this speculation proves true, it will be an empirical result of enormous importance.

The discovery that inference is involved in perception down to the level of sensory stimulation is not, of course, enough to show that intuitively subdoxastic states are beliefs. To get this conclusion we need the additional premise that inference is a relation among beliefs. Harman, as we saw in the last displayed quote above, endorses the premise and draws the conclusion. It is just here that my dissent comes in. Harman and I are agreed that inference likely relates states far removed from anything we would pre-theoretically call a belief. This fact, if it is a fact, puts considerable strain on our pre-theoretic views about beliefs. Harman would accommodate the strain by rejecting our intuitions on what sorts of states to count as beliefs. By contrast, I would accommodate the strain by simply rejecting the principle that inference is a relation exclusively among beliefs. By my lights, what the supposed discovery of inference in deep perceptual processes shows is not that intuitively subdoxastic states are actually beliefs, but rather that the domain of the inference relation includes other states in addition to beliefs.

There is something misleading in the account I have just given of the difference between Harman and myself. For it sounds as though the dispute is largely terminological. He wants to call subdoxastic states "beliefs" and preserve the principle that inference relates only beliefs; I want to renounce the principle and abjure the expanded extension of "belief." The issue, however, is not simply a terminological one. What is at stake is not whether we bloat the extension of "belief" to preserve a principle, but rather whether the old intuitive boundary between beliefs and subdoxastic states divides states which are in fact psychologically different. If it does, then following Harman's terminological proposal would simply make it necessary to coin some new term to denote the class of states we are now intuitively inclined to call "beliefs."

Harman nowhere addresses himself to the issue of the psychological importance of the belief-subdoxastic state distinction. However, in light of his proposed extension of "belief" to cover subdoxastic states and his failure to propose some other way of marking the boundary, I think we might plausibly attribute to him the view that the distinction is of small importance. Yet, as some of Harman's further remarks illustrate, this is not an easy position to espouse consistently. Thus consider the following dilemma. After defending the view that various (intuitively subdoxastic) states, including retinal stimulations, are beliefs because they are used "the way one uses beliefs in inference," Harman is in something of a quandary about just *what* beliefs they are. Just what belief are we to attribute to a perceiver, for example, when his retinal nerve is stimulated in a certain way? An obvious answer: the perceiver believes that his retinal nerve is being stimulated in that way. But, sensibly enough, Harman is unwilling to buy that answer. For he conjures the following objection:

The typical perceiver knows little psychology and nothing about stimulations of his retinal nerve. So if the data needed for his inference includes claims about his sensory stimulation, he does not believe the data. (1973: 185)

Harman is plainly troubled by the objection, and his efforts to parry are a bit bizarre. The perceiver, he concedes, does not have any beliefs *about* sensory stimulations. Rather, the sensory stimulations themselves are the beliefs; it is they which serve as data for perceptual inference

The data are not about sensory stimulations, they *are* sensory stimulations. . . .
Does [the perceiver] believe the data? He uses them in the way one uses beliefs in inference. So there is some reason to say that he believes them. (1973: 186)

Well and good. The stimulations are beliefs. But beliefs *that what*?

Sensory stimulations serve the perceiver as non-linguistic representations which cannot be easily put into words. . . .
In order to be able to express in words the input data, we would have to know much more about the system of representation and its functioning than we now know. Even then it might be impossible to find linguistic representations equivalent to the non-linguistic representations constituted by sensory stimulation. (1973: 186)

Now it is pretty clear that part of this reply is simply a bluff. Harman suggests that we might be able to express the content of sensory stimulations if only we knew more about the workings of the system. But it seems pretty plain that there is no sentence which will serve to express the content of retinal stimulations *any better* than a sentence asserting that the retina is being stimulated in a certain way. Indeed, any sentence S which might be proposed as a candidate for expressing the content of retinal stimulations would face just the same difficulties as a sentence specifying how the retina is being stimulated. To see this, consider for a moment why we are unwilling to say of a perceiver whose retina is being stimulated in a certain way that he *believes* it is being stimulated in that way. Harman's reply is that the typical perceiver knows little psychology and nothing about the stimulation of his retinal nerve. But why are we so sure of this? The answer, I think, is that if we were to attribute beliefs about retinal stimulations to a naive perceiver, they would be a most peculiar species of belief, for they would be beliefs to which the perceiver had no access and which were largely inferentially isolated from the remainder of his beliefs. The same would be true if we instead attributed to the perceiver the belief that p, where p is an arbitrary candidate for expressing the content of a retinal stimulation.

Harman's other strategy for parrying the problem that we cannot find suitable content sentences for retinal stimulations is to retreat into mysticism. Even after we have a decent understanding of the functioning of the perceptual system, "it might be impossible to find linguistic representations equivalent to the non-linguistic representations constituted by sensory stimulations" (1973: 186). Their content is so mysterious that it is not expressible by words. It is tempting here to ponder whether it could make any sense to say that a state represents something, but there is no saying what it represents. I shall, however, resist the temptation. For it seems to me that by retreating to this doctrine of the unspeakable, Harman has conceded the principal point that I have been arguing. The states for whose contents it is impossible "to find linguistic representation" are just those that we have been calling subdoxastic. So Harman has conceded, however obliquely, that there is an important difference between beliefs and subdoxastic states. But if Harman and I agree on this central point, serious differences remain in how to characterize the difference. For Harman, the difference turns on the linguistic expressibility of the contents of subdoxastic states. On my view, however, there is no particular problem in expressing the contents of subdoxastic states. Harman sees a problem because he insists that subdoxastic states are beliefs. But it is more than his intuition will tolerate to attribute to a subject the belief that p, where p expresses the content of the state. Thus he must postulate some mysterious unspeakable content. As I see it, the problem is not in finding a content sentence, but in failing to distinguish subdoxastic states from beliefs. Once the distinction has been recognized, we can assign quite ordinary contents to subdoxastic states without worrying that the subject fails to believe the content sentence.

We began this section with the concern that Harman's arguments appeared to show the distinction between beliefs and subdoxastic states is untenable. I think it fair to conclude that we have found the fault to lie not with the distinction but with the argument trying to undermine it.

8 Where does all this leave us? I believe we have a plausible case for the claim that the intuitive distinction between beliefs and subdoxastic states marks a real and psychologically interesting boundary. Moreover, it is a boundary that has been largely overlooked by contemporary work in cognitive simulation. The reasons for this neglect are not obvious. It would be my guess that, like Harman, many of those concerned with cognitive simulation have been so captivated with the promise of inferential accounts of the mechanisms underlying perception and thought that they have failed to note the rather special and largely isolated nature of the inferential processes between beliefs and subdoxastic states. Failure to take seriously the matter of access to consciousness likely has a less creditable explanation. Since the heyday of behaviorism, conscious awareness has had a bad name among many psychologists. And the attitude seems to persist even among those who have come to see behaviorism as a dead end.

If it is granted that the belief-subdoxastic state distinction is (at least *prima facie*) an important one, then we are left with an intriguing question. Why do inferential integration and access to consciousness run in tandem? Is this just an accident, or is there some underlying mechanism that accounts for both phenomena? My hunch is that it is more than an accident. But if I have inferred that view, the premises I have used are well hidden from conscious access.

Notes

1   Speakers might, for example, have a system of states which serves to store or internally represent each of the rules of the grammar. In judging whether a sentence is grammatical, the relevant psychological mechanism might try to produce a derivation of the sentence at hand, aided by some efficient derivation finding heuristic. If it succeeds, it sets in motion a process which ordinarily leads to an affirmative answer. I think this sort of "analysis by synthesis" strategy, though surely logical possibly, is wildly implausible as an empirical hypothesis. It does, however, have the advantage of being a particularly straightforward example of the way internally represented grammatical information might be exploited. For a much more subtle illustration of how grammatical information might be represented and utilized, cf. Winograd (1972).

2   There are a pair of assumptions being made here. First, I assume that the grammatical information stored by a competent speaker consists (in part) of rules of the speaker's grammar. As noted in fn. 1, I suspect this is a counterfactual assumption. Second, I assume that grammatical rules can be formulated in such a way that it makes sense to talk of believing a rule. More specifically, I am assuming that appending a formulation of a rule to '*S* believes that _____' produces a well-formed sentence.

3   For problem solving see Newell and Simon (1973); for some interesting work in inference, cf. Anderson and Bower (1974: ch. 13); for an account of perception which stresses the parallels between perceptual representation and inference on the one hand, and representation and inference among beliefs on the other hand, see Anderson and Bower (1974: ch. 8; also Moran (1973) and Pylyshyn (1973).

References

Anderson, J. and Bower, G., *Human Associative Memory*. Washington: John Wiley and Sons, 1974.

Austin, J.L., *Sense and Sensibilia*. New York: Oxford University Press, 1964.

Chomsky, N. and Katz, J., "What the linguist is talking about." *Journal of Philosophy* 71 (1974): 347–67.

Dretske, F., *Seeing and Knowing*. Chicago: University of Chicago Press, 1969.

Graves, C., Katz, J., *et al.*, "Tacit knowledge." *Journal of Philosophy* 70 (1973): 318–30.

Haber, R.N. and Hershenson, M., *The Psychology of Visual Perception*. New York: Holt, Rinehart, and Winston, 1973.

Harman, G., *Thought*. Princeton: Princeton University Press, 1973.

Hess, E.H., "Attitude and pupil size." *Scientific American* 212 (1965): 46–54.

—— "The role of pupil size in communication." *Scientific American* 233 (1975): 113–19.

Julesz, J., *The Cyclopean Eye*. New York: Academic Press, 1970.

Moran, T.P., "The symbolic imagery hypothesis: A production system model." Ph.D. Dissertation, Carnegie-Mellon University, 1973.

Newell, A. and Simon, H., *Human Problem Solving*. Englewood Cliffs: Prentice-Hall, 1973.

Pylyshyn, Z., "What the mind's eye tells the mind's brain: A critique of mental imagery." *Psychological Bulletin* 80 (1973): 1–24.

Stich. S.P., "What every speaker knows." *Philosophical Review* 80 (1971): 476–96.

—— "Competence and indeterminacy." In *Testing Linguistic Hypotheses*, Cohen, D. and Wirth, J.R., eds. Washington: John Wiley, 1975.

—— *From Folk Psychology to Cognitive Science: A Case Against Belief*. Cambridge, Mass.: MIT Press, 1983.

Winograd, T., "Understanding natural language." *Cognitive Psychology* 3 (1972): 1–191.

27

G. Evans, "Semantic Theory and Tacit Knowledge"

I

In his provocative paper, Crispin Wright threw down several challenges to philosophers like myself* who have been attracted by, and supposed themselves to be participating in, the enterprise of constructing a systematic theory of meaning for a natural language. I shall have time this evening to take up only one of his challenges, which I hope is the most important.

Professor Wright notes that those who are interested in constructing a theory of meaning for a natural language insist that it should be what he calls 'structure-reflecting'; as he says, all the interest of the theories or sub-theories which have been constructed lies in their capacity to exhibit the meanings of complex expressions as a function of the meanings of their parts. Wright then takes this 'structure-reflecting' requirement in one hand and examines various accounts of the nature of a theory of meaning which might justify its imposition. He considers three such accounts.

The first is this: the task of a theory of meaning is simply to enable one to state what each of the sentences of a language means. He argues, I think correctly, that if this is the task of a theory of meaning, the structure-reflecting requirement cannot be justified; indeed, and here again I agree with him, in the special case in which the language under study is included in the language in which the theory is being stated, the single axiom schema:

$$\text{True } (\bar{\varphi}) \equiv \varphi$$

will serve the purpose.

(Like Professor Wright, I will concentrate upon theories of meaning which yield statements of sentences' truth-conditions, since, as he says, his scepticism about theories of meaning arises equally for theories whose central notion is

---

*[Editor] Sections I, II, and IV of Evans's paper were originally written as a response to the paper by Crispin Wright cited in n. 1 on p. 591.

not that of truth but, say, warranted assertibility, or falsibility. In order to focus upon the question of structure, we can assume that no question is being raised about the empirical content of the *theorems* of the theory of meaning; the question is about the significance of their being derived from a finite set of principles (axioms) in a structure-revealing way.)

Wright argues that if the structure-reflecting requirement is to be justified, a theory of meaning must in some way or other be regarded as a theory of the competence of speakers of the language, but in what way? We can say that the theory states something which speakers of the language tacitly know, but what does this mean? Two interpretations provide the second and third accounts which Wright considers. One he finds relatively weak, and acceptable, but unable to justify the requirement; the other he finds inadequately explained and open to serious objection.

According to the weak sense of 'tacit knowledge', 'to attribute implicit knowledge of such a "theory" ... is to do no more than obliquely to describe their behaviour; it is to say that they behave in just the way which someone would behave who successfully tried to suit his behaviour to ... an explicit statement [of the theory]'.[1] Let us call two theories of meaning which attribute the same meanings to sentences of a language – which agree in their theorems – *extensionally equivalent* (by analogy with the notion of extensional equivalence applied to grammars). According to Wright, to suit one's behaviour to a theory of meaning is to suit one's behaviour to its theorems. Consequently, if the behaviour of native speakers is the same as one who suits his behaviour to the explicitly formulated theory T, it is the same as one who suits his behaviour to an explicit statement of any extensionally equivalent theory T. Hence, native speakers tacitly know all extensionally equivalent theories, whether those theories discern different structures in native sentences or, in the case of a theory formulated with a single axiom schema, do not discern structure in their sentences at all. So, while this weak notion of tacit knowledge is perfectly clear, it does not provide one with the basis for preferring one extensionally equivalent theory to another.

We come then to the third account which Wright considers. It would be quite unfair to complain that Wright did not make this third option terribly clear, for it is one of his points that is not very clear. But in the absence of an explicit statement, we must rest content with hints. The notion of tacit knowledge is richer, and allows for the idea of 'unconscious deployment of information', it is also capable of figuring in an *explanation* of a speaker's capacity to understand new sentences. Though this indicates the kind of direction in which Wright thinks one who seeks to justify the structure-reflecting requirement must be pushed, he expresses doubt about whether a genuine explanation could be provided by the use of the notion of tacit knowledge; to invoke tacit knowledge of a theory of meaning to explain a speaker's capacity to understand new sentences is vacuous, in the way in which explanations invoking the notion of a universal are vacuous. Secondly, he suggests that any such rich notion of tacit knowledge of a theory of meaning is only dubiously consistent with Wittgenstein's rule-following considerations:

> the thesis seems to involve thinking of mastery of the language as consisting in (unconscious) equipment with the information which systematically settles the content of so far unconstructed and unconsidered sentences. Such a conception is far from patently coherent with the repudiation of the objectivity of sameness of use involved in the scepticism about investigation-independence sketched above.[2]

Though it is not my intention to focus on this aspect of his paper, I am unsure how Wittgenstein's considerations, at least as interpreted by Wright, can threaten this, as yet unborn, third option. Professor Wright says that Wittgenstein's rule-following considerations:

> do not . . . impugn the legitimacy of at least the most basic purpose with which such a theory might be devised: that of securing a description of the use of . . . the object language of such a kind that to be apprised of that description would be to know how to participate in the use of . . . the language.[3]

Someone who knows a finite theory for an infinite language is in some sense in possession of information which *settles in advance* (allows him to predict) the meanings of as yet unconstructed sentences. It is unclear to me why those who wish to argue that speakers of an infinite language tacitly know a finite theory of meaning need suppose the theory to determine the meanings of unconstructed sentences in any stronger, or more objectionable, sense than the one Wright implicitly accepts in the passage I have just quoted.

However good or bad the reasons for Wright's pessimism might be, he certainly threw down a challenge, and I want to take it up. I want to try to explain how the structure-reflecting requirement might be justified. But I must immediately mention two limitations on my attempt. I do not pretend that it is the only possible way of replying to Professor Wright's challenge, nor do I think that it would command universal assent among theorists of meaning. For example, I am fairly sure that Donald Davidson would dissent from it, since, contrary to what Wright suggests, he has conspicuously avoided reference to the psychological states of language users in his explanation of the nature of a theory of meaning. Second, I propose to do merely what I say: to defend the enterprise on which the structure-reflecting requirement is a constraint. I do not propose to defend the claim that philosophical insights and benefits accrue from taking the enterprise seriously.

Those who have followed recent debates in grammatical theory will be aware that Wright's challenge to the theorist of meaning is very similar to Quine's challenge to the grammarian:

Implicit guidance is a moot enough idea to demand some explicit methodology. If it is to make sense to say that a native was implicitly guided by one system of rules rather than another, extensionally equivalent one, this sense must link up somehow with the native's dispositions to behave in observable ways in observable circumstances.[4]

However, in a way Wright's challenge is more radical, because it is not possible to formulate even a merely extensionally adequate grammar by the use of a single axiom schema. But this idea, that all a semantic theorist needs to say about English in English can be encapsulated in a single axiom scheme, must surely lead us to begin upon our task of meeting the challenge with a conviction that it can be met. Can it seriously be suggested that there is nothing to be said about the semantics of specific construction – of adverbs, tense, modality, intensional contexts, pronouns, quantifiers, proper names, definite descriptions, and the like? A good deal has already been said on these subjects by Frege, Russell, Davidson, Geach, Dummett, and many others, and though I can detect deficiencies in this work, they do not lead me to think that there are simply no questions of the kind these theorists are attempting to answer. Wright has criticized semantic theorists for ignoring the ideas of 'the most original philosophical thinker of the twentieth century', but it is surely equally deplorable if students of those ideas act as intellectual Luddites, dismissing the entirety of a sophisticated and developing intellectual tradition without a detailed consideration of its findings, and an alternative account of the enterprise to which the obviously compelling distinctions and observations it contains do properly belong: I do not say that Wright would himself join, or even encourage, the fanatics wrecking the machines, and I am prepared to concede that his challenge has not been squarely faced, but I should have liked to see a little more evidence that the questions he posed were 'expecting the answer "Yes"', rather than 'expecting the answer "No"'.

II

Let us begin by considering a little elementary and finite language which contains ten names, $a, b, c, \ldots$ and ten monadic predicates $F, G, H, \ldots$; in all, the language has 100 possible sentences. I consider this case partly for simplicity, but also in order to stress that the structure-reflecting requirement has nothing whatever to do with *finiteness*. The fact that a language has an infinite number of possible sentences is a sufficient but not necessary condition of its having semantically significant structure, as our little language will illustrate. (It is unfortunate that Chomsky's writings have led people to equate the *creativity* of language use with the *unboundedness* natural languages display. Linguistic creativity is manifested in the capacity to understand new sentences, and the speaker of a finite language such as the one I have described can manifest it.) I want to consider two possible theories of meaning for this language. T_1 has 100 axioms; one for each sentence of the language. Examples would be:

Fa is true iff John is bald
Fb is true iff Harry is bald

...

Ga is true iff John is happy
Gb is true iff Harry is happy.

T_1 treats each of the sentences as unstructured. T_2 on the other hand, has twenty-one axioms – one for each 'word' of the language, and a general, compositional one. Ten of the axioms are of the form:

a denotes John
b denotes Harry

and ten are of the form:

An object satisfies *F* iff it is bald
An object satisfies *G* iff it is happy.

The compositional axiom is:

A sentence coupling a name with a predicate is true iff the object denoted by the name satisfies the predicate.

One can derive from these twenty-one axioms a statement of the truth conditions of each of the 100 sentences of the language – the very statements which T_1 takes as axioms. T_2 treats a sentence like *Fa* as structured; it discerns two distinct elements in it: the name *a* and the predicate *F*. Thus, T_1 and T_2 are extensionally equivalent in our sense, and our question is: what can be meant by saying that the practice of speakers of the language shows that one of these is to be preferred to the other, or equivalently, that they tacitly know one of these theories rather than the other?

It is tempting to answer this question by saying that T_1 is a theory tacitly known by someone who has had to receive training with, or exposure to the practice with, each one of the 100 sentences taken individually – someone who had not realized, or who could make no use of the fact, that the same expressions occur in different sentences – whereas T_2 is tacitly known by someone who has the capacity to understand *new* sentences of this simple subject-predicate form (e.g. *Kc*), provided that he has been exposed to the practice with a sufficiency of sentences containing the name *c* and the predicate *K*. However, though this contains the essence of the answer, it will not do as it stands, since it may reasonably be objected that T_1 also comprises a statement of what *Kc* means, so that someone who tacitly knew T_1 would be able to understand it.

I suggest that we construe the claim that someone tacitly knows a theory of meaning as ascribing to that person a set of dispositions – one corresponding to each of the expressions for which the theory provides a distinct axiom. In the case of T_1, it is easy to see what these dispositions are: one tacitly knows T_1 iff one has 100 distinct dispositions, each one being a disposition to judge utterances of the relevant sentence type as having such-and-such truth conditions. It is more difficult to specify the dispositions which tacit knowledge of T_2 requires of a speaker, because they are interconnected. The only judgements which we are prepared to ascribe to speakers are judgements about the truth conditions of whole sentences – this, of course, is why we must speak of the knowledge of the axioms being tacit. However, if the subject tacitly knows T_2 we shall regard any such judgement as the exercise of two distinct dispositions. Consequently, the dispositions which tacit knowledge of T_2 requires can never be manifested singly. The dispositions must be interdefined, but though this makes the task of specifying the dispositions more difficult, it does not make it impossible.

For example we might say that a speaker U tacitly knows that the denotation of a is John iff he has a disposition such that:

($\Pi\Phi$) ($\Pi\psi$) if
  (i) U tacitly knows that an object satisfies Φ iff it is ψ
  (ii) U hears an utterance having the form $\Phi^\frown a$
     then U will judge the utterance is true iff John is ψ.

Connectedly, we say that a speaker U tacitly knows that an 'object satisfies F iff it is bald iff he has a disposition such that:

(Πx) ($\Pi\alpha$) if
  (i) U tacitly knows that the denotation of α is x,
  (ii) U hears an utterance having the form $F^\frown\alpha$,
     then U will judge that the utterance is true iff x is bald.

In these formulations, 'Π' is a universal substitutional quantifier, with variables having the following substitution classes: Φ, names of predicate expressions of the (object) language; α, names of names of the (object) language; ψ, predicate expressions of our language (the metalanguage); and x, proper names of our language.

Now, it is essential that the notion of a disposition used in these formulations be understood in a full-blooded sense. These statements of tacit knowledge must not be regarded as simple statements of regularity, for if they were, anyone who correctly judged the meanings of complete sentences would have a tacit knowledge of T_2. When we ascribe to something the disposition to V in circumstances C, we are claiming that there is a state S which, when taken together with C, provides a causal explanation of all the episodes of the subject's V-ing (in C). So we make the claim that there is a common explanation for all those episodes of V-ing. Understood in this way, the ascription of tacit knowledge of T_2 does not merely report upon the regularity in the way in which the subject reacts to sentences containing a given expression (for this regularity can be observed in the linguistic behaviour of someone for whom the sentence is unstructured). It involves the claim that there is a single state of the subject which figures in a causal explanation of why he reacts in this regular way to all the sentences containing the expression. Tacit knowledge of T_2 requires that there should be twenty such states of the subject – one corresponding to each expression of the language which the theory treats separately – such that the causal explanation of why the subject reacts in the way that he does to any sentence of the language involves two of these states, and any one of the states is involved in the explanation of the way he reacts to ten sentences containing a common element.

The difference between the ascription of tacit knowledge of T_1 and T_2 can be brought out diagrammatically, with the diagrams representing two extremely abstract and schematic psychological models of a subject's capacity to understand sentences. Tacit knowledge of T_1 and T_2 is incompletely represented in Figs. 27.1 and 27.2 respectively. Forget about the dotted lines for a

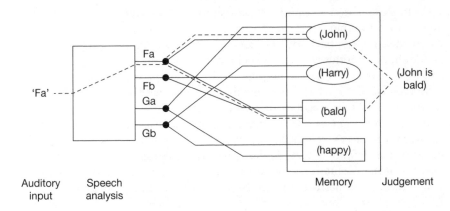

Figure 27.1

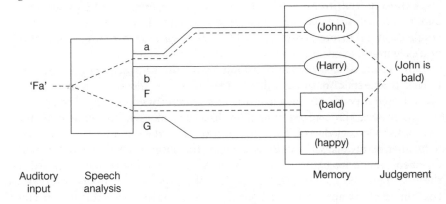

Figure 27.2

moment. You will observe that in the first model, there are two *independent* links between the speech-analysing device and the subject's store of knowledge of John (and in a full representation there would be ten such independent links), whereas in the second model, there is just one link between the speech-analysis device and the subject's store of knowledge of John. The dotted lines are intended to indicate what happens when the subject hears the sentence *Fa*. If you imagine dotted lines drawn to trace the consequences of the subject's hearing the sentence *Ga*, you will observe that in the former case they will not, and in the latter case they will, share a pathway with the dotted line already on the diagram. This is a representation of the fact that in the former case there is not, and in the latter case there is, a common factor which must be invoked in the explanation of the speaker's reaction to the two sentences.

It appears to me that there is a clear empirical difference between these two models of competence, and hence between tacit knowledge of T_1 and T_2 interpreted in the way I have suggested.

The decisive way to decide which model is correct is by providing a causal, presumably neurophysiologically based, explanation of comprehension. With such an explanation in hand, we can simply see whether or not there is an appeal to a common state or structure in the explanation of the subject's comprehension of each of the sentences containing the proper name *a*. However, even in the absence of such an explanation, we can have very good empirical reasons for preferring one model of competence to the other.

In the first place, we can examine the way in which the dispositions to react to sentences (the capacity to understand them) are acquired. We might find that the acquisition of the language progressed in quite definite ways, and involved a subject's acquiring the capacity to understand sentences he had never heard before. For example, suppose a subject had progressed in his mastery of the language to the point where he understood all of the sentences which could be constructed from the vocabulary *a*, *b*, *c*, *d*, *e*, and *F*, *G*, *H*, *I*, *J*. Suppose further that he is exposed to the sentences *Ff* and *Gf* in surroundings which, or with instructions which, made it clear what they mean. Whether this exposure leads to his acquiring the capacity to understand new sentences, and which new sentences he was able to understand, would cast very considerable light upon the structure of his competence with the language, both antecedent and subsequent to the introduction of new vocabulary.

If he acquired the capacity to understand the sentences *Hf*, *If*, *Jf*, never having heard them before (and no others), this would strongly confirm the second model of his competence, for this is exactly what it predicts. On the second model, the understanding of these sentences is consequential upon the subject's possession of dispositions specific to the expressions *H*, *I*, *J*, and *f*. Further, if the second model is correct, the subject's understanding of the fragment of the language without the new name *f* showed that he possessed the first three relevant dispositions, while the exposure to just two sentences containing the name *f* can suffice for the establishment of the fourth, provided the circumstances are such that it is clear what those sentences mean.

So, according to the second model, all the ingredients of understanding of some sentences are present before any of them have been heard, and they are specifically the sentences *Hf*, *If*, *Jf*.

The first model generates no predictions as to the understanding of unheard sentences. According to it, the understanding of each sentence is a separate capacity, and there is absolutely no reason why the inculcation of competence in the two sentences *Ff* and *Gf* should induce competence with any others. If it does so, this can only be accommodated on the first model by additional postulates, but why light dawns on the particular sentences *Hf*, *If*, *Jf*, rather than *Li* or *Mj*, must be left totally unexplained.

Thus, we can see more clearly what bearing the capacity to understand new sentences has upon the choice between T_1 and T_2. The fact that someone has the capacity to understand the unheard sentence *Hf* does not refute the ascription to him of tacit knowledge of T_1 *outright* – it just makes the ascription extremely implausible.

Evidence of a parallel kind can be derived from the way in which competence is lost. Suppose a subject is such that, if he loses his competence with any sentence of the form $\Phi^\frown a$ (while retaining his competence with some sentences of the form $\Phi^\frown \beta$), he simultaneously loses his competence with *every* sentence of that form. This would also favour the second model of the subject's competence, since this is, once again, what that model predicts. On the first model, however, it is *inexplicable* why the loss of the capacity to understand one sentence should drag the comprehension of other sentences with it. (Evidence of this kind would be equally valuable whether the loss of competence was simply due to the subject's forgetting the meanings of words, or to brain damage.)

There is evidence of a third kind which might be used to decide between the models, since they carry with them different accounts of sentence perception. The second model requires that the subject perceive the sentence *Fa*, for example, *as* structured, that is to say, as containing the expression *a*. There is a clear difference between perceiving a sentence which does in fact contain the expression *a*, and perceiving a sentence *as* containing the expression *a*. Consequently, we can regard as relevant to the decision between the two models the various psychological tests which have been devised for identifying perceived acoustic structure, for example, the click test originally devised by Ladefoged and Broadbent.[5]

Thus, it seems to me that Crispin Wright's challenge can be met. It is possible to link tacit knowledge of one theory (rather than one of its extensionally equivalent rivals) to 'the native's dispositions to behave in observable ways in observable situations'. But to do this, one must look further than just to the dispositions to respond to, or to use, whole sentences. It is possible that the scepticism which Wright expresses is due in a small way to the mistaken thought that facts of native usage which bear upon the content possessed by whole sentences are all the facts to which a theory of meaning can or need be sensitive.

Bearing in mind the interpretation of 'tacit knowledge' which I have proposed, let us briefly consider infinite languages. What would be involved in the tacit knowledge of the theory for such a language which is formulated with the use of a single axiom schema?

An axiom schema is not a theory; it is a compendious specification by their syntactic form of the sentences which do constitute the theory. In the case of an infinite language, there are an infinite number of such sentences. Someone would possess tacit knowledge of such a theory only if he possessed an infinite number of *distinct* linguistic dispositions: one corresponding to each of the sentences of the language. This we know no one can possess. I have concentrated upon the more challenging case of a finite language because it is important to stress the point that there can be compelling evidence that someone *does* not possess a battery of distinct dispositions other than the fact that no one *can* possess them, so that we may want to do for a speaker of a finite language what we are forced to do for a speaker of an infinite language.

Infinity in language results from recursiveness; syntactic and semantic rules which operate upon their own output. A standard clause for the recursive element 'and' runs like this:

> A sentence of the form S⌢'and'⌢S' is true iff S is true
> and S' is true

Generalizing the procedure used earlier, we can say that a speaker U tacitly knows this principle iff he has a disposition such that:

(ΠS) (ΠP) (ΠS') (ΠP') if:
  (i) U is disposed to judge that S is true iff P
 (ii) U is disposed to judge that S' is true iff P'
(iii) U hears an utterance having the form S⌢'and'⌢S',
      then U will judge that the utterance is true iff P and P'.

(The substitution classes for the variables S and S', and P and P', are names of sentences of the object language, and sentences of the metalanguage, respectively.) More difficult is the clause for an existential quantifier. It might run:

> A sentence of the form '$(\exists x)$'⌢Φ is true iff there is something y such that,
> letting β be its name, the sentence Φ^β/x is true.

This is a simplified 'Fregean' clause for an objectual quantifier.[6] 'Φ^β/x' abbreviates 'the result of substituting β for all occurrences of x in Φ'. Then we can say that U tacitly knows this principle iff he has a disposition such that:

($\Pi\Phi$) ($\Pi\psi$), if:
(i) ($\Pi\beta$) (Πx) (If U tacitly knows the denotation of β is x, then U is
    disposed to judge that the sentence Φ^β/x is true iff x is ψ)

(ii) U hears an utterance of the form '$(\exists x)$'$^\frown\Phi$ then U is disposed to judge that the utterance is true iff something is ψ.

(In this instance, the substitution class for Φ are structural-descriptive names of object-language propositional functions in the variable x.)

III

Professor Wright and I are agreed that tacit knowledge of the semantic rules of a language is a 'logical construction' out of the use of whole sentences. I have suggested that the idea that we may tacitly know one rather than another of two extensionally equivalent theories which differ in the amount of structure they discern in sentences leads one to the thought of a correspondence between the separable principles of a theory and a series of internal states of the subject, dispositionally characterized. Nevertheless, I would agree with Wright that to regard these states as states of knowledge or belief, that is to say, states of the same kind as are identified by the ordinary use of those words, is wrong and capable of leading to confusions of the kind he gestures at. To establish this point would require another paper. However, I shall say a brief word about it now, since I believe it is to this point, rather than the very idea of a psychological underpinning to the theory of meaning, that Wright's criticisms are legitimately directed.

There is no doubt in what the similarity between the states of tacit knowledge and the ordinary states of knowledge and belief is taken to consist. At the level of output, one who possesses the tacit knowledge that p is disposed to do and think some of the things which one who had the ordinary belief that p would be inclined to do and think (given the same desires). At the level of input, one who possesses the state of tacit knowledge that p will very probably have acquired that state as the result of exposure to usage which supports or confirms (though far from conclusively) the proposition that p, and hence in circumstances which might well induce in a rational person the ordinary belief that p. But these analogies are very far from establishing tacit knowledge as a species of belief. After all, similar analogies at the level of input and output exist between the state of a rat who avoids a certain food which has upset it in the past ('bait-shyness') on the one hand, and the belief that a man might have that a certain food is poisonous, on the other.

It is true that many philosophers would be prepared to regard the dispositional state of the rat as a belief. But such a view requires blindness to the fundamental differences which exist between the state of the rat and the belief of the man – differences which suggest that fundamentally different mechanisms are at work. We might begin with this disanalogy: the rat manifests the 'belief' in only one way – by not eating – whereas there is no limit to the ways in which the ordinary belief that something is poisonous might be manifested. The subject might manifest it by, for example, preventing someone else from eating the food, or by giving it to a hated enemy, or by committing suicide

587

with it. These variations stem from the different projects with which the belief may interact, but similar variations arise from combining the belief with other beliefs. It might, for example, lead to a subject's consuming a small amount of the food every day, when combined with the belief that the consumption of small doses of a poison renders one immune to its effects. (The existence of other beliefs induces a similar variability in the ways in which the belief that something is poisonous might be established.) It is of the essence of a belief state that it be at the service of many distinct projects, and that its influence on any project be mediated by other beliefs. The rat simply has a disposition to avoid a certain food; the state underlying this disposition is not a part of a system which would generate widely varying behaviour in a wide variety of situations according to the different projects and further 'beliefs' it may possess.

So, one who possesses a belief will typically be sensitive to a wide variety of ways in which it can be established (what it can be inferred from), and a wide variety of different ways in which it can be used (what can be inferred from it) – if we think of plans for intentional action as being generated from beliefs by the same kind of rational inferential process as yields further beliefs from beliefs. To have a belief requires one to appreciate its location in a network of beliefs; this is why Wittgenstein says, 'When we first begin to *believe* anything, what we believe is not a single proposition, it is a whole system of propositions. (Light dawns gradually over the whole.)'.[7] To think of beliefs in this way forces us to think of them as structured states; the subject's appreciation of the inferential potential of one belief (e.g. the belief that a *is F*) at least partly depending upon the same general capacity as his appreciation of the inferential potential of others (e.g. the belief that b *is F*). After all, the principle of an *inference*, of *reasoning*, can never be specific to the set of propositions involved.[8] Possession of this general capacity is often spoken of as mastery of a concept, and the point I am making is frequently made by saying that belief involves the possession of concepts (e.g. the concept of *poison*). Behind the idea of a system of beliefs lies that of a system of concepts, the structure of which determines the inferential properties which thoughts involving an exercise of the various component concepts of the system are treated as possessing. At the ground floor of the structure will be observational concepts whose possession requires the subject to be able to discriminate (in suitable favourable circumstances) instances of the concept. Inferential links connect these concepts with more theoretical concepts 'higher' in the structure, and they in their turn will be connected with concepts yet more remote from observation.

Concepts are exercised in the first instance in thoughts; beliefs may be regarded as dispositions to entertain thoughts in the 'believing mode' – i.e. to make judgements; if we think of belief in this way, we shall not be prepared to attribute to a subject the belief that a *is F* (for some particular object a, and property F) unless we can suppose the subject to be capable of entertaining the supposition (having the thought) that b *is F*, for every object b of which he has a conception. For example, we will not be inclined to explain a subject's actions by attributing to him the belief that *he* is F (e.g. he is in pain) unless we suppose him capable of entertaining the supposition with respect to individuals distinct from himself that they are F (e.g. that the person is in pain).[9] Now, it is true that the 'believing mode' of thought cannot be characterized without reference to its influence upon the subject's actions; the traditional accounts of belief which I am largely following went wrong in trying to identify the difference between judgement and mere thought in terms of some introspectible feature of accompaniment of the thought. A judgement is (*ceteris paribus*) a thought one acts upon (if a suitable plan for action is derived from it). But we are now far away from the rat's disposition to avoid certain food. For one thing, there is an enormous gap between belief (a disposition to judge that *p* when the question whether *p* is raised) and action. Even though a subject believes a substance is poisonous he may not slip it to an enemy he wants to kill and knows no other way to kill either because he 'didn't think of it' or because, having thought of it, he 'forgot' what to do when the time came.

Tacit knowledge of the syntactic and semantic rules of the language are not states of the same kinds as the states we identify in our ordinary use of the terms 'belief' and 'knowledge'. Possession of tacit knowledge is exclusively manifested in speaking and understanding a language; the information is not even potentially at the service of any other project of the agent, nor can it interact with any other beliefs of the agent (whether genuine beliefs or other tacit 'beliefs') to yield further beliefs. Such concepts as we use in specifying it are not concepts we need to suppose the subject to possess, for the state is inferentially insulated from the rest of the subject's thoughts and beliefs. There is thus no question of regarding the information being brought by the subject to bear upon speech and interpretation in rational processes of thought, or of making sense of the subject's continued possession of the information despite incorrect performance, due to his 'not thinking' of the rule at the appropriate time etc. Remarks which Wright makes ('unconscious deployment of information' etc.) suggest that he considers the proponent of his third option as holding that tacit knowledge is a real species of belief, but with all the relevant inferential processes made by the subject somehow taking place outside his ken. This is certainly a mysterious and confused position.

I disagree with Professor Wright only in denying that the proponent of a structure-reflecting theory of meaning need have anything to do with it.

IV

I come finally to the question of whether there is any sense in which the theorist of meaning provides an explanation of a speaker's capacity to understand new sentences. Now it is implicit in what has gone before that the notion of tacit knowledge of a structure-reflecting theory of meaning, explained as I have explained it, cannot be used to explain the capacity to understand new sentences. I have given a purely dispositional characterization of tacit knowledge, and though this does not just amount to a re-description of the speaker's capacities to understand sentences (including the new ones) what it provides, in addition to a description of those capacities, is not itself something that could be involved in an explanation of them. The surplus concerned the form which an explanation of the capacities would take, and to say that a group of phenomena have a common explanation is obviously not yet to say what the explanation is. So I agree with Wright when he writes:

> there is no reason to think that it is within the power of the sort of theory which we are considering to serve up anything which could rightly be considered an *explanation* of the infinitary character of competence with its object-language.[10]

But while I agree with this, I disagree with his claim that a proponent of structure-reflecting theories of meaning must somehow be committed to the view that they are providing an explanation of speakers' capacity to understand new sentences.

Nevertheless, I believe that there is a way of explaining a speaker's capacity to understand new sentences to which provision of a structure-reflecting theory of meaning is indispensable. For we can provide a genuine explanation of a speaker's capacity to understand a certain novel utterance by citing his exposure, in the past, to the elements of that sentence occurring in sentences whose meaning was, or was made, manifest. I envisage an explanatory chain like this:

Exposure to corpus of sentences containing parts of the given sentence being used in determinate ways		Complex set of dispositions = tacit knowledge of clauses in theory of meaning		Understanding of a given new sentence
	=>		=>	

This chain can be genuinely explanatory even though the last link of the chain by itself is not. The attribution to a subject of tacit knowledge of T_1 is neither more nor less explanatory of the capacity to understand the given new sentences than the attribution of T_2, but tacit knowledge of T_2 belongs in an explanation of the capacity to understand a new sentence because we understand how those dispositions might have been acquired as a result of exposure to the corpus of utterances which the subject has heard. Now, we can cite a subject's exposure to a corpus of utterances in explanation of his capacity to understand a new one only if we believe that the use of expressions in the new sentence is *in conformity with* their use in the previously heard corpus. Only in this case will we be able to show what set of dispositions the subject might have acquired which meets the two conditions: (1) exercising them yields the observed (and correct) interpretation of the new sentence; (2) they would have been exercised in, and hence could have been acquired by exposure to, the previous use. Consequently, when a capacity to understand novel sentences is observed, the theorist of meaning has an indispensable role to play in its explanation, since he must exhibit the regularity between the old and the new.

I have more or less deliberately spoken in terms which might well offend some of those present, for I believe that some of those present, though not, I think, Professor Wright, believe that Wittgenstein's arguments on rule-following show that the ambition to exhibit such regularity must be based upon some kind of mistake. Perhaps this is so, and if it is so, I hope that we shall hear tonight why it is so. Since I do not have time to discuss the arguments of such philosophers, let me end by addressing two connected questions to them.

> Is it their opinion that all capacities to understand novel sentences (to *know*, I stress, what they mean) are equally inexplicable, or do they believe that scope is provided for one kind of explanation of how it is that a speaker knows what a new sentence means when and only when it can be shown to contain elements which also occur in sentences with whose use he is already familiar?

On the assumption that their answer to my first question is 'Yes', I come to my second:

> Do they think that it is sufficient to provide an explanation of the kind which the occurrence of familiar expressions makes possible simply by showing that the new sentence does contain expressions which also occur in sentences with whose use he is already familiar, or do they believe, in view of the evident possibility of ambiguity, that something else must be provided? If so, how does this further part of the explanation differ from a statement of the regularity between the old use and the new?

Notes

1 C. Wright, 'Rule-following, objectivity and the theory of meaning', in S. Holtzman and C. Leich (eds), *Wittgenstein: To Follow a Rule* (London: Routledge and Kegan Paul, 1981), p. 110.
2 Ibid., p. 112.
3 Ibid., pp. 115–16.
4 W.V. Quine, 'Methodological reflections on current linguistic theory', in D. Davidson and G. Harman (eds), *Semantics of Natural Language* (Dordrecht: Reidel, 1972), pp. 442–54.
5 P. Ladefoged and D.E. Broadbent, 'Perception of sequences in auditory events', *Quarterly Journal of Experimental Psychology* 13 (1960), pp. 162–70. See also

J.A. Fodor and T.G. Bever, 'The psychological reality of linguistic segments', *Journal of Verbal Learning and Verbal Behaviour* 4 (1965), pp. 414–20.

6 For an account of the 'Fregean' approach to quantifiers, see my paper 'Pronouns, quantifiers and relative clauses (I)', *Canadian Journal of Philosophy* 7 (1977), pp. 467–536.

7 L. Wittgenstein, *On Certainty* (Oxford: Blackwell, 1969), sect. 141.

8 See T. Nagel, *The Possibility of Altruism* (Oxford: Clarendon Press, 1970), chap. 7.

9 See P.F. Strawson, *Individuals* (London: Methuen, 1959), chap. 3, sect. 4.

10 Wright, 'Rule-following', p. 113.

IIIE

THINKING AND LANGUAGE

28

G. Harman, "Language, Thought, and Communication"

I shall discuss two apparently conflicting views about our use of natural language. The first view, that language is used primarily in thought, has rarely been given explicit formulation but may be associated with the theories of Noam Chomsky, W. V. Quine, and Wilfrid Sellars. The second view, that language is used primarily in communication, has been explicitly put forward by J. A. Fodor and J. J. Katz and may also be associated (I think) with the theories of Paul Ziff and Donald Davidson. I shall describe each view and then try to say where I think the truth lies.

The view that language is used primarily in thought

Chomsky (1964) takes the primary function of language to be its use in the free expression of thought. He speaks approvingly of Humboldt's emphasis on the connection between language and thought, especially the way in which a particular language brings with it a world view that colours perception, thought, and feeling. According to Chomsky's description of Humboldt's view, to have a language is to have a system of concepts,

> and it is the place of a concept within this system (which may differ somewhat from speaker to speaker) that in part, determines the way in which the hearer understands a linguistic expression ... [T]he concepts so formed are systematically interrelated in an 'inner totality', with varying interconnections and structural relations ... This inner totality, formed by the use of language in thought, conception and expression of feeling, functions as a conceptual world interposed through the constant activity of the mind between itself and the actual objects, and it is within this system that a word obtains its value ... Consequently, a language should not be regarded merely, or primarily, as a means of communication ... and the instrumental use of language (its use for achieving concrete aims) is derivative and subsidiary. It is, for Humboldt, typical only of parasitic systems (e.g. ... the lingua franca along the Mediterranean coast). (1964: 58–9)

Now this view, that language is used primarily in thought, need not imply that all or even most thinking or theorizing is in some natural language. We may reasonably suppose that animals think, that children can think before they learn a natural language, and that speakers of a natural language can have thoughts they cannot express in language. The view is, rather, that anyone who fully learns a natural language can and does sometimes think in that language. More precisely, it is that some of a speaker's so-called propositional attitudes are to be construed as, at bottom, attitudes involving sentences of her language. A speaker of English may believe that the door is open by using the sentence, 'The door is open'. Another may fear that the door is open by being in a state of fear that involves that sentence. A third may think of the door's being open by adopting an appropriate attitude involving the sentence.

Strictly speaking, sentential attitudes involve sentences with one or another more or less detailed grammatical analysis. I shall return to this point near the end of this essay. For now, I shall speak loosely of sentential attitudes as attitudes involving sentences. (This is not to say that they are attitudes *toward* sentences. They are not attitudes *about* sentences.)

In this view, linguistic communication is the communication of thought. The parties involved typically communicate using the same language they use in thinking. The words used to communicate a thought are the same as those one 'says to oneself' when one has that thought. Linguistic communication does not typically require any complicated system of coding and decoding. Our usual translation scheme for understanding others is the identity relation. Words are used to communicate thoughts that would ordinarily be thought in those very words. It is true that allowance must sometimes be made for irony and other such devices; but in that case the thought communicated is some simple function of what would be normally communicated by a literal use of those words.

More precisely, linguistic communication typically involves communication of what is sometimes called 'propositional content'. A speaker says, 'The door is shut', 'Shut the door', 'Is the door shut?' or some such thing. He does so in part to get his hearer to think of the door's being shut. This first view holds that in such a situation, if communication is successful, the hearer will think of the door's being shut by adopting a state of mind that consists in part in a token of the sentence, 'The door is shut'. There is no claim that a person can think of the door's being shut *only* by using the sentence, 'The door is shut'. There are various ways in which a person might think of the door's being shut. But, normally, when a speaker successfully communicates in English by saying, 'The door is shut', etc., both speaker and hearer think of the door's being shut by using the English sentence, 'The door is shut'.

Even more precisely, sentential attitudes involve sentences with particular grammatical analyses. It is sufficient that the hearer should use the sentence uttered with the appropriate analysis. In this sense, linguistic communication does not typically make use of complex principles of coding and decoding and our usual translation scheme is the identity scheme. The hearer need only hear the sentence uttered as having the appropriate structural description and does not need to go on to translate the sentence, under that analysis, into anything else in order to understand it.

Proponents of the view that language is primarily used in thought can point out that, although one *can* use a natural language as a code, so that one's listeners would have to use complicated principles of decoding in order to understand what has been said, that is not an ordinary case of linguistic communication. They can also point out that, when a person learns a second language, she may at first have to treat the new language as a code; but hopefully the person soon learns to think directly in the second language and to communicate with other speakers of that language in the ordinary way, which does not involve complex coding and decoding or translation.

Furthermore, proponents can say, when a person thinks out loud, it is not always true that she has to find a linguistic way to express something that exists apart from language. Without language many thoughts and other psychological attitudes would not even be possible. In learning her first natural language, a child does not simply learn a code which she can use in communicating her thoughts to others and in decoding what they say. She acquires a system of representation in which she may express thoughts made possible by that very system. This is obvious when one acquires for the first time the language of a science or of mathematics. The claim is that it is no less true when one learns one's first natural language.

We now have a rough sketch of the view that language is used primarily in thought, I shall say more about that view below. Now I want to describe the apparently conflicting theory that communication provides the primary use of language.

The view that language is used primarily in communication

A compositional theory of meaning holds that a hearer determines what the meaning of an utterance is on the basis of her knowledge of the meaning of its parts and her knowledge of its syntactic structure. Such a view follows naturally from the picture of communication that takes it to involve complex coding and decoding. On that picture, to understand (the meaning of) a sentence is to know what (nonverbal) thought or thoughts the sentence encodes. Meanings are identified with the relevant thoughts. Hence the view is that to know the meaning of an expression is to know what meaning, i.e. thought, the code associates with that sentence. In this view, a general theory of meaning of a language is given by the principles of the code that defines the sound–meaning correspondence for the language. Because of the unbounded nature of language, these principles would have to be compositional or recursive.

The rules of coding and decoding are to be given by a grammar in a wide sense of this term. The grammar has three components, a syntactic component that connects a phonological component with a semantic component.

597

And as Katz describes it, '[W]hereas the phonological component provides a phonetic shape for a sentence, the semantic component provides a representation of that message which actual utterances having this phonetic shape convey to speakers of the language in normal speech situations' (1966b: 151). Katz adds that

> The hypothesis on which we will base our model of the semantic component is that the process by which a speaker interprets each of the infinitely many sentences is a compositional process in which the meaning of any syntactically compound constituent of a sentence is obtained as a function of the meanings of the parts of the constituent . . .
>
> This means that the semantic component will have two subcomponents: a *dictionary* that provides a representation of the meaning of each of the words in the language, and a system of *projection rules* that provide the combinatorial machinery for projecting the semantic representation for all supraword constituents in a sentence from the representations that are given in the dictionary for the meanings of the words in the sentence. (152–3)

Here meanings are to be identified with what Katz calls 'readings'. He continues,

> Projection rules operate on underlying phrase markers that are partially interpreted in the sense of having sets of readings assigned only to the lower level elements in them. They combine readings already assigned to constituents to form derived readings for constituents which, as yet, have had no readings assigned to them . . . Each constituent of an underlying phrase marker is thus assigned a set of readings, until the highest constituent, the whole sentence, is reached and assigned a set of readings, too. (164–5)

This theory would be appropriate as an account of the meaning of expressions in one language, e.g. Russian, given in another language taken to be antecedently understood, e.g., English. In that case one would want some general principles for translating Russian into English. Such principles would enable one to know the meaning of Russian expressions because one already knows (in the ordinary sense of this phrase) the meaning of the corresponding English expressions. Katz tries to make the same trick work in order to give an account of the meaning of sentences in English. In effect he envisages a theory that gives principles for translating from English into Mentalese. He thinks these principles are sufficient because one already knows Mentalese.

Meaning in Mentalese?

Katz's theory of communication is circular, if Mentalese is simply English used to think in. And, if Mentalese is not simply English used to think in, the theory simply shifts the problem back one step. How are we to give an account of meaning for Mentalese? We cannot continue forever to give as our theory of meaning a way to translate one system of representation into another. At some point a different account is needed. Katz's theory appears only to delay the moment of confrontation.

There are two distinct issues here. The first is the difficult quasi-empirical question whether thought is in the relevant sense verbal. Let us postpone discussion of that issue for a moment. The second issue is the methodological question whether a semantic theory may presuppose a theory of the nature of thought. Proponents of the view that language is primarily used for thought take semantics to be part of such a theory of the nature of thought. They argue, as it were, that semantics must be concerned in the first instance with the content of thoughts.

Katz assumes that no account need be given of the content of thoughts, as if Mentalese were intrinsically intelligible. That is exactly the sort of view Bloomfield (1933, 1955) attacked as 'mentalistic'. In an influential article, Katz (1966a) attempts to answer Bloomfield but only blurs the issue, since he never considers whether Bloomfield's criticisms of mentalism apply against a theory that assumes semantics can be unconcerned with the meaning of thoughts because of their supposed intrinsic intelligibility.

I argue that a theory of the meaning of messages must presuppose a theory of the content of thoughts. The former theory might resemble that proposed by Paul Grice. According to Grice (1957), the thought meant is the one the speaker intends the hearer to think the speaker has, by virtue of his recognition of the speaker's intention. However that may be, in normal linguistic communication speakers and hearers rely on a regular association between messages and thoughts. Those philosophers and linguists who think that language is used primarily in communication suppose that this association is between sentences in, for example, English (conceived under particular structural descriptions) and, as it were, sentences in Mentalese. Those who believe that language is used primarily in thought suppose that the association is a relatively trivial one, since the language used to communicate with is normally the same as that used to think with.

A theory of the content of thought might exploit the Humboldtian idea that the meaning of a linguistic expression is derived from its function in thought as determined by its place in one's total conceptual scheme. We might consider the influence of perception on thought, the role of inference in allowing one to pass from some thoughts to others, and the way thought leads to action. The resulting theory might be like that proposed in Sellars (1963). Sellars identifies the meaning of an expression with its (potential) role in the evidence-inference-action language game of thought. Similar theories have been proposed by various philosophers, e.g. Carnap (1936, 1937, 1956), Ayer (1936, 1940), and Hampshire (1959). And Quine (1960) has argued that meaning at this level admits of a special sort of indeterminacy.

According to proponents of the view that language is used primarily in thought, a compositional theory of meaning of the sort defended in Katz (1966b) provides neither an account of the meaning of language as used to think with nor an account of the meaning of language as used to communicate with. They claim that it cannot provide a theory of the meaning of thought, since a speaker does not understand the words he uses in thinking by assigning readings to them, and that it cannot provide a theory of the meaning of a message, since it treats a relatively simple problem of interpretation as if it were more complicated.

Composition and communication

Compositional theories of meaning assume that language is used primarily in communication. Davidson (1965) argues for compositionality as follows. He says, first, '[W]e are entitled to consider in advance of empirical study what we shall count as knowing a language, how we shall describe the skill or ability of a person who has learned to speak a language.' He wants to argue for the condition 'that we must be able to specify, in a way that depends effectively and solely on formal considerations, what every sentence means. With the right psychological trappings, our theory should equip us to say, for an arbitrary sentence, what a speaker of the language means by that sentence (or takes it to mean).' That last reference, to what a speaker takes the sentence to mean, sounds like Katz's view described above, which assumes that to give an account of meaning for some language is to say how a 'speaker–hearer' is able to correlate meanings, *qua* thoughts, with sentences. This suspicion is confirmed by Davidson's explicit argument for the compositional theory:

> These matters appear to be connected in the following informal way with the possibility of learning a language. When we can regard the meaning of each sentence as a function of a finite number of features of the sentence, we have an insight not only into what there is to be learned; we also understand how an infinite aptitude can be encompassed by finite accomplishments. Suppose on the other hand the language lacks this feature; then no matter how many sentences a would-be speaker learns to produce and understand, there will remain others whose meanings are not given by the rules already mastered. It is natural to say such a language is unlearnable. This argument depends, of course, on a number of empirical assumptions: for example, that we do not at some point suddenly acquire an ability to intuit the meanings of sentences on no rule at all; that each new item of vocabulary, or new grammatical rule takes some finite time to be learned; that man is mortal. (1965: 387–8)

This argument makes sense only in the presence of an assumption, which Davidson (1967) explicitly acknowledges, that 'speakers of a language can effectively determine the meaning or meanings of an arbitrary expression (if it has a meaning)', where that is understood to mean that a speaker (hearer) understands a sentence by translating it into its Mentalese counterpart (and where Mentalese is not the language used in communication). If speakers of a language can effectively determine the meaning of messages in ordinary linguistic communication by using the identity mapping of verbal message onto verbal thought, the assumption does not support Davidson's argument for a compositional theory of meaning.

In the end Davidson (1967) argues for a version of the theory that meaning is given by truth conditions. That is not very different from Katz's (1966b) theory. According to Katz, a speaker knows the meaning of sentences of his language because he has mastered the complicated rules that correlate sentences with thoughts. According to Davidson, a speaker knows the meaning of sentences of his language because he has mastered the complicated rules of a truth definition for his language that correlate sentences with truth conditions. Katz's theory is in trouble if the relevant thoughts are verbal. The same difficulty faces Davidson in a slightly different form, if the relevant knowledge of truth conditions is verbal. Katz would say that the speaker understands the sentence 'Snow is white' by virtue of the fact that he has correlated it with the thought that snow is white. Davidson would (presumably) say that the speaker understands that sentence by virtue of the fact that he knows it is true if and only if snow is white. The difficulty in either case is that the speaker needs some way to represent to himself snow's being white. If the relevant speaker uses the words 'Snow is white' to represent in the relevant way that snow is white, both Katz's and Davidson's theories are circular. And if speakers have available a form of Mentalese in which they can represent that snow is white, so that the two theories avoid circularity, there is still the problem of meaning for Mentalese.

The point is that no reason has been given for a compositional theory of meaning for any system of representation we think in, be it Mentalese or English. This point has obvious implications for linguistics, and for philosophy too, if only of a negative sort. For example, Davidson (1965) uses his theory in order to support objections to certain theories about the logical form of belief sentences. Since his argument for a compositional theory of meaning fails for the language one thinks in, those objections have no force against theories about the logical form of belief sentences used in thinking or theorizing.

Similar remarks apply to the compositional theory of meaning in Ziff (1960). Ziff asserts that '[T]he semantic analysis of an utterance consists in associating with it some set of conditions [and] the semantic analysis of a morphological element having meaning in the language consists in associating with it some set of conditions . . .' Very roughly speaking, the relevant conditions are those that must obtain if something is to be uttered without deviance from relevant nonsyntactic semantic regularities.

Ziff says, 'In formulating the theory presented here I have had but one objective in mind, viz. that of determining a method and a means of evaluating and choosing between competing analyses of words and utterances'. If 'analysis' here means 'philosophical analysis', Ziff's enterprise must be counted a success, especially in the light of his careful discussion of the analysis of the word 'good' in the final chapter. And since analysis is perhaps a kind of translation or decoding, it may be possible to defend a compositional theory of meaning as a compositional theory of analysis. (One must see that a proposed analysis of a word is adequate for various contexts and is consistent with analyses suggested for other words.)

But Ziff does not give quite that argument for a compositional theory of meaning; and the argument he does give indicates that he wants more from his theory than a way of evaluating philosophical analyses. His own argument seems to assume that a speaker understands sentences by virtue of being able to give analyses or explications of them. In Ziff (1960) the argument goes like this:

> In a general form, the principle of composition is absolutely essential to anything that we are prepared to call a natural language, a language that can be spoken and understood in the way any natural language can in fact be spoken or understood.
>
> How is it that one can understand what is said if what is said has not been said before? Any language whatever allows for the utterance of new utterances both by the reiteration of old ones and by the formation of new ones out of combinations of old elements. Hence any natural language whatever allows for the utterance of both novel utterance tokens and novel utterance types. If a new utterance is uttered and if the utterance is not then and there to be given an arbitrary explication, that one is able to understand what is said in or by uttering the utterance must in some way at least be partially owing to one's familiarity with the syntactic structure of the utterance. (61)

Ziff (1966) is more explicit:

> [P]art of what is involved in understanding an utterance is understanding what conditions are relevantly associated with the utterance . . .
>
> Someone says 'Hippopotami are graceful' and we understand what is said. In some cases we understand what is said without attending to the discourse the utterance has occurred in or without attending to the context of utterance. How do we do it?
>
> It seems reasonable to suppose that part of what is involved is this: Such an utterance is understood on the basis of its syntactic structure and morphemic constitution.
>
> Assuming that part of what is involved in understanding an utterance is understanding what conditions are relevantly associated with the utterance, this means that we take a certain set of conditions to be associated with such an utterance on the basis of its syntactic structure and morphemic constitution. (104–5)

To this the same remarks apply as to the theories of Katz and of Davidson. A speaker can *understand* that certain conditions are associated with an utterance and can take certain conditions to be associated with an utterance only if he has some way to represent to himself that the conditions are associated with the utterance. And even if the speaker uses Mentalese to represent utterance-conditions correlations, the problem of meaning is merely pushed back one step to Mentalese. Ziff fares no better than Katz or Davidson in showing that we need a compositional theory of meaning for the system of representation that we think with. If speakers of English think in English and we rely on that fact in communication, Ziff gives us no reason why we need a compositional theory of meaning for English.

Language used in thought

There are levels of meaning. A theory of the first level must account for the meaning of an expression as a function of its role in thought. A theory of the second level must account for the meaning of an expression used to communicate a thought. A theory of the second level must presuppose the first, since linguistic communication typically communicates a thought that can be expressed (roughly speaking) in the same words used for communication.

Katz and Fodor (1964) put forward a level two theory of meaning in communication. The theory is supposed to account for 'the way that speakers understand sentences'. That may suggest it is the sort of theory Grice (1957) tries to develop. But Katz and Fodor describe it as an account of the meaning or meanings a sentence has when taken in isolation from possible settings in actual discourse. In other words, their theory is restricted to giving an account of meaning for those cases in which the message communicates a thought that in an alternative view can be expressed in (roughly) the same words as those in which the message is expressed. Katz and Fodor say that an additional theory is needed to account for the interpretation or interpretations assigned when a sentence occurs in a particular setting. Furthermore, they argue that the latter theory must presuppose the one they present. Thus they come close to the distinction between levels one and two, and in a way they attempt to provide a theory of level one. Or rather, in their approach three theories are needed, although they do not acknowledge this. First, there is a theory of the content of thought, an account of content for whatever system of representation one uses to think with. Katz and Fodor say nothing about this theory, perhaps because they take thoughts to be intrinsically intelligible. On the alternative view, this theory is the most important part of the theory of meaning. Second, there is the theory Katz and Fodor describe that would associate sentences (under various structural descriptions) used in communication with meanings they have (in isolation from setting and discourse). This theory would associate sentences of English (with their structural descriptions) with 'readings' in the system of representation used in thinking. Katz and Fodor take this theory to be the central part of the theory of meaning, which amounts to a theory of how sentences in e.g. English are to be translated into Mentalese. The alternative view takes this part of the theory to be trivial, on the grounds that speakers of English think in English and can use what amounts to the identity scheme of translation. (I shall say more about this in a moment.) Third, there is the theory of the meaning of a message in a particular linguistic and nonlinguistic setting. Both sides agree that this is an important part of a theory of meaning and that it presupposes the other parts.

How are we to decide between a view like Katz and Fodor's, which takes language to be used primarily in communication, and the alternative which takes language to be used in thought? Katz (1967) claims that his and Fodor's semantic theory is needed in order to explain a great number of different things that cannot be explained on the alternative account, namely, 'semantic anomaly and ambiguity', 'synonymy, paraphrase, antonymy, semantic distinctness, semantic similarity, inclusion of senses, inconsistency, analyticity, contradiction, syntheticity, entailment, possible answers to a question, and so forth'. We have no right to reject their semantic theory unless we have some other method to explain or explain away the phenomena in question.

In the remainder of this essay I want to describe and defend one alternative method. I shall be concerned mainly with the level one theory of meaning, that is, the theory of the content of language used to think in. I shall say something about level two, which is concerned with the meaning of messages, only indirectly and in passing.

What is it for an expression to have a content on level one? It is certainly not that the relevant person, the 'thinker', can assign it one or more 'readings'. It is rather that she can use it in thought, i.e. that it has a role in her evidence-inference-action language game. She may be able to use the expression in direct perceptual reports. She must certainly be able to use it in (theoretical and practical) reasoning. She must be able to recognize implications involving the expression.

Sometimes an implication is formal. It depends only on the logical or grammatical form of relevant expressions and is not a function of nonlogical or nongrammatical vocabulary. In order to account for a person's ability to recognize such a formal implication, it is plausible to suppose that the sentences she uses in thought are grammatically structured. I shall return to this point in a moment. But first I note that it is not sufficient for full understanding of an expression that one be able to recognize formal implications involving that expression; at best this shows merely that one understands the expression as having a particular grammatical form. One must also be able to give paraphrases and notice implications that involve changes in nonlogical and nongrammatical vocabulary. One must be able to see what sentences containing the relevant expression imply, what they are equivalent to, etc.

It is here that Katz and others have thought that appeal must be made to meaning, to entailment by virtue of meaning, to equivalence by virtue of meaning, etc. Not so. The relevant notions of equivalence and of implication are ordinary ones: equivalence or implication with respect to one's background assumptions, where no distinctions need be made between analytic or synthetic background assumptions. One has an understanding of an expression to the extent that one can paraphrase sentences containing it, can make inferences involving such sentences, etc. It adds nothing to one's understanding if one can distinguish 'analytic' equivalences and implications from 'synthetic' ones. In fact, most people cannot do so. Only those who have been 'indoctrinated' can; and they are not the only ones who understand the language they think in.

It might be objected that sentences used in thinking are often ambiguous. How can we account for that – and for a person's ability to understand or interpret a sentence one way at one time and another way at another time? Can we account for it without assuming that she assigns an interpretation or 'reading' to the sentence in the way in which Katz suggests? Well, we can and we can't. An expression is ambiguous if a person can sometimes treat it as having one sort of role and at other times treat it as having a different role. Treated one way it admits of paraphrases it does not admit when treated the other way. This difference in paraphrasability represents the difference in interpretation; but recall that paraphrasability is relative to background knowledge and need not permit any analytic–synthetic distinction.

To account for the difference in the ways a person can use an ambiguous expression we must suppose that she does not simply view it as a sequence of words. She views it, or hears it, as having a particular syntactic structure and as containing words in one or another of their possible senses. Let us consider each of these things in turn.

Syntactically ambiguous sentences may be heard as having either of two (or more) different syntactic structures They are like lines on paper which may be seen as a staircase viewed from the back or from the front. Or they are like a group of dots that may be seen as two groups in one way or as two other groups in another way. Or they are like a figure that can be seen either as a duck or as a rabbit. The sentence, 'They are visiting philosophers,' may be understood in two different ways, depending on whether we take 'are visiting' together or 'visiting philosophers' together. We hear the sentence as admitting either of two groups of paraphrases, either 'They are philosophers who are visiting, etc. or 'They are visiting some philosophers', etc. Similarly, the sentence 'Visiting Philosophers can be unpleasant', differs in interpretation depending on its grammatical structure, although the difference is not simply a matter of grouping on the surface. It is rather a matter of the source of 'visiting philosophers'. Roughly speaking, it may come from 'someone visits philosophers' or from 'philosophers visit someone'. It is true that the average person is quite ignorant of the relevant linguistic principles. But that does not mean he fails to hear that sentence as having one or another of the indicated structures. A person can see lines on a page as forming one or another three-dimensional structure without knowing any geometry. In order to account for the way in which a person can deal with ambiguous sentences we must assume that in some sense she uses a sentence in thought with one or another syntactic structure. The same conclusion is needed in order to account for the formal inferences a person can make, quite apart from considerations of ambiguity.

Similarly, in order to account for the way in which a person deals with ambiguous words, we must assume that she distinguishes a word used in one sense from the same word used in another sense. But we can do that without assuming that she makes the distinction by assigning different readings to the word. She may mark the distinction in sentences by an arbitrary device as simple as a subscript. The inferences and paraphrases that are then permissible depend in general on the subscript selected (Harman 1966). One reason why no more is needed than a subscript is that the relevant sorts of inference and paraphrase are those possible by virtue of background information. Such background information itself must be 'stored' as sentences under certain structural descriptions including subscripted words. But a person can understand the expressions she uses without having divided her background information into a part that is true by 'definition' (the dictionary) and another part that is not true by definition (the encyclopaedia).

We think with sentences that have particular structural descriptions, where the subscripts that distinguish word senses are part of their structural descriptions. So-called propositional attitudes are structured sentential attitudes, where the relevant sentences have particular structural descriptions. In understanding what someone else says to us, we must determine the content of her utterance taken literally. It is sufficient that we should hear her words as having a particular syntactic structure. That is not to say that we come (even unconsciously) to know that it has a particular structure; and it is certainly not to say that we have knowledge of the principles that relate phonetic representations to structural descriptions. The situation is strictly analogous to other cases of perceiving something as something. We perceive a series of lines as making up a particular three-dimensional structure without explicitly thinking about that structure, indeed without knowing anything about geometrical structure. We can certainly do so without knowing rules that relate two-dimensional figures and three-dimensional structures.

Sounds reach a person's ears and, after physiological processes we know little about, she perceives or conceives a sentence with a particular structural description. Her understanding of that sentence is represented not by her having assigned it a 'reading' in Mentalese but rather by her being able to use the sentence with that structural description in her thought. If we like, we may still speak of 'decoding' here. One decodes certain sounds into a sentence plus structural description. But this is not enough for the sort of decoding that Katz refers to, namely, decoding into intrinsically intelligible Mentalese 'readings'.

I conclude that it is possible to give an account of how people understand sentences without postulating that a speaker understands sentences by assigning such readings to them.

Anomaly and synonymy

Katz and Fodor have one more argument. They claim that their semantic theory can account for a couple of things that it would be difficult to handle in any other way. First, Katz and Fodor (1964) argue that their theory can show how certain interpretations of a sentence that are grammatically possible are semantically ruled out, so that they can account for a certain amount of disambiguation with their theory. Second, Katz (1964, 1966b, 1967) argues that the theory shows how certain sentences are analytic, others contradictory, and still others synthetic, so that the theory can account for native speakers' intuitive judgements about analyticity, etc.

In reply, I say that there is no such thing as semantic anomaly and no such distinction as the analytic–synthetic distinction. To believe otherwise is to suffer from a lack of imagination.

For example, Katz and Fodor argue as follows:

> Now let S be the sentence *The paint is silent*. English speakers will at once recognize that this sentence is anomalous in some way. For example, they will distinguish it from such sentences as *The paint is wet* and *The paint is yellow* by applying to it such epithets as 'odd,' 'peculiar,' and 'bizarre' . . . Hence, another facet of the semantic ability of the speaker is that of detecting semantic anomalies. (1964: 402–3)

But I say that whatever anomaly there is in the phrase 'silent paint' arises from the fact that paints do not emit noise. If some paints did and some did not, 'silent paint' would not be anomalous. And that is to say that there is nothing peculiarly semantic about the anomaly. Its anomaly is a result of our general nonlinguistic knowledge of the world.

Again, Katz and Fodor (1964) argue that a theory that incorporates only the sort of considerations I have sketched above

> will not be able to distinguish the correct sense of 'seal' in 'One of the oil seals in my car is leaking' from such incorrect senses as 'a device bearing a design so made that it can impart an impression' or 'an impression made by such a device' or 'the material upon which the impression is made' or 'an ornamental or commemorative stamp' and so forth, since all of these senses can apply to nominal occurrences of 'seal' (409)

But, surely, it requires only a little imagination to see that 'seal' may have any of these senses, although in ordinary discourse it would be more likely to have the sense the authors have in mind (Bolinger 1965).

McCawley (1970) makes a similar point with respect to purported syntactic anomalies of a certain type

> Moreover, it appears incorrect to regard many so-called 'selectional violations' as not corresponding to possible messages, since many of them can turn up in reports of dreams:
>
> (2) I dreamed that my toothbrush was pregnant.
> (3) I dreamed that I poured my mother into an inkwell.

(4) I dreamed that I was a proton and fell in love with a shapely green-and-orange-striped electron.

or in reports of the beliefs of other persons:

(5) John thinks that electrons are green with orange stripes.
(6) John thinks that his toothbrush is trying to kill him.
(7) John thinks that ideas are physical objects and are green with orange stripes.

or in the speech of psychotics. While one might suggest that a paranoid who says things like

(8) My toothbrush is alive and is trying to kill me.

has different selectional restrictions from a normal person, it is pointless to do so, since the difference in 'selectional restriction' will correspond exactly to a difference in beliefs as to one's relationship with inanimate objects; a person who utters sentences such as (8) should be referred to a psychiatric clinic, not to a remedial English course.

McCawley's argument supports the conclusion that there is no real distinction between semantic anomaly and anomaly due to 'extralinguistic factors'.

Similar points apply to Katz's claims about analyticity, etc. First, the fact that people have 'intuitions' about analyticity shows at best that there is a distinction between 'seems analytic to certain people' and 'seems synthetic to them'. It does not show that there are sentences that are really analytic as opposed to others that are synthetic. The fact that people once had intuitions that some women were witches and others not, certainly fails to show that there were women that really were witches as opposed to others that were not.

Second, the intuitive distinction Katz and others make between analytic and synthetic truths is easily explained away without appeal to their semantic theory. People who have such intuitions suffer from a lack of imagination. The intuitions come from their inability to imagine that certain sentences are false. But as Putnam (1962), Moravcsik (1965), and others have pointed out, after a little practice such things can be imagined.

Final remarks

Consider the two views. On the first view, a person who speaks a natural language can think in that language and does not need to translate sentences conceived into some other system of representation, Mentalese. On this view, Mentalese incorporates one's natural language. On the second view, a person cannot think in language and must translate sentences of her language into Mentalese. The incorporation view has the advantage over the translation view that it provides a natural explanation of the way in which learning one's first language makes possible thoughts and other propositional attitudes one would not otherwise have. The translation view must add some special principle to account for this. Furthermore, the translation view suggests things that are false about anomaly, synonymy, etc.

It is difficult to see how, say, neurophysiological evidence could support one of the views against the other (except by pointing to further relatively behavioural phenomena to be explained). For, as descriptions of the mechanism of the brain, the two views must be taken to be descriptions of a fairly abstract sort. And it is not easy to see how any neurological mechanism that might account for the relevant behaviour and that could be interpreted as an instantiation of one of the descriptions could not also be interpreted as an instantiation of the other. So far then, I see no reason not to accept the incorporation view.

References

Ayer, A.J. (1936) *Language, Truth and Logic.* London: Gollancz.
—— (1940) *The Foundations of Empirical Knowledge.* London: Macmillan.
Bloomfield, L. (1933) *Language.* New York: Holt.
—— (1955) "Linguistic aspects of science." *International Encyclopedia of Unified Science.* Chicago, Ill.: University of Chicago Press.
Bolinger, D. (1965) "The atomization of meaning." *Language* 41: 555–73.
Carnap, R. (1936) "Testability and meaning", Pt. 1. *Philosophy of Science* 3: 419–71.
—— (1937) "Testability and meaning", Pt. 2. *Philosophy of Science* 4: 1–40.
—— (1956) "Meaning and synonymy in natural languages." In R. Carnap, *Meaning and Necessity*, 2nd edn. Chicago, Ill.: University of Chicago Press, 233–47.
Chomsky, N (1964) "Current issues in linguistic theory." In J. Fodor and J. Katz (eds.), *The Structure of Language.* Englewood Cliffs, N.J.: Prentice-Hall.
Davidson, D. (1965) "Theories of meaning and learnable languages." In Y. Bar-Hillel (ed.), *Logic, Methodology and Philosophy of Science: Proceedings of the 1964 International Congress.* Amsterdam: North-Holland.
—— (1967) "Truth and meaning." *Synthese* 17: 304–23.
Grice, H.P. (1957) "Meaning." *Philosophical Review* 66: 377–88.
Hampshire, S. (1959) *Thought and Action.* London: Chatto & Windus.
Harman, G (1966) "What an adequate grammar could do." *Foundations of Language* 2: 134–6.
Katz, J. (1964) "Analyticity and contradiction in natural language." In J. Fodor and J. Katz (eds), *The Structure of Language.* Englewood Cliffs, N.J.: Prentice-Hall.
—— (1966a) "Mentalism in lingustics." *Language* 40: 124–37.
—— (1966b) *The Philosophy of Language.* New York: Harper & Row.
—— (1967) "Some remarks on quine on analyticity." *Journal of Philosophy* 64: 35–52.
Katz, J. and Fodor, J. (1964) "The structure of semantic theory." In J. Fodor and J. Katz (eds), *The Structure of Language.* Englewood Cliffs, N.J.: Prentice-Hall.
McCawley, J.D. (1970). "Where do noun phrases come from?" In P.S. Rosenbaum (ed.), *Readings in English Transformational Grammar.* Waltham, Mass.: Ginn.
Moravcsik, J.M.E. (1965) "The analytic and the nonempirical." *Journal of Philosophy* 62: 421–3.

Putnam, H. (1962) "It ain't necessarily so." *Journal of Philosophy* 59: 658–71.

Quine, W.V. (1960) *Word and Object*. Cambridge, Mass.: MIT Press.

Sellars, W. (1963) "Some reflections on language games." In W. Sellars, *Science, Perception, and Reality*. London: Routledge & Kegan Paul.

Ziff, P. (1960) *Semantic Analysis*. Ithaca, N.Y.: Cornell University Press.

—— (1966) "On understanding 'Understanding utterances'." In P. Ziff, *Philosophic Turnings*. Ithaca, N.Y.: Cornell University Press.

29

P. Carruthers, "The Cognitive Functions of Language"

1 Introduction

Natural language looms large in the cognitive lives of ordinary folk. Although proportions vary, many people seem to spend a good deal of their waking activity engaged in "inner speech," with imaged natural language sentences occupying a significant proportion of the stream of their conscious mentality.

This bit of folk wisdom has been corroborated by Hurlburt (1990, 1993), who devised a method for sampling people's inner experience. Subjects wore headphones during the course of the day, through which they heard, at various intervals, a randomly generated series of bleeps. When they heard a bleep, they were instructed to immediately "freeze" what was passing through their consciousness at that exact moment and then make a note of it, before elaborating on it later in a follow-up interview. Although frequency varied widely, all normal (as opposed to schizophrenic) subjects reported experiencing inner speech on some occasions – with the minimum being 7 percent of occasions sampled, and the maximum being 80 percent. Most subjects reported inner speech on more than half of the occasions sampled. (The majority of subjects also reported the occurrence of visual images and emotional feelings – on between 0 percent and 50 percent of occasions sampled in each case.) Think about it: more than half of the total set of moments which go to make up someone's conscious waking life occupied with inner speech – that's well-nigh continuous!

Admittedly, the sample-sizes in Hurlburt's studies were small; and other interpretations of the data are possible. (Perhaps the reports of linguistically-clothed thoughts occurring at the time of the bleep were a product of *confabulation*, for example, reflecting people's naïve theory that thought *must* be in natural language. If so, this should be testable.) But let us suppose that inner verbalization is as ubiquitous as common-sense belief and Hulburt's data would suggest. Just what would all this inner verbalization be doing? What would be its function, or cognitive role? The naïve common-sense answer is that inner verbalization is constitutive of our thinking – it is that we think *by* talking to ourselves in inner speech (as well as by manipulating visual images,

611

etc.). Anyone who holds such a view endorses a version of what I shall call "the cognitive conception of language," which maintains that, besides its obvious communicative functions, language also has a direct role to play in normal human cognition (in thinking and reasoning).

Quite a different answer would be returned by most members of the cognitive science community, however. They endorse what I shall call "the (purely) communicative conception of language," according to which language is but an input-output system for central cognition. Believing that language is only a channel, *or conduit,* for transferring thoughts into and out of the mind, they are then obliged to claim that the stream of inner verbalization is more-or-less epiphenomenal in character. (Some possible minor cognitive roles for inner speech, which should nevertheless be acceptable to those adopting this perspective, will be canvassed later.) The real thinking will be going on elsewhere, in some other medium of representation.

One reason for the popularity of the communicative conception amongst cognitive scientists is that almost all now believe that language is a distinct input-output module of the mind (at least in *some* sense of "module," if not quite in Fodor's classic – 1983 – sense). And they find it difficult to see how the language faculty could *both* have this status *and* be importantly implicated in central cognition. But this reasoning is fallacious. Compare the case of visual imagination: Almost everyone now thinks that the visual system is a distinct input-module of the mind, containing a good deal of innate structure. But equally, most cognitive scientists now accept that visual *imagination* re-deploys the resources of the visual module for purposes of reasoning – for example, many of the same areas of the visual cortex are active when imagining as when seeing. (For a review of the evidence, see Kosslyn 1994.)

What is apparent is that central cognition can co-opt the resources of peripheral modules, activating some of their representations to subserve central cognitive functions of thinking and reasoning. The same is then possible in connection with language. It is quite consistent with language being an innately structured input and output module, that central cognition should access and deploy the resources of that module when engaging in certain kinds of reasoning and problem solving.

Note, too, that hardly anyone is likely to maintain that visual imagery is a mere epiphenomenon of central cognitive reasoning processes, playing no real role in those processes in its own right. On the contrary, it seems likely that there are many tasks which we cannot easily solve without deploying a visual (or other) image. For example, suppose you are asked (orally) to describe the shape which is enclosed within the capital letter "A." It seems entirely plausible that success in this task should require the generation of a visual image of that letter, from which the answer ("a triangle") can then be read off. So it appears that central cognition operates, in part, by co-opting the resources of the visual system to generate visual representations, which can be of use in solving a variety of spatial-reasoning tasks. And this then opens up the very real possibility that central cognition may also deploy the resources of the language system to generate representations of natural language sentences (in "inner speech"), which can similarly be of use in a variety of *conceptual* reasoning tasks.

There is at least one further reason why the cognitive conception of language has had a bad press within the cognitive science community in recent decades. (It continues to be popular in some areas of the social sciences and humanities, including philosophy.) This is that many of the forms of the thesis which have been defended by philosophers and by social scientists are implausibly strong, as we shall see in section 3 below. The unacceptability of these strong views has then resulted in *all* forms of the cognitive conception being tarred with the same brush.

A crucial liberalizing move, therefore, is to realize that the cognitive conception of language can come in many different strengths, each one of which needs to be considered separately on its own merits. In this paper I shall distinguish between some of the many different versions of the cognitive conception. I shall begin (in sect. 2) by discussing some weak claims concerning the cognitive functions of language that are largely uncontroversial. This will help to clarify just what (any interesting form of) the cognitive conception *is*, by way of contrast. I shall then (in sect. 3) consider some claims which are so strong that cognitive scientists are clearly right in rejecting them, before zeroing in on those which are both interesting and plausible (in sects. 4 and 5). I shall come to focus, in particular, on the thesis that natural language is the medium of inter-modular integration. This is a theoretical idea which has now begun to gather independent empirical support.

I should explain at the outset, however, that the thesis I shall be working towards is that it is natural language *syntax* which is crucially necessary for inter-modular integration. The hypothesis is that non-domain-specific thinking operates by accessing and manipulating the representations of the language faculty. More specifically, the claim is that non-domain-specific thoughts implicate representations in what Chomsky (1995) calls "logical form" (LF). Where these representations are *only* in LF, the thoughts in question will be non-conscious ones. But where the LF representation is used to generate a full-blown phonological representation (an imaged sentence), the thought will generally be conscious.[1]

I should emphasize that I shall not be claiming that syntax is logically required for inter-modular integration, of course. Nor shall I be claiming that only natural language syntax – with its associated recursive and hierarchical structures, compositionality, and generativity – could possibly play such a role in any form of cognition, human or not. Rather, my claim will be that syntax *does* play this role in human beings. It is a factual claim about the way in which our cognition happens to be structured, not an unrestricted modal claim arrived at by some sort of task-analysis.

I should also declare at the outset how I shall be using the word "thought" in this paper. Unless I signal otherwise, I intend all references to *thought* and *thinking* to be construed realistically. Thoughts are discrete, semantically-evaluable, causally-effective states, possessing component structure, and where those structures bear systematic relations to the structures of other, related, thoughts. So distinct thoughts have distinct physical realizations, which may be true or false, and which cause other such thoughts and behavior. And thoughts are built up out of component parts, where those parts belong to types which can be shared with other thoughts. It is not presupposed, however, that thoughts are borne by sentence-like structures. Although I shall be arguing that *some* thoughts are carried by sentences (namely, non-domain-specific thoughts which are carried by sentences of natural language), others might be carried by mental models or mental images of various kinds.

It is hugely controversial that there *are* such things as thoughts, thus construed, of course. And while I shall say a little in defense of this assumption below (in sect. 3.3), for the most part it is just that – an assumption – for present purposes. I can only plead that one can't do everything in one article, and that one has to start somewhere. Those who don't want to share this assumption should read what follows conditionally: if we *were* to accept that there are such things as realistically-construed thoughts, then how, if at all, should they be seen as related to natural language sentences?

Also, a word about the nature of the exercise before we proceed further. This article ranges over a great many specialist topics and literatures in a number of distinct disciplines. Of necessity, therefore, our discussion of any given subject must be relatively superficial, with most of the detail, together with many of the required qualifications and *caveats*, being omitted. Similarly, my arguments against some of the competitor theories have to be extremely brisk, and some quite large assumptions will have to get taken on board without proper examination. My goal, here, is just to map out an hypothesis space, using quite broad strokes, and then to motivate and discuss what I take to be the most plausible proposal within it.

2   Weak claims

Everyone will allow that language makes some cognitive difference. For example, everyone accepts that a human being with language and a human being without language would be very different, cognitively speaking. In this section I shall outline some of the reasons why.

2.1   *Language as the conduit of belief*

Everyone should agree that natural language is a necessary condition for human beings to be capable of entertaining at least some kinds of thought. Language is the conduit through which we acquire many of our beliefs and concepts, and in many of these cases we could hardly have acquired the component concepts in any other way. Concepts which have emerged out of many years of collective labor by scientists, for example – such as *electron*, *neutrino*, and *DNA* – would *de facto* be inaccessible to someone deprived of language. This much, at any rate, should be obvious. But all it really shows is that language is required for certain kinds of thought; not that language is actually involved in or is the representational vehicle of those thoughts.

It is often remarked, too, that the linguistic and cognitive abilities of young children will normally develop together. If children's language is advanced, then so will be their abilities across a range of tasks; and if children's language is delayed, then so will be their cognitive capacities. To cite just one item from a wealth of empirical evidence: Astington (1996) and Peterson and Siegal (1998) report finding a high correlation between language-ability and children's capacity to pass false-belief tasks, whose solution requires them to attribute, and reason from, the false belief of another person. Does this and similar data show that language is actually involved in children's thinking?

In the same spirit, we might be tempted to cite the immense cognitive deficits that can be observed in those rare cases where children grow up without exposure to natural language. Consider, for example, the cases of so-called "wolf children," who have survived in the wild in the company of animals, or of children kept by their parents locked away from all human contact (Malson 1972; Curtiss 1977). Consider, also, the cognitive limitations of profoundly deaf children born of hearing parents who have not yet learned to sign (Schaller 1991; Sacks 1989). These examples might be thought to show that human cognition is constructed in such away as to require the presence of natural language if it is to function properly.

But all that such data really show is, again, that language is a necessary condition for certain kinds of thought and types of cognitive process: not that it is actually implicated in those forms of thinking. And this is easily explicable from the standpoint of someone who endorses the standard cognitive science conception of language, as being but an input-output system for central cognition, or a mere communicative device. For language, in human beings, is a necessary condition of normal enculturation. Without language, there are many things which children cannot learn; and with delayed language, there are many things that children will learn only later. It is only to be expected, then, that cognitive and linguistic development should proceed in parallel. It does not follow that language is itself actually used in children's central cognition.

Another way of putting the point is that this proposed cognitive function of language is purely developmental – or diachronic – rather than synchronic. Nothing is said about the role of language in the cognition of adults, once a normal set of beliefs and concepts has been acquired. And the evidence from aphasia suggests that at least many aspects of cognition can continue to operate normally once language has been removed.

Aphasias come in many forms, of course, and in many different degrees of severity. And it is generally hard to know the extent of any collateral damage – that is, to know which other cognitive systems besides the language faculty may have been disabled as a result of the aphasia-causing brain-damage. But many patients with severe aphasia continue to be adept at visuo-spatial thinking, at least (Kertesz 1988), and many continue to manage quite well for themselves in their daily lives.

Consider, for example, the agrammatic aphasic man studied in detail by Varley (1998, 2002). He is incapable of either producing or comprehending sentences, and he also has considerable difficulty with vocabulary, particularly verbs. He has lost all mentalistic vocabulary ("belief," "wants," etc.), and his language system is essentially limited to nouns. Note that there is not a lot of explicit thinking that you can do using just nouns! (It should also be stressed that he has matching deficits of input and output, suggesting that it is the underlying system of linguistic knowledge which has been damaged.) Yet he continues to drive, and to have responsibility for the family finances. He is adept at communicating, using a mixture of single-word utterances and pantomime. And he has passed a range of tests of theory of mind (the standard battery of false-belief and deception tasks, explained using nouns and pantomime), as well as various tests of causal thinking and reasoning. It appears that, once language has done its developmental work of loading the mind with information, a good deal of adult cognition can thereafter survive its loss.

Since natural language is the conduit for many of our beliefs and for much of our enculturation, everyone should accept that language is immensely important for normal cognitive development. That language has this sort of cognitive function should be no news to anyone.[2]

2.2   *Language as sculpting cognition*

A stronger and more controversial thesis has been proposed and defended by some researchers over recent decades. This is that the process of language acquisition and enculturation does not merely serve to load the mind with beliefs and concepts, but actually sculpts our cognitive *processes* to some degree (Bowerman and Levinson 2001; Lucy 1992a, 1992b; Nelson 1996).[3]

For example, acquisition of Yucatec (as opposed to English) – in which plurals are rarely marked and many more nouns are treated grammatically as substance-terms like "mud" and "water" – leads subjects to see similarities amongst objects on the basis of material composition rather than shape (Lucy 1992b; Lucy and Gaskins 2001). And children brought up speaking Korean (as opposed to English) – in which verbs are highly inflected and massive noun ellipsis is permissible in informal speech – leads children to be much weaker at categorization tasks, but much better at means-ends tasks such as using a rake to pull a distant object towards them (Choi and Gopnik 1995; Gopnik 2001; Gopnik *et al.* 1996)

Fascinating as these data are, they do not, in themselves, support any version of the cognitive conception of language. This is because the reported effects of language on cognition are still entirely diachronic and developmental, rather than synchronic. The fact that acquiring one language as opposed to another causes subjects to attend to different things and to reason somewhat differently doesn't show that language itself is actually involved in people's thinking. Indeed, on the hypothesis proposed by Gopnik (2001), language-acquisition has these effects by providing evidence for a pre-linguistic theorizing capacity, which operates throughout development to construct children's systems of belief and inference.

2.3   Language as a cognitive scaffold

Other claims can be extracted from the work of Vygotsky (1934/1986), who argues that language and speech serve to scaffold the development of cognitive capacities in the growing child. Researchers working in this tradition have studied the self-directed verbalizations of young children – for example, observing the effects of their soliloquies on their behavior (Diaz and Berk 1992). They have found that children tend to verbalize more when task demands are greater, and that those who verbalize most tend to be more successful in problem-solving.

This claim of linguistic scaffolding of cognition admits, however, of a spectrum of readings. At its weakest, it says no more than has already been conceded above, that language may be a necessary condition for the acquisition of certain cognitive skills. At its strongest, on the other hand, the idea could be that language forms part of the functioning of the highest-level executive system – which would then make it a variant of the ideas to be discussed in sections 4 and 5 below.

Clark (1998) argues for a sort of intermediate-strength version of the Vygotskian idea, defending a conception of language as a cognitive *tool*. (Chomsky, too, has argued for an account of this sort. See his 1976, Ch. 2.) According to this view – which Clark labels "the supra-communicative conception of language" – certain extended processes of thinking and reasoning constitutively involve natural language. The idea is that language gets used, not just for communication, but also to augment human cognitive powers.

Thus by writing an idea down, for example, I can off-load the demands on memory, presenting myself with an object of further leisured reflection; and by performing arithmetic calculations on a piece of paper, I may be able to handle computational tasks which would otherwise be too much for me (and my short-term memory). In similar fashion, it may be that *inner* speech serves to enhance memory, since it is now well-established that the powers of human memory systems can be greatly extended by association (Baddeley 1988). Inner speech may thus facilitate complex trains of reasoning (Varley 1998).

Notice that according to this supra-communicative account, the involvement of language in thought only arises when we focus on a process of thinking or reasoning *extended over time*. So far as any given individual (token) thought goes, the account can (and does) buy into the standard input-output conception of language. It maintains that there is a neural episode which carries the content of the thought in question, where an episode of that type can exist in the absence of any natural language sentence and can have a causal role distinctive of the thought, but which in the case in question causes the production of a natural language representation. This representation can then have further benefits for the system of the sort which Clark explores (off-loading or enhancing memory).

According to stronger forms of the cognitive conception to be explored in later sections, in contrast, a particular tokening of an inner sentence is (sometimes) an inseparable part of the mental episode which carries the content of the thought-token in question. So there is no neural or mental event at the time which can exist distinct from that sentence, which can occupy a causal role distinctive of that sort of thought, and which carries the content in question; and so language is actually involved in (certain types of) cognition, even when our focus is on individual (token) thinkings.

In this section I have discussed two weak claims about the role of language (that language is necessary for the acquisition of many beliefs and concepts; and that language may serve as a cognitive tool, enhancing the range and complexity of our reasoning processes). These claims should be readily acceptable to most cognitive scientists. In addition, I have briefly introduced a more controversial thesis, namely that the acquisition of one or another natural language can sculpt our cognitive processes, to some degree. But this thesis relates only to the developmental, or diachronic, role of language. It says nothing about the role of language in adult cognition. We will in future focus on more challenging versions of the cognitive conception of language.

3   Strong claims

As is starting to emerge, the thesis that language has a cognitive function admits of a spectrum of readings. In this section I shall jump to the other end of that spectrum, considering forms of the cognitive conception of language which are too strong to be acceptable.

3.1   *Language as necessarily required for thought*

When the question of the place of natural language in cognition has been debated by philosophers the discussion has, almost always, been conducted *a priori* in universalist terms. Various arguments have been proposed for the claim that it is a conceptually necessary truth that *all* thought requires language, for example (Davidson 1975, 1982; Dummett 1981, 1989; McDowell 1994; Wittgenstein 1921, 1953). But these arguments all depend, in one way or another, upon an anti-realist conception of the mind – claiming, for instance, that since we cannot interpret anyone as entertaining any given fine-grained thought in the absence of linguistic behavior, such thoughts cannot even exist in the absence of such behavior (Davidson 1975). Since the view adopted in this paper – and shared by most cognitive psychologists – is quite strongly realist about thought, I do not propose to devote any time to such arguments.

Notice, too, that Davidson *et al.* are committed to denying that any non-human animals can entertain genuine thoughts, given that it is very doubtful whether any such animals are capable of understanding and using a natural language (in the relevant sense of "language," that is; see Pinker 1994; Premack 1986). This conclusion conflicts, not just with common-sense belief, but also with what can be discovered about animal cognition, both experimentally and by observation of their behavior in the wild (Allen and Bekoff 1997; Byrne 1995; de Waal 1982, 1996; Dickinson and Shanks 1995; Gallistel 1990; Hauser 2000; Povinelli 2000; Savage-Rumbaugh and Lewin 1994; Walker 1983). So not only are the arguments of Davidson *et al.* unsound, but we have independent reasons to think that their conclusion is false.

Dummett (1994) makes some attempt to accommodate this sort of point by distinguishing between concept-involving thoughts (which are held to be necessarily dependent upon language) and what he calls "proto-thoughts," which are what animals are allowed to possess. Proto-thoughts are said to consist of "visual images superimposed on the visually perceived scene," and are said to be possible only when tied to current circumstances and behavior. But such an account vastly underestimates the cognitive capacities of non-human animals, I believe. If an animal can decide whom to form an alliance with, or can calculate rates of return from different sources of food, or can notice and exploit the ignorance of another, then these things cannot be accounted for in Dummett's terms. And given that conceptual thinking of this sort is possible for animals, then he will be left without any principled distinction between animal thought and human thought.

I do not expect that these brief considerations will convince any of my philosophical opponents, of course; and they aren't meant to. Given the intended readership of this target article, their position is not really one that I need to take seriously. It is mentioned here just to set it aside, and (most important) in order that other, more plausible, versions of the cognitive conception of language shouldn't be confused with it.

I propose, therefore, to take it for granted that thought is conceptually independent of natural language, and that thoughts of many types can actually occur in the absence of such language. But this leaves open the possibility that some types of thought might *de facto* involve language, given the way in which human cognition is structured. It is on this – weaker but nevertheless still controversial – set of claims that I shall focus. Claims of this type seem to me to have been unjustly under-explored by researchers in the cognitive sciences; partly, no doubt, because they have been run together with the *a priori* and universalist claims of some philosophers, which have been rightly rejected.

619

3.2   The Joycean machine

Another overly strong form of cognitive conception of language – which has been endorsed by some philosophers and by many social scientists – is that language is, as a matter of fact, the medium of all human conceptual thinking. Most often it has been associated with a radical empiricism about the mind, according to which virtually all human concepts and ways of thinking, and indeed much of the very structure of the human mind itself, are acquired by young children from adults when they learn their native language – these concepts and structures differing widely depending upon the conceptual resources and structures of the natural language in question. This mind-structuring and social-relativist view of language is still dominant in the social sciences, following the writings early in this century of the amateur linguist Whorf (many of whose papers have been collected together in his 1956) – indeed, Pinker (1994) refers to it disparagingly as "the Standard Social Science Model" of the mind.

Perhaps Dennett (1991) is one of the clearest exponents of this view. He argues that human cognitive powers were utterly transformed following the appearance of natural language, as the mind became colonized by *memes* (ideas or concepts, which are transmitted, retained, and selected in a manner supposedly analogous to genes; see Dawkins 1976). Prior to the evolution of language, in this picture, the mind was a bundle of distributed connectionist processors – which conferred on early hominids some degree of flexibility and intelligence, but which were quite limited in their computational powers. The arrival of language then meant that a whole new – serial and compositionally structured – cognitive architecture could be programmed into the system.

This is what Dennett calls the *Joycean machine* (named after James Joyce's "stream of consciousness" writing). The idea is that there is a highest-level processor which runs on a stream of natural-language representations, utilizing learned connections between ideas and patterns of reasoning acquired in and through the acquisition of linguistic memes. According to this account, then, the concept-wielding mind is a kind of social construction, brought into existence through the absorption of memes from the surrounding culture. And in this view, the conceptual mind is both dependent upon, and constitutively involves, natural language.

Admittedly, what Dennet will actually *say* is that animals and pre-linguistic hominids are capable of thought, and engage in much intelligent thinking. But this is because he is not (in my sense) a realist about thoughts. On the contrary, he (like Davidson) is what is sometimes called an "interpretationalist" – he thinks that there is nothing more to thinking than engaging in behavior which is interpretable as thinking. Yet he does seem committed to saying that it is only with the advent of natural language that you get a kind of thinking which involves discrete, structured, semantically-evaluable, causally-effective states – that is, thoughts realistically construed.

Bickerton's proposals (1990, 1995) are somewhat similar, but more biological in flavor. He thinks that, before the evolution of language, hominid cognition was extremely limited in its powers. According to his view, these early forms of hominid cognition consisted largely of a set of relatively simple computational systems, underpinning an array of flexible but essentially behavioristic conditioned responses to stimuli. But then the evolution of language some 100,000 years ago involved a dramatic re-wiring of the hominid brain, giving rise to distinctively human intelligence and conceptual powers.[4]

Bickerton, like Dennett, allows that subsequent to the evolution of language the human mind would have undergone further transformations, as the stock of socially transmitted ideas and concepts changed and increased. But the basic alteration was coincident with, and constituted by, a biological alteration – namely, the appearance of an innately-structured language-faculty. For Bickerton is a nativist about language. (Indeed, his earlier work on the creolization of pidgin languages – 1981 – is often cited as part of an argument for the biological basis of language; see Pinker 1994.) And it is language which, he supposes, conferred on us the capacity for "off-line thinking" – that is, the capacity to think and reason about topics and problems in the abstract, independent of any particular sensory stimulus.

These strong views seem very unlikely to be correct. This is so for two reasons. First, they undervalue the cognitive powers of pre-linguistic children, animals, and earlier forms of hominid. Thus *Homo erectus* and archaic forms of *Homo sapiens*, for example, were able to survive in extremely harsh tundra environments, presumably without language (see below). It is hard to see how this could have been possible without a capacity for quite sophisticated planning and a good deal of complex social interaction (Mithen 1996). Second, the views of Dennett and Bickerton are inconsistent with the sort of central-process modularism which has been gaining increasing support in recent decades. According to this account, the mind contains a variety of conceptual modules – for mind-reading, for doing naïve physics, for reasoning about social contracts, and so on – which are probably of considerable ancestry, pre-dating the appearance of a modular language-faculty.[5] So hominids were already capable of conceptual thought and of reasoning in a complex, and presumably "off-line," fashion *before* the arrival of language.

In sections 3.3 and 3.4 following, I shall elaborate briefly on these points. But first, I want to consider a potential reply which might be made by someone sympathetic to Bickerton's position. For Bickerton actually thinks that earlier hominids probably used a form of "proto-language" prior to the evolution of syntax, similar to the language used by young children and to pidgin languages. (This is, in fact, a very plausible intermediate stage in the evolution of natural language.) It might be claimed, then, that insofar as hominids are capable of intelligent thought, this is only because those thoughts are framed in proto-language. So the view that thought is dependent upon language can be preserved.

Such a reply would, indeed, give Bickerton a little extra wiggle-room; but only a little. For as we shall see in section 3.3 below, a good deal of the evidence for hominid thinking is provided by the capacities of our nearest relatives, the great apes, who are known to lack even a proto-language (without a good deal of human enculturation and explicit training, at any rate; Savage-Rumbaugh and Lewin 1994). And some of the other evidence – for example, provided by hominid stone knapping – is not plausibly seen as underpinned by proto-language. Moreover, the various thought-generating central modules, to be discussed in section 3.4 below, are almost surely independent both of language and proto-language. So it remains the case that much hominid thought is independent even of proto-language.

3.3 *Hominid intelligence*

Since social intelligence is something that we share with the other great apes (especially chimpanzees), it is reasonable to conclude that the common ancestor of all apes – and so, by implication, all earlier forms of hominid – will also have excelled in the social domain. While it is still disputed whether chimpanzees have full-blown mind-reading, or "theory of mind," abilities, of the sort attained by a normal four-year-old child, it is not in dispute that the social behavior of great apes can be extremely subtle and sophisticated (Byrne 1995; Byrne and Whiten 1988, 1998; Povinelli 2000).

Two points are worth stressing in this context. One is that it is well-nigh impossible to see how apes can be capable of representing multiple, complex, and constantly changing social relationships (who is friends with whom, who has recently groomed whom, who has recently fallen out with whom, and so on) unless they are capable of structured propositional thought.[6] This is a development of what Horgan and Tienson (1996) call "the tracking argument for Mentalese" (i.e., an argument in support of the claim that thoughts are structured out of recombinable components). Unless the social thoughts of apes were composed out of elements variously representing individuals and their properties and relationships, then it is very hard indeed to see how they could do the sort of one-off learning of which they are manifestly capable. This surely requires separate representations for individuals and their properties and relations, so that the latter can be varied while the former are held constant. So (*contra* Dennett and Bickerton) we have reason to think that all earlier forms of hominid would have been capable of sophisticated conceptual thought (realistically construed), at least in the social domain.[7]

The second point to note is that the social thinking of apes seems sometimes to be genuinely strategic in nature, apparently involving plans that are executed over the course of days or months. Consider, for example, the way in which a band of male chimpanzees will set out quietly and in an organized and purposive manner toward the territory of a neighboring group, apparently with the intention, either of killing some of the males of that group, or of capturing some of its females, or both (Byrne 1995). Or consider the way in which a lower-ranking male will, over the course of a number of months, build up a relationship with the beta male, until the alliance is strong enough for them to cooperate in ousting the alpha male from his position (de Waal

1982). Presumably the thinking that would generate such long-term plans and strategies would have to be "off-line," in the sense of not being tied to or driven by current perceptions of the environment.

We can conclude, then, that all of our hominid ancestors would have had a sophisticated social intelligence. In addition, the stone-tool-making abilities of later species of *Homo erectus* indicate a sophisticated grasp of fracture dynamics and the properties of stone materials. Making stone tools isn't easy. It requires judgment, as well as considerable hand-eye coordination and upper-body strength. And since it uses a reductive technology (starting from a larger stone and reducing it to the required shape) it cannot be routinized in the way that (presumably) nest-building by weaver birds and dam-building by beavers can be. Stone knappers have to hold in mind the desired shape and plan two or more strikes ahead in order to work toward it using variable and unpredictable materials (Mithen 1996; Pelegrin 1993). Moreover, some of the very fine three-dimensional symmetries produced from about half-a-million years ago would almost certainly have required significant capacities for visual imagination – in particular, an ability to mentally rotate an image of the stone product which will result if a particular flake is struck off (Wynn 2000). And this is surely "off-line" thinking if anything is!

We can also conclude that early humans were capable of learning and reasoning about their natural environments with a considerable degree of sophistication. They were able to colonize much of the globe, ranging from Southern Africa to Northwestern Europe to Southeast Asia. And they were able to thrive in a wide variety of habitats (including extremely harsh marginal tundra environments), adapting their life-style to local – and sometimes rapidly changing circumstances (Mithen 1990, 1996). This again serves as a premise for a version of the "tracking argument," suggesting that early humans were capable of compositionally-structured thoughts about the biological as well as the social worlds.

3.4   The modular mind

The above claims about the cognitive powers of our early ancestors both support, and are in turn supported by, the evidence of modular organization in the minds of contemporary humans. According to this account, besides a variety of input and output modules (including, e.g., early vision, face-recognition, and language), the mind also contains a number of innately channeled conceptual modules, designed to process conceptual information concerning particular domains. Although these would not be modules in Fodor's classic (1983) sense, in that they wouldn't have proprietary transducers, might not have dedicated neural hardware, and might not be fully encapsulated, they would still be innately channeled dedicated computational systems, generating information in accordance with algorithms which are not shared with, nor accessible to, other systems.

623

Plausible candidates for such conceptual modules might include a naïve physics system (Baillargeon 1995; Leslie 1994; Spelke 1994; Spelke et al. 1995), a naïve psychology or "mind-reading" system (Baron-Cohen 1995; Carey 1985; Leslie 1994), a folk-biology system (Atran 1990, 1998, 2002), an intuitive number system (Dehaene 1997; Gallistel and Gelman 1992; Wynn 1990), a geometrical system for reorienting and navigating in unusual environments (Cheng 1986; Hermer and Spelke 1994, 1996) and a system for processing and keeping track of social contracts (Cosmides and Tooby 1992; Fiddick et al. 2000).

Evidence supporting the existence of at least the first two of these systems (folk-physics and folk-psychology) is now pretty robust. Very young infants already have a set of expectations concerning the behaviors and movements of physical objects, and their understanding of this form of causality develops very rapidly over the first year or two of life. And folk-psychological concepts and expectations also develop very early and follow a characteristic developmental profile. Indeed, recent evidence from the study of twins suggests that three-quarters of the variance in mind-reading abilities amongst three year olds is both genetic in origin and largely independent of the genes responsible for verbal intelligence, with only one quarter of the variance being contributed by the environment (Hughes and Plomin 2000).[8]

Now, of course the thesis of conceptual modularity is still highly controversial and disputed by many cognitive scientists. And I cannot pretend to have said enough to have established it here; nor is there the space to attempt to do so. This is going to be one of the large assumptions that I need to ask my readers to take on board as background to what follows. However, there is one sort of objection to conceptual modularity which I should like to respond to briefly here. This is that there simply hasn't been time for all of these modular systems to have evolved (or at any rate, not those of them that are distinctively human – geometry and folk-physics might be the exceptions).

Tomasello (1999) argues that the mere six million years or so since the hominid line diverged from the common ancestor of ourselves and chimpanzees is just too short a time for the processes of evolution to have sculpted a whole suite of conceptual modules. He thinks that explanations of distinctively-human cognition need to postulate just one – at most two – biological adaptations, in terms of which all the other cognitive differences between us and chimpanzees should be explained. His preferred option is theory of mind ability, which underpins processes of cultural learning and cultural accumulation and transmission. Others might argue in similar fashion that the only major biological difference is the language faculty (Perner, personal communication).

The premise of this argument is false, however; six million years is a lot of time, particularly if the selection pressures are powerful ones. (Only 10,000 years separate polar bears and grizzlies, for example.) And this is especially so when, as in the present case, many of the systems in question don't have to be built ab initio, but can result from a deepening and strengthening of pre-existing faculties. Thus theory of mind would surely have developed from some pre-existing social-cognition module; folk-biology from a pre-existing foraging system; and so on. In order to reinforce the point, one just has to reflect on the major, and multiple, physical differences between ourselves and chimpanzees – including upright gait, arm length, physical stature, brain size, nasal shape, hairlessness, whites of eyes, and so on. These, too, have all evolved – many of them independently, plainly – over the last six million years.

3.5   Taking stock

What has happened in the cognitive sciences in recent decades, then, is this. Many researchers have become increasingly convinced, by neuropsychological and other evidence, that the mind is more or less modular in structure, built up out of isolable, and largely isolated, components (Barkow *et al.* 1992; Fodor 1983; Gallistel 1990; Hirschfeld and Gelman 1994; Pinker 1997; Sacks 1985; Shallice 1988; Sperber *et al.* 1995). They have also become convinced that the structure and contents of the mind are substantially innate (Carey 1985; Fodor 1981, 1983; Spelke 1994), and that *language* is one such isolable and largely innate module (Chomsky 1988; Fodor 1983; Pinker 1994). There has then been, amongst cognitive scientists, a near-universal reaction against the cognitive conception of language, by running it together with the Whorfian hypothesis. Most researchers have assumed, without argument, that if they were to accept any form of cognitive conception of language, then that would commit them to Whorfian linguistic relativism and radical empiricism, and would hence be inconsistent with their well-founded beliefs in modularity and nativism (Pinker 1994).

It is important to see, however, that someone endorsing the cognitive conception of language does not *have* to regard language and the mind as cultural constructs, either socially determined or culturally relative. In fact, some form of cognitive conception of language can equally well be deployed along with a modularist and nativist view of language and mind. There is a range of positions intermediate between the input-output conception of language on the one hand and Whorfian relativism (the Standard Social Science Model) on the other, which deserve the attention of philosophers and cognitive scientists alike. These views are nativist as opposed to empiricist about language and much of the structure of the mind, but nevertheless hold that language is constitutively employed in many of our thoughts.

4   Language and conscious thinking

What is at stake, then, is the question whether language might be constitutively involved in *some* forms of human thinking. But which forms? In previous work I suggested that language might be the medium in which we conduct our *conscious propositional* thinking – claiming, that is, that inner speech might be the vehicle of conscious-conceptual (as opposed to conscious visuo-spatial) thinking (Carruthers 1996). This view takes seriously and literally the bit of folk-wisdom with which this paper began – namely, that much of our conscious thinking (namely, our propositional thinking) is conducted in inner speech.

Now, if the thesis here is that the cognitive role of language is *confined* to conscious thinking, then it will have to be allowed that much propositional thinking also takes place independently of natural language – for it would hardly be very plausible to maintain that there is no thinking but conscious thinking. And there are then two significant options regarding the relations between non-conscious language-independent thought, on the one hand, and conscious language-involving thinking, on the other. For either we would have to say that anything which we can think consciously, in language, can also be thought non-consciously, independently of language; or we would have to say that there are some thought-types which can only be entertained at all, by us, when tokened consciously in the form of an imaged natural language sentence.

Suppose that it is the first – weaker and more plausible – of these options that is taken. Then we had better be able to identify some element of the distinctive causal role of an imaged sentence that is sufficiently thought-like or inference-like for us to be able to say that the sentence in question is partly *constitutive of* the (conscious) tokening of the thought-type in question, rather than being merely *expressive* of it. For otherwise – if everything which we can think consciously, in language, we can also think non-consciously, without language – what is to block the conclusion that inner speech is merely the means by which we have access to our occurrent thoughts, without inner speech being in any sense constitutive of our thinking? (On this, at length, see Carruthers 1998b.)

There would seem to be just two distinct (albeit mutually consistent) possibilities here. One (implicit in Carruthers 1996) would be to propose a suitably weakened version of Dennett's *Joycean machine* hypothesis. While allowing (*contra* Dennett) that much conceptual thinking (realistically construed) and all conceptual thought-types are independent of language (in the sense of not being constituted by it), we could claim that there are certain learned habits and patterns of thinking and reasoning that are acquired linguistically, and then restricted to linguistic (and conscious) tokenings of the thoughts that they govern. It is surely plausible, for example, that exact long-division or multiplication can only be conducted consciously, in imaged manipulations of numerical symbols. Similarly, it may be that the result of taking a course in logic is that one becomes disposed to make transitions between sentences, consciously in language, where one would otherwise not have been disposed to make the corresponding transitions between the thoughts expressed. If these sorts of possibilities are realized, then we would have good reason to say of a token application of a particular inference-form, that the imaged natural language sentences involved are constitutive of the inference in question, since it could not have taken place without them.

A second possibility, is proposed and defended by Frankish (1998a, 1998b, 2004; see also Cohen 1993). This is that the distinctive causal role of inner speech is partly a function of our *decisions* to accept, reject, or act on the propositions which our imaged sentences express. I can frame a hitherto unconsidered proposition in inner speech and decide that it is worthy of acceptance, thereby committing myself to thinking and acting thereafter as if that sentence were true. Then provided that I remember my commitments and execute them, it will be *just as if* I believed the proposition in question. (In his published work, Frankish describes this level of mentality as the "virtual mind" and the beliefs in question as "virtual beliefs.") But, by hypothesis, I would never have come to believe what I do, nor to reason as I do reason, except via the tokening of sentences in inner speech. Frankish argues, in effect, that there is a whole level of mentality (which he now dubs "Supermind") which is constituted by our higher-order decisions and commitments to accept or reject propositions; and that language is constitutive of the thoughts and beliefs which we entertain at this level.

Such views have considerable plausibility; and it may well be that one, or other, or both of these accounts of the causal role of inner speech is correct. Indeed, the *dual process theory* of human reasoning developed over the years by Evans and colleagues (Evans and Over 1996; Wason and Evans 1975), and more recently by Stanovich (1999), combines elements of each of them. According to this account, in addition to a suite of computationally powerful, fast, and implicit reasoning systems (from our perspective, a set of conceptual modules), the mind also contains a slow, serial, and explicit reasoning capaciy, whose operations are conscious and under personal control, and which is said (by some theorists at least; e.g., Evans and Over 1996) to involve natural language. The emphasis here on learned rules in the operations of the explicit system is reminiscent of Dennett's "Joycean machine," whereas the stress on our having personal control over the operations of that system seems very similar to Frankish's conception of "supermind."

Not only is some form of dual-process theory plausible, but it should also be stressed that these accounts are independent of central-process modularism. Those who deny the existence of any conceptual modules can still accept that there is a level of thinking and reasoning which is both language-involving and conscious. It is surely plain, however, that none of the above accounts can amount to the most fundamental cognitive function of language once conceptual modularity is assumed.

Given conceptual modularity, then unless the above views are held together with the thesis to be developed in section 5 below – namely, that language provides the medium for inter-modular communication and non-domain-specific thinking – we can set their proponents a dilemma. Either they must claim that a domain-general architecture was in place prior to the evolution of language or they must allow that there was no significant domain-general cognition amongst hominids prior to the appearance of language and language-involving conscious thinking; and they must claim that such cognition still evolved as a distinct development, either at the same time or later. Since contemporary humans are manifestly capable of conjoining information across different domains in both their theoretical thought and their planning, then either pre-linguistic humans must already have had domain-general theoretical and practical reasoning faculties; or they must have evolved them separately at the same time or after the evolution of the language faculty (that is, if it isn't language itself which enables us to combine information across modules).

The problem with the first alternative, however – namely, that domain-general reasoning capacities pre-dated language – is that the evidence from cognitive archaeology suggests that this was not the case. For although the various sub-species of *Homo erectus* and archaic forms of *Homo sapiens* were smart, they were not *that* smart. Let me briefly elaborate.

As Mithen (1996) demonstrates at length and in detail, the evidence from archaeology is that the minds of early humans were in important respects quite unlike our own. While they successfully colonized diverse and rapidly changing environments, the evidence suggests that they were incapable of bringing together information across different cognitive domains. It seems that they could not (or did not) mix information from the biological world (utilized in hunting and gathering) with information about the physical world (used in tool making); and that neither of these sorts of information interacted with their social intelligence. Although they made sophisticated stone tools, they did not use those tools for specialized purposes (with different kinds of arrow-head being used for different kinds of game, for example); and they did not make tools out of animal products such as antler and bone. There is no sign of the use of artifacts as social signals in the form of body ornaments and such, which is ubiquitous in modern human cultures. And there is no indication of totemization or other sorts of linkages between social and animal domains, such as lion-man figurines, cave-paintings, or the burning of the dead with (presumably symbolic) animal parts – which all emerge onto the scene for the first time with modern humans. As Mithen summarizes the evidence, it would appear that early humans had sophisticated special intelligences, but that these faculties remained largely isolated from one another.

The problem with the second horn of the dilemma sketched above is just that it is hard to believe, either that a domain-general reasoning faculty might have evolved *after* the appearance of language some 100,000 years ago (in just the 20,000 years or so before the beginning of the dispersal of modern humans around the globe), or that language and domain-general capacities might have coevolved as distinct faculties. For as we shall see in section 5, the evolution of language would in any case have involved the language faculty taking inputs from, and sending outputs to, the various modular systems, if there wasn't already a domain-general system for it to be linked to. And it is hard to discern what the separate selection pressures might have been, which would have led to the development of two distinct faculties at about the same time (language and domain-general thought), when just one would serve.

5 Language as the medium of non-domain-specific thinking

The hypothesis that I particularly want to explore, then, is that natural language is the medium of non-domain-specific thought and inference. Versions of this hypothesis have been previously proposed by Carruthers (1996, 1998a), by Mithen (1996), and by Spelke and colleagues (Hermer-Vazquez *et al.*, 1999; Spelke and Tsivkin 2001; Spelke, 2002). I shall sketch the thesis itself, outline the existing experimental evidence in its support, and then (in the section following) consider some of its ramifications and possible elaborations. Finally (in sect. 7), I shall discuss what further evidence needs to be sought as a test of our thesis.

5.1 The thesis

The hypothesis in question assumes a form of central-process modularism. That is, it assumes that in addition to the various input and output modules (vision, face-recognition, hearing, language, systems for motor-control, etc.), the mind also contains a range of conceptual modules, which take conceptual inputs and deliver conceptual outputs. Evidence of various sorts has been accumulating in support of central-process modularism in recent decades (some of which has already been noted above). One line of support is provided by evolutionary psychologists, who have argued on both theoretical and empirical grounds that the mind contains a suite of domain-specific cognitive adaptations (Barkow *et al.*, 1992; Pinker 1997; Sperber 1996). But many who would not describe themselves as "evolutionary psychologists" have argued for a modular organization of central cognition, on developmental, psychological, and/or neuro-pathological grounds (Baron-Cohen 1995; Carey 1985; Carey and Spelke 1994; Gallistel 1990; Hauser and Carey 1998; Leslie 1994; Smith and Tsimpli 1995; Shallice 1988; Spelke 1994).

What cognitive resources were antecedently available, then, prior to the evolution of the language faculty? Taking the ubiquitous laboratory rat as a representative example, I shall assume that all mammals, at least, are capable of thought – in the sense that they engage in computations which deliver structured (propositional) belief-like states and desire-like states (Dickinson 1994; Dickinson and Balleine 2000). I shall also assume that these computations are largely carried out within modular systems of one sort or another (Gallistel 1990) – after all, if the project here is to show how cross-modular thinking in humans can emerge out of modular components, then we had better assume that the initial starting-state was a modular one. Furthermore, I shall assume that mammals possess some sort of simple non-domain-specific practical reasoning system, which can take beliefs and desires as input, and figure out what to do.

I shall assume that the practical reasoning system in animals (and perhaps also in us) is a relatively simple and limited-channel one. Perhaps it receives as input the currently-strongest desire and searches amongst the outputs of the various belief-generating modules for something which can be done in relation to the perceived environment which will satisfy that desire. So its inputs have the form DESIRE [Y] and BELIEF [IF X THEN Y], where X should be something for which an existing motor-program exists. I assume that the practical reasoning system is *not* capable of engaging in other forms of inference (generating new beliefs from old), nor of combining together beliefs from different modules; though perhaps it is capable of chaining together conditionals to generate a simple plan – for example, BELIEF [IF W THEN X], BELIEF [IF X THEN Y], → BELIEF [IF W THEN Y].

The central modules will take inputs from perception, of course. And my guess is that many of the beliefs and desires generated by the central modules will have partially indexical contents – thus a desire produced as output by the sex module might have the form, "I want to mate with *that* female," and a belief produced by the causal-reasoning module might have the form, "*That* caused *that*." So if the practical reasoning system is to be able to do anything with such contents, then it, too, would need to have access to the outputs of perception, to provide anchoring for the various indexicals. The outputs of the practical reasoning system are often likely to be indexical too, such as an intention of the form, "I'll go *that* way."

The inputs to central-process modules can presumably include not only conceptualized perceptions but also propositional descriptions (in the latter case deriving from linguistic input – for we surely use our mind-reading system, for example, when processing a description of someone's state of mind as well as when observing their behavior). And in some cases, too, the inputs to a module will include the outputs of other central-process modules; for we might expect that there will be cases in which modules are organized into some sort of hierarchy. But what of the *outputs* from central-process modules? Besides being directed to other modules (in some instances), and also to the practical reasoning system, where is the information which is generated by central-process modules normally sent? And in particular, is there some *non*-domain-specific central arena where all such information is collated and processed?

The hypothesis being proposed here is that there is such an arena, but one which crucially implicates natural language, and which cannot operate in the absence of such language. Moreover, the hypothesis is not just that our conscious propositional thinking involves language (as sketched in sect. 4 above), but that *all* non-domain-specific reasoning of a non-practical sort (whether conscious or non-conscious) is conducted in language. And as for the question of what a non-conscious tokening of a natural language sentence would be like, we can propose that it would be a representation stripped of all imagistic-phonological features, but still consisting of natural language lexical items and syntactic structures.

Chomsky (1995) has maintained, for example, that there is a level of linguistic representation which he calls "logical form" (LF), which is where the language faculty interfaces with central cognitive systems. We can then claim that all cross-modular thinking consists in the formation and manipulation of these LF representations. The hypothesis can be that all such thinking operates by accessing and manipulating the representations of the language faculty. Where these representations are *only* in LF, the thoughts in question will be non-conscious ones. But where the LF representation is used to generate a full-blown phonological representation (an imaged sentence), the thought will nomally be conscious. And crucially for my purposes, the hypothesis is that the language faculty has access to the outputs of the various central-process modules, in such a way that it can build LF representations which combine information across domains.

Let me say just a little more about the conscious/non-conscious distinction as it operates here. As I shall mention again in a moment language is both an input and an output module. Its production sub-system must be capable of receiving outputs from the conceptual modules in order to transform their creations into speech. And its comprehension sub-system must be capable of transforming heard speech into a format suitable for processing by those same conceptual modules. Now when LF representations built by the production sub-system are used to generate a phonological representation, in "inner speech," that representation will be consumed by the comprehension sub-system, and made available to central systems. One of these systems is a theory of mind module. And on the sort of higher-order theory of consciousness which I favor (Carruthers 2000), perceptual and imagistic states get to be phenomenally conscious by virtue of their availability to the higher-order thoughts generated by the theory of mind system (i.e., thoughts *about* those perceptual and imagistic states). So this is why inner speech of this sort is conscious: It is because it is available to higher-order thought.

The hypothesis, then, is that non-domain-specific, cross-modular, propositional thought depends upon natural language – and not just in the sense that language is a necessary condition for us to entertain such thoughts, but in the stronger sense that natural language representations are the bearers of those propositional thought-contents. So language is constitutively involved in (some kinds of) human thinking. Specifically, language is the vehicle of non-modular, non-domain-specific, conceptual thinking which integrates the results of modular thinking.

Before moving on to discuss the evidence in support of our thesis, consider one further question. Why does it have to be language, and not, for example, visual imagery that serves the integrative function? For visual images, too, can carry contents which cross modular domains. But such visual thinking will access and deploy the resources of a peripheral input module. It cannot, therefore, play a role in integrating information across conceptual modules, because the latter exist down-stream of the input-systems. Vision provides input to conceptual modules, and doesn't receive output from them. The language faculty, in contrast, while also "peripheral," has both input and output functions. (I shall return to this point again in sect. 6.2 below.) I would hypothesize, therefore, that in cases where visual images have cross-modular contents (and aren't memory images), they are always generated from some linguistic representation which originally served to integrate those contents.

5.2   The evidence

What evidence is there to support the hypothesis that natural language is the medium of inter-modular communication, or of non-domain-specific integrated thinking? Until recently, the evidence was mostly circumstantial. For example, one indirect line of argument in support of our thesis derives from cognitive archaeology, when combined with the evidence of contemporary central-process modularism (Mithen 1996). For as we noted above, it seems that we have significant evidence of cross-modular thought only following the emergence of contemporary humans some 100,000 years ago; whereas independent evidence suggests that language, too, was a late evolutionary adaptation, only finally emerging at about the same time (perhaps from an earlier stage of "proto-language" – Bickerton 1990, 1995). So the simplest hypothesis is that it is language which actually enables cross-modular thinking.

Another strand of indirect evidence can be provided if we take seriously the idea that the stream of inner verbalization is constitutive of (some forms of) thinking (Carruthers 1996). For as we saw in section 4, such views can only plausibly be held (given the truth of central-process modularism) together with the present hypothesis that language is the main medium of inter-modular communication.

Much more important, however, direct tests of (limited forms of) our hypothesis have now begun to be conducted. The most important of these is Hermer-Vazquez et al. (1999), which provides strong evidence that the integration of geometric properties with other sorts of information (color, smell, patterning, etc.) is dependent upon natural language. The background to their studies with human adults is the parent discovery of a *geometric module* in rats by Cheng (1986), as well as the discovery of a similar system in pre-linguistic human children (Hermer and Spelke 1994, 1996).

Cheng (1986) placed rats in a rectagonal chamber, and allowed them to discover the location of a food source. They were then removed from the chamber and disoriented, before being placed back into the box with the food now hidden. In each case there were multiple cues available – both geometric and non-geometric – to guide the rats in their search. For example, the different walls might be distinctively colored or patterned, one corner might be heavily scented, and so on. In fact in these circumstances the rats relied exclusively on geometric information, searching with equal frequency, for example, in the two geometrically-equivalent corners having a long wall on the left and a short wall on the right. Yet rats are perfectly well capable of noticing and remembering non-geometric properties of the environment and using them to solve other tasks. So it appears that, not only are they incapable of integrating geometric non-geometric information in these circumstances, but that geometric information takes priority.

(This makes perfectly good ecological-evolutionary sense. For in the rat's natural environment, overall geometrical symmetries in the landscape are extremely rare, and geometrical properties generally change only slowly with time; whereas object-properties of color, scent-markings, and so on will change with the weather and seasons. So a strong preference to orient by geometrical properties is just what one might predict.)

Hermer and Spelke (1994, 1996) found exactly the same phenomenon in pre-linguistic human children. Young children, too, rely exclusively on geometric information when disoriented in a rectangular room, and appear incapable of integrating geometrical with non-geometrical properties when searching for a previously seen but now-hidden object. Older children and adults are able to solve these problems without difficulty – for example, they go straight to the corner formed with a long wall to the left and a short blue wall to the right. It turns out that success in these tasks isn't directly corre-lated with age, nonverbal IQ, verbal working-memory capacity, vocabulary size, or comprehension of spatial vocabulary. In contrast, the only significant predictor of success in these tasks which could be discovered, was spontaneous use of spatial vocabulary conjoined with object-properties (e.g., 'It's left of the red one"). Even by themselves, these data strongly suggest that it is language which enables older children and adults to integrate geometric with non-geometric information into a single thought or memory.

Hermer-Vazquez et al. (1999) set out to test this idea with a series of dual-task experiments with adults. In one condition, subjects were required to solve one of these orientation problems while shadowing (i.e., repeating back) speech played to them through a set of headphones. In another condition, they were set the same problems while shadowing (with their hands) a *rhythm* played to them in their headphones. The hypothesis was that speech-shadowing would tie up the resources of the language faculty, whereas the rhythm-shadowing tasks would not; and great care was taken to ensure that the latter tasks were equally if not more demanding of the resources of working memory.

The results of these experiments were striking. Shadowing of speech severely disrupted subjects' capacity to solve tasks requiring integration of geometric with non-geometric properties. In contrast, shadowing of rhythm disrupted subjects' performance relatively little. Moreover, a follow-up experiment demonstrated that shadowing of speech didn't disrupt subjects' capacities to utilize non-geometric information *per se* – they were easily able to solve tasks requiring only memory for object-properties. So it would appear that it is language itself which enables subjects to conjoin geometric with non-geometric properties, just as the hypothesis that language is the medium of cross-modular thinking predicts.

Of course, this is just one set of experiments – albeit elegant and powerful – concerning the role of language in enabling information to be combined across just two domains (geometrical and object-properties). In which case, little direct support is provided for the more-demanding thesis that language serves as the vehicle of inter-modular integration in general. But the evidence does at least suggest that the more general thesis may be well worth pursing.

5.3   Challenging the data

The position taken by Hermer-Vazquez *et al.* (1999) has come under pressure from two different directions. First, there are claims that other species (chickens, monkeys) can integrate geometric and landmark information when disoriented (Gouteux *et al.* 2001; Vallortigara *et al.* 1990). And second, there is the finding that success in these tasks amongst young children is somewhat sensitive to the size of the room – in a larger room, significantly more young (four-year-old) children make the correct choice, utilizing both geometric and landmark information; and even more five- and six-year-old children are also able to make the correct choice (Learmonth *et al.* 2001, 2002).

To begin unpicking the significance of these new results, we need to return to some of the original claims. It is too strong to say that the original data with rats (Cheng 1986) showed the existence of a geometric module in that species. For rats can use landmark information when navigating in other circumstances. The fact is just that they don't use such information when disoriented. Nor is it established that rats *cannot* integrate geometric with landmark information. The fact is just that they *do not* utilize both forms of information when disoriented. So the data are consistent with the following model: there are no modules; rather, geometric and landmark information are both processed according to general-purpose algorithms and made available to some sort of practical reasoning system. But when disoriented, rats only pay attention to, and only make use of, the geometric information.

Even if one thinks (as I do) that other forms of evidence and other arguments make some sort of modularist architecture quite likely, the following proposal is still consistent with the data: both the geometric and landmark modules normally make their information available to some sort of practical reasoning system; but when disoriented, rats show a strong preference to make use *only* of the geometric information.

Equally, however, the fact that other species are able to solve these problems doesn't show that members of those species can integrate geometric with landmark information into a single belief or thought. For it is possible to solve these tasks by making use of the information sequentially. The problems can be solved by first re-orienting to the landmark, and then using geometric information to isolate the correct corner. So the data are consistent with the following modularist model: Both the geometric and landmark modules make their outputs available to a limited-channel practical reasoning system, where the latter doesn't have the inferential resources to integrate information from different modules; rather, it can only utilize that information sequentially, using a variety of heuristics (both innate and learned) in selecting the information to be used, and in what order. According to this view, the difference between monkeys and rats is just that the former utilize landmark information first, before using geometry; whereas the latter use geometry exclusively in these circumstances. Neither species may in fact be capable of integrating geometrical with landmark information.

(It is tempting to seek an adaptionist explanation of these species differences. Open-country dwellers such as rats and pre-linguistic humans may have an innate pre-disposition to rely only on geometric information when disoriented because such information alone will almost always provide a unique solution – given that rectagonal rooms don't normally occur in nature! Forest dwellers such as chickens and monkeys, in contrast, have an innate pre-disposition to seek for landmark information first, only using geometric information to navigate in relation to a known landmark. This is because geometric information is of limited usefulness in a forest – the geometry is just too complex to be useful in individuating a place in the absence of a landmark such as well-known fruit-tree.)

What of the new data concerning the effects of room size? Well, the first thing to say is that this data leaves intact the finding by Hermer-Vazquez *et al.* (1999) that the best predictor of success in children (in small room experiments) is productive use of left-right vocabulary. This suggests, both that language has something to do with their success, and that it is specifically syntax (the capacity to integrate different content-bearing items into a single thought) that is required. For if the role of language were simply to help fix the salience and importance of landmark information, one would expect that it should have been productive use of color vocabulary, rather than spatial vocabulary, which was the best predictor of success. For by hypothesis, after all, children are already disposed to use geometric information in reorienting; their problem is to make use of color information as well.

Equally untouched are the experiments with adults involving speech shadowing and rhythm shadowing, which found that the former greatly disrupts the capacity to use geometric and landmark information together, whereas the latter does not. These results, too, suggest that it is language which enables adults to integrate the two forms of information.

Why should room size have any effect upon children's performance, however? Here is one testable possibility, which is consistent with the theoretical framework of Hermer-Vazquez *et al.* (1999) and the present author. In a small room (4 feet by 6 feet) it requires but very little time and energy to select a corner and turn over a card. In a larger room (8 feet by 12 feet), in contrast, children have to take a few steps in order to reach a selected corner, giving them both a motive, and the time, to reflect. It may then be that the children who were able to succeed in the large-room condition were on the cusp of having the linguistic competence necessary to integrate geometric and landmark information. Perhaps they could do this, but only haltingly and with some effort. Then it is only to be expected that such children should succeed when given both the time and the motive to do so.

5.4   More data: Language and arithmetic

We have examined one set of data which provides strong support for a limited version of our thesis. Data is now available in one other domain – that of number. This comes from a recent bilingual training study conducted by Spelke and Tsivkin (2001). The background to this study is the discovery of numerical capacities in animals and human infants, of two different sorts. One is the capacity possessed by many different kinds of animal (including birds and fish) to represent the approximate numerosity of largish sets of items (Dehaene 1997; Gallistel 1990). This capacity is utilized especially in foraging, enabling animals to estimate rates of return from different food sources. The other numerical capacity is possessed by monkeys and human infants, at least. It is a capacity to represent the exact number of small sets of items (up to about four), keeping track of their number using simple forms of addition and subtraction (Gallistel and Gelman 1992; Hauser and Carey 1998).

The developmental hypothesis which forms the backdrop to Spelke and Tsivkin's study is that language-learning in human children – specifically, learning to pair number words with items in a set through the process of counting – builds upon these two pre-linguistic numerical capacities to enable humans to represent exact numbers of unlimited magnitude. But the developmental hypothesis could be interpreted in two ways. On one interpretation, the role of language is to load the child's mind with a set of language independent exact numerical concepts – so that, once acquired, the capacity to represent exact large magnitudes is independent of language. The other interpretation is that it is the numerical vocabulary of a specific natural language which forms the medium of exact-magnitude representation, in such a way that natural language is the vehicle of arithmetic thought. It is this latter interpretation which Spelke and Tsivkin (2001) set out to test.

They conducted three different bilingual arithmetic training experiments. In one experiment, bilingual Russian-English college students were taught new numerical operations; in another, they were taught new arithmetic equations; and in the third, they were taught new geographical and historical facts involving both numerical and non-numerical information. After learning a set of items in each of their two languages, subjects were tested for knowledge of those and of new items in both languages. In all three studies subjects retrieved information about exact numbers more effectively in the language in which they were trained on that information, and they solved trained problems more effectively than new ones. In contrast, subjects retrieved information about approximate numbers and about non-numerical (geographical or historical) facts with equal ease in their two languages, and their training on approximate number facts generalized to new facts of the same type.[9] These results suggest that one or another natural language is the vehicle of thought about exact numbers, but not for representing approximate numerosity (a capacity shared with other animals).

What we have, then, is the beginnings of evidence in support of our general thesis that natural language is the medium of inter-modular non-domain-specific thinking.

8 Conclusion*

This paper has reviewed a wide range of claims concerning the cognitive functions of language. At one extreme is the purely communicative (or input-output) conception of language, and at the other extreme is the claim that language is required for all propositional thought as a matter of conceptual necessity, with a variety of positions in between these two poles. Section 2 discussed some versions of the cognitive conception of language which are too weak to be of any deep interest; and section 3 considered some claims which are too strong to be acceptable. Section 4 expressed sympathy for a variety of "dual process" models of cognition, especially the claim that language is the vehicle of conscious-conceptual thinking. But it pointed out that to be plausible (given the truth of central-process modularisrn) such views must depend on the prior and more fundamental claim that language is the medium of cross-modular thought. This then became the focus of our enquiries in section 5.

In closing, however, let me provide a reminder of the *character* of the exercise we have undertaken. Almost every paragraph in this paper has contained claims which are still controversial to some degree, and yet there hasn't been the space to pursue those controversies or to defend my assumptions. This has been inevitable, given the array of theories we have considered, and the range of considerations and types of evidence which are relevant to their truth, drawn from a variety of academic disciplines. But then the task has only been to survey those theories, and to show that some of them are well enough motivated to warrant further investigation – not to nail down and conclusively establish a precisely formulated thesis. And in that task, I hope, the target article has succeeded.

Acknowledgments

My thanks to Colin Allen, José Bermudez, George Botterill, Daniel Dennett, Edouard Machery, David Papineau, Josef Perner, Michael Siegal, Liz Spelke, and an anonymous referee for *BBS* [*Behavioral and Brain Sciences*] for their comments on an earlier draft.

Notes

1 Philosophers and logicians should note that Chomsky's LF is very different from what *they* are apt to mean by "logical form." In particular, sentences of LF don't consist just in logical constants and quantifiers, variables, and dummy names.

*[Editor] Sections 6 and 7 omitted.

Rather they are constructed from lexical items drawn from the natural language in question. They are also syntactically structured, but regimented in such a way that all scope-ambiguities and the like are resolved, and with pronouns cross-indexed to their referents and so on. Moreover, the lexical items will be semantically interpreted, linked to whatever structures in the knowledge-base secure their meanings.

Note, too, that an appeal to LF isn't strictly necessary for the purposes of the main thesis of this article. I use it more by way of illustration, and for the sake of concreteness. All that is truly essential is that there should exist a separate mental faculty for processing natural language, with both input and output functions, and that this faculty should deal in structured representations.

2   Admittedly, developmental psychologists have – until very recently – tended to down-play the significance of testimony (and hence of language) in child development. Following Piaget, they have mostly viewed children as individualistic learners – acquiring information for themselves, and developing and testing theories in the light of the information acquired (e.g. Gopnik and Meltzoff 1997). See Harris (2002) who makes a powerful plea for the role of testimony to be taken much more seriously in accounts of child development.

3   This is, in fact, a weak version of the *Whorfian hypothesis*, to be discussed in its strongest form in section 3.2.

4   This date for the first appearance of fully-syntactic natural language seems to be quite widely adopted amongst cognitive archaeologists – see Mithen (1996) – so I, too, propose to accept it (albeit tentatively) in what follows. But it is, of course, still highly controversial. And it should be noted that at least some of the evidence for it turns on assumptions about the cognitive role of language.

5   Here and throughout the remainder of this article I shall use the term "module" loosely (following Smith and Tsimpli 1995, and others) especially when talking about central-process, or *conceptual*, modules. (Another option would have been to use the stylistically-barbaric term "quasi-module" throughout.) While these systems might not be modular in Fodor's classic (1983) sense – they will not have proprietary inputs, for example, and might not be fully encapsulated – they should be understood to conform to at least some of the main elements of Fodorian modularity. As I shall henceforward understand it, modules should be innately channeled (to some significant degree) and subject to characteristic patterns of breakdown; their operations might be mandatory and relatively fast; and they should process information relating to their distinctive domains according to their own specific algorithms.

6   Note that the computer programme *Chimp World* which successfully simulated chimpanzee behaviors and social structures without deploying higher-order thoughts nevertheless did employ structured propositional representations (Hughes 1993, reported in Povinelli 2000).

7   What is the status of arguments that take the form, "It is very hard to see how otherwise?" Do they merely reflect a lack of imagination on our part? Perhaps. But a more sympathetic gloss is that these are just standard arguments *to the best available explanation*. All theorizing, of course, in whatever discipline, has to work with those theories which can be imagined, or thought of, to explain the data. And it is often the case that there is only one theory which can be thought of to explain a given set of data.

8 How does this square with the data mentioned earlier, that there is nevertheless a substantial correlation between language ability and theory of mind in young children? Well, first, the Hughes and Plomin finding is that the genes for theory of mind and for verbal intelligence are not wholly independent of one another. And second, a quarter of the variance in theory of mind ability comes from the environment: and this may well be linguistically mediated in one way or another.

9 Note that geographical information isn't the same as geometric information; neither do the kinds of fact in question require integration with geometry. (Knowing that Paris is the capital of France doesn't need geometry.) So the finding that recall of geographical information is independent of language isn't inconsistent with the thesis that language is necessary to integrate geometric information with information of other kinds.

References

Allen, C. and Bekoff, M. (1997) *Species of Mind: The Philosophy and Psychology of Cognitive Ethology*. MIT Press.

Astington, J. (1996) "What is theoretical about the child's theory of mind?" In: *Theories of theories of mind*, ed. P. Carruthers and P. K. Smith. Cambridge University Press.

Atran, S. (1990) *Cognitive Foundations of Natural History: Towards an Anthropology of Science*. Cambridge University Press.

—— (1998) "Folk biology and the anthropology of science: Cognitive universals and cultural particulars." *Behavioral and Brain Sciences* 21: 547–68.

—— (2002) "An experimental approach to the cognitive basis of science: Universal and cultural factors in biological understanding." In: *The Cognitive Basis of Science*, ed. P. Carruthers, S. Stich, and M. Siegal. Cambridge University Press.

Baddeley, A. (1988) *Human Memory*. Erlbaum.

Baillargeon, R. (1995) "Physical reasoning in infancy." In: *The Cognitive Neurosciences*, ed. M. Gazzaniga. MIT Press.

Barkow, J., Cosmides, L. and Tooby, J. (eds) (1992) *The Adapted Mind*. MIT Press.

Baron-Cohen, S. (1995) *Mindblindness*. MIT Press.

Bickerton, D. (1981) *Roots of Language*. Ann Arbor.

—— (1990) *Language and Species*. University of Chicago Press.

—— (1995) *Language and Human Behavior*. University of Washington Press.

Bowerman, M. and Levinson, S. (eds) (2001) *Language Acquisition and Conceptual Development*. Cambridge University Press.

Byrne, R. (1995) *The Thinking Ape*. Oxford University Press.

Byrne, R. and Whiten, A. (eds) (1988) *Machiavellian Intelligence*. Oxford University Press.

—— (1998) *Machiavellian Intelligence II: Evaluations and Extensions*. Cambridge University Press.

Carey, S. (1985) *Conceptual Change in Childhood*. MIT Press.

Carey, S. and Spelke, E. (1994) "Domain-specific knowledge and conceptual change." In: *Mapping the Mind*, ed. L. Hirshfeld and S. Gelman. Cambridge University Press.

Carruthers, P. (1992) *Human Knowledge and Human Nature*. Oxford University Press.

—— (1996) *Language, Thought and Consciousness*. Cambridge University Press.

—— (1998a) "Thinking in language? Evolution and a modularist possibility." In: *Language and thought*, ed. P. Carruthers and J. Boucher. Cambridge University Press.

—— (1998b) Conscious thinking: Language or elimination? *Mind and Language* 13: 323–42.

—— (2000) *Phenomenal Consciousness: A Naturalistic Theory*. Cambridge University Press.

Cheng, K. (1986) "A purely geometric module in the rat's spatial representation." *Cognition* 23: 149–78.

Choi, S. and Gopnik, A. (1995) "Early acquisition of verbs in Korean: A cross-linguistic study." *Journal of Child Language* 22: 497–529.

Chomsky, N. (1976) *Reflections on language*. Temple Smith.

—— (1995) *The Minimalist Program*. MIT Press.

Clark, A. (1998) "Magic words: How language augments human computation." In: *Language and Thought*, ed. P. Carruthers and J. Boucher. Cambridge University Press.

Cohen, L.J. (1993) *An Essay on Belief and Acceptance*. Oxford University Press.

Cosmides, L. and Tooby, J. (1992) "Cognitive adaptations for social exchange." In: *The Adapted Mind*, ed. J. Barkow, L. Cosmides, and J. Tooby. Oxford University Press.

Curtiss, S. (1977) *Genie: A Psycholinguistic Study of a Modern-day Wild Child*. Academic Press.

Davidson, D. (1975) "Thought and talk." In: *Mind and Language*, ed. S. Guttenplan. Oxford University Press.

—— (1982) "Rational animals." In: *Actions and Events*, ed. E. Lepore and B. McLaughlin. Blackwell.

Dawkins, R. (1976) *The Selfish Gene*. Oxford University Press.

De Waal, F. (1982) *Chimpanzee Politics*. Jonathan Cape.

—— (1996) *Good Natured*. Harvard University Press.

Dehaene, S. (1997) *The Number Sense*. Oxford University Press.

Dennett, D. (1991) *Consciousness Explained*. Penguin Press.

Diaz K. and Berk, L. (eds) (1992) *Private Speech: From Social Interaction to Self-regulation*. Erlbaum.

Dickinson, A. (1994) "Instrumental conditioning." In: *Animal Learning and Cognition*, ed. N. Mackintosh. Academic Press.

Dickinson, A. and Balleine, B. (2000) "Causal cognition and goal-directed action." In: *The Evolution of Cognition*, ed. C. Heyes and L. Huber. MIT Press.

Dickinson, A. and Shanks, D. (1995) "Instrumental action and causal representation." In: *Causal cognition*, ed. D. Sperber, D. Premack, and A. Premack. Blackwell.

Dummett, M. (1981) *The interpretation of Frege's Philosophy*. Duckworth.

—— (1989) "Language and communication." In: *Reflections on Chomsky*, ed. A. George. Blackwell.

Evans, J. and Over, D. (1996) *Rationality and Reasoning*. Psychology Press.

Fodor, J. (1981) "The present status of the innateness controversy." In: *Representations*. Harvester Press.

—— (1983) *The Modularity of Mind*. MIT Press.

Frankish, K. (1998a) "Natural language and virtual belief." In: *Language and Thought*, ed. P. Carruthers and J. Boucher. Cambridge University Press.

—— (1998b) "A matter of opinion." *Philosophical Psychology* 11: 423–42.

—— (2004) *Mind and Supermind*. Cambridge: Cambridge University Press.

Gallistel, R. (1990) *The Organization of Learning*. MIT Press.

Gallistel, R. and Gelman, R. (1992) "Preverbal and verbal counting and computation." *Cognition* 44: 43–74.

Gopnik, A. (2001) "Theories, language and culture." In: *Language Acquisition and Conceptual Development*, ed. M. Bowerman and S. Levinson. Cambridge University Press.

Gopnik, A., Choi, S., and Baumberger, T. (1996) "Cross-linguistic differences in early semantic and cognitive development." *Cognitive Development* 11: 197–227.

Gopnik A. and Melzoff, A. (1997) *Words, Thoughts and Theories*. MIT Press.

Gouteux, S., Thinus-Blanc, C., and Vauclair, J. (2001) "Rhesus monkeys use geometric and non-geometric information during a reorientation task." *Journal of Experimental Psychology: Gen. Proc.* 130: 505–19.

Harris, P. (2002) "What do children learn from testimony?" In *The Cognitive Basis of Science*, ed. P. Carruthers, S. Stich, and M. Siegal. Cambridge University Press.

Hauser, M. (2000) *Wild Minds*. Penguin Press.

Hauser, M. and Carey, S. (1998) "Building a cognitive creature from a set of primitives." In: *The Evolution of Mind*, ed. D. Cummins and C. Allen. Oxford University Press.

Hermer, L. and Spelke, E. (1994) "A geometric process for spatial reorientation in young children." *Nature* 370: 57–59.

—— (1996) "Modularity and development: The case of spatial reorientation." *Cognition* 61: 195–232.

Hermer-Vazquez, L., Spelke, E., and Katsnelson, A. (1999) "Sources of flexibility in human cognition: Dual task studies of space and language." *Cognitive Psychology* 39: 3–36.

Hirschfeld, L. and Gelman, S. (eds) (1994) *Mapping the Mind: Domain Specificity in Cognition and Culture*. Cambridge University Press.

Horgan T. and Tienson, J. (1996) *Connectionism and Philosophy of Psychology*. MIT Press.

Hughes, C. and Plomin, R. (2000) "Individual differences in early understanding of mind: Genes, nonshared environment and modularity." In: *Evolution and the Human Mind*, ed. P. Carruthers and A. Chamberlain. Cambridge University Press.

Hughes, L. (1993) "ChimpWorld: A wind-tunnel for the social sciences." Ph.D. dissertation, Yale University.

Hurlburt, R. (1990) *Sampling Normal and Schizophrenic Inner Experience*. Plenum Press.

—— (1993) *Sampling Inner Experience with Disturbed Effect*. Plenum Press.

Kertesz, A. (1988) "Cognitive function in severe aphasia. In: *Thought Without Language*, ed. L. Weiskrantz. Oxford University Press.

Kosslyn, S. (1994) *Image and Brain*. MIT Press.

Learmonth, A., Nadel, L., and Newcombe, N. (2002) "Children's use of landmarks: Implications for modularity theory." *Psychological Science*.

Learmonth, A., Newcombe, N., and Huttenlocher J. (2001) "Toddlers' use of metric information and landmarks to reorient." *Journal of Experimental Child Psychology*, 80: 225–44.

Leslie, A. (1994) "ToMM, ToBY and Agency: Core architecture and domain specificity." In: *Mapping the Mind*, ed. L. Hirschfeld and S. Gelman. Cambridge University Press.

Lucy, J. (1992a) *Language, Diversity and Thought: A Reformulation of the Linguistic Relativity Hypothesis.* Cambridge University Press.

—— (1992b) *Grammatical Categories and Cognition: A Case-study of the Linguistic Relativity Hypothesis.* Cambridge University Press.

Lucy, J. and Gaskins, S. (2001) "Grammatical categories and development of classification preferences: A comparative approach." In: *Language Acquisition and Conceptual Development,* ed. M. Bowerman and S. Levinson. Cambridge University Press.

Malson, L. (1972) *Wolf Children and the Problem of Human Nature.* Monthly Review Press.

McDowell, J. (1994) *Mind and World.* MIT Press.

Mithen, S. (1990) *Thoughtful Foragers: A Study of Prehistoric Decision Making.* Cambridge University Press.

—— (1996) *The Prehistory of the Mind.* Thames Hudson.

Nelson, K. (1996) *Language in Cognitive Development: The Emergence of the Mediated Mind.* Cambridge University Press.

Pelegrin, J. (1993) "A framework for analyzing prehistoric stone tool manufacture and a tentative application of some early stone industries." In: *The Use of Tools by Human and Non-human Primates,* ed. A. Berthelet and J. Chavaillon. Oxford University Press.

Peterson, C. and Siegal, M. (1998) "Representing inner worlds: Theory of mind in autistic, deaf and normal hearing children." *Psychological Science* 9: 117–33.

Pinker, S. (1994) *The Language Instinct.* Penguin Press.

—— (1997) *How the Mind Works.* Penguin Press   [aPC, CP]

Povinelli, D. (2000) *Folk Physics for Apes.* Oxford University Press.

Sacks, O. (1985) *The Man who Mistook his Wife for a Hat.* Picador.

—— (1989) *Seeing Voices.* Picador.

Savage-Rumbaugh, S. and Lewin, R. (1994) *Kanzi: The Ape at the Brink of the Human Mind.* John Wiley.

Schaller, S. (1991) *A Man Without Words.* Summit Books.

Shallice, T. (1988) *From Neuropsychology to Mental Structure.* Cambridge University Press.

Smith, N. and Tsimpli, I.-M. (1995) *The Mind of a Savant: Language-learning and Modularity.* Blackwell.

Spelke, E. (1994) "Initial knowledge: Six suggestions." *Cognition* 50: 433–47.

Spelke, E. and Tsivkin, S. (2001) "Language and number: A bilingual training study." *Cognition* 78: 45–88.

—— (2002) "Developing knowledge of space: Core systems and new combinations." In: *Languages of the Brain,* eds A.M. Galaburda, S.M. Kosslyn, and Y. Christen. Harvard Univeristy Press.

Spelke, E., Vishton, P., and von Hofsten, C. (1995) "Object perception, object-directed action, and physical knowledge in infancy." In: *The Cognitive Neurosciences,* ed. M. Gazzaniga. MIT Press.

Sperber, D. (1996) *Explaining Culture: A Naturalistic Approach.* Blackwell.

Sperber, D. and Wilson, D. (1986) *Relevance: Communication and Cognition.* Blackwell. (Second edition, 1995.)

Tomasello, M. (1999) *The Cultural Origins of Human Cognition.* Harvard University Press.

Vallortigara, G., Zanforlin, M., and Pasti, G. (1990) "Geometric modules in animal's spatial representations: A test with chicks." *Journal of Comparative Psychology*, 104: 248–54.

Varley, R. (1998) "Aphasic language, aphasic thought." In: *Language and Thought*, ed. P. Carruthers and J. Boucher. Cambridge University Press.

—— (2002) "Science without grammar: Scientific reasoning in severe agrammatic aphasia." In: *The Cognitive Basis of Science*, ed. P. Carruthers, S. Stich, and M. Siegal. Cambridge University Press.

Vygotsky, L. (1934/1986) *Thought and Language*. Trans. Kozulin. MIT Press.

Walker, S.F. (1983) *Animal Thought*. London: Routledge and Kegan Paul.

Whorf, B.L. (1956) *Language, Thought, and Reality*. MIT Press.

Wittgenstein, L. (1921) *Tractatus Logico-philosophicus*. Routledge.

—— (1953) *Philosophical Investigations*. Blackwell.

Wynn, K. (1990) "Children's understanding of counting." *Cognition* 36: 155–93.

—— (1995) "Origins of mathematical knowledge." *Mathematical Cognition* 1: 35–60.

Wynn, T. (2000) "Symmetry and the evolution of the modular linguistic mind." In: *Evolution and the Human Mind*, ed. P. Carruthers and A. Chamberlain. Cambridge University Press.

30

J.L. Bermúdez, "Language and Thinking about Thoughts"

There are different conceptions of the relation between linguistic and nonlinguistic thought, and correspondingly of the scope and limits of nonlinguistic thought. These different conceptions fall naturally into two broad groups. At one extreme are views that seek to drive as much of a wedge as possible between linguistic and nonlinguistic thought. For example, there is the minimalist conception of nonlinguistic thought, according to which nonlinguistic creatures are capable only of an etiolated and imagistic type of thinking, the vehicles of which are "spatial images superimposed on spatial perceptions." If the minimalist conception is correct then it will provide us with a very clear sense of the differences between linguistic thought and nonlinguistic thought. So too would a view that goes naturally with the minimalist conception – the view, namely, that considerations of sense and mode of presentation can get no grip in the absence of language. But much of my book *Thinking without Words* (from which this chapter is extracted) is devoted to arguing that, initial appearances to the contrary, there is indeed room at the nonlinguistic level for the ascription of thoughts that have determinate content and compositional structure – and, more strongly, that such thoughts are indispensable for the purpose of psychological explanation. So where does this leave us? Are there any genuine differences at all between linguistic thought and nonlinguistic thought?

The principal claim of this chapter is that an important class of thoughts is in principle unavailable to nonlinguistic creatures. In the first section I briefly discuss some of the claims that have been made about how language can function as a cognitive tool. It emerges that many of these functions do not actually require a full-fledged language. If language is to have a distinctive, unique, and essential cognitive function, so that the difference between linguistic and nonlinguistic cognition is qualitative rather than merely quantitative, then we must look elsewhere. In section 2 I develop my own account of the contribution that language can make to cognition – and explain why it is a contribution that can only be made by language. The central claim is that all thinking that involves intentional ascent (roughly, all thinking that involves thinking about thoughts) requires the capacity to think about words.

1 Language as a cognitive tool

Andy Clark (1998) has usefully plotted out six fundamental respects in which language can function as a tool, enhancing, extending, and facilitating thought and cognition), as follows.[1]

1   *Memory augmentation.* The acquisition of a public language offers us powerful means of systematically storing data (not simply in written language but also in communicated oral traditions).
2   *Environmental simplification.* Applying linguistic labels is one way that the perceived environment can be broken down into persisting objects and properties.
3   *Coordination.* Language permits the mutual control of attention and resource allocation in coordinated activities.
4   *Transcending path-dependent learning.* The learning patterns of linguistic creatures are not constrained by the particular cognitive paths they have followed, since linguistic communication allows ordinary learning patterns to be circumvented and short-circuited.
5   *Control loops.* Language allows us to create control loops for our future behavior (by writing down plans that might be too complicated to keep in one's head, for example) as well as to register and respond to the instruction and regulation of others.
6   *Data manipulation and representation.* "Extended intellectual arguments and theses are almost always the product of brains acting in concert with multiple external resources. These resources enable us to pursue manipulations and juxtapositions of ideas and data which would quickly baffle the un-augmented brain" (Clark 1998: 173).

These are all, no doubt, important ways that language possession serves to extend and enhance thinking. But they do not, I think, mark types of thinking that are in principle available only to language-using creatures. As a first step in plotting out the scope of nonlinguistic thought, it will be useful to explore how several of the functions that Clark identifies can be carried out by nonlinguistic processes.

By "nonlinguistic process" I mean one or other of two things. On the one hand a process can be straightforwardly nonlinguistic in virtue of not relying on any symbols at all.[2] On the other a process can be nonlinguistic even though it is dependent on symbols, simply because it does not rely on the right sort of symbols. Of course, to describe a process as nonlinguistic in this second sense is hostage to a principled distinction between linguistic and nonlinguistic symbol systems, and I shall have some more to say about that shortly. First, though, consider how far one can get with the prosthetic functions of language at an entirely nonsymbolic level.

The mutual control of attention and resource allocation in coordinated social activities does not require the intervention of language. Coordination

645

requires a degree of communication, but this communication can perfectly well be nonsymbolic (hence, uncontroversially, nonlinguistic). It is well known, for example, that human infants engage from a very early age in sustained periods of coordinated activity with their caregivers. The process has aptly been called one of *affect attunement* (Stern 1985). It is a process of exploring and communicating emotional states through changes in facial expression, vocalizations, and gesture.

> Affect attunement is the performance of behaviors that express the quality of feeling of a shared affect state without imitating the exact behavioral expression of the inner state. . . . The reason attunement behaviors are so important is that true imitation does not permit the partners to refer to the internal state. It maintains the focus of attention on the forms of the external behaviors. Attunement behaviors, on the other hand, recast the event and shift the focus of attention to what is behind the behavior, to the quality of feeling that is being shared. (Stern 1985: 142)

In affect attunement, emotional states are communicated by being shared. The infant's participation in this sort of communication is intentional (as, of course, is the caregiver's), and the process of affect attunement is a type of coordinated activity in which there is a mutual control of resource allocation. Nonetheless, the process is not one of symbolic communication, because facial expressions and vocalizations are not *symbols* for the emotional states that are being communicated. The link between a scowl and a feeling of disagreeableness, for example, is expressive rather than symbolic. The behavioral manifestations of emotions and feelings cannot be divorced from the emotions and feelings that are being manifested. That is to say, the link between them is not arbitrary and conventional, which is the essence of the symbolic.

A further example of coordination without symbols comes with the well-studied dances carried out by worker honeybees (von Frisch 1967).[3] Although the details of the dances vary among the seven known species of the genus *Apis*, the basic principles are similar. Worker bees returning to the nest site after successful foraging land on the horizontal top of the nest and perform what has come to be known as a waggle dance to inform their fellow workers of the location of the food source. In the waggle dance the bee flies in a figure-of-eight pattern, moving its abdomen back and forth laterally on the straight line in between the two circles. Although there is of course a degree of error, the waggle dances communicate information about the direction, distance, and desirability of the food source. Each of these three dimensions of variation is correlated with a dimension of variation in the dance. The angle of the dance relative to the position of the sun indicates the direction of the food source. The duration of a complete figure-of-eight circuit indicates the distance to the food source (or rather the flying time to the food source, because it increases when the bees would have to fly into a headwind). And the vigor of the dance indicates the desirability of the food to be found. Variation in all three environmental features is preserved in the relevant dimensions of the bee dance.

The bee dance is an even clearer example than affect attunement of coordination in resource allocation – and, as in the affect attunement case, it does not seem appropriate to describe the coordination as resting on symbolic communication. The bee dance is nonsymbolic because it does not involve arbitrary signals. To appreciate the point, and in particular the distinction between arbitrary and iconic signals, it is worth making a small digression into the theory of signals. There can be no transfer of information without rules for the encoding and decoding of signals (Green and Marler 1979). Viewed in broad and abstract terms, the rules for the encoding of a signal govern the transformations that lead from stimuli received at the sensory surfaces to signaling behavior. The simplest such rules yield deterministic links from input to output, as when the signaling behavior is what is sometimes called an 'instinctive behavior pattern' or an 'innate releasing mechanism.' Newly hatched herring gulls, for example, are particularly sensitive to the sensory input correlated with the length, movement, and coloration of the adult herring gull's bill. A transformation rule maps this onto the chick's characteristic signaling behavior, vigorous pecking at the adult's bill tip (Tinbergen 1973). In this case the decoding signal is equally straightforward. The adult herring gull responds by feeding the chick. More complex signaling behaviors might involve a series of rules governing a series of transformations. In affect attunement, for example, there will be rules governing the extraction of various qualitative and quantitative aspects of vocal exclamations and gestures by the partner in the exchange; rules mapping those aspects onto an amodal 'common currency'; and rules that then generate responsive gestures or vocalizations (Stern 1985).

In an iconic signal system there is, for each dimension of variation in the relevant environmental feature (the distance of the food source in the honeybee case, for example), a single transformation rule mapping variation in that parameter onto variation in the relevant dimension of the signal. The receiver of the signal will decode the signal by an inverse mapping.[4] Signs are arbitrary, as opposed to iconic, when no such general and continuous rules exist to map variations in environmental parameters onto variations in signals. Each member of the signal set is linked to a particular environmental feature by specific assignments that can only be characterized one by one. Within the framework set by the distinction between arbitrary and iconic signals, it seems relatively uncontroversial, first, that the bee dances are iconic rather than arbitrary signaling practices and, second, that no practice that does not involve arbitrary signals can plausibly be described as linguistic.

The bee dances, then, clearly illustrate how coordination in resource allocation and communal activity can be achieved at the nonlinguistic level. They also illustrate how control loops can be created without language and, moreover, how path-dependent learning can be transcended. The whole point of the bee dances is that the vast majority of worker bees do not need to seek the food for themselves. The worker bees that remain in the hive can profit from the explorations of a small number of bees to circumvent the standard search procedures.

Imitative learning is perhaps the most fundamental way of overcoming path-dependence through permitting the social transmission of knowledge. Imitation is extremely widespread in the animal kingdom and is present in human infants more or less from birth (Meltzoff and Moore 1977, 1983). The most straightforward form of imitative learning is simple mimicry, of the sort that can be seen in the social transmission of bird songs and in neonatal imitation of facial expressions. In many species, individual birds deprived (e.g., by neonatal deafening or by being raised in isolation) of the opportunity to imitate the songs of conspecifics develop either only very rudimentary versions of the standard songs or radically abnormal songs (see, e.g. Marler 1970). At a more sophisticated level we can identify various types of mimetic learning, of different degrees of sophistication. It is known from studies of chimpanzee tool use, for example, that chimpanzees are skilled at learning about the dynamic properties of objects from observing them being manipulated by others (Boesch and Boesch 1992). There is some debate about whether tool-using chimpanzees are actually imitating patterns of behavior (Tomasello 1996), as opposed to picking up the dynamic affordances of objects and learning about features of the environment, but these clearly illustrate some form of the social transmission of knowledge.

The cognitive significance of mimetic learning within phylogeny has been recognized by Merlin Donald in his speculative reconstruction of the emergence of the modern mind (Donald 1991). Donald suggests that a long period of mimetic culture served as the bridge between the episodic form of cognition characteristic of the apes and earliest hominids and the language-based culture that emerged after the transition from the Middle Paleolithic to the Upper Paleolithic. He associates mimetic culture with a wide range of social cognitive phenomena that collectively served as an adaptive foundation for the evolutionary emergence of language. The enormous development in techniques of tool manufacture characteristic of the Middle Paleolithic period must have been linked with new means for the transmission of information across a community. From what we know of contemporary hunter-gatherer societies, the process of tool manufacture is very much a social process, and clearly dependent on successful communication among the participants (Reynolds 1993). If we follow the majority of archeologists in dating the emergence of linguistic communication after the Middle Paleolithic (Bickerton 1990, 1996; Lieberman 1984) then it is hard to see any alternative to group mimetic learning as the crucial cognitive mechanism underpinning complex tool manufacture. Mimesis can also plausibly be viewed as the foundation for the social expression of emotion – again a form of nonlinguistic communication that circumvents the path-dependence of language.

Returning to Clark's list of the instrumental cognitive functions served by language, the function of environmental simplification does not require any sort of communication, symbolic or otherwise. Human infants are born able to parse the perceived environment into object-like segments that are taken to obey certain basic higher-order physical principles. This is probably not enough, however, for the type of environmental simplification that Clark intends. His view, I suspect, is that the environmental simplification that language provides applies to a perceived environment that is already parsed into objects or object-like entities. Language does not enable us to perceive an environment composed of discrete and continuously existing objects in the way that many philosophers have argued.[5] What it allows us to do is to impose a simplified pattern that will allow us to make sense of the discrete and continuously existing objects that we encounter in perception and action.

Even when the function of environmental simplification is understood in this sense, however, it still seems clear that it can be achieved at the nonlinguistic level. It is at this point that it becomes pressing to say something about quite how "linguistic" and "nonlinguistic" are being understood here. There has been considerable discussion among philosophers, linguists, and psychologists as to what constitutes a language. Savage-Rumbaugh has argued, for example, that language emerges with the appearance of symbolic communication (Savage-Rumbaugh 1986). Most linguists, on the other hand, think that some form of grammar and syntactic structure is essential for a symbol system to count as a genuine language (Chomsky 1980). The majority of philosophers have followed the linguists in this respect (Bennett 1976), although David Lewis (1983) has proposed in a rather more inclusive spirit that languages are simply functions from expressions onto meanings. Confronted with this it is hard not to be pulled in two directions. On the one hand it is tempting to think that there is little point in trying to arbitrate in this debate. It is unclear what criteria we should use to judge any of these proposals. If we are trying to capture the essence of human language then it is clear where the answer lies – but our project is broader than that. The ordinary meaning of the word "language" is too vague to help us. After all, ordinary language allows us to talk freely of the language of architecture and the language of the body. But, on the other hand, it seems impossible to investigate the nature and scope of nonlinguistic thought without a demarcation line between the linguistic and the nonlinguistic.

I will adopt a middle way between these two extremes. A genuine language must allow for the formation of complex symbols from simple symbols. The essence of language is the combination of symbols with each other to express thoughts, taking thoughts to be complex entities that can be assessed for truth or falsity. The possibility of truth appears only with complex symbols. It emerges only when a state of affairs is asserted to be the case, and this requires, at a bare minimum, the combination of a naming symbol and a predicate symbol. A lexicon of simple symbols will not support communicative utterances that are assessable for truth or falsity (although they may, of course, be adequate to perform speech acts such as issuing injunctions). So complex symbolic systems allow the formation of complex symbols, symbols whose meaning is determined by the meaning of the symbols of which they are composed. That is to say, complex symbol systems display what is often known as *compositionality*, the possibility of recombining the members of a finite number of simple symbols to produce a range of complex symbols. This characteristic of complex symbol systems is frequently stressed in both philosophical and psychological discussions of language. It tends to be taken as a unitary phenomenon, but compositionality can be displayed in two fundamentally different ways, corresponding to two fundamentally different types of complex symbol systems.

In the first category, the category of sequentially complex symbol systems, complex symbols are formed in a purely additive or successive manner. Correlatively, understanding a sequentially complex symbol is a matter of successively understanding the simple symbols that make it up. A good example of such a sequentially complex symbol system comes with the communication systems spontaneously developed by very young children born deaf but whose parents do not use sign language to them. Such children tend without instruction to develop elementary signing systems employing combinations of two signs (Goldin-Meadow 1979). The two-sign combinations typically involve a pointing gesture combined with an action sign. An example might be pointing at a door combined with a turning gesture to signify that it should be opened. Pygmy chimpanzees, or bonobos (*Pan paniscus*), have acquired similar abilities (Greenfield and Savage-Rumbaugh 1990). It is clear that we are dealing here with the formation of complex symbols. In the given example, it is the formation of a complex symbol communicating an injunction – the injunction to open the door. But the mode of formation is extremely simple. The syntactic rules of the symbol system are such that the action sign (the turning gesture) can only be conjoined with a sign that picks out an object. There is no way of using the syntactical rules to build up further complex symbols.

In what might be termed a hierarchically complex symbol system, on the other hand, the logical and semantic relations between the components of a complex symbol cannot in every case be read off from the sequential ordering of simple symbols. The basic feature of a hierarchically complex symbolic system is that it possesses a hierarchically organized compositional semantics operating in such a way that understanding a complex symbol will not always be a matter of successively understanding the simple symbols that make it up. To get from a sequentially complex to a hierarchically complex symbol system we must lift the basic restriction that complex symbols can *only* be formed by combining a predicate symbol and the appropriate number of naming symbols. Hierarchically complex symbol systems possess a variety of mechanisms that allow the formation of complex symbols. Operators analogous to the definite and indefinite articles in English will allow the formation of complex names (i.e., definite and indefinite descriptions), while reiterable operators that apply to complete sentences will allow the formation of complex symbols compounded from sentences. The logical constants are a case in point, but so too are the operators indicating possibility and necessity and indeed tense.

Returning to the matter at hand, it seems plausible that the function of environmental simplification identified by Clark can be carried out by "labeling" environmental features with a simple symbol system. Environmental simplification does not require complex symbols (although of course it would be greatly enhanced by a complex symbol system) and hence does not require a language. A classic example of how this might work (and one that provides a further example of how the instrumental functions I have already considered can be effected at the nonlinguistic level) comes with the alarm calls of vervet monkeys (Cheney and Seyfarth 1990). Vervet monkeys have three alarm calls, each geared to a different category of predator – eagle, leopard, and snake. When vervets hear a particular alarm call they do not display an indiscriminate fear or avoidance response, but rather behave in ways appropriate to the predator to whose presence they have been alerted. When they hear the eagle alarm call, for example, they look up and scan the sky. Vervets also have two further calls, the "wrr" and "chutter" calls, which communicate the nearby presence of strange groups of vervets. According to Cheney and Seyfarth, vervet monkeys are more likely to issue alarm calls when there are close kin in the vicinity (1990: ch. 5). Something similar holds for the food signals issued by macaque monkeys, who seem to scan for members of their social group before issuing a food signal (Hauser and Marler 1993). Even if we assume that the vervet alarm calls are symbolic, they do not constitute a complex symbol system, since there is no scope for the formation of complex symbols. Yet it is clear that the alarm calls are serving a function of environmental simplification, and indeed permit the creation of control loops for regulating each individual's future behavior and the behavior of other members of the group.

Nor is it only in primates that we find such behaviors. A classic ethological example of environmental simplification and control loop creation comes with the ways that different species of birds hide caches of seeds at specific locations. Clark's nutcrackers are known to deploy multiple cues to identify the locations of nut caches. Experiments have shown that they are able to reidentify nut stores even when experimenters manipulate the most obvious landmarks (Balda and Turek 1984). In creating food stores, birds both simplify the environment in terms of markers that allow them to reidentify the caches and create control loops for future behavior in terms of a structure of inter-cache trajectories that will determine their movements when retrieving food.

As far as Clark's original list of six instrumental functions is concerned, therefore, it looks as if we can make sense of at least four of them operating at the nonlinguistic level. And the two that are left (memory augmentation and data manipulation) do not seem very likely candidates for marking a distinctive type of cognition only made available by the acquisition of language. There are all sorts of ways that nonlinguistic creatures can augment their limited memory capacities, some of which I have already considered in thinking about how path-dependent learning might be transcended at the nonlinguistic level. And data manipulation is a characteristic of all thought. The only differences between linguistic and nonlinguistic thought in either of these dimensions are likely to be differences of degree. It would seem, therefore, that if there indeed are any fundamental differences of type between linguistic and nonlinguistic cognition, they will lie elsewhere. In the next section I will turn to a fundamentally different type of argument for the distinctiveness of linguistic cognition.

2　Intentional ascent and semantic ascent

In the same article in which he puts forward the six instrumental functions of language, Andy Clark offers the following conjecture about the role of language in underpinning the distinctiveness of human cognition.

> Perhaps it is public language that is responsible for a complex of rather distinctive features of human thought – viz., our ability to display *second-order cognitive dynamics*. By second-order cognitive dynamics I mean a cluster of powerful capacities involving self-evaluation, self-criticism and finely honed remedial responses. Examples would include: recognizing a flaw in our own plan or argument, and dedicating further cognitive efforts to fixing it; reflecting on the unreliability of our own initial judgements in certain types of situation and proceeding with special caution as a result; coming to see why we reached a particular conclusion by appreciating the logical transitions in our own thought; thinking about the conditions under which we think best and trying to bring them about. The list could be continued, but the pattern should be clear. In all these cases we are effectively thinking about our own cognitive profiles or about specific thoughts. (Clark 1998: 177)

He explains how language makes these types of thought available in the following terms.

> It is easy to see in broad outline how this might come about. For as soon as we formulate a thought in words (or on paper), it becomes an object both for ourselves and for others. As an object it is the kind of thing we can have thoughts about. In creating the object we need have no thoughts about thoughts – but once it is there, the opportunity immediately exists to attend to it as an object in its own right. The process of linguistic formulation thus creates the stable structure to which subsequent thinkings attach. (Clark 1998: 177)

It seems to me that the basic idea Clark is putting forward is essentially correct. My aim in this section of the chapter will be to formulate the basic idea more precisely and to provide an argument to back it up.

Clark's explanation of the role language plays in second-order cognitive dynamics is incomplete, at least for my purposes. For one thing, all he really offers is an account of how, given that we have language, we are able to engage in second-order cognitive dynamics – whereas what we need is an argument that second-order cognitive dynamics can only be undertaken by language-using creatures. This links up directly with a more fundamental worry. The natural way to derive an argument for the necessity of language from Clark's suggestions would be to claim that language is required for thinking about our own thoughts. But this claim is hardly uncontroversial. It would be instantly denied, for example, by language of thought theorists. It is an integral part of the language of thought hypothesis that reflexive thinking is available in the language of thought. Once again we find ourselves caught in the familiar grey area between public languages and the language of thought. We need to investigate not simply whether some form of language is required but what type of language that must be.

The basic premise from which we need to start here is that reflexive thoughts can only be possible if the target thoughts have vehicles that allow them to be the objects of further thoughts. The question, then, is what form these vehicles must take. Broadly speaking, the candidates fall into two broad categories. They might be either personal-level vehicles or subpersonal vehicles. Any argument to show that reflexive thinking requires the target thoughts to be vehicled in a public language will have to establish, first, that the vehicles must be at the personal level and, second, that the only available vehicles at the personal level are public language sentences.

The plausibility of the first step in the argument emerges when we reflect that reflexive thinking will paradigmatically involve a direct and conscious cognitive access to the target thoughts. As the first passage quoted from Clark at the beginning of this section makes clear, typical examples of reflexive thinking might include evaluating evidential and inferential relations between thoughts. Such reflexive thinking involves having the target thoughts in mind – entertaining them consciously and considering how they relate to each other logically and evidentially. Yet it seems clear that we do not have the appropriate sort of direct and conscious cognitive access to subpersonal states. Second-order cognitive dynamics is a matter of the conscious regulation and policing of one's own thoughts – and we do not consciously regulate and police sentences in the language of thought. It might well be the case that certain types of hypothesis testing and refinement do take place at the subpersonal level. Something like this happens, according to Fodor, when we learn a language. Nothing I say is incompatible with that proposal, since my claim is simply that such processes would not count as instances of second-order cognitive dynamics. Nonetheless, one might want to question the proposal on other grounds, such as the availability of alternative models of language acquisition, particularly those developed within the connectionist tradition (for a survey of recent work see McLeod et al. 1998).

It is hard to see how a defender of the language of thought hypothesis could maintain that we do have conscious access to sentences in the language of thought, given that the language of thought hypothesis is a hypothesis about subpersonal cognitive architecture, not about the medium of conscious thought. It is generally accepted that subpersonal states are inferentially insulated from the conscious processes of cognitive evaluation and self-criticism. This is precisely the distinction between the personal and subpersonal levels (see, for example, Stich 1978). A fortiori, therefore, it follows that the vehicles of the thoughts that are the objects of what Clark calls second-order cognitive dynamics cannot be sentences in a subpersonal language of thought.[6]

There are versions of the language of thought hypothesis, however, that are not put forward purely as hypotheses about subpersonal cognitive architecture and hence are not directly blocked by this line of argument. Some authors have suggested that there might be a modular internal language in which thoughts are encoded for conscious consideration. This general approach would sit well with (although neither entails nor is entailed by) higher-order thought theories of consciousness (Rosenthal 1993). It seems to me, however, that this proposal lacks phenomenological plausibility. All the *propositional* thoughts that we consciously introspect, whether thoughts that come unbidden into our minds or thoughts that we consciously instigate and consider in solving a problem, take the form of sentences in a public language. We do, of course, engage in various types of nonsentential thinking – what might be termed thinking-how in contrast to thinking-that – and it is only mistaking nonpropositional thinking-how for propositional thinking-that that leads to the view that we can be aware of "pure" thoughts without any sentences featuring among the contents of introspection.[7] There are certain types of problem that we solve by manipulating mental images and exercising the visual imagination. And we are, of course, conscious of bodily sensations, emotional feelings, and other such qualitative states (although these are not properly described as types of thinking at all). But we are not, I think, ever conscious of *propositional* thoughts that do not have linguistic vehicles. When we are conscious of propositional thoughts we are conscious of imaged sentences.[8] What we introspect when we introspect our propositional thoughts in the manner required for the processes of second-order cognitive dynamics is inner speech.

This brings me to the second step of the argument. What needs to be shown is that public language sentences are the only possible personal-level vehicles for thoughts that are to be the objects of reflexive thinking. The conclusion so far is that sentences in the language of thought are not appropriate vehicles. The only way to proceed is by elimination – showing that there are no viable alternatives to public language sentences. How else might the representation relation work? There seem to be two possibilities. On the one hand representation might be secured symbolically through the complex symbols of a natural language (complex symbols being required since what are being represented are thoughts about states of affairs). A thought would be represented, therefore, through its linguistic expression and would appear as a potential object of thought *qua* linguistic entity. On the other hand, representation might be secured in an analogue manner, through some kind of pictorial model. On this conception of the vehicles of thought, which we find developed in different ways in mental models theory in the psychology of reasoning (originally proposed in Craik 1943 but most comprehensively developed in Johnson-Laird 1983) and in the conception of mental maps put forward by Braddon-Mitchell and Jackson (1996), the vehicle of a thought is a pictorial representation of the state of affairs being thought about.[9]

The idea of structural isomorphism is at the heart of both theories. Both mental models and maps are spatially isomorphic with what they represent. The relations (or at least some of them) holding between elements of the mental model/map can be mapped on to the relations holding between objects in the represented state of affairs. In this way representation is secured through the relations of exemplification and resemblance. The mental model/map represents a state of affairs by exemplifying the structure of that state of affairs – that is to say, by itself possessing a structure that resembles (at some suitable level of abstraction) the structure of the represented state of affairs. It does so, however, in a way that does not have an independently identifiable structure corresponding to the state of affairs exemplified. Braddon-Mitchell and Jackson put the point clearly.

> There is no natural way of dividing a map at its truth-assessable representational joints. Each part of a map contributes to the representational content of the whole map, in the sense that had that part of the map been different, the representational content of the whole would have been different. Change the bit of the map of the United States between New York and Boston, and you change systematically what the map says. This is part of what makes it true that the map is structured. However, there is no preferred way of dividing the map into basic representational units. There are many jigsaw puzzles you might make out of the map, but no single one would have a claim to have pieces that were all and only the most basic units. (Braddon-Mitchell and Jackson 1996: 171)

We need, therefore, to distinguish weak and strong senses in which a representational vehicle might be structured. In the weak sense there is structure whenever a structural isomorphism can be identified between the vehicle and what it represents. In the strong sense, however, structure requires the existence of basic representational units combined according to independently identifiable combinatorial rules. Natural language sentences (or for that matter sentences in the language of thought) are clearly structured in the strong sense, whereas mental maps/models only possess structure in the weak sense.

In mental models and maps, the representation relation will be secured through some combination of isomorphic resemblance and exemplification holding primarily between the model/map as a whole and the represented state of affairs as a whole and only derivatively at the level of the distinguishable elements of the map/model and state of affairs, respectively). There are important questions to ask about the nature, and even the possibility, of resemblance and exemplification-based representation – questions that go back to early criticisms of the British Empiricists (and that have arisen more recently in criticisms of the picture theory of the proposition offered by Ludwig Wittgenstein in the *Tractatus Logico-Philosophicus*). I shall prescind from these, however. There is a fundamental problem with either version of the analogue proposal as an account of how it is possible for thoughts to have vehicles that allow them to become the objects of further thoughts.

Second-order cognitive dynamics involves sensitivity to the inferential relations between thoughts, and we do not yet have an understanding of how images can be inferentially connected to each other. The problem once again derives from the intimate relation between inference and structure. There is a sense in which mental models and maps are structured, since they contain elements that can feature in further mental models/maps. Nonetheless, they do not seem to be structured in the right sort of way to permit the reflexive type of second-order cognitive dynamics under discussion. It will be helpful to take maps and mental models separately.

A canonical example of second-order cognitive dynamics might be coming to see the evidential basis for a particular belief and then evaluating the inferential transition made on that basis. One might realize that one has made an overly rash inductive generalization, or a faulty deductive inference. It is perfectly easy to see how there could be some very basic forms of inferential transition between maps. Such transitions might be modeled on broadly associationist lines, and it is the possibility of such transitions that enables maps to serve as guides to action. What is not possible, however, is for such transitions to be understood and evaluated in terms of either deductive validity or probabilistic support. Those very features of maps (their analogue nature and structural isomorphism with what they represent) that make them so useful for guiding action serve to make them inappropriate for the type of inferential evaluation characteristic of second-order cognitive dynamics. In order for such evaluation to take place, the maps must be interpreted in broadly propositional terms. We must interpret one map as expressing one proposition and the second as representing a further proposition, and then evaluate the inferential relations (be they deductive, inductive, or probabilistic) between those two propositions. Once again, our only understanding of how to do this rests on the two propositions being linguistically formulated.

Braddon-Mitchell and Jackson do not directly address this issue, but they do offer the following explanation of how maps can evolve over time in what is clearly intended to be an analogy with inferential transitions between linguistically vehicled representations.

Maps are physical entities whose structure can govern the way they evolve over time. When cartographers update maps or put two maps together to make one that incorporates all the information in a single map, these operations are governed in part by the structures of the maps they are working on. And in order to find a target, rockets use a kind of internal map that gets continually updated as new information comes in. In these rockets, later maps are causal products of earlier maps plus what comes in via the rocket's sensors. Hence map theorists can tell an essentially similar story to language of thought theorists about how thoughts evolve over time as a function of their propositional objects. (Braddon-Mitchell and Jackson 1996: 173)

There is a fundamental disanalogy here, however. The issue is not really about how thoughts evolve over time. In a very important sense individual thoughts quite simply do not evolve over time. It is systems of thought that evolve, and they do so as a function of the inferential relations between the thoughts that compose them. These inferential relations hold between distinct thoughts, and nothing that Braddon-Mitchell and Jackson say in this short passage gives us any way of understanding how we should understand inferential relations between distinct thoughts at the level of mental maps. The process of combining maps has only very limited analogies with the process of inferring one thought from another. We do not have, for example, any idea what a conditional map might look like – and consequently little understanding of how conditional reasoning might take place at the level of mental maps. A fortiori, therefore, there seems no sense in which we can understand second-order cognitive dynamics as applying to the inferential transitions between mental maps.

The situation is somewhat more complicated with mental models theory. How can mental models not be suitable targets for the type of reflexive thinking characteristic of second-order cognitive dynamics, given that mental models are explicitly proposed as providing a unified account of deductive, probabilistic, and modal reasoning (Johnson-Laird 1999)? It is important to be clear, however, about the precise claims of mental models theory. Mental models theory is proposed as an alternative to the so-called mental logic theory (Rips 1994), according to which reasoning is an exclusively syntactic matter grounded in formal rules of inference.[10] The key idea of mental models theory is that arguments are evaluated by the construction of mental models of the relevant premises. An argument is judged to be deductively valid if the conclusion holds in all the constructed models of the premises, probabilistically valid if it holds in most of the models, and so forth. The claim made is that this model of reasoning provides a better explanation of the patterns discovered in the experimental study of how subjects reason than the idea that reasoning involves the manipulation of sentential representations according to formal rules. Some of these patterns involve systematic susceptibility to formal fallacies, which it is obviously difficult to explain on the mental logic approach. Others are simply patterns in the time taken to carry out certain inferences, which advocates of the mental models approach claim is directly correlated with the number of models that the reasoner needs to construct (Johnson-Laird and Byrne 1991).

Mental models are indeed supposed to be structurally isomorphic to the states of affairs described in the premises. But like mental maps, their structure is derivative. It is derived from the premises that they are modeling. The models are constructed from constituents and properties that feature in the premise being modeled. And those premises are of course linguistic entities. It would be a mistake to think that mental models theory construes inference in terms of transitions between mental models – any more than a model-theoretic approach to the sentence calculus construes inference in terms of transitions between truth tables. Mental models theory construes inference as a matter of transitions between sententially encoded propositions. What is distinctive about it is that it construes those transitions between sententially encoded propositions as taking place in virtue of relations between analogue representations of the states of affairs portrayed in those sententially encoded propositions (as opposed to formal relations holding between the syntactic structures of the relevant sentences). Mental models theory is not a genuine alternative to the sentential conception of reasoning, since the whole idea of a mental model only makes sense within the framework of the sentential conception. Mental models theory offers a particular way of developing the sentential conception, not of supplanting it. Mental models are not the vehicles of inference, but rather, as their name suggests, models of those inferences.

By a process of elimination, therefore, we have reached the conclusion that thoughts can only be the objects of the type of reflexive thinking in which thoughts are the objects of thought if they have natural language vehicles. This is not, of course, to say that we cannot deploy mental maps and mental models. It is clear that we do, and it is highly likely that nonlinguistic creatures do as well. Nor is it to say that mental models and mental maps cannot be the objects of thought. It seems clear that we can think about mental models and mental maps as well as think by means of them. The point is that we cannot use mental maps or mental models for thinking about thoughts in the manner demanded by second-order cognitive dynamics. Natural language sentences are the only proxies that will permit thoughts to function as the objects of thought in this manner. To put the matter in the form of a slogan, there can be no intentional ascent without semantic ascent. We think about thoughts through thinking about the sentences through which those thoughts might be expressed. The significance of this thesis depends, however, on the types of thinking that constitutively involve intentional, and hence semantic, ascent. We began this section with Clark's programmatic suggestion that only language-users can be capable of the types of cognitive self-criticism and self-monitoring that he terms second-order cognitive dynamics. It turns out, however (see ch. 9 of Bermúdez 2003), that second-order cognitive dynamics is simply one species in the genus of reflexive thinking. Other varieties of reflexive thinking include logical thinking; the ascription of propositional attitudes to others; and domain-general thinking. These are all unavailable to nonlinguistic creatures, if the argument sketched above is sound.

Notes

1 As I will show hereafter, these six respects do not exhaust Clark's conception of the contribution that language can make to cognition.

2 I take it as uncontroversial that no system of communication can count as linguistic unless it involves symbols. The characteristic of symbols is that they are arbitrary as opposed to iconic signals (see further in the main text hereafter).

3 The bee dances have also received attention from philosophers. See Bennett 1964.

4 The definition of iconic signals just posed is significantly different from that suggested by Charles Sanders Peirce, who is usually credited with having first formulated the distinction between iconic and arbitrary signals (or rather, in his terms, between iconic and symbolic signs). Peirce defines an icon as a "Sign that represents its Object in resembling it" (1991: 270). He does not impose any requirement that continuous variation in the object be matched by continuous variation in the signal, and consequently takes as iconic signs that would not count as iconic on the criteria just outlined. For example, he holds that linguistic predicates are iconic as well as logical and mathematical proofs. Peirce's theory of signs is discussed in chapters 4 and 6 of Hookway 1985.

5 Consider, for example, the following two passages from Michael Dummett's book on Frege. "Our apprehension of reality as decomposable into discrete objects is the product of our application to an originally unarticulated reality of the conceptual apparatus embodied in our language" (Dummett 1973: 505). And: "Our ability to discriminate, within reality, objects of any particular kind results from our having learned to use expressions, names or general terms, with which are associated a criterion of identity which yields segments of reality of just that shape: we can, in principle, conceive of a language containing names and general terms with which significantly different criteria of identity were associated, and the speakers of such a language would view the world as falling apart into discrete objects in a different way from ourselves . . . For Frege, the world does not come to us articulated in any way; it is we who, by the use of our language (or by grasping the thoughts expressed in that language), impose a structure on it" (1973: 503–504).

6 Nothing I say is intended to be incompatible with the substantive claims made by the theorists in the language of thought tradition. In particular, it may well be the case (as Fodor suggests) that the understanding of public language sentences involves in some sense translating them into the language of thought. My point is simply that reflexive thinking (in the sense in which I am understanding it, namely, as involving, e.g., the evaluation of epistemic links between propositions) is directed at the public language sentences rather than at the sentences in the language of thought that give their meaning.

7 The point was well put by Wittgenstein, who has plausible things to say about what is going on when it seems to one that one is introspecting a thought that is not sententially vehicled: "What happens when we make an effort – say in writing a letter – to find the right expression for our thoughts? – This phrase

compares the process to one of translating or describing: the thoughts are already there (perhaps were there in advance) and we merely look for their expression. This picture is more or less appropriate in different cases. – But can't all sorts of things happen here? – I surrender to a mood and the expression *comes*. Or a picture occurs to me and I try to describe it. Or an English expression occurs to me and I try to hit on the corresponding German one. Or I make a gesture and ask myself: What words correspond to this gesture? And so on." (Wittgenstein 1953, sec. 335). For further discussion of Wittgenstein's complex views on the relation between language and thought see Budd 1989, chs. 5 and 6.

8　Peter Carruthers, who proposes that all domain-general cognition consists in the formation and manipulation of linguistic representations at the level of what Chomsky terms logical form, nonetheless thinks that we cannot be conscious of these "stripped down" linguistic representations (Carruthers 1996). We are only conscious of sentences with the full complement of natural language phonological and structural features from which the level of logical form is an abstraction.

9　I will count mental models theory as a conception of pictorial models even though the two notions cannot be straightforwardly mapped onto each other. It is true that mental models, as proposed by Johnson-Laird, are intended to be semiperceptual states that resemble the situations they represent. Nonetheless, there is a crucial ambiguity in mental models theory. On the one hand the manipulation of mental models is supposed to take place in working memory, the contents of which are generally thought to be open to conscious access and report. On the other hand it seems clear that introspection will have little role to play in deciding the issue between mental logic and mental models as far as the psychology of reasoning is concerned. To the extent that mental models theory is a theory of the subpersonal mechanisms of thought, it will be correspondingly of less use as a theoretical account of how thoughts might be vehicled in a way that would allow them to be the objects of further reflexive thinking.

10　The difference between the mental logic and mental models theories is frequently compared to that between proof-theoretic and model-theoretic approaches in logic.

References

Balda, R.P. and Turek, R.J.(1984) "Memory in birds." In H.L. Roitblat, T.G. Bever, and H.S. Terrace, *Animal Cognition*. Hillsdale, N.J.: Lawrence Erlbaum.

Bennett, J. (1976) *Linguistic Behaviour*. Cambridge: Cambridge University Press.

Bickerton, D. (1990) *Language and Species*. Chicago: Chicago University Press.

—— (1996) *Language and Human Behaviour*. London: UCL Press.

Boesch, C. and Boesch, H. (1992) "Transmission aspects of tool use in wild chimpanzees." In T. Ingold and K.R. Gibson, *Tools, Language and Intelligence: Evolutionary Implications*. Oxford: Oxford University Press.

Braddon-Mitchell, D. and Jackson, F. (1996) *Philosophy of Mind and Cognition*. Oxford: Blackwell.

Budd, M. (1989) *Wittgenstein's Philosophy of Psychology*. London: Routledge.

Carruthers, P. (1996) *Language, Thought, and Consciousness*. Cambridge: Cambridge University Press.

Cheney, D.L. and Seyfarth, R.M. (1990) *How Monkeys See the World*. Chicago: University of Chicago Press.

Chomsky, N.(1980) *Rules and Representations*. Oxford: Blackwell.

Clark, A. (1998) "Magic words: How language augments human cognition." In P. Carruthers and J. Boucher (eds), *Language and Thought: Interdisciplinary Themes*. Cambridge: Cambridge University Press.

Craik, M. (1943) *The Nature of Explanation*. Cambridge: Cambridge University Press.

Donald, M. (1991) *Origins of the Modern Mind*. Cambridge, Mass.: Harvard University Press.

Dummett, M. (1973) *Frege: Philosophy of Language*. London: Duckworth.

von Frisch, K. (1967) *The Dance Language and Orientation of Bees*. Cambridge, Mass.: Harvard University Press.

Green, S. and Marler, P.M. (1979) "The analysis of animal communication." In P.M. Marler and J.C. Vanderbergh (eds), *Handbook of Behavioral Neurobiology*, Vol. III: *Social Behavior and Communication*. New York: Plenum Press.

Goldin-Meadow, S. (1979) "Structure in a manual communication system developed without a language model: Language without a helping hand." In H.A. Whiter (ed.), *Studies in Neurolinguistics*, Vol. 4. New York: Academic Press.

Greenfield, P.M. and Savage-Rumbaugh, E.S. (1990) "Grammatical combination in Pan Paniscus: Processes of learning and invention in the evolution and development of language." In S. Taylor-Parker and K.R. Gibson (eds), *Language and Intelligence in Monkeys and Apes*. Cambridge: Cambridge University Press.

Hauser, M.S. and Marler, P. (1993) "Food calls in rhesus macaques (Macaca mulata) I & II." *Behavioral Ecology* 4: 194–205, 206–12.

Hookway, C. (1985) *Peirce*. London: Routledge.

Johnson-Laird, P. (1983) *Mental Models*. Cambridge: Cambridge University Press.

—— (1999) "Mental models". In R.A. Wilson and F.C. Keil (eds), *The MIT Encyclopedia of the Cognitive Sciences*. Cambridge, Mass.: MIT Press.

Johnson-Laird, P. and Byrne, R.M.J. (1991) *Deduction*. Hillsdale, N.J.: Erlbaum.

Lewis, D. (1983) "Language and Languages." In *Philosophical Papers Vol. 1*. Cambridge: Cambridge University Press.

Lieberman, P. (1984) *The Biology and Evolution of Language*. Cambridge, Mass.: Harvard University Press.

McLeod, P., Plunkett, K., and Rolls, E.T. (1998) *Introduction to Connectionist Modelling of Cognitive Processes*. Oxford: Oxford University Press.

Marler, P. (1970) "A comparative approach to vocal learning: Song development in white-crowned sparrows." *Journal of Comparative and Physiological Psychology* 71 (Supplement): 1–25.

Meltzoff, A.N. and Moore, M.K. (1977) "Imitation of facial and manual gestures by human neonates." *Science* 198: 75–8.

—— (1983) "Newborn infants imitate adult facial gestures." *Child Development* 54: 702–9.

Peirce, C.S. (1991) *Peirce on Signs: Writings on Semiotics*. Chapel Hill: University of Carolina Press.

Reynolds, P.C. (1993) "The complementation theory of language and tool use." In K.R. Gibson and T. Ingold (eds), *Tools, Language and Cognition in Human Evolution*. Cambridge: Cambridge University Press.

Rips, L. (1994) *The Psychology of Proof*. Cambridge, Mass.: MIT Press.

Rosenthal, D.M. (1993) "Thinking that one thinks." In M. Davies and G.W. Humphreys (eds), *Consciousness*. Oxford: Blackwell.

Savage-Rumbaugh, E.S. (1986) *Ape Language: From Conditioned Response to Symbol*. New York: Columbia University Press.

Stern, D. (1985) *The Interpersonal World of the Infant*. New York: Academic Press.

Stich, S. (1978) "Beliefs and subdoxastic states." *Philosophy of Science* 45: 499–518.

Tinbergen, N. (1973) *The Animal in Its World*. Cambridge, Mass.: Harvard University Press.

Tomasello, M. (1996) "Do apes ape?" In C. Heyes and B.G. Galef, *Social Learning in Animals: The Roots of Culture*. New York: Academic Press.

Wittgenstein, L. (1953) *Philosophical Investigations*. Translated by G.E.M. Anscombe. Oxford: Blackwell.

INDEX

Related titles from Routledge

Philosophy of Psychology

José Luis Bermúdez

'Philosophers of psychology and philosophically minded psychologists are in need of just this kind of introductory book. I would recommend this material both for pedagogy and as a place for scholars to turn to for a refresher.'

Joe Cruz, Williams College, USA

'An outstanding introductory text in philosophy of psychology that lends itself readily to use in a variety of courses. It will, in addition, constitute an independent, substantive contribution to philosophy of psychology and philosophy of mind.'

David Rosenthal, City University of New York, USA

Philosophy of Psychology is an introduction to philosophical problems that arise in the scientific study of cognition and behaviour.

José Luis Bermúdez introduces the philosophy of psychology as an interdisciplinary exploration of the nature and mechanisms of cognition. *Philosophy of Psychology* charts out four influential 'pictures of the mind' and uses them to explore central topics in the philosophical foundations of psychology, including the relation between different levels of studying the mind/brain; the nature and scope of psychological explanation; the architecture of cognition; and the relation between thought and language.

An introductory chapter looks at what the philosophy of psychology is, tracing its historical background and exploring its relationship to philosophy of mind and to psychology itself. Further chapters cover all the core concepts and themes found in undergraduate courses in philosophy of psychology.

ISBN10: 0–415–27594–6 (hbk)
ISBN10: 0–415–27595–4 (pbk)

ISBN13: 978–0–415–27594–1 (hbk)
ISBN13: 978–0–415–27595–8 (pbk)

Available at all good bookshops
For ordering and further information please visit:
www.routledge.com

Related titles from Routledge

Metaphysics: Contemporary Readings

Michael J. Loux

'This anthology has many excellent features: the choice of readings is very good, mixing in an interesting way established and much-anthologised classics with new material.'
Tim Crane, University College London

This comprehensive anthology draws together leading philosophers writing on the big topics in metaphysics. Each section is prefaced by an introduction that guides the student into each topic. This is a highly accessible and user-friendly text which gives a broad-ranging exploration of the subject. The readings are carefully picked to complement Michael Loux's textbook *Metaphysics: A Contemporary Introduction*, which is now in its third edition.

ISBN10: 0–415–26108–2 (hbk)
ISBN10: 0–415–26109–0 (pbk)

ISBN13: 978–0–415–26108–1 (hbk)
ISBN13: 978–0–415–26109–8 (pbk)

Available at all good bookshops
For ordering and further information please visit:
www.routledge.com

Related titles from Routledge

Philosophy of Mind 2nd edition
John Heil

'I thought that the first edition of this book was excellent. I recommend it strongly to my own students. Even so, I think that the main changes made by John Heil in this second edition make it better still.'
E. J. Lowe, Durham University

'This book is at the right level of difficulty and is well-written. By this I don't just mean that it is clear but that it makes the subject come alive; a student reading it should get a feeling for why the topic is important, even exciting.'
Barry Dainton, University of Liverpool

Philosophy of Mind: A Contemporary Introduction is a comprehensive and accessible survey of main themes, positions and debates in philosophy of mind. John Heil introduces and discusses the major topics in succinct, user-friendly, self-contained chapters.

This revised and updated edition includes expanded chapters on eliminativism, qualia, and the representational theory of mind, and an entirely new chapter on property dualism. There are annotated suggestions for further reading at the end of each chapter, updated to include recent material and internet resources.

ISBN10: 0–415–28355–8 (hbk)
ISBN10: 0–415–28356–6 (pbk)

ISBN13: 978–0–415–28355–7 (hbk)
ISBN13: 978–0–415–28356–4 (pbk)

Available at all good bookshops
For ordering and further information please visit:
www.routledge.com